LIFE CONTINGENCIES

LIFE CONTINGENCIES

BY

E. F. SPURGEON, F.I.A.

CAMBRIDGE

Published for the Institute of Actuaries

AT THE

UNIVERSITY PRESS

1932

CAMBRIDGE UNIVERSITY PRESS
Cambridge, New York, Melbourne, Madrid, Cape Town,
Singapore, São Paulo, Delhi, Tokyo, Mexico City

Cambridge University Press
The Edinburgh Building, Cambridge CB2 8RU, UK

Published in the United States of America by Cambridge University Press, New York

www.cambridge.org
Information on this title: www.cambridge.org/9781107648098

First published by the authority and on behalf of the
Institute of Actuaries, by C. & E. Layton, 1922
First paperback edition 2011

A catalogue record for this publication is available from the British Library

ISBN 978-1-107-64809-8 Paperback

INTRODUCTION

PART II of the Text Book of the Institute of Actuaries, dealing with the Theory of Life Contingencies, was first issued in 1887. This work, for which the Institute must ever be indebted to its distinguished author Mr George King, did more than simplify the progress of the actuarial student to his desired goal; it systematised and co-ordinated the presentation of the complex theory with which it dealt, thus elevating to the status of a definite branch of scientific knowledge a subject which, though fully ripe for such recognition, had up to that time suffered from the disadvantage of comparative inaccessibility.

During the long period which has elapsed since the Text Book was first published considerable changes have been made in the educational course prescribed by the Institute; in particular the value to the actuarial student of a competent knowledge of the elements of the Differential and Integral Calculus has been more fully realised and these subjects are now included in the mathematical course with which the training of the student begins. To secure a consistent educational scheme it has therefore been found necessary to re-arrange the volume hitherto entitled Part II of the Text Book and to bring into greater prominence those mathematical demonstrations which were formerly treated as subjects of optional study. The theoretical basis of these demonstrations is now included in the mathematical text book which is issued as a separate work, and certain chapters of the old Text Book, Part II, are omitted from the present Volume which thus deals exclusively with the theory of actuarial science so far as relates to Life Contingencies.

These are the principal changes introduced, but the opportunity has also been taken to make certain alterations which bring the work more fully into conformity with modern requirements. At the request of the Council the compilation of the new treatise was undertaken by Mr E. F. Spurgeon who brought to his task the indispensable qualifications of long experience as a Tutor and a conspicuous gift of exposition. The resulting Volume is issued by the Council in the belief that it will fully meet the needs of students and promote the attainment of those high professional qualifications which are connoted by the Fellowship of the Institute of Actuaries.

A. W. W.

May 1922.

AUTHOR'S PREFACE

In the preparation of this Volume and in determining the order in which the various subjects should be dealt with, special attention has been directed to the following considerations, namely,

(i) That the student should, at an early stage of his work, acquire a sound knowledge of the *principles* of the construction of Mortality Tables, and of the evaluation of Annuities and Assurances, *on the simplest possible basis.*

(ii) That in applying these principles to the more intricate parts of his work, the student should automatically revise his knowledge of the earlier portions, on a sound grasp of which so much depends.

(iii) That such information on practical points as will be of assistance to the student in his more advanced studies should, where possible, be given, even though at times these may not be strictly within the limits of Part II of the Institute Examinations.

The Book has been divided into three parts:—Part I deals with Mortality Tables and Single-Life Functions; Part II with Functions involving two or more lives; and Part III with those subjects which could not conveniently be fitted into either of the earlier parts.

In Part I it was essential that the first subject dealt with should be the Mortality Table, and in the second chapter it was deemed advisable to proceed directly to Mortality Tables constructed from Life Assurance Statistics, with particular reference to Select Tables. This enables us, in Chapter III, to deal at once with Single-Life Annuities payable annually, Single-Life Assurances payable at the end of the year of death and Annual Premiums based on Select Tables. In Chapter IV, Premium Conversion Tables are dealt with; and in Chapter V, varying Annuities and Assurances and Premiums for special classes of assurances with reference to many practical points. Chapter VI deals with the values of Single-Life Policies subject to annual Premiums.

It will be seen that by taking the subjects in this order the student will, by the end of Chapter VI, have acquired a knowledge of all the principles involved in the calculation of probabilities and in the evaluation of Annuities and Assurances, on the basis of *Single Life Annual Functions*, all the later work being an extension or modification of the matters dealt with in these Chapters. As a result of this arrangement, we are able in a single chapter (Chapter VII) to dispose of Annuities and Premiums payable more frequently than once a year, together with the values of policies subject to such premiums. In Chapters VIII and IX Assurances payable at the moment of death and Complete Single-Life Annuities are discussed.

Chapter X, dealing with Life Office Valuations, has been included in order to avoid the difficulty which Part II students have met with in the past, namely, that they have acquired a knowledge of Policy Values only to find that in their later work Policy Values, as such, are seldom used.

In order to prepare for subjects included in Part II of the Book it now becomes necessary, in Chapter XI, to consider Makeham's Law of Mortality, and in Chapter XII to deal with statistical applications of the Mortality Table and the Expectation of Life.

In Part II, when considering Joint-Life and Contingent Probabilities, Joint-Life and Last-Survivor Annuities and Assurances, and Contingent Assurances, the student will be merely extending the principles studied in the first few chapters.

Part III consists of two chapters only. In Chapter XX (Construction of Tables) the advantage of the Arithmometer has been emphasised and it has been considered necessary again to include a plate of a machine showing a particular calculation, the description of the machine being taken word for word from the old Text Book. In Chapter XXI the question of Tables involving two or more causes of decrement has been introduced in the simplest possible manner.

At the end of the Volume it was considered advisable to include, firstly, a Mortality Table based on population data (The English Life Table, No. 8), secondly, a Select Life Table (The $O^{[NM]}$) and thirdly, the H^M Table (Makeham Graduation) because of its value for instructional purposes. The Tables of Monetary Functions on the basis of the English Life Table, No. 8, which have not previously been published, have been supplied entirely by the Prudential Assurance Company; the Tables based on the $O^{[NM]}$ experience have been taken from those published by the Institute of Actuaries and Faculty of Actuaries jointly; and those based on the H^{M} experience from the old Text Book Part II.

It has been a distinct advantage to have a great part of the work already mapped out by Mr George King in the old Text Book, and to have been able to make use of his collection of symbols and expressions in such chapters as that relating to Compound Survivorship Annuities and Assurances. It would have added very materially to the work of preparation of the present volume had these not been available.

In conclusion I wish to express my high appreciation of the very valuable assistance rendered to me by Messrs W. W. Williamson, F.I.A., and C. C. Barrett, F.I.A., both in criticising my manuscript and in reading the proofs. If this book prove of the value to students and to the profession which I hope, their exceedingly helpful criticisms and suggestions will have contributed thereto in no small degree.

E. F. S.

AUTHOR'S PREFACE TO SECOND EDITION

In the Second Edition of this book the plan adopted in the First Edition has been retained.

The principal alterations are, the transfer from Chapter IV 13 to Chapter III 26 of the remarks concerning the comparison of premiums calculated on the basis of select and aggregate tables respectively, the revision of Chapter VI 44 and 45 and the addition of paragraph 14 to Chapter XXI.

Advantage has, of course, been taken of the opportunity afforded of correcting errors and misprints which appeared in the First Edition, and some slight changes in wording have also been made.

E. F. S.

AUTHOR'S PREFACE TO THIRD EDITION

THE principal alterations in the Third Edition occur in Chapters V and X. In Chapter V, paragraph 34 (Options) has been redrafted in order to introduce more "practical" formulae, and paragraph 36 (Deferred Assurances with Return of Premiums) has been slightly altered for a similar reason. In Chapter X, paragraphs 3 to 11 have been redrafted in order to bring out more clearly, for the benefit of students, the actual bases of the formulae employed in practice; no alteration in principle is, however, involved.

Various suggestions have been received that extracts from papers and notes published during the last few years should be included in the Third Edition. These have been carefully considered, but as only slight variations of the application of principles already dealt with in this book were involved, it was not deemed advisable to increase the size of the work by their inclusion.

The Author desires to express his very great appreciation of the assistance he has received in the preparation of the Third Edition from Messrs W. F. Gardner, F.I.A., and G. A. Hosking, F.I.A., who have, indeed, undertaken practically the whole of the task of examining the suggestions received, in addition to themselves making recommendations concerning various points which had come before them in the course of their tutorial work.

E. F. S.

TABLE OF CONTENTS

PART I

CHAPTERS I TO XII

MORTALITY TABLES

SINGLE-LIFE PROBABILITIES OF LIFE AND DEATH

SINGLE-LIFE ANNUITIES AND ASSURANCES

STATISTICAL APPLICATION OF THE MORTALITY TABLE

CHAPTER I (Pages 1—18)

THE MORTALITY TABLE—MORTALITY TABLES CONSTRUCTED FROM POPULATION STATISTICS

CHAPTER II (Pages 19—30)

MORTALITY TABLES CONSTRUCTED FROM LIFE ASSURANCE STATISTICS—SELECT LIFE TABLES

CHAPTER III (Pages 31—59)

SINGLE-LIFE ANNUITIES AND ASSURANCES. ANNUAL PREMIUMS

CHAPTER IV (Pages 60—67)

RELATION BETWEEN ASSURANCES AND ANNUITIES. PREMIUM CONVERSION TABLES

CHAPTER V (Pages 68—94)

VARYING SINGLE-LIFE ANNUITIES AND ASSURANCES. OFFICE PREMIUMS AND SPECIAL CLASSES OF ASSURANCES

CHAPTER VI (Pages 95—127)

VALUES OF SINGLE-LIFE POLICIES SUBJECT TO ANNUAL PREMIUMS

CHAPTER VII (Pages 128—150)

SINGLE-LIFE ANNUITIES AND PREMIUMS PAYABLE MORE FREQUENTLY THAN ONCE A YEAR. VALUES OF SINGLE-LIFE POLICIES SUBJECT TO PREMIUMS PAYABLE MORE FREQUENTLY THAN ONCE A YEAR

CHAPTER VIII (Pages 151—160)

SINGLE-LIFE ASSURANCES PAYABLE AT ANY OTHER MOMENT THAN AT THE END OF THE YEAR OF DEATH

CHAPTER IX (Pages 161—171)

COMPLETE SINGLE-LIFE ANNUITIES

CHAPTER X (Pages 172—190)

LIFE OFFICE VALUATIONS

CHAPTER XI (Pages 191—202)

MATHEMATICAL REPRESENTATION OF THE LAW OF MORTALITY; GOMPERTZ'S AND MAKEHAM'S LAWS

CHAPTER XII (Pages 203—220)

STATISTICAL APPLICATIONS OF THE MORTALITY TABLE

PART II

CHAPTERS XIII TO XIX

FUNCTIONS INVOLVING TWO OR MORE LIVES
PROBABILITIES OF LIFE AND DEATH
JOINT-LIFE AND LAST SURVIVOR ANNUITIES AND ASSURANCES
CONTINGENT ASSURANCES
REVERSIONARY ANNUITIES

CHAPTER XIII (Pages 223—237)

JOINT-LIFE AND SURVIVORSHIP PROBABILITIES

CHAPTER XIV (Pages 238—252)

CONTINGENT PROBABILITIES

CHAPTER XV (Pages 253—276)

JOINT-LIFE ANNUITIES. ANNUITIES PAYABLE UNTIL THE DEATH OF THE LAST SURVIVOR OF TWO OR MORE LIVES

CHAPTER XVI (Pages 277—290)

JOINT-LIFE AND LAST-SURVIVOR ASSURANCES. COMPLETE JOINT-LIFE AND LAST-SURVIVOR ANNUITIES

CHAPTER XVII (Pages 291—320)

CONTINGENT ASSURANCES

CHAPTER XVIII (Pages 321—340)

REVERSIONARY ANNUITIES

CHAPTER XIX (Pages 341—354)

COMPOUND SURVIVORSHIP ANNUITIES AND ASSURANCES

PART III

CHAPTERS XX AND XXI

CONSTRUCTION OF TABLES

TABLES INVOLVING TWO OR MORE CAUSES OF DECREMENT AND FUNCTIONS DEPENDENT THEREON

CHAPTER XX (Pages 357—380)

CONSTRUCTION OF TABLES

CHAPTER XXI (Pages 381—394)

TABLES INVOLVING TWO OR MORE CAUSES OF DECREMENT

TABLES

PART I

CHAPTERS I TO XII

MORTALITY TABLES
SINGLE-LIFE PROBABILITIES OF LIFE AND DEATH
SINGLE-LIFE ANNUITIES AND ASSURANCES
STATISTICAL APPLICATION OF THE MORTALITY TABLE

CHAPTER I

THE MORTALITY TABLE. MORTALITY TABLES CONSTRUCTED FROM POPULATION STATISTICS

1. The Mortality Table is the instrument by means of which are measured the probabilities of life and the probabilities of death. It is the object of this chapter to give a clear idea of the formation of such a table, the first step being an explanation of the functions the values of which it contains and of the symbols employed to represent these functions.

The English Life Table No. 8, printed on pages 398–399, consists of a mortality table with the addition of columns of the values of certain functions not essential to the calculation of the probabilities of life and death, though useful in other directions. Reference should be made to this table as each function is discussed.

2. The number living. l_x represents the number of persons who, according to the mortality table, attain precise age x in any year of time. This number is not obtained by actual enumeration of persons who reach age x, but is calculated on the basis of observations (in the manner described in paragraph 7) so that the values of l_x, for all values of x included in the table, bear the proper relation to each other.

In this chapter a table based on the experience of the general population, commencing with an *assumed* number of births, l_0, occurring in any year of time (which, for convenience, will be taken as a calendar year), will alone be considered.

In the suffix of l, it is convenient to limit the use of x to integral ages, and to employ another letter, such as t or n, where required, to denote the addition of either an integral or fractional number of years of age. Thus l_{x+t} will denote the number of persons who in any year attain precise age $x+t$, x being an integer and t either an integer or a fraction. These l_{x+t} persons are the survivors of those born in a year $x+t$ years ago; they are also the survivors of the l_{x+t-1} persons who attained age $x+t-1$

in the previous year, or of the l_{x+t-2} persons who attained age $x+t-2$ two years previously, and so on.

3. L_x represents the number living between ages x and $x+1$ as disclosed by an enumeration of the assumed population represented in the Mortality Table at a certain moment of time (e.g. midnight on a specified date).

As the basis of all calculations dependent on the mortality table, the assumption is made that the births occurring in any year are uniformly distributed over that year. If, therefore, a very large number (l_0) of births occur in a year, the number occurring in a moment of time (dt) will be $l_0 dt$.

Similarly, if l_0 births have occurred every year over a large number of years, and the number and distribution of the deaths have been the same throughout that period, there will at any moment of time be $l_{x+t}dt$ persons living of precise age $x+t$, these being the survivors of the $l_0 dt$ births which occurred exactly $x+t$ years before.

A census of the assumed population taken at a moment of time will disclose a number of persons of every fractional age, the number living between ages x and $x+1$ being $\int_0^1 l_{x+t}dt$, which, as has been stated above, is represented by L_x. Thus

$$L_x = \int_0^1 l_{x+t}dt \qquad \text{(1)}.$$

4. Deaths. d_x represents the number, out of l_x persons attaining precise age x, who die before reaching age $x+1$. Thus

$$d_x = l_x - l_{x+1} \qquad \text{(2)}.$$

5. Rate of Mortality. q_x represents the probability that a person of exact age x will die within one year following the attainment of that age. This is called the *Rate of Mortality*.

Since, out of l_x persons who attain precise age x, d_x die before reaching age $x+1$, it follows that

$$q_x = \frac{d_x}{l_x} \qquad \text{(3)}.$$

6. From the relationship $L_x = \int_0^1 l_{x+t}dt$, if l_x followed a definite mathematical law, for example, if l_x were known to be a function of the nth degree, L_x could be evaluated exactly.

As a rule l_x does not follow directly any law of this nature, but if the assumption be made that the deaths in the year of age x to $x+1$ are equally distributed over that year of age, it will be seen that

$$\left.\begin{aligned} L_x &= \int_0^1 l_{x+t}\,dt \\ &= \int_0^1 (l_x - t d_x)\,dt \\ &= l_x - \tfrac{1}{2} d_x \\ &= l_{x+\frac{1}{2}} \\ &= \tfrac{1}{2}(l_x + l_{x+1}) \end{aligned}\right\} \quad \ldots\ldots\ldots\ldots (4).$$

This relationship is of great importance. As will be seen later, the employment of the infinitesimal calculus materially facilitates the solving of problems involving life contingencies, but owing to l_x not following any definite mathematical law, it is generally necessary, for the purpose of actual evaluation, to fall back on the assumption that $L_x = l_{x+\frac{1}{2}} = \frac{1}{2}(l_x + l_{x+1})$.

7. From the definition of a Mortality Table given in the first paragraph, it follows that the value of such a table depends on its ability to supply the necessary ratios representing such probabilities of life and death as may be required. The actual numbers in the l_x and d_x columns are only of importance in so far as they bear the correct proportion to each other and facilitate the calculation of probabilities of life and death and of the values of monetary functions dependent thereon.

If, therefore, we have the value of q_x for every age from 0 upwards, we can commence with any convenient radix, say 100,000 births ($=l_0$), and multiply this number by q_0, so obtaining $l_0 q_0 = d_0$ the number of deaths between ages 0 and 1.

Subtracting the value of d_0 from l_0, we obtain l_1, the number out of the 100,000 births who survive to age 1; and again multiplying l_1 by q_1, the value of d_1 is obtained.

Subtracting d_1 from l_1, the value of l_2 is obtained: and so on, until we reach an age ω, where $l_\omega = 0$, ω being used in this connection to represent the *limiting age* of the table; that is, the year of age on which the last survivor enters but does not complete.

The *radix* of a mortality table is the number of persons assumed to be alive at some age convenient for the purpose of constructing the l_x and other columns by means of the ratios derived from actual observations. It is generally most convenient that this age should be the youngest age in the table, though this is not essential. In the English Life Table No. 8 (see page 398) the radix is 1,000,000 births; in the $O^{[NM]}$ Table (see page 440) 100,000 living at age 20, the youngest age in the table; but in the case of the H^M Table (as printed on page 410) the radix is 100,000 at age 10, though the table was afterwards taken back to age 0.

8. In practice, when dealing with the mortality experience of the population of a country or district, the data available consist generally of

(*a*) Census returns giving the number of persons living at the time of the census in each year of age. In some instances this number may be available only for groups of ages.

(*b*) The number of deaths occurring in each year of age in each calendar year as shown by the death registers.

The returns of one or more censuses may be employed, the simplest case and the only one that need be considered here being that in which the returns of one census only are utilised to give the values of L'_x, and the death registers for a small and equal number of years on either side of the date of the census utilised to give a value of d'_x for each age, these symbols being accented to indicate that the numbers they represent are not the numbers finally appearing in the Mortality Table.

The death registers will give the number of deaths in the year of age x to $x+1$ occurring in a year, but neither the death registers nor the census returns will give directly the number of persons attaining precise age x amongst whom these deaths occurred.

It thus becomes necessary to utilise the ratio $\frac{d_x}{L_x}$ which is called the *Central Death Rate* and is represented by m_x.

Making the assumption referred to in paragraph 6, that the deaths in the year of age x to $x+1$ are uniformly spread over that year of age, we have

$$m_x = \frac{d_x}{L_x} \quad \dots\dots\dots\dots (5)$$

$$= \frac{d_x}{l_x - \frac{1}{2}d_x}$$

$$\left.\begin{aligned} &= \frac{2q_x}{2-q_x} \\ \text{or} \qquad q_x &= \frac{2m_x}{2+m_x} \end{aligned}\right\} \qquad \text{.........................(6).}$$

If, therefore, the values of m_x at each age be obtained from the data supplied by the census returns and the death registers, the value of q_x can be derived therefrom for each age; and commencing with any convenient number for l_0, the values of l_x and d_x for all ages can be obtained in the manner indicated in paragraph 7.

The table is thus constructed from actual observations of as recent a date as possible, and, for the purpose of employing it in connection with various actuarial problems, the assumption is made that the conditions disclosed will for practical purposes be sufficiently accurate as a guide to the future.

9. Probability of surviving one year. The probability that a person of exact age x will survive one year is represented by p_x.

Out of l_x persons of exact age x, l_{x+1} survive to age $x+1$: therefore

$$p_x = \frac{l_{x+1}}{l_x} \qquad \text{............................(7).}$$

Since a person aged x must either survive one year or die within that year, $p_x + q_x = 1$.

On the assumption that the deaths in the year of age x to $x+1$ are uniformly spread over that year,

$$\begin{aligned} p_x &= \frac{l_{x+\frac{1}{2}} - \frac{1}{2}d_x}{l_{x+\frac{1}{2}} + \frac{1}{2}d_x} \\ &= \frac{2-m_x}{2+m_x} \qquad \text{..........................(8).} \end{aligned}$$

It will therefore be seen that, given the value of m_x at each age, the value of p_x (instead of q_x) can be obtained. Commencing at age 0 with a radix of l_0 we can then take $l_0 \times p_0 = l_1$, $l_1 \times p_1 = l_2$ and so on, thus constructing a table of l_x. The values of d_x can then be ascertained by means of the relation $d_x = l_x - l_{x+1}$.

10. From the foregoing discussion it will be realised that in the construction of a Mortality Table it is necessary, having given the number of deaths in any year of age x to $x+1$, that some means be found of ascertaining, or estimating, the number of persons who reached age x amongst whom these deaths occurred: in other words, we must have both d_x and l_x (or d_x and L_x) derived from observations, in order to obtain the ratio $\frac{d_x}{l_x} = q_x$.

In the Mortality Table the l_x and d_x columns are so related that one can be found from the other, and this in the past led some investigators into the error of enumerating the deaths in a community in each year of age, during a period of one year or a number of years, and, by successive addition from the oldest to the youngest age, constructing therefrom a column intended to represent the number living at each age corresponding to the tabulated number of deaths.

The fallacy in this method can be seen by taking an extreme case and assuming that for some special reason, as for example the opening of a Home of Rest, there is such an influx of old lives into a district that there are at some particular period 100 persons of each age from 85 to 90, that at age 91 the number living is 10, and that the numbers at higher ages are approximately those which would be obtained by multiplying successively by p_{91}, p_{92}... etc. as shown by the English Life Table No. 8. It will be assumed that these are the numbers at exact ages and that the mortality experience in the district, including the recent immigrants, is during the following year in agreement with that shown by the English Life Table No. 8.

The following table shows the number living at each age at the commencement of the year, the number of deaths in a year and the result of constructing a table by enumeration of the deaths only without regard to the number of persons amongst whom these deaths occurred.

Age (1)	Actual number living (2)	Deaths (3)	Assumed l_x by adding actual deaths (4)	Resultant q_x col. (3) ÷ col. (4) (5)	Actual q_x English Life Table No. 8 (6)
85	100	20	151	·13245	·19911
86	100	21	131	·16031	·21196
87	100	23	110	·20909	·22626
88	100	24	87	·27586	·24208
89	100	26	63	·41270	·25840
90	100	27	37	·72973	·27395
91 & upwards	28	10	—	—	—

It is evident from this extreme case that migration alone must render a table based solely on the enumeration of deaths valueless.

Moreover, even if there were no migration, the number of births is not the same in successive years. Suppose, for example, the number of births during the last year prior to the extraction of the particulars of deaths was double the number fifty years previously. It is evident that the number of deaths at the infantile ages cannot be taken in conjunction with the numbers at ages over 50, which occur amongst the survivors from the births of over 50 years ago.

The construction of a table from death registers alone could, in fact, only be correct provided the population had been stationary over a period at least equal to the age of the oldest survivor: that is, provided that over that period the number and distribution of the deaths had been the same each year, the number of deaths each year being equal to the number of births, and that the population had not been disturbed by migration. It is clear that no community in existence satisfies these conditions.

11. In the practical compilation of a mortality table it is often found that the rates of mortality disclosed by the observations are very irregular from age to age and that errors frequently occur in statements of ages. It consequently becomes necessary to review the data very carefully and to adopt a system of graduation of the results in order to secure a more uniform progression of the rates of mortality, while at the same time retaining any outstanding features disclosed by the statistics. This graduation may be described as the endeavour to arrive at the true law of mortality underlying the rough results disclosed by the data.

It is beyond the scope of this work to discuss the various methods of graduation which can be employed, and reference is only made to it in order that the student shall not form the opinion that this chapter deals with anything more than the bare principles of the compilation of a mortality table from census returns and death registers.

12. The English Life Table No. 8—Males—(see p. 398) was constructed from data supplied by census returns and death registers in England and Wales. The enumeration of the population as disclosed by the census of 1911 (2nd April 1911) was employed in conjunction with the particulars of deaths obtained from the death registers for the years 1910 to 1912 inclusive.

The central point of the three years 1910, 1911 and 1912 is 1st July 1911, and an adjustment was made to determine the corresponding population at that date, this adjustment being based on the rate of increase or decrease of the population in quinquennial age groups as disclosed by a comparison of the census of 1911 with that of 1901.

By taking, in quinquennial age groups, the ratio of the number of deaths per annum to the population, the value of m_x was obtained for the central age of each group, and thence the rate of mortality by means of the formula $q_x = \frac{2m_x}{2+m_x}$. The intervening values of q_x were then obtained by interpolation.

The enumeration of the number living during the first six years of life was found to be unreliable and for these ages special methods had to be employed.

Full details of the methods adopted are given in the "Supplement to the Seventy-Fifth Annual Report of the Registrar-General of Births, Deaths and Marriages in England and Wales—Part I Life Tables."

13. Having explained the functions, the values of which are given in the Mortality Table, we can now proceed to the calculation of various probabilities of survival or death of a single life. Numerical examples are given on page 17.

(i) ${}_np_x$ represents the probability that a person of exact age x will survive n years. Since out of l_x persons of exact age x, l_{x+n} survive to age $x+n$; we have

$$ {}_np_x = \frac{l_{x+n}}{l_x} \quad \text{.........................(9).}$$

It will also be seen that

$$ {}_np_x = \frac{l_{x+1}}{l_x} \times \frac{l_{x+2}}{l_{x+1}} \times \frac{l_{x+3}}{l_{x+2}} \times \ldots \times \frac{l_{x+n}}{l_{x+n-1}} $$
$$ = p_x \times p_{x+1} \times p_{x+2} \times \ldots \times p_{x+n-1}. $$

Again,
$$ {}_{n+t}p_x = \frac{l_{x+n+t}}{l_x} $$
$$ = \frac{l_{x+n}}{l_x} \times \frac{l_{x+n+t}}{l_{x+n}} $$
$$ = {}_np_x \times {}_tp_{x+n}. $$

(ii) $_{n|}q_x$ represents the probability that a person of exact age x will die in the $(n+1)$th year from the present time. Out of l_x persons aged x, d_{x+n} die between ages $x+n$ and $x+n+1$: therefore

$$_{n|}q_x = \frac{d_{x+n}}{l_x} \quad \text{......................(10).}$$

Or we may argue as follows: the probability that a person now aged x will survive n years is $_np_x$; and the probability that, having reached that age, he will die within one year is q_{x+n}. The probability that a person aged x will die in the $(n+1)$th year is, therefore,

$$_np_x \times q_{x+n} = \frac{l_{x+n}}{l_x} \cdot \frac{d_{x+n}}{l_{x+n}} = \frac{d_{x+n}}{l_x}$$

as before.

Again, the probability in question is evidently the difference between the probability that a person aged x will survive n years and the probability that he will survive $n+1$ years.

That is,
$$_{n|}q_x = {_np_x} - {_{n+1}p_x}$$
$$= \frac{l_{x+n} - l_{x+n+1}}{l_x} = \frac{d_{x+n}}{l_x}.$$

(iii) The probability that a person aged x will die *within* n years from the present time is represented by the symbol $_{|n}Q_x$. Of l_x persons aged x, l_{x+n} survive to age $x+n$ and the number who die before reaching that age is $l_x - l_{x+n}$. It follows, therefore, that

$$_{|n}Q_x = \frac{l_x - l_{x+n}}{l_x}$$
$$= 1 - {_np_x} \quad \text{.........................(11),}$$

the latter form being obviously correct since a person must either survive n years or die within that period.

It is evident also that

$$_{|n}Q_x = \sum_{t=0}^{t=n-1} {_{t|}q_x}$$
$$= \frac{1}{l_x} \sum_{t=0}^{t=n-1} d_{x+t}$$
$$= \frac{l_x - l_{x+n}}{l_x}$$

as before.

(iv) ${}_{n|m}Q_x$ represents the probability that a person aged x will die during a period of m years, which period commences to run on the expiration of n years from the present time.

Out of l_x persons now aged x, l_{x+n} survive to age $x+n$ and of these $l_{x+n} - l_{x+n+m}$ die during the following m years; the probability required is, therefore,

$$\left.\begin{aligned} {}_{n|m}Q_x &= \frac{l_{x+n} - l_{x+n+m}}{l_x} \\ &= {}_np_x - {}_{n+m}p_x \end{aligned}\right\} \quad \ldots\ldots\ldots\ldots\ldots(12).$$

This probability also can be obtained from the product of two separate probabilities; since, ${}_np_x$ being the probability that a person now aged x will survive n years, and ${}_{|m}Q_{x+n}$ the probability that a person who has reached age $x+n$ will die within m years, it follows that

$${}_{n|m}Q_x = {}_np_x \times {}_{|m}Q_{x+n} = \frac{l_{x+n}}{l_x} \cdot \frac{l_{x+n} - l_{x+n+m}}{l_{x+n}} = \frac{l_{x+n} - l_{x+n+m}}{l_x}$$

as before.

Again

$$\begin{aligned} {}_{n|m}Q_x &= \sum_{t=n}^{t=n+m-1} {}_{t|}q_x \\ &= \frac{1}{l_x} \sum_{t=n}^{t=n+m-1} d_{x+t} \\ &= \frac{l_{x+n} - l_{x+n+m}}{l_x}. \end{aligned}$$

14. The notation employed in connection with these probabilities should be carefully considered.

When the term to which the probability relates is one year this is not specifically indicated in the symbol. Thus we write ${}_np_x$ for all values of n other than unity (whether integral or fractional), but simply p_x when we wish to denote the probability of surviving one year.

Similarly, in the case of ${}_{n|}q_x$, since the probability refers to death occurring in one year (i.e. the $(n+1)$th), the figure "1" is omitted from the symbol; but here the bar after the "n" indicates that the period of one year is deferred n years.

The use of the symbol q is limited to "one-year" probabilities, the symbol Q being employed to denote probabilities of death occurring in periods other than one year.

It is convenient to represent the phrase "a person aged x" by

(x), and this will be adopted throughout the remainder of this volume.

15. The Force of Mortality. Before proceeding further it is necessary that the function known as the Force of Mortality, a most important function in connection with the subject of Life Contingencies, shall be considered.

Out of l_x persons aged x, $l_{x+\frac{1}{m}}$ survive to age $x+\frac{1}{m}$, the number dying in the first $\frac{1}{m}$th part of a year following age x being $l_x - l_{x+\frac{1}{m}}$, and the probability of a person aged x dying in that $\frac{1}{m}$th part of a year being $\frac{l_x - l_{x+\frac{1}{m}}}{l_x}$.

If this probability be multiplied by m, the result will be a nominal annual rate of mortality based on the assumption that during each $\frac{1}{m}$th part of the year the probability of death was exactly the same. This nominal annual rate is

$$\frac{l_x - l_{x+\frac{1}{m}}}{l_x} \times m = \frac{l_x - l_{x+\frac{1}{m}}}{\frac{1}{m}\, l_x}.$$

If now m be indefinitely increased so that $\frac{1}{m}$ approaches the limit "0," the limiting value of this last expression will be $-\frac{1}{l_x}\cdot\frac{dl_x}{dx}$.

This limiting value is called the *Force of Mortality*, and is represented by μ_x. Thus

$$\left.\begin{aligned} \mu_x &= -\frac{1}{l_x}\cdot\frac{dl_x}{dx} \\ &= -\frac{d \log_e l_x}{dx} \end{aligned}\right\} \qquad \text{..................(13).}$$

The force of mortality, μ_x, is thus the nominal annual rate of mortality based on the assumption that the intensity of mortality remained the same at every moment during the year of age x to $x+1$ as it was during the moment following the attainment of age x.

A year is taken as the most convenient unit of time for measuring this force: the function employed in actual calculations is the probability of death occurring at each successive moment of time.

16. Since $\mu_x = -\frac{1}{l_x} \cdot \frac{dl_x}{dx}$, it follows that

$-dl_x = l_x \mu_x dx$ represents the number of deaths occurring at the moment of attaining age x (out of l_x persons alive at that age);

$-\frac{dl_x}{l_x} = \mu_x dx$ represents the probability that a person of exact age x will die *at that moment.*

Similarly, $l_{x+t}\mu_{x+t}dt$ represents the number of deaths occurring at moment of age $x+t$, whence, d_x being the number of deaths occurring between ages x and $x+1$, it follows that

$$d_x = \int_0^1 l_{x+t}\mu_{x+t}dt \qquad (14),$$

and

$$\left. \begin{aligned} q_x &= \frac{1}{l_x}\int_0^1 l_{x+t}\mu_{x+t}dt \\ &= \int_0^1 {}_tp_x \mu_{x+t}dt \end{aligned} \right\} \qquad (15).$$

Equations (14) and (15) can easily be seen to be correct algebraically by writing $l_{x+t}\mu_{x+t}dt = -dl_{x+t}$.

Equation (14) was arrived at in the first place by general reasoning, and equation (15) can be obtained in the same way.

The probability that a person aged x will survive to time t being ${}_tp_x$, and the probability that, having reached age $x+t$, he will die at that moment of age being $\mu_{x+t}dt$, it follows that the probability that (x) will die at moment of age $x+t$ is ${}_tp_x\mu_{x+t}dt$. Integrating this expression within the limits $t=0$ and $t=1$, the result is the probability that (x) will die within one year. That is,

$$q_x = \int_0^1 {}_tp_x \mu_{x+t}dt$$

as before.

If the function ${}_tp_x\mu_{x+t}dt$ be integrated between the limits 0 and ∞, the result is the total probability that (x) will die, which is a certainty. Thus

$$Q_x = \int_0^\infty {}_tp_x \mu_{x+t}dt = 1.$$

Beyond the "limiting age" there are no survivors (according to the table) and the value of ${}_tp_x$ where $x+t \geqq \omega$ is accordingly zero.

It is, therefore, immaterial whether the integral for the value of Q_x be written $\int_0^\infty {}_tp_x\mu_{x+t}dt$ or $\int_0^{\omega-x} {}_tp_x\mu_{x+t}dt$.

If the limits be taken as $t=n$ to $t=n+1$ the result is

$$\begin{aligned} {}_{n|}q_x &= \int_n^{n+1} {}_tp_x\mu_{x+t}dt \\ &= -\frac{1}{l_x}\int_n^{n+1}\frac{dl_{x+t}}{dt}dt \\ &= \frac{l_{x+n}-l_{x+n+1}}{l_x} \\ &= \frac{d_{x+n}}{l_x} \end{aligned}$$

as in equation (10), and if the integration be from $t=n$ to $t=n+m$,

$$\begin{aligned} {}_{n|m}Q_x &= \int_n^{n+m} {}_tp_x\mu_{x+t}dt \\ &= \frac{l_{x+n}-l_{x+n+m}}{l_x} \end{aligned}$$

as in equation (12).

17. Various formulae can be obtained for the approximate value of μ_x in terms of the functions l_x and d_x.

Employing the approximate form of the differential coefficient

$$\frac{df(x)}{dx} = \tfrac{1}{2}\{f(x+1)-f(x-1)\},$$

we have

$$\begin{aligned} \mu_x &= -\frac{1}{l_x}\cdot\frac{dl_x}{dx} \\ &= \frac{l_{x-1}-l_{x+1}}{2l_x} \quad\text{..........(16)} \\ &= \frac{d_{x-1}+d_x}{2l_x} \quad\text{..........(17)}, \end{aligned}$$

which formulae assume l_x to be a function of the second degree.

Assuming l_x to be a function of the fourth degree, the value of μ_x can be expressed as follows:

Let $$l_x = a + bx + cx^2 + dx^3 + ex^4,$$

where a, b, c, d and e are constants.

Then $$\frac{dl_x}{dx} = b + 2cx + 3dx^2 + 4ex^3,$$

and when $x=0$, $\frac{dl_0}{dx}=b.$

$$
\begin{aligned}
\text{Also}\qquad l_{-1}&=a-\ \ b+\ c-\ \ d+\ \ e,\\
l_{+1}&=a+\ \ b+\ c+\ \ d+\ \ e,\\
\therefore\ l_{-1}-l_{+1}&=\ -\ 2b\qquad -\ 2d \qquad\ldots\ldots\ldots\ldots(\alpha).\\
l_{-2}&=a-\ 2b+4c-\ 8d+16e,\\
l_{+2}&=a+\ 2b+4c+\ 8d+16e,\\
\therefore\ l_{-2}-l_{+2}&=\ -\ 4b\qquad -16d \qquad\ldots\ldots\ldots\ldots(\beta).
\end{aligned}
$$

Multiplying (α) by 8,

$$8(l_{-1}-l_{+1})=\ -16b\qquad -16d \qquad\ldots\ldots\ldots\ldots(\gamma)$$

and subtracting (β) from (γ)

$$8(l_{-1}-l_{+1})-(l_{-2}-l_{+2})=\ -12b.$$

$$
\begin{aligned}
\text{Whence}\qquad \mu_0&=-\frac{1}{l_0}\cdot\frac{dl_0}{dx}\\
&=-\frac{1}{l_0}\cdot b\\
&=\frac{8(l_{-1}-l_{+1})-(l_{-2}-l_{+2})}{12l_0}\\
&=\frac{7(d_{-1}+d_0)-(d_{-2}+d_{+1})}{12l_0}.
\end{aligned}
$$

Therefore, also,

$$
\begin{aligned}
\mu_x&=\frac{8(l_{x-1}-l_{x+1})-(l_{x-2}-l_{x+2})}{12l_x}\ \ldots\ldots\ldots\ldots\ldots(18)\\
&=\frac{7(d_{x-1}+d_x)-(d_{x-2}+d_{x+1})}{12l_x}\ \ \ldots\ldots\ldots\ldots(19).
\end{aligned}
$$

Other approximate expressions can be obtained from the relation

$$\mu_x=-\frac{1}{l_x}\cdot\frac{dl_x}{dx}\ \ =-\frac{1}{l_x}(\Delta l_x-\tfrac{1}{2}\Delta^2 l_x+\tfrac{1}{3}\Delta^3 l_x-\ldots),$$

or from

$$
\begin{aligned}
\mu_x&=-\frac{d\log_e l_x}{dx}=-(\Delta\log_e l_x-\tfrac{1}{2}\Delta^2\log_e l_x+\tfrac{1}{3}\Delta^3\log_e l_x-\ldots)\\
&=\operatorname{colog}_e p_x-\tfrac{1}{2}\Delta\operatorname{colog}_e p_x+\tfrac{1}{3}\Delta^2\operatorname{colog}_e p_x-\ldots,
\end{aligned}
$$

stopping, in either case, at any selected order of differences.

18. Another form of the relationship between $\operatorname{colog}_e p_x$ and the force of mortality is the following:

$$\mu_x = -\frac{d \log_e l_x}{dx},$$

$$\therefore \quad \log_e l_x = -\int \mu_x dx + (\text{constant}),$$

$$\left.\begin{aligned} \operatorname{colog}_e p_x &= \log_e l_x - \log_e l_{x+1} \\ &= \int_0^1 \mu_{x+t} dt \\ &= \mu_{x+\frac{1}{2}} \text{ approx.} \end{aligned}\right\} \quad \ldots\ldots\ldots\ldots\ldots(20).$$

If, therefore, it be assumed that $\mu_{x+\frac{1}{2}} = \frac{1}{2}(\mu_x + \mu_{x+1})$, it is a simple matter to find any required value of p_x or q_x from a table of values of μ_x.

For example, in the H^M Table (Makeham Graduation)

$$\mu_{50} = {\cdot}01542 \text{ and } \mu_{51} = {\cdot}01631.$$

Taking $\mu_{50\frac{1}{2}} = \frac{1}{2}(\mu_{50} + \mu_{51}) = {\cdot}01587,$

we have $\mu_{50\frac{1}{2}} = \operatorname{colog}_e p_{50} = {\cdot}01587,$

$\therefore$ to the base "10," $\operatorname{colog} p_{50} = {\cdot}01587 \times {\cdot}4343$

$$= {\cdot}00688,$$

$$\therefore \quad \log p_{50} = \bar{1}{\cdot}99312$$

$$p_{50} = {\cdot}98428$$

$$q_{50} = {\cdot}01572$$

which is the value in the table.

19. A point that may present some difficulty at first sight is that the force of mortality at certain ages is, in some tables (the $O^{[NM]}$ Ultimate Table on pages 448–449 is an example), shown as unity or greater than unity and yet persons survive to older ages. The difficulty arises from the fact that μ_x is a purely nominal annual measure and may (and does) exceed unity while the effective rate of mortality is still less than unity.

Using again the approximation $\mu_{x+\frac{1}{2}} = \operatorname{colog}_e p_x$, if we write $\mu_{x+\frac{1}{2}} = 1$, we shall find that $q_x = {\cdot}63212$ only. If $q_x = 1$, any life surviving at age x is, on the basis of the mortality table, certain to die within the following year.

In the last year of age shown in the mortality table, when $q_x = 1$, all the survivors at the beginning of the year of age die in a period of less than one year, and the nominal annual rate of mortality based on that period must be greater than unity. Similarly, there must be a time in that year when the force of mortality exceeds unity.

Again, at age 0, if the number dying each day continued the same as during the first day succeeding birth, all the children born would have died long before a year had elapsed. If, therefore, we take as an approximation to the force of mortality at age 0,

$$\mu_0 = \frac{l_0 - l_{\frac{1}{365}}}{l_0} \times 365,$$

it is clear that this force (in this case, the nominal annual rate of mortality based on the assumption that the risk of dying on each day from age 0 to age 1 remained the same) will exceed unity.

20. Considering the differential coefficient of L_x we have

$$\begin{aligned}\frac{dL_x}{dx} &= \frac{d}{dx}\int_0^1 l_{x+t}\,dt \\ &= \int_0^1 \left(\frac{d}{dx}\,l_{x+t}\right) dt \\ &= l_{x+1} - l_x \\ &= -d_x \quad \text{.............................(21)},\end{aligned}$$

whence it follows that

$$\begin{aligned}m_x &= \frac{d_x}{L_x} \\ &= -\frac{1}{L_x}\cdot\frac{dL_x}{dx} \quad \text{.......................(22)}.\end{aligned}$$

If L_x be taken as equal to $l_{x+\frac{1}{2}}$, we have

$$\begin{aligned}m_x &= -\frac{1}{l_{x+\frac{1}{2}}}\cdot\frac{dl_{x+\frac{1}{2}}}{dx} \\ &= \mu_{x+\frac{1}{2}} \quad \text{.............................(23)}.\end{aligned}$$

We thus arrive at the conclusion that approximately

$$\text{colog}_e\, p_x = m_x = \mu_{x+\frac{1}{2}}.$$

It will be observed that, in accordance with formula (20), we have also

$$\text{colog}_e\, {}_np_x = \int_0^n \mu_{x+t}\,dt,$$

$$\therefore\quad {}_np_x = e^{-\int_0^n \mu_{x+t}\,dt}$$

21. It is interesting to compare the results of differentiating the function ${}_tp_x$ with regard to each of the variables x and t:

$$\frac{d\,{}_tp_x}{dx} = \frac{d}{dx}\frac{l_{x+t}}{l_x}$$

$$= \frac{l_x \dfrac{dl_{x+t}}{dx} - l_{x+t}\dfrac{dl_x}{dx}}{(l_x)^2}$$

$$= {}_tp_x(\mu_x - \mu_{x+t}) \qquad\qquad (24),$$

and

$$\frac{d\,{}_tp_x}{dt} = \frac{1}{l_x}\cdot\frac{dl_{x+t}}{dt}$$

$$= -\,{}_tp_x\mu_{x+t} \qquad\qquad (25).$$

Formulae (24) and (25) (particularly the former) are of great practical value in the later work.

EXAMPLES

The following are examples of the application of Mortality Tables.

Ex. 1. On the basis of the English Life Table No. 8 find the probability that a man aged 30 will

(*a*) survive to age 40;

(*b*) die before reaching age 50;

(*c*) die in his 50th year (i.e. between ages 49 and 50);

(*d*) die between ages 40 and 50.

(*a*) $${}_{10}p_{30} = \frac{l_{40}}{l_{30}} = \frac{716727}{762227} = \cdot 94031;$$

(*b*) $${}_{\overline{20}|}Q_{30} = 1 - {}_{20}p_{30} = 1 - \frac{643333}{762227} = \cdot 15598;$$

(*c*) $${}_{19|}q_{30} = \frac{d_{49}}{l_{30}} = \frac{9074}{762227} = \cdot 01190;$$

(*d*) $${}_{10|10}Q_{30} = \frac{l_{40} - l_{50}}{l_{30}} = \frac{716727 - 643333}{762227} = \cdot 09629.$$

Ex. 2. Find the value of μ_{40} by means of the values given in the l_x column of the English Life Table No. 8.—Males.

$$\mu_{40} = \frac{l_{39} - l_{41}}{2l_{40}}$$

$$= \frac{722284 - 710914}{2(716727)}$$

$$= \cdot 00793,$$

or
$$\mu_{40} = \frac{8(l_{39} - l_{41}) - (l_{38} - l_{42})}{12l_{40}}$$

$$= \frac{8(722284 - 710914) - (727603 - 704817)}{12(716727)}$$

$$= \cdot 00793.$$

CHAPTER II

MORTALITY TABLES CONSTRUCTED FROM LIFE ASSURANCE STATISTICS. SELECT LIFE TABLES

1. In the first chapter the mortality table considered was one constructed from data supplied by census returns and death registers of the general population of a Country or District, but for purposes of Life Assurance, as a basis for the calculation of premiums, the valuation of life assurance contracts, and other kindred purposes, mortality tables are constructed from the experience of assured lives.

Such tables can be constructed by a process similar to that employed in the first chapter, but in order to bring out clearly the special features of tables based on assurance data different methods will now be described.

2. With the information available in a Life Office, by assuming an exact age (whether integral or fractional) for each life at entry into the experience (such as, for example, that a person's nearest integral age at the date he effects a policy of life assurance is his exact age at that date), the rate of mortality, q_x, can be obtained directly from the data without the employment of the function m_x.

3. The experience on which the table is based should be such as is most likely to represent the experience of the future, and should, therefore, be limited to a recent period consisting of a comparatively small number of years.

The table can be constructed from the records of one or of several Life Offices, and can be based on the experience of one or of several classes of Life Assurance. In order to simplify the discussion of the principles on which such a table could be compiled, the following conditions will be assumed:

(i) That the records of a single Life Office only are utilised.

(ii) That the experience is limited to Whole-Life Assurances, that is, assurances under which the sums assured are payable at death only.

(iii) That the observations are limited to a period of 20 years, which period will be referred to as the "period of observations."

(iv) That the nearest integral age of the life assured at the time the contract of assurance is entered into is assumed to be the exact age at that date.

(v) That there are no terminations of assurances otherwise than by death: that is, that every person entering into the experience is under observation until the end of the period of observations or until death if occurring during that period.

(vi) That the youngest age for which the experience is to be extracted is age 20.

4. The books of the Office will supply the number of assurances effected at each (assumed) exact age and will also show the number of deaths occurring in any year of assurance—that is, in any year dating from the date of the assurance contract—and the number of persons who survive each such year. The age at entry being the assumed exact age the assumed life years will coincide with the "Assurance" or "Policy" years.

5. In compiling the table the number living at age x employed in the calculation of q_x is known as the number "exposed to risk" and is represented by E_x. The number of deaths between ages x and $x+1$ disclosed by the observations is represented by θ_x.

6. Since the object in view is the ascertainment of the value q_x —the probability that a person aged x will die within a year following the attainment of that age—only those lives which reached age x during the period of observations with the chance of surviving a full year during that period will be included in the experience. In other words, E_x will be the number of persons who reached age x during, but not later than twelve months before the expiration of, the period of observations, and θ_x must be the number of deaths occurring amongst these E_x persons within twelve months after attainment of age x. Then

$$q_x = \frac{\theta_x}{E_x}.$$

7. This method will be employed separately for each age from 20 upwards. Assuming q_{20} to have been obtained, E_{21} will be the

number of persons who attained age 21 at any time during, but not later than twelve months before the end of, the period of observations, and θ_{21} will be the number of deaths occurring between ages 21 and 22 amongst these E_{21} persons. Then

$$q_{21} = \frac{\theta_{21}}{E_{21}}.$$

8. It will be observed that E_{21} is not the number of survivors at the end of a year of the E_{20} persons aged 20 dealt with in the calculation of q_{20}. Persons who attained age 21 in the first year of the period of observations and those who effected policies at age 21 during that period are included in the group E_{21} but are not included in E_{20}: and, on the other hand, those who were included in E_{20} but who attained age 21 during the last year of the period of observations are excluded from the number exposed to risk at age 21.

Similarly, in dealing with age 22, E_{22} will not represent the number of survivors from the E_{20} and E_{21} persons observed at ages 20 and 21.

At this stage we are only concerned with the calculation of the values of q_x, and so long as the essential condition that θ_x and E_x bear the proper relation to each other is satisfied, it is not necessary that E_x, E_{x+1}, etc., should be related in any way, though it is evident that the great majority of the persons under observation will be included in two or more of these groups.

9. Having in this manner ascertained the value of q_x for each age from 20 onwards, any convenient radix for l_{20} (100,000 say) can be assumed, and by means of the values of q_x the entire mortality table can be constructed in the manner indicated in Chap. I 7.

10. Tables constructed in this manner, in which all the lives of a given attained age are grouped together for the purpose of ascertaining their Mortality experience, are known as *Aggregate Tables*.

11. Select Life Tables. In practice, lives assured under Whole-Life policies are as a rule medically examined at the time of proposing for assurance, and are thus selected or "select" lives from that point of view. This selection results in the exclusion of unhealthy lives and in the selection of a body of lives which, for the first few years after entry, experience, as a whole, lighter mortality than would be experienced by a more general body of lives.

Tables of mortality known as *Select Life Tables* are accordingly constructed to show the effect of this selection*.

12. Select Tables show the mortality experienced in each year from entry (i.e. from the date of assurance) amongst persons of a particular age at entry, the age at entry being distinguished by being enclosed in square brackets: thus $[x]$. The number of years elapsed since entry is denoted by an addition to the suffix not enclosed in brackets: thus $[x]+t$.

13. Bearing in mind the conditions laid down in paragraph 6, in the compilation of the mortality table based on the experience of Select Lives,

$E_{[x]}$ represents the number of persons who entered at age x as select lives, at such time that the whole of the first year of assurance must fall within the period of observations,

$E_{[x]+1}$ represents the number of persons who entered at age x, and who completed their first year of assurance at such time that the whole of the second year of assurance must fall within the period of observations,

and generally,

$E_{[x]+t}$ represents the number of persons who entered at age x, and who completed their tth year of assurance at such time that the whole of the $(t+1)$th year must fall within the period of observations.

Similarly, the numbers of deaths occurring in the first, second ...$(t+1)$th years after entry, amongst the $E_{[x]}$, $E_{[x]+1} \dots E_{[x]+t}$ exposed to risk in the first, second ...$(t+1)$th years, are represented by $\theta_{[x]}$, $\theta_{[x]+1} \dots \theta_{[x]+t}$ respectively, and the corresponding rates of mortality by $q_{[x]}$, $q_{[x]+1} \dots q_{[x]+t}$ respectively. Then

$$q_{[x]+t} = \frac{\theta_{[x]+t}}{E_{[x]+t}}.$$

14. The records of the Office will give the number of persons who effected whole-life assurances at age x and the number of those who died in the first, second ... years of assurance.

* "Selection" may arise from causes other than medical examination, and the methods employed in paragraphs 13 to 22 can be applied to any body of data in which the experience of each individual can be traced from "entry" to "exit."

If the observations be limited as before to a period of 20 years, the number of lives who entered at age x during, but not later than twelve months before the end of, that period will give $E_{[x]}$; and the number of these who died in the first year of assurance, $\theta_{[x]}$. Then

$$q_{[x]} = \frac{\theta_{[x]}}{E_{[x]}}.$$

15. The number of persons who entered at age x, whether during the period of observations or in the year before, but who completed one year of assurance during, but not later than twelve months before the end of, that period, will give $E_{[x]+1}$; and the number of these who died in the second year of assurance, $\theta_{[x]+1}$. Then

$$q_{[x]+1} = \frac{\theta_{[x]+1}}{E_{[x]+1}}.$$

Here, also, $E_{[x]+1}$ does not represent the number of survivors out of the $E_{[x]}$ employed to obtain $q_{[x]}$.

As in the case of Aggregate Tables, however, this is of no importance, since all we are concerned with at the moment is to obtain the proper values of $q_{[x]}$, $q_{[x]+1}$ ... etc., and this will be effected if we ensure that the numerator of the fraction (θ) is in each case the number of deaths in one year amongst the lives included in the denominator (E), and that each life included in the denominator had, at the commencement of the year of assurance under consideration, a chance of completing that year before the termination of the period of observations.

16. To obtain $q_{[x]+2}$, $E_{[x]+2}$ will include all those who effected assurances at age x whether during or before the period of observations, and who completed the second year of assurance during, but not less than twelve months before the end of, that period; and $\theta_{[x]+2}$, the number of these $E_{[x]+2}$ persons who died in the third year of assurance; and so on.

17. It is found that the effect of selection, so far as improving the mortality experience of a body of selected lives is concerned, wears off after a small number of years, and after the end of this period the lives may be considered to be subject to a rate of mortality dependent only on the age attained.

Taking the period during which selection has some effect on the mortality experience (which will be referred to as the "Select

Period") as n years, the rate of mortality will be found in the manner indicated in paragraphs 13 to 16 for each of the first n years in respect of each age at entry; that is, $q_{[x]}$, $q_{[x]+1}$ ... $q_{[x]+n-1}$.

18. The lives which remain in insurance n years or more will then be grouped together according to attained ages, regardless of their ages at entry or the duration of their assurances, and, on the basis of their experience after n years of assurance, a mortality table will be constructed in the manner explained in paragraphs 6 to 10 in connection with Aggregate Tables.

This table excluding the experience of the "Select Period" is called the *Ultimate Table.*

If the "Select Period" be taken as five years, the youngest age at entry being 20, the first age in the Ultimate Table will be 25.

19. For the Ultimate Table, therefore, following the method laid down in paragraphs 6 to 10, the number who attained each integral age during, but not later than twelve months before the end of, the period of observations will give E_{25}, E_{26} ... etc., the number of deaths amongst these lives in each year of age will give θ_{25}, θ_{26} ..., and the values of q_{25}, q_{26} ... will then be obtained from the equations

$$q_{25}=\frac{\theta_{25}}{E_{25}},\quad q_{26}=\frac{\theta_{26}}{E_{26}}\ \ldots \text{etc.}$$

It will be seen that the E_{25} to be utilised in connection with the calculation of q_{25} will consist of survivors of entrants at ages not exceeding 20; E_{26} will consist of survivors of entrants at ages not exceeding 21; E_{27} of entrants at ages up to 22; and so on. As in the other instances E_{27}, for example, does not consist of the survivors of the E_{25} and E_{26} persons exposed to risk at ages 25 and 26.

Since the values in the Ultimate Table depend only on the age attained without reference to the age of selection, square brackets do not appear in the suffixes.

20. Having obtained all the rates of mortality required for the construction of the table, the youngest age at entry being 20, a convenient radix for $l_{[20]}$ (100,000 say) is assumed, and the entire mortality table for entrants at this age is constructed by means of the values of $q_{[20]}$, $q_{[20]+1}$ ... $q_{[20]+4}$ derived from "Select" data, and of q_{25}, q_{26} ... etc. derived from the "Ultimate" data.

21. Proceeding to age at entry 21, it is necessary that the number of survivors at the end of five years from the assumed number of entrants at this age shall be l_{26} as shown by the "Ultimate" Table.

This is effected by working backwards from l_{26} with the aid of the values of $p_{[21]+4}$, $p_{[21]+3}$ ... $p_{[21]}$. Thus

$$l_{[21]+4} = \frac{l_{26}}{p_{[21]+4}}; \quad l_{[21]+3} = \frac{l_{[21]+4}}{p_{[21]+3}}; \quad \ldots \; l_{[21]} = \frac{l_{[21]+1}}{p_{[21]}}.$$

In this way a number is obtained for $l_{[21]}$ such that, after the end of five years of assurance, the figures in the "Ultimate" Table can be utilised for all purposes.

A similar plan is then followed for age 22 at entry, working backwards from l_{27}, and so on for other ages.

The advantages of such an arrangement will become apparent in the chapters dealing with monetary values based on Select Tables.

22. The entire "l" column being thus constructed, the "d" column is obtained by differencing the values of "l." Thus

$$d_{[x]} = l_{[x]} - l_{[x]+1},$$
$$d_{[x]+1} = l_{[x]+1} - l_{[x]+2},$$
$$\ldots\ldots\ldots\ldots\ldots\ldots$$

When the "Select Period" is taken as five years,

$$d_{[x]+4} = l_{[x]+4} - l_{x+5},$$

and in the Ultimate Table

$$d_{x+n} = l_{x+n} - l_{x+n+1}.$$

The mistake is sometimes made of taking $d_{[x]}$ as equal to the difference between $l_{[x]}$ and $l_{[x+1]}$, but as $l_{[x+1]}$ bears no direct relation to $l_{[x]}$ this is clearly incorrect.

The final arrangement of the columns will be seen by reference to the tables printed on pages 440 and 442.

23. It is beyond the scope of this chapter to discuss the various methods which can be employed in the extraction and compilation of the mortality experience of assured lives; all that has been attempted is to take the simplest possible method and on this basis to give a clear idea of the qualities of such tables, particularly of "Select" Tables.

In order, however, to avoid confusion in later work, it may be remarked that the manner in which the entry age is dealt with and the assumptions arising therefrom must vary according to the nature of the data available, and actuaries may hold different opinions as to the most suitable method of handling the data. Moreover, in practice, withdrawals occur during the period of observations through the lapse or surrender of policies, and a certain number of lapsed policies are revived. All these cases require special treatment which will vary according to the information available as regards date of lapse, surrender, etc.; and the results obtained from the original data will require graduation. These points, however, do not affect the *principles* which have alone been dealt with in this chapter.

24. In 1893 the Institute of Actuaries and the Faculty of Actuaries in Scotland formed a Joint Committee for the purpose of compiling the experience of a number of British Offices. The experience dealt with was limited to the thirty years 1863 to 1893, and the resulting tables were published at various times from 1899 to 1903, since when additional useful tables have been prepared and published by various actuaries.

The details of the methods employed in the construction of these tables are set out in the volume "British Offices Life Tables 1893—Account of Principles and Methods" published in 1903. It is only necessary here to make brief reference to the more important tables representing the mortality experience of assured lives.

The aggregate table based on the experience of the whole-life participating assurances (that is, assurances with a right to share in the profits) is known as the O^{M} Table, and the Select Table based on the same experience as the $O^{[M]}$.

A second aggregate table, the $O^{M(5)}$, was also constructed on the basis of the experience of this body of lives, but excluding the first five years of assurance. This table, which is known as a "Truncated Table," differs from an Ultimate Table in that, in its construction, a life was only included once in respect of each period of observation, but for the Select and Ultimate Tables, each life insured under two or more policies was included once in respect of each age at entry.

In the $O^{[M]}$ Table the "Select Period" was taken as ten years, and it has been found more convenient for the purposes of this volume to include the $O^{[NM]}$ Table, based on the experience of non-participating whole-life assurances, in connection with which the "Select Period" was taken as five years. This table is printed on pages 439 to 450 and the values of monetary functions dependent thereon on the following pages.

25. In the l_x column of the $O^{[NM]}$ Table the last few values are less than unity: which, at first sight, would appear to suggest that a fraction of a person was living at each of the ages 102 to 105. This, however, should not cause any difficulty if it be borne in mind that l_x is in reality only a commutation function, that is, a function which enables us to commute the values of other functions, and that it is of no importance whether it is represented by a whole number or a fraction so long as it bears the proper ratio to the other numbers in the column.

At ages 102 to 105 the values of μ_x are greater than unity, an example of the point referred to in Chap. I 19.

26. Reference should also be made here to the "Institute of Actuaries Life Tables" published by the Institute of Actuaries under this title in 1872. These tables are based on the experience of twenty British Offices to the end of 1863, the most important table being the H^M (Healthy Males)—Aggregate Table—which, as regraduated by Mr George King for the earlier Text-book on Life Contingencies, appears on pages 410–411 of this volume. This table which is referred to in this book as the H^M Table (Makeham Graduation) differs slightly from the original owing to the different methods of graduation adopted.

27. Practical Application of Select Tables. When using Select Tables it is evident that as the lives entering at age $[x]$ first come under observation at that age, it is not possible to use any formula which includes a term with a suffix such as $[x]-n$. Such a suffix has no meaning since there are no data available prior to age $[x]$.

Such formulae as (16) to (19) of Chapter I for the force of mortality cannot, therefore, be employed to ascertain the value of $\mu_{[x]}$.

Approximate values of $\mu_{[x]}$ can be obtained by means of the relation

$$\mu_{[x]} = -\frac{1}{l_{[x]}} \cdot \frac{dl_{[x]}}{dx}$$

$$= -\frac{1}{l_{[x]}} (\Delta l_{[x]} - \tfrac{1}{2}\Delta^2 l_{[x]} + \tfrac{1}{3}\Delta^3 l_{[x]} - \ldots),$$

or

$$\mu_{[x]} = -\frac{d \log_e l_{[x]}}{dx}$$

$$= \frac{1}{M} (\text{colog}_{10}\, p_{[x]} - \tfrac{1}{2}\Delta\, \text{colog}_{10}\, p_{[x]} + \tfrac{1}{3}\Delta^2\, \text{colog}_{10}\, p_{[x]} - \ldots),$$

where M is the modulus of the common logarithms and $= \cdot 43429448$. A more satisfactory method would be to ascertain the number of lives select at age x dying, say, within one week of effecting their assurances, and to take the value of $\mu_{[x]}$ as approximately

$$\frac{l_{[x]} - l_{[x]+\frac{1}{52}}}{l_{[x]}} \times 52.$$

As the lives were examined at the time, or shortly before, the policies were issued, it is evident that $\mu_{[x]}$ must be very small, and the approximation to its value based on the risk of death during the first week after selection will be greater than the true value.

28. When dealing with probabilities of survival or death, the "Select Period" being assumed to be five years, the values of functions employed with a duration of less than five years must all relate to the same age at entry: when the duration is five years or more the ultimate values are employed. Thus

$${}_n p_{[x]} = \frac{l_{[x]+n}}{l_{[x]}} \text{ if } n < 5 \text{ or } \frac{l_{x+n}}{l_{[x]}} \text{ if } n \geqq 5,$$

$${}_{n|}q_{[x]} = \frac{d_{[x]+n}}{l_{[x]}} \text{ if } n < 5 \text{ or } \frac{d_{x+n}}{l_{[x]}} \text{ if } n \geqq 5,$$

$${}_{|n}Q_{[x]} = \frac{l_{[x]} - l_{[x]+n}}{l_{[x]}} \text{ if } n < 5 \text{ or } \frac{l_{[x]} - l_{x+n}}{l_{[x]}} \text{ if } n \geqq 5,$$

$${}_{n|m}Q_{[x]} = \frac{l_{[x]+n} - l_{[x]+n+m}}{l_{[x]}} \text{ if } n + m < 5$$

$$= \frac{l_{[x]+n} - l_{x+n+m}}{l_{[x]}} \text{ if } n < 5 \text{ and } n + m \geqq 5$$

$$= \frac{l_{x+n} - l_{x+n+m}}{l_{[x]}} \text{ if } n \geqq 5.$$

EXAMPLES

Ex. 1. By means of the values of l in the O[NM] Table, find approximate values of $\mu_{[40]}$, $\mu_{[40]+1}$ and $\mu_{[40]+4}$.

It will be advisable first to set out the differences of $l_{[40]}$, $l_{[40]+1}$ etc

	Δ	Δ^2	Δ^3	Δ^4
$l_{[40]} = 84188$	-549	-166	38	-7
$l_{[40]+1} = 83639$	-715	-128	31	1
$l_{[40]+2} = 82924$	-843	-97	32	
$l_{[40]+3} = 82081$	-940	-65		
$l_{[40]+4} = 81141$	-1005			
$l_{45} = 80136$				

Formulae involving the differences of l as far as the third will be the most suitable.

$$\mu_{[40]} = -\frac{1}{l_{[40]}}(\Delta l_{[40]} - \tfrac{1}{2}\Delta^2 l_{[40]} + \tfrac{1}{3}\Delta^3 l_{[40]})$$

$$= \frac{1}{84188}(549 - 83 - 13)$$

$$= \cdot 00538.$$

$$\mu_{[40]+1} = -\frac{1}{l_{[40]+1}}(\Delta l_{[40]+1} - \tfrac{1}{2}\Delta^2 l_{[40]+1} + \tfrac{1}{3}\Delta^3 l_{[40]+1})$$

$$= \frac{1}{83639}(715 - 64 - 10)$$

$$= \cdot 00766.$$

If formula (16) of Chapter I be employed the result is

$$\mu_{[40]+1} = \frac{l_{[40]} - l_{[40]+2}}{2l_{[40]+1}}$$

$$= \frac{84188 - 82924}{2(83639)}$$

$$= \cdot 00756.$$

For $\mu_{[40]+4}$ we can employ any of the formulae of Chapter I. Thus

$$\mu_{[40]+4} = \frac{l_{[40]+3} - l_{45}}{2l_{[40]+4}}$$

$$= \frac{82081 - 80136}{2(81141)}$$

$$= \cdot 01199,$$

or
$$\mu_{[40]+4} = \frac{8(l_{[40]+3} - l_{45}) - (l_{[40]+2} - l_{46})}{12 l_{[40]+4}}$$
$$= \frac{8(82081 - 80136) - (82924 - 79095)}{12(81141)}$$
$$= \cdot 01204.$$

The values shown by the table are $\mu_{[40]} = \cdot 00534$, $\mu_{[40]+1} = \cdot 00764$ and $\mu_{[40]+4} = \cdot 01204$. These depend on a particular mathematical formula which will be referred to in Chapter XI.

The suffixes of the terms employed should be carefully noted. Where the duration is five or more years, the age attained is inserted without reference to the age at entry, in accordance with the principles laid down in this chapter.

Ex. 2. On the basis of the $O^{[NM]}$ Table, find the values of the following probabilities:

(*a*) that a select life aged 30 will die before reaching age 40;

(*b*) that a life which entered at age 30, and has been assured for exactly two years, will die between ages 34 and 40.

$$(a) \quad {}_{|10}Q_{[30]} = 1 - {}_{10}p_{[30]}$$
$$= 1 - \frac{l_{40}}{l_{[30]}}$$
$$= 1 - \frac{84924}{92529}$$
$$= \cdot 08219.$$

$$(b) \quad {}_{2|6}Q_{[30]+2} = \frac{l_{[30]+4} - l_{40}}{l_{[30]+2}}$$
$$= \frac{89991 - 84924}{91472}$$
$$= \cdot 05539.$$

CHAPTER III

SINGLE-LIFE ANNUITIES AND ASSURANCES. ANNUAL PREMIUMS

1. In the calculation of monetary values based on the mortality table the assumption is tacitly made, in every instance, that there are sufficient cases, that is, sufficient individuals or contracts, to form an average.

2. Thus, the question "What is the present value of a sum of 1 payable to a person now aged x on his attaining age $x+t$?" is equivalent to the question "What is the contribution that each of l_x persons now aged x must make to a fund which, accumulated at interest, will provide the sum of 1 to be paid to each of the l_{x+t} survivors t years hence?"

In the latter case, the amount payable t years hence will be l_{x+t}, and the present value of this is $v^t l_{x+t}$. The amount to be contributed by each of the l_x persons is, therefore,

$$\frac{v^t l_{x+t}}{l_x} \text{ or } v^t {}_tp_x.$$

This question can be looked at in another way. The present value of a sum, the payment of which depends upon a contingency, is the present value of the sum taken as a certainty multiplied by the probability of its being received. The value of 1 payable t years hence if (x) be then alive is thus $v^t {}_tp_x$.

A sum payable only in the event of a life surviving a definite period is called an *Endowment*, or sometimes a *Pure Endowment*, the present value of an endowment of 1 payable to (x) if he survive t years being represented by ${}_tE_x$ or $A_{x:\overset{1}{\overline{t|}}}$, the "1" over the "$\overline{t|}$" in the latter symbol denoting that, for the sum of 1 to become payable, the term of t years must end before the death of (x).

Thus $$ {}_tE_x \text{ or } A_{x:\overset{1}{\overline{t|}}} = v^t {}_tp_x \quad \text{.....................(1).}$$

3. Annuities. A *Life Annuity*, often called simply an *Annuity*, is a series of payments depending on the continuance of a given life or combination of lives.

The simplest form of annuity is that consisting of the payment of 1 at the end of each year of life that (x) completes; the value of which is evidently the value of a series of endowments of 1 payable at the end of 1, 2, 3, etc., years, if (x) be alive.

Using the symbol a_x to represent this value, we have, from equation (1), giving t the values 1, 2, 3, etc.,

$$\left.\begin{aligned} a_x &= \sum_{t=1}^{t=\infty} v^t {}_tp_x \\ &= \frac{1}{l_x} \sum_{t=1}^{t=\infty} v^t l_{x+t} \end{aligned}\right\} \quad \text{..........................(2).}$$

When the first payment is to be made at the end of the first interval, in this case a year, the annuity is said to be an *immediate annuity*.

An *annuity-due* is an annuity under which a payment is made at the commencement of each interval that (x) enters upon, and if payable yearly at the rate of 1 per annum for the whole of the life of (x) is represented by $\mathbf{a}_x$. Thus

$$\left.\begin{aligned} \mathbf{a}_x &= \sum_{t=0}^{t=\infty} v^t {}_tp_x \\ &= 1 + a_x \end{aligned}\right\} \quad \text{..............................(3).}$$

It will also be seen that

$$\begin{aligned} a_x &= \sum_{t=0}^{t=\infty} v^{t+1} {}_{t+1}p_x \\ &= vp_x \sum_{t=0}^{t=\infty} v^t {}_tp_{x+1} \\ &= vp_x \mathbf{a}_{x+1} \quad \text{..............................(4).} \end{aligned}$$

An annuity depending on a single life is sometimes referred to as a *single-life annuity* to distinguish it from one depending on a combination of two or more lives.

4. A *Deferred Annuity* is one the first payment of which is deferred for a stated period. For example, "What is the value of an annuity of 1 payable annually to (x), deferred n years?"

Since under an immediate annuity, payable annually, the first payment would be made at the end of the first year, under the annuity deferred n years, the first payment would be made at the end of $n+1$ years, provided (x) be then alive. This annuity is represented by ${}_{n|}a_x$.

Thus
$$
\begin{aligned}
{}_{n|}a_x &= \sum_{t=n+1}^{t=\infty} v^t {}_t p_x \\
&= \frac{1}{l_x} \sum_{t=n+1}^{t=\infty} v^t l_{x+t} \\
&= v^n \frac{l_{x+n}}{l_x} \cdot \frac{1}{l_{x+n}} \sum_{t=1}^{t=\infty} v^t l_{x+n+t} \\
&= v^n {}_n p_x \cdot a_{x+n} \qquad \text{.............................(5).}
\end{aligned}
$$

The last expression is clearly correct, since at age $x+n$ the value of the annuity will be a_{x+n}, and the deferred annuity is thus equivalent to an endowment of a_{x+n} payable at the end of n years, if (x) be then alive.

In this case the annuity is said to be *entered upon* at the end of n years.

5. For the value of a *Temporary Annuity* of 1 for n years payable annually to (x), which is represented by ${}_{|n}a_x$ or $a_{x:\overline{n|}}$, we have
$$
\begin{aligned}
a_{x:\overline{n|}} &= \sum_{t=1}^{t=n} v^t {}_t p_x \\
&= \frac{1}{l_x} \sum_{t=1}^{t=n} v^t l_{x+t} \\
&= \frac{1}{l_x} \sum_{t=1}^{t=\infty} v^t l_{x+t} - \frac{1}{l_x} \sum_{t=n+1}^{t=\infty} v^t l_{x+t} \\
&= a_x - {}_{n|}a_x \qquad \text{.................................(6),}
\end{aligned}
$$
the latter expression showing, as is self-evident, that the value of this annuity is the difference between the values of the whole-life annuity and of the deferred annuity.

6. The value of a *Deferred Temporary Annuity* can be obtained in a similar manner; thus, the value of an annuity payable during the lifetime of (x) for a term not exceeding m years, to be entered upon at the end of n years from the present time, is
$$
\begin{aligned}
{}_{n|m}a_x &= \sum_{t=n+1}^{t=n+m} v^t {}_t p_x \\
&= \frac{1}{l_x} \sum_{t=n+1}^{t=n+m} v^t l_{x+t} \\
&= {}_{n|}a_x - {}_{n+m|}a_x \qquad \text{....................(7).}
\end{aligned}
$$

7. Reverting to equation (2), if both the numerator and denominator be multiplied by v^x, the resulting expression is

$$a_x = \frac{1}{v^x l_x} \sum_{t=1}^{t=\infty} v^{x+t} l_{x+t}$$

$$= \frac{1}{D_x} \sum_{t=1}^{t=\infty} D_{x+t},$$

where $D_x = v^x l_x$,

$$= \frac{N_{x+1}}{D_x} \quad \text{.................................(8)},$$

where $N_{x+1} = \sum_{t=1}^{t=\infty} D_{x+t}$.

Similarly,
$$a_{x+n} = \frac{1}{l_{x+n}} \sum_{t=1}^{t=\infty} v^t l_{x+n+t}$$

$$= \frac{1}{v^{x+n} l_{x+n}} \sum_{t=1}^{t=\infty} v^{x+n+t} l_{x+n+t}$$

$$= \frac{1}{D_{x+n}} \sum_{t=1}^{t=\infty} D_{x+n+t}$$

$$= \frac{N_{x+n+1}}{D_{x+n}} \quad \text{..............................(9)}.$$

8. By tabulating $D_x = v^x l_x$ and $N_x = \sum_{t=0}^{t=\infty} D_{x+t}$ for all ages, therefore, we have a convenient method of calculating the values of any single-life annuities that may be required.

The values of D and N are accordingly calculated on the basis of all Mortality Tables which are used to any extent in connection with Life Assurance and Annuity calculations, the values being arranged in columns called *Commutation Columns* as in the tables at the end of this volume.

It will be observed that the values of D and N have no meaning whatever in themselves; they are only aids to enable us more readily to calculate the values of annuities and other benefits.

9. Employing Commutation Columns to ascertain the values of the other kinds of Life Annuities already dealt with, it will at once be seen that

$$\text{a}_x = \frac{1}{D_x} \sum_{t=0}^{t=\infty} D_{x+t} = \frac{N_x}{D_x} \quad \text{...................................(10)},$$

$$_{|n}a_x = \frac{1}{D_x} \sum_{t=1}^{t=n} D_{x+t} = \frac{1}{D_x} \sum_{t=1}^{t=\infty} D_{x+t} - \frac{1}{D_x} \sum_{t=n+1}^{t=\infty} D_{x+t} = \frac{N_{x+1} - N_{x+n+1}}{D_x}$$

$$\text{............(11)},$$

$$_{n|}a_x = \frac{1}{D_x}\sum_{t=n+1}^{t=\infty} D_{x+t} = \frac{N_{x+n+1}}{D_x} \quad\text{.....................(12),}$$

$$_{n|m}a_x = \frac{1}{D_x}\sum_{t=n+1}^{t=n+m} D_{x+t} = \frac{N_{x+n+1} - N_{x+n+m+1}}{D_x} \quad\text{......(13).}$$

Also in the case of the Endowment,

$$A_{x:\overset{1}{\overline{n}|}} = \frac{D_{x+n}}{D_x} \quad\text{...(14).}$$

10. In paragraph 3 reference was made to a single-life annuity-due payable for the whole of life. In a similar manner there can be *Temporary Annuities-due* or *Deferred Annuities-due.*

A *Temporary Annuity-due* of 1 per annum payable annually to (x) for n years, $|_n\mathbf{a}_x$ or $\mathbf{a}_{x:\overline{n}|}$, is one under which the first payment is made at once, the remaining $n-1$ payments being made at the commencement of successive years provided (x) be still alive.

Thus
$$\begin{aligned}\mathbf{a}_{x:\overline{n}|} &= \frac{1}{D_x}\sum_{t=0}^{t=n-1} D_{x+t} \\ &= \frac{N_x - N_{x+n}}{D_x} \quad\text{........................(15)} \\ &= 1 + \frac{N_{x+1} - N_{x+n}}{D_x} \\ &= 1 + a_{x:\overline{n-1}|} \quad\text{........................(16).}\end{aligned}$$

In the case of a *Deferred Annuity-due*, the period of deferment being n years, the first payment is to be made at the commencement of the $(n+1)$th year.

Thus
$$\begin{aligned}_{n|}\mathbf{a}_x &= v^n\,{}_np_x \cdot \mathbf{a}_{x+n} \\ &= \frac{D_{x+n}}{D_x}\cdot\frac{N_{x+n}}{D_{x+n}} \\ &= \frac{N_{x+n}}{D_x} \quad\text{..............................(17),}\end{aligned}$$

which is evidently equal to $_{n-1|}a_x$.

11. Before proceeding further it should be observed that until comparatively recent years the function $N_x = \sum_{t=1}^{t=\infty} D_{x+t}$ was employed, and where this is tabulated care must be taken not to confuse N_x with N_x.

For example $a_x = \frac{N_x}{D_x}$, and it was originally to make this expression symmetrical that $N_x = \sum_{t=1}^{t=\infty} D_{x+t}$ was adopted. When, however, Select Tables received attention it was found impossible to employ "N," since, for the value of an annuity-due of 1 payable to a select life aged x, this would necessitate using the suffix $[x]-1$, whereas the life only came under observation at age $[x]$. As will be seen later the annuity-due is very generally required in connection with problems of Life Assurance.

Apart from the symbol at the head of the column it is easy to determine which form has been employed, either by differencing any two successive values or by considering the last value,

$$D_{\omega-1} = \mathbb{N}_{\omega-1} = N_{\omega-2}.$$

The form $\mathbb{N}$ is generally known as the "initial" form and N as the "terminal" form of commutation columns.

The most important tables at the present time in connection with which the older form N was used are the "Institute of Actuaries Life Tables" (H^M etc.); the form $\mathbb{N}_x$ has however been adopted in the tables based on the H^M experience printed at the end of this volume. In the later British Offices experience (O^M etc.) the symbol $\mathbb{N}$ was employed throughout.

12. Commutation Tables based on Select Tables are constructed in precisely the same manner as those dealt with in the last few paragraphs, the age at entry and number of years elapsed since entry being denoted in the suffixes to the symbols D and $\mathbb{N}$ as in the case of $l, d, q \ldots$ mentioned in Chapter II.

Thus, assuming the "select period" to be five years,

$$D_{[x]} = v^x l_{[x]},$$

$$D_{[x]+t} = v^{x+t} l_{[x]+t} \text{ if } t < 5,$$

$$D_{x+t} = v^{x+t} l_{x+t} \text{ if } t \geqq 5,$$

$$\mathbb{N}_{[x]} = \sum_{t=0}^{t=4} D_{[x]+t} + \sum_{t=5}^{t=\infty} D_{x+t},$$

$$\mathbf{a}_{[x]} = \frac{\mathbb{N}_{[x]}}{D_{[x]}},$$

$$a_{[x]} = \frac{\mathbb{N}_{[x]+1}}{D_{[x]}},$$

$$
{}_{n|}a_{[x]} = \begin{cases} \dfrac{N_{[x]+n+1}}{D_{[x]}} \text{ if } n+1<5 \\ \text{or} \\ \dfrac{N_{x+n+1}}{D_{[x]}} \text{ if } n+1 \geqq 5. \end{cases}
$$

13. The value is frequently required of an annuity of 1 per annum to (x) under which the first payment is to be made a fraction—say $\frac{1}{k}$th—of a year hence.

Since ${}_{0|}\mathrm{a}_x = \mathrm{a}_x$ and ${}_{1|}\mathrm{a}_x = \mathrm{a}_x - 1$, if the value required be obtained by first difference interpolation, the result is

$$
\left.\begin{aligned} {}_{\frac{1}{k}|}\mathrm{a}_x &= \mathrm{a}_x - \frac{1}{k} \\ &= a_x + \left(1 - \frac{1}{k}\right) \end{aligned}\right\} \quad \text{..................(18).}
$$

This is the formula most generally used in practice, but a more accurate one is easily obtained as follows:

$$
\begin{aligned}
{}_{\frac{1}{k}|}\mathrm{a}_x &= \sum_{t=0}^{t=\infty} v^{t+\frac{1}{k}} {}_{t+\frac{1}{k}}p_x \\
&= \frac{1}{l_x} \sum_{t=0}^{t=\infty} v^{t+\frac{1}{k}} l_{x+t+\frac{1}{k}} \\
&= \frac{1}{D_x} \sum_{t=0}^{t=\infty} D_{x+t+\frac{1}{k}} \\
&= \frac{1}{D_x} \sum_{t=0}^{t=\infty} \left[D_{x+t} + \frac{1}{k} \Delta D_{x+t} + \frac{\frac{1}{k}\left(\frac{1}{k}-1\right)}{\lfloor 2} \Delta^2 D_{x+t} \right. \\
&\qquad \left. + \frac{\frac{1}{k}\left(\frac{1}{k}-1\right)\left(\frac{1}{k}-2\right)}{\lfloor 3} \Delta^3 D_{x+t} + \dots \right] \\
&= \mathrm{a}_x - \frac{1}{k} + \frac{k-1}{2k^2} \frac{\Delta D_x}{D_x} - \frac{(k-1)(2k-1)}{6k^3} \frac{\Delta^2 D_x}{D_x} + \dots \quad \text{...(19),}
\end{aligned}
$$

the practical formula being obtained by neglecting terms involving ΔD_x, $\Delta^2 D_x$ ... etc.

As examples of the practical formula we have,

when $k=4$, ${}_{\frac{1}{4}|}\mathrm{a}_x = \mathrm{a}_x - \frac{1}{4} = a_x + \frac{3}{4}$,

when $k=2$, ${}_{\frac{1}{2}|}\mathrm{a}_x = \mathrm{a}_x - \frac{1}{2} = a_x + \frac{1}{2}$.

For a temporary annuity under which the first payment is to be made $\frac{1}{k}$ of a year hence, we have

$$
\begin{aligned}
{}_{\frac{1}{k}|}\mathbf{a}_{x:\overline{n}|} &= \frac{1}{D_x}\sum_{t=0}^{t=n-1} D_{x+t+\frac{1}{k}} \\
&= \mathbf{a}_{x:\overline{n}|} - \frac{1}{k}\left(1 - \frac{D_{x+n}}{D_x}\right) + \frac{k-1}{2k^2}\frac{\Delta D_x - \Delta D_{x+n}}{D_x} - \dots \quad \text{.....(20)},
\end{aligned}
$$

or, neglecting terms involving ΔD_x, $\Delta^2 D_x$ etc.,

$$
\begin{aligned}
{}_{\frac{1}{k}|}\mathbf{a}_{x:\overline{n}|} &= \mathbf{a}_{x:\overline{n}|} - \frac{1}{k}\left(1 - \frac{D_{x+n}}{D_x}\right) \quad \text{.....................(21)} \\
&= \mathbf{a}_{x:\overline{n}|} - \frac{1}{k}\left(1 - a_{x:\overline{n}|} + a_{x:\overline{n-1}|}\right) \\
&= \left(1 - \frac{1}{k}\right)\mathbf{a}_{x:\overline{n}|} + \frac{1}{k}a_{x:\overline{n}|} \quad \text{.....................(22)},
\end{aligned}
$$

which again is the expression most commonly used in practice.

Formulae (20), (21), and (22) can also be obtained from the relationship

$$
{}_{\frac{1}{k}|}\mathbf{a}_{x:\overline{n}|} = {}_{\frac{1}{k}|}\mathbf{a}_x - \frac{D_{x+n}}{D_x}\cdot{}_{\frac{1}{k}|}\mathbf{a}_{x+n}.
$$

As examples of formulae (21) and (22) we have,

when $k=4$,
$$
\begin{aligned}
{}_{\frac{1}{4}|}\mathbf{a}_{x:\overline{n}|} &= \mathbf{a}_{x:\overline{n}|} - \tfrac{1}{4}\left(1 - \frac{D_{x+n}}{D_x}\right) \\
&= \tfrac{3}{4}\mathbf{a}_{x:\overline{n}|} + \tfrac{1}{4}a_{x:\overline{n}|},
\end{aligned}
$$

when $k=2$,
$$
\begin{aligned}
{}_{\frac{1}{2}|}\mathbf{a}_{x:\overline{n}|} &= \mathbf{a}_{x:\overline{n}|} - \tfrac{1}{2}\left(1 - \frac{D_{x+n}}{D_x}\right) \\
&= \tfrac{1}{2}\left(\mathbf{a}_{x:\overline{n}|} + a_{x:\overline{n}|}\right).
\end{aligned}
$$

14. The following table giving the expressions for the values of the various single-life annuities dealt with in this chapter is included for convenience of reference.

EXPRESSIONS FOR SINGLE-LIFE ANNUITY VALUES. LIFE AGED x

Aggregate Mortality Table

Type of Annuity	Symbol	In terms of ${}_tp_x$	In terms of D_x	In terms of N and D
Whole-life	a_x	$\sum_{t=1}^{t=\infty} v^t {}_tp_x$	$\frac{1}{D_x}\sum_{t=1}^{t=\infty} D_{x+t}$	$\frac{N_{x+1}}{D_x}$
Whole-life annuity-due	$\mathbf{a}_x$ $(=1+a_x)$	$\sum_{t=0}^{t=\infty} v^t {}_tp_x$	$\frac{1}{D_x}\sum_{t=0}^{t=\infty} D_{x+t}$	$\frac{N_x}{D_x}$
Temporary (n years) ...	$\vert_n a_x$ or $a_{x:\overline{n}\vert}$	$\sum_{t=1}^{t=n} v^t {}_tp_x$	$\frac{1}{D_x}\sum_{t=1}^{t=n} D_{x+t}$	$\frac{N_{x+1}-N_{x+n+1}}{D_x}$
Temporary annuity-due (n payments)	$\vert_n \mathbf{a}_x$ or $\mathbf{a}_{x:\overline{n}\vert}$ $(=1+a_{x:\overline{n-1}\vert})$	$\sum_{t=0}^{t=n-1} v^t {}_tp_x$	$\frac{1}{D_x}\sum_{t=0}^{t=n-1} D_{x+t}$	$\frac{N_x-N_{x+n}}{D_x}$
Deferred (n years) ...	${}_n\vert a_x$	$\sum_{t=n+1}^{t=\infty} v^t {}_tp_x$	$\frac{1}{D_x}\sum_{t=n+1}^{t=\infty} D_{x+t}$	$\frac{N_{x+n+1}}{D_x}$
Deferred annuity-due (n years)	${}_n\vert \mathbf{a}_x$ $(={}_{n-1}\vert a_x)$	$\sum_{t=n}^{t=\infty} v^t {}_tp_x$	$\frac{1}{D_x}\sum_{t=n}^{t=\infty} D_{x+t}$	$\frac{N_{x+n}}{D_x}$
Deferred n years, then temporary for m years	${}_n\vert_m a_x$	$\sum_{t=n+1}^{t=n+m} v^t {}_tp_x$	$\frac{1}{D_x}\sum_{t=n+1}^{t=n+m} D_{x+t}$	$\frac{N_{x+n+1}-N_{x+n+m+1}}{D_x}$
Deferred n years, then temporary annuity-due (m payments)	${}_n\vert_m \mathbf{a}_x$ $(={}_{n-1}\vert_m a_x)$	$\sum_{t=n}^{t=n+m-1} v^t {}_tp_x$	$\frac{1}{D_x}\sum_{t=n}^{t=n+m-1} D_{x+t}$	$\frac{N_{x+n}-N_{x+n+m}}{D_x}$

15. It sometimes happens in practice that the value of a_x is required at a rate of interest for which tables of annuity-values are not available, and the question arises as to which is the best method of approximating to the required value without undue labour.

The method generally employed is to interpolate by means of a finite difference formula between such values of a_x as are known or to make use of the ratio between annuity-values based on another mortality table. For example, if the value of a_{30} be required at $3\frac{1}{4}$ per cent. by a mortality table for which tables of a_x are available at 3 per cent. and $3\frac{1}{2}$ per cent., an approximation to the required value might be obtained by taking $a_{30(3\frac{1}{4}\%)} = \frac{1}{2}(a_{30(3\%)} + a_{30(3\frac{1}{2}\%)})$: or if there should be a second mortality table for which a_x is tabulated at 3 per cent. and $3\frac{1}{4}$ per cent., the value might be derived from the expression $a_{30(3\%)} \times \dfrac{a'_{30(3\frac{1}{4}\%)}}{a'_{30(3\%)}}$, where a' is based on the second table.

An alternative method which gives very good results may be explained as follows:

If it be required to find the value of a_x at rate i, find first the value of n' for which at rate i' $(=i-k$ say$)$ $a'_x = a_{\overline{n'}|}$ and the value of n'' for which at rate i'' $(=i+h$ say$)$ $a''_x = a_{\overline{n''}|}$, then the term of the annuity-certain for which, at rate i, $a_x = a_{\overline{n}|}$ is

$$n' - \frac{k}{h+k}(n' - n'').$$

For example, assume that the value of a_{20} by the H^{M} Table (Makeham graduation) at $3\frac{1}{2}$ per cent. is required, but the tables of a_x are only available at 3 per cent. and 4 per cent.

Here
$$a_{20}^{3\%} = 22{\cdot}064 = a_{\overline{n'}|}^{3\%},$$
$$a_{20}^{4\%} = 18{\cdot}662 = a_{\overline{n''}|}^{4\%}.$$

By reference to tables of annuities-certain it is found by first difference interpolation between the tabulated values that $n' = 36{\cdot}693$ and $n'' = 34{\cdot}990$. Therefore $n = \frac{1}{2}(n' + n'') = 35{\cdot}843$, and

$$a_{20}^{3\frac{1}{2}\%} = a_{\overline{35{\cdot}843}|}^{3\frac{1}{2}\%}$$
$$= 20{\cdot}245,$$

which is the true value.

If we had taken $a_{20}^{3\frac{1}{2}\%} = \frac{1}{2}(a_{20}^{3\%} + a_{20}^{4\%})$, the result would have been 20·363, showing clearly that this method is not satisfactory when the difference between the rates of interest for which a_x is tabulated is so great as 1 per cent.

16. Temporary and Whole-Life Assurances. A contract of Life Assurance is one securing the payment of a specified sum on the death of a person, called the Life Assured, the simplest case being one under which the sum assured is payable at the end of a year provided (x) has died in that period.

In accordance with the principle laid down in the first paragraph of this chapter, the question "What is the value of an assurance of 1 payable at the end of a year if (x) die during that year?" is equivalent to the problem "If an Office enter into a contract to pay a unit at the end of one year in respect of each one of l_x persons now aged x who dies in the year, how much must the Office receive from or in respect of each of the l_x persons?"

The amount to be provided at the end of the year is d_x, its present value being vd_x, and the amount to be paid by each of the l_x persons is, therefore, $\frac{vd_x}{l_x} = vq_x$.

Representing the value of this temporary life assurance for one year by $|_1A_x$ or $A^{\,1}_{x:\overline{1}|}$, we have

$$|_1A_x \text{ or } A^{\,1}_{x:\overline{1}|} = vq_x \quad \text{.....................(23).}$$

In this case also the contract may be looked at from another point of view. The probability of the sum becoming payable in respect of any one of the persons is q_x, and the present value of the amount to be paid taken as a certainty is v: the value of the assurance is, therefore, vq_x.

In the symbol $A^{\,1}_{x:\overline{1}|}$ the "1" is placed over the age to denote that the sum assured will only become payable provided (x) die before the expiration of the period.

17. Unless the contrary is expressed or implied it is usual to assume, in calculating the values of assurances, that the sum assured is payable *at the end of the year of death.* This is not the condition of practice, but, as will be seen later (Chap. VIII), it is a simple matter to make a sufficiently accurate adjustment to provide for payment at any other time, as, for example, immediately on proof of death.

18. If the term of the Temporary Life Assurance be n years, the problem is "What is the amount to be received by the Office from each of l_x persons aged x to provide a fund which, accumulated at interest, will enable a payment of 1 to be made at the end of the year of death in respect of each of those persons who die during the n years?"

The amount to be provided at the end of the first year will be d_x; at the end of the second year, d_{x+1}; at the end of the third year, d_{x+2}, and so on; the amount at the end of the nth year being d_{x+n-1}. The present value of all these payments is $\sum_{t=0}^{t=n-1} v^{t+1} d_{x+t}$, and the amount to be received from each of the l_x persons is, therefore, $\frac{1}{l_x} \sum_{t=0}^{t=n-1} v^{t+1} d_{x+t}$.

Thus

$$\left.\begin{aligned} {}_{|n}A_x \text{ or } A^{1}_{x:\overline{n}|} &= \frac{1}{l_x} \sum_{t=0}^{t=n-1} v^{t+1} d_{x+t} \\ &= \sum_{t=0}^{t=n-1} v^{t+1}\, {}_{t|}q_x \end{aligned}\right\} \quad \text{............(24)},$$

the latter expression being again obtainable by considering the value of a sum the payment of which is dependent on a contingency.

19. The argument employed in the last paragraph can clearly be extended to the case of an Assurance of 1 payable at the end of the year of death of (x) whenever that may happen. This is called a *Whole-Life Assurance*, its value being represented by A_x.

Thus

$$\left.\begin{aligned} A_x &= \frac{1}{l_x} \sum_{t=0}^{t=\infty} v^{t+1} d_{x+t} \\ &= \sum_{t=0}^{t=\infty} v^{t+1}\, {}_{t|}q_x \end{aligned}\right\} \quad \text{..................(25)}.$$

20. Commutation Columns similar to those referred to in connection with annuities can be employed to assist in the calculation of the values of Assurances.

Considering the value of A_x, multiplying both numerator and denominator of formula (25) by v^x, we have

$$A_x = \frac{1}{v^x l_x} \sum_{t=0}^{t=\infty} v^{x+t+1} d_{x+t}$$

$$= \frac{1}{D_x} \sum_{t=0}^{t=\infty} C_{x+t},$$

where $C_{x+t} = v^{x+t+1} d_{x+t}$,

$$= \frac{M_x}{D_x} \quad \text{.............................(26)},$$

where $M_x = \sum_{t=0}^{t=\infty} C_{x+t}$.

Expressing the values of the temporary assurances already discussed by means of these Commutation Symbols, we have

$$A^1_{x:\overline{1|}} = \frac{C_x}{D_x} \quad \text{.............................(27)},$$

$$A^1_{x:\overline{n|}} = \frac{1}{D_x} \sum_{t=0}^{t=n-1} C_{x+t}$$

$$= \frac{M_x - M_{x+n}}{D_x} \quad \text{....................(28)}.$$

21. The value of a *Deferred* Whole-Life Assurance of 1 payable at the end of the year of death of (x), provided this occur after the expiration of a period of n years from the present time, is

$${}_{n|}A_x = \frac{1}{D_x} \sum_{t=n}^{t=\infty} C_{x+t}$$

$$= \frac{M_{x+n}}{D_x} \quad \text{........................(29)},$$

which formula can also be obtained from the equation

$${}_{n|}A_x = v^n {}_n p_x A_{x+n}.$$

Similarly the value of a *Deferred Temporary* Assurance, deferred n years and then to run for m years, is

$${}_{n|m}A_x = \frac{1}{D_x} \sum_{t=n}^{t=n+m-1} C_{x+t}$$

$$= \frac{M_{x+n} - M_{x+n+m}}{D_x} \quad \text{..............(30)},$$

which can be obtained from the equation

$${}_{n|m}A_x = v^n {}_n p_x \cdot {}_{|m}A_{x+n}.$$

22. The sum, whether single or periodical, payable in consideration of an assurance is usually called a *Premium*. Thus A_x, $|_n A_x$, $_n|A_x$ etc. are the *Single Premiums* for the respective contracts of assurance of 1 on the life of (x).

23. When Select Tables are employed, assuming the "select period" to be five years,

$$C_{[x]+t} = v^{x+t+1} d_{[x]+t} \text{ if } t < 5,$$

$$C_{x+t} = v^{x+t+1} d_{x+t} \text{ if } t \geqq 5,$$

$$M_{[x]} = \sum_{t=0}^{t=4} C_{[x]+t} + \sum_{t=5}^{t=\infty} C_{x+t}.$$

And the expressions for the values of the various assurances already referred to are

$$A^{\ 1}_{[x]:\overline{1|}} = \frac{C_{[x]}}{D_{[x]}},$$

$$A^{\ 1}_{[x]:\overline{n|}} = \begin{cases} \dfrac{M_{[x]} - M_{[x]+n}}{D_{[x]}} & \text{if } n < 5, \\ \dfrac{M_{[x]} - M_{x+n}}{D_{[x]}} & \text{if } n \geqq 5, \end{cases}$$

$$A_{[x]} = \frac{M_{[x]}}{D_{[x]}},$$

$$_n|A_{[x]} = \begin{cases} \dfrac{M_{[x]+n}}{D_{[x]}} & \text{if } n < 5, \\ \dfrac{M_{x+n}}{D_{[x]}} & \text{if } n \geqq 5, \end{cases}$$

$$_{n|m}A_{[x]} = \begin{cases} \dfrac{M_{[x]+n} - M_{x+n+m}}{D_{[x]}} & \text{if } n < 5 \text{ and } n+m \geqq 5, \\ \dfrac{M_{x+n} - M_{x+n+m}}{D_{[x]}} & \text{if } n \geqq 5. \end{cases}$$

24. Endowment Assurances. An Endowment Assurance is one under which the sum assured is payable in the event of the death of the life assured during a stated period, or at the end of this period if the life survive until that time. It is thus a combination of a Temporary Assurance and a Pure Endowment.

Representing the value of, or Single Premium for, an n-year Endowment Assurance on (x) for a sum of 1 by $A_{x:\overline{n}|}$, we have

$$A_{x:\overline{n}|} = \frac{1}{l_x}\left\{\sum_{t=0}^{t=n-1} v^{t+1} d_{x+t} + v^n l_{x+n}\right\}$$

$$= \frac{1}{D_x}\left\{\sum_{t=0}^{t=n-1} C_{x+t} + D_{x+n}\right\}$$

$$= \frac{M_x - M_{x+n} + D_{x+n}}{D_x} \quad\text{..................(31),}$$

which expression could have been obtained from the equation $A_{x:\overline{n}|} = A^1_{x:\overline{n}|} + A_{x:\overset{1}{\overline{n}|}}$ by substituting for the terms on the right-hand side the values given in formulae (28) and (14) of this chapter.

On the basis of Select Tables

$$A_{[x]:\overline{n}|} = \begin{cases} \dfrac{M_{[x]} - M_{[x]+n} + D_{[x]+n}}{D_{[x]}} & \text{if } n < 5, \\[2ex] \dfrac{M_{[x]} - M_{x+n} + D_{x+n}}{D_{[x]}} & \text{if } n \geqq 5. \end{cases}$$

25. The value of an Endowment Assurance on the life of (x) deferred n years (n being greater than the "select period") and then to run for m years is

$$_{n|}A_{[x]:\overline{m}|} = \frac{1}{D_{[x]}}\left\{\sum_{t=n}^{t=n+m-1} C_{x+t} + D_{x+n+m}\right\}$$

$$= \frac{M_{x+n} - M_{x+n+m} + D_{x+n+m}}{D_{[x]}}.$$

26. Premiums based on Select Tables. In order not to confuse the arguments employed in arriving at the formulae for the Single Premiums for Assurances these formulae have been obtained on the basis of Aggregate Tables, the expressions applicable to Select Tables being given afterwards.

Calculations of premiums to be charged by Life Offices are now almost invariably made on the basis of Select Tables, and from this point, therefore, the formulae will be given, unless otherwise stated, on the assumption that such tables are employed and that the "Select Period" is five years. The corresponding expressions for Aggregate Tables only differ from those for Select Tables by the omission of the square brackets enclosing the age at entry.

This must not, however, be taken to imply that all existing tables of premiums appearing in the prospectuses of Life Offices are based on Select Tables. Many of these have been a long time in operation and were in the first instance calculated on the basis of Aggregate Tables.

When Aggregate Tables are employed, the premiums as compared with those based on Select Tables are reduced at the younger ages on account of the rate of mortality at older ages being diminished by the inclusion of select lives entering at those ages: the premiums at older ages are higher through the rate of mortality being increased by the inclusion of lives which entered many years before, but are now unhealthy lives. As compared with those based on Select Tables, therefore, premiums calculated by Aggregate Tables are too low at the younger ages and too high at the older ages.

27. Annual Premiums. Instead of paying a single premium, the proposer for an assurance generally prefers to pay a smaller premium annually, or at more frequent intervals, the first being paid immediately and a further premium at the commencement of each succeeding interval. It is now proposed to deal with annual premiums.

In order to calculate the net annual premium required in any particular case it is necessary to bear in mind that the value to be received by the Office for the assurance must be the same, on the average, as when a single premium is paid.

28. If $P^{1}_{[x]:\overline{n|}}$ represent the net annual premium to be paid at the commencement of each year during which the contract remains in force, for a temporary assurance of 1 on the life of (x) for n years, the value at the outset of these annual premiums is $P^{1}_{[x]:\overline{n|}}\,\mathrm{a}_{[x]:\overline{n|}}$, which must be equal to the value of the assurance, i.e. the single premium, $A^{1}_{[x]:\overline{n|}}$.

Thus $$P^{1}_{[x]:\overline{n|}}\,\mathrm{a}_{[x]:\overline{n|}} = A^{1}_{[x]:\overline{n|}},$$

whence
$$\left.\begin{aligned} P^{1}_{[x]:\overline{n|}} &= \frac{A^{1}_{[x]:\overline{n|}}}{\mathrm{a}_{[x]:\overline{n|}}} \\ &= \frac{M_{[x]} - M_{[x]+n}}{N_{[x]} - N_{[x]+n}} \text{ if } n < 5 \\ &= \frac{M_{[x]} - M_{x+n}}{N_{[x]} - N_{x+n}} \text{ if } n \geqq 5 \end{aligned}\right\} \quad \ldots\ldots\ldots(32).$$

29. To obtain the annual premium, $P_{[x]}$, payable throughout life for a whole-life assurance of 1 on the life of (x), we have

$$P_{[x]}\,a_{[x]} = A_{[x]},$$

$$\left.\begin{aligned}\therefore\quad P_{[x]} &= \frac{A_{[x]}}{a_{[x]}}\\ &= \frac{M_{[x]}}{N_{[x]}}\end{aligned}\right\}\quad\ldots\ldots\ldots\ldots\ldots\ldots\ldots(33).$$

30. For a deferred assurance the annual premium is generally payable from the date of the contract to the termination of the assurance. Thus, the annual premium (P*), for a temporary assurance on (x) deferred n years and then to run for m years, will be found from the equation

$$P a_{[x]:\overline{n+m}|} = {}_{n|}A^{1}_{[x]:\overline{m}|},$$

whence

$$\left.\begin{aligned}P &= \frac{{}_{n|}A^{1}_{[x]:\overline{m}|}}{a_{[x]:\overline{n+m}|}}\\ &= \frac{M_{[x]+n} - M_{x+n+m}}{N_{[x]} - N_{x+n+m}}\quad\left(\begin{matrix}\text{if} & n < 5\\ \text{and } & n+m \geqq 5\end{matrix}\right)\\ &= \frac{M_{x+n} - M_{x+n+m}}{N_{[x]} - N_{x+n+m}}\qquad \text{if } n \geqq 5\end{aligned}\right\}\ldots\ldots(34).$$

Similarly, for the deferred whole-life assurance, the period of deferment being n years,

$$P a_{[x]} = {}_{n|}A_{[x]},$$

$$\left.\begin{aligned}\therefore\quad P &= \frac{{}_{n|}A_{[x]}}{a_{[x]}}\\ &= \frac{M_{[x]+n}}{N_{[x]}}\quad \text{if } n < 5\\ &= \frac{M_{x+n}}{N_{[x]}}\quad \text{if } n \geqq 5\end{aligned}\right\}\quad\ldots\ldots\ldots\ldots\ldots(35).$$

31. Representing the annual premium, payable throughout the duration of the contract, for an n-year endowment assurance of 1 on the life of (x), by $P_{[x]:\overline{n}|}$, we have

$$P_{[x]:\overline{n}|}\,a_{[x]:\overline{n}|} = A_{[x]:\overline{n}|},$$

whence

$$\left.\begin{aligned}P_{[x]:\overline{n}|} &= \frac{A_{[x]:\overline{n}|}}{a_{[x]:\overline{n}|}}\\ &= \frac{M_{[x]} - M_{x+n} + D_{x+n}}{N_{[x]} - N_{x+n}}\end{aligned}\right\}\ldots\ldots\ldots\ldots(36),$$

assuming $n \geqq 5$.

* N.B. P (without suffix) is used as a general symbol for the premium when there is no convenient symbol embodying an indication of the nature of the assurance.

The symbol for the annual premium payable for n years for a pure endowment of 1 receivable by (x) at the end of n years, if he be then alive, is $P_{[x]:\overset{1}{\overline{n|}}}$, and it follows that, assuming $n \geqq 5$,

$$\left.\begin{aligned} P_{[x]:\overset{1}{\overline{n|}}} &= \frac{A_{[x]:\overset{1}{\overline{n|}}}}{a_{[x]:\overline{n|}}} \\ &= \frac{D_{x+n}}{N_{[x]} - N_{x+n}} \end{aligned}\right\} \quad \ldots\ldots\ldots\ldots\ldots\ldots(37).$$

From equation (36) it will be seen that

$$\begin{aligned} P_{[x]:\overline{n|}} &= \frac{A^{1}_{[x]:\overline{n|}} + A_{[x]:\overset{1}{\overline{n|}}}}{a_{[x]:\overline{n|}}} \\ &= P^{1}_{[x]:\overline{n|}} + P_{[x]:\overset{1}{\overline{n|}}}, \end{aligned}$$

which again demonstrates that an endowment assurance is a combination of a temporary assurance and a pure endowment.

Endowment Assurances are seldom granted for terms of less than ten years.

32. For an Endowment Assurance deferred n years and then to run for m years, the premium being payable throughout the full period of $n+m$ years, the annual premium is

$$\left.\begin{aligned} P &= \frac{{}_{n|}A_{[x]:\overline{m|}}}{a_{[x]:\overline{m+n|}}} \\ &= \frac{M_{[x]+n} - M_{x+n+m} + D_{x+n+m}}{N_{[x]} - N_{x+n+m}} \end{aligned}\right\} \quad \ldots\ldots\ldots\ldots\ldots(38),$$

assuming $n < 5$ and $n + m \geqq 5$. If $n \geqq 5$, the square brackets enclosing the age at entry would be omitted in $M_{[x]+n}$.

33. Limited Payment Policies. Assurances are frequently granted by Life Offices under which the maximum number of annual premiums payable is specified in the contract.

A Whole-Life Assurance, for example, may be granted subject to annual premiums limited to t payments, the premiums being payable annually in advance during the life of the assured, or for the period of t years, whichever is the shorter. If the assured survive beyond the t years, no further premiums are payable.

In calculating the amount of the net annual premium to be charged for such a contract on the life of (x), the sum assured being 1, the principle indicated in paragraph 27 of this chapter must be applied.

Thus, employing Select Tables and representing the annual premium by ${}_tP_{[x]}$, we have

$$ {}_tP_{[x]}\,a_{[x]:\overline{t|}} = A_{[x]}, $$

$$ \left.\begin{aligned} \therefore\ {}_tP_{[x]} &= \frac{A_{[x]}}{a_{[x]:\overline{t|}}} \\ &= \frac{M_{[x]}}{N_{[x]} - N_{[x]+t}} \end{aligned}\right\} \quad \ldots\ldots\ldots\ldots\ldots(39). $$

34. To ascertain the annual premiums limited to t payments for a temporary assurance for n years $(t < n)$ on the life of (x), ${}_tP^{\,1}_{[x]:\overline{n|}}$, and for an endowment assurance on the life of (x) for a similar period, ${}_tP_{[x]:\overline{n|}}$, we have

$$ \left.\begin{aligned} {}_tP^{\,1}_{[x]:\overline{n|}} &= \frac{A^{\,1}_{[x]:\overline{n|}}}{a_{[x]:\overline{t|}}} \\ &= \frac{M_{[x]} - M_{[x]+n}}{N_{[x]} - N_{[x]+t}} \end{aligned}\right\} \quad \ldots\ldots\ldots\ldots\ldots\ldots\ldots\ldots(40), $$

and

$$ \left.\begin{aligned} {}_tP_{[x]:\overline{n|}} &= \frac{A_{[x]:\overline{n|}}}{a_{[x]:\overline{t|}}} \\ &= \frac{M_{[x]} - M_{[x]+n} + D_{[x]+n}}{N_{[x]} - N_{[x]+t}} \end{aligned}\right\} \quad \ldots\ldots\ldots\ldots\ldots(41). $$

35. The tables of formulae for single and annual premiums on pages 50 and 51 are added for convenience of reference.

SINGLE-LIFE ASSURANCES

SELECT TABLES

SINGLE PREMIUMS. AGE x

Type of Assurance	Reference paragraph	Net Single Premiums: Symbol	In terms of ${}_{t\vert}q_{[x]}$	In terms of C and D	In terms of M and D
Temporary (n years)	18	${\vert}_n A_{[x]}$ or $A^{1}_{[x]\overline{n\vert}}$	$\sum_{t=0}^{t=n-1} v^{t+1}{}_{t\vert}q_{[x]}$	$\frac{1}{D_{[x]}}\sum_{t=0}^{t=n-1} C_{[x]+t}$	$\frac{M_{[x]}-M_{[x]+n}}{D_{[x]}}$
Deferred Temporary	21	${}_{n\vert m}A_{[x]}$ or ${}_{n\vert}A^{1}_{[x]\overline{m\vert}}$	$\sum_{t=n}^{t=n+m-1} v^{t+1}{}_{t\vert}q_{[x]}$	$\frac{1}{D_{[x]}}\sum_{t=n}^{t=n+m-1} C_{[x]+t}$	$\frac{M_{[x]+n}-M_{[x]+n+m}}{D_{[x]}}$
Whole-life	19	$A_{[x]}$	$\sum_{t=0}^{t=\infty} v^{t+1}{}_{t\vert}q_{[x]}$	$\frac{1}{D_{[x]}}\sum_{t=0}^{t=\infty} C_{[x]+t}$	$\frac{M_{[x]}}{D_{[x]}}$
Deferred Whole-life	21	${}_{n\vert}A_{[x]}$	$\sum_{t=n}^{t=\infty} v^{t+1}{}_{t\vert}q_{[x]}$	$\frac{1}{D_{[x]}}\sum_{t=n}^{t=\infty} C_{[x]+t}$	$\frac{M_{[x]+n}}{D_{[x]}}$
Endowment Assurance	24	$A_{[x]\overline{n\vert}}$ $(=A^{1}_{[x]\overline{n\vert}}+A_{[x]\overline{n\vert}}^{\;\;1})$	$\sum_{t=0}^{t=n-1} v^{t+1}{}_{t\vert}q_{[x]}+v^{n}{}_{n}p_{[x]}$	$\frac{1}{D_{[x]}}\left(\sum_{t=0}^{t=n-1} C_{[x]+t}+D_{[x]+n}\right)$	$\frac{M_{[x]}-M_{[x]+n}+D_{[x]+n}}{D_{[x]}}$
Deferred Endowment Assurance	25	${}_{n\vert}A_{[x]\overline{m\vert}}$	$\sum_{t=n}^{t=n+m-1} v^{t+1}{}_{t\vert}q_{[x]}+v^{n+m}{}_{n+m}p_{[x]}$	$\frac{1}{D_{[x]}}\left(\sum_{t=n}^{t=n+m-1} C_{[x]+t}+D_{[x]+n+m}\right)$	$\frac{M_{[x]+n}-M_{[x]+n+m}+D_{[x]+n+m}}{D_{[x]}}$

NOTE. When the suffix of any term includes n, $n+m$ or t and this is greater than the "select period" the square brackets are omitted: e.g. when the "select period" is 5 years, $\sum_{t=0}^{t=\infty} C_{[x]+t}=\sum_{t=0}^{t=4} C_{[x]+t}+\sum_{t=5}^{t=\infty} C_{x+t}$ (see paragraph 23).

SINGLE-LIFE ASSURANCES

SELECT TABLES

ANNUAL PREMIUMS. AGE x

Type of Assurance	Net Annual Premiums Payable throughout duration of contract				Net Annual Premiums Limited to t payments			
	Reference paragraph	Symbol	In terms of A and a	In terms of Commutation Symbols	Reference paragraph	Symbol	In terms of A and a	In terms of Commutation Symbols
Temporary (n years)	28	$P^{1}_{[x]\overline{n}\|}$	$\frac{A^{1}_{[x]\overline{n}\|}}{a_{[x]\overline{n}\|}}$	$\frac{M_{[x]}-M_{[x]+n}}{N_{[x]}-N_{[x]+n}}$	33	${}_{t}P^{1}_{[x]\overline{n}\|}$	$\frac{A^{1}_{[x]\overline{n}\|}}{a_{[x]\overline{t}\|}}$	$\frac{M_{[x]}-M_{[x]+n}}{N_{[x]}-N_{[x]+t}}$
Deferred Temporary	30		$\frac{{}_{n\|}A^{1}_{[x]\overline{m}\|}}{a_{[x]\overline{m+n}\|}}$	$\frac{M_{[x]+n}-M_{[x]+n+m}}{N_{[x]}-N_{[x]+n+m}}$			$\frac{{}_{n\|}A^{1}_{[x]\overline{m}\|}}{a_{[x]\overline{t}\|}}$	$\frac{M_{[x]+n}-M_{[x]+n+m}}{N_{[x]}-N_{[x]+t}}$
Whole-life	29	$P_{[x]}$	$\frac{A_{[x]}}{a_{[x]}}$	$\frac{M_{[x]}}{N_{[x]}}$	33	${}_{t}P_{[x]}$	$\frac{A_{[x]}}{a_{[x]\overline{t}\|}}$	$\frac{M_{[x]}}{N_{[x]}-N_{[x]+t}}$
Deferred Whole-life	30		$\frac{{}_{n\|}A_{[x]}}{a_{[x]}}$	$\frac{M_{[x]+n}}{N_{[x]}}$			$\frac{{}_{n\|}A_{[x]}}{a_{[x]\overline{t}\|}}$	$\frac{M_{[x]+n}}{N_{[x]}-N_{[x]+t}}$
Endowment Assurance	31	$P_{[x]\overline{n}\|}$	$\frac{A_{[x]\overline{n}\|}}{a_{[x]\overline{n}\|}}$	$\frac{M_{[x]}-M_{[x]+n}+D_{[x]+n}}{N_{[x]}-N_{[x]+n}}$	33	${}_{t}P_{[x]\overline{n}\|}$	$\frac{A_{[x]\overline{n}\|}}{a_{[x]\overline{t}\|}}$	$\frac{M_{[x]}-M_{[x]+n}+D_{[x]+n}}{N_{[x]}-N_{[x]+t}}$
Deferred Endowment Assurance	32		$\frac{{}_{n\|}A_{[x]\overline{m}\|}}{a_{[x]\overline{m+n}\|}}$	$\frac{M_{[x]+n}-M_{[x]+n+m}+D_{[x]+n+m}}{N_{[x]}-N_{[x]+n+m}}$			$\frac{{}_{n\|}A_{[x]\overline{m}\|}}{a_{[x]\overline{t}\|}}$	$\frac{M_{[x]+n}-M_{[x]+n+m}+D_{[x]+n+m}}{N_{[x]}-N_{[x]+t}}$

NOTE. When the suffix of any term includes n, $n+m$ or t and this is greater than the "select period" the square brackets are omitted.

36. Numerical Examples on the basis of the H^M Table. We have shown mathematically that a_x is the present value of an annuity on the life of (x); that is, that if l_x annuities be granted on lives all aged x, each at the price a_x, the fund so formed, with its interest at the assumed rate, will be sufficient to provide the payments of the annuities as they fall due; and when the last life fails, the fund too will be exhausted. The mathematical reasoning is quite conclusive, but a numerical example may possibly assist to convey conviction to some minds. The principle is the same whatever age we assume for the lives, but the work will be shortened if we take an advanced age, 90. On the basis of the H^M Table (Makeham Graduation) the value at 3 per cent. interest of an annuity on a life aged 90 is 1·685961, and the number living at age 90 is 1273. The total fund at the outset to provide the annuities will, therefore, be 2146·228.

The following table shows the operation of the fund:

(1) Year	(2) Fund at commencement of year	(3) Interest earned in year	(4) Sum of (2) and (3)	(5) Amount paid to surviving annuitants at end of year	(6) Fund at end of year
1	2146·228	64·387	2210·615	871	1339·615
2	1339·615	40·188	1379·803	575	804·803
3	804·803	24·144	828·947	366	462·947
4	462·947	13·888	476·835	222	254·835
5	254·835	7·645	262·480	129	133·480
6	133·480	4·004	137·484	71	66·484
7	66·484	1·995	68·479	37	31·479
8	31·479	·944	32·423	19	13·423
9	13·423	·403	13·826	9	4·826
10	4·826	·145	4·971	4	·971
11	·971	·029	1·000	1	·000
12	...	...	...	...	...

The second column of the foregoing table shows the amount of the fund at the beginning of each year, and the third column the interest earned thereon in the year. In column (4) appears the amount of the fund at the end of the year just before the payment of the annuities then due. The fifth column gives the amount that has to be paid out at the end of each year in respect of the annuities, and the sixth column the remaining balance of the fund.

It is seen that the fund decreases year by year, until at the end of eleven years it is completely exhausted, the last annuitant living eleven years to receive the annuity, but dying before the end of the twelfth year.

37. The two following tables supply a similar illustration for whole-life assurance premiums, the first treating of single, and the second of annual premiums.

In the case of the first, it is supposed that 1273 persons aged 90 assure their lives for 1 each at a single premium of ·921768. The fund receives an annual increment of interest at 3 per cent., and at the end of each year 1 has to be paid out for each death that has occurred in the year. It will be seen that the fund steadily diminishes, until at the end of 12 years it has become completely exhausted.

The second table is very similar, but perhaps more instructive. Besides the increment of interest, the fund is increased by an annual income from premiums, each survivor having to pay in a premium of ·34318 at the beginning of each year. In this case it will be observed that the fund does not diminish from the beginning. On the contrary, it shows a tendency at the commencement to increase: in fact, if we were to prepare a table for a young age at entry, say 20, we should find that for many years the fund would continue to grow, and only when the surviving lives became advanced in age would the fund begin to diminish. This elementary illustration shows that it is not a proof that an insurance company is prosperous when its investments are accumulating. Even with growing funds it may be steadily advancing towards insolvency, because, although there may be an increase of assets, it may be less than that required under normal conditions such as are assumed in the table. On the other hand, the assurance fund of an old company may be dwindling, and yet the company may in reality be accumulating surplus wealth.

SUFFICIENCY OF SINGLE PREMIUM

Single Premium = ·921768

(1) Year	(2) Fund at commencement of year	(3) Interest earned in year	(4) Sum of (2) and (3)	(5) Claims	(6) Fund at end of year
1	1173·4107	35·2023	1208·6130	402	806·6130
2	806·6130	24·1984	830·8114	296	534·8114
3	534·8114	16·0443	550·8557	209	341·8557
4	341·8557	10·2557	352·1114	144	208·1114
5	208·1114	6·2434	214·3548	93	121·3548
6	121·3548	3·6408	124·9956	58	66·9956
7	66·9956	2·0099	69·0055	34	35·0055
8	35·0055	1·0501	36·0556	18	18·0556
9	18·0556	·5417	18·5973	10	8·5973
10	8·5973	·2579	8·8552	5	3·8552
11	3·8552	·1157	3·9709	3	·9709
12	·9709	·0291	1·0000	1	·0000

SUFFICIENCY OF ANNUAL PREMIUM

Annual Premium = ·34318

(1) Year	(2) Fund at commencement of year	(3) Premium paid at commencement of year	(4) Sum of (2) and (3)	(5) Interest earned in year	(6) Sum of (4) and (5)	(7) Claims	(8) Fund at end of year
1	000·0000	436·8681	436·8681	13·1060	449·9741	402	47·9741
2	47·9741	298·9098	346·8839	10·4065	357·2904	296	61·2904
3	61·2904	197·3285	258·6189	7·7586	266·3775	209	57·3775
4	57·3775	125·6039	182·9814	5·4894	188·4708	144	44·4708
5	44·4708	76·1860	120·6568	3·6198	124·2766	93	31·2766
6	31·2766	44·2702	75·5468	2·2664	77·8132	58	19·8132
7	19·8132	24·3658	44·1790	1·3254	45·5044	34	11·5044
8	11·5044	12·6977	24·2021	·7262	24·9283	18	6·9283
9	6·9283	6·5204	13·4487	·4036	13·8523	10	3·8523
10	3·8523	3·0886	6·9409	·2083	7·1492	5	2·1492
11	2·1492	1·3727	3·5219	·1057	3·6276	3	·6276
12	·6276	·3432	·9708	·0292	1·0000	1	·0000

EXAMPLES

Ex. 1. Calculate, on the basis of the $O^{[NM]}$ Table at $3\frac{1}{2}$ per cent., the net annual premiums for the following assurances on (35):

(*a*) Whole-life Assurance.

(*b*) Whole-life Assurance, premiums limited to 15 payments.

(*c*) Endowment Assurance for 20 years.

(*d*) Endowment Assurance for 20 years, premiums limited to 10 payments.

(*e*) Deferred Temporary Assurance: the assurance to commence at age 40 and then to continue for 5 years.

(*a*) $$P_{[35]} = \frac{A_{[35]}}{\mathbf{a}_{[35]}} = \frac{M_{[35]}}{N_{[35]}} = \frac{10153{\cdot}39}{485132} = {\cdot}02093.$$

(*b*) $${}_{15}P_{[35]} = \frac{A_{[35]}}{\mathbf{a}_{[35]:\overline{15}|}} = \frac{M_{[35]}}{N_{[35]} - N_{50}} = \frac{10153{\cdot}39}{485132 - 187022}$$
$$= \frac{10153{\cdot}39}{298110} = {\cdot}03406.$$

(*c*) $$P_{[35]:\overline{20}|} = \frac{A_{[35]:\overline{20}|}}{\mathbf{a}_{[35]:\overline{20}|}} = \frac{M_{[35]} - M_{55} + D_{55}}{N_{[35]} - N_{55}}$$
$$= \frac{10153{\cdot}39 - 5943 + 10228}{485132 - 126719} = \frac{14438{\cdot}39}{358413}$$
$$= {\cdot}04029.$$

(*d*) $${}_{10}P_{[35]:\overline{20}|} = \frac{A_{[35]:\overline{20}|}}{\mathbf{a}_{[35]:\overline{10}|}} = \frac{M_{[35]} - M_{55} + D_{55}}{N_{[35]} - N_{45}}$$
$$= \frac{10153{\cdot}39 - 5943 + 10228}{485132 - 264592} = \frac{14438{\cdot}39}{220540}$$
$$= {\cdot}06547.$$

(*e*) $$\frac{{}_{5|}A^{\ 1}_{[35]:\overline{5}|}}{\mathbf{a}_{[35]:\overline{10}|}} = \frac{M_{40} - M_{45}}{N_{[35]} - N_{45}} = \frac{9184{\cdot}11 - 8094{\cdot}11}{485132 - 264592}$$
$$= \frac{1090}{220540} = {\cdot}00493.$$

Ex. 2. Find the numbers living at ages 20 to 23 if, at 4 per cent., $a_{20} = 18{\cdot}662$, $a_{21} = 18{\cdot}520$, $a_{22} = 18{\cdot}379$, $a_{23} = 18{\cdot}238$, $a_{24} = 18{\cdot}095$, and $l_{24} = 93691$.

To answer this question the formula to be used is

$$a_x = vp_x(1 + a_{x+1}),$$

or

$$p_x = \frac{(1+i)\,a_x}{1 + a_{x+1}}.$$

x	a_x	$(1\cdot04)\,a_x$	$1+a_{x+1}$	$\frac{\text{col. (3)}}{\text{col. (4)}}=p_x$	$l_x=\frac{l_{x+1}}{p_x}$
(1)	(2)	(3)	(4)	(5)	(6)
20	18·662	19·40848	19·520	·99429	96064
21	18·520	19·26080	19·379	·99390	95515
22	18·379	19·11416	19·238	·99356	94932
23	18·238	18·96752	19·095	·99332	94321
24	18·095	—	—	—	93691

The divisions required to complete columns (5) and (6) were carried out on the arithmometer. If an arithmometer were not available, logarithms would be employed. Thus

$$\log p_x = \log(1\cdot04) + \log a_x - \log(1 + a_{x+1}),$$

the work being arranged as follows:

x	a_x	$\log a_x$	col. (3) $+\log(1\cdot04)$	$\log(1+a_{x+1})$	col. (4) $-$ col. (5) $=\log p_x$ $=\Delta \log l_x$	$\log l_x$ $=\log l_{x+1}$ $-\log p_x$	l_x
(1)	(2)	(3)	(4)	(5)	(6)	(7)	(8)

Ex. 3. Supposing Commutation Tables given at various rates of interest, find an expression for the value of $\mathbf{a}_{30}$, on the assumption that interest will be at $3\frac{1}{2}$ per cent. for ten years and will fall not lower than 2 per cent. by steps of $\frac{1}{2}$ per cent. at the end of each ten years.

The expression required is

$$\underset{3\frac{1}{2}\%}{\left(\frac{N_{30}-N_{40}}{D_{30}}\right)} + \underset{3\frac{1}{2}\%}{\frac{D_{40}}{D_{30}}} \cdot \underset{3\%}{\left(\frac{N_{40}-N_{50}}{D_{40}}\right)} + \underset{3\frac{1}{2}\%}{\frac{D_{40}}{D_{30}}} \cdot \underset{3\%}{\frac{D_{50}}{D_{40}}} \cdot \underset{2\frac{1}{2}\%}{\left(\frac{N_{50}-N_{60}}{D_{50}}\right)}$$

$$+ \underset{3\frac{1}{2}\%}{\frac{D_{40}}{D_{30}}} \cdot \underset{3\%}{\frac{D_{50}}{D_{40}}} \cdot \underset{2\frac{1}{2}\%}{\frac{D_{60}}{D_{50}}} \cdot \underset{2\%}{\mathbf{a}_{60}}.$$

Ex. 4. The value is required at rate of interest i of an annuity-due of 1 per annum to accumulate during the life of (x) at rate j.

This question can be dealt with in four different ways.

Firstly: if (x) die in the $(n+1)$th year from the present time the accumulations of the annuity payments will amount to $(1+j)\,s_{\overline{n+1}|\,(j)}$. The probability of (x) dying in the $(n+1)$th year is ${}_{n|}q_x$, and the present value of the accumulation of the annuity payments conditional on his dying in that year is

$$v^{n+1}\,{}_{n|}q_x(1+j)\,s_{\overline{n+1}|(j)}.$$

The value of the accumulations of the annuity payments at the end of the year of death of (x) whenever that may happen is

$$\begin{aligned}
&\sum_{n=0}^{n=\infty} v^{n+1}\,{}_{n|}q_x(1+j)\,s_{\overline{n+1}|(j)}\\
&\quad=\sum_{n=0}^{n=\infty} v^{n+1}\,{}_{n|}q_x(1+j)\,.\,\frac{(1+j)^{n+1}-1}{j}\\
&\quad=\frac{1+j}{j}\sum_{n=0}^{n=\infty}{}_{n|}q_x\left\{\left(\frac{1+j}{1+i}\right)^{n+1}-v^{n+1}\right\}\\
&\quad=\frac{1+j}{j}\sum_{n=0}^{n=\infty}{}_{n|}q_x\left\{\left(\frac{1}{1+\mathrm{J}}\right)^{n+1}-v^{n+1}\right\}\\
&\quad=\frac{1+j}{j}(\mathrm{A}'_x-\mathrm{A}_x),
\end{aligned}$$

where J is such a rate of interest that $\dfrac{1}{1+\mathrm{J}}=\dfrac{1+j}{1+i}$, or $\mathrm{J}=\dfrac{i-j}{1+j}$, A'_x is calculated at rate J and A_x at rate i.

If $j=i$, that is, if the annuity payments are to be accumulated at the rate of interest at which the annuity value is calculated, the expression becomes

$$\frac{1+i}{i}(1-\mathrm{A}_x)=1+a_x.$$

Secondly: assuming l_x persons purchased such annuities at age x, the present value of the accumulations of the annuities in respect of the deaths in the $(n+1)$th year will be

$$v^{n+1}d_{x+n}(1+j)\,s_{\overline{n+1}|(j)},$$

whence, by giving n the values 0 to ∞, the amounts for the successive years are seen to be as follow:

1st year		$vd_x(1+j)$,
2nd „	$v^2d_{x+1}(1+j)\,s_{\overline{2}|}$	$=v^2d_{x+1}\{(1+j)+(1+j)^2\}$,
3rd „	$v^3d_{x+2}(1+j)\,s_{\overline{3}|}$	$=v^3d_{x+2}\{(1+j)+(1+j)^2+(1+j)^3\}$
....	....	....
$(n+1)$th „	$v^{n+1}d_{x+n}(1+j)\,s_{\overline{n+1}|}$	$=v^{n+1}d_{x+n}\{(1+j)+(1+j)^2+\ldots+(1+j)^{n+1}\}$

The sum of all these expressions is

$$\begin{aligned}(1+j)&(vd_x+v^2d_{x+1}+v^3d_{x+2}+\dots)\\&+(1+j)^2(v^2d_{x+1}+v^3d_{x+2}+\dots)\\&+(1+j)^3(v^3d_{x+2}+\dots)\\&\text{and so on,}\end{aligned}$$

whence, dividing by l_x, and multiplying both numerator and denominator by v^x, we have for the value required

$$\frac{1}{D_x}\{(1+j)M_x+(1+j)^2M_{x+1}+\dots+(1+j)^{n+1}M_{x+n}+\dots\}.$$

Thirdly: by rearranging the terms set out in the second method we can write the value of the accumulations of the amounts thus:

$$\begin{aligned}\frac{1}{l_x}\{(1+j)\,vd_x&+(1+j)^2v^2d_{x+1}+(1+j)^3v^3d_{x+2}+\dots\\&+(1+j)\;v^2d_{x+1}+(1+j)^2v^3d_{x+2}+\dots\\&+(1+j)\;v^3d_{x+2}+\dots\\&\text{etc.}\},\end{aligned}$$

whence, writing $\qquad (1+j)\,v=\dfrac{1+j}{1+i}=\dfrac{1}{1+J}$,

and accenting symbols involving rate of interest J, we have

$$\begin{aligned}\frac{1}{l_x}\Big\{v'\,d_x&+v'^2d_{x+1}+v'^3d_{x+2}+\dots\\&+\frac{1}{1+j}\,v'^2d_{x+1}+\frac{1}{1+j}\,v'^3d_{x+2}+\dots\\&+\frac{1}{(1+j)^2}\,v'^3d_{x+2}+\dots\text{etc.}\Big\}.\end{aligned}$$

Multiplying numerator and denominator by v'^x, the expression becomes

$$\begin{aligned}\frac{1}{D'_x}\Big\{M'_x&+\frac{1}{1+j}\,M'_{x+1}+\frac{1}{(1+j)^2}\,M'_{x+2}+\dots\\&+\frac{1}{(1+j)^n}\,M'_{x+n}+\dots\Big\}.\end{aligned}$$

Fourthly: again rearranging the terms, we can write the expression as follows:

$$\begin{aligned}\frac{1}{l_x}&\left\{v'd_x+v'^2d_{x+1}\left(1+\frac{1}{1+j}\right)+v'^3d_{x+2}\left(1+\frac{1}{1+j}+\frac{1}{(1+j)^2}\right)+\dots\right\}\\&=\frac{1}{D'_x}\left\{C'_x+C'_{x+1}\mathrm{a}_{\overline{2}|}+C'_{x+2}\mathrm{a}_{\overline{3}|}+\dots+C'_{x+n}\mathrm{a}_{\overline{n+1}|}+\dots\right\},\end{aligned}$$

where accented symbols are again calculated at rate J and $\mathbf{a}_{\overline{2}|}$, $\mathbf{a}_{\overline{3}|}$ etc. at rate j.

Ex. 5. If l_x annuities-due on the lives of persons all aged x be allowed to accumulate at compound interest at rate i, and each person at his death draws the accumulated amount of his particular annuity, what amount, on the average, will be paid out at each death?

Out of l_x annuitants now aged x, there will be d_{x+n} deaths in the $(n+1)$th year, and in respect of each of these the sum to be paid out will be $(1+i)\, s_{\overline{n+1}|}$. Giving n the values 0, 1, 2, etc., the amounts to be paid out will be found to be, in successive years,

$$d_x(1+i),$$
$$d_{x+1}\{(1+i)+(1+i)^2\},$$
$$d_{x+2}\{(1+i)+(1+i)^2+(1+i)^3\},$$
$$\cdots\cdots\cdots\cdots\cdots\cdots\cdots\cdots$$
$$d_{x+n}\{(1+i)+(1+i)^2+(1+i)^3+\ldots+(1+i)^{n+1}\},$$
etc., etc.,

the total being

$$l_x(1+i)+l_{x+1}(1+i)^2+l_{x+2}(1+i)^3+\ldots+l_{x+n}(1+i)^{n+1}+\ldots \text{ etc.}$$

Dividing this total by l_x, the average of the amounts paid out is

$$\frac{1}{l_x}\sum_{t=0}^{t=\infty} l_{x+t}(1+i)^{t+1}.$$

It is evident that, if a number of calculations of such amounts had to be made, it would be a simple matter to construct suitable commutation columns to assist in the work.

Ex. 6. If, as in Ex. 5, the l_x annuities-due are to be accumulated, but at each death the same amount is to be paid out, what will this uniform death benefit be if the fund so formed is to be exactly exhausted by the payment on the last death?

Since an annual premium of P_x will secure a payment of 1 at the end of the year of death, by simple proportion a payment of 1 at the commencement of each year by each of the l_x persons still surviving will allow the sum of $\frac{1}{P_x}$ to be paid.

CHAPTER IV

RELATION BETWEEN ASSURANCES AND ANNUITIES. PREMIUM CONVERSION TABLES

1. In the preceding chapter Assurances and Annuities were dealt with separately, but it will be advisable to consider the extent to which they depend upon each other, and to demonstrate various formulae showing their relationship, all of which hold whether Aggregate or Select Tables are employed.

If there are two annuities, under one of which the sum of 1 is payable at the end of each year of life that (x) enters upon, and under the other the sum of 1 is payable at the end of each year that (x) completes, the difference between the values of these two annuities will be the value of the sum of 1 payable at the end of the year that (x) enters upon but does not complete; i.e., A_x.

The value of the first annuity is $v\mathbf{a}_x$, and of the second, a_x. Thus

$$A_x = v\mathbf{a}_x - a_x \quad \text{.......................(1).}$$

2. If there are two temporary annuities, each of n payments, under one of which the sum of 1 is payable at the end of each of n years that (x) enters upon, and under the other that sum is payable at the end of each of the n years that (x) completes, the difference between the values of these two annuities will be the value of 1 payable at the end of the year (x) enters upon but does not complete, provided his death occurs during the n years; i.e., $A^{1}_{x:\overline{n}|}$.

Thus $$A^{1}_{x:\overline{n}|} = v\mathbf{a}_{x:\overline{n}|} - a_{x:\overline{n}|} \quad \text{.................(2).}$$

If, however, the second of these annuities run for $n-1$ years only, then if (x) survive the n years the unit will be payable under the first annuity and will not be deducted under the second, the condition as regards payment in the event of the death of (x) during the n years being the same as before. In this case, therefore, the difference between the values of the two annuities will be $A^{1}_{x:\overline{n}|} + v^n{}_np_x = A_{x:\overline{n}|}$.

Thus $$A_{x:\overline{n}|} = v\mathbf{a}_{x:\overline{n}|} - a_{x:\overline{n-1}|} \quad \text{.................(3).}$$

3. Substituting in the formulae

$$P_x = \frac{A_x}{\mathbf{a}_x},\quad P^1_{x:\overline{n|}} = \frac{A^1_{x:\overline{n|}}}{\mathbf{a}_{x:\overline{n|}}}\quad \text{and}\quad P_{x:\overline{n|}} = \frac{A_{x:\overline{n|}}}{\mathbf{a}_{x:\overline{n|}}}$$

the expressions for the respective Single Premiums found in the last two paragraphs, corresponding expressions for the values of the Annual Premiums are obtained, namely

$$P_x = v - \frac{a_x}{\mathbf{a}_x} \quad \text{..........................(4)},$$

$$P^1_{x:\overline{n|}} = v - \frac{a_{x:\overline{n|}}}{\mathbf{a}_{x:\overline{n|}}} \quad \text{.......................(5)},$$

$$P_{x:\overline{n|}} = v - \frac{a_{x:\overline{n-1|}}}{\mathbf{a}_{x:\overline{n|}}} \quad \text{.....................(6)}.$$

4. The relations between the Commutation Functions employed in connection with Assurances and those employed in connection with Annuities naturally follow the same general principles as the relations between the functions themselves. Thus

$$\begin{aligned} C_x &= v^{x+1} d_x \\ &= v^{x+1}(l_x - l_{x+1}) \\ &= vD_x - D_{x+1} \quad \text{..........................(7)}, \end{aligned}$$

$$\begin{aligned} M_x &= \sum_{t=0}^{t=\infty} C_{x+t} \\ &= \sum_{t=0}^{t=\infty} (vD_{x+t} - D_{x+t+1}) \\ &= vN_x - N_{x+1} \quad \text{..........................(8)}. \end{aligned}$$

Similarly for Select Tables,

$$C_{[x]} = vD_{[x]} - D_{[x]+1},$$
$$M_{[x]} = vN_{[x]} - N_{[x]+1}.$$

5. Let us now consider the investment of a unit in the purchase of an annuity to (x).

This sum will purchase an annuity-due, payable during the life of (x), of a year's interest payable in advance (i.e. d), the value of which is $d\mathbf{a}_x$; and at the end of the year of death of (x) the unit will remain intact, no interest being then due. The value of a unit payable at the end of the year of death of (x) being A_x, it follows that

$$1 = d\mathbf{a}_x + A_x,$$

whence

$$A_x = 1 - d(1 + a_x) \quad \text{......................(9)}.$$

A similar formula holds in the case of endowment assurances, the equation being

$$A_{x:\overline{n}|} = 1 - d\,(1 + a_{x:\overline{n-1}|}) \quad \text{...............(10)},$$

and in every case in which the sum assured is certainly payable at the end of one year after the last payment of the annuity. Where, however, this condition does not hold, as, for example, in the case of temporary assurances and limited payment policies, the value of the assurance cannot be expressed in this form.

Formulae (9) and (10) are also readily obtainable from formulae (1) and (3).

6. Premium Conversion Tables. The formula $A = 1 - d\,(1 + a)$ is of great importance. It is independent of the age of the life assured and of the mortality table on which the annuity value is based, being dependent only on the rate of interest. If we know the value of "a" and the rate of interest, these are all that are required to ascertain the corresponding value of the assurance. Moreover, if successive values of the annuity proceed by a constant difference, Δa, it is evident that ΔA will be constant also: algebraically,

$$A = 1 - d\,(1 + a),$$

$$A + \Delta A = 1 - d\,(1 + a + \Delta a),$$

$$\therefore \quad \Delta A = -d\Delta a.$$

It is, therefore, a simple matter to construct a table known as a "Single Premium Conversion Table" by means of which, for a given rate of interest, if the value of "a" be known, the corresponding value of "A" can be found by inspection.

Starting with an initial value of $a = 0$, and assuming $\Delta a = \cdot 01$, we have,

$$\begin{array}{lll} \text{when } a = 0, & A_{(0)} & = 1 - d = v, \\ \quad ,, \quad a = \cdot 01, & A_{(\cdot 01)} & = A_{(0)} - \cdot 01d, \\ \quad ,, \quad a = \cdot 02, & A_{(\cdot 02)} & = A_{(\cdot 01)} - \cdot 01d, \\ \qquad \text{etc.,} & & \qquad \text{etc.,} \end{array}$$

where $A_{(\cdot 01)}$, $A_{(\cdot 02)}$, etc. represent the assurance values corresponding to the annuity values ·01, ·02, etc.

It will be seen that the method of constructing the table is exceedingly simple, since, having determined the initial value, if $\Delta a = \cdot 01$, all that is required is constantly to deduct $d\Delta a = \cdot 01d$.

It is, however, necessary, when a constant quantity is deducted at each step in this way, to take precautions against an accumulation of error occurring as a result of the limitation in the number of places of decimals retained. For this purpose, it will be sufficient to work to two or three places of decimals more than are required in the final table, to insert a check value at, say, every 10th or 15th value beforehand by means of the fundamental formula $A = 1 - d(1 + a)$, and to watch the value of the figures discarded in the final "cutting down" to the number of places required in the table.

7. Single Premium Conversion Tables for rates of interest 3, $3\frac{1}{2}$, and 4 per cent., commencing with $a = 1$ and proceeding by a constant $\Delta a = \cdot 1$, are printed on pages 474 to 476. The integer contained in the value of the annuity is given at the left-hand side and the first decimal place at the top.

The method of using the tables is precisely similar to the method of using tables of logarithms, but it may be an advantage to give the following example:

Let it be required to find at $3\frac{1}{2}$ per cent. the single premium corresponding to an annuity value of 16·042. Reference to the table on page 475 shows that

for annuity value 16·0 the Single Premium = ·42512
" 16·1 " = ·42174

Δ = ·00338
·42
·00142

therefore, for annuity value 16·042 the Single Premium = ·42370.

It will be found on reference to the O[NM] Table at $3\frac{1}{2}$ per cent. (page 472) that $a_{[40]} = 16·042$ and $A_{[40]} = ·42369$.

8. Dividing formulae (9) and (10) by the annuity values $\mathbf{a}_x$ and $\mathbf{a}_{x:\overline{n}|}$ respectively, corresponding expressions for the annual premiums are obtained. Thus

$$P_x = \frac{1}{1 + a_x} - d \quad \text{.........................(11)},$$

$$P_{x:\overline{n}|} = \frac{1}{1 + a_{x:\overline{n-1}|}} - d \quad \text{..................(12)}.$$

If, therefore, the value of "a" and the rate of interest be known, the annual premium also can be ascertained without reference to the table of mortality or the age of the life assured. The differences of P are, however, of a more complex nature than the differences of "A," for if "a" increase by Δa, we have

$$P = \frac{1}{1+a} - d,$$

$$P + \Delta P = \frac{1}{1+a+\Delta a} - d,$$

whence
$$\Delta P = \frac{1}{1+a+\Delta a} - \frac{1}{1+a}$$

$$= \Delta \frac{1}{1+a},$$

the quantities by the successive addition of which the values of P will be formed thus being the differences of the reciprocals of $1+a$.

It is not, however, a difficult matter to construct an "Annual Premium Conversion Table" by means of which, for a given rate of interest, the value of the annuity being known, the corresponding annual premium can be obtained by inspection. If for this table we commence with $a = 0$, and, as before, assume $\Delta a = {\cdot}01$, we have,

$$\text{when } a = 0, \qquad P_{(0)} = 1 - d = v,$$

$$\text{,, } \quad a = {\cdot}01, \quad P_{({\cdot}01)} = P_{(0)} + \left(\frac{1}{1{\cdot}01} - 1\right),$$

$$\text{,, } \quad a = {\cdot}02, \quad P_{({\cdot}02)} = P_{({\cdot}01)} + \left(\frac{1}{1{\cdot}02} - \frac{1}{1{\cdot}01}\right),$$

etc. etc.

In this case there is no accumulation of error arising from the deduction of a constant quantity, but in order to ensure accuracy it is advisable to insert periodical check values calculated by means of the original formula, $P = \frac{1}{1+a} - d$, and also to work to at least one place of decimals more than are required for the final table.

9. Annual Premium Conversion Tables for rates of interest 3, 3½ and 4 per cent., commencing with $a = 1$ and proceeding by a constant $\Delta a = {\cdot}1$, are also printed on pages 474 to 476, the arrangement and method of use being the same as in the case of the Single Premium Conversion Table.

The following examples may be taken:

By the O[NM] Table at 3½ per cent. the value of $a_{[35]}$ is 17·266, and entering the 3½ per cent. Conversion Table we have,

$$
\begin{aligned}
\text{when } a = 17{\cdot}2,\quad & \mathrm{P} = {\cdot}02113 \\
,,\quad a = 17{\cdot}3,\quad & \mathrm{P} = {\cdot}02083 \\
& \Delta = {\cdot}00030 \\
& \qquad\quad {\cdot}66 \\
& \quad {\cdot}00020
\end{aligned}
$$

Therefore, when $a = 17{\cdot}266$, $\mathrm{P} = {\cdot}02093$, which is the value of $\mathrm{P}_{[35]}$ obtained in Chap. III Ex. 1.

Again, by the same table, at 3½ per cent.

$$a_{[35]:\overline{19}|} = \frac{\mathrm{N}_{[35]+1} - \mathrm{N}_{55}}{\mathrm{D}_{[35]}} = 12{\cdot}495,$$

and by reference to the 3½ per cent. Conversion Table,

$$
\begin{aligned}
\text{when } a = 12{\cdot}4,\quad & \mathrm{P} = {\cdot}04081 \\
,,\quad a = 12{\cdot}5,\quad & \mathrm{P} = {\cdot}04026 \\
& \Delta = {\cdot}00055 \\
& \qquad\quad {\cdot}95 \\
& \quad {\cdot}00052
\end{aligned}
$$

Therefore, when $a = 12{\cdot}495$, $\mathrm{P} = {\cdot}04029$, which is the value of $\mathrm{P}_{[35]:\overline{20}|}$ found in Chap. III Ex. 1.

10. It will be noticed that as $\Delta\mathrm{P} = \Delta \dfrac{1}{1+a}$, Δa being constant, the differences of the annual premiums are independent of the rate of interest, so that, having been calculated for one rate, the same differences can be employed in the construction of annual premium conversion tables based on other rates of interest.

11. If $\mathrm{P}_{(i)}$ and $d_{(i)}$ represent the annual premium and rate of discount at rate of interest i, and $\mathrm{P}_{(j)}$ and $d_{(j)}$ the annual premium and rate of discount at rate j, P in each case being the annual premium corresponding to an annuity value of "a,"

$$\mathrm{P}_{(i)} = \frac{1}{1+a} - d_{(i)},$$

$$\mathrm{P}_{(j)} = \frac{1}{1+a} - d_{(j)},$$

whence $$\mathrm{P}_{(i)} - \mathrm{P}_{(j)} = d_{(j)} - d_{(i)},$$

or $$\mathrm{P}_{(i)} = \mathrm{P}_{(j)} + (d_{(j)} - d_{(i)}).$$

If, therefore, the annual premium corresponding to an annuity value at one rate of interest be known, the annual premium corresponding to *the same annuity value* at any other rate of interest can be found by simply adding or deducting the difference between the rates of discount. If $j > i$, an addition must be made to $P_{(j)}$ to obtain $P_{(i)}$; if $j < i$ a deduction must be made; the annual premium decreasing with an increase in the rate of interest.

For example, if the 3 per cent. Annual Premium Conversion Table be entered with 17·266, the resulting annual premium is ·02562 which differs from the $3\frac{1}{2}$ per cent. premium by (·02562 − ·02093) ·00469, which is also the difference between the rate of discount corresponding to a rate of interest of 3 per cent. (·029126) and the rate of discount corresponding to a rate of interest of $3\frac{1}{2}$ per cent. (·033816).

12. Premium Conversion Tables were first prepared by William Orchard and printed in 1856, but the volume most used at the present time is that published in 1893 by Messrs Rothery and Ryan. Orchard's Tables commence with $a = 0$, Rothery and Ryan's with $a = 1$; both proceed on the basis of $\Delta a = \cdot 01$ and give the single or annual premium to five places of decimals. The tables printed on pages 474 to 476 commence with $a = 1$ and proceed on the basis of $\Delta a = \cdot 1$.

The use of Premium Conversion Tables is not limited to Single-Life Assurances. They can be utilised in connection with any functions where the argument and the result are so related that, in the one case, $A = 1 - d(1 + a)$ and, in the other, $P = \dfrac{1}{1+a} - d$.

13. From formulae (11) and (12) it will be seen that the values of the whole-life and temporary annuities-due can be expressed in the following convenient form:

$$\ddot{a}_x = \frac{1}{P_x + d} \quad \text{.........................(13)},$$

$$\ddot{a}_{x:\overline{n}|} = \frac{1}{P_{x:\overline{n}|} + d} \quad \text{.....................(14)},$$

and expressing $\mathbf{a}_x$ and $\mathbf{a}_{x:\overline{n}|}$ in the same formulae in terms of D and N, we have

$$P_x = \frac{D_x}{N_x} - d \quad\text{..........................(15)},$$

$$P_{x:\overline{n}|} = \frac{D_x}{N_x - N_{x+n}} - d \quad\text{..................(16)}.$$

CHAPTER V

VARYING SINGLE-LIFE ANNUITIES AND ASSURANCES. OFFICE PREMIUMS AND SPECIAL CLASSES OF ASSURANCES

1. In the annuities dealt with in the preceding chapters, each payment was of the same amount, and under the assurances the sum assured was uniform throughout the duration of each contract. In this chapter it is proposed to deal with annuity and assurance contracts under which the annuity payments and the sums assured vary.

2. Dealing first with annuities, it is necessary to introduce a new Commutation Function, namely:

$$\mathbb{S}_x = \sum_{t=0}^{t=\infty} \mathrm{N}_{x+t}$$

$$= \sum_{t=0}^{t=\infty} (t+1)\,\mathrm{D}_{x+t},$$

whence

$$\mathbb{S}_{x+1} = \sum_{t=1}^{t=\infty} \mathrm{N}_{x+t}$$

$$= \sum_{t=1}^{t=\infty} t\mathrm{D}_{x+t}.$$

These relations between $\mathbb{S}$, N and D must be carefully considered. If the limits be taken between 0 and $n-1$ instead of 0 and ∞, the result is

$$\sum_{t=0}^{t=n-1} (t+1)\,\mathrm{D}_{x+t} = \mathrm{D}_x + 2\mathrm{D}_{x+1} + 3\mathrm{D}_{x+2} + \ldots + n\mathrm{D}_{x+n-1}$$

$$= \mathrm{N}_x + \mathrm{N}_{x+1} + \mathrm{N}_{x+2} + \ldots + \mathrm{N}_{x+n-1} - n\mathrm{N}_{x+n}$$

$$= \mathbb{S}_x - \mathbb{S}_{x+n} - n\mathrm{N}_{x+n}.$$

3. The value of an Increasing Annuity-due payable annually for n years subject to (x) surviving, the first payment being 1, the second 2, and so on, the last payment being n, is represented by $(\mathrm{I}\mathbf{a})_{x:\overline{n|}}$, its value being

$$(\mathrm{I}\mathbf{a})_{x:\overline{n|}} = \sum_{t=0}^{t=n-1} (t+1)\,v^t\,{}_tp_x$$

$$= \frac{1}{\mathrm{D}_x} \sum_{t=0}^{t=n-1} (t+1)\,\mathrm{D}_{x+t}$$

$$= \frac{1}{\mathrm{D}_x} \{\mathbb{S}_x - \mathbb{S}_{x+n} - n\mathrm{N}_{x+n}\} \quad \ldots\ldots\ldots\ldots(1).$$

If the annuity-due is to commence with a payment of 1, successive payments increasing by 1 per annum for the whole of life of (x), its value is

$$(\mathrm{I}\mathbf{a})_x = \frac{1}{\mathrm{D}_x}\sum_{t=0}^{t=\infty}(t+1)\,\mathrm{D}_{x+t}$$
$$= \frac{\mathbb{S}_x}{\mathrm{D}_x} \quad \text{..(2).}$$

The values of the corresponding annuities, the first payment to be made at the end of the first year, are

$$(\mathrm{I}a)_{x:\overline{n|}} = \frac{1}{\mathrm{D}_x}\sum_{t=1}^{t=n} t\mathrm{D}_{x+t}$$
$$= \frac{1}{\mathrm{D}_x}\left\{\sum_{t=1}^{t=n}\mathrm{N}_{x+t} - n\mathrm{N}_{x+n+1}\right\}$$
$$= \frac{1}{\mathrm{D}_x}\{\mathbb{S}_{x+1} - \mathbb{S}_{x+n+1} - n\mathrm{N}_{x+n+1}\} \text{.........(3),}$$

and $$(\mathrm{I}a)_x = \frac{\mathbb{S}_{x+1}}{\mathrm{D}_x} \quad \text{..(4).}$$

4. It has been mentioned in Chap. III 11 that until comparatively recent years the symbol $\mathrm{N}_x = \sum_{t=1}^{t=\infty}\mathrm{D}_{x+t}$ was employed, N_x only coming into use with the development of Select Tables. In connection with N_x, S_x was employed, the relation being

$$\mathrm{S}_x = \sum_{t=0}^{t=\infty}\mathrm{N}_{x+t}$$
$$= \sum_{t=1}^{t=\infty} t\mathrm{D}_{x+t},$$

which in paragraph 2 has been shown to be equal to $\mathbb{S}_{x+1}$.

5. If the value be required of a decreasing annuity-due, under which the first payment is n, each successive payment being less than the preceding one by 1, terminating with the nth payment, we have

$$\frac{1}{\mathrm{D}_x}\{n\mathrm{D}_x + (n-1)\,\mathrm{D}_{x+1} + (n-2)\,\mathrm{D}_{x+2} + \ldots + \mathrm{D}_{x+n-1}\}$$
$$= \frac{1}{\mathrm{D}_x}\left\{n\,(\mathrm{N}_x - \mathrm{N}_{x+n}) - \sum_{t=1}^{t=n-1} t\mathrm{D}_{x+t}\right\}$$
$$= \frac{1}{\mathrm{D}_x}\{n\,(\mathrm{N}_x - \mathrm{N}_{x+n}) - (\mathbb{S}_{x+1} - \mathbb{S}_{x+n} - (n-1)\,\mathrm{N}_{x+n})\}$$
$$= \frac{1}{\mathrm{D}_x}\{n\mathrm{N}_x - (\mathbb{S}_{x+1} - \mathbb{S}_{x+n+1})\} \quad \text{..................................(5).}$$

If the first payment of this annuity were to be made at the end of the first year, the other conditions remaining the same, the value would be

$$\frac{1}{D_x}\{nN_{x+1}-(\mathbb{S}_{x+2}-\mathbb{S}_{x+n+2})\} \quad \text{..............(6).}$$

6. An annuity might be payable to (x) during the whole of his life, commencing with a payment of 1 at the end of the first year, successive payments increasing by 1 per annum until the nth payment of "n," from which time the payments are to be uniform at that amount. The value of such an annuity will be

$$\frac{1}{D_x}\left\{\sum_{t=1}^{t=n} tD_{x+t}+nN_{x+n+1}\right\}$$

$$=\frac{1}{D_x}\{\mathbb{S}_{x+1}-\mathbb{S}_{x+n+1}\} \quad \text{..........................(7).}$$

Similarly, a decreasing annuity to (x) may commence with a payment of n at the end of the first year, successive payments decreasing by 1 until the annual payment becomes 1, at which it is to continue for the remainder of the life of (x). The value of this annuity will be

$$\frac{1}{D_x}\{nN_{x+1}-(\mathbb{S}_{x+2}-\mathbb{S}_{x+n+1})\} \quad \text{..............(8),}$$

which expression should be carefully compared with formula (6), the different suffixes of $\mathbb{S}$ being particularly noted.

7. The annual increase or decrease in the annuity payments can, of course, be any suitable amount. For example, the value of an annuity payable annually during the life of (x), of which the first payment is h, successive payments increasing or decreasing by k per annum until the nth year (i.e. $n-1$ increases or decreases), the payments thereafter remaining constant, is

$$\frac{1}{D_x}\{hN_{x+1}\pm k(\mathbb{S}_{x+2}-\mathbb{S}_{x+n+1})\} \quad \text{..............(9).}$$

8. Turning to the question of assurances with varying sums assured, it is again necessary to introduce a new Commutation Function, namely,

$$R_x=\sum_{t=0}^{t=\infty} M_{x+t}$$

$$=\sum_{t=0}^{t=\infty}(t+1)\,C_{x+t},$$

whence
$$R_{x+1} = \sum_{t=1}^{t=\infty} M_{x+t}$$
$$= \sum_{t=1}^{t=\infty} tC_{x+t}.$$

The relations between C, M and R are precisely similar to those existing between D, N and S.

Thus
$$\sum_{t=0}^{t=n-1} (t+1)\, C_{x+t} = R_x - R_{x+n} - nM_{x+n}.$$

9. The value of an Increasing Temporary Assurance on the life of (x) for n years, the sum assured being 1 in the first year, 2 in the second year, and so on until it becomes n in the nth year, the sum assured being payable at the end of the year of death, $(IA)^{1}_{x:\overline{n}|}$, is
$$(IA)^{1}_{x:\overline{n}|} = \frac{1}{D_x} \sum_{t=0}^{t=n-1} (t+1)\, C_{x+t}$$
$$= \frac{1}{D_x} \{R_x - R_{x+n} - nM_{x+n}\} \quad \text{............(10)},$$
and the value of a similar whole-life assurance increasing throughout the life of (x)
$$(IA)_x = \frac{1}{D_x} \sum_{t=0}^{t=\infty} (t+1)\, C_{x+t}$$
$$= \frac{R_x}{D_x} \quad \text{.......................................(11)}.$$

10. If the value be required of a decreasing assurance on the life of (x), the sum assured, payable at the end of the year of death, being n in the first year, decreasing by 1 each year until the nth year, at the end of which the assurance ceases, we have
$$\frac{1}{D_x} \{nC_x + (n-1)\, C_{x+1} + (n-2)\, C_{x+2} + \ldots + C_{x+n-1}\}$$
$$= \frac{1}{D_x} \{nM_x - (R_{x+1} - R_{x+n+1})\} \quad \text{..............................(12)}.$$

11. The value of a whole-life assurance on the life of (x) payable at the end of the year of death, the sum assured being 1 in the first year, 2 in the second year, and so on, increasing by 1 per annum until it reaches n, at which sum it is to remain uniform, is
$$\frac{1}{D_x} \{R_x - R_{x+n}\} \quad \text{.....................(13)}.$$

12. The increase or decrease in the sum assured may be of any amount. For example, the value of a whole-life assurance on the life of (x) commencing with a sum assured of h, and increasing or decreasing by k per annum until the nth year (i.e. $(n-1)$ increases or decreases), thereafter remaining constant, is

$$\frac{1}{D_x}\{hM_x \pm k(R_{x+1} - R_{x+n})\} \quad \ldots\ldots\ldots\ldots\ldots(14).$$

13. In connection with Select Tables, exactly similar relations hold between D, N and $\mathbb{S}$ and between C, M and R as in the case of Aggregate Tables. It is not thought necessary to show in detail the alterations in the suffixes of the various symbols which must be made in applying the formulae to values of annuities and assurances based on such tables.

It will also be seen that

$$\begin{aligned} R_x &= \sum_{t=0}^{t=\infty} (vN_{x+t} - N_{x+t+1}) \\ &= v\mathbb{S}_x - \mathbb{S}_{x+1}. \end{aligned}$$

14. The value of a series of payments of uniformly increasing amount can be found from the values, at different rates of interest, of a series of payments of uniform amount. If B represent the value of a series of annual payments of s, and IB represent the value of a series of annual payments the first payment being s and the successive payments increasing annually by s, we have

$$\begin{aligned} \frac{dB}{di} &= \frac{d}{di}\sum_{t=1}^{t=\infty} sv^t \\ &= -sv\sum_{t=1}^{t=\infty} tv^t \\ &= -v\,(\mathrm{I}B). \end{aligned}$$

$$\begin{aligned} \therefore\ (\mathrm{I}B) &= -(1+i)\frac{dB}{di} \\ &= -(1+i)\frac{1}{\Delta i}\{\Delta B - \tfrac{1}{2}\Delta^2 B + \tfrac{1}{3}\Delta^3 B - \ldots\}. \end{aligned}$$

Thus, in the case of assurances and annuities, we can write

$$\begin{aligned} (\mathrm{IA})_x &= -(1+i)\frac{dA_x}{di} \\ &= -(1+i)\frac{1}{\Delta i}\{\Delta A_x - \tfrac{1}{2}\Delta^2 A_x + \tfrac{1}{3}\Delta^3 A_x - \ldots\}, \end{aligned}$$

and

$$\begin{aligned} (\mathrm{I}a)_x &= -(1+i)\frac{da_x}{di} \\ &= -(1+i)\frac{1}{\Delta i}\{\Delta a_x - \tfrac{1}{2}\Delta^2 a_x + \tfrac{1}{3}\Delta^3 a_x - \ldots\}, \end{aligned}$$

where if $\Delta i = \cdot 005$, ΔA_x at $3\,\%_0 = A_x^{3\frac{1}{2}\%} - A_x^{3\%}$: i.e. the variable is the rate of interest.

As an example, let it be required to find the value of $(IA)_{35}$ by the H^M Table (Makeham Graduation) at 3 per cent. interest.

$$(IA)_{35} = -\frac{1\cdot 03}{\cdot 005}(\Delta A_{35} - \tfrac{1}{2}\Delta^2 A_{35}) \text{ approx.}$$

$$= -\frac{1\cdot 03}{\cdot 005}\{A_{35}^{3\frac{1}{2}\%} - A_{35}^{3\%} - \tfrac{1}{2}(A_{35}^{4\%} - 2A_{35}^{3\frac{1}{2}\%} + A_{35}^{3\%})\}$$

$$= -\frac{1\cdot 03}{\cdot 005}\{\cdot 37949 - \cdot 42873 - \tfrac{1}{2}(\cdot 33768 - 2 \times \cdot 37949 + \cdot 42873)\}$$

$$= 10\cdot 910.$$

By the ordinary formula

$$(IA)_{35} = \frac{R_{35}}{D_{35}}$$

$$= \frac{337103\cdot 68}{30612}$$

$$= 11\cdot 010.$$

15. Participating or With-Profit Policies. A participating or with-profit assurance is one entitled to participate in the profits of the Office issuing the policy, such participation being by way of a bonus, the most popular form of declaring a bonus at the present time (1932) being as an addition to the sum assured, payable when the sum assured itself becomes payable. This is known as a "Reversionary Bonus," and can be either a "Uniform" (or "Simple") Reversionary Bonus which is declared as a percentage of the original sum assured, or a "Compound" Reversionary Bonus, which is declared as a percentage of the sum assured *plus* any bonuses already attaching to the policy.

In the case of an Office which values its life assurance contracts quinquennially, it is customary to declare a bonus in respect of the past quinquennium, which immediately attaches to the policy as part of the sum assured, and an interim bonus—frequently at a somewhat lower rate—which will be paid only in the event of the sum assured becoming payable during the ensuing quinquennium. In each case the declaration is at a certain rate per annum, the number of years bonus attaching to a policy being in proportion to the number of annual premiums paid.

The practice of Offices varies as regards the details of their bonus conditions to such an extent that it is impossible to indicate any definite rule as to the relation between the amounts of the quinquennial and interim bonuses.

In calculating the premiums for with-profit assurances a rate of bonus somewhat less than that which it is hoped to distribute is frequently assumed as part of the benefit assured, profits from various sources being relied upon to provide the balance.

16. Uniform Reversionary Bonus. It is required to find the net annual premium for a whole-life assurance of 1 on the life of (x) on the assumption of a uniform reversionary bonus of b per annum declared quinquennially and an interim bonus of b' per annum. The policy is to be entitled to a year's bonus immediately on payment of the first annual premium.

Representing the net annual premium by P, and assuming the "select period" to be five years, we have

$$P = \frac{1}{N_{[x]}} \left\{ \begin{array}{l} M_{[x]} + b'\{R_{[x]} - R_{x+5} - 5M_{x+5}\} + 5bM_{x+5} \\ \quad + b'\{R_{x+5} - R_{x+10} - 5M_{x+10}\} + 5bM_{x+10} \\ \quad + b'\{R_{x+10} - R_{x+15} - 5M_{x+15}\} + 5bM_{x+15} \\ \qquad \text{etc.} \qquad \text{etc.} \qquad \text{etc.} \end{array} \right\}$$

$$= \frac{1}{N_{[x]}} \left\{ \begin{array}{l} M_{[x]} + 5b\{M_{x+5} + M_{x+10} + \ldots\} \\ \quad + b'\{R_{[x]} - 5(M_{x+5} + M_{x+10} + \ldots)\} \end{array} \right\} \quad \ldots\ldots(15).$$

If $b = b'$, that is, if the interim bonus is to be at the same rate as the quinquennial bonus, the formula becomes

$$P = \frac{1}{N_{[x]}}(M_{[x]} + bR_{[x]}) \quad \ldots\ldots\ldots\ldots\ldots\ldots(16).$$

If the policy is not to participate in the declaration of bonuses until it has been five years in force, the last portion of the numerator in formula (15) will become $b'\{R_{x+5} - 5(M_{x+10} + M_{x+15} + \ldots)\}$ and in formula (16), $b(5M_{x+5} + R_{x+5})$ must be substituted for $bR_{[x]}$.

17. For the net annual premium for an Endowment Assurance of 1 on the life of (x) for n years on the assumption of a uniform reversionary bonus of b per annum, declared quinquennially, and an interim bonus of b' per annum, the policy to be entitled to a bonus immediately on payment of the first annual premium, n being a multiple of 5, the formula is

$$P = \frac{1}{N_{[x]} - N_{x+n}} \left\{ \begin{array}{l} M_{[x]} - M_{x+n} + D_{x+n} \\ \quad + 5b\,\{M_{x+5} + M_{x+10} + \ldots + M_{x+n}\} \\ \qquad\qquad - nb\,M_{x+n} + nbD_{x+n} \\ \quad + b'\,\{R_{[x]} - R_{x+n} \\ \qquad - 5\,(M_{x+5} + M_{x+10} + \ldots + M_{x+n})\} \end{array} \right\} \quad \ldots\ldots\ldots\ldots(17),$$

or if $b' = b$,

$$P = \frac{1}{N_{[x]} - N_{x+n}} \left\{ \begin{array}{l} M_{[x]} - M_{x+n} + D_{x+n} \\ \quad + b\,(R_{[x]} - R_{x+n} - nM_{x+n} + nD_{x+n}) \end{array} \right\} \quad \ldots\ldots\ldots\ldots(18).$$

If the policy is not to participate in profits until it has been five years in force, the last portion of the numerator in formula (17) must be altered to

$$b'\,[R_{x+5} - R_{x+n} - 5\,(M_{x+10} + M_{x+15} + \ldots + M_{x+n})],$$

and the second expression in the numerator of formula (18) to

$$b\,[5M_{x+5} + R_{x+5} - R_{x+n} - nM_{x+n} + nD_{x+n}].$$

18. Compound Reversionary Bonuses. To ascertain the net annual premium for a whole-life assurance of 1 on the life of (x) similar to that dealt with in paragraph 16, the quinquennial bonuses, however, being compound reversionary bonuses, we have

$$P = \frac{1}{N_{[x]}} \left\{ \begin{array}{l} (M_{[x]} - M_{x+5}) + (1 + 5b)\,(M_{x+5} - M_{x+10}) \\ \qquad + (1 + 5b)^2\,(M_{x+10} - M_{x+15}) + \ldots \text{ etc.} \\ \qquad + b'\,(R_{[x]} - R_{x+5} - 5M_{x+5}) \\ \qquad + b'\,(1 + 5b)\,(R_{x+5} - R_{x+10} - 5M_{x+10}) \\ \qquad + b'\,(1 + 5b)^2\,(R_{x+10} - R_{x+15} - 5M_{x+15}) + \ldots \text{ etc.} \end{array} \right\} \quad \ldots\ldots\ldots\ldots(19),$$

or if $b' = b$,

$$P = \frac{1}{N_{[x]}} \left\{ \begin{array}{l} M_{[x]} + b\,(R_{[x]} - R_{x+5}) \\ \qquad + b\,(1 + 5b)\,(R_{x+5} - R_{x+10}) + \ldots \text{ etc.} \end{array} \right\} \ldots\ldots\ldots(20).$$

If no interim bonus be given during the first five years, the term

$$b'\,(R_{[x]} - R_{x+5} - 5M_{x+5})$$

must be omitted from formula (19), and in formula (20) $5bM_{x+5}$ must be substituted for $b\,(R_{[x]} - R_{x+5})$.

19. For the annual premium for the corresponding endowment assurance for n years, we have

$$P = \frac{1}{N_{[x]} - N_{x+n}} \times \left\{ \begin{array}{l} (M_{[x]} - M_{x+5}) + (1+5b)(M_{x+5} - M_{x+10}) \\ \qquad + (1+5b)^2 (M_{x+10} - M_{x+15}) + \dots \\ + (1+5b)^{\frac{n-5}{5}} (M_{x+n-5} - M_{x+n}) + (1+5b)^{\frac{n}{5}} D_{x+n} \\ + b'(R_{[x]} - R_{x+5} - 5M_{x+5}) \\ \qquad + b'(1+5b)(R_{x+5} - R_{x+10} - 5M_{x+10}) \\ + b'(1+5b)^2 (R_{x+10} - R_{x+15} - 5M_{x+15}) + \dots \\ \qquad + b'(1+5b)^{\frac{n-5}{5}} (R_{x+n-5} - R_{x+n} - 5M_{x+n}) \end{array} \right\} \quad \dots\dots\dots\dots(21).$$

If $b' = b$ the formula becomes

$$P = \frac{1}{N_{[x]} - N_{x+n}} \times \left\{ \begin{array}{l} M_{[x]} + b(R_{[x]} - R_{x+5}) + b(1+5b)(R_{x+5} - R_{x+10}) \\ \qquad + b(1+5b)^2 (R_{x+10} - R_{x+15}) + \dots \\ \qquad + b(1+5b)^{\frac{n-5}{5}} (R_{x+n-5} - R_{x+n}) + (1+5b)^{\frac{n}{5}} (D_{x+n} - M_{x+n}) \end{array} \right\} \quad \dots\dots\dots\dots(22).$$

If no interim bonus be given during the first five years of the assurance, the term $b'(R_{[x]} - R_{x+5} - 5M_{x+5})$ must be omitted from formula (21), and in formula (22) $5bM_{x+5}$ must be substituted for $b(R_{[x]} - R_{x+5})$.

20. In the case of an Office making annual valuations and declaring annual bonuses which vest immediately, the formulae to be employed for whole-life and endowment assurances when simple reversionary bonuses are dealt with are (16) and (18) respectively.

When compound reversionary bonuses are taken into account, the bonuses compounding annually, the formulae become, for a whole-life assurance,

$$\frac{1}{N_{[x]}} \{(1+b)C_{[x]} + (1+b)^2 C_{[x]+1} + (1+b)^3 C_{[x]+2} + \dots + (1+b)^{n+1} C_{x+n} + \dots\} \quad \dots\dots\dots\dots\dots\dots(23),$$

and for an endowment assurance

$$\frac{1}{N_{[x]} - N_{x+n}} \{(1+b) C_{[x]} + (1+b)^2 C_{[x]+1} + \dots + (1+b)^n C_{x+n-1} + (1+b)^n D_{x+n}\} \dots\dots\dots(24).$$

21. A good approximation to the net premium for a participating policy with reversionary bonuses compounding annually can be obtained by taking the Single Premium calculated at a rate of interest less, by the assumed rate of bonus, than that at which the net premium is calculated, and dividing by the annuity-due calculated at the latter rate. For example, if the bonuses be treated as compounding yearly, the present value at 4 per cent. of a whole-life assurance of 1 with a compound reversionary bonus of 30*s.* per cent. may be represented thus:

$$\frac{1}{D_{[x]}}\{1{\cdot}015\,C_{[x]}+(1{\cdot}015)^2\,C_{[x]+1}+\ldots+(1{\cdot}015)^{n+1}\,C_{x+n}+\ldots\}$$

$$=\frac{1}{l_{[x]}}\left\{\frac{1{\cdot}015}{1{\cdot}04}\,d_{[x]}+\left(\frac{1{\cdot}015}{1{\cdot}04}\right)^2 d_{[x]+1}+\ldots+\left(\frac{1{\cdot}015}{1{\cdot}04}\right)^{n+1} d_{x+n}+\ldots\right\},$$

but $\frac{1{\cdot}015}{1{\cdot}04}=\frac{1}{1{\cdot}02463}=\frac{1}{1{\cdot}025}$ approximately, and substituting the latter value we have

$$\frac{1}{l_{[x]}}\left\{\frac{1}{1{\cdot}025}\,d_{[x]}+\left(\frac{1}{1{\cdot}025}\right)^2 d_{[x]+1}+\ldots+\left(\frac{1}{1{\cdot}025}\right)^{n+1} d_{x+n}+\ldots\right\}$$

$$=A_{[x]} \text{ at } 2\tfrac{1}{2}\ {}^\circ\!/_\circ,$$

which must be divided by $a_{[x]}$ at 4 per cent. to obtain the required annual premium. The formula for the annual premium thus becomes

$$\frac{A_{[x]}^{(2\frac{1}{2}\,{}^\circ\!/_\circ)}}{a_{[x]}^{(4\,{}^\circ\!/_\circ)}}.$$

If the rate of bonus assumed in the calculations were 20*s.* per cent., then since $\frac{1{\cdot}01}{1{\cdot}04}=\frac{1}{1{\cdot}0297}=\frac{1}{1{\cdot}03}$ approximately, the value of the sum assured and bonuses would be similarly $A_{[x]}$ at 3 per cent., and the net premium would be given by the formula

$$\frac{A_{[x]}^{(3\,{}^\circ\!/_\circ)}}{a_{[x]}^{(4\,{}^\circ\!/_\circ)}}.$$

Similar expressions clearly hold in the case of Endowment Assurances.

These formulae have been obtained on the assumption that the bonuses compound annually, but in practice they can also be used with a sufficient degree of accuracy when the bonuses compound quinquennially, provided the interim rate of bonus is the same as the quinquennial rate and is declared from the inception of the policy.

22. Guaranteed Bonus Policies. In calculating the annual premiums for policies under which a certain rate of bonus is guaranteed, the full bonus guaranteed is treated as part of the benefit. Such policies do not, as a rule, participate in any bonuses beyond those stated in the contract, and, on the other hand, these are not reduced in the event of the bonuses declared on the ordinary with-profit policies being smaller. In other words, the sum assured, though varying, is determined at the outset, and the policies really become non-participating.

If a minimum rate is guaranteed, to be increased in the event of the bonus declared on ordinary participating policies being greater, the premiums should contain an addition to provide for this guarantee.

23. Varying Sum Assured and Varying Premium. The following example is added in order to demonstrate that the theoretical net premium can easily be ascertained whatever the variations in the sum assured and premiums.

An Office is asked to issue an Endowment Assurance for a term of 25 years, on the life of (x), the sum assured commencing at £100, and increasing by £2 per annum, the sum of £150 being payable at the end of the term if (x) be then alive. The net premium payable is to increase annually by one-tenth of the first premium for five years, the sixth and subsequent premiums being of uniform amount. What is the amount of the initial net annual premium?

Assuming a "select period" of five years, if P represent the initial net annual premium,

$$\text{Value of Benefit} = \frac{1}{D_{[x]}}\{100(M_{[x]} - M_{x+25}) + 2(R_{[x]+1} - R_{x+25} - 24M_{x+25}) + 150D_{x+25}\},$$

$$\text{Value of Premiums} = \frac{P}{D_{[x]}}\{N_{[x]} + \cdot 1(\mathbb{S}_{[x]+1} - \mathbb{S}_{x+6}) - 1\cdot 5N_{x+25}\}.$$

Whence

$$P = \frac{100M_{[x]} + 2(R_{[x]+1} - R_{x+25}) - 148M_{x+25} + 150D_{x+25}}{N_{[x]} + \cdot 1(\mathbb{S}_{[x]+1} - \mathbb{S}_{x+6}) - 1\cdot 5N_{x+25}}.$$

It is not necessary to continue examples of this kind.

24. Office Premiums. The premiums so far considered are known as *net* premiums, these being the premiums that will just suffice to meet the claims for payment of the sums assured at the end of the year of death, or on the maturity of the policies, on the assumptions that the mortality experienced is exactly that shown by the mortality table on which the premiums are based, the rate of interest earned on the accumulations of the premiums is that assumed in their calculation, and no expenses are incurred in connection with the contracts of assurance.

In practice these conditions do not hold, the mortality experienced and rate of interest earned differ from those assumed in calculating the premiums, and the Office granting the assurances incurs expense in connection with its business and desires also to make a profit on the transactions.

In order to meet these varying circumstances, it is the practice, in calculating the Office Premiums to be charged, to assume a rate of interest which the Office can confidently expect to earn throughout the duration of the contracts, and to make an addition to the premium—called the Loading—to provide for expenses, profits and contingencies. The table of mortality is generally selected so as to provide as nearly as possible for the mortality expected to be experienced, and different tables may be employed for different classes of assurances.

In connection with the addition to provide for expenses, allowance must be made for (*a*) Initial Expenses—i.e. expenses, such as medical examination, the commission allowed to an agent on introduction of new business and the cost of placing the case on the books of the Office, and (*b*) Renewal Expenses, consisting of the commission payable to an agent on payment of the renewal premiums and the cost of preparation and despatch of the renewal notice and receipt and of recording the premium payments.

It is usual to allow for Initial Expenses by means of an addition proportionate to the sum assured spread over the whole of the premiums; for the constant renewal expenses by a small addition to each premium; and for commission by the addition of a percentage calculated on (*a*) the net premium increased by these constants or on (*b*) the Office premium.

Thus, if the addition to provide for initial expenses be k per cent. of the sum assured, the addition for constant renewal expense

l per cent. of the sum assured, and the percentage addition, m per cent. of the premium increased by the two constants, then, if $P'_{[x]}$ be the Office premium for a Whole-Life Assurance of 1 on the life of (x),

$$P'_{[x]} = \left(P_{[x]} + \frac{\cdot 01k}{\mathbf{a}_{[x]}} + \cdot 01l\right)(1 + \cdot 01m).$$

If the percentage addition be calculated on the gross premium the formula becomes

$$P'_{[x]} = \left(P_{[x]} + \frac{\cdot 01k}{\mathbf{a}_{[x]}} + \cdot 01l\right)\frac{1}{1 - \cdot 01m}.$$

For participating assurances the net premium inserted in each of these expressions would be the net premium to provide for the sum assured *plus* bonuses at a rate somewhat lower than that at which it is hoped bonuses will actually be declared. This addition for prospective bonuses will provide a margin for fluctuations and it may, therefore, be considered advisable to reduce the percentage addition as compared with that employed in the calculation of premiums for non-participating assurances.

The formulae as they stand are scarcely suitable for short term assurances in connection with which a large initial commission is not generally allowed.

The calculation of Office premiums is dealt with at some length in papers by Mr H. Moir (*Transactions of the Faculty of Actuaries*, Vol. 2) and Mr F. J. Cameron (*Journal of the Institute of Actuaries*, Vol. 48).

25. Office Premiums for Limited Payment Policies. In Chapter III 33, the formulae for the net premiums for Limited Payment policies were obtained.

In practice the premiums payable under these policies are generally calculated by redistributing the value of the annual premiums actually charged by the Office. Thus, to arrive at the Office premium payable for a whole-life assurance of 1 on the life of (x), the premiums being limited to t annual payments, the expression employed will be

$$_tP'_{[x]} = \frac{P'_{[x]}\mathbf{a}_{[x]}}{\mathbf{a}_{[x]:\overline{t}|}},$$

$_tP'_{[x]}$ and $P'_{[x]}$ being Office premiums.

The premiums will be paid up under such a contract at an earlier date than when $P'_{[x]}$ is payable, and if the same rate of interest were employed in the calculation as was adopted in arriving at $P'_{[x]}$ there would be a distinct gain in interest. This calculation is consequently frequently made on the basis of a slightly higher rate of interest.

26. Instalment Policies. The nominal sum assured under a policy may, by the contract, be made payable by instalments instead of in a lump sum, the actual sum assured thus being the value of an annuity of the instalments.

For example, if in the case of a whole-life assurance on the life of (x), instead of a single payment of 1 being assured, this sum is to be paid by n annual instalments, first payment at the end of the year of death, the sum assured must be taken as $\frac{1}{n}\,\mathrm{a}_{\overline{n|}}$ and the net and Office premiums respectively will be $P_{[x]}\frac{1}{n}\,\mathrm{a}_{\overline{n|}}$ and $P'_{[x]}\frac{1}{n}\,\mathrm{a}_{\overline{n|}}$.

Similarly, for an endowment assurance for t years, subject to the same condition as regards the sum assured, the net and Office premiums will be $P_{[x]:\overline{t|}}\cdot\frac{1}{n}\,\mathrm{a}_{\overline{n|}}$ and $P'_{[x]:\overline{t|}}\cdot\frac{1}{n}\,\mathrm{a}_{\overline{n|}}$ respectively.

In the case of an Endowment Assurance, a further condition may be attached that, if the life survive the term of the contract, the annuity of $\frac{1}{n}$ is to be payable for n years certain and so long thereafter as (x) may live. In this case the sum assured must be taken as

$$\frac{1}{n}\left\{\mathrm{a}_{\overline{n|}}+\frac{D_{x+t+n}}{D_{x+t}}\,\mathrm{a}_{x+t+n}\right\}$$

on the maturity of the policy, but $\frac{1}{n}\,\mathrm{a}_{\overline{n|}}$ if death occur before maturity, and the premium must therefore be specially calculated.

Where this condition attaches the policies are called *Continuous Instalment Policies*.

27. Debenture Policies. A *Debenture Policy* is one containing the condition that when a claim arises the sum assured shall be retained by the Office for a term of, say, n years, interest at the rate of, say, j per unit. per annum being allowed in the meantime.

If the premiums are calculated at rate i, the sum assured must be treated as $v^n + ja_{\overline{n}|} = 1 + (j-i)\,a_{\overline{n}|}$, where v^n and $a_{\overline{n}|}$ are calculated at rate i, and the premiums required obtained by multiplying the premiums for assurances of 1 by this increased sum assured.

The net annual premium for a whole-life assurance subject to this condition would thus be $P_{[x]}\{1+(j-i)\,a_{\overline{n}|}\}$ and the Office premium $P'_{[x]}\{1+(j-i)\,a_{\overline{n}|}\}$: for an endowment assurance for t years the net premium would be $P_{[x]:\overline{t}|}\{1+(j-i)\,a_{\overline{n}|}\}$ and the Office premium $P'_{[x]:\overline{t}|}\{1+(j-i)\,a_{\overline{n}|}\}$: and so on.

It is clear that the Office can guarantee any rate of interest required if the sum assured and premiums be dealt with in this manner.

28. Double Endowment Assurances. A double endowment assurance is one under which the sum payable on the life assured surviving to the maturity of the policy is twice that payable in the event of earlier death.

For a double endowment assurance for n years on the life of (x), the sum payable on death within the term of n years being 1, and on maturity of the policy, 2, the net annual premium required is

$$\left.\begin{aligned}&\frac{A_{[x]:\overline{n}|} + A_{[x]:\overset{1}{\overline{n}|}}}{\text{a}_{[x]:\overline{n}|}}\\ &= \frac{M_{[x]} - M_{[x]+n} + 2D_{[x]+n}}{N_{[x]} - N_{[x]+n}}\end{aligned}\right\} \quad\ldots\ldots\ldots\ldots\ldots(25).$$

It should be noted that if a table showing a heavier rate of mortality be employed as a basis for the calculation of premiums, the premiums for double endowment assurances may be diminished instead of increased as would be the case with whole-life assurances and ordinary endowment assurances. This arises from the consequent reduction in the pure endowment portion of the premium being greater than the increase in the temporary assurance portion.

29. Assurances subject to Increasing Premiums. An Ascending-Scale policy is one under which the premium payable during the earlier years (usually the first five) is less than that payable during the remainder of the period covered by the policy.

In calculating the net premiums to be charged for a whole-life assurance of £100 on the life of (x) to which this condition as regards the premiums applies, we can proceed as follows:

$$\text{Value of Benefit} = 100A_{[x]},$$
$$\text{,, Premiums} = P(a_{[x]} + k_5|a_{[x]}),$$

where P is the net premium payable during the first five years, $P(1+k)$ being payable thereafter.

Equating the value of the net premiums to the value of the benefit assured, we obtain

$$P = \frac{100M_{[x]}}{N_{[x]} + kN_{x+5}} \quad \text{....................(26).}$$

In practice, however, the value of the Office premiums would most probably be redistributed by the formula

$$P' = \frac{100P'_{[x]}a_{[x]}}{a_{[x]} + k_5|a_{[x]}} \quad \text{....................(27),}$$

$P'_{[x]}$ being the Office annual premium for the whole-life assurance, and P' the annual premium payable during the first five years under the Ascending-Scale policy. In some circumstances the premiums under such a policy might be loaded more heavily than the level premium, and the formula would have to be adjusted accordingly.

Similarly, if the premium during the first five years were to be greater than that payable from the commencement of the sixth year onwards, the value of the level Office premiums payable throughout the duration of the contract would be redistributed by the annuity value $a_{[x]} - k_5|a_{[x]}$.

Under a Whole-Life Ascending-Scale policy the premium payable after five years should not be greater than the tabular Office premium for a whole-life assurance at age $x+5$; as otherwise a healthy life would drop the original policy and effect a new whole-life assurance at the lower premium, and the Office would thus, in effect, be granting a whole-life assurance, from the commencement, at an inadequate premium as well as incurring the heavy initial expense twice over.

The Ascending-Scale premiums to be charged for Endowment Assurance and other classes of policies are calculated in the same manner.

30. Assurances with Return of Premiums. Assurances are sometimes issued with the condition that all premiums paid are to be returned to the assured or his representative when the sum assured becomes payable.

Since the Office premium is to be returned, it is necessary, before the calculation of the premium is made, to determine the loadings to be added to the net premiums. For the purposes of demonstration, it will be sufficient to assume that

$$A' = (A + c)(1 + k) \text{ and } P' = (P + c)(1 + k),$$

where A and P are net single and annual premiums respectively and A′ and P′ the corresponding Office premiums.

To find the single premium for a whole-life assurance of 1 on the life of (x), the premium paid to be returned with the sum assured; that is, the sum assured being in reality $(1 + A')$ instead of 1; we have

$$\text{Value of Benefit} = A_{[x]}(1 + A')$$
$$= A_{[x]}\{1 + (A + c)(1 + k)\},$$
$$\text{Single Premium} = A,$$

whence
$$A = \frac{A_{[x]}\{1 + c(1 + k)\}}{1 - A_{[x]}(1 + k)} \quad \text{............(28)};$$

and the Office Single Premium,

$$A' = (A + c)(1 + k)$$
$$= \frac{A_{[x]} + c}{1 - A_{[x]}(1 + k)}(1 + k) \quad \text{.........(29)}.$$

In the expression for the value of the Benefit the return of the Office premium is allowed for as a liability, but only the net premium can be taken credit for as a payment on the asset side. At the outset it must be assumed that the loading to the premium is exactly absorbed in the purposes for which it is added, and if it be not so absorbed, the balance will show as a profit at the Company's valuation.

31. If an annual premium, P′, is to be paid for an assurance similar to that dealt with in the last paragraph the Benefit will consist of (*a*) the uniform assurance of the sum assured of 1, the value of which is $A_{[x]}$; and (*b*) an increasing whole-life assurance commencing at P′ and increasing by P′ per annum, the value of which is $P'(IA)_x$ or $P'\frac{R_{[x]}}{D_{[x]}}$.

Thus:

$$\text{Value of Benefit} = A_{[x]} + (P+c)(1+k)(IA)_{[x]},$$

$$\text{,, Premiums} = Pa_{[x]},$$

whence

$$\left.\begin{aligned} P &= \frac{A_{[x]} + c(1+k)(IA)_{[x]}}{a_{[x]} - (1+k)(IA)_{[x]}} \\ &= \frac{M_{[x]} + c(1+k)R_{[x]}}{N_{[x]} - (1+k)R_{[x]}} \end{aligned}\right\} \text{......(30)}$$

and

$$P' = \frac{M_{[x]} + cN_{[x]}}{N_{[x]} - (1+k)R_{[x]}}(1+k) \text{ ......(31).}$$

32. In the case of an Endowment Assurance of 1 on the life of (x) for n years subject to annual premiums payable throughout the duration of the contract, the premiums paid may be returnable:

(*a*) Only in the event of a claim arising under the policy through the death of the assured,

(*b*) Only in the event of the policy maturing by the life assured surviving to the end of the term, or

(*c*) In either event.

If P represent the net annual premium for such a policy, then, assuming n to be greater than the "select period," in case (*a*)

$$P \,.\, a_{[x]:\overline{n|}} = A_{[x]:\overline{n|}} + (P+c)(1+k)(IA)^{1}_{[x]:\overline{n|}},$$

whence

$$\left.\begin{aligned} P &= \frac{A_{[x]:\overline{n|}} + c(1+k)(IA)^{1}_{[x]:\overline{n|}}}{a_{[x]:\overline{n|}} - (1+k)(IA)^{1}_{[x]:\overline{n|}}} \\ &= \frac{(M_{[x]} - M_{x+n} + D_{x+n}) + c(1+k)(R_{[x]} - R_{x+n} - nM_{x+n})}{(N_{[x]} - N_{x+n}) - (1+k)(R_{[x]} - R_{x+n} - nM_{x+n})} \end{aligned}\right\} \text{...(32),}$$

and

$$P' = \frac{(M_{[x]} - M_{x+n} + D_{x+n}) + c(N_{[x]} - N_{x+n})}{(N_{[x]} - N_{x+n}) - (1+k)(R_{[x]} - R_{x+n} - nM_{x+n})}(1+k) \text{ ...(33).}$$

In case (*b*) $nA_{[x]:\overset{\;1}{\overline{n|}}}\left(= n\dfrac{D_{x+n}}{D_{[x]}}\right)$ must be substituted for $(IA)^{1}_{[x]:\overline{n|}}$ on the Benefit side of the equation, and the formulae become

$$P = \frac{(M_{[x]} - M_{x+n} + D_{x+n}) + c(1+k)nD_{x+n}}{(N_{[x]} - N_{x+n}) - (1+k)nD_{x+n}} \text{ ....(34),}$$

and

$$P' = \frac{(M_{[x]} - M_{x+n} + D_{x+n}) + c(N_{[x]} - N_{x+n})}{(N_{[x]} - N_{x+n}) - (1+k)nD_{x+n}}(1+k) \text{............(35).}$$

In case (c) the Benefit side of the equation is

$$A_{[x]:\overline{n|}} + (P + c)(1 + k)\{(IA)^{1}_{[x]:\overline{n|}} + nA_{[x]:\overline{n|}}^{\;\;\;1}\}$$

and the formulae become

$$P = \frac{(M_{[x]} - M_{x+n} + D_{x+n}) + c(1+k)(R_{[x]} - R_{x+n} - nM_{x+n} + nD_{x+n})}{(N_{[x]} - N_{x+n}) - (1+k)(R_{[x]} - R_{x+n} - nM_{x+n} + nD_{x+n})} \quad \text{............(36)},$$

and

$$P' = \frac{(M_{[x]} - M_{x+n} + D_{x+n}) + c(N_{[x]} - N_{x+n})}{(N_{[x]} - N_{x+n}) - (1+k)(R_{[x]} - R_{x+n} - nM_{x+n} + nD_{x+n})}(1+k) \quad \text{............(37)}.$$

33. The simplest and most common case of a policy with return of premiums is that of a Pure Endowment, most frequently Children's Endowments.

The theoretical premium for a pure endowment payable to (x) on his attaining age $x + n$, all premiums to be returned in the event of death within this period, is as follows:

For the Single Premium

$$A = \frac{1}{D_{[x]}}\{D_{x+n} + (A + c)(1 + k)(M_{[x]} - M_{x+n})\},$$

whence
$$A = \frac{D_{x+n} + c(1 + k)(M_{[x]} - M_{x+n})}{D_{[x]} - (1 + k)(M_{[x]} - M_{x+n})} \quad \text{..................(38)};$$

the Office premium being

$$A' = \frac{D_{x+n} + cD_{[x]}}{D_{[x]} - (1 + k)(M_{[x]} - M_{x+n})}(1 + k) \quad \text{............(39)}.$$

For the annual premium payable throughout the n years, we have

$$Pa_{x:\overline{n|}} = A_{x:\overline{n|}}^{\;\;\;1} + (P + c)(1 + k)(IA)^{1}_{x:\overline{n|}},$$

whence
$$P = \frac{D_{x+n} + c(1 + k)(R_{[x]} - R_{x+n} - nM_{x+n})}{(N_{[x]} - N_{x+n}) - (1+k)(R_{[x]} - R_{x+n} - nM_{x+n})} \quad \text{......(40)},$$

and the Office premium

$$P' = \frac{D_{x+n} + c(N_{[x]} - N_{x+n})}{(N_{[x]} - N_{x+n}) - (1 + k)(R_{[x]} - R_{x+n} - nM_{x+n})}(1 + k) \quad \text{...(41)}.$$

A little consideration of a contract of this kind, however, will show that, if death occur, the only profit accruing to the Office is that portion of the interest on the premiums received which is not absorbed by expenses. It is, therefore, scarcely worth while to introduce the element of mortality into the calculation, and if this be excluded the problem becomes "What annual premium will, after deduction of expenses, amount to 1 in n years?" the contract thus being treated as a Sinking Fund or Capital Redemption Assurance.

If P represent the net annual premium for such a policy, the amount of the endowment being 1,

$$P = \frac{1}{(1+i)\,s_{\overline{n}|}}.$$

The method of calculation adopted in practice would, however, probably be as follows:

If P′ be the Office premium for an endowment of 1 payable at the end of n years if the life survive that term, and after payment of expenses—such as agent's commission—which can be considered to be a percentage of the premium, kP' is left, and the "constant" expenses are m per cent. of the sum assured, then

$$(kP' - \cdot 01m)(1+i)\,s_{\overline{n}|} = 1,$$

whence

$$P' = \frac{1}{k}\left\{\frac{1}{(1+i)\,s_{\overline{n}|}} + \cdot 01m\right\} \quad \ldots(42).$$

It may be remarked that the loading in such cases is usually very light, and little, if any, profit is made on this class of policy. These contracts are, however, generally considered desirable from the Office point of view, particularly when granted on the lives of children, because of the possibility of a fresh policy being taken out by the recipient of the endowment.

34. Options. Assurances are sometimes granted under which the assured can at certain periods exercise an option to effect an assurance at the tabular Office premium without undergoing a fresh medical examination. The question, therefore, arises as to how the value of this option is to be calculated.

What then is the net present value of the option to (x), now a select life, to effect a whole-life assurance at the tabular Office rate at age $x+n$ without undergoing a fresh medical examination?

The tabular Office premium that will be paid under the policy will be $P'_{[x+n]}$, but as at age $x+n$ the life will be no longer "select" the premium he should pay is $P'_{[x]+n}$ (i.e. a premium calculated on a similar basis to the Office tabular premium). The net value of the option can, therefore, be taken as the present value of an annuity, deferred n years, of the difference between these two premiums.

If the net single premium for this option be presented by ${}_{n}|O_{[x]}$, we have

$$
\begin{aligned}
{}_{n}|O_{[x]} &= (P'_{[x]+n} - P'_{[x+n]})\,{}_{n}|a_{[x]} \\
&= (P'_{[x]+n} - P'_{[x+n]})\frac{N_{[x]+n}}{D_{[x]}} \quad \text{............(43).}
\end{aligned}
$$

If the option be to effect a temporary assurance for a term of r years, the expression becomes

$$
{}_{n}|O^{\;1}_{[x]:\overline{r}|} = (P'^{\;1}_{[x]+n:\overline{r}|} - P'^{\;1}_{[x+n]:\overline{r}|})\frac{N_{[x]+n} - N_{[x]+n+r}}{D_{[x]}} \text{...(44).}
$$

As already indicated such options are usually attached to contracts for other assurances, the net addition to be made to the annual premium being found by dividing by the appropriate temporary annuity value.

35. Deferred Assurances with Return of Premiums. Deferred Assurances are sometimes granted on the lives of children with the condition that all premiums paid shall be returned in the event of the child's death before the benefit is entered upon, the same annual premium being payable throughout the entire duration of the contract.

Considering a deferred whole-life assurance of 1 on the life of (x), the age at which the risk commences being $x+n$, the theoretical net annual premium can be ascertained from the formula

$$
\begin{aligned}
P &= \frac{1}{a_{[x]}}\{{}_{n}|A_{[x]} + P'(IA)^{\;1}_{[x]:\overline{n}|}\} \\
&= \frac{1}{N_{[x]}}\{M_{x+n} + P'(R_{[x]} - R_{x+n} - nM_{x+n})\},
\end{aligned}
$$

or writing

$$
P' = (P+c)(1+k),
$$

$$
P = \frac{M_{x+n} + c(1+k)(R_{[x]} - R_{x+n} - nM_{x+n})}{N_{[x]} - (1+k)(R_{[x]} - R_{x+n} - nM_{x+n})} \quad \text{.........(45),}
$$

whence

$$
P' = \frac{M_{x+n} + cN_{[x]}}{N_{[x]} - (1+k)(R_{[x]} - R_{x+n} - nM_{x+n})}(1+k) \text{......(46).}
$$

In practice, however, this contract can be treated as regards the period of deferment as a pure endowment with return of premiums, the amount of the endowment being the value of an annuity, from age $x+n$ onwards, of the difference between the premium that would be charged for a new assurance at age $x+n$ and the premium actually payable.

36. If $P'_{[x+n]}$ represent the Office tabular premium for a whole-life assurance of 1 on the life of $(x+n)$ and P' represent the premium payable under the deferred assurance, the value at age $x+n$ of an annuity of the difference between these two premiums will be $(P'_{[x+n]} - P')\,\mathbf{a}_{[x]+n}$, the life assured being at that time no longer select. Since the Office premium employed in this calculation is based on the assumption that the life assured *is* select, a further addition of $(P'_{[x]+n} - P'_{[x+n]})\,\mathbf{a}_{[x]+n}$ should be made to provide for the difference in the premium due to the life having been "select" at age x since when n years have elapsed.

P' being the Office premium to be charged under the contract, this can be dealt with as indicated in paragraph 33 in connection with pure endowments, with the result that

Value of Benefit at end of n years

$$=\{(P'_{[x+n]} - P') + (P'_{[x]+n} - P'_{[x+n]})\}\,\mathbf{a}_{[x]+n},$$

Value of Premiums at end of n years

$$=(kP' - \cdot 01m)(1+i)\,s_{\overline{n}|},$$

the net premium only being taken into account on the premium side. Whence

$$P' = \frac{\{P'_{[x+n]} + (P'_{[x]+n} - P'_{[x+n]})\}\,\mathbf{a}_{[x]+n} + \cdot 01m\,(1+i)\,s_{\overline{n}|}}{k\,(1+i)\,s_{\overline{n}|} + \mathbf{a}_{[x]+n}} \quad \ldots(47).$$

If considered necessary further loading can be imposed by substituting $(P'_{[x]+n} - P'_{[x+n]})(1+\cdot 01l)$, where l is the percentage loading required, for $(P'_{[x]+n} - P'_{[x+n]})$.

Since the formula is based on Office premiums it can easily be modified so as to apply to endowment assurances, limited-payment policies, and also to with-profit assurances. In the last mentioned case bonuses would commence to accrue from the date of commencement of the risk, that is from age $x+n$.

37. Discounted Bonus Policies. A class of assurance that was at one time very popular is that under which the premiums are reduced in anticipation of future bonuses. The premiums for such policies are generally based on the full with-profit premiums of the Office, from which the annual value of the bonuses anticipated forms a deduction.

The rate of bonus anticipated should be materially less than that which it is expected the Office will be able to declare, and the condition should be attached to the contract that if the bonuses actually declared exceed the rate anticipated the policy shall share in the excess, while if the rate declared fall short of the rate discounted either the sum assured shall be reduced or the premium increased.

The rate of interest employed in discounting future bonuses should be not less than that earned on the invested funds or at which the Office is prepared to grant loans on the security of its policies. The higher the rate of interest employed the smaller will be the reduction of premium. If the Office anticipates a long period of low yields on investments and discounts the bonuses at a rate rather higher than that provided by other securities, and provided bonuses can be maintained at a rate higher than that discounted, such policies supply an attractive investment yielding a very satisfactory rate of interest, with no expense attaching thereto.

When, however, higher yields are obtainable on sound investments, and a time of general depreciation in values accompanied by high expense rates occurs, discounted bonus policies offer no attraction from the Company's point of view and may prove a difficult problem for settlement between the Office and the assured, who will probably object to his sum assured being reduced or his premium increased in spite of any conditions attaching to his assurance.

38. If Simple Reversionary Bonus additions be discounted, and it be assumed that both the quinquennial and interim bonuses are at rate b, interim bonuses being declared only after the first five years, the reduction of the tabular with-profit whole-life premium (assuming a "select period" of five years) will be obtained by the formula

$$\frac{b(5M_{x+5}+R_{x+5})}{N_{[x]}}.$$

39. If Compound Reversionary Bonuses be discounted at the same rate b and subject to the same condition as regards interim bonuses, the reduction of the tabular with-profit premium will be given by the formula

$$\frac{1}{N_{[x]}}\{5bM_{x+5} + b(1+5b)(R_{x+5} - R_{x+10}) + b(1+5b)^2(R_{x+10} - R_{x+15}) + \ldots \text{etc.}\}.$$

These two expressions are of the same form as the additions made to the net premiums in paragraphs 16 and 18 respectively for similar bonuses.

As regards the discounting of *Compound* Reversionary Bonuses, it has been argued that as the bonuses do not remain attached to the policy to earn additional bonuses, allowance cannot be made for the "compounding" when ascertaining the reduction to be made from the full with-profit premium. It is argued that only *Simple* reversionary bonus additions can be taken into account. The second formula given above assumes that compound bonuses are discounted: if the other opinion be held the first formula will be employed.

The corresponding expressions for endowment assurances, and for whole-life assurances when other conditions as regards the declaration of the bonuses apply, can be seen by examining the additions to allow for bonuses made in the formulae in paragraphs 16 to 19 inclusive.

40. If the Office declare a quinquennial cash bonus as a percentage of the premiums paid during the quinquennium and a percentage KP′ be discounted, the reduction of premium to be allowed in the case of a whole-life assurance will be, assuming the "select period" to be five years,

$$5KP' . \frac{1}{N_{[x]}}\{D_{x+5} + D_{x+10} + D_{x+15} + \ldots\},$$

which, if we assume

$$5D_{x+5} = D_{[x]+3} + D_{[x]+4} + D_{x+5} + D_{x+6} + D_{x+7} \text{ approx.},$$

can be written $$KP' . \frac{N_{[x]+3}}{N_{[x]}}.$$

41. Mortality Experience of Different Classes of Assurance. The mortality experience amongst lives assured under various classes of policies differs materially, and indicates that, however carefully a Life Office may select lives to be insured, there is also selection against the Office. A person who has reason to think that his standard of health is below the average may prefer a whole-life assurance under which the premium is smaller, thus securing greater protection for his annual outlay, while a healthier individual may prefer an endowment assurance, in order to make provision for old age as well as protection for his dependants.

In the British Offices Experience it was found that, generally speaking, the higher the rate of premium the lighter was the mortality. The experience was extracted for various classes of assurances. The $O^{[M]}$ and $O^{[NM]}$ have already been mentioned, and it is only necessary here to refer to one other table, the $O^{[EM]}$, based on the experience of single-life endowment assurances. A comparison of these three tables shows that $\overset{O^{[EM]}}{q}_{[x]+n} < \overset{O^{[M]}}{q}_{[x]+n} < \overset{O^{[NM]}}{q}_{[x]+n}$: that is, as the premium charged diminished, the rate of mortality increased.

During the period to which this experience relates, however, Endowment Assurances formed a comparatively small part of the business of the Offices which supplied particulars of their policies, whereas since that period there has been a very rapid growth in the demand for this class of assurance, the new business effected in recent years containing a far greater number of Endowment Assurances than of any other type of policy. It is probable that, as a result, the later experience of lives under this class will be similar to that under whole-life assurances.

EXAMPLES

Ex. 1. If the net single premium for a whole-life policy for £100 at a given age is £32. 8*s*., the corresponding net level yearly premium £1. 12*s*. 5*d*. and the corresponding net yearly premium reducible by 50 per cent. after ten years £2. 5*s*. 8*d*., find the net single premium on the same basis for a ten-year endowment assurance for £100.

By the question

$$100\mathrm{A}_x = 32{\cdot}4,$$

$$100\mathrm{P}_x = 1{\cdot}6208\dot{3},$$

and $$2{\cdot}2\dot{8}3\,(\mathbf{a}_x - \tfrac{1}{2}\,{}_{10|}\mathbf{a}_x) = 100\mathrm{A}_x = 32{\cdot}4.$$

To ascertain $\mathbf{a}_x$, we have

$$\mathbf{a}_x = \frac{A_x}{P_x} = \frac{32{\cdot}4}{1{\cdot}6208\dot{3}} = 19{\cdot}990,$$

$$\therefore \quad 2{\cdot}28\dot{3}\ {}_{10|}\mathbf{a}_x = 2\,\{2{\cdot}28\dot{3}\,(19{\cdot}990) - 32{\cdot}4\}$$
$$= 26{\cdot}488,$$

and
$$ {}_{10|}\mathbf{a}_x = 11{\cdot}601.$$

It is required to find $A_{x:\overline{10|}} = 1 - d\mathbf{a}_{x:\overline{10|}}$, the values of d and $\mathbf{a}_{x:\overline{10|}}$ thus being required,

$$d = \frac{1 - A_x}{\mathbf{a}_x} = \frac{1 - {\cdot}324}{19{\cdot}990} = {\cdot}03382,$$

$$\mathbf{a}_{x:\overline{10|}} = \mathbf{a}_x - {}_{10|}\mathbf{a}_x$$
$$= 8{\cdot}389,$$

$$\therefore \quad A_{x:\overline{10|}} = 1 - {\cdot}03382\,(8{\cdot}389)$$
$$= {\cdot}71628.$$

The net single premium for a ten-year endowment assurance for £100 is therefore £71. 12*s*. 7*d*. say.

Ex. 2. The annual premium for a whole-life policy is ·04 for five years and ·02 thereafter, or ·0475 for five years and ·0175 thereafter. Find the uniform annual whole-life premium.

Also find the annual premium for an endowment assurance payable at the end of five years or previous death in terms of ${}_5P_x$ and d.

From the question we can write at once:

$$P_x\mathbf{a}_x = {\cdot}04\mathbf{a}_{x:\overline{5|}} + {\cdot}02\,{}_{4|}a_x = {\cdot}0475\,\mathbf{a}_{x:\overline{5|}} + {\cdot}0175\,{}_{4|}a_x.$$

From the second and third of these expressions,

$${\cdot}0025\,{}_{4|}a_x = {\cdot}0075\,\mathbf{a}_{x:\overline{5|}},$$

$$\therefore \quad {}_{4|}a_x = 3\mathbf{a}_{x:\overline{5|}}.$$

Also
$$\mathbf{a}_x = \mathbf{a}_{x:\overline{5|}} + {}_{4|}a_x$$
$$= 4\mathbf{a}_{x:\overline{5|}}.$$

Therefore
$$P_x\mathbf{a}_x = {\cdot}04\mathbf{a}_{x:\overline{5|}} + {\cdot}02\,{}_{4|}a_x$$
$$= {\cdot}04\,(\tfrac{1}{4}\mathbf{a}_x) + {\cdot}02\,(\tfrac{3}{4}\mathbf{a}_x),$$

whence
$$P_x = {\cdot}01 + {\cdot}015$$
$$= {\cdot}025.$$

For the second part of the question, we have:

$$\begin{aligned} P_{x:\overline{5}|} &= \frac{1}{a_{x:\overline{5}|}} - d \\ &= \frac{1 - d a_{x:\overline{5}|}}{a_{x:\overline{5}|}} \\ &= \frac{1 - d a_x}{a_{x:\overline{5}|}} + \frac{3 d a_{x:\overline{5}|}}{a_{x:\overline{5}|}} \quad \text{since } a_{x:\overline{5}|} = \tfrac{1}{4} a_x \\ &= {}_5P_x + 3d. \end{aligned}$$

Ex. 3. A man aged 35 wishes to be allowed to pay a premium of $P_{[30]}$ for a whole-life assurance, and is prepared to have his sum assured reduced by 30X in the first year, 29X in the second year, and so on, the deduction from the sum assured decreasing by X per annum. Find an approximate value of X by $O^{[NM]}$ at 3 per cent.

Here we must take

$$P_{[30]} \cdot a_{[35]} = A_{[35]} - \frac{X}{D_{[35]}} \{30 M_{[35]} - R_{[35]+1} + R_{66}\}$$

or

$$\begin{aligned} X &= \frac{M_{[35]} - P_{[30]} N_{[35]}}{30 M_{[35]} - R_{[35]+1} + R_{66}} \\ &= \frac{13581{\cdot}33 - 11671{\cdot}76}{407439{\cdot}9 - 285320{\cdot}16} \\ &= {\cdot}0156. \end{aligned}$$

The question asks for an approximate value, which can be obtained more simply by assuming a constant deduction of 15X. Then

$$\begin{aligned} X &= \frac{M_{[35]} - P_{[30]} N_{[35]}}{15 (M_{[35]} - M_{65})} \\ &= {\cdot}0154. \end{aligned}$$

It should be pointed out that

$$R_{[35]+1} = M_{[35]+1} + M_{[35]+2} + \dots + M_{[35]+4} + \sum_{40}^{\omega} M_x.$$

CHAPTER VI

VALUES OF SINGLE-LIFE POLICIES SUBJECT TO ANNUAL PREMIUMS

1. Policy Values. At the time a policy of assurance is issued, the value of the net premiums exactly equals the value of the benefit assured. In connection with a Whole-Life or an Endowment Assurance, however, as the policy continues in force, the time at which the sum assured is to be paid draws nearer, and the value of the assurance increases. On the other hand, the number of premiums remaining to be paid becomes smaller and the value of future premiums decreases. The value of the assurance will thus exceed the value of future premiums, or in other words the premiums to be received in future will not suffice to meet the claim when it arises, and the Office must have in hand a sum, known as the Value of the Policy, sufficient to meet the difference. The only source from which this sum can be derived is the premiums already paid together with interest earned thereon.

In calculating the value of a policy, as in connection with all other monetary values based on the Mortality Table, the assumption is tacitly made that there is a sufficient number of assurances to supply the average experience of the mortality table employed.

The formulae for the values of the various policies considered in this chapter will be given on the basis of Select Tables, the suffix of any symbol involving duration t being written $[x]+t$. The square brackets enclosing the age at entry must be omitted when the value of a function is taken from the "Ultimate" portion of a Select Table, or when an Aggregate Table is used.

2. In the case of a whole-life assurance of 1, subject to annual premiums, effected t years ago (t being integral) on a life then aged x, the value of the sum assured is now $A_{[x]+t}$, and the value of the remaining premiums, including the $(t+1)$th premium now due, is $P_{[x]}\mathbf{a}_{[x]+t}$. Representing the value of the policy by ${}_tV_{[x]}$, we have

$$ {}_tV_{[x]} = A_{[x]+t} - P_{[x]}\mathbf{a}_{[x]+t} \quad \ldots\ldots\ldots\ldots\ldots\ldots(1).$$

3. The value of an endowment assurance is obtained in a similar manner. Assuming the term of the assurance to be n years and that it was effected t years ago on a life then aged x, the present age is $x+t$, the remaining period of the assurance is $n-t$ years and there are $n-t$ premiums (including the one just due) remaining to be paid.

The value of the sum assured is therefore $A_{[x]+t:\overline{n-t}|}$ and of the future premiums $P_{[x]:\overline{n}|}\cdot \mathbf{a}_{[x]+t:\overline{n-t}|}$; whence, representing the value of the policy by ${}_tV_{[x]:\overline{n}|}$, we have

$$ {}_tV_{[x]:\overline{n}|}=A_{[x]+t:\overline{n-t}|}-P_{[x]:\overline{n}|}\cdot \mathbf{a}_{[x]+t:\overline{n-t}|} \quad \text{.........(2).}$$

4. The method adopted in the last two paragraphs of ascertaining the value of the policy by reference to the future is called the "Prospective Method." As has been stated, however, the only source from which the policy value can have been accumulated is the past premiums, and it will be instructive to consider these accumulations and to ascertain the value by what is known as the "Retrospective Method."

Assuming $l_{[x]}$ whole-life assurances effected on lives all aged x at entry, the sum assured in each case being 1, the amount in hand at the end of the first year of assurance will be

$$P_{[x]}l_{[x]}(1+i)-d_{[x]},$$

since there will have been $l_{[x]}$ premiums paid at the commencement of the year, and $d_{[x]}$ deaths during the year, on each of which 1 would have to be paid, it being assumed that claims are paid at the end of the year of death. At the end of the second year the sum in hand will be

$$\{l_{[x]}P_{[x]}(1+i)-d_{[x]}\}(1+i)+\{l_{[x]+1}P_{[x]}(1+i)-d_{[x]+1}\}$$
$$=P_{[x]}\{l_{[x]}(1+i)^2+l_{[x]+1}(1+i)\}-\{d_{[x]}(1+i)+d_{[x]+1}\},$$

and similarly at the end of t years, the sum in hand from the accumulations of past premiums, after allowing for the payment of claims, will be

$$P_{[x]}\{l_{[x]}(1+i)^t+l_{[x]+1}(1+i)^{t-1}+\ldots+l_{[x]+t-1}(1+i)\}$$
$$\qquad -\{d_{[x]}(1+i)^{t-1}+d_{[x]+1}(1+i)^{t-2}+\ldots+d_{[x]+t-1}\}$$
$$=\frac{1}{v^{x+t}}\{P_{[x]}(D_{[x]}+D_{[x]+1}+\ldots+D_{[x]+t-1})$$
$$\qquad -(C_{[x]}+C_{[x]+1}+\ldots+C_{[x]+t-1})\}.$$

Whence, dividing by $l_{[x]+t}$, the number of survivors at the end of the t years, we have as the amount in hand for each survivor, or the value of each policy,

$$ {}_tV_{[x]} = \frac{1}{D_{[x]+t}} \{P_{[x]}(N_{[x]} - N_{[x]+t}) - (M_{[x]} - M_{[x]+t})\} \quad ......(3). $$

The form of the expression for the retrospective value of an endowment assurance will be exactly the same as that for the value of a whole-life assurance, since the same number of premiums will have been accumulated, and the same number of claims paid: the only difference is in the amount of the net premium.

Thus

$$ {}_tV_{[x]:\overline{n}|} = \frac{1}{D_{[x]+t}} \{P_{[x]:\overline{n}|}(N_{[x]} - N_{[x]+t}) - (M_{[x]} - M_{[x]+t})\} \quad ...(4). $$

5. So long as net functions only are used and the policy values are based on the mortality table and the rate of interest employed in calculating the net premiums, the prospective and retrospective methods give identical policy values.

Considering the whole-life policy value by the retrospective method, and remembering that $P_{[x]}N_{[x]} = M_{[x]}$,

$$ \begin{aligned} {}_tV_{[x]} &= \frac{1}{D_{[x]+t}} \{P_{[x]}(N_{[x]} - N_{[x]+t}) - (M_{[x]} - M_{[x]+t})\} \\ &= \frac{1}{D_{[x]+t}} \{M_{[x]+t} - P_{[x]}N_{[x]+t}\} \\ &= A_{[x]+t} - P_{[x]}a_{[x]+t}, \end{aligned} $$

the prospective value.

Similarly, for an endowment assurance, since

$$ P_{[x]:\overline{n}|}(N_{[x]} - N_{[x]+n}) = M_{[x]} - M_{[x]+n} + D_{[x]+n}, $$

$$ \begin{aligned} {}_tV_{[x]:\overline{n}|} &= \frac{1}{D_{[x]+t}} \{P_{[x]:\overline{n}|}(N_{[x]} - N_{[x]+t}) - (M_{[x]} - M_{[x]+t})\} \\ &= \frac{1}{D_{[x]+t}} \{P_{[x]:\overline{n}|}(N_{[x]} - N_{[x]+n} + N_{[x]+n} - N_{[x]+t}) \\ &\quad - (M_{[x]} - M_{[x]+n} + D_{[x]+n}) + (M_{[x]+t} - M_{[x]+n} + D_{[x]+n})\} \\ &= A_{[x]+t:\overline{n-t}|} - P_{[x]:\overline{n}|}a_{[x]+t:\overline{n-t}|}. \end{aligned} $$

6. The policy values for limited payment whole-life and endowment assurances on the life of (x), the sum assured being 1 and the premiums limited to k payments, are represented by ${}^k_tV_{[x]}$ and ${}^k_tV_{[x]:\overline{n}|}$ respectively.

For the whole-life assurance, by the prospective method

$$\left.\begin{aligned} {}^k_tV_{[x]} &= A_{[x]+t} - {}_kP_{[x]}\, a_{[x]+t:\overline{k-t}|} \quad \text{when } t < k \\ &= A_{[x]+t} \qquad\qquad\qquad\quad\;\; \text{,,} \quad t \geqq k \end{aligned}\right\} \quad \text{.........(5)},$$

and by the retrospective method

$$\left.\begin{aligned} {}^k_tV_{[x]} &= \frac{1}{D_{[x]+t}}\{{}_kP_{[x]}(N_{[x]} - N_{[x]+t}) - (M_{[x]} - M_{[x]+t})\} \text{ when } t<k \\ &= \frac{1}{D_{[x]+t}}\{{}_kP_{[x]}(N_{[x]} - N_{[x]+k}) - (M_{[x]} - M_{[x]+t})\} \quad \text{,,} \quad t \geqq k \end{aligned}\right\} \text{...(6)}.$$

For an endowment assurance, by the prospective method

$$\left.\begin{aligned} {}^k_tV_{[x]:\overline{n}|} &= A_{[x]+t:\overline{n-t}|} - {}_kP_{[x]:\overline{n}|}\, a_{[x]+t:\overline{k-t}|} \quad \text{when } t < k \\ &= A_{[x]+t:\overline{n-t}|} \qquad\qquad\qquad\qquad \text{,,} \quad t \geqq k \end{aligned}\right\} \quad \text{...............(7)},$$

and by the retrospective method

$$\left.\begin{aligned} {}^k_tV_{[x]:\overline{n}|} &= \frac{1}{D_{[x]+t}}\{{}_kP_{[x]:\overline{n}|}(N_{[x]} - N_{[x]+t}) - (M_{[x]} - M_{[x]+t})\} \text{ when } t<k \\ &= \frac{1}{D_{[x]+t}}\{{}_kP_{[x]:\overline{n}|}(N_{[x]} - N_{[x]+k}) - (M_{[x]} - M_{[x]+t})\} \quad \text{,,} \quad t \geqq k \end{aligned}\right\} \text{(8)}.$$

With regard to the retrospective policy value when the duration "t" is greater than k, the number of premiums payable, the expression for the accumulation of the premiums, excluding the claims, takes the form $P\,\dfrac{N_{[x]} - N_{[x]+k}}{D_{[x]+t}}$. The total accumulation to time k of the premiums paid by $l_{[x]}$ original entrants or the survivors of these is $l_{[x]+k}P\,\dfrac{N_{[x]} - N_{[x]+k}}{D_{[x]+k}}$ and, no further premiums being payable, this sum must be accumulated for $(t-k)$ years and divided amongst the $l_{[x]+t}$ survivors. That is,

$$P\,\frac{N_{[x]} - N_{[x]+k}}{D_{[x]+k}} \times (1+i)^{t-k} \times \frac{l_{[x]+k}}{l_{[x]+t}}$$

$$= P\,\frac{N_{[x]} - N_{[x]+k}}{D_{[x]+t}}.$$

In each of the cases given in this paragraph the prospective policy value can readily be shown to be identical with that found by the retrospective method.

7. It is only when the net premiums by the mortality table and at the rate of interest employed in the valuation are used that the prospective and retrospective policy values are identical. If in place of the net premium, $P' (= P + \phi)$ be taken into account (ϕ being positive); by the prospective method, a larger premium will be taken credit for and the policy value will consequently be reduced; whereas, by the retrospective method, larger premiums will have been accumulated, and the policy value will be increased. Thus for a whole-life assurance, the policy value where the premium $P + \phi$ is valued is, prospectively,

$$\begin{aligned} &A_{[x]+t} - (P_{[x]} + \phi)\, a_{[x]+t} \\ &= {}_tV_{[x]} - \phi a_{[x]+t}, \end{aligned}$$

and retrospectively,

$$\begin{aligned} &\frac{1}{D_{[x]+t}} \{(P_{[x]} + \phi)(N_{[x]} - N_{[x]+t}) - (M_{[x]} - M_{[x]+t})\} \\ &\qquad = {}_tV_{[x]} + \phi \frac{N_{[x]} - N_{[x]+t}}{D_{[x]+t}}. \end{aligned}$$

If on the other hand the premium valued be less than the net premium, say $P - \phi$, the policy value becomes, prospectively,

$${}_tV_{[x]} + \phi a_{[x]+t},$$

and retrospectively, $\quad {}_tV_{[x]} - \phi \dfrac{N_{[x]} - N_{[x]+t}}{D_{[x]+t}}.$

A similar argument clearly holds with endowment assurance and other classes of policies.

8. In order to avoid repetition it will be taken for granted, unless otherwise stated, that each of the policies dealt with in the following paragraphs is for a sum assured of 1 on the life of (x), and that where a pure endowment, temporary assurance or endowment assurance is being considered, the full term of the contract is n years.

It may perhaps be pointed out that in practice the prospective method of valuing policies is employed except occasionally in the case of special classes of policies which are more easily valued by the retrospective method.

9. Policy Values at Fractional Durations. Annual Premiums. The values of policies subject to annual premiums at durations which include a fraction of a year are most readily obtained by interpolation.

In order to obtain the value of a policy subject to annual premiums at duration $t+\frac{1}{s}$, it must be remembered that, as at this time the number of premiums paid will be $t+1$, the interpolation must be made between the values at duration t with $t+1$ premiums paid—i.e. ${}_tV_{[x]}+P_{[x]}$—and at duration $t+1$, with the same number of premiums paid—i.e. ${}_{t+1}V_{[x]}$. Thus for a whole-life assurance,

$$\begin{aligned}{}_{t+\frac{1}{s}}V_{[x]} &= ({}_tV_{[x]}+P_{[x]})+\frac{1}{s}\{{}_{t+1}V_{[x]}-({}_tV_{[x]}+P_{[x]})\}\\ &= {}_tV_{[x]}+\frac{1}{s}({}_{t+1}V_{[x]}-{}_tV_{[x]})+\left(1-\frac{1}{s}\right)P_{[x]} \quad\text{......(9).}\end{aligned}$$

If the interpolation had been made between ${}_tV_{[x]}$ (t premiums paid) and ${}_{t+1}V_{[x]}$ ($t+1$ premiums paid) the result would have been the value at duration $t+\frac{1}{s}$ with $t+\frac{1}{s}$ premiums paid: which would not fit the case.

A numerical example may make the point clearer, while at the same time demonstrating the simplicity of the interpolation in practice.

Let us suppose that ${}_3V_x = \cdot068$, ${}_4V_x=\cdot091$, $P_x=\cdot030$, and it is required to find the value of ${}_{3\frac{1}{4}}V_x$. We have

$$\begin{aligned}{}_{3\frac{1}{4}}V_x &= {}_3V_x+\tfrac{1}{4}({}_4V_x-{}_3V_x)+\tfrac{3}{4}P_x\\ &= \cdot068+\tfrac{1}{4}(\cdot023)+\tfrac{3}{4}(\cdot030)\\ &= \cdot096.\end{aligned}$$

From expression (9) it is seen that in addition to the value that would be obtained by interpolating between ${}_tV_{[x]}$ and ${}_{t+1}V_{[x]}$ there must be kept in hand a portion of the year's premium corresponding to the period still to elapse before another premium becomes payable.

10. An alternative method of arriving at the value of ${}_{t+\frac{1}{s}}V_{[x]}$, involving the use of the practical annuity-value

$${}_{1-\frac{1}{s}|}a_{x+t+\frac{1}{s}} = a_{x+t+\frac{1}{s}}-\left(1-\frac{1}{s}\right),$$

is as follows:

$$
\begin{aligned}
{}_{t+\frac{1}{s}}V_{[x]} &= {}^{*}A_{[x]+t+\frac{1}{s}} - P_{[x]}.{}_{1-\frac{1}{s}}|a_{[x]+t+\frac{1}{s}} \\
&= \left\{A_{[x]+t} + \frac{1}{s}(A_{[x]+t+1} - A_{[x]+t})\right\} \\
&\qquad - P_{[x]}\left\{a_{[x]+t} + \frac{1}{s}(a_{[x]+t+1} - a_{[x]+t}) - \left(1-\frac{1}{s}\right)\right\} \\
&= {}_tV_{[x]} + \frac{1}{s}({}_{t+1}V_{[x]} - {}_tV_{[x]}) + \left(1-\frac{1}{s}\right)P_{[x]},
\end{aligned}
$$

as before.

11. For the value of an endowment assurance at duration $t+\frac{1}{s}$ we have

$$
\begin{aligned}
{}_{t+\frac{1}{s}}V_{[x]:\overline{n|}} &= ({}_tV_{[x]:\overline{n|}} + P_{[x]:\overline{n|}}) + \frac{1}{s}\{{}_{t+1}V_{[x]:\overline{n|}} - ({}_tV_{[x]:\overline{n|}} + P_{[x]:\overline{n|}})\} \\
&= {}_tV_{[x]:\overline{n|}} + \frac{1}{s}({}_{t+1}V_{[x]:\overline{n|}} - {}_tV_{[x]:\overline{n|}}) + \left(1-\frac{1}{s}\right)P_{[x]:\overline{n|}} \quad \ldots(10).
\end{aligned}
$$

12. If the number of premiums payable be limited to k, the values of the whole-life and endowment assurances respectively at time $t+\frac{1}{s}\left(t+\frac{1}{s}<k\right)$ will be

$$
{}^{k}_{t+\frac{1}{s}}V_{[x]} = {}^{k}_{t}V_{[x]} + \frac{1}{s}({}^{k}_{t+1}V_{[x]} - {}^{k}_{t}V_{[x]}) + \left(1-\frac{1}{s}\right){}_kP_{[x]} \quad \ldots\ldots(11),
$$

and

$$
{}^{k}_{t+\frac{1}{s}}V_{[x]:\overline{n|}} = {}^{k}_{t}V_{[x]:\overline{n|}} + \frac{1}{s}({}^{k}_{t+1}V_{[x]:\overline{n|}} - {}^{k}_{t}V_{[x]:\overline{n|}}) + \left(1-\frac{1}{s}\right){}_kP_{[x]:\overline{n|}} \quad \ldots\ldots(12).
$$

13. Values of Participating Policies. In obtaining the value of an ordinary participating policy, as the assured has no title to bonuses not yet declared, it is only necessary to consider those already attached to the policy, and to value these as an addition to the sum assured. Thus in the case of a whole-life assurance, the sum assured being S and reversionary bonuses added thereto being B, the value will be

$$
\begin{aligned}
&(S+B)\,A_{[x]+t} - SP_{[x]}a_{[x]+t} \\
&= S\,.\,{}_tV_{[x]} + BA_{[x]+t}.
\end{aligned}
$$

Similarly, for an endowment assurance for the same sum assured and with the same bonus additions, the value will be

$$
S\,.\,{}_tV_{[x]:\overline{n|}} + BA_{[x]+t:\overline{n-t|}}.
$$

* A theoretical point which arises in connection with this function is discussed in Chap. VIII 16.

14. In the case of a guaranteed bonus, the whole of the benefit assured, including both existing and future bonuses, must be valued. For example, the value of a whole-life policy for £100 effected on the life of (x) ten years ago, with a guaranteed simple reversionary bonus of £2 per cent. per annum, is

$$120\,A_{x+10} + 2\,(IA)_{x+10} - Pa_{x+10},$$

P being the net premium to provide for the full benefit assured, including the guaranteed bonus.

15. Pure Endowment Policy Values. The value at the end of t years of an endowment of 1 payable on (x) attaining age $x+n$ secured by an annual premium $P_{[x]:\overset{1}{\overline{n|}}}$ is

$$ {}_tV_{[x]:\overset{1}{\overline{n|}}} = A_{[x]+t:\overset{1}{\overline{n-t|}}} - P_{[x]:\overset{1}{\overline{n|}}}\,a_{[x]+t:\overline{n-t|}} \text{ prospectively} \ldots(13)$$

$$= \frac{P_{[x]:\overset{1}{\overline{n|}}}(N_{[x]} - N_{[x]+t})}{D_{[x]+t}} \quad \text{retrospectively}\ldots\ldots\ldots(14),$$

the retrospective value consisting of the accumulations of the premiums, no claims having occurred.

Since

$$P_{[x]:\overset{1}{\overline{t|}}} = \frac{D_{[x]+t}}{N_{[x]} - N_{[x]+t}}$$

it follows from formula (14) that ${}_tV_{[x]:\overset{1}{\overline{n|}}} = \dfrac{P_{[x]:\overset{1}{\overline{n|}}}}{P_{[x]:\overset{1}{\overline{t|}}}}$.

16. When the endowment is granted with return of premiums in the event of death before attainment of the endowment age, representing the net premium by P and the Office premium by P′, the value is, prospectively,

$$A_{[x]+t:\overset{1}{\overline{n-t|}}} + \frac{P'}{D_{[x]+t}}\{tM_{[x]+t} + R_{[x]+t} - R_{[x]+n} - nM_{[x]+n}\} - Pa_{[x]+t:\overline{n-t|}}$$

and retrospectively

$$\frac{1}{D_{[x]+t}}\{P\,(N_{[x]} - N_{[x]+t}) - P'\,(R_{[x]} - R_{[x]+t} - tM_{[x]+t})\} \quad (15).$$

These two formulae give identical results. The numerator of the retrospective value can be rewritten as follows:

$$P\,(N_{[x]} - N_{[x]+n} + N_{[x]+n} - N_{[x]+t})$$
$$+ P'\,(tM_{[x]+t} + R_{[x]+t} - R_{[x]+n} - nM_{[x]+n})$$
$$- P'\,(R_{[x]} - R_{[x]+n} - nM_{[x]+n}),$$

the terms $PN_{[x]+n}$ and $P'(R_{[x]+n} - nM_{[x]+n})$ having been added and subtracted.

And since

$$P(N_{[x]} - N_{[x]+n}) = D_{[x]+n} + P'(R_{[x]} - R_{[x]+n} - nM_{[x]+n}),$$

the expression reduces to

$$D_{[x]+n} + P'(tM_{[x]+t} + R_{[x]+t} - R_{[x]+n} - nM_{[x]+n}) - P(N_{[x]+t} - N_{[x]+n}),$$

which is the numerator of the expression for the prospective value.

If mortality be neglected, the value is simply

$$P(1+i)\, s_{\overline{t}|}.$$

17. Deferred Assurances. For the value at the end of t years of a whole-life assurance on (x), deferred n years $(t < n)$, no benefit or return of premiums being granted in the event of (x) dying during the period of deferment, and P being the net premium payable throughout the duration of the policy, the expression is

$$_{n-t|}A_{[x]+t} - Pa_{[x]+t} = \frac{1}{D_{[x]+t}}\{M_{[x]+n} - PN_{[x]+t}\}.$$

If the deferred assurance be granted with return of premiums in the event of (x) dying before the assurance becomes effective, the amount which the Office should have in hand at the end of n years, namely $(P_{[x]+n} - P)\,\mathbf{a}_{[x]+n} = A_{[x]+n} - P\mathbf{a}_{[x]+n}$, which can be represented by V′, can be treated as the amount of a pure endowment falling in on the assured reaching age $x+n$, and the policy valued by the method shown in paragraph 16.

If mortality during the period of deferment be ignored the value at the end of t years $(t < n)$ becomes

$$P(1+i)\, s_{\overline{t}|}.$$

After the assurance is entered upon (i.e. where $t > n$) the value is

$$A_{[x]+t} - Pa_{[x]+t},$$

the contract being then a whole-life assurance subject to a special net premium.

18. Endowment Assurances with Return of Premiums. The prospective formula for the value at the end of t years of an endowment assurance with return of premiums when the sum assured is payable, is

$$\left.\begin{aligned}&\frac{1}{D_{[x]+t}}\{M_{[x]+t}-M_{[x]+n}+D_{[x]+n}\\&\qquad+P'(tM_{[x]+t}+R_{[x]+t}-R_{[x]+n}-nM_{[x]+n}+nD_{[x]+n})\\&\qquad-P(N_{[x]+t}-N_{[x]+n})\}\\&\text{and the retrospective value}\\&\frac{1}{D_{[x]+t}}\{P(N_{[x]}-N_{[x]+t})-(M_{[x]}-M_{[x]+t})\\&\qquad-P'(R_{[x]}-R_{[x]+t}-tM_{[x]+t})\}\end{aligned}\right\}\ldots(16),$$

P and P′ being respectively the net and Office premiums for the special assurance.

It is clear from a comparison of the prospective and retrospective formulae (16) that the retrospective method is generally the simpler for use in valuing assurances with return of premiums.

If the premiums are returnable only in the event of death during the n years, the expression for the value of the policy by the retrospective method is the same as formula (16) if the values of P and P′ be those for the particular benefit involved.

But if the premiums are returnable only in the event of the assured surviving to the end of the period of the contract, there will not have been any claims for the return of premiums, and the expression for the policy value takes the form

$$\frac{P(N_{[x]}-N_{[x]+t})-(M_{[x]}-M_{[x]+t})}{D_{[x]+t}}.$$

19. Instalment and Debenture Policies. In valuing a policy under which the sum assured is payable by instalments or the payment of the sum assured is deferred, interest being allowed in the meantime, the ordinary policy values can be employed provided they are multiplied by the factor representing the value, as at the time the claim arises, of the benefit assured.

Thus for a policy on the life of (x) under which the nominal sum assured of 1 is payable by m equal annual instalments payable in advance, the value is

for a whole-life assurance $\quad {}_tV_{[x]}\times\frac{1}{m}\ddot{a}_{\overline{m}|}$,

for an endowment assurance $\quad {}_tV_{[x]:\overline{n}|}\times\frac{1}{m}\ddot{a}_{\overline{m}|}$.

Similarly with debenture policies, for which the sum assured would be taken as $1 + (j - i)\, a_{\overline{m}|}$.

20. Double Endowment Assurances. A double endowment assurance being a combination of an ordinary endowment assurance and a pure endowment, its value at the end of t years, the sum assured being 1 at death or 2 at maturity, is

$$ {}_tV_{[x]:\overline{n}|} + {}_tV_{[x]:\overset{1}{\overline{n}|}}. $$

21. In connection with all the classes of policies so far considered in this chapter, the policy values immediately before successive premiums become due normally increase with the duration until the sum assured becomes payable. The risk of the Office having to pay the sum assured is an increasing one, and the premium, being uniform, is in the early years more than sufficient to cover the current risk. There is thus a margin left which is kept in hand and accumulated at interest to provide that part of the increased risk in later years not covered by the current premiums. Under an endowment assurance the policy values immediately before successive premiums become due increase until at the end of the term the value is equal to the sum assured; under a whole-life assurance the value must similarly increase until at age $\omega - 1$ it closely approximates to the sum assured, which (according to the Mortality Table) must become payable during the following year. In order that this condition may hold the premium and interest together must each year be more than sufficient to meet the current risk.

In the case of a temporary assurance the conditions are different. Assuming, for example, an assurance for ten years; in the early years the premium charged will be more than sufficient to cover the risk and the reserve will increase, but shortly after the middle of the term the premium and interest will fall short of being sufficient to cover the risk, so that part of the reserve also will be absorbed, and the policy value will thus decrease each year until at the end of the term it vanishes, the assurance then terminating.

22. Temporary Assurances. The value of a temporary assurance can be obtained by either the prospective or the retrospective method, these methods giving, as in other cases, identical results when net functions are employed. Thus,

$$\left.\begin{aligned} &\text{Prospectively} \quad {}_tV^{\,1}_{[x]:\overline{n}|} = A^{\,1}_{\overline{[x]+t}:\overline{n-t}|} - P^{\,1}_{[x]:\overline{n}|}\, a_{[x]+t:\overline{n-t}|}, \\ &\text{Retrospectively} \quad = \frac{P^{\,1}_{[x]:\overline{n}|}(N_{[x]} - N_{[x]+t}) - (M_{[x]} - M_{[x]+t})}{D_{[x]+t}} \end{aligned}\right\} \ldots(17).$$

23. The progress of the values of whole-life, temporary assurance, pure endowment, and endowment assurance policies is clearly shown in the following Tables A to D.

Table A deals with Whole-Life Assurances on lives aged 30 at entry, on the basis of the H^M Table (Makeham Graduation), for a period of 10 years from entry, and is divided into two parts, showing, on the assumption of 89,685 policies, the progress of the assurance fund ascertained by the retrospective and prospective methods respectively.

In Tables B, C and D the term of the contracts is taken as 10 years, the same number of policies effected on lives aged 30 being assumed, but it has not been thought necessary to subdivide these tables to show the progress of the fund by both the retrospective and prospective methods. At the end of each year the endowment assurance fund is exactly equal to the sum of the pure endowment and temporary assurance funds, as must result from the relation existing between these classes of policies.

In these tables the columns of policy-values will enable the student to test his knowledge of the methods of calculating policy-values by an Aggregate Table (the H^M) by means of the formulae obtained in this chapter.

Table A

Showing the progress of a Fund formed by the Contributions of 89,685 *Members, each assuring for the Whole of Life at Age* 30 *for* 1, *at an Annual Premium of* ·01873208.—*Interest* 3 *per cent.*

Retrospective Method

(1) Year n	(2) Fund at Commencement of Year	(3) Premiums paid at Commencement of Year	(4) Sum of (2) and (3)	(5) Interest earned in Year	(6) Sum of (4) and (5)	(7) Claims in Year	(8) Fund at End of Year	(9) Survivors at End of Year	(10) (8) ÷ (9) $= {}_nV_{30}$	(11) Year n
1	0000·000	1679·987	1679·987	50·400	1730·387	691	1039·387	88994	·01168	1
2	1039·387	1667·043	2706·430	81·193	2787·623	700	2087·623	88294	·02364	2
3	2087·623	1653·930	3741·553	112·247	3853·800	709	3144·800	87585	·03590	3
4	3144·800	1640·649	4785·449	143·564	4929·013	719	4210·013	86866	·04847	4
5	4210·013	1627·181	5837·194	175·116	6012·310	729	5283·310	86137	·06133	5
6	5283·310	1613·525	6896·835	206·905	7103·740	742	6361·740	85395	·07450	6
7	6361·740	1599·626	7961·366	238·841	8200·207	756	7444·207	84639	·08795	7
8	7444·207	1585·465	9029·672	270·890	9300·562	770	8530·562	83869	·10171	8
9	8530·562	1571·041	10101·603	303·048	10404·651	786	9618·651	83083	·11577	9
10	9618·651	1556·317	11174·968	335·249	11510·217	806	10704·217	82277	·13010	10

TABLE A (*continued*)

Showing the Liability for each Year under the Policies of 89,685 *Persons, each assuring at Age* 30 *for* 1, *at an Annual Premium of* ·01873208.—*Interest* 3 *per cent.*

Prospective Method

(1) Year n	(2) Survivors at End of Year	(3) A_{30+n}	(4) Value of Total Sums Assured	(5) Amount of Premiums just due	(6) $(1+a_{30+n})$	(7) Value of Future Premiums	(8) (4) − (7), being Total Liability	(9) Liability under each Contract $={}_nV_{30}$	(10) Year n
0	89685	·3914073	35103·363	1679·987	20·89502	35103·363	0·000	·00000	0
1	88994	·3985152	35465·462	1667·043	20·65098	34426·072	1039·390	·01168	1
2	88294	·4057968	35829·423	1653·930	20·40098	33741·793	2087·630	·02364	2
3	87585	·4132592	36195·307	1640·649	20·14477	33050·497	3144·810	·03590	3
4	86866	·4209031	36562·169	1627·181	19·88233	32352·150	4210·019	·04847	4
5	86137	·4287360	36930·033	1613·525	19·61340	31646·711	5283·322	·06133	5
6	85395	·4367460	37295·925	1599·626	19·33839	30934·191	6361·734	·07450	6
7	84639	·4449344	37658·803	1585·465	19·05725	30214·603	7444·200	·08795	7
8	83869	·4533089	38018·564	1571·041	18·76973	29488·015	8530·549	·10171	8
9	83083	·4618647	38373·105	1556·317	18·47598	28754·482	9618·623	·11577	9
10	82277	·4705851	38718·330	1541·219	18·17658	28014·090	10704·240	·13010	10

TABLE B

Showing the progress of a Fund formed by the Contributions of 89,685 *Members, each assuring for* 1 *at age* 30 *for* 10 *Years only, at an Annual Premium of* ·00826797.—*Interest* 3 *per cent.*

(1) Year n	(2) Funds at Commencement of Year	(3) Premiums paid at Commencement of Year	(4) Sum of (2) and (3)	(5) Interest earned in Year	(6) Sum of (4) and (5)	(7) Claims in Year	(8) Funds at End of Year	(9) Policy Value ${}_nV^1_{30:\overline{10}\rvert}$
1	00·000	741·511	741·511	22·245	763·756	691	72·756	·00082
2	72·756	735·800	808·556	24·256	832·812	700	132·812	·00150
3	132·812	730·010	862·822	25·885	888·707	709	179·707	·00205
4	179·707	724·150	903·857	27·116	930·973	719	211·973	·00244
5	211·973	718·204	930·177	27·905	958·082	729	229·082	·00266
6	229·082	712·176	941·258	28·238	969·496	742	227·496	·00266
7	227·496	706·042	933·538	28·006	961·544	756	205·544	·00243
8	205·544	699·791	905·335	27·160	932·495	770	162·495	·00194
9	162·495	693·425	855·920	25·678	881·598	786	95·598	·00115
10	95·598	686·927	782·525	23·475	806·000	806	00·000	·00000

TABLE C

Showing the progress of a Fund formed by the Contributions of 89,685 *Members, each taking out an Endowment of* 1, *at age* 30, *payable at the end of* 10 *Years, at an Annual Premium of* ·08043157.—*Interest* 3 *per cent.*

(1) Year n	(2) Funds at Commencement of Year	(3) Premiums paid at Commencement of Year	(4) Sum of (2) and (3)	(5) Interest earned in Year	(6) Funds at End of Year	(7) Policy Value ${}_nV_{30:\overline{10}\rvert}^{\ \ 1}$
1	000·000	7213·505	7213·505	216·405	7429·910	·08349
2	7429·910	7157·927	14587·837	437·635	15025·472	·17017
3	15025·472	7101·625	22127·097	663·813	22790·910	·26021
4	22790·910	7044·599	29835·509	895·065	30730·574	·35378
5	30730·574	6986·769	37717·343	1131·520	38848·863	·45101
6	38848·863	6928·134	45776·997	1373·310	47150·307	·55214
7	47150·307	6868·454	54018·761	1620·563	55639·324	·65737
8	55639·324	6807·649	62446·973	1873·411	64320·384	·76692
9	64320·384	6745·716	71066·100	2131·984	73198·084	·88103
10	73198·084	6682·497	79880·581	2396·419	82277·000	1·00000

TABLE D

Showing the progress of a Fund formed by the Contributions of 89,685 *Members, each effecting an Endowment Assurance Policy for* 1, *at age* 30, *payable at the end of* 10 *Years or on previous death, at an Annual Premium of* ·08869954.—*Interest* 3 *per cent.*

(1) Year n	(2) Funds at Commencement of Year	(3) Premiums paid at Commencement of Year	(4) Interest earned in Year	(5) Sum of (2), (3) and (4)	(6) Claims in Year	(7) Funds at End of Year	(8) Policy Value $_nV_{30:\overline{10}\rvert}$
1	000·000	7955·016	238·650	8193·666	691	7502·666	·08431
2	7502·666	7893·727	461·891	15858·284	700	15158·284	·17167
3	15158·284	7831·635	689·698	23679·617	709	22970·617	·26226
4	22970·617	7768·749	922·181	31661·547	719	30942·547	·35622
5	30942·547	7704·973	1159·425	39806·945	729	39077·945	·45367
6	39077·945	7640·310	1401·548	48119·803	742	47377·803	·55480
7	47377·803	7574·496	1648·569	56600·868	756	55844·868	·65980
8	55844·868	7507·440	1900·571	65252·879	770	64482·879	·76886
9	64482·879	7439·141	2157·662	74079·682	786	73293·682	·88218
10	73293·682	7369·424	2419·894	83083·000	806	82277·000	1·00000

24. Various alternative formulae for $_tV_{[x]}$ can be obtained from the prospective value. Thus

$$_tV_{[x]} = A_{[x]+t} - P_{[x]}\text{a}_{[x]+t} \quad \ldots\ldots\ldots\ldots\ldots\ldots(18)$$

$$= 1 - (P_{[x]} + d)\,\text{a}_{[x]+t} \quad \ldots\ldots\ldots\ldots\ldots\ldots(19)$$

$$(\text{since } A_{[x]+t} = 1 - d\,\text{a}_{[x]+t})$$

$$= 1 - \frac{\text{a}_{[x]+t}}{\text{a}_{[x]}} \text{ or } 1 - \frac{1 + a_{[x]+t}}{1 + a_{[x]}} \quad \ldots\ldots\ldots(20)$$

$$\left(\text{since } P_{[x]} + d = \frac{1}{\text{a}_{[x]}}\right)$$

$$= \frac{\text{a}_{[x]} - \text{a}_{[x]+t}}{\text{a}_{[x]}} \quad \ldots\ldots\ldots\ldots\ldots\ldots\ldots\ldots(21)$$

$$= \frac{A_{[x]+t} - A_{[x]}}{1 - A_{[x]}} \quad \ldots\ldots\ldots\ldots\ldots\ldots\ldots(22),$$

since from $A_{[x]} = 1 - d\,\text{a}_{[x]}$ it follows that $\text{a}_{[x]} = \dfrac{1 - A_{[x]}}{d}$.

Again, from the original formula

$$ {}_tV_{[x]} = A_{[x]+t}\left(1 - \frac{P_{[x]}a_{[x]+t}}{A_{[x]+t}}\right) $$

$$ = A_{[x]+t}\left(1 - \frac{P_{[x]}}{P_{[x]+t}}\right) \quad \text{.....................(23),} $$

or

$$ {}_tV_{[x]} = (P_{[x]+t} - P_{[x]})\, a_{[x]+t} \quad \text{.....................(24)} $$

$$ (\text{since } A_{[x]+t} = P_{[x]+t}\, a_{[x]+t}) $$

$$ = \frac{P_{[x]+t} - P_{[x]}}{P_{[x]+t} + d} \quad \text{..............................(25).} $$

The expressions here given for the value ${}_tV_{[x]}$ can all be obtained by general reasoning. It will be sufficient to give two examples.

If a unit be invested in the purchase of an annuity payable annually in advance during the life of (x), the annual payment will be $\frac{1}{a_{[x]}}$ or $P_{[x]} + d$, and the premium $P_{[x]}$ being available at the beginning of each year will secure a policy to provide the return of the unit at the end of the year of death of (x). At the end of t years, if the unit were payable immediately, its value would be 1, but payment is deferred during the life of (x), for which period the annuity of $P_{[x]} + d$ continues payable, its value being $(P_{[x]} + d)\, a_{[x]+t}$. Deducting this value from the unit the value of the policy is

$$ 1 - (P_{[x]} + d)\, a_{[x]+t}. $$

Again, if a person aged $[x] + t$ desired to take out a whole-life assurance on his own life he would have to pay a premium of $P_{[x]+t}$, the value of all the premiums payable under the contract being $P_{[x]+t}\, a_{[x]+t}$. If, however, $([x] + t)$ holds a policy effected t years ago at a premium of $P_{[x]}$, the value of the remaining premiums is $P_{[x]}a_{[x]+t}$, and the amount by which this falls short of the value of the premiums to be paid for a similar policy at his present age is the value of his existing policy. That is

$$ (P_{[x]+t} - P_{[x]})\, a_{[x]+t}. $$

25. Expressions similar to those given in paragraph 24 for the value of a whole-life assurance can be obtained for the value of an endowment assurance. Thus

$$ {}_t V_{[x]:\overline{n}|} = A_{[x]+t:\overline{n-t}|} - P_{[x]:\overline{n}|}\, \mathbf{a}_{[x]+t:\overline{n-t}|} \quad \ldots\ldots\ldots\ldots\ldots(26)$$

$$ = 1 - (P_{[x]:\overline{n}|} + d)\, \mathbf{a}_{[x]+t:\overline{n-t}|} \quad \ldots\ldots\ldots\ldots\ldots(27)$$

$$ = 1 - \frac{\mathbf{a}_{[x]+t:\overline{n-t}|}}{\mathbf{a}_{[x]:\overline{n}|}} \text{ or } 1 - \frac{1 + a_{[x]+t:\overline{n-t-1}|}}{1 + a_{[x]:\overline{n-1}|}} \quad \ldots\ldots(28)$$

$$ = \frac{\mathbf{a}_{[x]:\overline{n}|} - \mathbf{a}_{[x]+t:\overline{n-t}|}}{\mathbf{a}_{[x]:\overline{n}|}} \quad \ldots\ldots\ldots\ldots\ldots(29)$$

$$ = \frac{A_{[x]+t:\overline{n-t}|} - A_{[x]:\overline{n}|}}{1 - A_{[x]:\overline{n}|}} \quad \ldots\ldots\ldots\ldots\ldots(30).$$

Also from the original formula

$$ {}_t V_{[x]:\overline{n}|} = A_{[x]+t:\overline{n-t}|} \left(1 - \frac{P_{[x]:\overline{n}|}\, \mathbf{a}_{[x]+t:\overline{n-t}|}}{A_{[x]+t:\overline{n-t}|}}\right)$$

$$ = A_{[x]+t:\overline{n-t}|} \left(1 - \frac{P_{[x]:\overline{n}|}}{P_{[x]+t:\overline{n-t}|}}\right) \quad \ldots\ldots\ldots\ldots\ldots(31)$$

$$ = (P_{[x]+t:\overline{n-t}|} - P_{[x]:\overline{n}|})\, \mathbf{a}_{[x]+t:\overline{n-t}|} \quad \ldots\ldots\ldots\ldots\ldots(32)$$

$$ = \frac{P_{[x]+t:\overline{n-t}|} - P_{[x]:\overline{n}|}}{P_{[x]+t:\overline{n-t}|} + d} \quad \ldots\ldots\ldots\ldots\ldots(33).$$

26. Policy Values by different Mortality Tables. A mortality table exhibiting a higher rate of mortality does not necessarily give higher policy values. For example, from the expression

$$ {}_t V_x = 1 - \frac{\mathbf{a}_{x+t}}{\mathbf{a}_x},$$

it will be seen that if the rate of mortality below age $x+t$ be increased, but above that age remain unaltered, the value of $\mathbf{a}_x$ is diminished, that of $\mathbf{a}_{x+t}$ remaining the same, the fraction $\frac{\mathbf{a}_{x+t}}{\mathbf{a}_x}$ is increased, and the whole-life policy value is diminished.

On the other hand, if the mortality from age $x+t$ onwards only be increased, both $\mathbf{a}_{x+t}$ and $\mathbf{a}_x$ are reduced in value, but the reduction in the value of $\mathbf{a}_{x+t}$ is greater proportionately than in that of $\mathbf{a}_x$. The fraction $\frac{\mathbf{a}_{x+t}}{\mathbf{a}_x}$ is therefore diminished and the policy value increased.

27. Whether a policy value by one mortality table is greater or less than that by another table depends, therefore, not on the actual rates of mortality exhibited by the two tables, but on the progression in these rates.

If there are two mortality tables T and T′ and the letters a, V, etc. relate to table T and accented letters a', V′, etc. to table T′, then

$$ {}_t V_x >=< {}_t V'_x,$$

according as $1 - \frac{a_{x+t}}{a_x} >=< 1 - \frac{a'_{x+t}}{a'_x}$,

" $\frac{a'_{x+t}}{a'_x} >=< \frac{a_{x+t}}{a_x}$,

" $\frac{a_x}{a'_x} >=< \frac{a_{x+t}}{a'_{x+t}}$.

If, therefore, the values of the ratio $\frac{a_x}{a'_x}$ be calculated for all values of x, a simple inspection of the results will show the ages at entry and durations for which table T will give greater or smaller whole-life policy values than table T′.

Similarly for Endowment Assurances,

$${}_tV_{x:\overline{n}|} >=< {}_tV'_{x:\overline{n}|},$$

according as $1 - \frac{a_{x+t:\overline{n-t}|}}{a_{x:\overline{n}|}} >=< 1 - \frac{a'_{x+t:\overline{n-t}|}}{a'_{x:\overline{n}|}}$,

" $\frac{a'_{x+t:\overline{n-t}|}}{a'_{x:\overline{n}|}} >=< \frac{a_{x+t:\overline{n-t}|}}{a_{x:\overline{n}|}}$,

" $\frac{a_{x:\overline{n}|}}{a'_{x:\overline{n}|}} >=< \frac{a_{x+t:\overline{n-t}|}}{a'_{x+t:\overline{n-t}|}}$.

If therefore the ratio $\frac{a_{x:\overline{n}|}}{a'_{x:\overline{n}|}}$ be calculated for all values of x and n, a simple inspection of the results, $x + n$ being constant, will show the ages at entry and durations for which table T will give greater or smaller endowment assurance policy values than table T′.

28. The following tables of the ratios of the whole-life and temporary annuities-due, in the latter case ceasing at age 60, by the H^M and O^M Tables illustrate the use of the method of comparing the policy values by different tables.

COMPARISON OF WHOLE-LIFE POLICY VALUES

Values of $\frac{a_x^{(H^M)}}{a'^{(O^M)}_x}$ *at 3 per cent.*

x	$\frac{a_x}{a'_x}$	x	$\frac{a_x}{a'_x}$	x	$\frac{a_x}{a'_x}$
20	·9720	45	·9888	70	·9804
25	·9778	50	·9895	75	·9739
30	·9813	55	·9890	80	·9792
35	·9850	60	·9870	—	—
40	·9881	65	·9860	—	—

where $\quad {}_nV_x$ by H^M Table $> = <$ ${}_nV_x$ by O^M Table

if
$$\frac{\mathbf{a}_x}{\mathbf{a}'_x} > = < \frac{\mathbf{a}_{x+n}}{\mathbf{a}'_{x+n}}.$$

As an example, for a policy effected at age 40, since

$$\frac{\mathbf{a}_{40}}{\mathbf{a}'_{40}} < \frac{\mathbf{a}_{50}}{\mathbf{a}'_{50}}, \quad {}_{10}V_{40}^{(H^M)} < {}_{10}V_{40}^{(O^M)},$$

but as
$$\frac{\mathbf{a}_{40}}{\mathbf{a}'_{40}} > \frac{\mathbf{a}_{60}}{\mathbf{a}'_{60}}, \quad {}_{20}V_{40}^{(H^M)} > {}_{20}V_{40}^{(O^M)}.$$

Similarly the value of a policy effected at age 20 is always less by the H^M than by the O^M Table, but that of a policy taken out at age 50 is always greater by the former table.

Comparison of Endowment Assurance Policy Values

Policies maturing at age 60

Values of $\dfrac{\mathbf{a}^{(H^M)}_{x:\overline{60-x}|}}{\mathbf{a}'^{(O^M)}_{x:\overline{60-x}|}}$ *at* 3 *per cent.*

x	$\dfrac{\mathbf{a}_{x:\overline{60-x}\|}}{\mathbf{a}'_{x:\overline{60-x}\|}}$	x	$\dfrac{\mathbf{a}_{x:\overline{60-x}\|}}{\mathbf{a}'_{x:\overline{60-x}\|}}$
20	·9756	40	·9935
25	·9816	45	·9951
30	·9855	50	·9971
35	·9896	55	·9989

This table shows that for all ages at entry and durations the values of endowment assurances maturing at age 60 are less by the H^M Table than by the O^M Table.

29. In paragraph 27 it was shown that

$${}_tV_x = {}_tV'_x,$$

provided
$$\frac{\mathbf{a}_x}{\mathbf{a}'_x} = \frac{\mathbf{a}_{x+t}}{\mathbf{a}'_{x+t}}.$$

If, therefore, $\mathbf{a}_x = (1+k)\,\mathbf{a}'_x$ for all values of x, the two tables will always give equal whole-life policy values. Investigating this relationship we find that, if

$$\mathbf{a}_x = (1+k)\,\mathbf{a}'_x,$$

then since
$$\mathbf{a}'_x = 1 + a'_x$$
$$= 1 + vp'_x \,.\, \mathbf{a}'_{x+1}$$
$$= 1 + vp'_x \frac{\mathbf{a}_{x+1}}{1+k},$$
$$\mathbf{a}_x = (1+k)\left\{1 + vp'_x \frac{\mathbf{a}_{x+1}}{1+k}\right\}$$
$$= (1+k) + vp'_x \frac{a_x}{vp_x},$$
or
$$a_x = k + \frac{p'_x}{p_x} a_x,$$
$$\therefore \quad p'_x = p_x\left(1 - \frac{k}{a_x}\right),$$
whence
$$q'_x = 1 - p_x\left(1 - \frac{k}{a_x}\right)$$
$$= q_x + \frac{kp_x}{a_x}$$
$$= q_x + \frac{k}{v\mathbf{a}_{x+1}}$$
$$= q_x + \frac{c}{\mathbf{a}_{x+1}},$$
where c is a constant and equals $\frac{k}{v}$.

Since the value of $\mathbf{a}_{x+1}$ normally decreases as the age increases, the condition under which two tables will give equal policy values is that the rates of mortality at successive ages under one table shall be capable of being derived from those of the other table by an addition which increases with the age, the addition at any particular age being of the form $\frac{c}{\mathbf{a}_{x+1}}$. If, in proportion to the rate of increase in this quantity, the addition to the rate of mortality be greater at the younger ages, the policy values by table T′ will be smaller than those by table T; if the addition be proportionately greater at the older ages, the policy values by table T′ will be greater than by table T.

If, for example, a *constant* addition be made to the rate of mortality at all ages it is clear that, as compared with the increasing addition $\frac{c}{\mathbf{a}_{x+1}}$, the constant addition will be proportionately greater at the younger ages and less at the higher ages, thus diminishing policy values. If on the other hand a constant deduction be made from the value of q at all ages the *decrease* will be proportionately greater at the younger ages and the increase in the rate of mortality from age to age will be too rapid to give equal policy values and these values will accordingly be increased.

These points will be discussed more fully in Chapter X.

30. Surrender Values. All Life Offices are prepared, after a certain number of premiums have been paid, or after a policy has been a stated number of years in force, to grant a cash surrender value for the cancelment of the contract. The value allowed is something less than the reserve or policy value held by the Office, and may be a proportion of that reserve or the policy value calculated at a higher rate of interest than that employed in the periodical valuations.

In connection with whole-life assurances it is generally a condition that three years' premiums must have been paid before a surrender value can be granted, and there is frequently a guarantee that this value shall then be not less than one-fourth or one-third of the premiums paid or sometimes a higher percentage of the premiums paid excluding the first.

For endowment assurances and limited payment policies the number of premiums that must be paid before a surrender value attaches to a policy is reduced by some Offices to two or even one.

The practice of companies, however, varies and these examples must be taken only as a general indication of the conditions under which surrender values are granted in the United Kingdom at the present time (1932).

31. Free or Paid-up Policies. A Free Policy is a policy free from all future premiums. Thus, a policy subject to the payment of a single premium or a limited number of periodical premiums, after the payment of premiums has ceased, might be considered a free policy, but in practice this name is limited to assurances granted in lieu of policies subject to periodical premiums on the latter being given up, or surrendered, to the Office. The symbol "W" is employed to denote a free policy.

In the following paragraphs the formulae for the net free policy values are given; in practice, the amount of the free policy in the case of whole-life assurances is generally based on the surrender value, and in the case of limited payment policies and endowment assurances is frequently that proportion of the original sum assured which the number of premiums paid bears to the total number payable under the contract.

32. A whole-life assurance was effected t years ago on a life then aged x at a premium of $P_{[x]}$. What is the amount of the free policy that can now be granted?

There are two simple methods of arriving at this amount:

(1) The value of the existing assurance is ${}_tV_{[x]}$, the present age of the assured being $[x]+t$. The amount of the free policy that can now be granted is the sum assured payable at the death of $([x]+t)$ which will be secured by the payment of ${}_tV_{[x]}$ as a single premium. This amount is

$$ {}_tW_{[x]} = \frac{{}_tV_{[x]}}{A_{[x]+t}} \quad \text{........................(34).} $$

(2) If the life now aged $[x]+t$ desired to effect a new whole-life assurance of 1 on his own life, the annual premium he should pay is $P_{[x]+t}$. If he continued to pay $P_{[x]}$ this premium would secure a sum assured of $\frac{P_{[x]}}{P_{[x]+t}}$, leaving a balance of sum assured of $1-\frac{P_{[x]}}{P_{[x]+t}}$ to be provided by the sum in hand from past premiums, that is, by the policy value. The free policy which can now be granted is, therefore,

$$ {}_tW_{[x]} = 1 - \frac{P_{[x]}}{P_{[x]+t}} \quad \text{.....................(35).} $$

Formulae (34) and (35) must clearly, from the arguments employed, give identical results; and that this is so is easily shown algebraically,

$$ \frac{{}_tV_{[x]}}{A_{[x]+t}} = \frac{A_{[x]+t} - P_{[x]}a_{[x]+t}}{A_{[x]+t}} $$

$$ = 1 - \frac{P_{[x]}}{P_{[x]+t}}. $$

33. By similar reasoning, for an endowment assurance for n years which has been t years in force, the free policy that can be granted is

$$ {}_tW_{[x]:\overline{n}|} = \frac{{}_tV_{[x]:\overline{n}|}}{A_{[x]+t:\overline{n-t}|}} \quad \text{.....................(36),} $$

or

$$ {}_tW_{[x]:\overline{n}|} = 1 - \frac{P_{[x]:\overline{n}|}}{P_{[x]+t:\overline{n-t}|}} \text{..................(37),} $$

these two expressions giving the same result.

34. In order that the formula $1-\frac{P}{P_t}$ may be employed, it is necessary that the reasoning employed in paragraph 32 shall be appropriate to the particular case in question.

Thus for a temporary assurance

$$ {}_tW^{\,1}_{[x]:\overline{n}|} = 1 - \frac{P^{\,1}_{[x]:\overline{n}|}}{P^{\,1}_{[x]+t:\overline{n-t}|}} \quad\text{.................(38)}, $$

for a pure endowment

$$ {}_tW_{[x]:\overset{1}{\overline{n}|}} = 1 - \frac{P_{[x]:\overset{1}{\overline{n}|}}}{P_{[x]+t:\overset{1}{\overline{n-t}|}}} \quad\text{.................(39)}, $$

for a whole-life limited payment policy

$$ {}^k_tW_{[x]} = 1 - \frac{{}_kP_{[x]}}{{}_{k-t}P_{[x]+t}} \quad\text{.................(40)}. $$

The method of applying the policy value as a single premium in order to determine the sum assured under a free policy is, however, applicable to all classes of policies.

35. The following is an example of the grant of a free policy in lieu of a more complicated contract.

It is required to find the free policy which can be granted for the surrender of an n-year endowment assurance effected t years ago on a life then aged (x), with the condition that all premiums paid are to be returned with the sum assured at death or maturity.

The value of the original policy at the end of t years is, by the retrospective method,

$$ \frac{1}{D_{[x]+t}}\{P(N_{[x]}-N_{[x]+t})-(M_{[x]}-M_{[x]+t})-P'(R_{[x]}-R_{[x]+t}-tM_{[x]+t})\}, $$

where

$$ P=\frac{(M_{[x]}-M_{[x]+n}+D_{[x]+n})+c(1+k)(R_{[x]}-R_{[x]+n}-nM_{[x]+n}+nD_{[x]+n})}{(N_{[x]}-N_{[x]+n})-(1+k)(R_{[x]}-R_{[x]+n}-nM_{[x]+n}+nD_{[x]+n})}, $$

and the Office premium

$$ P'=(P+c)(1+k). $$

Representing the policy value by V, the sum assured by the Free Policy will be

$$ \frac{V}{A_{[x]+t:\overline{n-t}|}} $$

$$ =\frac{P(N_{[x]}-N_{[x]+t})-(M_{[x]}-M_{[x]+t})-P'(R_{[x]}-R_{[x]+t}-tM_{[x]+t})}{M_{[x]+t}-M_{[x]+n}+D_{[x]+n}}. $$

The premiums paid will not be returned with the sum assured under the free policy.

The formula $1 - \frac{P}{P_t}$ cannot be applied to a case of this kind.

36. In the case of a participating policy, the bonuses added to the sum assured are already free of any payment of premium, and the free policy which can be allowed relative to the sum assured alone can therefore be calculated by means of the formula $1 - \frac{P}{P_t}$, the full existing bonuses being added thereto.

For a guaranteed bonus policy, this being, as indicated in Chapter V 22, in reality a non-participating policy with a varying sum assured, the formula $1 - \frac{P}{P_t}$ cannot be employed to ascertain the free policy.

37. Alterations of Policies. Life Offices are frequently asked to have policies altered so as better to suit the requirements of the assured.

The most frequent kind of alteration is from whole-life to endowment assurance. Let us suppose that a person who effected a whole-life assurance for a sum assured of unity t years ago at age x now desires the policy converted into an endowment assurance for the same amount to mature at age $x + n$. The problem is to find the annual premium that must be paid for the remainder of the term.

Dealing first with net functions only, the premium can be ascertained in the following ways:

(1) If an endowment assurance had been taken out in the first place on the life aged x to mature at age $x+n$, a premium of $P_{[x]:\overline{n|}}$ would have been paid, and the Office would have in hand at the end of t years a sum of ${}_tV_{[x]:\overline{n|}}$. A whole-life assurance having been effected, it actually has in hand ${}_tV_{[x]}$. The assured must, therefore, pay annually for the next $n-t$ years, in addition to the premium of $P_{[x]:\overline{n|}}$, such a sum as will be equal in present value to the difference between ${}_tV_{[x]:\overline{n|}}$ and ${}_tV_{[x]}$.

The annual premium required is, therefore,

$$P_{[x]:\overline{n|}} + \frac{{}_tV_{[x]:\overline{n|}} - {}_tV_{[x]}}{\mathrm{a}_{[x+t]:\overline{n-t|}}},$$

where, in view of the nature of the alteration, the life assured is treated as being still a "select" life.

(2) If an endowment assurance of unity were effected now, the age of the life being $x+t$, to mature at age $x+n$, the annual premium to be paid would be $P_{[x+t]:\overline{n-t}|}$. But the Office actually has a sum of ${}_tV_{[x]}$ in hand and can, therefore, afford to reduce the premium by the annual equivalent of this sum: that is, to charge a premium of

$$P_{[x+t]:\overline{n-t}|} - \frac{{}_tV_{[x]}}{\mathbf{a}_{[x+t]:\overline{n-t}|}}.$$

38. In practice, further points arise for consideration. Under Method (1), if for $P_{[x]:\overline{n}|}$ we substitute the Office tabular premium $P'_{[x]:\overline{n}|}$ the additional charge to cover the difference between ${}_tV_{[x]:\overline{n}|}$ and ${}_tV_{[x]}$ must be loaded to provide for a certain amount of expenses; commission, for example, being payable on the total premium.

Under Method (2), on the other hand, if the Office premium $P'_{[x+t]:\overline{n-t}|}$ be substituted for the net premium, the Office will make a profit, since the premium contains loading for initial and renewal expenses, whereas the initial expenses are not incurred at the time of alteration and renewal commission will not be paid on the amount $\dfrac{{}_tV_{[x]}}{\mathbf{a}_{[x+t]:\overline{n-t}|}}$.

39. When the policies are "with profits" allowance must be made for the difference between the value of the existing bonus additions under the new terms and their value under the whole-life assurance.

40. When the life assured is not considered to be still a "select" life, or when an aggregate table is used, and only net functions are considered, a perfectly general plan for all alterations of policies is to equate the policy value immediately before the alteration to the value immediately after the alteration, and solve for the quantity—such as the new premium—to be determined.

In the case dealt with in paragraph 37 for instance, if P be the net premium to be paid in future, this can be determined by the following equation:

$$\begin{aligned} {}_tV_{[x]} &= A_{x+t:\overline{n-t}|} - P\mathbf{a}_{x+t:\overline{n-t}|} \\ &= (A_{x+t:\overline{n-t}|} - P_{[x]:\overline{n}|}\,\mathbf{a}_{x+t:\overline{n-t}|}) + (P_{[x]:\overline{n}|} - P)\,\mathbf{a}_{x+t:\overline{n-t}|}, \end{aligned}$$

$$\therefore\quad P - P_{[x]:\overline{n}|} = \frac{{}_tV_{[x]:\overline{n}|} - {}_tV_{[x]}}{\mathbf{a}_{x+t:\overline{n-t}|}},$$

or $$P = P_{[x]:\overline{n}|} + \frac{{}_tV_{[x]:\overline{n}|} - {}_tV_{[x]}}{a_{x+t:\overline{n-t}|}},$$

as in Method (1) of paragraph 37; or

$${}_tV_{[x]} = A_{x+t:\overline{n-t}|} - Pa_{x+t:\overline{n-t}|},$$

$$\therefore\ P = \frac{A_{x+t:\overline{n-t}|} - {}_tV_{[x]}}{a_{x+t:\overline{n-t}|}} = P_{x+t:\overline{n-t}|} - \frac{{}_tV_{[x]}}{a_{x+t:\overline{n-t}|}},$$

as in Method (2) of paragraph 37.

In this case Methods (1) and (2) give identical results, but they do not do so when the life is treated as being still select.

For practical purposes it then becomes necessary to consider the question of expenses, etc.

41. A somewhat similar case to that discussed in paragraph 37 is where the assured under an endowment assurance wishes the policy to mature at an earlier age than that stated in the original contract. Let us suppose that an endowment assurance was effected t years ago at age x to mature at age $x+n$, and it is now desired to make the maturity age $x+m$ $(m<n)$. The premium to be paid for the remaining $m-t$ years can be ascertained as follows:

$$(1)\quad P_{[x]:\overline{m}|} + \frac{{}_tV_{[x]:\overline{m}|} - {}_tV_{[x]:\overline{n}|}}{a_{[x+t]:\overline{m-t}|}},$$

$$(2)\quad P_{[x+t]:\overline{m-t}|} - \frac{{}_tV_{[x]:\overline{n}|}}{a_{[x+t]:\overline{m-t}|}}.$$

The points discussed in paragraph 38 also arise for consideration in this case.

42. If it be desired that the future premiums under a whole-life assurance, instead of being payable throughout life, shall be limited to t payments, the premium to be paid will be ascertained by redistributing the value of the premiums (net or Office) payable under the original assurance: that is, by taking

$$\frac{P_{[x]}\,a_{[x+n]}}{a_{[x+n]:\overline{t}|}}.$$

The life is assumed to be select as otherwise he would not wish to pay the higher premium so brought out.

If, on the other hand, the period during which the premiums are payable under a limited payment policy is to be extended, the annual premium being thus reduced, the calculation will be made in a similar manner, but evidence of good health must be obtained before the alteration is permitted.

43. An Office is sometimes asked to apply the cash value of bonus additions to limit the number of future premiums payable under a policy. Take the case of a whole-life assurance, effected t years ago on a life then aged x, the sum assured being S and the bonus additions B. The cash value of the bonus additions is BA_{x+t}. If it be assumed that y is the age at which premiums will cease after the alteration has been effected, the loss to the Office (to be covered by the cash value of the bonuses) will consist of the value of a deferred annuity of the premium, first payment at age y, that is $SP_{[x]}\dfrac{N_y}{D_{x+t}}$. We thus have

$$BA_{x+t} = SP_{[x]}\frac{N_y}{D_{x+t}},$$

whence
$$N_y = \frac{BM_{x+t}}{SP_{[x]}}.$$

The age y must then be determined by reference to a table of the values of N_x. It will generally be fractional, and it will be for the Office to decide whether a fractional premium shall be paid in the last year or whether such an amount ot bonus shall be surrendered as to give an exact age for y.

44. The cash value of the bonus additions might similarly be applied to convert a whole-life assurance into an endowment assurance, in which case consideration must be given to the different values of future bonuses before and after conversion.

Suppose that the loading added to the annual premiums for both whole-life and endowment assurances includes provision for an annual simple reversionary bonus of b per unit of the sum assured, so that, at age x, under a whole-life contract, the bonus loading is $b_{[x]} = \dfrac{b\,(IA)_{[x]}}{\mathbf{a}_{[x]}}$.

Then, if the existing bonus additions amount to B, the value of the whole-life policy, taking future bonuses into account, will be, at the end of t years,

$$(S+B)\,A_{x+t} + Sb\,(IA)_{x+t} - S\,[P_{[x]} + b_{[x]}]\,\mathbf{a}_{x+t}.$$

If y be the age at which the endowment assurance is to mature, the value of the policy after conversion into an endowment assurance by surrender of B, the existing bonuses, will be

$$SA_{x+t:\overline{y-x-t}|} + Sb\,(IA)_{x+t:\overline{y-x-t}|} - S\,(P_{[x]} + b_{[x]})\,a_{x+t:\overline{y-x-t}|},$$

and these two expressions must be equal. Hence

$$BA_{x+t} = \frac{SN_y}{D_{x+t}}[d + P_{[x]} + b_{[x]}] + Sb\,[(IA)_{x+t:\overline{y-x-t}|} - (IA)_{x+t}]$$

$$= \frac{SN_y}{D_{x+t}}[d + P_{[x]} + b_{[x]}] + Sb\,\frac{(y-x-t)\,dN_y - R_y}{D_{x+t}},$$

from which, with the aid of tables of N_x and R_x, y can be found by trial.

The last expression shows that the loss to the Office is (a deferred annuity of the interest on the sum assured, the annual premium and the original bonus loading) *plus* (a deferred annuity of the interest on the $y-x-t$ bonuses to be added between the ages $x+t$ and y) *minus* (the present value of the bonuses originally due after age y but which will not accrue under the endowment assurance).

45. If the bonus additions to an endowment assurance effected t years ago on a life then aged x for a period of n years are to be applied to limit the number of future premiums, the formula to be employed will be

$$BA_{x+t:\overline{n-t}|} = SP_{[x]:\overline{n}|}\,\frac{N_y - N_{x+n}}{D_{x+t}},$$

whence

$$N_y = \frac{B\,(M_{x+t} - M_{x+n} + D_{x+n})}{SP_{[x]:\overline{n}|}} + N_{x+n}.$$

If, however, they are to be applied to accelerate the date of maturity of the policy, a plan similar to that employed in paragraph 44 must be employed.

Thus, if b per unit of the sum assured be the simple reversionary bonus provided for in the loading, the actual loading to the premium under the original policy be represented by $b_{[x]:\overline{n}|}$, and y' the new maturity age, the expression employed will be

$$BA_{x+t:\overline{n-t}|} = S\,\frac{N_{y'} - N_{x+n}}{D_{x+t}}[d + P_{[x]:\overline{n}|} + b_{[x]:\overline{n}|}]$$
$$+ Sb\,[(IA)_{x+t:\overline{y'-x-t}|} - (IA)_{x+t:\overline{n-t}|}]$$
$$= S\,\frac{N_{y'} - N_{x+n}}{D_{x+t}}[d + P_{[x]:\overline{n}|} + b_{[x]:\overline{n}|}]$$
$$+ \frac{Sb}{D_{x+t}}[(y'-x-t)\,d\,(N_{y'} - N_{x+n})$$
$$- \{R_{y'} - R_{x+n} - (x+n-y')(M_{x+n} - D_{x+n})\}].$$

The loss to the Office in this case is (a deferred temporary annuity of the interest on the sum assured, the annual premium and the original bonus loading) *plus* (a deferred temporary annuity of the interest on the $y'-x-t$ bonuses to be added between ages $x+t$ and y') *minus* (the value of the bonuses which would have been added to the sum assured between the ages y' and $x+n$ but which will not now accrue).

EXAMPLES

Ex. 1. On the basis of the $O^{[NM]}$ Table at 3 per cent., calculate the values of ${}_8V_{[30]}$ and ${}_8V_{[30]}$.

$$\begin{aligned}{}_8V_{[30]} &= A_{[30]+8} - P_{[30]}\,a_{[30]+8}\\ &= \cdot 41991 - \cdot 01901 \times 19\cdot 916\\ &= \cdot 04131,\\ {}_8V_{[30]} &= A_{38} - P_{[30]}\,a_{38}\\ &= \cdot 45976 - \cdot 01901 \times 18\cdot 548\\ &= \cdot 10716.\end{aligned}$$

Ex. 2. Find the value at 3 per cent. interest of a whole-life policy for £1250 effected at age 30 which has been 20 years in force and to which a reversionary bonus of £500 is attached, having given that $P_{30} = \cdot 0179$ and $P_{50} = \cdot 0373$.

This question is included simply as an example for which one of the more unusual formulae for the value of a whole-life policy must be used.

The value is

$$\begin{aligned} & 1750A_{50} - 1250P_{30}\,.\,a_{50}\\ &= (1750P_{50} - 1250P_{30})\,a_{50}\\ &= \frac{1750P_{50} - 1250P_{30}}{P_{50} + d}\\ &= 645\cdot 8.\end{aligned}$$

Ex. 3. An assurance on the life of (x) is payable at the end of $n+t$ years if (x) be then alive, or at his death should this occur during the last t years of this period. If (x) die during the first n years the premiums paid are to be returned.

Assuming an Aggregate Mortality Table, find expressions for

(*a*) the annual premium payable for n years only;

(*b*) the value of the policy by the prospective and retrospective methods at the end of $n+m$ years, and prove that these values are identical ($m < t$).

The Office premium "P′" is obtained from the net premium "P" by the equation $P'=(P+c)(1+k)$.

(*a*) Value of Benefit $=\dfrac{1}{D_x}[(M_{x+n}-M_{x+n+t}+D_{x+n+t})$
$$+P'(R_x-R_{x+n}-nM_{x+n})],$$

" Premiums $=\dfrac{P}{D_x}(N_x-N_{x+n})$,

therefore

$$P=\frac{(M_{x+n}-M_{x+n+t}+D_{x+n+t})+c(1+k)(R_x-R_{x+n}-nM_{x+n})}{(N_x-N_{x+n})-(1+k)(R_x-R_{x+n}-nM_{x+n})},$$

and

$$P'=\frac{(M_{x+n}-M_{x+n+t}+D_{x+n+t})+c(N_x-N_{x+n})}{(N_x-N_{x+n})-(1+k)(R_x-R_{x+n}-nM_{x+n})}(1+k).$$

(*b*) The value of the policy at the end of $n+m$ years is, by the prospective method,

$$A_{x+n+m:\overline{t-m|}}=\frac{M_{x+n+m}-M_{x+n+t}+D_{x+n+t}}{D_{x+n+m}},$$

and by the retrospective method

$$\frac{1}{D_{x+n+m}}\{P(N_x-N_{x+n})-(M_{x+n}-M_{x+n+m})$$
$$-P'(R_x-R_{x+n}-nM_{x+n})\}$$
$$=\frac{1}{D_{x+n+m}}\{P(N_x-N_{x+n})-(M_{x+n}-M_{x+n+t}+D_{x+n+t})$$
$$-P'(R_x-R_{x+n}-nM_{x+n})+(M_{x+n+m}-M_{x+n+t}+D_{x+n+t})\}$$
$$=\frac{M_{x+n+m}-M_{x+n+t}+D_{x+n+t}}{D_{x+n+m}},\text{ the prospective value.}$$

Ex. 4. An endowment assurance policy is effected on a life aged x, payable at the end of 25 years or at previous death, with the condition that the premium payable during the first five years shall be the ordinary whole-life premium, the premium payable thereafter being correspondingly increased.

On the basis of select tables, assuming the "select period" to be five years, give an expression for the net premium during the remaining 20 years.

Find also the value of the policy at the end of ten years (1) by the retrospective method, and (2) by the prospective method, and show that the two expressions are equal.

$$\text{Value of Benefit} = A_{[x]:\overline{25}|}.$$

If P^u be the ultimate net premium,

$$\text{Value of Premiums} = P_{[x]} \,.\, a_{[x]:\overline{5}|} + P^u \,.\, {}_5|a_{[x]:\overline{20}|},$$

whence
$$P^u = \frac{A_{[x]:\overline{25}|} - P_{[x]}\, a_{[x]:\overline{5}|}}{{}_5|a_{[x]:\overline{20}|}}$$
$$= \frac{M_{[x]} - M_{x+25} + D_{x+25} - P_{[x]}(N_{[x]} - N_{x+5})}{N_{x+5} - N_{x+25}}$$
$$= \frac{P_{[x]} N_{x+5} - M_{x+25} + D_{x+25}}{N_{x+5} - N_{x+25}}.$$

At the end of ten years the policy value is:

(*a*) by the retrospective method,

$$\frac{1}{D_{x+10}}\{P_{[x]}(N_{[x]} - N_{x+5}) + P^u(N_{x+5} - N_{x+10}) - (M_{[x]} - M_{x+10})\};$$

(*b*) by the prospective method,

$$A_{x+10:\overline{15}|} - P^u a_{x+10:\overline{15}|}$$
$$= \frac{1}{D_{x+10}}\{M_{x+10} - M_{x+25} + D_{x+25} - P^u(N_{x+10} - N_{x+25})\}.$$

The retrospective value can be written, by adding and subtracting similar terms, as follows:

$$\frac{1}{D_{x+10}}\{P_{[x]}(N_{[x]} - N_{x+5}) + P^u(N_{x+5} - N_{x+25}) - P^u(N_{x+10} - N_{x+25})$$
$$- (M_{[x]} - M_{x+25} + D_{x+25}) + (M_{x+10} - M_{x+25} + D_{x+25})\}$$
$$= \frac{1}{D_{x+10}}\{M_{x+10} - M_{x+25} + D_{x+25} - P^u(N_{x+10} - N_{x+25})\},$$

which is the prospective value; since from the formula for the value of P^u, it is evident that

$$P_{[x]}(N_{[x]} - N_{x+5}) + P^u(N_{x+5} - N_{x+25}) = M_{[x]} - M_{x+25} + D_{x+25}.$$

Ex. 5. A child's deferred assurance is effected at age 5 subject to annual premiums payable throughout life, the sum assured being payable at death after age 21. In the event of death before age 21 the premiums paid are returnable without interest.

Find the value of the assurance

(*a*) at the end of 10 years,

(*b*) " " 25 " .

In accordance with Chap. V 33 the mortality of the child before age 21 can be ignored.

The net annual premium being represented by P, we have

$$P = \frac{A_{21}}{s_{\overline{17}|} + a_{21}}.$$

The value of the policy is

(*a*) at the end of 10 years, $P(s_{\overline{11}|} - 1)$,

(*b*) " " 25 " $A_{30} - P\mathbf{a}_{30}$.

As indicated in Chap. V 36 the more practical method would be to take, where P′ is the Office premium,

$$(kP' - {\cdot}01m)(1+i)\,s_{\overline{16}|} = (P'_{[21]} - P')\,\mathbf{a}_{21},$$

$$\therefore\ P' = \frac{P'_{[21]} \cdot \mathbf{a}_{21} + {\cdot}01m\,(1+i)\,s_{\overline{16}|}}{k\,(1+i)\,s_{\overline{16}|} + \mathbf{a}_{21}},$$

to which an addition might also be made to allow for the fact that in taking the Office premium $P'_{[21]}$ the assumption is tacitly made that the life is still select at that age.

The policy values would then be ascertained in the same manner as above, putting $P = (kP' - {\cdot}01m)$.

Ex. 6. A man now aged 40 effected five years ago a whole-life assurance for £500, the number of annual premiums being limited to a maximum of 20. He now desires to alter it to an endowment assurance maturing at age 55 for a reduced amount at the same annual premium. Find the amount of the endowment assurance on the basis of the H^M 3 per cent. table and net premiums.

In this case the same premium and the same number of premiums will be payable under the revised as under the original contract. All that is required, therefore, is to reduce the sum assured in the ratio of the single premium for a whole-life assurance on the life of (40) to that for an endowment assurance on the life of (40) maturing at age 55.

The amount of the revised endowment assurance will, therefore, be

$$500 \times \frac{A_{40}}{A_{40:\overline{15}|}}$$

$$= 500 \times \frac{M_{40}}{M_{40} - M_{55} + D_{55}}$$

$$= 500 \times \frac{11869}{11869 - 8111 + 13098}$$

$$= 352.$$

CHAPTER VII

SINGLE-LIFE ANNUITIES AND PREMIUMS PAYABLE MORE FREQUENTLY THAN ONCE A YEAR. VALUES OF SINGLE-LIFE POLICIES SUBJECT TO PREMIUMS PAYABLE MORE FREQUENTLY THAN ONCE A YEAR

1. Annuities and Premiums payable fractionally throughout the year. So far we have dealt only with annuities and premiums payable annually. In practice, both annuities and premiums are often payable at more frequent intervals and it is, therefore, necessary to investigate the modifications that must be made in the formulae already obtained to allow for this difference in the times of payment.

What then is the value of an annuity of 1 per annum payable during the life of (x) by instalments of $\frac{1}{m}$ at the end of successive $\frac{1}{m}$ths of each year?

Representing the value of this annuity by $a_x^{(m)}$ we have

$$a_x^{(m)} = \frac{1}{m} \sum_{t=1}^{t=\infty} v^{\frac{t}{m}} {}_{\frac{t}{m}}p_x$$

$$= \frac{1}{m} \frac{1}{D_x} \sum_{t=1}^{t=\infty} D_{x+\frac{t}{m}}$$

$$= \frac{1}{D_x}\left[\sum_{t=1}^{t=\infty} D_{x+t} + \frac{m-1}{2m} D_x + \frac{m^2-1}{12m^2}\frac{dD_x}{dx} - \dots\right]$$

$$= a_x + \frac{m-1}{2m} + \frac{m^2-1}{12m^2}\frac{1}{D_x}\frac{dD_x}{dx} \text{ approx.}$$

$$= a_x + \frac{m-1}{2m} - \frac{m^2-1}{12m^2}(\mu_x + \delta) \quad \text{.......................(1)},$$

since $\quad \frac{1}{D_x}\frac{dD_x}{dx} = \frac{d \log D_x}{dx} = \frac{d}{dx}\log l_x + \frac{d}{dx}\log v^x = -(\mu_x + \delta).$

Or, if we write $\frac{dD_x}{dx} = \frac{1}{2}(D_{x+1} - D_{x-1})$ approximately,

$$a_x^{(m)} = a_x + \frac{m-1}{2m} - \frac{m^2-1}{12m^2}\frac{D_{x-1} - D_{x+1}}{2D_x} \quad \text{...............(2).}$$

An alternative expression can be obtained thus:

$$a_x^{(m)} = \frac{1}{D_x}\frac{1}{m}\sum_{t=1}^{t=\infty} D_{x+\frac{t}{m}}$$

$$= \frac{1}{D_x}\left[\sum_{t=1}^{t=\infty} D_{x+t} + \frac{m-1}{2m}D_x + \frac{m^2-1}{12m^2}\Delta D_x - \frac{m^2-1}{24m^2}\Delta^2 D_x + \text{... etc.}\right]$$

$$= a_x + \frac{m-1}{2m} + \frac{m^2-1}{12m^2}\frac{\Delta D_x - \frac{1}{2}\Delta^2 D_x}{D_x} \text{ approx.}$$

$$= a_x + \frac{m-1}{2m} - \frac{m^2-1}{12m^2}\frac{3D_x - 4D_{x+1} + D_{x+2}}{2D_x} \quad \text{...........(3).}$$

2. It will be seen from formulae (1) to (3) that if the terms involving the successive differences or differential coefficients of D_x be neglected the resulting approximation to the value of $a_x^{(m)}$ is in each case

$$a_x^{(m)} = a_x + \frac{m-1}{2m} \quad \text{........................(4).}$$

This approximation is the one most commonly used in practice, it being generally unnecessary to employ a more accurate value.

On the basis of the H^M Table and 3 per cent. interest the value of the term $\frac{m^2-1}{12m^2}(\mu_x + \delta)$ when $m = 4$ is ·0029 when $x = 30$, and ·0046 when $x = 60$.

3. The corresponding value of the annuity-due payable at $m$thly intervals is

$$\text{a}_x^{(m)} = \frac{1}{m} + a_x^{(m)},$$

whence, using the practical approximation for $a_x^{(m)}$,

$$\left.\begin{aligned} \text{a}_x^{(m)} &= a_x + \frac{m+1}{2m} \\ &= \text{a}_x - \frac{m-1}{2m} \end{aligned}\right\} \quad \text{.....................(5).}$$

4. The value of a temporary annuity of 1 per annum payable to (x) for n years by instalments of $\frac{1}{m}$ at the end of successive $\frac{1}{m}$ ths of each year, provided (x) be still alive, is

$$a^{(m)}_{x:\overline{n}|} = \frac{1}{D_x}\frac{1}{m}\sum_{t=1}^{t=mn} D_{x+\frac{t}{m}}$$

$$= \frac{1}{D_x}\left[\sum_{t=1}^{t=n} D_{x+t} + \frac{m-1}{2m}(D_x - D_{x+n}) + \frac{m^2-1}{12m^2}\left(\frac{dD_x}{dx} - \frac{dD_{x+n}}{dx}\right) - \dots\right]$$

$$= a_{x:\overline{n}|} + \frac{m-1}{2m}\left(1 - \frac{D_{x+n}}{D_x}\right) - \frac{m^2-1}{12m^2}\left\{(\mu_x + \delta) - \frac{D_{x+n}}{D_x}(\mu_{x+n} + \delta)\right\} \text{ approx.} \quad \dots(6),$$

or, neglecting terms involving differential coefficients,

$$a^{(m)}_{x:\overline{n}|} = a_{x:\overline{n}|} + \frac{m-1}{2m}\left(1 - \frac{D_{x+n}}{D_x}\right) \quad \dots\dots\dots\dots(7).$$

Formulae (6) and (7) can also be obtained from the relationship

$$a^{(m)}_{x:\overline{n}|} = a^{(m)}_x - \frac{D_{x+n}}{D_x} a^{(m)}_{x+n}.$$

For the corresponding annuity-due we have

$$\mathbf{a}^{(m)}_{x:\overline{n}|} = \frac{1}{m} + a^{(m)}_{x:\overline{n-\frac{1}{m}}|}$$

$$= \mathbf{a}^{(m)}_x - \frac{D_{x+n}}{D_x}\mathbf{a}^{(m)}_{x+n}$$

$$\left.\begin{aligned} &= \mathbf{a}_{x:\overline{n}|} - \frac{m-1}{2m}\left(1 - \frac{D_{x+n}}{D_x}\right) \\ &= a_{x:\overline{n}|} + \frac{m+1}{2m}\left(1 - \frac{D_{x+n}}{D_x}\right) \end{aligned}\right\} \quad \dots\dots\dots\dots\dots(8).$$

It does not appear necessary to set out the formulae for $a^{(m)}_{x:\overline{n}|}$ corresponding to formulae (2) and (3).

5. To find the value of an annuity of 1 per annum payable m times a year during the life of (x), the first payment to be made

at the end of $\frac{1}{t}$th of a year $\left(\frac{1}{t} < \frac{1}{m}\right)$, we have

$$\begin{aligned}
{}_{\frac{1}{t}|}\mathrm{a}_x^{(m)} &= \frac{1}{m}\sum_{r=0}^{r=\infty} v^{\frac{1}{t}+\frac{r}{m}}\;{}_{\frac{1}{t}+\frac{r}{m}}p_x \\
&= \frac{1}{\mathrm{D}_x}\cdot\frac{1}{m}\sum_{r=0}^{r=\infty} \mathrm{D}_{x+\frac{1}{t}+\frac{r}{m}} \\
&= \frac{1}{\mathrm{D}_x}\cdot\frac{1}{m}\sum_{r=0}^{r=\infty}\left(\mathrm{D}_{x+\frac{r}{m}} + \frac{m}{t}\Delta\mathrm{D}_{x+\frac{r}{m}} + \frac{\frac{m}{t}\left(\frac{m}{t}-1\right)}{\underline{|2}}\Delta^2\mathrm{D}_{x+\frac{r}{m}} + \dots\right)
\end{aligned}$$

where $\Delta\mathrm{D}_x = \mathrm{D}_{x+\frac{1}{m}} - \mathrm{D}_x$

$$= \mathrm{a}_x^{(m)} - \frac{1}{t} + \frac{t-m}{2t^2}\,\frac{\Delta\mathrm{D}_x}{\mathrm{D}_x} + \text{etc.} \quad\dots\dots(9),$$

or, ignoring terms involving $\Delta\mathrm{D}_x$, $\Delta^2\mathrm{D}_x$ ... etc., where $\frac{1}{t} < \frac{1}{m}$,

$${}_{\frac{1}{t}|}\mathrm{a}_x^{(m)} = \mathrm{a}_x^{(m)} - \frac{1}{t} \quad\dots\dots(10).$$

It follows that, for the corresponding temporary annuity value,

$$\begin{aligned}
{}_{\frac{1}{t}|}\mathrm{a}_{x:\overline{n}|}^{(m)} &= \frac{1}{\mathrm{D}_x}\cdot\frac{1}{m}\sum_{r=0}^{r=mn-1}\mathrm{D}_{x+\frac{1}{t}+\frac{r}{m}} \\
&= \frac{1}{\mathrm{D}_x}\cdot\frac{1}{m}\sum_{r=0}^{r=mn-1}\left[\mathrm{D}_{x+\frac{r}{m}} + \frac{m}{t}\Delta\mathrm{D}_{x+\frac{r}{m}} + \frac{\frac{m}{t}\left(\frac{m}{t}-1\right)}{\underline{|2}}\Delta^2\mathrm{D}_{x+\frac{r}{m}} + \dots\right]
\end{aligned}$$

where $\Delta\mathrm{D}_x = \mathrm{D}_{x+\frac{1}{m}} - \mathrm{D}_x$

$$= \mathrm{a}_{x:\overline{n}|}^{(m)} + \frac{1}{t}\cdot\frac{\mathrm{D}_{x+n}-\mathrm{D}_x}{\mathrm{D}_x} - \frac{t-m}{2t^2}\,\frac{\Delta\mathrm{D}_{x+n}-\Delta\mathrm{D}_x}{\mathrm{D}_x} + \text{etc.}\dots(11),$$

or, ignoring terms after the second,

$$\begin{aligned}
{}_{\frac{1}{t}|}\mathrm{a}_{x:\overline{n}|}^{(m)} &= \mathrm{a}_{x:\overline{n}|}^{(m)} - \frac{1}{t}\left(1 - \frac{\mathrm{D}_{x+n}}{\mathrm{D}_x}\right) \\
&= \mathrm{a}_{x:\overline{n}|}^{(m)} - \frac{1}{t}\left\{1 - m\left(a_{x:\overline{n}|}^{(m)} - a_{x:\overline{n-\frac{1}{m}}|}^{(m)}\right)\right\} \\
&= \mathrm{a}_{x:\overline{n}|}^{(m)} - \frac{m}{t}\left\{\mathrm{a}_{x:\overline{n}|}^{(m)} - a_{x:\overline{n}|}^{(m)}\right\} \\
&= \left(1-\frac{m}{t}\right)\mathrm{a}_{x:\overline{n}|}^{(m)} + \frac{m}{t}\,a_{x:\overline{n}|}^{(m)} \quad\dots\dots(12).
\end{aligned}$$

As an example of formula (12) if $m = 4$ and $t = 8$,

$${}_{\frac{1}{8}|}\mathrm{a}_{x:\overline{n}|}^{(4)} = \tfrac{1}{2}\left(\mathrm{a}_{x:\overline{n}|}^{(4)} + a_{x:\overline{n}|}^{(4)}\right).$$

6. In practice when an annuity is payable m times a year, and the next payment is due, or can be assumed to be due, exactly half of an interval hence, it is usual to assume that its value is the mean between the $m$thly annuity-due and the ordinary $m$thly immediate annuity. That is

$$_{\frac{1}{2m}|}\mathbf{a}_x^{(m)} = \tfrac{1}{2}(\mathbf{a}_x^{(m)} + a_x^{(m)}) \qquad\qquad (13),$$

and

$$_{\frac{1}{2m}|}\mathbf{a}_{x:\overline{n}|}^{(m)} = \tfrac{1}{2}(\mathbf{a}_{x:\overline{n}|}^{(m)} + a_{x:\overline{n}|}^{(m)}) \qquad\qquad (14).$$

The example given in paragraph 5 is a particular case of this last expression when $m = 4$.

By inserting the practical approximations for the values of $\mathbf{a}_x^{(m)}$ and $a_x^{(m)}$ in formula (13) we have

$$_{\frac{1}{2m}|}\mathbf{a}_x^{(m)} = \tfrac{1}{2}\left(a_x + \frac{m+1}{2m} + a_x + \frac{m-1}{2m}\right)$$

$$= a_x + \tfrac{1}{2} \qquad\qquad (15),$$

whatever the value of m; an expression which could have been obtained directly from formula (10) by writing $t = 2m$.

7. Expressed in Commutation Symbols the formulae for the various annuities discussed in this chapter become, using the practical approximations only,

$$a_x^{(m)} = \frac{N_{x+1} + \dfrac{m-1}{2m} D_x}{D_x}$$

$$\mathbf{a}_x^{(m)} = \frac{N_x - \dfrac{m-1}{2m} D_x}{D_x}$$

$$a_{x:\overline{n}|}^{(m)} = \frac{(N_{x+1} - N_{x+n+1}) + \dfrac{m-1}{2m}(D_x - D_{x+n})}{D_x}$$

$$\mathbf{a}_{x:\overline{n}|}^{(m)} = \frac{(N_x - N_{x+n}) - \dfrac{m-1}{2m}(D_x - D_{x+n})}{D_x}$$

$$_{\frac{1}{t}|}\mathbf{a}_x^{(m)} = \frac{N_x - \left(\dfrac{m-1}{2m} + \dfrac{1}{t}\right) D_x}{D_x}$$

$$_{\frac{1}{t}|}\mathbf{a}_{x:\overline{n}|}^{(m)} = \frac{(N_x - N_{x+n}) - \left(\dfrac{m-1}{2m} + \dfrac{1}{t}\right)(D_x - D_{x+n})}{D_x}.$$

All these formulae are applicable to Select Tables, if the necessary alterations be made in the suffixes.

8. Continuous Annuities. A Continuous Annuity is one payable by infinitely small instalments at infinitely small intervals throughout each year. The value of such an annuity of 1 per annum to (x) for the whole of life, $\bar{a}_x$, is

$$\begin{aligned}\bar{a}_x &= \int_0^\infty v^t \, {}_tp_x \, dt \\ &= \frac{1}{D_x}\int_0^\infty D_{x+t}\, dt \\ &= \frac{1}{D_x}\left\{\sum_{t=1}^{t=\infty} D_{x+t} + \tfrac{1}{2}D_x + \tfrac{1}{12}\frac{dD_x}{dx} - \dots\right\} \\ &= a_x + \tfrac{1}{2} - \tfrac{1}{12}(\mu_x + \delta) \text{ approx.} \quad \dots\dots\dots\dots(16) \\ &= a_x + \tfrac{1}{2} - \tfrac{1}{12}\frac{D_{x-1} - D_{x+1}}{2D_x} \text{ approx.} \quad \dots\dots\dots\dots(17).\end{aligned}$$

If the last term be neglected, we have the approximation to the value of $\bar{a}_x$ usually employed in practice; namely

$$\left.\begin{aligned}\bar{a}_x &= a_x + \tfrac{1}{2} \\ &= \text{a}_x - \tfrac{1}{2}\end{aligned}\right\} \quad \dots\dots\dots\dots(18).$$

Formulae (16), (17) and (18) can also be obtained by making m infinitely great in formulae (1), (2) and (4) respectively.

It will be observed that the expression $a_x + \frac{1}{2}$ is used as the approximate value of three different annuities, namely ${}_{\frac{1}{2}|}\text{a}_x$, ${}_{\frac{1}{2m}|}\text{a}_x^{(m)}$ and $\bar{a}_x$.

9. The value of a continuous temporary life annuity to (x) for n years is

$$\bar{a}_{x:\overline{n}|} = \bar{a}_x - \frac{D_{x+n}}{D_x}\bar{a}_{x+n}$$

$$\left.\begin{aligned}&= a_{x:\overline{n}|} + \tfrac{1}{2}\left(1 - \frac{D_{x+n}}{D_x}\right) \\ &= \tfrac{1}{2}\left(\text{a}_{x:\overline{n}|} + a_{x:\overline{n}|}\right)\end{aligned}\right\} \quad \dots\dots\dots\dots(19),$$

which is sometimes represented by $\frac{1}{2} + a_{x:\overline{n-\frac{1}{2}}|}$, the value of $a_{x:\overline{n-\frac{1}{2}}|}$ being taken as $\frac{1}{2}(a_{x:\overline{n-1}|} + a_{x:\overline{n}|})$.

10. If $\overline{N}_x$ represent the numerator of the expression for the value of the continuous annuity, $\bar{a}_x$, it follows that $\bar{a}_x = \frac{\overline{N}_x}{D_x}$, and

$$\overline{N}_x = \int_0^\infty D_{x+t}\,dt,$$

whence

$$\frac{d\overline{N}_x}{dx} = \frac{d}{dx}\int_0^\infty D_{x+t}\,dt$$

$$= \int_0^\infty \frac{d}{dx} D_{x+t}\,dt$$

$$= \int_0^\infty \frac{d}{dt} D_{x+t}\,dt$$

$$= -D_x \quad \text{.........................(20).}$$

In practice $\overline{N}_x$ would be taken as equal to $N_x - \frac{1}{2}D_x$, thus complying with the usual practical approximation

$$\bar{a}_x = a_x - \tfrac{1}{2}$$

$$= \frac{N_x - \frac{1}{2}D_x}{D_x} \quad \text{....................(21).}$$

In obtaining formula (1) it was shown that

$$\frac{1}{D_x}\frac{dD_x}{dx} = -(\mu_x + \delta),$$

$$\therefore \frac{dD_x}{dx} = -D_x(\mu_x + \delta) \quad \text{..................(22),}$$

and

$$\frac{d\bar{a}_x}{dx} = \frac{d}{dx}\frac{\overline{N}_x}{D_x}$$

$$= \frac{D_x \frac{d}{dx}\overline{N}_x - \overline{N}_x \frac{d}{dx} D_x}{(D_x)^2}$$

$$= \frac{-(D_x)^2 + \overline{N}_x \,.\, D_x(\mu_x + \delta)}{(D_x)^2}$$

$$= \bar{a}_x(\mu_x + \delta) - 1 \quad \text{..........................(23).}$$

11. In connection with annuity values the practical assumption is sometimes made that a constant addition of ·01 to the rate of mortality at all ages is equivalent to an increase of 1 per cent. in the rate of interest.

From the relation

$$\frac{d \log D_x}{dx} = -(\mu_x + \delta),$$

it is evident that if an addition be made to either μ_x or δ, the effect on the value of $\log D_x$ (or of D_x) will be the same. Thus a constant addition to the *force* of mortality is equivalent to a constant addition to the *force* of interest, from which it follows that the assumption mentioned can be adopted without great loss of accuracy.

If the corresponding value of A_x or P_x were required it would be necessary, with the new value of a_x, to make the calculation or enter a premium conversion table at the original rate of interest.

12. Premiums payable m times a year. In the calculation of premiums payable m times a year, it is again necessary to bear in mind the principle laid down in Chap. III 27, that, so far as net functions are concerned, at the inception of an assurance the value of the periodical premiums to be paid must equal the value of the sum assured.

If $P_{[x]}^{(m)}$ represent the net premium per annum to be paid for an assurance of 1 on the life of (x), $\frac{1}{m} P_{[x]}^{(m)}$ being payable in advance at the commencement of each $\frac{1}{m}$th of a year that (x) enters upon, the value of the premiums to be received is $P_{[x]}^{(m)} \mathbf{a}_{[x]}^{(m)}$.

It follows, therefore, that

$$P_{[x]}^{(m)} \mathbf{a}_{[x]}^{(m)} = A_{[x]},$$

$$P_{[x]}^{(m)} = \frac{A_{[x]}}{\mathbf{a}_{[x]}^{(m)}} = \frac{A_{[x]}}{\mathbf{a}_{[x]} - \frac{m-1}{2m}} \text{ approx.}$$

since by formula (5) $\mathbf{a}_x^{(m)} = \mathbf{a}_x - \frac{m-1}{2m}$ approx.,

whence
$$P_{[x]}^{(m)} = \frac{P_{[x]}}{1 - \frac{m-1}{2m}(P_{[x]} + d)} \quad \text{..............(24)},$$

since $\frac{1}{\mathbf{a}_{[x]}} = P_{[x]} + d$.

By means of formula (24), if the rate of interest on which the premiums are based be known, $P_{[x]}^{(m)}$ can readily be obtained from

$P_{[x]}$. The premium payable at the beginning of each $\frac{1}{m}$th part of a year is $\frac{1}{m} \cdot \frac{P_{[x]}}{1 - \frac{m-1}{2m}(P_{[x]} + d)}$.

13. The relation between $P_{[x]}$ and $P_{[x]}^{(m)}$ can be expressed in the following form, namely

$$P_{[x]}^{(m)} = P_{[x]} + \frac{m-1}{2m} P_{[x]}^{(m)} (P_{[x]} + d) \quad \text{............(25).}$$

Considering the difference between the values of $P_{[x]}$ and $P_{[x]}^{(m)}$, $P_{[x]}^{(m)}$ must exceed $P_{[x]}$ on account of (*a*) the possible loss of premium in the year of death, and (*b*) the loss of interest on those portions of the year's premium, payment of which is deferred.

As regards (*a*), if death occur in the first $\frac{1}{m}$th part of a year, $\frac{m-1}{m} P_{[x]}^{(m)}$ of that year's premium will remain unpaid; if death occur in the second $\frac{1}{m}$th part of the year, $\frac{m-2}{m} P_{[x]}^{(m)}$ will remain unpaid; and so on. The probability that death will occur in any particular $\frac{1}{m}$th part of the year, on the assumption of a uniform distribution of deaths over that year, being $\frac{1}{m}$, it follows that the average loss of premiums in the year of death would, on this assumption, be

$$P_{[x]}^{(m)} \cdot \frac{1}{m} \left[\frac{m-1}{m} + \frac{m-2}{m} + \dots + \frac{1}{m} \right]$$

$$= \frac{m-1}{2m} P_{[x]}^{(m)},$$

and the premium to provide for the payment of this sum on the death of (x) is approximately

$$\frac{m-1}{2m} P_{[x]}^{(m)} \cdot P_{[x]}.$$

As regards (*b*) the loss of interest on the final payment is $\frac{1}{m} P_{[x]}^{(m)} \cdot \frac{m-1}{m} d$, on the last payment but one $\frac{1}{m} P_{[x]}^{(m)} \cdot \frac{m-2}{m} d$, the total loss of interest being

$$\frac{1}{m} P_{[x]}^{(m)} \left[\frac{m-1}{m} + \frac{m-2}{m} + \dots + \frac{1}{m}\right] d$$

$$= \frac{m-1}{2m} P_{[x]}^{(m)} . d.$$

The total addition to be made to $P_{[x]}$ to obtain $P_{[x]}^{(m)}$ is therefore, approximately,

$$\frac{m-1}{2m} P_{[x]}^{(m)} (P_{[x]} + d).$$

14. In the case of an Endowment Assurance

$$P_{[x]:\overline{n}|}^{(m)} = \frac{A_{[x]:\overline{n}|}}{a_{[x]:\overline{n}|}^{(m)}}$$

$$= \frac{A_{[x]:\overline{n}|}}{a_{[x]:\overline{n}|} - \frac{m-1}{2m}\left(1 - \frac{D_{x+n}}{D_{[x]}}\right)}$$

$$= \frac{P_{[x]:\overline{n}|}}{1 - \frac{m-1}{2m}(P_{[x]:\overline{n}|} + d - P_{[x]:\overset{1}{\overline{n}|}})}$$

$$= \frac{P_{[x]:\overline{n}|}}{1 - \frac{m-1}{2m}(P^{1}_{[x]:\overline{n}|} + d)} \quad\dots\dots\dots\dots\dots\dots\dots\dots(26),$$

the premium payable at the beginning of each $\frac{1}{m}$th part of the year being $\frac{1}{m} P_{[x]:\overline{n}|}^{(m)}$.

In the form corresponding to formula (25)

$$P_{[x]:\overline{n}|}^{(m)} = P_{[x]:\overline{n}|} + \frac{m-1}{2m} P_{[x]:\overline{n}|}^{(m)} (P^{1}_{[x]:\overline{n}|} + d) \quad \dots\dots(27).$$

This expression can be explained verbally in the manner adopted in paragraph 13 in connection with Whole-Life Assurances, except that the addition for loss of premium in this case involves a temporary assurance only.

15. The corresponding premium for the Whole-Life Limited Payment Policy is

$${}_tP_{[x]}^{(m)} = \frac{A_{[x]}}{a_{[x]:\overline{t}|}^{(m)}}$$

$$= \frac{{}_tP_{[x]}}{1 - \frac{m-1}{2m}(P^{1}_{[x]:\overline{t}|} + d)} \quad\dots\dots\dots\dots\dots(28),$$

and for the Limited Payment Endowment Assurance

$$
{}_tP^{(m)}_{[x]:\overline{n}|} = \frac{A_{[x]:\overline{n}|}}{a^{(m)}_{[x]:\overline{t}|}}
$$

$$
= \frac{{}_tP_{[x]:\overline{n}|}}{1 - \frac{m-1}{2m}(P^{\;1}_{[x]:\overline{t}|} + d)} \quad \ldots\ldots\ldots\ldots\ldots(29),
$$

the premiums payable at the commencement of each $\frac{1}{m}$th part of a year being $\frac{1}{m}\cdot{}_tP^{(m)}_{[x]}$ and $\frac{1}{m}\cdot{}_tP^{(m)}_{[x]:\overline{n}|}$ respectively.

16. The premiums dealt with in paragraphs 12 to 15 are called *true* premiums payable m times a year, in order to distinguish them from *instalment* premiums which are subject to the condition that any part of the year's premium unpaid at the death of the life assured shall be deducted from the sum payable under the policy.

17. When Instalment premiums are charged the total premium payable each year is, in effect, an annual premium payable by instalments, and in its calculation (ignoring the slight difference introduced by the fact that, in the year of death, certain of the later instalments are not received at their due dates) it is only necessary to make an addition to the annual premium to provide for interest on the deferred instalments.

If $P^{[m]}_{[x]}$ represent the yearly premium payable by *instalments* m times a year for a whole-life assurance of 1 on the life of (x), the value at the beginning of each year of the instalments to be paid in that year must be equal to the annual premium.

Thus
$$
P_{[x]} = P^{[m]}_{[x]}\,.\,a^{(m)}_{\overline{1}|} = \frac{1}{m}P^{[m]}_{[x]}\,.\sum_{t=0}^{t=m-1} v^{\frac{t}{m}}
$$

$$
= \frac{1}{m}P^{[m]}_{[x]}\,.\sum_{t=0}^{t=m-1}\left(1 - \frac{t}{m}d\right) \text{ approx.}
$$

$$
= P^{[m]}_{[x]}\left\{1 - \frac{m-1}{2m}d\right\},
$$

whence
$$
P^{[m]}_{[x]} = \frac{P_{[x]}}{1 - \frac{m-1}{2m}d} \quad \ldots\ldots\ldots\ldots\ldots\ldots\ldots\ldots\ldots(30).
$$

The analogy of this expression to formula (24) is evident.

18. In this case a precisely similar argument applies to Limited Payment Policies and Endowment Assurances. Thus

$$ {}_tP_{[x]}^{[m]} = \frac{{}_tP_{[x]}}{1 - \frac{m-1}{2m}d} \quad \text{..................(31)},$$

$$ P_{[x]:\overline{n}|}^{[m]} = \frac{P_{[x]:\overline{n}|}}{1 - \frac{m-1}{2m}d} \quad \text{..................(32)},$$

and

$$ {}_tP_{[x]:\overline{n}|}^{[m]} = \frac{{}_tP_{[x]:\overline{n}|}}{1 - \frac{m-1}{2m}d} \quad \text{..................(33)}.$$

In these cases also the premium payable at the commencement of each $\frac{1}{m}$th part of a year is $\frac{1}{m}$th of the above expressions.

In practice, in addition to loss of interest and premiums the additional trouble and expense involved in the more frequent collection of premiums have to be considered, with the result that the theoretical premiums $P^{(m)}$ and $P^{[m]}$ are seldom used, the Office annual premium generally being increased by a fixed percentage, as for example $2\frac{1}{2}$ or 3 per cent. in half-yearly and 5 per cent. in quarterly cases, whether the premiums are charged as true or instalment premiums.

19. When premiums are payable weekly or monthly as in Industrial Life Assurances they are calculated as if they were payable continuously, continuous annuities being employed.

The practical approximation to the value of an annuity-due of 1 per annum during the life of (x), payable weekly, is $a_x + \frac{53}{104}$ and payable monthly, $a_x + \frac{13}{24}$, neither of which values differs to any material extent from $a_x + \frac{1}{2}$, the value employed for $\bar{a}_x$.

Thus the premium per annum, $\bar{P}_x$, payable at infinitesimal intervals throughout each year (or in practice by weekly or monthly instalments) for a whole-life assurance of 1 on the life (x) is

$$\bar{P}_x = \frac{A_x}{\bar{a}_x} \quad \text{..(34)},$$

the corresponding premium for an n-year endowment assurance on (x) being

$$\left.\begin{aligned} \bar{P}_{x:\overline{n}|} &= \frac{A_{x:\overline{n}|}}{\bar{a}_{x:\overline{n}|}} \\ &= \frac{A_{x:\overline{n}|}}{\frac{1}{2}(\mathrm{a}_{x:\overline{n}|} + a_{x:\overline{n}|})} \text{ approx.} \end{aligned}\right\} \quad \text{...........(35)}.$$

Other expressions for continuous premiums can be obtained by making m infinitely great in formulae (24) to (33).

20. Values of Policies subject to true premiums payable m times a year. The value of a whole-life assurance subject to "true" premiums payable m times a year, which has been t years in force (t being integral), is represented by ${}_tV^{(m)}_{[x]}$ and is found as follows:

$$
\begin{aligned}
{}_tV^{(m)}_{[x]} &= A_{[x]+t} - P^{(m)}_{[x]}\mathbf{a}^{(m)}_{[x]+t} \quad \text{......(36)}\\
&= A_{[x]+t} - P^{(m)}_{[x]}\left(\mathbf{a}_{[x]+t} - \frac{m-1}{2m}\right)\\
&= A_{[x]+t} - \left\{P_{[x]} + \frac{m-1}{2m}P^{(m)}_{[x]}(P_{[x]}+d)\right\}\mathbf{a}_{[x]+t} + \frac{m-1}{2m}P^{(m)}_{[x]}\\
&= (A_{[x]+t} - P_{[x]}\mathbf{a}_{[x]+t}) + \frac{m-1}{2m}P^{(m)}_{[x]}\{1-(P_{[x]}+d)\,\mathbf{a}_{[x]+t}\}\\
&= {}_tV_{[x]}\left(1 + \frac{m-1}{2m}P^{(m)}_{[x]}\right) \quad \text{......(37).}
\end{aligned}
$$

This result may be explained verbally: By accepting premiums payable m times a year instead of yearly the Office runs the risk of losing part of the year's premium in the year of death. Assuming a uniform distribution of deaths over the year of age, the probability that death occurs in any one $\frac{1}{m}$th part of the year is $\frac{1}{m}$. If the life fail in the first $\frac{1}{m}$th part, the loss is $\frac{m-1}{m}P^{(m)}_{[x]}$; if in the second $\frac{1}{m}$th part $\frac{m-2}{m}P^{(m)}_{[x]}$ and so on, there being no loss if death occur in the last $\frac{1}{m}$th part of the year. The average loss in the year of death is, therefore,

$$
\begin{aligned}
&\frac{1}{m}P^{(m)}_{[x]}\left\{\frac{m-1}{m} + \frac{m-2}{m} + \dots + \frac{1}{m}\right\}\\
&= \frac{m-1}{2m}P^{(m)}_{[x]},
\end{aligned}
$$

and the Office must treat this as part of the sum assured and reserve in hand ${}_tV_{[x]}\cdot\frac{m-1}{2m}P^{(m)}_{[x]}$ in addition to ${}_tV_{[x]}$.

21. The difference between ${}_tV^{(m)}_{[x]}$ and ${}_tV_{[x]}$ is small. It is greatest when m is infinite and the premiums are payable momently. For example, at age 30, by the O[NM] Table at 3 per cent. interest $P_{[30]} = \cdot 01947$ and, at age 60, $\bar{P}_{[60]} = \cdot 06159$. Therefore

$$_t\bar{V}_{[30]} = {_tV_{[30]}} \times 1{\cdot}00974 \text{ and } {_tV_{[60]}} = {_tV_{[60]}} \times 1{\cdot}03080.$$

In half-yearly cases

$$_tV^{(2)}_{[30]} = {_tV_{[30]}} \times 1{\cdot}00482 \text{ and } {_tV^{(2)}_{[60]}} = {_tV_{[60]}} \times 1{\cdot}01505:$$

in quarterly cases

$$_tV^{(4)}_{[30]} = {_tV_{[30]}} \times 1{\cdot}00726 \text{ and } {_tV^{(4)}_{[60]}} = {_tV_{[60]}} \times 1{\cdot}02285.$$

For practical purposes it is usual to discard the difference and to write in all cases

$$_tV^{(m)}_{[x]} = {_tV_{[x]}} \quad \text{.......................(38).}$$

22. In the case of an endowment assurance, subject to *true* premiums payable m times a year,

$$_tV^{(m)}_{[x]:\overline{n|}} = A_{[x]+t:\overline{n-t|}} - P^{(m)}_{[x]:\overline{n|}}\, a^{(m)}_{[x]+t:\overline{n-t|}} \quad \text{.............................(39)}$$

$$= A_{[x]+t:\overline{n-t|}} - P^{(m)}_{[x]:\overline{n|}} \left\{ a_{[x]+t:\overline{n-t|}} - \frac{m-1}{2m}\left(1 - \frac{D_{[x]+n}}{D_{[x]+t}}\right)\right\}$$

$$= A_{[x]+t:\overline{n-t|}} - \left\{ P_{[x]:\overline{n|}} + \frac{m-1}{2m} P^{(m)}_{[x]:\overline{n|}} (P^{\;1}_{[x]:\overline{n|}} + d)\right\} a_{[x]+t:\overline{n-t|}}$$
$$+ \frac{m-1}{2m} P^{(m)}_{[x]:\overline{n|}} \left(1 - \frac{D_{[x]+n}}{D_{[x]+t}}\right)$$

$$= (A_{[x]+t:\overline{n-t|}} - P_{[x]:\overline{n|}}\, a_{[x]+t:\overline{n-t|}}) + \frac{m-1}{2m} P^{(m)}_{[x]:\overline{n|}} \{1 - d\,a_{[x]+t:\overline{n-t|}}$$
$$- A_{[x]+t:\overline{n-t|}}^{\;\;1} - P^{\;1}_{[x]:\overline{n|}}\, a_{[x]+t:\overline{n-t|}}\}$$

$$= {_tV_{[x]:\overline{n|}}} + \frac{m-1}{2m} P^{(m)}_{[x]:\overline{n|}} \cdot {_tV^{\;1}_{[x]:\overline{n|}}} \quad \text{.........................(40),}$$

since

$$1 - d\,a_{[x]+t:\overline{n-t|}} - A_{[x]+t:\overline{n-t|}}^{\;\;1} = A_{[x]+t:\overline{n-t|}} - A_{[x]+t:\overline{n-t|}}^{\;\;1} = A^{\;1}_{\overline{[x]+t}:\overline{n-t|}}.$$

The reserve to cover the possible loss of premium, arising from the fact that premiums are payable m times a year, must in this case be that for a temporary assurance only.

Here also it is usual to discard the second term and, where t is an integer, to write

$$_tV^{(m)}_{[x]:\overline{n|}} = {_tV_{[x]:\overline{n|}}} \quad \text{.......................(41).}$$

23. In connection with the values of policies subject to true $m$thly premiums, at durations involving *a fraction of a year*, two distinct cases arise. In the first place, if the fractional duration is an exact number of $\frac{1}{m}$th parts of the year; that is, if the policy value be required exactly at the end of a premium period, the next premium being just due; interpolation can be made between the policy values at the beginning and end of the year, assuming a premium in each case to be just due. On the other hand, if the value be required at some period during a premium interval, the interpolation must be between the policy value at the beginning of the interval allowing for a premium having *just been paid*, and the value at the end of the interval when another premium is *just due*, thus assuming the same number of premiums paid in each case.

24. If in the case of a whole-life assurance subject to true $m$thly premiums the value is required at duration $t+\frac{r}{m}$ years, when $t+\frac{r}{m}$ years' premiums will have been paid, the interpolation can be made between ${}_tV_{[x]}^{(m)}$ (t years' premiums paid) and ${}_{t+1}V_{[x]}^{(m)}$ ($t+1$ years' premiums paid). When, however, the value is required at time $t+\frac{r}{m}+\frac{1}{sm}$, this method cannot be employed, the number of yearly premiums paid being, not $t+\frac{r}{m}+\frac{1}{sm}$, but $t+\frac{r+1}{m}$. In this case, therefore, it is necessary to interpolate between ${}_{t+\frac{r}{m}}V_{[x]}^{(m)}+\frac{1}{m}P_{[x]}^{(m)}$ and ${}_{t+\frac{r+1}{m}}V_{[x]}^{(m)}$, both of which allow for $t+\frac{r+1}{m}$ years' premiums having been paid.

Algebraically, we have

$$
\begin{aligned}
{}_{t+\frac{r}{m}}V_{[x]}^{(m)} &= {}_tV_{[x]}^{(m)}+\frac{r}{m}({}_{t+1}V_{[x]}^{(m)}-{}_tV_{[x]}^{(m)}) \\
&= \left\{{}_tV_{[x]}+\frac{r}{m}({}_{t+1}V_{[x]}-{}_tV_{[x]})\right\}\left(1+\frac{m-1}{2m}P_{[x]}^{(m)}\right) \quad \ldots(42),
\end{aligned}
$$

and

$$
\begin{aligned}
{}_{t+\frac{r}{m}+\frac{1}{sm}}V_{[x]}^{(m)} &= \left({}_{t+\frac{r}{m}}V_{[x]}^{(m)}+\frac{1}{m}P_{[x]}^{(m)}\right)+\frac{1}{s}\left\{{}_{t+\frac{r+1}{m}}V_{[x]}^{(m)}-\left({}_{t+\frac{r}{m}}V_{[x]}^{(m)}+\frac{1}{m}P_{[x]}^{(m)}\right)\right\} \\
&= {}_{t+\frac{r}{m}}V_{[x]}^{(m)}+\frac{1}{s}({}_{t+\frac{r+1}{m}}V_{[x]}^{(m)}-{}_{t+\frac{r}{m}}V_{[x]}^{(m)})+\left(\frac{1}{m}-\frac{1}{sm}\right)P_{[x]}^{(m)} \\
&\qquad\qquad \ldots\ldots\ldots\ldots(43).
\end{aligned}
$$

But since $\qquad {}_{t+\frac{r+1}{m}}V_{[x]}^{(m)} = {}_tV_{[x]}^{(m)}+\frac{r+1}{m}({}_{t+1}V_{[x]}^{(m)}-{}_tV_{[x]}^{(m)})$,

and $\qquad {}_{t+\frac{r}{m}}V_{[x]}^{(m)} = {}_tV_{[x]}^{(m)}+\frac{r}{m}({}_{t+1}V_{[x]}^{(m)}-{}_tV_{[x]}^{(m)})$,

$$\frac{1}{s}({}_{t+\frac{r+1}{m}}V_{[x]}^{(m)}-{}_{t+\frac{r}{m}}V_{[x]}^{(m)})=\frac{1}{sm}({}_{t+1}V_{[x]}^{(m)}-{}_tV_{[x]}^{(m)}).$$

Therefore

$$_{t+\frac{r}{m}+\frac{1}{sm}}V^{(m)}_{[x]} = {}_tV^{(m)}_{[x]} + \left(\frac{r}{m}+\frac{1}{sm}\right)({}_{t+1}V^{(m)}_{[x]} - {}_tV^{(m)}_{[x]}) + \left(\frac{1}{m}-\frac{1}{sm}\right)P^{(m)}_{[x]}$$

$$= \left\{{}_tV_{[x]} + \left(\frac{r}{m}+\frac{1}{sm}\right)({}_{t+1}V_{[x]} - {}_tV_{[x]})\right\}\left(1+\frac{m-1}{2m}P^{(m)}_{[x]}\right)$$

$$+\left(\frac{1}{m}-\frac{1}{sm}\right)P^{(m)}_{[x]} \quad\text{...........(44).}$$

Formula (42) can be obtained from the prospective formula for the policy value: thus, on the basis of an aggregate table, on which basis the formula will be the same as by a select table except for the omission of the brackets enclosing the letter x,

$$_{t+\frac{r}{m}}V^{(m)}_x = {}^*A_{x+t+\frac{r}{m}} - P^{(m)}_x \,.\, a^{(m)}_{x+t+\frac{r}{m}}$$

$$= A_{x+t+\frac{r}{m}} - \left\{P_x + \frac{m-1}{2m}P^{(m)}_x(P_x+d)\right\}\left(a_{x+t+\frac{r}{m}} - \frac{m-1}{2m}\right)$$

$$= \left\{A_{x+t} + \frac{r}{m}(A_{x+t+1} - A_{x+t})\right\} - P_x\left\{a_{x+t} + \frac{r}{m}(a_{x+t+1} - a_{x+t})\right\}$$

$$-\frac{m-1}{2m}P^{(m)}_x \,.\, \frac{a_{x+t+\frac{r}{m}}}{a_x} + \frac{m-1}{2m}P^{(m)}_x$$

$$= \left\{{}_tV_x + \frac{r}{m}({}_{t+1}V_x - {}_tV_x)\right\}\left(1+\frac{m-1}{2m}P^{(m)}_x\right),$$

since $\dfrac{m-1}{2m}P^{(m)}_x\left(1-\dfrac{a_{x+t+\frac{r}{m}}}{a_x}\right) = \dfrac{m-1}{2m}P^{(m)}_x\left\{{}_tV_x + \dfrac{r}{m}({}_{t+1}V_x - {}_tV_x)\right\}.$

Similarly for formula (44)

$$_{t+\frac{r}{m}+\frac{1}{sm}}V^{(m)}_x = {}^*A_{x+t+\frac{r}{m}+\frac{1}{sm}} - P^{(m)}_x \,.\, {}_{\frac{1}{m}-\frac{1}{sm}|}a^{(m)}_{x+t+\frac{r}{m}+\frac{1}{sm}}$$

$$= A_{x+t+\frac{r}{m}+\frac{1}{sm}} - \left\{P_x + \frac{m-1}{2m}P^{(m)}_x(P_x+d)\right\}$$

$$\times\left\{a_{x+t+\frac{r}{m}+\frac{1}{sm}} - \frac{m-1}{2m}\right\} + \left(\frac{1}{m}-\frac{1}{sm}\right)P^{(m}_x$$

$$= (A_{x+t+\frac{r}{m}+\frac{1}{sm}} - P_x a_{x+t+\frac{r}{m}+\frac{1}{sm}})$$

$$+\frac{m-1}{2m}P^{(m)}_x\left(1-\frac{a_{x+t+\frac{r}{m}+\frac{1}{sm}}}{a_x}\right) + \left(\frac{1}{m}-\frac{1}{sm}\right)P^{(m)}_x$$

$$= \left\{{}_tV_x + \left(\frac{r}{m}+\frac{1}{sm}\right)({}_{t+1}V_x - {}_tV_x)\right\}\left(1+\frac{m-1}{2m}P^{(m)}_x\right)$$

$$+\left(\frac{1}{m}-\frac{1}{sm}\right)P^{(m)}_x.$$

* A theoretical point which arises in connection with this function is discussed in Chap. VIII 16.

It is evident that the simpler method of obtaining these values is by interpolation.

In practice, in both the policy values obtained in this paragraph, the reserve for possible loss of premiums in the year of death would be discarded, the values thus becoming

$$_{t+\frac{r}{m}}V_{[x]}^{(m)} = {}_tV_{[x]} + \frac{r}{m}({}_{t+1}V_{[x]} - {}_tV_{[x]}) \text{ ....(45)},$$

and

$$_{t+\frac{r}{m}+\frac{1}{sm}}V_{[x]}^{(m)} = {}_tV_{[x]} + \left(\frac{r}{m}+\frac{1}{sm}\right)({}_{t+1}V_{[x]} - {}_tV_{[x]}) + \left(\frac{1}{m}-\frac{1}{sm}\right)P_{[x]} \text{ (46)}.$$

In the latter expression, since a payment of premium is not due for the balance $\left(\frac{1}{m}-\frac{1}{sm}\right)$ of the premium interval, this proportion of the year's premium is kept in hand: it will be noticed also that $P_{[x]}$ is used as approximately equal to $P_{[x]}^{(m)}$.

The following example will demonstrate the practical method of calculation.

Given ${}_3V_x = \cdot068$, ${}_4V_x = \cdot091$, $P_x = \cdot030$, find, without going into any refinements, values for ${}_{3\frac{1}{4}}V_x$, ${}_{3\frac{1}{4}}V_x^{(2)}$, ${}_{3\frac{1}{4}}V_x^{(4)}$.

$$\begin{aligned}
{}_{3\frac{1}{4}}V_x &= {}_3V_x + \tfrac{1}{4}({}_4V_x - {}_3V_x) + \tfrac{3}{4}P_x \\
&= \cdot096, \text{ (as obtained in Chap. VI 9)} \\
{}_{3\frac{1}{4}}V_x^{(2)} &= {}_3V_x + \tfrac{1}{4}({}_4V_x - {}_3V_x) + \tfrac{1}{4}P_x \\
&= \cdot081, \\
{}_{3\frac{1}{4}}V_x^{(4)} &= {}_3V_x + \tfrac{1}{4}({}_4V_x - {}_3V_x) \\
&= \cdot074.
\end{aligned}$$

It will be observed that ${}_{3\frac{1}{4}}V_x > {}_{3\frac{1}{4}}V_x^{(2)} > {}_{3\frac{1}{4}}V_x^{(4)}$. It is evident that this must be so because, in respect of the current assurance year, in the first case the full premium has been paid, in the second there is half a year's premium still to be paid, and in the third three-quarters of the year's premium remains to be paid.

A word of warning may perhaps be given here as to the danger of confusing the values of ${}_{t+\frac{r}{m}}V_{[x]}$ and ${}_{t+\frac{r}{m}}V_{[x]}^{(m)}$. The mistake is frequently made of assuming ${}_{t+\frac{r}{m}}V_{[x]}$ to be equal to

$${}_tV_{[x]} + \frac{r}{m}({}_{t+1}V_{[x]} - {}_tV_{[x]}),$$

which, as has been shown, is the expression for the value of ${}_{t+\frac{r}{m}}V_{[x]}^{(m)}$. A comparison of formulae (9) of Chap. VI and (45) of this chapter shows that

$${}_{t+\frac{r}{m}}V_{[x]} = {}_{t+\frac{r}{m}}V_{[x]}^{(m)} + \left(1 - \frac{r}{m}\right) P_{[x]}.$$

This danger will be avoided if the necessity of keeping in hand that part of the year's premium corresponding to the period which has to elapse before another premium becomes due be borne in mind: this necessity arises in the case of ${}_{t+\frac{r}{m}}V_{[x]}$ which is subject to annual premiums, but not in the case of ${}_{t+\frac{r}{m}}V_{[x]}^{(m)}$ which refers to a policy under which, at time $t+\frac{r}{m}$, a $\frac{1}{m}$thly premium payment is just due.

25. For the value of an endowment assurance subject to true $m$thly premiums

$$\begin{aligned}{}_{t+\frac{r}{m}}V_{[x]:\overline{n}|}^{(m)} &= {}_tV_{[x]:\overline{n}|} + \frac{r}{m}\left({}_{t+1}V_{[x]:\overline{n}|} - {}_tV_{[x]:\overline{n}|}\right)\\ &\quad + \frac{m-1}{2m} P_{[x]:\overline{n}|}^{(m)} \left\{{}_tV_{[x]:\overline{n}|}^{1} + \frac{r}{m}\left({}_{t+1}V_{[x]:\overline{n}|}^{1} - {}_tV_{[x]:\overline{n}|}^{1}\right)\right\} \quad \ldots(47),\end{aligned}$$

$$\begin{aligned}{}_{t+\frac{r}{m}+\frac{1}{sm}}V_{[x]:\overline{n}|}^{(m)} &= {}_tV_{[x]:\overline{n}|} + \left(\frac{r}{m} + \frac{1}{sm}\right)\left({}_{t+1}V_{[x]:\overline{n}|} - {}_tV_{[x]:\overline{n}|}\right)\\ &\quad + \frac{m-1}{2m} P_{[x]:\overline{n}|}^{(m)} \left\{{}_tV_{[x]:\overline{n}|}^{1} + \left(\frac{r}{m} + \frac{1}{sm}\right)\left({}_{t+1}V_{[x]:\overline{n}|}^{1} - {}_tV_{[x]:\overline{n}|}^{1}\right)\right\}\\ &\quad + \left(\frac{1}{m} - \frac{1}{sm}\right) P_{[x]:\overline{n}|}^{(m)} \quad \ldots\ldots\ldots\ldots(48),\end{aligned}$$

the reserve for possible loss of premiums being as before that for a temporary assurance.

Again discarding the reserve for possible loss of premiums, and in the latter case writing $P_{[x]:\overline{n}|}$ as approximately equal to $P_{[x]:\overline{n}|}^{(m)}$ the formulae become, for practical purposes,

$${}_{t+\frac{r}{m}}V_{[x]:\overline{n}|}^{(m)} = {}_tV_{[x]:\overline{n}|} + \frac{r}{m}\left({}_{t+1}V_{[x]:\overline{n}|} - {}_tV_{[x]:\overline{n}|}\right) \quad \ldots\ldots\ldots\ldots(49),$$

$$\begin{aligned}{}_{t+\frac{r}{m}+\frac{1}{sm}}V_{[x]:\overline{n}|}^{(m)} &= {}_tV_{[x]:\overline{n}|} + \left(\frac{r}{m} + \frac{1}{sm}\right)\left({}_{t+1}V_{[x]:\overline{n}|} - {}_tV_{[x]:\overline{n}|}\right)\\ &\quad + \left(\frac{1}{m} - \frac{1}{sm}\right) P_{[x]:\overline{n}|} \quad \ldots\ldots\ldots\ldots(50).\end{aligned}$$

26. Values of Policies subject to Instalment Premiums. In paragraphs 20 to 25 the values of whole-life and endowment assurances subject to "true" premiums payable m times a year have been considered: it is now proposed to deal with the corresponding values when "instalment" premiums are charged.

Dealing first with whole-life assurances, on the assumption of a uniform distribution of deaths, if premiums are payable m times a year, the average amount of premium to be deducted from the sum assured is $\frac{m-1}{2m}P^{[m]}$, which at once suggests that in ascertaining the value of a policy subject to instalment premiums, the sum assured may be treated as $1-\frac{m-1}{2m}P^{[m]}$. Thus,

$$
\begin{aligned}
{}_tV^{[m]}_{[x]} &= A_{[x]+t}\left(1-\frac{m-1}{2m}P^{[m]}_{[x]}\right)-P^{[m]}_{[x]}a^{(m)}_{[x]+t} \quad \ldots\ldots\ldots\ldots(51)\\
&= A_{[x]+t}-\frac{m-1}{2m}P^{[m]}_{[x]}(1-d\mathbf{a}_{[x]+t})-P^{[m]}_{[x]}\left(\mathbf{a}_{[x]+t}-\frac{m-1}{2m}\right)\\
&= A_{[x]+t}+\frac{m-1}{2m}P^{[m]}_{[x]}\,.\,d\mathbf{a}_{[x]+t}-\left\{P_{[x]}+\frac{m-1}{2m}P^{[m]}_{[x]}\,.\,d\right\}\mathbf{a}_{[x]+t}\\
&= {}_tV_{[x]} \quad \ldots\ldots\ldots\ldots\ldots\ldots\ldots\ldots(52).
\end{aligned}
$$

The policy is, in fact, subject to annual premiums payable by instalments, so that, in ascertaining its value, since the loss of interest on the deferred instalments is counteracted by the increased amount of the premium paid each year, the policy can at a policy anniversary be treated as if the ordinary annual premium were payable. When the policy value is required at a date between two policy anniversaries, allowance must be made for the fact that, instead of the annual premium having been received in full, there may be certain instalments of the current year's premium still to be received.

If the value be required at time $t+\frac{r}{m}$, a payment of premium being just due, there will be $1-\frac{r}{m}$ of the current year's premium still to be received and it will not be necessary to allow in the expression for the policy value for this proportion of the year's premium to be kept in hand. The expression thus becomes

$$
{}_{t+\frac{r}{m}}V^{[m]}_{[x]} = {}_tV_{[x]}+\frac{r}{m}({}_{t+1}V_{[x]}-{}_tV_{[x]}) \quad \ldots\ldots\ldots\ldots(53).
$$

When the value is required at a date between two premium payments, for example at time $t+\frac{r}{m}+\frac{1}{sm}$, that proportion of the annual premium corresponding to the time to run until the next instalment of premium becomes payable must be kept in hand and the expression becomes

$$_{t+\frac{r}{m}+\frac{1}{sm}}V_{[x]}^{[m]} = {}_tV_{[x]} + \left(\frac{r}{m}+\frac{1}{sm}\right)({}_{t+1}V_{[x]} - {}_tV_{[x]}) + \left(\frac{1}{m}-\frac{1}{sm}\right)P_{[x]} \qquad \ldots\ldots\ldots\ldots(54).$$

Formulae (53) and (54) are identical with those obtained for policy values at similar durations when true premiums are payable, but the student should notice carefully the different adjustments made in the two cases. Formulae (53) and (54) should, moreover, in view of the arguments employed in deducing them, be compared with formula (9) of Chapter VI substituting $\frac{r}{m}$ and $\frac{r}{m}+\frac{1}{sm}$ respectively for $\frac{1}{s}$.

27. For Endowment Assurances subject to instalment premiums

$${}_tV_{[x]:\overline{n}|}^{[m]} = A_{\overset{1}{[x]+t}:\overline{n-t}|}\left(1-\frac{m-1}{2m}P_{[x]:\overline{n}|}^{[m]}\right) + A_{[x]+t:\overset{1}{\overline{n-t}|}} - P_{[x]:\overline{n}|}^{[m]}\,a_{[x]+t:\overline{n-t}|}^{(m)} \qquad \ldots\ldots\ldots\ldots(55)$$

$$= A_{[x]+t:\overline{n-t}|} - \frac{m-1}{2m}P_{[x]:\overline{n}|}^{[m]}A_{\overset{1}{[x]+t}:\overline{n-t}|} - P_{[x]:\overline{n}|}^{[m]}\left\{a_{[x]+t:\overline{n-t}|} - \frac{m-1}{2m}\left(1-\frac{D_{[x]+n}}{D_{[x]+t}}\right)\right\}$$

$$= A_{[x]+t:\overline{n-t}|} - \left\{P_{[x]:\overline{n}|} + \frac{m-1}{2m}P_{[x]:\overline{n}|}^{[m]}\,.\,d\right\}a_{[x]+t:\overline{n-t}|}$$

$$+\frac{m-1}{2m}P_{[x]:\overline{n}|}^{[m]}\{1 - A_{[x]+t:\overset{1}{\overline{n-t}|}} - A_{\overset{1}{[x]+t}:\overline{n-t}|}\}$$

$$= A_{[x]+t:\overline{n-t}|} - P_{[x]:\overline{n}|}\,a_{[x]+t:\overline{n-t}|}$$

$$= {}_tV_{[x]:\overline{n}|} \qquad \ldots\ldots\ldots\ldots\ldots\ldots\ldots\ldots\ldots\ldots\ldots\ldots\ldots\ldots(56).$$

Similarly

$$_{t+\frac{r}{m}}V_{[x]:\overline{n}|}^{[m]} = {}_tV_{[x]:\overline{n}|} + \frac{r}{m}({}_{t+1}V_{[x]:\overline{n}|} - {}_tV_{[x]:\overline{n}|}) \qquad \ldots\ldots\ldots\ldots\ldots(57),$$

and

$$_{t+\frac{r}{m}+\frac{1}{sm}}V_{[x]:\overline{n}|}^{[m]} = {}_tV_{[x]:\overline{n}|} + \left(\frac{r}{m}+\frac{1}{sm}\right)({}_{t+1}V_{[x]:\overline{n}|} - {}_tV_{[x]:\overline{n}|}) + \left(\frac{1}{m}-\frac{1}{sm}\right)P_{[x]:\overline{n}|} \qquad \ldots\ldots(58).$$

28. Values of Limited Payment Policies at fractional durations etc. It will perhaps be an advantage if the values of limited payment policies corresponding to the values of ordinary whole-life and endowment assurances dealt with in paragraphs 20 to 25 be set out, though it is not thought necessary to reproduce the method of obtaining them.

Thus

$$\left.\begin{aligned} {}^k_tV^{(m)}_{[x]} &= {}^k_tV_{[x]} + \frac{m-1}{2m}\cdot {}_kP^{(m)}_{[x]}\cdot {}_tV^{\ 1}_{[x]:\overline{k|}} \\ &= {}^k_tV_{[x]} \text{ approx.} \end{aligned}\right\} \quad\text{.........................(59)},$$

$$\left.\begin{aligned} {}^k_tV^{(m)}_{[x]:\overline{n|}} &= {}^k_tV_{[x]:\overline{n|}} + \frac{m-1}{2m}\cdot {}_kP^{(m)}_{[x]:\overline{n|}}\cdot {}_tV^{\ 1}_{[x]:\overline{k|}} \\ &= {}^k_tV_{[x]:\overline{n|}} \text{ approx.} \end{aligned}\right\} \quad\text{..................(60)},$$

$$\left.\begin{aligned} {}^{\ \ k}_{t+\frac{r}{m}}V^{(m)}_{[x]} &= {}^k_tV_{[x]} + \frac{r}{m}\left({}^{\ k}_{t+1}V_{[x]} - {}^k_tV_{[x]}\right) \\ &\quad + \frac{m-1}{2m}\cdot {}_kP^{(m)}_{[x]}\left\{{}_tV^{\ 1}_{[x]:\overline{k|}} + \frac{r}{m}\left({}_{t+1}V^{\ 1}_{[x]:\overline{k|}} - {}_tV^{\ 1}_{[x]:\overline{k|}}\right)\right\} \\ &= {}^k_tV_{[x]} + \frac{r}{m}\left({}^{\ k}_{t+1}V_{[x]} - {}^k_tV_{[x]}\right) \text{ approx.} \end{aligned}\right\} \quad (61),$$

$$\left.\begin{aligned} {}^{\ \ k}_{t+\frac{r}{m}}V^{(m)}_{[x]:\overline{n|}} &= {}^k_tV_{[x]:\overline{n|}} + \frac{r}{m}\left({}^{\ k}_{t+1}V_{[x]:\overline{n|}} - {}^k_tV_{[x]:\overline{n|}}\right) \\ &\quad + \frac{m-1}{2m}\cdot {}_kP^{(m)}_{[x]:\overline{n|}}\left\{{}_tV^{\ 1}_{[x]:\overline{k|}} + \frac{r}{m}\left({}_{t+1}V^{\ 1}_{[x]:\overline{k|}} - {}_tV^{\ 1}_{[x]:\overline{k|}}\right)\right\} \\ &= {}^k_tV_{[x]:\overline{n|}} + \frac{r}{m}\left({}^{\ k}_{t+1}V_{[x]:\overline{n|}} - {}^k_tV_{[x]:\overline{n|}}\right) \text{ approx.} \end{aligned}\right\} \quad (62).$$

The formulae for ${}^{\ \ \ \ \ \ \ k}_{t+\frac{r}{m}+\frac{1}{sm}}V^{(m)}_{[x]}$ and ${}^{\ \ \ \ \ \ \ k}_{t+\frac{r}{m}+\frac{1}{sm}}V^{(m)}_{[x]:\overline{n|}}$ respectively will be similar to formulae (61) and (62), $\left(\frac{r}{m}+\frac{1}{sm}\right)$ being substituted for $\frac{r}{m}$, and the term $\left(\frac{1}{m}-\frac{1}{sm}\right){}_kP^{(m)}_{[x]}$ or $\left(\frac{1}{m}-\frac{1}{sm}\right){}_kP^{(m)}_{[x]:\overline{n|}}$ being added.

In practice special points arise for consideration in reference to part of the loading of the premiums being kept in hand to provide for the expenses attaching to the policies after the payment of premiums has ceased. These are dealt with in Chapter X.

EXAMPLES

Ex. 1. A man now aged 40 ten years ago invested £1000 in the purchase of an annuity payable half-yearly. He now wishes the future payments to be made quarterly.

On the basis of the H^M Table at 3 per cent., what was the amount of the half-yearly payment, and what quarterly payment will be made in future? Net functions only.

The half-yearly payment is

$$\frac{1}{2} \cdot \frac{1000}{a_{30} + \frac{1}{4}}$$

$$= \frac{1}{2} \cdot \frac{1000}{19{\cdot}895 + {\cdot}25}$$

$$= 24{\cdot}82 \text{; say, £24. 16s. 5d.}$$

The value of future payments is

$$2 \times 24{\cdot}82\,(a_{40} + \tfrac{1}{4})$$

$$= 2 \times 24{\cdot}82\,(17{\cdot}177 + {\cdot}25) = 865{\cdot}08,$$

and the quarterly payment to be made in future will be

$$\frac{1}{4} \cdot \frac{865{\cdot}08}{a_{40} + \frac{3}{8}} = \frac{1}{4} \cdot \frac{865{\cdot}08}{17{\cdot}552} = 12{\cdot}32 \text{; say, £12. 6s. 5d.}$$

Ex. 2. Find the value by the $O^{[NM]}$ 3 per cent. Table of an annuity of £400 per annum payable half-yearly for 20 years certain, the half-yearly payment to be reduced to £150 after the first death and £100 after the second death of two lives aged 30 and 40 if such deaths occur during the term of the annuity.

Consideration of this problem shows that it can be looked upon as an annuity certain of £200 for 20 years with an additional £100 so long as (30) lives during the 20 years and a further £100 so long as (40) lives during that period, all the annuities being payable half-yearly.

The value is, therefore,

$$200\,a^{(2)}_{\overline{20}|} + 100\,a^{(2)}_{[30]:\overline{20}|} + 100\,a^{(2)}_{[40]:\overline{20}|}$$

$$= 100\left[2a_{\overline{20}|} \times \frac{i}{j_{(2)}} + \frac{1}{D_{[30]}}\{N_{[30]+1} - N_{51} + \tfrac{1}{4}(D_{[30]} - D_{50})\}\right.$$

$$\left. + \frac{1}{D_{[40]}}\{N_{[40]+1} - N_{61} + \tfrac{1}{4}(D_{[40]} - D_{60})\}\right]$$

$$= 100\,[2 \times 14{\cdot}8775 \times 1{\cdot}00744$$

$$+ \tfrac{1}{38121}\{753{,}889 - 233{,}036 + \tfrac{1}{4}(38121 - 17007)\}$$

$$+ \tfrac{1}{25808}\{441{,}378 - 102{,}255 + \tfrac{1}{4}(25808 - 10121)\}]$$

$$= 5707{\cdot}41.$$

Ex. 3. Find on the basis of the $O^{[NM]}$ Table at $3\frac{1}{2}$ per cent. the true net quarterly premium and the quarterly instalment premium for

(*a*) a whole-life assurance on (30),

(*b*) an endowment assurance on (30) for a term of 15 years.

(i) True quarterly premiums:

$$(a)\qquad \tfrac{1}{4}P^{(4)}_{[30]}=\frac{1}{4}\,\frac{P_{[30]}}{1-\frac{3}{8}(P_{[30]}+d)}$$

$$=\frac{1}{4}\,\frac{\cdot 01788}{1-\frac{3}{8}(\cdot 01788+\cdot 03382)}$$

$$=\cdot 00456,$$

$$(b)\quad \tfrac{1}{4}P^{(4)}_{[30]:\overline{15}|}=\frac{1}{4}\,\frac{P_{[30]:\overline{15}|}}{1-\frac{3}{8}(P^{\;1}_{[30]:\overline{15}|}+d)}$$

$$=\frac{1}{4}\,\frac{\cdot 05455}{1-\frac{3}{8}(\cdot 00887+\cdot 03382)}$$

$$=\cdot 01386.$$

(ii) Instalment quarterly premiums:

$$(a)\qquad \tfrac{1}{4}P^{[4]}_{[30]}=\frac{1}{4}\,\frac{P_{[30]}}{1-\frac{3}{8}d}$$

$$=\frac{1}{4}\,\frac{\cdot 01788}{1-\frac{3}{8}(\cdot 03382)}$$

$$=\cdot 00453,$$

$$(b)\quad \tfrac{1}{4}P^{[4]}_{[30]:\overline{15}|}=\frac{1}{4}\,\frac{P_{[30]:\overline{15}|}}{1-\frac{3}{8}d}$$

$$=\frac{1}{4}\,\frac{\cdot 05455}{1-\frac{3}{8}(\cdot 03382)}$$

$$=\cdot 01381.$$

CHAPTER VIII

SINGLE-LIFE ASSURANCES PAYABLE AT ANY OTHER MOMENT THAN AT THE END OF THE YEAR OF DEATH

1. In the preceding chapters it has been assumed that, where the payment of the sum assured depended on the death of the life assured, such payment would be made at the end of the year of death. In practice the sum due is, as a rule, paid immediately on proof of death and of the title of the claimant, and it becomes necessary, therefore, to investigate the modifications to be made in the formulae already obtained to allow for this condition. Where "select" symbols are employed the formulae apply also to aggregate tables with the omission of the brackets round the age at entry.

2. The symbols for the single premiums for the various classes of assurances, where the sum assured is payable at the *moment of death*, differ from those employed in earlier chapters only by the insertion of a "bar" over the letter A: thus $\bar{A}$.

Since the probability of a select life aged x dying at moment of time t after that age is ${}_tp_{[x]}\,\mu_{[x]+t}\,dt$, it follows that the present value of 1 payable immediately on the death of $[x]$ in the event of his dying at the moment of age $x+t$ is $v^t\,{}_tp_{[x]}\,\mu_{[x]+t}\,dt$, and the value of an assurance of 1 payable at the moment of death of $[x]$ if this occur within a period of n years is

$$\begin{aligned}\bar{A}^{1}_{[x]:\overline{n}|} &= \int_0^n v^t\,{}_tp_{[x]}\,\mu_{[x]+t}\,dt \\ &= -\frac{1}{l_{[x]}}\int_0^n v^t\,\frac{dl_{[x]+t}}{dt}\,dt \\ &= -\frac{1}{l_{[x]}}\left[v^t\,l_{[x]+t} - \int v^t \log_e v\,l_{[x]+t}\,dt\right]_{t=0}^{t=n} \\ &= 1 - v^n\,{}_np_{[x]} - \delta\bar{a}_{[x]:\overline{n}|} \quad\ldots\ldots(1),\end{aligned}$$

since $$-\log_e v = \delta \text{ and } \frac{1}{l_{[x]}}\int_0^n v^t\,l_{[x]+t}\,dt = \bar{a}_{[x]:\overline{n}|}.$$

3. The value of a whole-life assurance of 1 payable at the moment of death of (x) is

$$\bar{A}_{[x]} = \int_0^\infty v^t \, {}_tp_{[x]} \, \mu_{[x]+t} \, dt$$
$$= 1 - \delta\bar{a}_{[x]} \quad \text{.............................(2)},$$

since when $t = \infty$, $v^t \, l_{[x]+t}$ vanishes.

4. In the case of an endowment assurance, for n years, since this is a combination of a temporary assurance and a pure endowment, we have

$$\bar{A}_{[x]:\overline{n}|} = \int_0^n v^t \, {}_tp_{[x]} \, \mu_{[x]+t} \, dt + v^n \, {}_np_{[x]}$$
$$= 1 - \delta\bar{a}_{[x]:\overline{n}|} \quad \text{..........................(3)}.$$

5. Formulae (2) and (3) can be obtained by general reasoning. The investment of a unit will produce a continuous annuity of the force of interest, δ, payable during the life of $[x]$, the value of which is $\delta\bar{a}_{[x]}$, and the unit will remain intact at his death. The value of a unit payable at the moment of death of $[x]$ being $\bar{A}_{[x]}$, we have

$$1 = \delta\bar{a}_{[x]} + \bar{A}_{[x]},$$
$$\therefore \quad \bar{A}_{[x]} = 1 - \delta\bar{a}_{[x]}.$$

Similar reasoning obviously applies to the case of an endowment assurance, or of any contract where the interest is, or can be assumed to be, payable momently, and the sum assured is payable immediately the annuity ceases.

6. Alternative formulae for $\bar{A}^1_{x:\overline{n}|}$ and $\bar{A}_x$ (i.e. on the assumption of an Aggregate Table) can be obtained by considering the differential coefficient of the continuous annuity with regard to x. Thus

$$\frac{d\bar{a}_{x:\overline{n}|}}{dx} = \frac{d}{dx}\int_0^n v^t \, {}_tp_x \, dt$$
$$= \int_0^n v^t \left(\frac{d}{dx}\, {}_tp_x\right) dt$$
$$= \int_0^n v^t \, {}_tp_x \, (\mu_x - \mu_{x+t}) \, dt \qquad \text{(see Chap. I 21)}$$
$$= \mu_x \bar{a}_{x:\overline{n}|} - \bar{A}^1_{x:\overline{n}|},$$

whence

$$\bar{A}^1_{x:\overline{n}|} = \mu_x \bar{a}_{x:\overline{n}|} - \frac{d\bar{a}_{x:\overline{n}|}}{dx}$$
$$= \mu_x \bar{a}_{x:\overline{n}|} + \tfrac{1}{2}\left(\bar{a}_{x-1:\overline{n}|} - \bar{a}_{x+1:\overline{n}|}\right) \text{ approx. } \ldots\text{(4)}.$$

Similarly, commencing with $\frac{d\bar{a}_x}{dx}$ we obtain the formula

$$\bar{A}_x = \mu_x \bar{a}_x - \frac{d\bar{a}_x}{dx}$$

$$= \mu_x \bar{a}_x + \tfrac{1}{2}(\bar{a}_{x-1} - \bar{a}_{x+1}) \text{ approx.} \quad \ldots\ldots\ldots\ldots\ldots(5).$$

7. Again

$$\bar{A}^{\,1}_{x:\overline{n}|} = \frac{1}{l_x}\int_0^n v^t\, l_{x+t}\, \mu_{x+t}\, dt$$

$$= \frac{1}{l_x}\int_0^n v^t\, l_{x+t}\, \frac{l_{x-1+t} - l_{x+1+t}}{2l_{x+t}}\, dt \quad \text{approx.}$$

$$= \tfrac{1}{2}\left[\frac{l_{x-1}}{l_x}\int_0^n v^t \frac{l_{x-1+t}}{l_{x-1}}\, dt - \frac{l_{x+1}}{l_x}\int_0^n v^t \frac{l_{x+1+t}}{l_{x+1}}\, dt\right]$$

$$= \tfrac{1}{2}\left(\frac{\bar{a}_{x-1:\overline{n}|}}{p_{x-1}} - p_x \bar{a}_{x+1:\overline{n}|}\right) \quad \ldots\ldots\ldots\ldots\ldots\ldots(6).$$

Similarly

$$A_x = \tfrac{1}{2}\left(\frac{\bar{a}_{x-1}}{p_{x-1}} - p_x \bar{a}_{x+1}\right) \quad \ldots\ldots\ldots\ldots\ldots\ldots(7).$$

Formulae (4), (5), (6) and (7) are not applicable to select tables: in order to obtain corresponding expressions that can be employed in connection with such tables it would be necessary to adopt an approximation to the differential coefficient of $\bar{a}$, or to the value of μ, which does not involve an age earlier than x.

8. Considering formulae (2) and (3) it will be seen that the relation $\bar{A} = 1 - \delta\bar{a}$ is independent of the age of the life assured and of the rate of mortality involved, and consequently, if the value of $\bar{a}$ and the rate of interest be known, the value of the corresponding single premium $\bar{A}$ can be ascertained.

It follows, therefore, that tables can be constructed, similar to those discussed in Chapter IV, by means of which, the value of $\bar{a}$ and the *rate* of interest being given, the value of $\bar{A}$ can be obtained by inspection. Such a table for rate of interest 3 per cent. is printed on page 477 of this volume.

It should be noted that in order to obtain the value of $\bar{A}_{x:\overline{n}|}$ this table must be entered with the annuity value $\bar{a}_{x:\overline{n}|}$ whereas the Single Premium Conversion Table discussed in Chapter IV must, in order to obtain $A_{x:\overline{n}|}$, be entered with $a_{x:\overline{n-1}|}$.

9. It has been mentioned in Chapter III that tables of premiums are frequently calculated by employing functions which

assume that the sum assured is payable at the end of the year of death, no adjustment being definitely made to provide for immediate payment of claims. The values of assurances including this provision are, however, often required, and in order to simplify their calculation, monetary values are based on the assumption of a uniform distribution of deaths over each integral year of age.

If the deaths occurring in a year of age be uniformly distributed over that year, they can be taken, on the average, as occurring in the middle of the year. If, therefore, the sum assured be payable at the moment of death, it will, on the average, be paid six months earlier than was assumed in the expressions for A_x, etc. obtained in Chapters III and IV. We can, therefore, write $\bar{A} = A(1+i)^{\frac{1}{2}}$.

Thus in the case of whole-life and temporary assurances respectively, we have

$$\bar{A}_{[x]} \doteq A_{[x]}(1+i)^{\frac{1}{2}} \quad \text{......................(8)},$$

and

$$\bar{A}^{\,1}_{[x]:\overline{n}|} = A^{\,1}_{[x]:\overline{n}|}(1+i)^{\frac{1}{2}} \quad \text{......................(9)}.$$

In the case of an endowment assurance this adjustment for the immediate payment of claims does not affect the pure endowment portion, with the result that

$$\bar{A}_{[x]:\overline{n}|} = A^{\,1}_{[x]:\overline{n}|}(1+i)^{\frac{1}{2}} + A_{[x]:\overset{\,1}{\overline{n}|}} \quad \text{...........(10)}.$$

This assumption enables the commutation functions discussed in Chapter III to be employed in connection with continuous assurances, the values of which expressed in commutation functions are

$$\bar{A}_{[x]} = \frac{M_{[x]}(1+i)^{\frac{1}{2}}}{D_{[x]}},$$

$$\bar{A}^{\,1}_{[x]:\overline{n}|} = \frac{(M_{[x]} - M_{[x]+n})(1+i)^{\frac{1}{2}}}{D_{[x]}},$$

$$\bar{A}_{[x]:\overline{n}|} = \frac{(M_{[x]} - M_{[x]+n})(1+i)^{\frac{1}{2}} + D_{[x]+n}}{D_{[x]}}.$$

In order not to have to write $(1+i)^{\frac{1}{2}}$ in every case, a "bar" is inserted over the commutation symbol when it is desired to indicate that the provision for the immediate payment of claims is to be included. Thus

$$\left.\begin{aligned} \bar{C}_{[x]} &= C_{[x]}(1+i)^{\frac{1}{2}} \\ \bar{M}_{[x]} &= M_{[x]}(1+i)^{\frac{1}{2}} \\ \bar{R}_{[x]} &= R_{[x]}(1+i)^{\frac{1}{2}} \end{aligned}\right\} \text{......................(11)}.$$

In practice it is sufficiently accurate to employ $1+\frac{1}{2}i$ in place of $(1+i)^{\frac{1}{2}}$.

10. In applying the methods adopted in this chapter to deferred assurances, and deferred temporary assurances, it is only necessary to bear in mind the relations

$$_{n|}\overline{A}_{[x]} = \frac{D_{[x]+n}}{D_{[x]}}\overline{A}_{[x]+n},$$

$$_{n|m}\overline{A}_{[x]} = \frac{D_{[x]+n}}{D_{[x]}}\cdot {}_{|m}\overline{A}_{[x]+n}.$$

11. Periodical premiums for continuous assurances may be payable yearly or at more frequent intervals.

Denoting the fact that the assurance is payable at the moment of death by writing $^{(\infty)}P$ in place of P, it follows that, for a whole-life assurance,

$$\left.\begin{aligned} {}^{(\infty)}P_{[x]} &= \frac{\overline{A}_{[x]}}{a_{[x]}} = P_{[x]}(1+i)^{\frac{1}{2}} \\ {}^{(\infty)}P^{(m)}_{[x]} &= \frac{\overline{A}_{[x]}}{a^{(m)}_{[x]}} = P^{(m)}_{[x]}(1+i)^{\frac{1}{2}} \\ {}^{(\infty)}\overline{P}_{[x]} &= \frac{\overline{A}_{[x]}}{\overline{a}_{[x]}} = \overline{P}_{[x]}(1+i)^{\frac{1}{2}} \end{aligned}\right\} \quad \ldots\ldots\ldots\ldots\ldots(12),$$

and for an endowment assurance

$$\left.\begin{aligned} {}^{(\infty)}P_{[x]:\overline{n}|} &= \frac{\overline{A}_{[x]:\overline{n}|}}{a_{[x]:\overline{n}|}} = P^{1}_{[x]:\overline{n}|}(1+i)^{\frac{1}{2}} + P_{[x]:\overline{n}|}^{\ \ 1} \\ {}^{(\infty)}P^{(m)}_{[x]:\overline{n}|} &= \frac{\overline{A}_{[x]:\overline{n}|}}{a^{(m)}_{[x]:\overline{n}|}} = P^{(m)\,1}_{[x]:\overline{n}|}(1+i)^{\frac{1}{2}} + P^{(m)\ \ 1}_{[x]:\overline{n}|} \\ {}^{(\infty)}\overline{P}_{[x]:\overline{n}|} &= \frac{\overline{A}_{[x]:\overline{n}|}}{\overline{a}_{[x]:\overline{n}|}} = \overline{P}^{1}_{[x]:\overline{n}|}(1+i)^{\frac{1}{2}} + \overline{P}_{[x]:\overline{n}|}^{\ \ 1} \end{aligned}\right\} \quad \ldots\ldots(13).$$

12. If we write $\overline{A}_x = 1-\delta\overline{a}_x$ and $\overline{A}_{x:\overline{n}|} = 1-\delta\overline{a}_{x:\overline{n}|}$, the formulae for $^{(\infty)}\overline{P}_{[x]}$ and $^{(\infty)}\overline{P}_{[x]:\overline{n}|}$ become respectively

$$\left.\begin{aligned} {}^{(\infty)}\overline{P}_{[x]} &= \frac{1}{\overline{a}_{[x]}} - \delta \\ {}^{(\infty)}\overline{P}_{[x]:\overline{n}|} &= \frac{1}{\overline{a}_{[x]:\overline{n}|}} - \delta \end{aligned}\right\} \quad \ldots\ldots\ldots\ldots\ldots\ldots(14).$$

With the aid of the expression $^{(\infty)}\overline{P} = \frac{1}{\overline{a}} - \delta$, continuous annual premium conversion tables can be constructed precisely similar to those discussed in Chapter IV for annual functions.

Such a table for rate of interest 3 per cent., extracted from Rothery and Ryan's Premium Conversion Tables, appears on page 477 of this volume. It must however be clearly understood that the result of entering this table with the value of a continuous annuity is to obtain the corresponding premium per annum payable momently for an assurance payable at the moment of death.

13. When the sum assured is payable at the moment of death and the *annual* premium to provide for such immediate payment is taken into account the formula for the value of a whole-life policy becomes

$$\bar{A}_{[x]+t} - {}^{(\infty)}P_{[x]}\, a_{[x]+t}$$
$$= {}_tV_{[x]}(1+i)^{\frac{1}{2}}.$$

The corresponding expression for a temporary assurance is

$$\bar{A}_{\overset{1}{[x]+t}:\overline{n-t}|} - {}^{(\infty)}P_{\overset{1}{[x]}:\overline{n}|}\, a_{[x]+t:\overline{n-t}|}$$
$$= {}_tV_{\overset{1}{[x]}:\overline{n}|}(1+i)^{\frac{1}{2}},$$

and for an endowment assurance

$$\bar{A}_{[x]+t:\overline{n-t}|} - {}^{(\infty)}P_{[x]:\overline{n}|}\, a_{[x]+t:\overline{n-t}|}$$
$$= \{A_{\overset{1}{[x]+t}:\overline{n-t}|}(1+i)^{\frac{1}{2}} + A_{[x]+t:\overset{1}{\overline{n-t}|}}\} - \{P_{\overset{1}{[x]}:\overline{n}|}(1+i)^{\frac{1}{2}} + P_{[x]:\overset{1}{\overline{n}|}}\}\, a_{[x]+t:\overline{n-t}|}$$
$$= {}_tV_{\overset{1}{[x]}:\overline{n}|}(1+i)^{\frac{1}{2}} + {}_tV_{[x]:\overset{1}{\overline{n}|}}.$$

14. $\bar{M}_x$ has been taken as equal to $M_x(1+i)^{\frac{1}{2}}$ but it would be more correctly represented theoretically in the form

$$\int_0^\infty v^{x+t} l_{x+t}\mu_{x+t}\,dt,$$

whence

$$\frac{d\bar{M}_x}{dx} = \frac{d}{dx}\int_0^\infty D_{x+t}\mu_{x+t}\,dt$$
$$= \int_0^\infty \left(\frac{d}{dx}D_{x+t}\mu_{x+t}\right)dt$$
$$= \int_0^\infty \frac{d}{dt}D_{x+t}\mu_{x+t}\,dt$$
$$= -D_x\mu_x \qquad (15).$$

From which it follows that

$$\frac{d\overline{A}_x}{dx} = \frac{d}{dx}\frac{\overline{M}_x}{D_x}$$

$$= \frac{D_x \frac{d}{dx}\overline{M}_x - \overline{M}_x \frac{d}{dx} D_x}{(D_x)^2}$$

$$= \frac{-(D_x)^2 \mu_x + \overline{M}_x . D_x (\mu_x + \delta)}{(D_x)^2}$$

$$= \overline{A}_x (\mu_x + \delta) - \mu_x \quad \text{.......................(16).}$$

The similarity of formulae (15) and (16) to formulae (20) and (23) of Chap. VII should be carefully noted.

15. Assurances under which the sum assured is payable at the end of the $\frac{1}{m}$th interval of a year (e.g. half-year or quarter) in which (x) dies are not often met with in practice, but it may be an advantage theoretically to examine the formulae to be employed in their calculation.

$A_{[x]}^{(m)}$ represents the Single Premium for a whole-life assurance of 1 on the life of (x) payable at the end of that $\frac{1}{m}$th interval of a year, measured from the date of the contract, in which (x) dies.

The investment of a unit will purchase an annuity-due of $f_{(m)}$, the nominal rate of discount convertible m times a year, during the life of (x), the unit remaining intact at the end of that $\frac{1}{m}$th part of a year in which (x) dies. Thus

$$1 = f_{(m)}\, \mathrm{a}_{[x]}^{(m)} + A_{[x]}^{(m)},$$

$$\therefore \quad A_{[x]}^{(m)} = 1 - m\left(1 - v^{\frac{1}{m}}\right) \mathrm{a}_{[x]}^{(m)} \quad \text{...............(17).}$$

If in this formula m be indefinitely increased, we have at once $\overline{A}_{[x]} = 1 - \delta \overline{a}_{[x]}$ (formula (2) of this chapter).

16. Assuming a uniform distribution of deaths over each integral year of age, and accordingly over each $\frac{1}{m}$th part of that year, the deaths occurring in any such $\frac{1}{m}$th part will on the average occur in the middle of it, and the sum assured by $A^{(m)}_{[x]}$ will, therefore, be payable $\frac{1}{2m}$ of a year later than in the case of $\bar{A}_{[x]}$.

Thus $$A^{(m)}_{[x]} = \bar{A}_{[x]}(1+i)^{-\frac{1}{2m}} = A_{[x]}(1+i)^{\frac{1}{2}-\frac{1}{2m}} \quad \text{......(18).}$$

For example, if $m=2$, $A^{(2)}_{[x]} = A_{[x]}(1+i)^{\frac{1}{4}}$,

$m=4$, $A^{(4)}_{[x]} = A_{[x]}(1+i)^{\frac{3}{8}}$.

Looking at this question from another point of view, if there are nm assurances each of $\frac{1}{m}$ payable at the end of that $\frac{1}{m}$th part of a year in which (x) dies, they will on the assumption of a uniform distribution of deaths over each year of age, n being sufficiently large, be equivalent to n assurances of $s^{(m)}_{\overline{1}|}$ payable at the end of the year of death. Therefore

$$A^{(m)}_{[x]} = A_{[x]} s^{(m)}_{\overline{1}|} = A_{[x]} \frac{i}{j_{(m)}} \quad \text{..................(19).}$$

If m be indefinitely increased, this expression becomes

$$\bar{A}_{[x]} = A_{[x]} \frac{i}{\delta} \quad \text{.......................(20).}$$

It may be noted that the policy value at the top of page 101 should strictly be

$${}_{t+\frac{1}{s}}V_{[x]} = A^{\left(1-\frac{1}{s}\right)}_{\overset{1}{\overline{[x]+t+\frac{1}{s}}}:\overline{1-\frac{1}{s}}|} + {}_{1-\frac{1}{s}|}A_{[x]+t+\frac{1}{s}} - P_{[x]} \cdot {}_{1-\frac{1}{s}|}\mathbf{a}_{[x]+t+\frac{1}{s}}$$

in order to allow for the fact that the sum assured is payable at the end of the policy year in which death occurs. A similar point arises in two formulae on page 143.

17. An interesting point arises in connection with increasing assurances payable at the moment of death. It has been shown in Chap. V 9, that $(IA)_x = \frac{R_x}{D_x}$, and, on the assumption of a uniform distribution of deaths over each year of age, if the sum assured is to be paid at the moment of death, we can write

$$(IA)_x(1+i)^{\frac{1}{2}} = \frac{R_x(1+i)^{\frac{1}{2}}}{D_x} = \frac{\bar{R}_x}{D_x}.$$

If we employ the calculus in connection with an increasing whole-life assurance on the life of (x), we have

$$(I\bar{A})_x = \int_0^\infty t v^t {}_tp_x \mu_{x+t} dt,$$

under which the sum assured commences at "0" and is continuously increasing throughout the life of (x).

Examining this last expression, if recourse be made to the assumption of a uniform distribution of deaths over each year of age, so that the deaths occur on the average in the middle of the year, the result will be that if death occur in the first year the sum payable will on the average be $\frac{1}{2}$, if death occur in the second year $1\frac{1}{2}$, if in the third year $2\frac{1}{2}$, and so on: in each case less by $\frac{1}{2}$ than the sum that would be paid at the same time under the assurance represented by $(IA)_x(1+i)^{\frac{1}{2}}$, which, though payable at the moment of death, commences at 1 and increases by yearly increments of 1. It follows, therefore, that $(IA)_x(1+i)^{\frac{1}{2}}$ exceeds $(I\overline{A})_x$ approximately by the value of a continuous assurance of $\frac{1}{2}$. In symbols,

$$(IA)_x(1+i)^{\frac{1}{2}} = (I\overline{A})_x + \tfrac{1}{2}\overline{A}_x.$$

The introduction of the calculus and the consequent employment of $(I\overline{A})_x$ often simplifies the solution of a problem, but for its final evaluation it is generally necessary to employ the usual commutation functions and consequently to substitute for $(I\overline{A})_x$ the expression $[(IA)_x - \frac{1}{2}A_x](1+i)^{\frac{1}{2}}$.

18. It has been shown in Chapter VII 8, that

$$\bar{a}_x = \frac{1}{D_x}\int_0^\infty D_{x+t}\,dt,$$

whence, we have

$$\begin{aligned}
\bar{a}_x &= \frac{1}{D_x}\int_0^\infty D_{x+t}\left(\frac{dt}{dt}\right)dt \\
&= \frac{1}{D_x}\left[tD_{x+t} - \int t\,\frac{dD_{x+t}}{dt}\,dt\right]_{t=0}^{t=\infty} \\
&= \frac{1}{D_x}\left[tD_{x+t} + \int tD_{x+t}\,(\mu_{x+t}+\delta)\,dt\right]_{t=0}^{t=\infty} \\
&= \frac{1}{D_x}\left(\int_0^\infty tD_{x+t}\,\mu_{x+t}\,dt + \delta\int_0^\infty tD_{x+t}\,dt\right) \\
&= (I\overline{A})_x + \delta\,(I\bar{a})_x,
\end{aligned}$$

or $$(I\overline{A})_x = \bar{a}_x - \delta\,(I\bar{a})_x.$$

EXAMPLES

Ex. 1. By means of the H^M Table at 3 per cent. find the value of $\bar{A}_{30}$ by three methods.

$$\bar{A}_{30} = A_{30}(1{\cdot}015) = {\cdot}39141\,(1{\cdot}015) = {\cdot}39728;$$

$$\bar{A}_{30} = A_{30} \times \frac{i}{\delta} = {\cdot}39141\,(1{\cdot}01493) = {\cdot}39725;$$

$$\bar{A}_{30} = 1 - \delta\bar{a}_{30} = 1 - {\cdot}02956\,(20{\cdot}395) = {\cdot}39712.$$

In practice the first form is used.

Ex. 2. On the basis of the $O^{[NM]}$ Table at $3\frac{1}{2}$ per cent. find the annual premium for the following assurances, on a life aged (30), in each case making provision for the immediate payment of claims:

(*a*) Temporary assurance for 10 years.

(*b*) Endowment assurance for 15 years.

(*c*) Double endowment assurance for 15 years.

(*a*) $$\frac{M_{[30]} - M_{40}}{N_{[30]} - N_{40}}(1{\cdot}0175) = \frac{11402{\cdot}88 - 9184{\cdot}11}{637657 - 362706}(1{\cdot}0175) = {\cdot}00821,$$

(*b*) $$\frac{(M_{[30]} - M_{45})(1{\cdot}0175) + D_{45}}{N_{[30]} - N_{45}}$$

$$= \frac{(11402{\cdot}88 - 8094{\cdot}11)(1{\cdot}0175) + 17042}{637657 - 264592} = {\cdot}05471,$$

(*c*) $$\frac{(M_{[30]} - M_{45})(1{\cdot}0175) + 2D_{45}}{N_{[30]} - N_{45}} = {\cdot}10039.$$

CHAPTER IX

COMPLETE SINGLE-LIFE ANNUITIES

1. A *Complete* or *Apportionable* annuity of 1 per annum payable m times a year during the life of (x) is one under which a payment of $\frac{1}{m}$ is made at the end of each $\frac{1}{m}$th part of a year that (x) survives, and an additional payment at the death of (x) of an amount proportionate to the time elapsed between the date of the last payment and the date of death. An annuity under which this proportionate payment to the date of death is not made is known as a *curtate* annuity, and a complete annuity is, therefore, equivalent to a curtate annuity with the addition of the proportionate payment to be made at the death of the annuitant.

2*. The value of the curtate annuity is $a_x^{(m)}$. The adjustment to be made for the proportionate payment to the death of (x) would be a regularly increasing assurance during the whole of life (payable at the moment of death) but that at each $\frac{1}{m}$ of a year a payment of annuity is received, and the assurance must, therefore, be decreased at the end of each interval by $\frac{1}{m}$. The present value of the regularly increasing assurance is $\frac{1}{\mathrm{D}_x}\int_0^\infty \overline{\mathrm{M}}_{x+t}\,dt$ and the deductions are $\frac{1}{m}\frac{\overline{\mathrm{M}}_{x+\frac{1}{m}}}{\mathrm{D}_x}$, $\frac{1}{m}\frac{\overline{\mathrm{M}}_{x+\frac{2}{m}}}{\mathrm{D}_x}$; etc.

Representing the value of the complete annuity to (x) by $\mathring{a}_x^{(m)}$, we have

$$\mathring{a}_x^{(m)} = a_x^{(m)} + \frac{1}{\mathrm{D}_x}\left\{\int_0^\infty \overline{\mathrm{M}}_{x+t}\,dt - \frac{1}{m}\sum_{t=1}^{t=\infty}\cdot\overline{\mathrm{M}}_{x+\frac{t}{m}}\right\} \quad \text{.........(1).}$$

Applying the approximate integration formula

$$\int_0^\infty f(h)\,dh = \frac{1}{m}\sum_{t=1}^{t=\infty} f\left(\frac{t}{m}\right) + \frac{1}{2m}f(0) + \frac{1}{12m^2}\frac{df(0)}{dt} - \text{etc.}$$

* N.B. The methods employed in paragraphs 2 to 5 are taken from a Note by W. P. Elderton in *J. I. A.* Vol. 43, p. 99.

to the term $\int_0^\infty \overline{\text{M}}_{x+t}dt$, formula (1) becomes

$$\mathring{a}_x^{(m)} = a_x^{(m)} + \frac{1}{\text{D}_x}\left\{\frac{1}{m}\sum_{t=1}^{t=\infty}\overline{\text{M}}_{x+\frac{t}{m}} + \frac{1}{2m}\overline{\text{M}}_x + \frac{1}{12m^2}\frac{d\overline{\text{M}}_x}{dx} - \frac{1}{m}\sum_{t=1}^{t=\infty}\overline{\text{M}}_{x+\frac{t}{m}}\right\}$$

$$= a_x^{(m)} + \frac{1}{2m}\overline{\text{A}}_x - \frac{\mu_x}{12m^2} \quad\text{.........(2)},$$

since $\frac{\overline{\text{M}}_x}{\text{D}_x} = \overline{\text{A}}_x$ and $\frac{1}{\text{D}_x}\cdot\frac{d\overline{\text{M}}_x}{dx} = -\mu_x$.

The last term of this formula being very small can be neglected, and in practice the value of the second term is frequently taken as $\frac{1}{2m}\text{A}_x$, A_x being employed as a sufficiently accurate approximation to $\overline{\text{A}}_x$.

For practical purposes, therefore, the formula becomes

$$\mathring{a}_x^{(m)} = a_x + \frac{m-1}{2m} + \frac{1}{2m}\text{A}_x(1 + \tfrac{1}{2}i) \quad\text{.........(3a)},$$

or

$$\mathring{a}_x^{(m)} = a_x + \frac{m-1}{2m} + \frac{1}{2m}\text{A}_x \quad\text{.........(3b)}.$$

If the annuity be payable yearly, its value is $\mathring{a}_x = a_x + \frac{1}{2}\text{A}_x(1 + \frac{1}{2}i)$ or $\mathring{a}_x = a_x + \frac{1}{2}\text{A}_x$.

3. Since $a_x^{(m)} = \frac{1}{m}\cdot\frac{1}{\text{D}_x}\sum_{t=1}^{t=\infty}\text{D}_{x+\frac{t}{m}}$, formula (1) can be written

$$\mathring{a}_x^{(m)} = \frac{1}{\text{D}_x}\left\{\frac{1}{m}\sum_{t=1}^{t=\infty}(\text{D} - \overline{\text{M}})_{x+\frac{t}{m}} + \int_0^\infty \overline{\text{M}}_{x+t}dt\right\} \quad\text{......(4)}.$$

Applying the formula

$$\frac{1}{m}\sum_{t=1}^{t=\infty} f\left(\frac{t}{m}\right) = \int_0^\infty f(h)\,dh - \frac{1}{2m}f(0) - \frac{1}{12m^2}\frac{df(0)}{dt} + \ldots$$

to the first term of this equation, we have

$$\mathring{a}_x^{(m)} = \frac{1}{\text{D}_x}\left\{\int_0^\infty (\text{D} - \overline{\text{M}})_{x+t}dt - \frac{1}{2m}(\text{D} - \overline{\text{M}})_x - \frac{1}{12m^2}\frac{d(\text{D} - \overline{\text{M}})_x}{dx} + \int_0^\infty \overline{\text{M}}_{x+t}dt\right\}$$

$$= \bar{a}_x - \frac{1}{2m}\delta\bar{a}_x + \frac{\delta}{12m^2},$$

since $\frac{1}{\text{D}_x}\int_0^\infty \text{D}_{x+t}dt = \bar{a}_x$; $\frac{(\text{D} - \overline{\text{M}})_x}{\text{D}_x} = 1 - \overline{\text{A}}_x = \delta\bar{a}_x$;

and $\frac{d(\text{D} - \overline{\text{M}})_x}{dx} = -\delta\text{D}_x$.

$$\therefore\quad \mathring{a}_x^{(m)} = \bar{a}_x\left(1 - \frac{\delta}{2m}\right) + \frac{\delta}{12m^2} \quad\text{.........(5)}.$$

In formula (5) the last term is small and is usually neglected, the result being another simple formula frequently employed in practice, namely

$$\mathring{a}_x^{(m)} = (\tfrac{1}{2} + a_x)\left(1 - \frac{\delta}{2m}\right) \quad \text{..................(6).}$$

If the annuity be payable yearly,

$$\mathring{a}_x = (\tfrac{1}{2} + a_x)\left(1 - \frac{\delta}{2}\right).$$

4. Formula (6) can be derived very simply from formula (3a) if $\bar{A}_x$ be retained instead of $A_x(1+\frac{1}{2}i)$. Since $a_x + \frac{1}{2} = \bar{a}_x$ and $\bar{A}_x = 1 - \delta\bar{a}_x$, we have

$$\begin{aligned}\mathring{a}_x^{(m)} &= a_x + \frac{m-1}{2m} + \frac{1}{2m}\bar{A}_x \\ &= \bar{a}_x - \frac{1}{2m}(1 - \bar{A}_x) \\ &= \bar{a}_x\left(1 - \frac{\delta}{2m}\right).\end{aligned}$$

5. Again, applying the formula

$$\int_0^\infty f(h)\,dh = \frac{1}{m}\sum_{t=1}^{t=\infty} f\left(\frac{t}{m}\right) + \frac{1}{2m}f(0) + \frac{1}{12m^2}\Delta f(0) - \frac{1}{24m^2}\Delta^2 f(0)$$

to eliminate the integral in formula (1), the value of the complete annuity becomes

$$\begin{aligned}\mathring{a}_x^{(m)} &= a_x^{(m)} + \frac{1}{D_x}\left\{\frac{1}{m}\sum_{t=1}^{t=\infty}\bar{M}_{x+\frac{t}{m}} + \frac{1}{2m}\bar{M}_x + \frac{1}{12m^2}\Delta\bar{M}_x - \frac{1}{24m^2}\Delta^2\bar{M}_x \right. \\ &\qquad \left. - \frac{1}{m}\sum_{t=1}^{t=\infty}\bar{M}_{x+\frac{t}{m}}\right\} \\ &= a_x^{(m)} + \frac{1}{2m}\bar{A}_x + \frac{1}{12m^2}\frac{\Delta\bar{M}_x}{D_x} \text{ approx.} \\ &= a_x^{(m)} + \frac{1}{2m}\bar{A}_x - \frac{1}{12m^2}\bar{A}^1_{x:\overline{1|}} \quad \text{..................................(7),}\end{aligned}$$

where $$\bar{A}^1_{x:\overline{1|}} = \frac{1}{D_x}(\bar{M}_x - \bar{M}_{x+1}) = \frac{C_x(1+i)^{\frac{1}{2}}}{D_x} = v^{\frac{1}{2}}q_x,$$

and applying the expression

$$\frac{1}{m}\sum_{t=1}^{t=\infty} f\left(\frac{t}{m}\right) = \int_0^\infty f(h)\,dh - \frac{1}{2m}f(0) - \frac{1}{12m^2}\Delta f(0) + \dots \text{ etc.}$$

to the first term of formula (4) we have

$$\mathring{a}_x^{(m)} = \frac{1}{D_x}\left\{\int_0^\infty (D-\overline{M})_{x+t}\,dt - \frac{1}{2m}(D-\overline{M})_x - \frac{1}{12m^2}\Delta(D-\overline{M})_x + \int_0^\infty \overline{M}_{x+t}\,dt\right\}$$

$$= \bar{a}_x\left(1-\frac{\delta}{2m}\right) + \frac{\delta}{12m^2}(\bar{a}_x - vp_x\,\bar{a}_{x+1})$$

$$= \bar{a}_x\left(1-\frac{\delta}{2m}\right) + \frac{\delta}{12m^2}\bar{a}_{x:\overline{1}|} \quad \text{.......................(8).}$$

Formulae (7) and (8) are not of practical importance.

6. The values of temporary complete annuities are found most easily by taking the value of the complete whole life annuity less the value of a similar deferred annuity. Thus

$$\mathring{a}_{x:\overline{n}|}^{(m)} = \mathring{a}_x^{(m)} - \frac{D_{x+n}}{D_x}\mathring{a}_{x+n}^{(m)}$$

$$= \left(a_x + \frac{m-1}{2m} + \frac{1}{2m}A_x\right) - \frac{D_{x+n}}{D_x}\left(a_{x+n} + \frac{m-1}{2m} + \frac{1}{2m}A_{x+n}\right)$$

$$= a_{x:\overline{n}|} + \frac{m-1}{2m}\left(1-\frac{D_{x+n}}{D_x}\right) + \frac{1}{2m}A^1_{x:\overline{n}|} \quad \text{.....................(9),}$$

corresponding to formula (3 b); or

$$\mathring{a}_{x:\overline{n}|}^{(m)} = \bar{a}_{x:\overline{n}|}\left(1-\frac{\delta}{2m}\right) + \frac{\delta}{12m^2}\left(1-\frac{D_{x+n}}{D_x}\right) \quad \text{.........(10)}$$

$$= \left\{a_{x:\overline{n}|} + \tfrac{1}{2}\left(1-\frac{D_{x+n}}{D_x}\right)\right\}\left(1-\frac{\delta}{2m}\right) \quad \text{.........(11),}$$

corresponding to formulae (5) and (6).

7. The continuous assurance, $\overline{A}_x$, can be expressed in terms of the complete annuity.

If a unit be invested at rate i, it will produce an annuity of i payable annually together with the accrued portion of a year's interest to the death of (x)—the present value of the interest being approximately $i\mathring{a}_x$—and will remain intact at the death of (x).

Thus $$1 = i\mathring{a}_x + \overline{A}_x,$$

whence $$\overline{A}_x = 1 - i\mathring{a}_x \quad \text{.......................(12).}$$

8. In Chapter III 3 an annuity-due was described as an annuity under which a payment is made at *the beginning of each interval that* (x) *enters upon.* Since, therefore, each payment relates to the succeeding interval there can, in this case, be no question of a proportionate payment to the moment of death of the annuitant; in other words, there is no such thing as a *complete annuity-due.*

9. The following table gives the values of $\mathring{a}_{30}$ and $\mathring{a}_{60}$ on the basis of the H^M Table at 3 per cent. interest by the formulae obtained in this chapter, the values being given to five places of decimals, though annuity values are generally tabulated to three places of decimals only. The differences between the results of the various formulae are greatest when the annuity is payable yearly, and it is not necessary therefore for purposes of comparison to tabulate the values of annuities payable more frequently.

Where the symbol $\bar{A}_x$ has been retained this has been taken as equal to $1-\delta\bar{a}_x$, where $\bar{a}_x = a_x + \frac{1}{2} - \frac{1}{12}(\mu_x+\delta)$: this value of $\bar{a}_x$ has also been employed where the symbol $\bar{a}_x$ has been retained.

No. of formula	Formula for $\mathring{a}_x^{(m)}$	Formula for $\mathring{a}_x$	$\mathring{a}_{30}$	$\mathring{a}_{60}$
(2)	$a_x^{(m)} + \frac{1}{2m}\bar{A}_x - \frac{\mu_x}{12m^2}$	$a_x + \frac{1}{2}\bar{A}_x - \frac{\mu_x}{12}$	20·09300	10·56265
(3 a)	$a_x + \frac{m-1}{2m} + \frac{1}{2m}A_x(1+\frac{1}{2}i)$	$a_x + \frac{1}{2}A_x(1+\frac{1}{2}i)$	20·09366	10·56509
(3 b)	$a_x + \frac{m-1}{2m} + \frac{1}{2m}A_x$	$a_x + \frac{1}{2}A_x$	20·09073	10·56004
(5)	$\bar{a}_x\left(1-\frac{\delta}{2m}\right) + \frac{\delta}{12m^2}$	$\bar{a}_x\left(1-\frac{\delta}{2}\right) + \frac{\delta}{12}$	20·09300	10·56264
(6)	$(\frac{1}{2}+a_x)\left(1-\frac{\delta}{2m}\right)$	$(\frac{1}{2}+a_x)\left(1-\frac{\delta}{2}\right)$	20·09359	10·56500

10. A type of annuity sometimes met with in practice is one under which an Office guarantees that the annuity shall continue in any event until the payments amount to the purchase price.

Representing the net value of such an annuity, payable m times a year to (x), by A, and the purchase price by A′, the contract can be valued in two parts: (a) an annuity certain for A′ years;

(b) an annuity on the life of (x) deferred A′ years. The net value will then be given by the expression

$$A = a^{(m)}_{\overline{A'}|} + \frac{D_{x+A'}}{D_x}\mathring{a}^{(m)}_{x+A'} \qquad \text{.....................(13)},$$

by means of which, A′ being a function of A, the value must be found by trial. (See Example 5.)

11. Instead of the condition mentioned in paragraph 10, the contract might contain a clause that on the death of the annuitant before the total payments amount to the purchase price, the balance of that price shall be paid to the deceased's estate.

Taking the case of a complete annuity payable m times a year to (x), with this condition, and representing the net value by S, and the purchase price by S′, where $\cdot 9S' = S$; the contract can be dealt with in two parts as follows:

(a) A complete annuity to (x) payable m times a year, the value of which is

$$\mathring{a}^{(m)}_x = a_x + \frac{m-1}{2m} + \frac{1}{2m}\bar{A}_x.$$

(b) A decreasing temporary assurance, the sum assured commencing at S′ and decreasing momently as the amount *paid and accrued* under the complete annuity increases, until the end of a period of S′ years.

The value of this portion is

$$\int_0^{S'} (S'-t)\, v^t {}_tp_x\, \mu_{x+t}\, dt$$
$$= S'\bar{A}^{1}_{x:\overline{S'}|} - (I\bar{A})^{1}_{x:\overline{S'}|}$$
$$= S'A^{1}_{x:\overline{S'}|}(1+i)^{\frac{1}{2}} - \{(IA)^{1}_{x:\overline{S'}|} - \tfrac{1}{2}A^{1}_{x:\overline{S'}|}\}(1+i)^{\frac{1}{2}}$$
$$= \frac{1}{D_x}\{(S'+\tfrac{1}{2})(\bar{M}_x - \bar{M}_{x+S'}) - (\bar{R}_x - \bar{R}_{x+S'} - S'\bar{M}_{x+S'})\}$$
$$= \frac{1}{D_x}\{\tfrac{1}{2}(\bar{M}_x - \bar{M}_{x+S'}) + S'\bar{M}_x - \bar{R}_x + \bar{R}_{x+S'}\}.$$

Combining the two portions we have

$$S = \frac{1}{D_x}\left\{N_{x+1} + \frac{m-1}{2m}D_x + \frac{1}{2m}\bar{M}_x + \tfrac{1}{2}(\bar{M}_x - \bar{M}_{x+S'}) + S'\bar{M}_x - \bar{R}_x + \bar{R}_{x+S'}\right\}$$

$$= \frac{N_{x+1} + \frac{m-1}{2m}D_x + \frac{1}{2m}\bar{M}_x + \tfrac{1}{2}(\bar{M}_x - \bar{M}_{x+S'}) - \bar{R}_x + \bar{R}_{x+S'}}{D_x - \frac{10}{9}\bar{M}_x} \qquad \text{...(14)}.$$

By means of which expression the value of S and S′ must be found by trial. For practical purposes M_x and R_x would be used in place of $\overline{M}_x$ and $\overline{R}_x$.

If the annuity be payable yearly, the expression can be slightly simplified, as follows:

$$S = \frac{N_{x+1} + \overline{M}_x - \frac{1}{2}\overline{M}_{x+S'} - \overline{R}_x + \overline{R}_{x+S'}}{D_x - \frac{10}{9}\overline{M}_x}$$

$$= \frac{N_{x+1} - \overline{R}_{x+1} + \overline{R}_{x+S'+1} + \frac{1}{2}\overline{M}_{x+S'}}{D_x - \frac{10}{9}\overline{M}_x}$$

$$= \frac{N_{x+1} - R_{x+1} + R_{x+S'+1} + \frac{1}{2}M_{x+S'}}{D_x - \frac{10}{9}M_x} \text{ approximately} \ldots (15),$$

writing M_x and R_x in place of $\overline{M}_x$ and $\overline{R}_x$ respectively.

If the annuity were to be curtate and payable yearly, with the same condition as regards the return of the balance of the purchase money, the value of the first part would be a_x, and of the second part

$$\frac{1}{D_x}\{S'C_x + (S'-1)\,C_{x+1} + (S'-2)\,C_{x+2} + \ldots + (S'-S')\,C_{x+S'}\}$$

$$= \frac{1}{D_x}\{S'M_x - (R_{x+1} - R_{x+S'+1})\},$$

the total value being

$$S = \frac{1}{D_x}\{N_{x+1} + S'M_x - R_{x+1} + R_{x+S'+1}\}$$

$$= \frac{N_{x+1} - R_{x+1} + R_{x+S'+1}}{D_x - \frac{10}{9}M_x}.$$

A comparison of this expression with formula (15) shows that the adjustment to provide for the annuity being complete consists of the addition of the value of the assurance of $\frac{1}{2}$ from age $x + S'$ onwards. It can make no difference whether the proportion to the date of death before the total payments amount to S′ is paid under the complete annuity portion of the contract or under the condition for the payment of the balance of the purchase money (See Example 6.)

EXAMPLES

The following examples will illustrate the practical application of the values of complete annuities.

Ex. 1. Find the value of $\mathring{a}^{(4)}_{[48]+2}$ on the basis of the $O^{[NM]}$ Mortality Table with 3 per cent. interest.

$$\begin{aligned}\mathring{a}^{(4)}_{[48]+2} &= a_{[48]+2} + \tfrac{3}{8} + \tfrac{1}{8}A_{[48]+2}\\ &= 13{\cdot}746 + {\cdot}375 + \tfrac{1}{8}({\cdot}5705)\\ &= 14{\cdot}192.\end{aligned}$$

The value of $A_{[48]+2}$ is found by entering the 3 per cent. single premium conversion table with $a_{[48]+2}$, the latter value being obtainable from the table on page 458.

If the last term be taken as $\tfrac{1}{8}\bar{A}_{[48]+2} = \tfrac{1}{8}A_{[48]+2}\,(1{\cdot}015)$, the result is 14·193.

Ex. 2. If £100 be invested in the purchase of a complete life annuity to (70) payable quarterly, what will be the amount of each quarterly payment? Assume H^M Table at 3 per cent., and that a loading of 10 per cent. of the gross price is added to the net value of the annuity.

The net purchase price is £90, and the quarterly payment, using three places of decimals only, is

$$\begin{aligned}\frac{1}{4}\cdot\frac{90}{\mathring{a}^{(4)}_{70}} &= \frac{1}{4}\cdot\frac{90}{a_{70} + \tfrac{3}{8} + \tfrac{1}{8}A_{70}}\\ &= \frac{1}{4}\cdot\frac{90}{6{\cdot}656 + {\cdot}375 + \tfrac{1}{8}({\cdot}777)}\\ &= 3{\cdot}156,\end{aligned}$$

or

$$\begin{aligned}\frac{1}{4}\cdot\frac{90}{\mathring{a}^{(4)}_{70}} &= \frac{1}{4}\cdot\frac{90}{(1-\tfrac{\delta}{8})\,(\tfrac{1}{2} + a_{70})}\\ &= \frac{1}{4}\cdot\frac{90}{{\cdot}9963 \times 7{\cdot}156}\\ &= 3{\cdot}155.\end{aligned}$$

The quarterly payment would, therefore, be £3. 3*s.* 1*d.*

Ex. 3. A curtate annuity of £100 per annum is payable half yearly to a man now aged 55. The annuitant desires the annuity to be payable quarterly with a proportionate payment to the date of death. On the basis of the H^M Table at 3 per cent., what will be the amount of each quarterly payment?

The payment just due will be made on the old basis, and the value of future payments is $100a_{55}^{(2)}$. The amount of each quarterly payment in future will be

$$\frac{1}{4}\cdot\frac{100a_{55}^{(2)}}{\mathring{a}_{55}^{(4)}}=\frac{1}{4}\cdot\frac{100\left(a_{55}+\frac{1}{4}\right)}{a_{55}+\frac{3}{8}+\frac{1}{8}\mathrm{A}_{55}}$$

$$=\frac{1}{4}\cdot\frac{100\,(12\cdot072+\cdot25)}{12\cdot072+\cdot375+\frac{1}{8}(\cdot61927)}$$

$$=24\cdot595 \qquad \text{say } £24.\ 11s.\ 10d.,$$

or, the quarterly payment $=\dfrac{1}{4}\cdot\dfrac{100\left(a_{55}+\frac{1}{4}\right)}{\left(1-\frac{\delta}{8}\right)\left(a_{55}+\frac{1}{2}\right)}$

$$=\frac{1}{4}\cdot\frac{100\,(12\cdot072+\cdot25)}{\left(1-\dfrac{\cdot029559}{8}\right)(12\cdot072+\cdot5)}$$

$$=24\cdot594. \qquad £24.\ 11s.\ 10d.$$

The payment would be taken at the next lower penny.

Ex. 4. A company grants a complete annuity of £100 per annum payable by quarterly instalments to a life aged 60 with the special condition that if the life die within 4 years from the granting of the annuity the company will, on payment of £200, grant a similar annuity to another life aged 60 at the date of death of the annuitant with the same special condition, and so on indefinitely.

What should be the net purchase price for the annuity by the $\mathrm{H^M}$ 3 per cent. Table?

The value of the ordinary complete annuity to a life aged 60 is $100\mathring{a}_{60}^{(4)}$.

Let the purchase price required be P, then the company must be so placed at the death of (60) within four years that it then has P in hand to cover the granting of a similar contract. As £200 is to be paid in cash it is necessary to provide under the contract for the assurance of P − 200.

We thus have

$$\mathrm{P}=100\mathring{a}_{60}^{(4)}+|_4\bar{\mathrm{A}}_{60}\,(\mathrm{P}-200),$$

$$\therefore\quad \mathrm{P}=\frac{100\mathring{a}_{60}^{(4)}-200|_4\bar{\mathrm{A}}_{60}}{1-|_4\bar{\mathrm{A}}_{60}}$$

$$=\frac{100\,\{10\cdot2235+\cdot375+\cdot08414\,(1\cdot015)\}-200\,(\cdot1179)\,(1\cdot015)}{1-\cdot1179\,(1\cdot015)}$$

$$=1187. \qquad £1187.$$

Ex. 5. It is required to find on the basis of the H^M Table at 3 per cent. the value of an immediate annuity of 1 per annum payable half-yearly during the life of (60), with the condition that the annuity is to continue in any event until the payments amount to the purchase price. The purchase price is to be the net value with an addition of 10 per cent. of the gross value.

In this case

$$A = a^{(2)}_{\overline{\frac{1}{\cdot 9}A}|} + \frac{D_{60+\frac{1}{\cdot 9}A}}{D_{60}} \mathring{a}^{(2)}_{60+\frac{1}{\cdot 9}A}.$$

It is convenient to take trial values of the gross price as this enables us to employ integral terms and ages.

As a first trial value, let $\frac{1}{\cdot 9}A = 15$, then

$$\begin{aligned} A &= a_{\overline{15}|} \times \frac{i}{j_{(2)}} + \frac{D_{75}}{D_{60}}(a_{75} + \tfrac{1}{4} + \tfrac{1}{4}A_{75}) \\ &= 11{\cdot}938\,(1{\cdot}00744) + \frac{2789{\cdot}2}{9987{\cdot}6}(5{\cdot}074 + {\cdot}25 + \tfrac{1}{4} \times {\cdot}823) \\ &= 12{\cdot}027 + 1{\cdot}544 \\ &= 13{\cdot}571. \end{aligned}$$

Whence $$\frac{1}{\cdot 9}A = 15{\cdot}079.$$

As a second trial value, let $\frac{1}{\cdot 9}A = 16$, then

$$\begin{aligned} A &= a_{\overline{16}|} \times \frac{i}{j_{(2)}} + \frac{D_{76}}{D_{60}}(a_{76} + {\cdot}25 + \tfrac{1}{4}A_{76}) \\ &= 12{\cdot}5611\,(1{\cdot}00744) + \frac{2447{\cdot}9}{9987{\cdot}6}(4{\cdot}782 + {\cdot}25 + \tfrac{1}{4} \times {\cdot}832) \\ &= 12{\cdot}655 + 1{\cdot}284 \\ &= 13{\cdot}939. \end{aligned}$$

Whence $$\frac{1}{\cdot 9}A = 15{\cdot}488.$$

If the correct value be $15 + x$, we have

$$\begin{aligned} 15 + x &= 15{\cdot}079 + x\,(15{\cdot}488 - 15{\cdot}079), \\ {\cdot}591x &= {\cdot}079, \\ x &= {\cdot}134. \end{aligned}$$

The Purchase Price is therefore 15·134 = £15. 2*s*. 9*d*., the price being taken to the next higher penny.

The first trial in this case gave a result so close to the trial value, that in practice it would be sufficient to take the value as, say, £15. 2*s*. 6*d*. The method of interpolation has been included, however, in order to show the complete process of calculation.

Since the purchase price is not an integral number of yearly payments, the condition would probably be attached to the contract that in the event of death during the first fifteen years, a payment of £1 would continue to be made at the end of each year up to and including the fifteenth year and that at the end of the sixteenth year there would be a final payment of 2*s*. 9*d*. In practice the annuity would not be for £1 per annum, and the final payment would not be so small.

Ex. 6. It is required to find the purchase price, on the basis of the H^M Table at 3 per cent., of an immediate annuity of 1 payable yearly during the life of (60) with the condition that if (60) die before the payments amount to the price given the balance of the price shall be paid to his executors. The purchase price is to be the net value with an addition of 10 per cent. of the gross value.

Employing formula (15) we have

$$S = \frac{N_{61} - R_{61} + R_{61+S'} + \frac{1}{2}M_{60+S'}}{D_{60} - \frac{10}{9}M_{60}}.$$

As a first trial value, take $S' = 16$, then

$$S = \frac{102106 - 77314 + 10134 + \frac{1}{2}(2036)}{9988 - \frac{10}{9}(6723)}$$

$$= \frac{35944}{2518}$$

$$= 14{\cdot}275.$$

Whence $S' = 15{\cdot}861.$

This result is sufficiently close for practical purposes to take the value as 16.

CHAPTER X

LIFE OFFICE VALUATIONS

1. Life Office Valuations. In the periodical valuation of the contracts of a Life Assurance Company, policies are generally valued in groups.

If there were a large number of Whole-Life Assurances on lives whose exact age at the date of the valuation was y, the total sum assured by all these policies combined being S, the total bonus additions B, and the total net annual premiums $S\mathrm{P}$, all falling due immediately, the value of this group of assurances would be

$$(S+B)\,\mathrm{A}_y - S\mathrm{P}\mathbf{a}_y \quad \text{.....................(1),}$$

assuming the Office to value its policies by an Aggregate Table.

The most scientific method of valuing Whole-Life Assurances is by means of a Select Table, but as a very large number of groups, according to ages at entry and duration of the assurances, would be required, the work involved would be prohibitive. Various suggestions for making valuations by means of Select Tables without the necessity of using this large number of groups have appeared in the *Journal of the Institute of Actuaries*, and the *Transactions of the Faculty of Actuaries*, but as a sufficiently accurate valuation can be made by an Aggregate Table, or by a combination of Aggregate Tables, and the Actuary can always tell which way any error lies, and approximately its extent, these are still generally employed by Life Offices.

Valuations are most frequently made as at December 31st of the valuation year, and it must be understood in what follows that this date is taken.

2. The grouping of the policies according to the age attained involves some assumption as to the method of determining this age as at the Valuation date, and since premiums are charged at the age next birthday or for the next higher half or quarter age at the time policies are effected, which age may be attained during the calendar year of entry or after the end of that year, a further decision must be made as to the net premium to be valued.

The practice of Offices in both these respects varies considerably. For example, an Office may assume that the age next birthday at entry is attained on the average on the following 31st December, the net premium for that age being valued: or an Office may make the same assumption as to the age at 31st December but value the net premium for the nearest age at the date of entry: or the premium may be taken as that for the nearest age at entry and the valuation age as the nearest age at the valuation date: and so on.

The last-mentioned method has been found to be very accurate in its results and for the sake of example will be assumed in the following paragraphs.

3. Once the net premium applicable to a policy has been decided upon and recorded, and the method of ascertaining the valuation age determined, all the policies in force at the date of valuation of the same valuation age are grouped together, and the total sum assured, total bonus additions, and total net premiums ascertained.

The records of a Life Office are so arranged that the number of policies to be valued, with the corresponding totals of the sums assured, premiums, etc., for any particular group, can be ascertained by taking the number in the same group at the last valuation, adding particulars of the new assurances effected during the valuation period and deducting particulars of such items as claims, policies lapsed and surrendered, etc., during that period.

Considering Whole-Life Assurances only, the valuation age for any one group will increase from year to year, and it is convenient, therefore, to head the group "Office Year of Birth" which is constant, the Office Year of Birth being that year which, deducted from the valuation year, will give the valuation age: or, in other words, the year at the end of which the valuation age would be "0".

4. The valuation of the Sums Assured and Bonus Additions presents no difficulties, the totals for age y being simply multiplied by A_y, but since policies are effected at all periods of the year and the valuation is made at a fixed date, namely December 31st, in valuing the premiums the date of the next premium payment must be considered.

5. In order to arrive at the formulae to be employed in the valuation of the premiums, individual policies will first be considered.

If, in the case of a policy subject to annual premiums, the period to elapse between the date of the valuation and the date of the next policy anniversary be $\frac{k}{m}+t$ $\left(\text{i.e. } k \text{ periods of } \frac{1}{m} \text{ of a year plus a period } t, \text{ where } t<\frac{1}{m}\right)$ the annuity by which the premiums will be valued is

$$_{\frac{k}{m}+t|}a_y = a_y - \left(\frac{k}{m}+t\right) \text{.....................(2).}$$

In the case of a policy subject to premiums payable m times a year, with the same period to elapse before the next policy anniversary, provided true premiums $(P_x^{(m)})$ be valued, the annuity to be employed is

$$_{t|}a_y^{(m)} = a_y - \left(\frac{m-1}{2m}+t\right)$$

$$= {}_{\frac{k}{m}+t|}a_y + \left(\frac{k}{m} - \frac{m-1}{2m}\right) \text{.................(3).}$$

In applying these formulae to the valuation of the premiums under a group of policies, if the business be evenly distributed over the year, so that the average date of the policy anniversaries falls in the middle of the year, the average value of $\frac{k}{m}$ is $\frac{m-1}{2m}$ and the annuity value ${}_{\frac{k}{m}+t|}\mathrm{a}_y$ can be applied to both annual and $m$thly premiums. Moreover, since in this case $\frac{k}{m}+t=\frac{1}{2}$ it follows that $t=\frac{1}{2m}$ and the formula becomes

$$ {}_{\frac{1}{2m}|}\mathrm{a}_y^{(m)} = \mathrm{a}_y - \tfrac{1}{2} = a_y + \tfrac{1}{2} \quad \text{..................(4)}, $$

whatever the value of m.

If the period to elapse between the valuation date and the average date of the policy anniversaries be more than 6 months (as is usually the case in practice), the average value of $\frac{k}{m}$ will be $> \frac{m-1}{2m}$ and the annuity value given by formula (3) exceeds that applicable to annual premiums by a small positive amount. If, therefore, the annuity value ${}_{\frac{k}{m}+t|}\mathrm{a}_y$ be employed for $m$thly cases as well as for annual cases, the value of the premiums will be slightly understated. The undervaluing of the premiums, however, results in the liability being overvalued and is, therefore, on the safe side.

6. If the half-yearly and quarterly premiums charged are *instalment* premiums, these are equivalent, as from any policy anniversary, to annual premiums. As from the next anniversary, therefore, annual premiums can be valued by the annuity applicable to such premiums; but as the unpaid instalments for the current assurance year are certainly receivable, they can with sufficient accuracy be added. The value of the instalment premiums will, therefore, be

$$ \mathrm{P} \cdot {}_{\frac{k}{m}+t|}\mathrm{a}_y + \frac{k}{m}\,\mathrm{P}^{[m]} \quad \text{....................(5)}, $$

where P is the annual premium and $\frac{k}{m}\mathrm{P}^{[m]}$ the actual outstanding instalments of the current year's instalment premium.

7. The method of valuing all the premiums by the annuity applicable to the annual premiums is generally adopted in practice.

If, for example, the average date of the policy anniversaries fall at the end of the eighth month from the valuation date, the annuity value to be used for all the premiums will be

$$_{\frac{8}{12}|}\text{a}_y = \text{a}_y - \tfrac{2}{3} = a_y + \tfrac{1}{3} \text{..................... (6).}$$

Some offices further simplify their valuation arrangements by inserting the annual net premium, P_x, even when premiums are payable at more frequent intervals than annually, with the result that, since $P_x^{(m)} > P_x$, the liability is further overstated.

In the case of instalment premiums, the annual premiums would be valued by formula (6), and the outstanding instalments of the net premium for the current policy year added thereto.

8. Valuation of Endowment Assurances. If Endowment Assurances were grouped like Whole-Life Assurances, according to the age attained, there would be in each group policies with many different periods to run before maturity, which would have to be valued by different assurance and annuity factors. Consequently, as the value of a temporary life annuity does not vary much with variations in the age, it is the common practice to group the policies according to the nearest or integral unexpired term and to ascertain a "mean valuation age*" for each group.

Assuming the policies to be grouped according to the integral unexpired term, say n years, and that on the average the policy anniversary falls $\frac{k}{m}+t$ of a year after the valuation date, the factor by means of which the Sums Assured and Bonuses are valued is $A_{y:\overline{n+\frac{k}{m}+t}|}$, where y is the mean valuation age.

9. In order to arrive at the formulae to be employed in the valuation of the premiums, the method adopted in paragraph 5 will

* The methods of obtaining the "mean valuation age" are dealt with in Chap. XI 14.

again be used, individual policies being first considered, and the period to elapse before the next policy anniversary being in each case taken as $\frac{k}{m}+t$.

If the policy be subject to annual premiums, the formula to be employed is

$$_{\frac{k}{m}+t|}a_{y:\overline{n}|}=a_{y:\overline{n}|}-\left(\frac{k}{m}+t\right)\left(1-\frac{D_{y+n}}{D_y}\right)\text{ ....(7).}$$

If the policy be subject to premiums payable m times a year, assuming true premiums, the formula is

$$_{t|}a^{(m)}_{y:\overline{n+\frac{k}{m}}|}=a^{(m)}_{y:\overline{n+\frac{k}{m}}|}-t\left(1-\frac{D_{y+n}}{D_y}\right)\text{ approx.}$$

$$=a_{y:\overline{n}|}-\left(\frac{m-1}{2m}+t\right)\left(1-\frac{D_{y+n}}{D_y}\right)+\frac{k}{m}\frac{D_{y+n}}{D_y}\text{ approx.}$$

$$={}_{\frac{k}{m}+t|}a_{y:\overline{n}|}+\left(\frac{k}{m}-\frac{m-1}{2m}\right)\left(1-\frac{D_{y+n}}{D_y}\right)+\frac{k}{m}\frac{D_{y+n}}{D_y}\text{ ...(8).}$$

In applying these formulae to the valuation of premiums under a group of policies, if the business be evenly distributed over the year so that the average date of the policy anniversaries falls in the middle of the year, the average value of $\frac{k}{m}$ is $\frac{m-1}{2m}$ and the second term of formula (8) vanishes.

If the period to elapse between the valuation date and the average date of the policy anniversaries be more than six months (as is usually the case in practice), the average value of $\frac{k}{m}$ will be $>\frac{m-1}{2m}$; if therefore the second term of formula (8) be neglected, the annuity value appropriate to $m$thly premiums would be slightly understated, and the reserve in respect of such policies slightly overstated.

It follows that, if true premiums payable m times a year are charged, they can be valued with sufficient accuracy for practical purposes by the same annuity as the annual premiums, provided the portions of the current year's premiums outstanding at the date of valuation, multiplied by $\frac{D_{y+n}}{D_y}$, be added. If it be decided to neglect this adjustment, the reserve will be further strengthened.

10. If the half-yearly and quarterly premiums charged for Endowment Assurances are "Instalment" premiums, assuming the same integral unexpired term and same time to elapse on the average before the next policy anniversary, the annuity values to be employed in the valuation of the premiums will be:

For annual cases

$$_{\frac{k}{m}+t|}\mathbf{a}_{y:\overline{n}|} = \mathbf{a}_{y:\overline{n}|} - \left(\frac{k}{m}+t\right)\left(1-\frac{D_{y+n}}{D_y}\right) \quad \text{.........(9)},$$

and for $m$thly cases

$$_{t|}\mathbf{a}^{[m]}_{y:\overline{n+\frac{k}{m}}|} = \left(1-\frac{m-1}{2m}d\right) \cdot {}_{t|}\mathbf{a}_{y:\overline{n+\frac{k}{m}}|} \text{ approx.}$$

$$= \left(1-\frac{m-1}{2m}d\right)\left\{\mathbf{a}_{y:\overline{n+\frac{k}{m}}|} - t\left(1-\frac{D_{y+n}}{D_y}\right)\right\} \text{ approx.}$$

$$= \left(1-\frac{m-1}{2m}d\right)\left\{\mathbf{a}_{y:\overline{n}|} + \frac{k}{m}\frac{D_{y+n}}{D_y} - t\left(1-\frac{D_{y+n}}{D_y}\right)\right\} \text{ approx.}$$

$$\left(1-\frac{m-1}{2m}d\right)\left\{\mathbf{a}_{y:\overline{n}|} - \left(\frac{k}{m}+t\right)\left(1-\frac{D_{y+n}}{D_y}\right) + \frac{k}{m}\right\}$$

$$= \left(1-\frac{m-1}{2m}d\right)\left\{{}_{\frac{k}{m}+t|}\mathbf{a}_{y:\overline{n}|} + \frac{k}{m}\right\} \text{ approx. ....(10).}$$

But this is the annuity value with which to value the "Instalment" premium,

$$P^{[m]}_{x:\overline{n}|} = \frac{P_{x:\overline{n}|}}{1-\frac{m-1}{2m}d},$$

whence $\quad P^{[m]}_{x:\overline{n}|} \cdot {}_{t|}\mathbf{a}^{[m]}_{y:\overline{n+\frac{k}{m}}|} = P_{x:\overline{n}|} \cdot {}_{\frac{k}{m}+t|}\mathbf{a}_{y:\overline{n}|} + \frac{k}{m} P_{x:\overline{n}|} \quad \text{.........(11)},$

and it will make little difference if the second term of this formula be taken as $\frac{k}{m} P^{[m]}_{x:\overline{n}|}$.

In this case, therefore, the simplest method is to value the annual premium for every policy by the annuity value applicable to such premiums, and, for cases subject to instalment premiums payable m terms a year, to add to the value thus obtained the actual outstanding instalments of the current year's premium.

If true $m$thly premiums are valued as instalment premiums the error introduced is negligible, and in practice the simpler method of this paragraph can be adopted even where the half-yearly and quarterly premiums charged by the Office are "true" premiums.

11. To take a practical example, assuming as in paragraph 7 that the average policy anniversary falls at the end of the eighth month, and that policies are grouped according to the integral unexpired term, say n years, the factor by means of which the sums assured and bonuses are valued is $A_{y:\overline{n+\frac{2}{3}}|}$, where y is the mean valuation age.

For the annual premiums, there will be n payments to be made, so that the annuity to be employed to value these will be

$$_{\frac{2}{3}}|\mathbf{a}_{y:\overline{n}|} = \mathbf{a}_{y:\overline{n}|} - \tfrac{2}{3}\left(1 - \frac{D_{y+n}}{D_y}\right) \text{..............(12).}$$

In the case of true $m$thly premiums, it is clear from paragraph 9 that this annuity value may be used provided the portions of the current year's premiums outstanding at the date of valuation, multiplied by $\frac{D_{y+n}}{D_y}$, be added. If it be decided to neglect this adjustment, the reserve will be further strengthened.

In the case of instalment premiums, the annual premiums will be valued by formula (12) and the outstanding instalments of the net annual premiums for the current policy year added thereto.

12. The method of valuation of whole-life and endowment assurances so far dealt with takes into account the net premium on the basis of the mortality table employed for the valuation, and is known as a "net premium valuation." It may, however, be more suitable to the circumstances of a particular Office to determine what portion of the loading (i.e. the addition for expenses, etc.) should be retained for future expenses and contingencies, and to value the Office premium less this proportion of the loading.

This is generally referred to as a gross premium valuation, the premium valued being derived from the gross premium.

In the case of a Whole-Life Assurance, if ϕ_x represent the loading added to the net premium, so that $P'_x = P_x + \phi_x$, the ordinary formula for the net premium value of the policy can be written

$$ {}_tV_x = A_{x+t} - P'a_{x+t} + \phi a_{x+t} \quad \text{..............(13)}, $$

showing that a definite provision is made for future expenses by keeping in hand the value of all the future loadings. If only part of this loading, say $k\phi_x$, be retained, the result is

$$ \left. \begin{array}{ll} & A_{x+t} - P'a_{x+t} + k\phi a_{x+t} \\ \text{or} & A_{x+t} - (P' - k\phi)\, a_{x+t} \end{array} \right\} \text{.....................(14)}. $$

Similar arguments and formulae clearly apply also to Endowment Assurances.

A young Office at its first quinquennial valuation, in view of the heavy initial expenses it has experienced, the loading for which is spread over the whole duration of the assurances, might be considered justified in anticipating, or taking credit for, some of the future loading in this way and valuing a premium *greater* than the net premium by the table, and at the rate of interest, employed in the valuation; and this course would also be followed if a Company were being valued in order to determine whether its position was one of bare solvency, the loading kept in hand being simply that which was deemed sufficient to cover future expenses.

Again, in some Companies the premiums charged for Whole-Life non-participating assurances have been reduced to less than the net premiums by the table, and at the rate of interest, employed in the valuation of participating assurances; and in such cases it is evident that if the two classes be valued by the same mortality table and at the same rate of interest, credit cannot be taken in the case of the non-participating policies for the full net premium. It thus becomes necessary to value the Office premium less some provision for future expenses, the premium valued being less than the net premium, or to value the non-participating assurances at a higher rate of interest.

13. Valuation of Limited Payment Policies. The value of a Limited Payment Whole-Life Assurance at the end of t years $(t<k)$ is

$$
\begin{aligned}
{}_t^kV_x &= A_{x+t} - {}_kP_x \, . \, \mathbf{a}_{x+t:\overline{k-t|}} \\
&= A_{x+t} - {}_kP_x \, . \, \mathbf{a}_{x+t} + {}_kP_x \frac{N_{x+k}}{D_{x+t}} \quad \ldots\ldots\ldots\ldots\ldots\ldots(15).
\end{aligned}
$$

If these assurances be grouped according to the valuation age or Office year of birth, the sums assured and bonuses will be valued as for ordinary Whole-Life Assurances by the factor A_{x+t}. The factor for the valuation of the premiums is $\left(\mathbf{a}_{x+t} - \frac{N_{x+k}}{D_{x+t}}\right)$, the first term being the ordinary Whole-Life annuity-due and the second cancelling that part of the annuity-due that would fall after the cessation of premium payments. The numerator of this second term is constant, k being the number of premiums payable, whereas the denominator, depending on the valuation age, varies.

By the simple expedient of tabulating ${}_kP_xN_{x+k}$ at the time the policy is effected, and at each valuation up to the time the premiums cease, dividing this by D_y, where y is the valuation age, the value of the second term is easily ascertained.

14. There is, however, another point to be considered. The expression given above makes no allowance for expenses after the premiums have ceased, which arise from the assurance being retained on the Office books, and, if participating, in connection with the periodical declaration of bonus; such provision must therefore be made by the addition of another term.

The extent of this provision is a point to be determined by the Actuary of the Company (the Whole-Life loading less commission would appear to be a suitable quantity), but if this be represented by ϕ_x, the formula becomes

$$A_{x+t} - {}_kP_x \, . \, \mathbf{a}_{x+t} + \frac{({}_kP_x + \phi_x)\, N_{x+k}}{D_{x+t}} \quad \ldots\ldots\ldots\ldots(16),$$

or for the group for valuation age y, assuming the next premium due on the average eight months hence,

$$(S+B)\, A_y - S \, . \, {}_kP\, (\tfrac{1}{3} + a_y) + \frac{\Sigma\, ({}_kP + \phi)\, N_{x+k}}{D_y} \ldots\ldots(17).$$

When premiums have ceased, that is when $y \geqq x+k$, this expression becomes

$$(S+B)\, A_y + \Sigma\phi \, . \, \mathbf{a}_y \quad \ldots\ldots\ldots\ldots\ldots\ldots(18).$$

15. In connection with the valuation of Limited Payment Endowment Assurance Policies two different terms have to be dealt with, namely, the term at the end of which the policy will mature if the life survive, and the term for which the premiums are payable.

A method frequently adopted is to value the premiums according to the age attained (i.e. valuation age) as shown in paragraph 13; and to group the policies afresh according to the integral or nearest unexpired term and then ascertain a mean age on the basis of which to value the sums assured and bonuses. By this method the net liability can only be arrived at for the entire class of assurances and not for different groups.

As in the case of Limited Payment Whole-Life Assurances a special reserve of loading must be made for expenses (and profits, in participating assurances) after the payment of premiums has ceased.

16. Profit or Loss of a Life Office. If each of $l_{[x]}$ persons aged $[x]$ effects a Whole-Life Assurance on his own life, the number of survivors at the end of t years will, on the basis of the mortality table, be $l_{[x]+t}$, and the value of each of their policies will be ${}_tV_{[x]}$. Also, in connection with each policy there will be a net premium of $P_{[x]}$ due, and if all these premiums be paid immediately the fund in hand will be $l_{[x]+t}({}_tV_{[x]}+P_{[x]})$. Examining this expression, we have

$$\begin{aligned} l_{[x]+t}({}_tV_{[x]}+P_{[x]}) &= l_{[x]+t}\left\{1-\frac{\mathrm{a}_{[x]+t}}{\mathrm{a}_{[x]}}+\frac{1}{\mathrm{a}_{[x]}}-d\right\} \\ &= l_{[x]+t}\left\{v-\frac{a_{[x]+t}}{\mathrm{a}_{[x]}}\right\} \\ &= v\,.\,l_{[x]+t}\left\{1-\frac{p_{[x]+t}\,.\,\mathrm{a}_{[x]+t+1}}{\mathrm{a}_{[x]}}\right\} \\ &= v\,.\,l_{[x]+t}\left\{1-p_{[x]+t}(1-{}_{t+1}V_{[x]})\right\} \end{aligned}$$

or $$l_{[x]+t}({}_tV_{[x]}+P_{[x]})(1+i)=d_{[x]+t}+l_{[x]+t+1}\,.\,{}_{t+1}V_{[x]} \quad \text{......(19)}.$$

This last expression shows that the total reserve in hand at the commencement of a year, together with the net premiums then due, both accumulated at interest, will just suffice to pay the sum of 1 at the end of the year for each of the $d_{[x]+t}$ deaths occurring during the year, and also to provide the reserve required at the end of the year in respect of each of the survivors.

It is evident that a similar expression holds in the case of Aggregate Tables which, as already stated, are generally employed in Life Office Valuations.

17. If ΣV and ΣP represent the total reserve and total premiums all due immediately for all the Whole-Life Assurances in force at the beginning of a year, ΣD the *expected* amount of the claims, assumed to be payable at the end of the year, and ΣV_1 the reserve *expected* to be necessary at the end of the year, then

$$(\Sigma V + \Sigma P)(1 + i) = \Sigma D + \Sigma V_1,$$

where i is the rate of interest employed in the valuation.

Or, if $\Sigma\phi$ be the total loading on the premiums,

$$\Sigma[V + (P' - \phi)](1 + i) = \Sigma D + \Sigma V_1,$$

or $$\Sigma[V + (P' - \phi)](1 + i) - \Sigma D - \Sigma V_1 = 0 \quad \text{.........(20)},$$

which indicates that if the actual experience in the year coincides with the assumptions made in the valuation there will be neither a profit nor a loss on the year's working, the claims, expenses and reserves at the end of the year being exactly provided for.

18. If it be assumed that, in practice, premiums, expenses and claims (which in this case will include surrenders) are uniformly spread over the year, the expression to be considered becomes

$$\Sigma V(1 + i') + \Sigma(P' - E)(1 + \tfrac{1}{2}i') - \Sigma D'(1 + \tfrac{1}{2}i') - \Sigma V'_1 \quad \text{...(21)},$$

where ΣE represents the actual expenses, $\Sigma D'$ the actual claims during the year, and i' the actual rate of interest earned, ΣV and $\Sigma V'_1$ being calculated at the valuation rate i.

If this expression have a positive value, that is, if the reserves and premiums (less the actual expenses) accumulated at the rate of interest earned provide more than sufficient to meet the claims (also for comparison accumulated to the end of the year) and the actual reserves which the Office finds it necessary to hold at the end of the year, this value is the profit on the year's working. If the expression have a negative value, this (taken positively) is the loss on the year's working.

19. In the case of assurances under which no further premiums are payable, the net reserve at the beginning of the year is the Single Premium; and this accumulated at the valuation rate of interest will exactly provide in theory for the payment of the expected claims and for the reserves expected to be required at the end of the year. That is

$$l_{[x]+t} \cdot A_{[x]+t}(1+i) = d_{[x]+t} + l_{[x]+t+1} \cdot A_{[x]+t+1} \quad \ldots\ldots(22).$$

The expression to be considered in practice is

$$(\Sigma A + \Sigma EV)(1+i') - \Sigma(D+E)(1+\tfrac{1}{2}i') - (\Sigma A_1 + \Sigma EV_1) \ldots(23),$$

where ΣA is the net reserve and ΣEV the special reserve for expenses at the beginning of the year; ΣA_1 and ΣEV_1 the corresponding items at the end of the year; ΣD the actual claims; ΣE the actual expenses and i' the rate of interest earned.

20 In paragraphs 15 to 19, reference has been made to Whole-Life Assurances only, but it is evident that the arguments employed are equally applicable to all classes of policies. The expressions dealt with give the total profit on the year's working: in practice this profit is split up into its component parts in order that the Office shall know the sources from which it is mainly derived. A discussion of the sources of surplus would, however, be beyond the scope of this work.

21. Formula (19) can be expressed in the form

$$({}_tV_{[x]} + P_{[x]})(1+i) = q_{[x]+t} + p_{[x]+t} \cdot {}_{t+1}V_{[x]},$$

or in more general form

$$\left.\begin{aligned}(V+P)(1+i) &= q \,.\, S + p \,.\, V_1 \\ &= V_1 + q\,(S - V_1)\end{aligned}\right\} \ldots\ldots\ldots\ldots(24),$$

where S is the sum assured by the policy or group of policies.

This formula assumes that claims are payable at the end of the year, and the second form employed shows that the Office will then have in hand V_1 in respect of each policy in force at the commencement of the year, together with $(S - V_1)$, in addition, in respect of each claim. The difference between the sum assured and the policy value at the end of the year, $(S - V_1)$, is the amount of the "Death Strain at Risk," the term $q(S - V_1)$ giving the value of the "Expected Death Strain," that is the amount the Office expects to have to provide, in addition to the increased policy value for each case, in order to meet the claims. The

"Actual Death Strain" is ascertained from the experience during the year and a comparison of the actual with the expected strain provides a means of measuring the profit or loss from mortality.

A comparison of the expected and actual deaths, so often mentioned in the reports of Life Offices, is no guide to the profit or loss from mortality, since the actual number of deaths may be less than the expected and yet, owing to their incidence (e.g. a large proportion of recently effected assurances against which only small reserves are held), may be such that there is an actual loss from mortality.

22. Turning again to the equation

$$(V+P)(1+i)=V_1+q(S-V_1),$$

if a different basis of valuation, denoted by accented symbols, give identical Policy Values, the following equation will subsist,

$$(V+P')(1+i')=V_1+q'(S-V_1),$$

whence

$$(V+P)(i'-i)+(P'-P)(1+i')=(q'-q)(S-V_1) \quad \ldots(25),$$

which equation may be called the "Equation of Equilibrium*."

23. The verbal explanation of the "Equation of Equilibrium" is simple. If two sets of Policies, securing identical benefits and giving equal Policy Values, be conceived to be worked out side by side on different bases (which may be distinguished as the "Normal" and the "Special"), the financial working of the year under consideration must differ as follows: The Special Basis Policies will receive the Excess† Premium increased by a year's interest at the special rate, and will also earn Excess Interest on the Normal Initial Reserve. These additional receipts must be exactly sufficient to provide at the end of the year the Excess Claims and the Excess Reserves, the total of which may be termed the "Excess Strain."

* The discussion in paragraphs 22 to 31 based on the "Equation of Equilibrium" is taken from a paper on the "Changes in pure premium policy values consequent upon variations in the Rate of Interest or Rate of Mortality..." by G. J. Lidstone (*J.I.A.* Vol. 39).

† The "excess" may be either positive or negative, and the word is used as an abbreviated expression for the algebraical difference between the accented and non-accented functions.

24. The Equation of Equilibrium may also be put in the form

$$(P' - P)(1 + i') = (q' - q)(S - V_1) - (V + P)(i' - i),$$

that is, if the Special Policy Values are equal to the Normal Policy Values, the Accumulated Excess Premium must each year be equal to the [Excess Strain – Excess Interest].

If, however, the Special Basis be such that the [Excess Strain – Excess Interest] varies in comparison with the accumulated Excess Premium, instead of being always equal to that quantity, the Special Policy Values will differ from the Normal Policy Values. The difference between the Excess Premium and the [Excess Strain – Excess Interest], which may be called the Remainder, must be accumulated at interest with benefit of survivorship. Just as a Reserve-value itself arises from the circumstance that a uniform Premium is paid for a varying risk, thus requiring the Surplus Premium in the early years to be accumulated to form a Reserve for future years in which the current risk will be greater than the premium: so when two different bases of valuation are compared, a uniform Excess Premium is paid to cover a varying Excess Outgo, and the difference between these two items has to be accumulated to form a Special Reserve Fund which will meet similar differences in the reverse direction in subsequent years.

At the outset the value of the Excess Premium must exactly equal the value of the Excess Outgo: the assurance ultimately working itself out in either case. If each individual Value of the Remainder be zero, the two bases give identical policy values; but if this value be at first $\frac{\text{positive}}{\text{negative}}$ it must afterwards be $\frac{\text{negative}}{\text{positive}}$ in order that the positive and negative elements shall cancel each other by the time the Reserve (Special or Normal) becomes unity (or for temporary assurances, zero).

25. Suppose the Remainder commences by being $\frac{\text{positive}}{\text{negative}}$, passes through the value zero and thereafter becomes $\frac{\text{negative}}{\text{positive}}$. Then up to the zero the Special Fund built up by the accumulations of the Remainder must be $\frac{\text{positive}}{\text{negative}}$ (because it consists of $\frac{\text{positive}}{\text{negative}}$ elements) and it must continually increase in numerical value: after the zero point this Fund must diminish (through the introduction of elements of the contrary sign) until it reaches zero at the limiting age. The special fund cannot in the given conditions become $\substack{\text{negative}\\ \text{positive}}$ after reaching zero, for if it did the $\substack{\text{negative}\\ \text{positive}}$ value would be increased by the subsequent $\substack{\text{negative}\\ \text{positive}}$ values of the "Remainder" and could not ultimately become zero, as it must in fact do. Therefore the special fund must be $\substack{\text{positive}\\ \text{negative}}$ throughout, and hence the Special Policy Values must always be $\substack{\text{greater}\\ \text{less}}$ than the Normal Policy Values.

26. The above reasoning shows:

(1) That if the "Remainder" be *constant*, its value must be zero and the two sets of Policy Values will be equal throughout;

(2) That if the Remainder be first *positive* and then change permanently to *negative* (which it will certainly do if its value be continually *decreasing*), the Special Policy Values will be the *higher* throughout.

(3) That if the Remainder be first *negative* and then change permanently to *positive* (which it will certainly do if its value be continually *increasing*), the Special Policy Values will be *smaller* throughout.

Now since the Remainder is equal to

[Accumulated Excess Premium] *minus* [Excess Strain – Excess Interest],

i.e. $[(P' - P)(1 + i')] - [(q' - q)(S - V_1) - (i' - i)(V + P)]$,

it will (provided i' be constant) be equal to zero throughout, or continually increasing, or continually decreasing, according as the [Excess Strain – Excess Interest] be constant, decreasing or increasing. Thus if the [Excess Strain – Excess Interest] be called the Critical Function, the Special Policy Values will be (1) equal to, or (2) always greater than, or (3) always less than, the Normal Policy Values, if the Critical Function be (1) constant, (2) continually increasing, or (3) continually decreasing; provided that the special rate of interest be constant.

27. Effect of a change in the Rate of *Interest*, the Rate of Mortality remaining unchanged:

Putting $q' = q$ in the Equation of Equilibrium, there results

$$(V + P)(i' - i) + (P' - P)(1 + i') = 0,$$

or

$$(P' - P)(1 + i') = -(V + P)(i' - i),$$

that is to say, the Excess Premium accumulated at the Special Rate must be numerically equal, but of opposite sign, to the Excess Interest on the Initial Normal Reserve, which includes the Normal Premium. The Critical Function instead of consisting of the [Excess Strain − Excess Interest] becomes [− Excess Interest].

If the constant value of $i - i'$ be $\begin{array}{c}\text{negative}\\ \text{positive}\end{array}$ and if $(V + P)$ increase algebraically from year to year, the Critical Function $(V + P)(i - i')$ will be $\begin{array}{c}\text{decreasing}\\ \text{increasing}\end{array}$ algebraically, and the Special Policy Values will be $\begin{array}{c}\text{less}\\ \text{greater}\end{array}$ than the Normal Policy Values.

Thus, whatever the form of benefit, a constant $\begin{array}{c}\text{increase}\\ \text{decrease}\end{array}$ in the fixed rate of interest will $\begin{array}{c}\text{diminish}\\ \text{increase}\end{array}$ the Policy Values, provided the Normal Policy Values are always increasing algebraically from year to year.

In the case of an ordinary Whole-Life Policy the condition that $(V + P)$ shall be continually increasing will be satisfied if a_x constantly diminish as x increases.

28. Effect of Variations in the Rate of *Mortality*, the Rate of Interest remaining unchanged:

Putting $i = i'$ in the Equation of Equilibrium there results

$$(P' - P)(1 + i) = (q' - q)(S - V_1),$$

which expresses that if the Normal Basis and the Special Basis produce identical Policy Values, the Excess Premium accumulated to the end of the year must provide the Excess Claims then payable *plus* the Excess Reserves for the continuing policies.

It follows from this relation that the excess mortality must be such that

$$q' - q = \frac{(P' - P)(1 + i)}{S - V_1}.$$

In the case of a Whole-Life Assurance effected at age x, this becomes for the nth year

$$q'-q=(1+i)(\mathrm{P}'-\mathrm{P})\frac{1+a_x}{1+a_{x+n}},$$

showing that the excess mortality must be proportional to $\frac{1}{1+a_{x+n}}$, a result already established in Chapter VI 29.

The essential point is, however, that the excess mortality is inversely proportional to the Death Strain at Risk: i.e. $(S-\mathrm{V}_1)$. Hence if any given difference in the rate of mortality leave Policy Values unchanged, any multiple of that difference, whether added to or subtracted from the normal rate of mortality, will also leave Policy Values unchanged.

If the Excess Mortality be such that the expression

$$(\mathrm{P}'-\mathrm{P})(1+i)-(q'-q)(S-\mathrm{V}_1)$$

is not always zero, then the Special Reserves will differ from the Normal Reserves, the Critical Function being $(q'-q)(S-\mathrm{V}_1)$, the Excess Strain.

29. Suppose that $(q'-q)$ has a fixed value: that is, that the Special Rates of Mortality are derived from the Normal Rates by the addition of a constant. If $(S-\mathrm{V}_1)$ be continually diminishing, as in Whole-Life and Endowment Assurances, the Excess Strain $(q'-q)(S-\mathrm{V}_1)$ will be continually $\begin{matrix}\text{decreasing}\\ \text{increasing}\end{matrix}$ algebraically according as $q'-q$ is $\begin{matrix}\text{positive}\\ \text{negative}\end{matrix}$, and the Special Reserves will be $\begin{matrix}\text{less}\\ \text{greater}\end{matrix}$ than the Normal Reserves. Thus a constant $\begin{matrix}\text{increase}\\ \text{decrease}\end{matrix}$ in the rate of mortality will $\begin{matrix}\text{diminish}\\ \text{increase}\end{matrix}$ the Policy Values provided $(S-\mathrm{V}_1)$ is constantly decreasing from year to year. (See Chap. VI 29.)

30. Now let the rate of mortality be increased or diminished in a constant ratio; i.e. let $q'-q=kq$. Then if q, and therefore kq, or $q'-q$, be continually increasing and $(1-\mathrm{V}_1)$ continually decreasing, the product $kq(1-\mathrm{V}_1)$ may *prima facie* be either increasing or decreasing.

From equation (19)

$$q(1-\mathrm{V}_1)=\mathrm{P}(1+i)+\mathrm{V}(1+i)-\mathrm{V}_1;$$

$$\begin{aligned}\therefore\quad \Delta[q(1-\mathrm{V}_1)]&=(1+i)\Delta\mathrm{V}-\Delta\mathrm{V}_1\\ &=i\Delta\mathrm{V}-\Delta^2\mathrm{V}\end{aligned}$$

whence, in the case of an ordinary Whole-Life Assurance,

$$\Delta\,[q\,(1-V_1)] = (P+d)\,(\Delta^2 a - i\Delta a).$$

Therefore,

$$\Delta\,[q\,(1-V_1)] \text{ is } +,\ 0 \text{ or } - \text{ as } \Delta^2 a - i\Delta a \text{ is } +,\ 0 \text{ or } -,$$

i.e. as $$\Delta^2 a >=< i\Delta a.$$

Thus $kq\,(1-V_1)$ or $(q'-q)\,(1-V_1)$ will be increasing, constant or diminishing, according as $\Delta^2 a >=< i\Delta a$, and it will have the same sign as k because $(1-V_1)$ must necessarily be positive. Hence, if $\Delta^2 a$ be always $\substack{\text{greater}\\ \text{less}}$ than $i\Delta a$, the Excess Strain will be algebraically $\substack{\text{increasing}\\ \text{decreasing}}$ and the Special Reserves will be $\substack{\text{greater}\\ \text{less}}$ than the Normal Reserves.

Thus for ordinary Whole-Life Policies the effect of increasing or diminishing the rate of mortality by a constant percentage will be to change Policy Values in the same direction or in the reverse direction, according as $\Delta^2 a$ is $\substack{\text{greater}\\ \text{less}}$ than $i\Delta a$.

31. Next take the case in which the Excess Mortality is such that $p' = (1+k)\,p$, where k is any constant, positive or negative: then $q'-q = p-p' = -kp$. If p be always decreasing in numerical value, $q'-q$ or $-kp$ will be so too: and if $(S-V_1)$ have a continually diminishing value, $(q'-q)\,(S-V_1)$—the Excess Strain—will always be diminishing in numerical value, and will always have the same sign as $q'-q$; i.e. the opposite sign to k. Thus the Excess Strain, which in this case is the Critical Function, will have a continually $\substack{\text{increasing}\\ \text{decreasing}}$ value according as k is $\substack{\text{positive}\\ \text{negative}}$. It has been shown that under these conditions the Special Reserves will be $\substack{\text{greater}\\ \text{less}}$ than the Normal Reserves. Thus the effect of $\substack{\text{increasing}\\ \text{diminishing}}$ p by a constant percentage will be to $\substack{\text{increase}\\ \text{diminish}}$ the Policy Values provided that $(S-V_1)$ be always positive and that p and $(S-V_1)$ be continually decreasing.

CHAPTER XI

MATHEMATICAL REPRESENTATION OF THE LAW OF MORTALITY. GOMPERTZ'S AND MAKEHAM'S LAWS

1. Efforts have been made at various times to find a simple mathematical law which, while reproducing the mortality experienced by any body of lives with a sufficient degree of accuracy, will simplify the evaluation of the more complicated monetary functions dependent thereon.

2. The two most important laws propounded are those known respectively as "Gompertz's Law," and "Makeham's Law," the latter being a modification of the former.

Without reproducing the reasoning by which Gompertz arrived at his formula, it may be stated that his assumption is that the risk of dying, that is, the force of mortality, increases in geometrical progression throughout life; or, expressed algebraically, that

$$\mu_x = \mathrm{B}c^x \quad \text{.............................(1)},$$

where B and c are constants.

From this expression, since $\mu_x = -\dfrac{d \log_e l_x}{dx}$, it follows that

$$-\log_e l_x = \int \mathrm{B}c^x \, dx$$

or

$$\log_e l_x = -\frac{\mathrm{B}c^x}{\log_e c} + \log_e k,$$

where $\log_e k$ is the constant introduced in integration.

Writing $-\dfrac{\mathrm{B}}{\log_e c} = \log_e g$, we have

$$\log_e l_x = c^x \log_e g + \log_e k,$$

whence

$$l_x = kg^{c^x} \quad \text{.................................(2)}.$$

3. In a paper which appeared in the *Journal of the Institute of Actuaries* in January 1860, Makeham discussed Gompertz's formula and introduced a modification which has the effect of making the formula apply, with wonderful closeness, to many mortality tables from about age 20 to the utmost limits of life.

By Gompertz's Law, since $l_{x+t} = kg^{c^{x+t}}$ and $l_x = kg^{c^x}$, it follows that

$$ {}_tp_x = g^{c^x(c^t-1)}; $$

$$ \therefore \quad \log {}_tp_x = c^x(c^t-1)\log g \quad \text{.................(3)}. $$

In this expression the coefficient of c^x is negative and constant, and the logarithm of the probability that a life aged x will live t years thus decreases geometrically with the increase in x.

Examining various mortality tables for the period of life from age 20 to age 80, Makeham showed that the logarithm of the probability of living t years can be more accurately represented if we add to the geometrical progression above given a constant negative term, the magnitude of which is determined by the length of the interval t. Writing for that constant term, $t \log s$, we have

$$ \begin{aligned} \log {}_tp_x &= t\log s + c^x(c^t-1)\log g \\ &= \log k + (x+t)\log s + c^{x+t}\log g \\ &\quad - \log k - x\log s - c^x \log g, \end{aligned} $$

where $\log k + (x+t)\log s + c^{x+t}\log g = \log l_{x+t}$

and $\log k + x\log s + c^x\log g = \log l_x$.

From this value of $\log l_x$ it follows that

$$ l_x = ks^x g^{c^x} \quad \text{..........................(4)}. $$

The formula for the force of mortality at age x is in this case

$$ \begin{aligned} \mu_x &= -\frac{d\log_e l_x}{dx} \\ &= -\log_e s - c^x\log_e c \,.\, \log_e g \quad \text{..............(5)}, \end{aligned} $$

whence, writing

$$ -\log_e s = \mathrm{A} \quad \text{and} \quad -\log_e c \,.\, \log_e g = \mathrm{B}, $$

$$ \mu_x = \mathrm{A} + \mathrm{B}c^x \quad \text{........................(6)}, $$

where A, B and c are constants.

In effect, therefore, Makeham proceeded a stage further than Gompertz and assumed that the force of mortality consisted of two parts, the one constant and the other increasing in geometrical progression throughout life.

From formula (4) it follows that, by Makeham's Law,

$$ {}_tp_x = s^t g^{c^x(c^t-1)} \quad \text{........................(7)}. $$

4. It is of some interest to examine the relation between the values of the Continuous Assurance and the Continuous Annuity under Makeham's Law:

$$\begin{aligned}\bar{A}_x &= \int_0^\infty v^t\,{}_tp_x\,\mu_{x+t}\,dt \\ &= \int_0^\infty v^t\,{}_tp_x\,(A + Bc^{x+t})\,dt \\ &= A\bar{a}_x + Bc^x \int_0^\infty (vc)^t\,{}_tp_x\,dt \\ &= A\bar{a}_x + (\mu_x - A)\,\bar{a}'_x \quad\ldots\ldots(8),\end{aligned}$$

where $\bar{a}'_x$ is calculated at a rate of interest j such that $vc = v_j$ or

$$j = \frac{1+i}{c} - 1.$$

In the case of a table following Gompertz's Law the corresponding equation would be $\bar{A}_x = \mu_x \bar{a}'_x$.

As will be seen in later chapters, Makeham's Law of Mortality is of extreme importance in connection with the values of functions depending on two or more lives.

5. If it be known that a particular table follows Makeham's Law, but the values of the constants are not known, these can be ascertained from any four equidistant values of $\log l_x$. Thus

$$\left.\begin{aligned}\log l_x &= \log k + x \log s + c^x \log g \\ \log l_{x+t} &= \log k + (x+t) \log s + c^{x+t} \log g \\ \log l_{x+2t} &= \log k + (x+2t) \log s + c^{x+2t} \log g \\ \log l_{x+3t} &= \log k + (x+3t) \log s + c^{x+3t} \log g\end{aligned}\right\} \ldots\ldots(\alpha).$$

Differencing both sides of these equations twice, we have

$$\left.\begin{aligned}\Delta \log l_x &= t \log s + c^x (c^t - 1) \log g \\ \Delta \log l_{x+t} &= t \log s + c^{x+t} (c^t - 1) \log g \\ \Delta \log l_{x+2t} &= t \log s + c^{x+2t} (c^t - 1) \log g\end{aligned}\right\} \ldots\ldots(\beta),$$

and

$$\left.\begin{aligned}\Delta^2 \log l_x &= c^x (c^t - 1)^2 \log g \\ \Delta^2 \log l_{x+t} &= c^{x+t} (c^t - 1)^2 \log g\end{aligned}\right\} \ldots\ldots(\gamma).$$

Whence

$$\frac{\Delta^2 \log l_{x+t}}{\Delta^2 \log l_x} = c^t,$$

or

$$\log\{\Delta^2 \log l_{x+t}\} - \log\{\Delta^2 \log l_x\} = t \log c \quad\ldots\ldots(\delta).$$

The values on the left-hand side of equation (δ) being obtainable from the original data, $\log c$ can be found. Inserting the value of c in equation (γ), we arrive at the value of $\log g$; and proceeding similarly in succession to the equations (β) and (α), we obtain the values of the other two constants.

6. The Table given on pages 410–411—the H^M Table (Makeham Graduation)—strictly follows Makeham's Law from age 28 upwards, the values of the constants being as follow:

$$\log c = \cdot 0396569,$$
$$\log g = -\cdot 0004568 = \bar{1}\cdot 9995432,$$
$$\log s = -\cdot 0026893 = \bar{1}\cdot 9973107,$$
$$\log k = 5\cdot 0404723.$$

In the table as finally printed the radix has been taken as 100,000 at age 10, with the result that above that age the value of l_x contains five figures only. It is evident, therefore, that taking four equidistant values of l_x will not reproduce values of the constants correct to seven places of decimals, but the resulting values will be very close to those given.

It will be observed that both $\log g$ and $\log s$ are negative, and this point must be borne in mind in the course of the work.

For ages below 28 Makeham's Law did not apply to the H^M Table with a sufficient degree of accuracy, and special means of graduation were consequently employed for this portion of the Table.

7. When the values of the Makeham constants are known the construction of the table of values of l_x can be proceeded with as follows:

$$\log l_x = \log k + x \log s + c^x \log g,$$
$$\therefore \quad \log p_x = \Delta \log l_x = \log s + c^x (c-1) \log g,$$

and

$$\operatorname{colog} p_x = -\log s + c^x (c-1)(-\log g),$$
$$\therefore \quad \Delta \operatorname{colog} p_x = c^x (c-1)^2 (-\log g),$$
$$\log (\Delta \operatorname{colog} p_x) = x \log c + 2 \log (c-1) + \log(-\log g),$$
$$\Delta \log (\Delta \operatorname{colog} p_x) = \log c.$$

The work can conveniently be arranged in columns thus:

(1) x	(2) log (Δ colog p_x)	(3) Δ colog p_x	(4) colog p_x	(5) log p_x $=\Delta \log l_x$	(6) log l_x	(7) l_x
20						
21						
22						
⋮						

If the first age be 20, the first value in column (2) will be calculated by means of the expression

$$20 \log c + 2 \log (c-1) + \log (-\log g),$$

the values for higher ages being obtained by successive additions of log c. The whole of column (2) or any section of it can then be automatically checked by the formula

$$\log (\Delta \operatorname{colog} p_{20}) + n \log c = \log (\Delta \operatorname{colog} p_{20+n}).$$

The values in column (3) are obtained by extraction of the natural numbers for the logarithms in column (2), a process which can only be checked by the work being carried out in duplicate by independent operators, or by going through the reverse process of again extracting the logarithms.

For column (4) the first value is calculated by means of the expression $-\log s + c^{20}(c-1)(-\log g)$, and the values for higher ages by the successive additions of the values in column (3). Here also a check is provided by taking

$$\operatorname{colog} p_{20} + \sum_{20}^{20+n} \Delta \operatorname{colog} p_x = \operatorname{colog} p_{20+n+1}.$$

Passing from colog p_x to log p_x is a simple process which will be checked by working in duplicate, this step providing the values of $\Delta \log l_x$ to be employed in the construction of column (6).

The first value of l_x and thence of log l_x will be taken as any convenient value, the column of log l_x constructed by successive additions of $\Delta \log l_x$, and the values for the last column obtained by extraction of the natural numbers of which the logarithms appear in column (6), each stage of the work being adequately checked.

8*. If a curve be drawn whose ordinates are $-\frac{dl_x}{dx}=\mu_x l_x$ or $(\mu l)_x$ (which may be called the "Curve of Deaths") the ordinates of this curve corresponding to half ages will, to a close degree of approximation, be proportional to the values of d_x (since $(\mu l)_{x+\frac{1}{2}}=d_x-\frac{1}{24}\Delta^2 d_x$ very nearly), and if Makeham's Law be assumed, the shape of this curve can be investigated and the age at which the number of deaths will be a maximum or a minimum ascertained.

To examine the shape of the curve, remembering that $\mu_x=A+Bc^x$, we have

$$\frac{d}{dx}(\mu l)_x=\mu_x\frac{dl_x}{dx}+l_x\frac{d\mu_x}{dx}$$

$$=-l_x\left\{(\mu_x)^2-\frac{d}{dx}(A+Bc^x)\right\}$$

$$=-l_x\{(\mu_x)^2-Bc^x\log_e c\}$$

$$=-l_x\{(\mu_x)^2-\mu_x\log_e c+A\log_e c\}\ \ldots\ldots(\alpha),$$

since $Bc^x=\mu_x-A$.

Also
$$\frac{d^2}{dx^2}(\mu l)_x=-\frac{d}{dx}l_x\{(\mu_x)^2-Bc^x\log_e c\}$$

$$=-l_x\{2\mu_x Bc^x\log_e c-Bc^x(\log_e c)^2\}$$

$$-\{(\mu_x)^2-Bc^x\log_e c\}\frac{dl_x}{dx}\quad\ldots\ldots(\beta).$$

Now in order that there may be a maximum or a minimum point,

$$\frac{d}{dx}(\mu l)_x=-l_x\{(\mu_x)^2-\mu_x\log_e c+A\log_e c\}=0,$$

or since l_x is not zero,

$$(\mu_x)^2-\mu_x\log_e c+A\log_e c=0,$$

whence
$$\mu_x=\frac{\log_e c\pm\sqrt{(\log_e c)^2-4A\log_e c}}{2}$$

$$=\log_e c\,\frac{1\pm\sqrt{1-\dfrac{4A}{\log_e c}}}{2}\quad\ldots\ldots\ldots\ldots(\gamma).$$

* The "Curve of Deaths" was first discussed in a paper "On the Curve of deaths when the Force of Mortality is expressed by Makeham's Law" by D. C. Fraser (*J.I.A.* Vol. 45, p. 476).

Considering the second differential coefficient of $(\mu l)_x$: when μ_x has one of the values necessary for the curve to have a maximum or minimum value, the second term of expression (β) becomes 0 and

$$\therefore \frac{d^2}{dx^2}(\mu l)_x = -l_x\{2\mu_x Bc^x \log_e c - Bc^x(\log_e c)^2\}$$

$$= -l_x Bc^x \log_e c \left\{\log_e c\left(1 \pm \sqrt{1-\frac{4A}{\log_e c}}\right) - \log_e c\right\}$$

$$= -l_x Bc^x (\log_e c)^2 \left(\pm\sqrt{1-\frac{4A}{\log_e c}}\right) \quad \text{..............}(\delta).$$

Now if

$$\mu_x = \log_e c \frac{1+\sqrt{1-\frac{4A}{\log_e c}}}{2},$$

since 4A is positive and less than $\log_e c$, $\frac{d^2(\mu l)_x}{dx^2}$ is negative, and the curve of deaths reaches a maximum point: if, however,

$$\mu_x = \log_e c \frac{1-\sqrt{1-\frac{4A}{\log_e c}}}{2},$$

$\frac{d^2(\mu l)_x}{dx^2}$ is positive, and the curve reaches a minimum point.

9. The values of μ_x which give maximum and minimum points in the curve of deaths may be expressed more simply as follows:

From (γ) taking the *positive* value of the second term, that is, the value of μ which gives a maximum value to μl, we have

$$2\mu = \log_e c\left\{1 + \left(1 - \frac{4A}{\log_e c}\right)^{\frac{1}{2}}\right\}$$

$$= \log_e c\left\{1 + \left(1 - \frac{2A}{\log_e c} - \frac{2A^2}{(\log_e c)^2}\right)\right\} \text{ approximately,}$$

neglecting powers of $\frac{4A}{\log_e c}$ higher than the second.

Whence $$\mu = \log_e c - A - \frac{A^2}{\log_e c}.$$

The $O^{M(5)}$ Table and the H^M Table, as printed at the end of this volume from age 28 onwards, both follow Makeham's Law. In both these tables $\mu_{x+\frac{1}{2}} = \log_e c - A - \frac{A^2}{\log_e c}$, approximately, when $x = 73$, and at that age d_x has a maximum value.

Turning to the consideration of the minimum value of d_x we are limited to the $O^{M(5)}$ Table, since the H^M does not follow Makeham's Law at that part of the table at which the smallest number of deaths may be expected to occur.

In this case

$$2\mu_x = \log_e c \left\{1 - \left(1 - \frac{2A}{\log_e c} - \frac{2A^2}{(\log_e c)^2}\right)\right\} \text{ approx.,}$$

whence $\mu_x = A + \dfrac{A^2}{\log_e c}$ approx.

In the $O^{M(5)}$ Table, $\mu_{x+\frac{1}{2}} = A + \dfrac{A^2}{\log_e c}$ approximately when $x = 15$, and the number of deaths is smallest at that age.

10. It has been shown in Chap. VII 11 that, as regards annuity values, a constant increase in the force of mortality has the same effect as the same constant increase in the force of interest. If under Makeham's Law the constant to be added be taken as $-\log_e f$ where f is a positive fraction, and $-\log_e f$ is consequently positive, the Makeham formula becomes

$$\mu'_x = -(\log_e s + \log_e f) - (\log_e g \,.\, \log_e c)\, c^x,$$

whence $\qquad l'_x = ks^x f^x g^{c^x} = f^x l_x,$

and $\qquad {}_tp'_x = f^t \,.\, {}_tp_x.$

For the value of the annuity we, therefore, have

$$a'_x = \sum_{t=1}^{t=\infty} v^t \,.\, f^t \,.\, {}_tp_x$$

$$= a_{x(j)},$$

$a_{x(j)}$ being calculated at a rate of interest j such that

$$\frac{1}{1+j} = \frac{f}{1+i}, \text{ or } j = \frac{1+i}{f} - 1.$$

As f is a positive fraction, j is greater than i.

11. If in the formula $\mu_x = A + Bc^x$, the constant B be increased, this is equivalent to a constant addition to the age x. For if the increased value of this constant be Bc^h the resulting formula is $A + Bc^{x+h}$ which is equal to μ_{x+h}.

12. When Makeham's Law is applied to Select Tables, as in the case of the $O^{[NM]}$ Table, modifications have to be introduced during the "select period." The value of $\log c$ remains constant for all ages and durations, but log g, log s and log k vary with the duration until the "Ultimate" stage is reached.

The value of $\log_e l_{[x]+t}$ will be less than the value of $\log_e l_{x+t}$ on account of the extent to which the duration falls short of five years, and we can, therefore, assume

$$\log_e l_{[x]+t} = \log_e l_{x+t} - \int_t^5 \phi(t) \, . \, dt - \int_t^5 \psi(t) \, . \, c^{x+t} \, dt \quad \ldots(9),$$

where $\phi(t)$ and $\psi(t)$ are functions the values of which must be determined.

From this relationship it can be shown that

$$\mu_{[x]+t} = \mathrm{A}_t + \mathrm{B}_t \, . \, c^{x+t} \quad \ldots\ldots\ldots\ldots\ldots\ldots\ldots(10),$$

where the values of A_t and B_t vary with t.

In the case of the $\mathrm{O}^{[\mathrm{NM}]}$ Table,

$$\mathrm{A}_t = \mathrm{A} - m(5-t)^3,$$
$$\mathrm{B}_t = \mathrm{B}[1 - \{a(5-t)^2 + b(5-t)^3\}].$$

13. Makeham's Law is sometimes called Makeham's *First* Modification of Gompertz's Law, in view of the fact that Makeham investigated a further development of the mathematical formula for the force of mortality, which is referred to as Makeham's *Second* Development of Gompertz's Law. This development consisted of the further assumption that the force of mortality may consist of three elements, one a constant, another increasing in arithmetical progression throughout life, and the third increasing in geometrical progression throughout life. That is, algebraically,

$$\mu_x = \mathrm{A} + \mathrm{H}x + \mathrm{B}c^x \quad \ldots\ldots\ldots\ldots\ldots\ldots(11).$$

From this expression,

$$\log_e l_x = -\mathrm{A}x - \mathrm{H}\frac{x^2}{2} - \mathrm{B}\frac{c^x}{\log_e c} + \log_e k,$$

whence, writing

$$-\mathrm{A} = \log_e s, \quad -\frac{\mathrm{H}}{2} = \log_e w \quad \text{and} \quad -\frac{\mathrm{B}}{\log_e c} = \log_e g,$$

$$\log_e l_x = x \log_e s + x^2 \log_e w + c^x \log_e g + \log_e k.$$

$$\therefore \quad l_x = k s^x w^{x^2} g^{c^x} \quad \ldots\ldots\ldots\ldots\ldots\ldots\ldots\ldots\ldots\ldots(12).$$

In this case

$${}_tp_x = s^t \, . \, w^{2tx+t^2} \, . \, g^{c^x(c^t-1)},$$

and $\quad \log {}_tp_x = t \log s + (2tx + t^2) \log w + c^x(c^t - 1) \log g \quad \ldots(13).$

As is to be expected from formulae (12) and (13) this second modification of Gompertz's Law results in expressions that are far too complicated to be of practical use.

Mean Age for Valuation of Endowment Assurances in Groups

14. In Chapter X 8 reference was made to the grouping of endowment assurances for valuation according to the nearest or the integral unexpired term, a mean Valuation age being calculated for each group; but the method of ascertaining this mean valuation age was not dealt with.

A mean age can be obtained in various ways, as, for example, (*a*) by simply adding the ages of the lives assured together, and dividing by the number of lives; (*b*) by multiplying the sum assured at each age by the age and dividing by the total sum assured, thus weighting the ages in proportion to the amount assured; (*c*) dealing as in (*b*) with the sums assured and premiums separately, thus obtaining separate "weighted" mean ages for the valuation of sums assured and premiums respectively, or (*d*) the method now to be explained which is generally referred to as "Lidstone's Z Method."

Methods (*a*) to (*c*) do not produce nearly so accurate valuation results as Method (*d*).

The Z method is very fully discussed by Mr G. J. Lidstone in papers printed in the *Journal of the Institute of Actuaries*, Vols. 34 and 38, and it is only proposed here to give sufficient information to enable the student to understand its use in practice.

Since $A_{x:\overline{n}|} = 1 - d(1 + a_{x:\overline{n-1}|})$ it is evident that a mean age can be found by reference to the annuity values at the various ages appearing in a group of policies, and that if these values be weighted according to the sums assured by the respective policies the resulting mean ages should give very satisfactory results. The problem, therefore, resolves itself into finding a suitable method of ascertaining the mean age on the basis of the equation

$$a_{y:\overline{n}|}[S_x + S_{x+1} + \ldots] = S_x a_{x:\overline{n}|} + S_{x+1} a_{x+1:\overline{n}|} + \ldots \qquad \ldots\ldots(\alpha),$$

where $S_x, S_{x+1}, \ldots$ are the sums assured at the ages $x, x+1, \ldots$ in a group of policies with an unexpired term of n years, and y is the mean valuation age required for that group.

As this equation stands, the products $S_x a_{x:\overline{n}|}$, $S_{x+1} . a_{x+1:\overline{n}|}$, etc. would have to be formed at each valuation and it became necessary, therefore, to examine the form of the differences of $a_{x:\overline{n}|}$ to ascertain a more suitable method.

Assuming Makeham's Law and dealing with $\frac{d}{dx}\bar{a}_{x:\overline{n}|}$ instead of $\Delta_x a_{x:\overline{n}|}$, we have

$$\begin{aligned}\frac{d}{dx}\bar{a}_{x:\overline{n}|} &= \frac{d}{dx}\int_0^n v^t {}_tp_x\, dt\\ &= \int_0^n v^t {}_tp_x (\mu_x - \mu_{x+t})\, dt\\ &= -\mathrm{B}c^x \int_0^n v^t (c^t - 1)\, {}_tp_x\, dt.\end{aligned}$$

The general tendency of the value of the definite integral contained in this expression is to diminish with increasing rapidity as the age increases, and if it be assumed that it decreases in geometrical progression (which assumption is not theoretically exact but is sufficiently accurate) it follows that the differential coefficients and therefore the first differences of $a_{x:\overline{n}|}$ are increasing in geometrical progression with a common ratio r, say, which is less than c. The annuity values will, therefore, be approximately of the form $\alpha - \beta r^x$.

Employing this form in expression (α) we have

$$(\alpha - \beta r^y)\,\Sigma S_x = S_x(\alpha - \beta r^x) + S_{x+1}(\alpha - \beta r^{x+1}) + \dots,$$

whence $\quad r^y \Sigma S_x = \Sigma S_x r^x.$

If the mean age were found from this expression as it stands, it would be necessary, for each policy, to obtain the product $S_x r^x$ at each valuation; but if this product can be made to depend on the maturity age it will be constant for the whole duration of the assurance. If n be the number of years from the valuation date to the end of the financial year in which the policies will mature, and if we multiply both sides of the last equation by r^n we shall have

$$r^{y+n}\Sigma S_x = \Sigma S_x r^{x+n},$$

or

$$r^{\mathrm{M}'}\Sigma S_x = \Sigma S_x r^{\mathrm{M}},$$

where $x+n$ or M is the age at the end of the year of maturity (a constant), and $y+n$ or M′ is what may be called the mean "Maturity Age."

The value of $S \times r^M$ will be constant for each policy and can be found and recorded once and for all at the inception of the assurance.

It will evidently make no difference if $S \times r^M$ be multiplied by a constant factor, say r^k, giving $S \times r^M \times r^k$, provided the value of M be determined by entering inversely a table of the same function; and it is desirable to do this in order to reduce the size of the quantities to be operated on. If therefore we put $k = -55$, and write $S \times r^{M-55} = Z_M$, we have

$$r^{M'-55} \Sigma S_x = \Sigma S_x r^{M-55} = \Sigma Z_M,$$

and $$\text{Mean value of Z per unit assured} = \frac{\Sigma Z_M}{\Sigma S_x}.$$

If, therefore, a table of Z_M be constructed showing the value of Z for each maturity age, by entering this table inversely with the mean value of Z_M for the group of policies, the mean value of M is obtained; whence, by deducting n, we have

$$y = \text{Mean valuation age} = (\text{Mean value of M}) - n.$$

There still remains the important point, "What is the value of r?" It has been mentioned that with a Makeham Table this value is really slightly less than c, but after investigation it was found that for tables following Makeham's Law, the value of c was sufficiently accurate, and being slightly on the side of increasing the mean age and therefore increasing the reserves to be held by the Office, this value was adopted.

For other tables a rough graduation by Makeham's formula for the ages most important to endowment assurances will generally give a suitable indication of the value of c that should be employed, and this method was actually adopted by Mr Lidstone in reference to the O^M Table.

CHAPTER XII

STATISTICAL APPLICATIONS OF THE MORTALITY TABLE

1. In the First Chapter it was pointed out that the value of a mortality table depends on its ability to supply the ratios necessary for the solution of problems dependent on the contingencies of life; and that the table, as finally printed, assumes a stationary population supported by l_0 births each year (or by l_x entrants at the youngest age x) and entirely free from emigration or immigration.

It is proposed in this chapter to extend the investigation of questions depending on the contingencies of life, not involving the operation of interest, the general plan being, firstly, to employ the figures of the stationary population and, secondly, to modify the calculations or results thus obtained in such a way as to fit them to the actual population to which the question relates.

2. The symbol L_x has been employed to represent the number of persons living in a stationary community between the ages x and $x+1$ at any moment of time. Similarly, T_x represents the number of persons aged x *and upwards* living at any moment of time in such a community.

Thus $$T_x = \sum_{t=0}^{t=\infty} L_{x+t} = \int_0^\infty l_{x+t}\,dt \quad\ldots\ldots(1)$$

$$= \sum_{t=1}^{t=\infty} l_{x+t} + \tfrac{1}{2}l_x + \tfrac{1}{12}\Delta l_x - \tfrac{1}{24}\Delta^2 l_x + \ldots$$

$$= \sum_{t=1}^{t=\infty} l_{x+t} + \tfrac{1}{2}l_x \text{ approx.} \quad\ldots\ldots(2),$$

neglecting terms involving Δl_x, $\Delta^2 l_x$, ..., etc.

Formula (2) can also be obtained by assuming $L_x = \frac{1}{2}(l_x + l_{x+1})$ which, as was pointed out in Chapter I 6, would be strictly correct if there were a uniform distribution of births over every year of time and a uniform distribution of deaths over the year of age x to $x+1$.

3. In Chapter I 20, it was shown that $\frac{dL_x}{dx} = -d_x$. Similarly

$$\frac{dT_x}{dx} = \frac{d}{dx}\int_0^\infty l_{x+t}\,dt$$

$$= \int_0^\infty \frac{d}{dx} l_{x+t}\,dt$$

$$= -l_x \quad \ldots\ldots\ldots\ldots\ldots\ldots\ldots\ldots\ldots(3).$$

4. The total population in the stationary community represented by the mortality table is $T_0 = \sum_{x=0}^{x=\infty} L_x$.

In order that the community may remain stationary, if there are to be l_0 births each year, there must also be l_0 deaths each year, and the ratio of the annual number of births or of the annual number of deaths to the population is therefore $\frac{l_0}{T_0}$.

Similarly, each year l_x persons attain age x, amongst whom d_x die in a year; l_{x+1} attain age $(x+1)$ amongst whom d_{x+1} die in a year, and so on. The number of deaths annually between ages x and $x+n$ is, therefore, $d_x + d_{x+1} + d_{x+2} + \ldots + d_{x+n-1} = l_x - l_{x+n}$.

The population at any moment of time between ages x and $x+n$ is $\int_0^n l_{x+t}dt = T_x - T_{x+n}$, and the ratio of the annual number of deaths between ages x and $x+n$ to the population between those ages is, therefore, $\frac{l_x - l_{x+n}}{T_x - T_{x+n}}$. If $n = 1$ this becomes $\frac{d_x}{L_x} = m_x$, the central death rate.

5. By the H^M Mortality Table given on pages 410–411, the proportion of deaths to the population for the whole community is $\frac{127\,283}{6{,}082{,}031} = {\cdot}020928$ or about 21 per thousand. The proportion for the population aged less than 50 is

$$\frac{l_0 - l_{50}}{T_0 - T_{50}} = \frac{127{,}283 - 72{,}795}{6{,}082{,}031 - 1{,}475{,}603} = \frac{54{,}488}{4{,}606{,}428} = {\cdot}011829$$

or not quite 12 per thousand, while the proportion for the population aged 50 and upwards is $\frac{l_{50}}{T_{50}} = \frac{72{,}795}{1{,}475{,}603} = {\cdot}049332$ or over 49 per thousand. These figures show that if from any cause there is an unusual proportion of young persons in a community, the ratio of deaths to population will be diminished; but it does not follow that, therefore, the members of that community enjoy unusual longevity.

This point is of some importance because a favourite method of displaying vital statistics is to tabulate the number of deaths per annum per thousand of the total population. If two communities are similarly constituted as regards the proportionate number living in each year of age, it may give a sufficiently accurate idea of the relative salubrity of the districts in which they are placed, if the rates of mortality per thousand of population be compared. Thus, if we were to take the rate of mortality per thousand in London, and compare it with the rate of mortality per thousand in Edinburgh, we should probably not fall into a great mistake. But if the distribution of the population as regards age were very different,—if, for instance, a great many persons in the prime of life were to migrate from one community to the other, leaving behind them a large proportion of elderly persons, among whom the rate of mortality is normally heavy,—it would be inadmissible any longer to compare the rates of mortality per thousand. The community which had lost members by emigration would show a higher death rate, on account of the greater average age of the remaining population, than the community which had received the migrants. Such are the relative positions of Britain and some of her Colonies. The average number of annual deaths per thousand of population in Victoria, Australia, was 16·6 during the years 1853 to 1878, and 22·1 in England and Wales during the years 1850 to 1874; but, for the reasons explained above, these figures do not tell us whether Victoria or England is the more healthy. To form a just comparison we must ascertain the rate of mortality at each age.

6. Expectation of Life:—"What is the average number of years lived after age x, by each of the l_x persons who attain that age?"

Considering completed $\frac{1}{m}$th parts of years; of l_x persons aged x, $l_{x+\frac{1}{m}}$ survive $\frac{1}{m}$ of a year after age x, $l_{x+\frac{2}{m}}$ survive a further $\frac{1}{m}$ of a year and so on, the total number of *years* lived after age x by all the l_x persons being $\frac{1}{m}\sum_{t=1}^{t=\infty} l_{x+\frac{t}{m}}$; which, when m is indefinitely increased, becomes $\int_0^\infty l_{x+t}\,dt$. The number of years lived by the l_x persons after age x, every moment being counted, is thus $\int_0^\infty l_{x+t}\,dt$, and the average number required is

$$\frac{\int_0^\infty l_{x+t}\,dt}{l_x} = \frac{T_x}{l_x}.$$

This function is known as the *Complete Expectation of Life* and is represented by $\mathring{e}_x$. Therefore

$$\mathring{e}_x = \frac{T_x}{l_x} = \frac{\int_0^\infty l_{x+t}\,dt}{l_x} \quad \text{......................(4).}$$

7. If the question were "What is the average number of complete years of life lived after age x by each of l_x persons attaining that age?" the answer would be

$$\frac{\sum_{t=1}^{t=\infty} l_{x+t}}{l_x} = \sum_{t=1}^{t=\infty} {}_tp_x.$$

This is called the *Curtate Expectation of Life* and is represented by e_x. Thus

$$e_x = \frac{\sum_{t=1}^{t=\infty} l_{x+t}}{l_x} = \frac{T_x - \frac{1}{2}l_x}{l_x} \text{ approx.}$$

$$= \mathring{e}_x - \tfrac{1}{2} \quad \text{........................(5).}$$

The relation $\mathring{e}_x = e_x + \frac{1}{2}$ is a very convenient one. It can readily be arrived at by general reasoning on the assumption of a uniform distribution of deaths over each year of age; since, e_x being the average number of complete years of life lived after age x, on this assumption each of the l_x persons will on the average live $\frac{1}{2}$ a year in the year of death, thus giving $\frac{1}{2} + e_x$ as the *complete* expectation of life.

The term "expectation of life" appears to have been given to this function, because if it were known that the mortality experience of the past, as shown by the table, will exactly be reproduced in the future, $\mathring{e}_x$ would be the average number of years that the l_x persons could be expected to live after age x.

8. The average number of years lived after age x being $\mathring{e}_x$ it follows that the average age at death of the persons who attain age x is $x + \mathring{e}_x = x + \dfrac{T_x}{l_x}$.

Putting $x = 0$ the average age at death in the community is found to be $\mathring{e}_0 = \dfrac{T_0}{l_0}$.

9. The temporary complete expectation of life for n years, $|_n\mathring{e}_x$, is

$$\frac{\int_0^n l_{x+t}\,dt}{l_x} = \frac{T_x - T_{x+n}}{l_x} = \mathring{e}_x - {}_n|\mathring{e}_x \quad \text{..............(6)},$$

where ${}_n|\mathring{e}_x$ is the deferred expectation of life and is equal to ${}_np_x\mathring{e}_{x+n}$.

On the assumption that $\mathring{e}_x = \frac{1}{2} + e_x$

$$ {}_n|\mathring{e}_x = {}_np_x\left(\tfrac{1}{2} + e_{x+n}\right),$$

$$|_n\mathring{e}_x = \left(\tfrac{1}{2} + e_x\right) - {}_np_x\left(\tfrac{1}{2} + e_{x+n}\right)$$

$$= |_ne_x + \tfrac{1}{2}\left(1 - {}_np_x\right) \quad \text{..................(7)},$$

or multiplying by l_x

$$l_x|_n\mathring{e}_x = l_x \,.\, |_ne_x + \tfrac{1}{2}\left(l_x - l_{x+n}\right),$$

which formula demonstrates that in arriving at $|_n\mathring{e}_x$, having given the value of $|_ne_x$, half a year is added in respect of each death occurring during the n years, this being the period which, on the assumption of a uniform distribution of deaths, is lived in the year of death, on the average, by each of these persons.

10. If the question be asked "What is the average age at death of those persons who die between ages x and $x + n$?", this will be obtained by adding to the age x the average number of years lived by those who die in the n years following the attainment of that age. The number $\int_0^n l_{x+t}\,dt$ includes the n years lived by each of the l_{x+n} survivors, and to obtain the total number of years lived after age x by those who die between ages x and $x + n$, nl_{x+n} must be deducted, giving $\int_0^n l_{x+t}\,dt - nl_{x+n} = T_x - T_{x+n} - nl_{x+n}$.

The number of deaths between these ages is $l_x - l_{x+n}$, the average number of years lived by each of these persons after age x thus being $\dfrac{T_x - T_{x+n} - nl_{x+n}}{l_x - l_{x+n}}$, and the average age at death

$$x + \frac{T_x - T_{x+n} - nl_{x+n}}{l_x - l_{x+n}}.$$

Dealing with this question from another point of view, the number of deaths occurring at time t following age x is $l_{x+t}\mu_{x+t}\,dt$. As each of these persons lived t years after age x, the total number of years lived by all of them together since that age is $tl_{x+t}\,\mu_{x+t}\,dt$. If the integral of this function between the limits $t=0$ and $t=n$ be taken this will give the total number of years lived after age x by those persons who die between ages x and $x+n$. That is

$$\begin{aligned}\int_0^n tl_{x+t}\,\mu_{x+t}\,dt &= -\int_0^n t\frac{dl_{x+t}}{dt}\,dt \\ &= -\left[tl_{x+t} - \int l_{x+t}\,dt\right]_{t=0}^{t=n} \\ &= \int_0^n l_{x+t}\,dt - nl_{x+n} \\ &= T_x - T_{x+n} - nl_{x+n}.\end{aligned}$$

Dividing this number by the number of persons dying between ages x and $x+n$ and adding x, the result is the average age at death of those persons who die between ages x and $x+n$, namely $x + \dfrac{T_x - T_{x+n} - nl_{x+n}}{l_x - l_{x+n}}$, as before.

11. The method adopted in the last paragraph may also be employed to ascertain the complete expectation of life at age x; for if the limits of the integral be taken as 0 and ∞ (instead of the superior limit being n) the result will be the total number of years lived after age x by those (out of the l_x persons of that age) who die after its attainment. But *all* the l_x persons must die after age x and the average number of years lived after that age is, therefore,

$$\begin{aligned}\mathring{e}_x &= \frac{1}{l_x}\int_0^\infty tl_{x+t}\,\mu_{x+t}\,dt \\ &= \frac{1}{l_x}\int_0^\infty l_{x+t}\,dt \\ &= \frac{T_x}{l_x},\end{aligned}$$

as already obtained in paragraph 6.

12. It has been stated that the average age at death of the l_x persons aged x will be $x + \mathring{e}_x$. Now it will be found on reference to a mortality table that the higher the age, x, from which we count, the greater will be the average age at death. Thus, by the H^M Table, at age 10, the average age at death is 60·257 years; at age 20, it is 62·101; at age 30, it is 64·726; and at age 60, it is 73·808. This fact exposes a fallacy which is very often current. It is frequently stated by shallow reasoners that some profession, such as that of the lawyer, must be conducive to longevity; or that some class in society, such as the peerage, must be peculiarly long-lived; because the average age at death of the members of the profession or class is much higher than that of the general population. But the general population starts from age 0; and, starting from age 0, the average age at death, if the mortality were to follow the table, would be only 47·784 years; whereas a peer does not become a peer until the death of his predecessor, when he himself is perhaps 30, 40, or even 50 or 60 years of age; or until he is created a peer, when also he is usually advanced in life. The peer then does not become a peer until he is, on the average, say, 40 years of age; so that, measured by the same table as the general population, the average age of peers at death should be about 67 or 68 years.

In the same way, a lawyer does not enter the profession until he reaches manhood; and usually, it is not until many years later that he attains sufficient eminence for his death to be commented upon. Therefore, even if the rate of mortality among lawyers be not more favourable than among the general population, the average age at death of those whose deaths attract notice must be greater.

To compare the average ages at death of different classes or groups of persons does not prove anything, unless we know the average ages at which the persons come under observation, so as to be able to make allowances for differences in this respect. In order to form a correct idea of the relative mortality of different classes of persons, we must, as indicated in paragraph 5, ascertain and compare the rate of mortality at each age in each class.

13. It has been shown in paragraph 8 that the average age at death of a stationary population supported by births alone is

$$\mathring{e}_0 = \frac{T_0}{l_0}.$$

What will be the effect n years hence on the average age at death if there be an annual influx of $\frac{1}{k}l_x$ persons aged x?

The average age at death of the l_0 deaths occurring each year among the original population is $\mathring{e}_0$, and the sum of their ages at death is $l_0\mathring{e}_0 = T_0$.

The immigration being spread uniformly over each year the problem can be dealt with on the assumption that on the average all the $\frac{1}{k}l_x$ immigrants in any one year join the community at exact age x exactly in the middle of the year. When, therefore, the question is asked, "What is the effect of this immigration on the average age at the end of n years?" we can answer it on the basis of the average age at death during the year $n - \frac{1}{2}$ to $n + \frac{1}{2}$.

During that year the number of deaths amongst the immigrants will be $\frac{1}{k}(l_x - l_{x+n})$ and their average age at death

$$x + \frac{T_x - T_{x+n} - nl_{x+n}}{l_x - l_{x+n}}$$

(see paragraph 10), the sum of the ages at death of the immigrants who die in the year being

$$\frac{1}{k}(l_x - l_{x+n})\left(x + \frac{T_x - T_{x+n} - nl_{x+n}}{l_x - l_{x+n}}\right).$$

The total sum of the ages at death amongst the population, including the immigrants, is, therefore,

$$T_0 + \frac{1}{k}(l_x - l_{x+n})\left(x + \frac{T_x - T_{x+n} - nl_{x+n}}{l_x - l_{x+n}}\right),$$

and the total number of deaths is $l_0 + \frac{1}{k}(l_x - l_{x+n})$. The average age at death will, therefore, be

$$\frac{T_0 + \frac{1}{k}(l_x - l_{x+n})\left(x + \frac{T_x - T_{x+n} - nl_{x+n}}{l_x - l_{x+n}}\right)}{l_0 + \frac{1}{k}(l_x - l_{x+n})}.$$

14. A somewhat more difficult question is, "What is the average age at death of the present members aged x and upwards of the stationary community represented by the Mortality Table?"

The average age at death of these persons will be

$x +$ (average past life-time since age x) + (average future life-time).

Consider first the *total* past life-time since age x of the T_x persons aged x and upwards. The $l_{x+t}\,dt$ persons of exact age $x+t$ have lived exactly t years, that is, altogether $tl_{x+t}\,dt$ years, since age x; and the total number of years lived since that age by all the T_x persons is, therefore,

$$\int_0^\infty tl_{x+t}\,dt = -\int_0^\infty t\frac{dT_{x+t}}{dt}\,dt$$
$$= -\left[tT_{x+t} - \int T_{x+t}\,dt\right]_{t=0}^{t=\infty}$$
$$= \int_0^\infty T_{x+t}\,dt,$$

which may be represented by Y_x.

The *average* past life-time since age x is therefore $\frac{Y_x}{T_x}$.

Considering now the future life-time, the future life-time of l_{x+t} persons aged $x+t$ is $\int_t^\infty l_{x+n}\,dn = T_{x+t}$ and consequently the total future life-time of $\int_0^\infty l_{x+t}\,dt\,(=T_x)$ persons is $\int_0^\infty T_{x+t}\,dt = Y_x$.

The average future life-time is thus $\frac{Y_x}{T_x}$.

The average age at death of the T_x members of the community at present living of age x and upwards is therefore $x + \frac{2Y_x}{T_x}$.

In the same manner as T_x was taken as approximately equal to $\sum_{t=1}^{t=\infty} l_{x+t} + \frac{1}{2}l_x$, so also we can assume $Y_x = \sum_{t=1}^{t=\infty} T_{x+t} + \frac{1}{2}T_x$ approx.

If $x=0$, the average age at death of the present members of the community is seen to be $\frac{2Y_0}{T_0}$.

15. In connection with certain problems that arise in practice it is convenient to have a table giving for each age the value of $\sum_{t=1}^{t=\infty} l_{x+t}$, which value is generally represented by N'_x. This function is not really essential, because if it be assumed that $L_x = \frac{1}{2}(l_x + l_{x+1})$, it follows that $N'_x = T_x - \frac{1}{2}l_x$, whence, having a column of values of T_x, the sum of the values in the l_x column from age $x+1$ upwards is readily ascertained.

The function N'_x has, however, been tabulated for both the H^M (Makeham Graduation) Table and the English Life Table No. 8, but is not included in the tables at the end of this volume.

It will be observed that $e_x = \frac{N'_x}{l_x}$.

16. The following relation between $\mathring{e}_x$ and μ_x should be noted:

$$\begin{aligned}\frac{d\mathring{e}_x}{dx} &= \frac{d}{dx}\int_0^\infty {}_tp_x\,dt\\ &= \int_0^\infty \frac{d}{dx}\,{}_tp_x\,dt\\ &= \int_0^\infty {}_tp_x\,(\mu_x - \mu_{x+t})\,dt\\ &= \mu_x\mathring{e}_x - 1,\\ \therefore\quad \mu_x &= \frac{1}{\mathring{e}_x} + \frac{1}{\mathring{e}_x}\frac{d\mathring{e}_x}{dx}\\ &= \frac{1}{\mathring{e}_x}\{1 + \tfrac{1}{2}(\mathring{e}_{x+1} - \mathring{e}_{x-1})\} \quad \text{approx.}\end{aligned}$$

17. An erroneous notion not infrequently met with is that, in calculating the values of life annuities, the life may be represented by a term certain equal to the expectation of life. It is easy to prove, however, that the value of a life annuity is less than the value of an annuity certain for the curtate expectation.

Let there be l_x quantities of which d_x are equal to v, d_{x+1} equal to v^2, d_{x+2} to v^3 and so on. The arithmetic mean of these quantities is

$$\frac{vd_x + v^2d_{x+1} + v^3d_{x+2} + \dots}{l_x}$$
$$= A_x,$$

and the geometric mean is

$$v^{(d_x+2d_{x+1}+3d_{x+2}+\dots)\frac{1}{l_x}}$$
$$= v^{1+e_x}.$$

But as the arithmetic mean of a number of positive quantities is greater than the geometric mean, it follows that

$$A_x > v^{1+e_x},$$

$$\therefore\quad 1 - d(1 + a_x) > 1 - d(1 + a_{\overline{e_x}|}),$$

whence $$a_{\overline{e_x}|} > a_x.$$

18. The term of the annuity certain which is equal to the whole-life annuity can be ascertained by solving for n in the equation

$$a_x = \frac{1-v^n}{i},$$

whence we obtain $$n = -\frac{\log(1-ia_x)}{\log(1+i)}.$$

Expanding n as far as first powers of i only, remembering that a_x is a function of i, we have

$$-\log(1-ia_x) = ia_x + \frac{(ia_x)^2}{2} + \frac{(ia_x)^3}{3} + \dots$$

$$= i\sum_{t=1}^{t=\infty}(1+i)^{-t}\,{}_tp_x + \tfrac{1}{2}i^2\left\{\sum_{t=1}^{t=\infty}(1+i)^{-t}\,{}_tp_x\right\}^2 + \dots$$

or for convenience writing Σ for $\sum\limits_{t=1}^{t=\infty}$

$$= i\left(\Sigma\,{}_tp_x - i\,\Sigma t\,{}_tp_x + i^2\,\Sigma\frac{t(t+1)}{\underline{|2}}\,{}_tp_x - \dots\right)$$

$$+ \tfrac{1}{2}i^2(\Sigma\,{}_tp_x)^2 + \dots \text{ etc.}$$

$$= i\Sigma\,{}_tp_x - i^2\,\Sigma t\,{}_tp_x + \frac{i^2}{2}(\Sigma\,{}_tp_x)^2 - \dots \quad \dots\dots\dots\dots(\alpha),$$

also $$\log(1+i) = i - \frac{i^2}{2} + \frac{i^3}{3} - \dots \text{ etc.} \quad \dots\dots\dots(\beta).$$

Whence dividing (α) by (β), we have

$$n = \Sigma\,{}_tp_x + i\,\{\tfrac{1}{2}\Sigma\,{}_tp_x - \Sigma t\,{}_tp_x + \tfrac{1}{2}(\Sigma\,{}_tp_x)^2\} \text{ approx.}$$

$$= e_x - i\left\{\frac{1}{l_x}\sum_{t=1}^{t=\infty} t\,l_{x+t} - \tfrac{1}{2}e_x(e_x+1)\right\} \text{ approx.}$$

But $$\sum_{t=1}^{t=\infty} t l_{x+t} = \tfrac{1}{2}\mathrm{N}'_x + \sum_{t=1}^{t=\infty}\mathrm{T}_{x+t}$$

$$= \tfrac{1}{2}\mathrm{T}_x + \sum_{t=1}^{t=\infty}\mathrm{T}_{x+t} + \tfrac{1}{2}(\mathrm{N}'_x - \mathrm{T}_x)$$

$$= \mathrm{Y}_x - \tfrac{1}{4}l_x,$$

and $$\tfrac{1}{2}e_x(e_x+1) = \tfrac{1}{2}(e_x^2 + e_x)$$

$$= \tfrac{1}{2}\{(\tfrac{1}{2}+e_x)^2 - \tfrac{1}{4}\}$$

$$= \tfrac{1}{2}(\mathring{e}_x)^2 - \tfrac{1}{8},$$

$$\therefore \quad n = e_x - i\left\{\frac{\mathrm{Y}_x}{l_x} - \tfrac{1}{8} - \tfrac{1}{2}(\mathring{e}_x)^2\right\} \text{ approx.}$$

EXAMPLES

The application of the principles discussed in this chapter will be shown by the following series of examples.

Ex. 1. A Bank employs 300 clerks: they enter at age 18 at a salary of £30 per annum which is increased £10 a year to a maximum of £300: at age 60 they retire on a pension. Assuming that 10 per cent. leave the Bank after exactly five years' service and that after twenty years' service, 5 per cent. are promoted from the clerical staff to higher positions, how would you proceed to find the ultimate state of the clerical staff in the following particulars?—

(a) Total annual sum payable in salaries.

(b) Number superannuated each year.

(c) Number of pensioners on the books.

The first step is to ascertain the staff that would be employed if there were l_{18} entrants. This number is

$$\sum_{x=18}^{x=22} L_x + \cdot 9 \sum_{x=23}^{x=37} L_x + \cdot 9 \times \cdot 95 \sum_{x=38}^{x=59} L_x$$

$$= (T_{18} - T_{23}) + \cdot 9\,(T_{23} - T_{38}) + \cdot 855\,(T_{38} - T_{60})$$

$$= T_{18} - \cdot 1T_{23} - \cdot 045T_{38} - \cdot 855T_{60}$$

$$= X, \text{ say.}$$

The withdrawal of 10 per cent. of the staff at the end of five years is allowed for by multiplying the figures given by the mortality table by ·9 from age 23 onwards. At age 38, 5 per cent. are promoted, but as 10 per cent. previously withdrew this leaves 95 per cent. of 90 per cent. of L_x at age 38 and upwards.

The withdrawals and promotions in practice would not all take place at fixed periods as indicated in the question, but it has evidently been found that these changes occur at such periods and in such numbers as to be approximately equivalent to 10 per cent. at the end of five years and 5 per cent. at the end of twenty years respectively. Where such assumptions can be made without material loss of accuracy a large amount of work is, of course, saved.

The number of clerks employed being 300, the method to be adopted in answering the question will be to ascertain the numbers required on the assumption of l_{18} entrants, or a staff of X, and then to reduce the results in the proportion $\frac{300}{X}$.

(*a*) The total annual sum payable in salaries is:

$$\frac{300}{X}[30L_{18}+40L_{19}+\ldots+70L_{22}$$
$$+\cdot 9\,(80L_{23}+90L_{24}+\ldots+220L_{37})$$
$$+\cdot 855\,\{230L_{38}+240L_{39}+\ldots+300\,(L_{45}+L_{46}+\ldots+L_{59})\}]$$
$$=\frac{300}{X}\left[\left(30T_{18}+10\sum_{x=19}^{x=22}T_x-70T_{23}\right)+\cdot 9\left(80T_{23}+10\sum_{x=24}^{x=37}T_x-220T_{38}\right)\right.$$
$$\left.+\cdot 855\left(230T_{38}+10\sum_{x=39}^{x=45}T_x-300T_{60}\right)\right].$$

(*b*) If there were l_{18} entrants and a staff of X, the number superannuated each year would be $\cdot 855 l_{60}$.

The number required is, therefore,

$$\cdot 855 l_{60}\times\frac{300}{X}.$$

(*c*) With a staff of X, the number of pensioners on the books at any particular time would be $\cdot 855 T_{60}$.

The number required is, therefore,

$$\cdot 855 T_{60}\times\frac{300}{X}.$$

In (*c*) the number required is the number that would be given by a census at any particular time.

Ex. 2. A Company's Staff consisting of 1000 men who all enter at age 20 has reached a stationary condition.

Assuming (1) in the first three years of service, 15 per cent. of **those attaining age 21 resign at that age, 10 per cent.** resign at age **22 and 5** per cent. at age 23, after which there are no resignations.

(2) 10 per cent. of those attaining age 55 retire at that age, 40 per cent. retire at age 60 and 100 per cent. at age 65.

(3) H^M mortality, find:

(*a*) The number resigning each year.

(*b*) The number of pensioners.

If there were l_{20} entrants each year the staff would be

$$L_{20}+\cdot 85L_{21}+\cdot 85\times\cdot 9L_{22}+\cdot 85\times\cdot 9\times\cdot 95\,(T_{23}-T_{55})$$
$$+\cdot 85\times\cdot 9\times\cdot 95\,\{\cdot 9\,(T_{55}-T_{60})+\cdot 9\times\cdot 6\,(T_{60}-T_{65})\}$$
$$=L_{20}+\cdot 85L_{21}+\cdot 765L_{22}+\cdot 72675\,\{T_{23}-\cdot 1T_{55}-\cdot 36T_{60}-\cdot 54T_{65}\}$$
$$=2{,}473{,}777.$$

By the question the staff is 1000, and the numbers obtained for (*a*) and (*b*) on the basis of l_{20} entrants or a staff of 2,473,777 must therefore be reduced in the ratio $\frac{1000}{2,473,777}$.

(*a*) The number resigning each year will be

$$\frac{1000}{2,473,777}\{\cdot15l_{21}+\cdot1\times\cdot85l_{22}+\cdot05\times\cdot9\times\cdot85l_{23}\}$$
$$=\frac{1000}{2,473,777}(26004)$$
$$=10\cdot5.$$

This result means that the number will be 10 or 11 (say 10 and 11 in alternate years) averaging 10·5 per annum.

(*b*) The number of pensioners: that is, the number disclosed by a census will be

$$\frac{1000}{2,473,777}\times\cdot72675\times\{\cdot1T_{55}+\cdot4\times\cdot9T_{60}+\cdot6\times\cdot9T_{65}\}$$
$$=\frac{1000}{2,473,777}\times\cdot72675\times697491$$
$$=205.$$

Ex. 3. A staff, including both those in active service and those who have been pensioned, is represented, just after a year's entrants have joined the staff and a year's retirements have taken place, by the l_x column from age 20 onwards, and has reached a stationary condition.

Retirement on pension takes place at exact ages 61 to 65, and there are *no withdrawals* except by death. The proportion of those in active service at each age who retire at that age and the corresponding pensions are as follows:

Age	Proportion of those in active service at each age who then retire	Amount of Pension (assume payable momently)
61	One-tenth	£140
62	One-sixth	£160
63	One-third	£180
64	One-half	£200
65	All	£220

Assuming that the mortality among pensioners is the same as among those in active service at corresponding ages, *find expressions* for the following, just after a year's retirements have taken place:

(1) The total number of pensioners.

(2) The total pensions payable in a year.

(3) The sum (ignoring interest) of all future payments in respect of existing pensions.

The number of persons pensioned each year will be

$$\frac{1}{10}l_{61} + \frac{1}{6}\cdot\frac{9}{10}l_{62} + \frac{1}{3}\cdot\frac{5}{6}\cdot\frac{9}{10}l_{63} + \frac{1}{2}\cdot\frac{2}{3}\cdot\frac{5}{6}\cdot\frac{9}{10}(l_{64} + l_{65})$$
$$= \frac{1}{20}(2l_{61} + 3l_{62} + 5l_{63} + 5l_{64} + 5l_{65}).$$

(1) The total number of pensioners is required just after a year's retirements have taken place, and as it is clear from the question that the conditions are such that it may with sufficient accuracy be assumed that these take place at a definite time *and* at exact ages, the l_x and N'_x columns must be used.

Of those who retired each year at age 61, there are now persons surviving at all (exact) ages 61 and over, the total number being $\frac{1}{10}N'_{60}$.

The total number of pensioners is therefore

$$\frac{1}{20}(2N'_{60} + 3N'_{61} + 5N'_{62} + 5N'_{63} + 5N'_{64})$$
$$= \frac{1}{20}(2l_{61} + 5l_{62} + 10l_{63} + 15l_{64} + 20N'_{64}).$$

(2) In ascertaining the total amount of pensions payable in the year regard must be paid to the fact that these are to be treated as payable momently. It is, therefore, necessary to employ the L_x and T_x columns.

The amount required is

$$\frac{1}{20}\{140 \times 2T_{61} + 160 \times 3T_{62} + 180 \times 5T_{63} + 200 \times 5T_{64} + 220 \times 5T_{65}\}$$
$$= 14T_{61} + 24T_{62} + 45T_{63} + 50T_{64} + 55T_{65}.$$

(3) Of the $\frac{1}{10}l_{61}$ persons who have just retired at age 61, $\frac{1}{10}l_{62}$ will receive a full year's pension in the first year, and $\frac{1}{10}d_{61}$ will on the average receive half a year's pension: the total payable in the first year in respect of these retirements will thus be $\frac{140}{10}(l_{62} + \frac{1}{2}d_{61}) = 14L_{61}$. Similarly, in respect of this year's retirements at age 61, the amount payable in the second year will be $14L_{62}$: and so on.

Thus the future pensions payable in respect of the $\frac{1}{10}l_{61}$ persons who have just retired will be $14\sum_{x=61}^{x=\omega-1} L_x = 14T_{61}$.

The amount payable in respect of the persons who retired at age 61 a year earlier will be $14T_{62}$: and so on, the total amount of all future pensions in respect of persons who have retired at age 61 being $14\sum_{x=61}^{x=\omega-1} T_x$.

Applying similar arguments to the number of persons who have retired at ages 62 to 65, the sum required is found to be

$$14\sum_{x=61}^{x=\omega-1} T_x + 24\sum_{x=62}^{x=\omega-1} T_x + 45\sum_{x=63}^{x=\omega-1} T_x + 50\sum_{x=64}^{x=\omega-1} T_x + 55\sum_{x=65}^{x=\omega-1} T_x.$$

Ex. 4. A Society issues each year 1000 endowment assurances for £100 each on lives aged 40, 250 of the policies effected each year maturing at age 55, 500 at age 60, and 250 at age 65. When the Society reaches a stationary condition, what will be the total number of policies in force, and what sum will be paid each year (*a*) in respect of death claims, and (*b*) in respect of policies maturing?

Give numerical answers, assuming that each year's new assurances are *equally distributed throughout the year*, that there are *no withdrawals* and that the mortality is in accordance with the $O^{[NM]}$ Table.

If there were $l_{[40]}$ assurances effected each year of which $\frac{1}{4}l_{[40]}$ matured at age 55, $\frac{1}{2}l_{[40]}$ at age 60, and $\frac{1}{4}l_{[40]}$ at age 65, the number of policies in force would be

$$\begin{aligned}&\tfrac{1}{4}(T_{[40]} - T_{55}) + \tfrac{1}{2}(T_{[40]} - T_{60}) + \tfrac{1}{4}(T_{[40]} - T_{65})\\ &= T_{[40]} - \tfrac{1}{4}T_{55} - \tfrac{1}{2}T_{60} - \tfrac{1}{4}T_{65}.\end{aligned}$$

The number of assurances effected each year being 1000, the number of policies in force will be

$$\begin{aligned}&\frac{1000}{l_{[40]}}\{T_{[40]} - \tfrac{1}{4}T_{55} - \tfrac{1}{2}T_{60} - \tfrac{1}{4}T_{65}\}\\ &= 17383.\end{aligned}$$

The amount that will be paid each year in respect of death claims is

$$\begin{aligned}&100 \times \frac{1000}{l_{[40]}}\{\tfrac{1}{4}(l_{[40]} - l_{55}) + \tfrac{1}{2}(l_{[40]} - l_{60}) + \tfrac{1}{4}(l_{[40]} - l_{65})\}\\ &= 100 \times \frac{1000}{l_{[40]}}\{l_{[40]} - \tfrac{1}{4}l_{55} - \tfrac{1}{2}l_{60} - \tfrac{1}{4}l_{65}\}\\ &= 29700 \ldots\ldots\ldots\ldots\ldots\ldots\ldots\ldots\ldots (a),\end{aligned}$$

and the amount in respect of policies maturing

$$100 \times \frac{1000}{l_{[40]}} \{\tfrac{1}{4} l_{55} + \tfrac{1}{2} l_{60} + \tfrac{1}{4} l_{65}\}$$
$$= 70300 \quad \ldots\ldots\ldots\ldots\ldots\ldots\ldots\ldots\ldots\ldots\ldots\ldots(b).$$

It will be observed that $(a)+(b)=100\times1000$ as must be the case, since for the Society to be in a stationary condition there must be 1000 claims each year.

Ex. 5. In a population hitherto stationary, the *birth-rate* begins to increase at the rate of 1 per cent. per annum. How would you determine the population at the end of the first, second, third ...... etc. years of this increased birth-rate?

The "Birth-Rate" is presumably the ratio of the number of births during a year to the population in the middle of that year.

Let l', l'', l''' represent the additional number of births in the first, second and third years respectively: that is, the number by which the births in these years exceed l_0. Then

Population at the end of the First Year of Increase

$$= T_0 + \frac{l'}{l_0} L_0.$$

Population at the end of the Second Year of Increase

$$= T_0 + \frac{l'}{l_0} L_1 + \frac{l''}{l_0} L_0.$$

Population at the end of the Third Year of Increase

$$= T_0 + \frac{l'}{l_0} L_2 + \frac{l''}{l_0} L_1 + \frac{l'''}{l_0} L_0.$$

etc.

In order to determine l', l'', l''', etc., we have

Birth-rate in First Year of Increase

$$= (1{\cdot}01)\frac{l_0}{T_0} = \frac{l_0 + l'}{T_0 + \frac{1}{2}\frac{l'}{l_0} L_0}.$$

Birth-rate in Second Year of Increase

$$= (1{\cdot}01)^2\frac{l_0}{T_0} = \frac{l_0 + l''}{T_0 + \frac{l'}{l_0} l_1 + \frac{1}{2}\frac{l''}{l_0} L_0}.$$

Birth-rate in Third Year of Increase

$$= (1{\cdot}01)^3\frac{l_0}{T_0} = \frac{l_0 + l'''}{T_0 + \frac{l'}{l_0} l_2 + \frac{l''}{l_0} l_1 + \frac{1}{2}\frac{l'''}{l_0} L_0}.$$

etc.

Considering the first year of increase, there will in the middle of the year be a population of T_0 *plus* the number living of the *extra* births in the first half of the year. If we dealt with l' births evenly distributed over the whole year, there would at the end of the year be $\frac{l'}{l_0} L_0$ of these surviving: up to the middle of the year there will have been $\frac{1}{2}l'$ of these extra births, and we can take the number of these alive at that time as $\frac{1}{2}\frac{l'}{l_0} L_0$.

The population at the middle of the year will thus be

$$T_0 + \frac{1}{2}\frac{l'}{l_0} L_0.$$

In the middle of the second year there will be (*a*) the original population of T_0, (*b*) the survivors of the extra births in the previous year, and (*c*) the survivors of the extra births occurring in the first half of the current year.

As regards (*b*), since the births were uniformly distributed over the year, we may consider, with sufficient accuracy, that they all occurred in the middle of the year. The number surviving in the middle of the second year will, therefore, be $\frac{l'}{l_0} \times l_1$.

For (*c*) the number is $\frac{1}{2}\frac{l''}{l_0} L_0$.

The total population in the middle of the second year is, therefore,

$$T_0 + \frac{l'}{l_0} \times l_1 + \frac{1}{2}\frac{l''}{l_0} \times L_0,$$

and so on for other years.

PART II

CHAPTERS XIII TO XIX

FUNCTIONS INVOLVING TWO OR MORE LIVES

PROBABILITIES OF LIFE AND DEATH

JOINT-LIFE AND LAST SURVIVOR ANNUITIES AND ASSURANCES

CONTINGENT ASSURANCES

REVERSIONARY ANNUITIES

CHAPTER XIII

JOINT AND SURVIVORSHIP PROBABILITIES

1. In order to obtain a clear view of the application of Mortality Tables to functions dependent on the existence of two or more lives, it is necessary to commence with an examination of the methods by which various probabilities of death or survival for different combinations of lives can be evaluated.

2. The first question that presents itself is, "What is the probability that two persons, one aged x and the other aged y, will both survive n years?" Since the probability of (x) surviving n years is ${}_np_x$, and of (y) so surviving, ${}_np_y$, and these are independent events, the probability that both (x) and (y) will survive n years is ${}_np_x \times {}_np_y$. This probability is denoted by ${}_np_{xy}$. Thus

$${}_np_{xy} = {}_np_x \times {}_np_y = \frac{l_{x+n}}{l_x} \cdot \frac{l_{y+n}}{l_y} \quad \ldots\ldots\ldots\ldots\ldots(1).$$

Similarly, the probability that m persons aged $w, x, y, z \ldots$ respectively will all survive n years is

$${}_np_{wxyz\ldots(m)} = {}_np_w \times {}_np_x \times {}_np_y \times {}_np_z \times \ldots (m \text{ factors}) \ \ldots(2).$$

3. The probability that *neither* of two lives (x) and (y) will survive n years, or that both will die within n years, is represented by ${}_{|n}Q_{\overline{xy}}$, the bar over the suffix denoting that the life of the survivor (i.e. the longer period) must fail within the n years.

The probability that (x) will die within n years is ${}_{|n}Q_x = 1 - {}_np_x$, and that (y) will so die, ${}_{|n}Q_y = 1 - {}_np_y$, and these being independent events the probability required is

$$\begin{aligned} {}_{|n}Q_{\overline{xy}} &= {}_{|n}Q_x \times {}_{|n}Q_y \\ &= (1 - {}_np_x)(1 - {}_np_y) \quad \ldots\ldots\ldots\ldots\ldots\ldots(3). \end{aligned}$$

If $n = 1$, this formula becomes $q_{\overline{xy}} = q_x \times q_y$.

This also can be extended to any number of lives. Thus

$${}_{|n}Q_{\overline{wxyz\ldots(m)}} = (1 - {}_np_w)(1 - {}_np_x)(1 - {}_np_y) \ldots (m \text{ factors})\ldots(4).$$

4. The probability that *one only* of the lives (x) and (y) will survive n years, and the other die within that period, is the sum of two separate probabilities, namely, (i) that (x) will survive and

(y) fail; and (ii) that (y) will survive and (x) fail. This probability being represented by ${}_np_{\overline{xy}}^{[1]}$ we have

$$\begin{aligned}{}_np_{\overline{xy}}^{[1]} &= {}_np_x(1-{}_np_y)+{}_np_y(1-{}_np_x)\\ &= {}_np_x+{}_np_y-2{}_np_{xy} \quad\quad (5).\end{aligned}$$

5. The probability that *at least* one of the lives (x) and (y) will survive n years is the sum of three probabilities, namely, (i) that (x) will survive and (y) fail, (ii) that (y) will survive and (x) fail, and (iii) that both will survive. Representing this probability by ${}_np_{\overline{xy}}$, we have

$$\begin{aligned}{}_np_{\overline{xy}} &= {}_np_x(1-{}_np_y)+{}_np_y(1-{}_np_x)+{}_np_{xy}\\ &= {}_np_x+{}_np_y-{}_np_{xy} \quad\quad (6).\end{aligned}$$

Looking at this last problem from another point of view, since either both lives must fail within n years, or at least one must survive that period, the sum of the probabilities of these two events is unity (i.e. ${}_{n|}Q_{\overline{xy}}+{}_np_{\overline{xy}}=1$), and the probability that at least one will survive is the complement of the probability that both lives fail within the n years, that is

$$\begin{aligned}{}_np_{\overline{xy}} &= 1-{}_{n|}Q_{\overline{xy}}\\ &= {}_np_x+{}_np_y-{}_np_{xy} \text{ as before.}\end{aligned}$$

6. The probability that the joint existence of (x) and (y) will fail within n years (i.e. that the first death will occur or that at least one life will fail within that period) is the complement of the probability that both will survive n years, and is represented by ${}_{n|}Q_{xy}$. Thus

$${}_{n|}Q_{xy}=1-{}_np_{xy} \quad\quad (7).$$

If $n=1$ this becomes the probability that the joint existence of the lives (x) and (y) will fail within one year; that is,

$$\begin{aligned}q_{xy} &= 1-p_{xy}\\ &= \frac{l_{xy}-l_{x+1:y+1}}{l_{xy}}.\end{aligned}$$

If the numerator of this expression be denoted by d_{xy} it is seen that $d_{xy}=l_{xy}-l_{x+1:y+1}$.

The difference between the relation of l_{xy} to l_x and l_y, and of d_{xy} to d_x and d_y, must be carefully noted:

$$l_{xy}=l_x\times l_y, \text{ but } d_x\times d_y=(l_x-l_{x+1})(l_y-l_{y+1}),$$

which as just proved is *not* equal to d_{xy}.

7. Probabilities relating to the $(t+1)$th year (two lives). The probability that the joint lives (x) and (y) will fail in the $(t+1)$th year, that is, that the first death amongst these two lives will occur in that year, is represented by ${}_{t|}q_{xy}$.

The value of this is obtained by taking the product of two probabilities, (i) that both lives will survive to the beginning of the $(t+1)$th year, and (ii) that, both lives having so survived, the joint lives will fail in that year. That is,

$$\begin{aligned} {}_{t|}q_{xy} &= {}_tp_{xy}\,(1 - p_{x+t:y+t}) \\ &= {}_tp_{xy} - {}_{t+1}p_{xy} \quad \text{.......................(8).} \end{aligned}$$

Expressing this in terms of the l and d columns, we have

$${}_{t|}q_{xy} = \frac{l_{x+t:y+t} - l_{x+t+1:y+t+1}}{l_{xy}} = \frac{d_{x+t:y+t}}{l_{xy}}.$$

8. The probability that *both* the lives (x) and (y) will fail in the $(t+1)$th year is the product of the two independent probabilities that, firstly, (x) and, secondly, (y) will die in that year. That is,

$${}_{t|}q_x \times {}_{t|}q_y = \frac{d_{x+t}}{l_x} \times \frac{d_{y+t}}{l_y} \quad \text{..................(9).}$$

9. The probability that the survivor of (x) and (y) will die in the $(t+1)$th year is represented by ${}_{t|}q_{\overline{xy}}$. In this case it is not essential that both lives survive to the beginning of the $(t+1)$th year, since even if one of the lives fail before the commencement of that year the survivor may die in the year. There are, in fact, three probabilities involved, namely:

(i) That (x) will die before the end of the tth year and (y) in the $(t+1)$th year, i.e.

$$(1 - {}_tp_x)\,{}_{t|}q_y = (1 - {}_tp_x)({}_tp_y - {}_{t+1}p_y);$$

(ii) That (y) will die before the end of the tth year and (x) in the $(t+1)$th year, i.e.

$$(1 - {}_tp_y)\,{}_{t|}q_x = (1 - {}_tp_y)({}_tp_x - {}_{t+1}p_x);$$

and (iii) That both (x) and (y) will die in the $(t+1)$th year, i.e.

$${}_{t|}q_x \times {}_{t|}q_y = ({}_tp_x - {}_{t+1}p_x)({}_tp_y - {}_{t+1}p_y).$$

The sum of these three probabilities is

$$\begin{aligned} {}_{t|}q_{\overline{xy}} &= ({}_tp_x + {}_tp_y - {}_tp_{xy}) - ({}_{t+1}p_x + {}_{t+1}p_y - {}_{t+1}p_{xy}) \\ &= {}_tp_{\overline{xy}} - {}_{t+1}p_{\overline{xy}} \quad \text{....................................(10),} \end{aligned}$$

which is clearly correct, since the probability required is the probability that the survivor of (x) and (y) will be alive at the commencement of the $(t+1)$th year *less* the probability that the survivor will be alive at the end of that year.

Since $({}_tp_x - {}_{t+1}p_x) = {}_{t|}q_x$, the expression for ${}_{t|}q_{\overline{xy}}$ can be put in the form

$$ {}_{t|}q_{\overline{xy}} = {}_{t|}q_x + {}_{t|}q_y - {}_{t|}q_{xy} \quad \text{.................(11).}$$

If $t=0$, this becomes $q_{\overline{xy}} = q_x + q_y - q_{xy}$, which alternative form could have been obtained from formula (3) as follows:

$$\begin{aligned} {}_{|n}Q_{\overline{xy}} &= (1 - {}_np_x)(1 - {}_np_y) \\ &= 1 - {}_np_x - {}_np_y + {}_np_{xy} \\ &= (1 - {}_np_x) + (1 - {}_np_y) - (1 - {}_np_{xy}) \\ &= {}_{|n}Q_x + {}_{|n}Q_y - {}_{|n}Q_{xy}. \end{aligned}$$

Whence, putting $n=1$,

$$q_{\overline{xy}} = q_x + q_y - q_{xy}.$$

10. The student should carefully note the difference between the three probabilities respectively represented by ${}_{t|}q_{xy}$, ${}_{t|}q_x \times {}_{t|}q_y$ and ${}_{t|}q_{\overline{xy}}$; and that though $q_{\overline{xy}}$ can be expressed in two ways, $q_x \times q_y$ and $q_x + q_y - q_{xy}$, the deferred probability ${}_{t|}q_{\overline{xy}}$ can only be expressed in the latter form.

11. The probability that (x) will die in the $(t+1)$th year being ${}_{t|}q_x$, the probability that he will not die in that year is $1 - {}_{t|}q_x$, and the probability that neither (x) nor (y) will die in the $(t+1)$th year is

$$(1 - {}_{t|}q_x)(1 - {}_{t|}q_y) \quad \text{.....................(12).}$$

12. The probability that one *at least* of the two lives will fail in the $(t+1)$th year is the complement of the probability that neither will fail in that year. That is

$$\begin{aligned} &1 - (1 - {}_{t|}q_x)(1 - {}_{t|}q_y) \\ &= {}_{t|}q_x + {}_{t|}q_y - {}_{t|}q_x \times {}_{t|}q_y \quad \text{.................(13).} \end{aligned}$$

This expression could also have been obtained by considering the problem in detail, the probability required being the sum of three distinct probabilities, namely:

(i) That (x) will die in the $(t+1)$th year and (y) will not die in that year: that is,

$${}_{t|}q_x(1 - {}_{t|}q_y).$$

(ii) That (y) will die in the $(t+1)$th year and (x) will not die in that year: that is,

$$_{t|}q_y(1 - {_{t|}q_x});$$

and (iii) That both (x) and (y) will die in that year: that is,

$$_{t|}q_x \times {_{t|}q_y}.$$

The sum of these three expressions is

$$_{t|}q_x + {_{t|}q_y} - {_{t|}q_x} \times {_{t|}q_y},$$

as before.

13. Alternative methods of obtaining $|_nQ_{xy}$, etc. The expressions for the probabilities represented by $|_nQ_{xy}$ and $|_nQ_{\overline{xy}}$ can be obtained by summing the values of $_{t|}q_{xy}$ and $_{t|}q_{\overline{xy}}$ respectively for all values of t from 0 to $n-1$. Thus

$$\begin{aligned} |_nQ_{xy} &= \sum_{t=0}^{t=n-1} {_{t|}q_{xy}} \\ &= \sum_{t=0}^{t=n-1} ({_tp_{xy}} - {_{t+1}p_{xy}}) \\ &= 1 - {_np_{xy}} \text{ as in formula (7).} \end{aligned}$$

Also

$$\begin{aligned} |_nQ_{\overline{xy}} &= \sum_{t=0}^{t=n-1} {_{t|}q_{\overline{xy}}} \\ &= \sum_{t=0}^{t=n-1} ({_{t|}q_x} + {_{t|}q_y} - {_{t|}q_{xy}}) \\ &= (1 - {_np_x}) + (1 - {_np_y}) - (1 - {_np_x} \times {_np_y}) \\ &= (1 - {_np_x})(1 - {_np_y}) \text{ as in formula (3).} \end{aligned}$$

14. When the probability the value of which is required refers to a period of years (say m) deferred for a number of years (say n), the formulae become

$$\begin{aligned} {_{n|m}Q_{xy}} &= \sum_{t=n}^{t=n+m-1} {_{t|}q_{xy}} \\ &= \left.\begin{aligned} &{_np_{xy}} - {_{n+m}p_{xy}} \\ &= |_{m+n}Q_{xy} - |_nQ_{xy} \end{aligned}\right\} \quad \ldots\ldots\ldots\ldots(14), \end{aligned}$$

and

$$\begin{aligned} {_{n|m}Q_{\overline{xy}}} &= \sum_{t=n}^{t=n+m-1} {_{t|}q_{\overline{xy}}} \\ &= {_{n|m}Q_x} + {_{n|m}Q_y} - {_{n|m}Q_{xy}} \quad \ldots\ldots\ldots\ldots(15). \end{aligned}$$

In the latter case we *cannot* write ${_{n|m}Q_{\overline{xy}}} = {_{n|m}Q_x} \times {_{n|m}Q_y}$, because in order that the *survivor* shall die between the end of the nth and the end of the $(n+m)$th year it is not necessary that both (x) and (y) shall be alive at the commencement of this period.

15. Probabilities involving three lives. The expressions for probabilities involving three or more lives can be obtained in the same manner as for two lives. It may be of assistance to include the following example.

Of three lives (x), (y) and (z), find the probability that in the ($t+1$)th year from the present time,

(a) one and one only will die,

(b) exactly two will die,

(c) at least one will die.

(a) $$_{t|}q_x(1-{}_{t|}q_y)(1-{}_{t|}q_z)+{}_{t|}q_y(1-{}_{t|}q_x)(1-{}_{t|}q_z)+{}_{t|}q_z(1-{}_{t|}q_x)(1-{}_{t|}q_y).$$

(b) $$_{t|}q_x\times{}_{t|}q_y(1-{}_{t|}q_z)+{}_{t|}q_x\times{}_{t|}q_z(1-{}_{t|}q_y)+{}_{t|}q_y\times{}_{t|}q_z(1-{}_{t|}q_x).$$

(c) $$1-(1-{}_{t|}q_x)(1-{}_{t|}q_y)(1-{}_{t|}q_z).$$

These expressions at first sight appear complicated but are actually in the most suitable form for evaluation, if we write

$$_{t|}q_x=\frac{d_{x+t}}{l_x},\quad {}_{t|}q_y=\frac{d_{y+t}}{l_y}\quad\text{and}\quad {}_{t|}q_z=\frac{d_{z+t}}{l_z}.$$

16. Probabilities involving any number of lives. If there are m lives all aged x, the probability that r designated lives will survive t years and the remaining $m-r$ lives will fail to survive that period is $({}_tp_x)^r(1-{}_tp_x)^{m-r}$; and since r lives can be selected in $\binom{m}{r}$ ways, the probability that exactly r lives out of the m will survive t years and the rest fail to survive that period is

$$\binom{m}{r}({}_tp_x)^r(1-{}_tp_x)^{m-r}$$

$$=\frac{\lfloor m}{\lfloor r\,\lfloor m-r}({}_tp_x)^r\left\{1-(m-r)\,{}_tp_x+\frac{(m-r)(m-r-1)}{\lfloor 2}({}_tp_x)^2-\frac{(m-r)(m-r-1)(m-r-2)}{\lfloor 3}({}_tp_x)^3+\dots\right\}$$

$$=\frac{\lfloor m}{\lfloor r\,\lfloor m-r}({}_tp_x)^r-\frac{\lfloor m}{\lfloor r+1\,\lfloor m-r-1}(r+1)({}_tp_x)^{r+1}+\frac{\lfloor m}{\lfloor r+2\,\lfloor m-r-2}\frac{(r+1)(r+2)}{\lfloor 2}({}_tp_x)^{r+2}-\dots$$

$$=\binom{m}{r}({}_tp_x)^r-(r+1)\binom{m}{r+1}({}_tp_x)^{r+1}+\frac{(r+1)(r+2)}{\lfloor 2}\binom{m}{r+2}({}_tp_x)^{r+2}-\dots.$$

If now m lives of different ages be substituted for m lives of equal age, $\binom{m}{r}({}_tp_x)^r$ will become the sum of the probabilities of r lives surviving t years for all combinations of r lives that can be made out of the m lives of unequal age. Representing this by Z^r, the probability that out of the m lives of unequal age (say, w, x, y, z ... (m lives)) exactly r lives will survive t years, the remaining $(m-r)$ failing during that period, is

$$\mathrm{Z}^r - (r+1)\,\mathrm{Z}^{r+1} + \frac{(r+1)(r+2)}{\underline{|2}}\,\mathrm{Z}^{r+2} - \dots$$
$$= \frac{\mathrm{Z}^r}{(1+\mathrm{Z})^{r+1}}.$$

This probability is represented by ${}_tp_{\overline{wxyz...(m)}}^{[r]}$, the square brackets enclosing the letter r denoting that *exactly* the number of survivors is under consideration. We therefore have

$${}_tp_{\overline{wxyz...(m)}}^{[r]} = \frac{\mathrm{Z}^r}{(1+\mathrm{Z})^{r+1}} \quad \text{.................(16).}$$

If $m=2$ and $r=1$, the ages being x and y,

$$\mathrm{Z} = {}_tp_x + {}_tp_y \text{ and } \mathrm{Z}^2 = {}_tp_{xy}.$$

Whence
$$ {}_tp_{\overline{xy}}^{[1]} = \frac{\mathrm{Z}}{(1+Z)^2} = \mathrm{Z} - 2\mathrm{Z}^2$$
$$= {}_tp_x + {}_tp_y - 2\,{}_tp_{xy},$$

as in formula (5).

Applying the formula to the probability that of four lives aged w, x, y and z respectively, exactly two will survive,

$$\mathrm{Z} = {}_tp_w + {}_tp_x + {}_tp_y + {}_tp_z,$$
$$\mathrm{Z}^2 = {}_tp_{wx} + {}_tp_{wy} + {}_tp_{wz} + {}_tp_{xy} + {}_tp_{xz} + {}_tp_{yz},$$
$$\mathrm{Z}^3 = {}_tp_{wxy} + {}_tp_{wxz} + {}_tp_{wyz} + {}_tp_{xyz},$$
$$\mathrm{Z}^4 = {}_tp_{wxyz},$$

and
$$ {}_tp_{\overline{wxyz}}^{[2]} = \frac{\mathrm{Z}^2}{(1+\mathrm{Z})^3}$$
$$= \mathrm{Z}^2 - 3\mathrm{Z}^3 + 6\mathrm{Z}^4$$
$$= {}_tp_{wx} + {}_tp_{wy} + {}_tp_{wz} + {}_tp_{xy} + {}_tp_{xz} + {}_tp_{yz}$$
$$- 3\,({}_tp_{wxy} + {}_tp_{wxz} + {}_tp_{wyz} + {}_tp_{xyz}) + 6\,{}_tp_{wxyz}.$$

17. The probability that out of m lives of unequal ages, *at least* r will survive, is the sum of the probabilities that exactly r, exactly $r+1$, etc., up to m lives will survive.

Representing this probability by ${}_tp_{\overline{wxyz\ldots(m)}}^{\;r}$, we have

$$
\begin{aligned}
{}_tp_{\overline{wxyz\ldots(m)}}^{\;r} &= {}_tp_{\overline{wxyz\ldots(m)}}^{\;[r]} + {}_tp_{\overline{wxyz\ldots(m)}}^{\;[r+1]} + \ldots \text{ etc.} \\
&= \frac{Z^r}{(1+Z)^{r+1}} + \frac{Z^{r+1}}{(1+Z)^{r+2}} + \frac{Z^{r+2}}{(1+Z)^{r+3}} + \ldots \\
&= \frac{Z^r}{(1+Z)^r} \quad\ldots\ldots\ldots\ldots\ldots\ldots\ldots\ldots(17),
\end{aligned}
$$

the series being summed to infinity since the terms which would involve more than m lives are necessarily zero.

Applying this formula to the case where $m=4$ and $r=2$, we have

$$
\begin{aligned}
{}_tp_{\overline{wxyz}}^{\;2} &= \frac{Z^2}{(1+Z)^2} \\
&= Z^2 - 2Z^3 + 3Z^4 \\
&= {}_tp_{wx} + {}_tp_{wy} + {}_tp_{wz} + {}_tp_{xy} + {}_tp_{xz} + {}_tp_{yz} \\
&\qquad - 2\,({}_tp_{wxy} + {}_tp_{wxz} + {}_tp_{wyz} + {}_tp_{xyz}) + 3\,{}_tp_{wxy}
\end{aligned}
$$

and when $m=2$ and $r=1$,

$$
\begin{aligned}
{}_tp_{\overline{xy}} &= \frac{Z}{1+Z} \\
&= Z - Z^2 \\
&= {}_tp_x + {}_tp_y - {}_tp_{xy},
\end{aligned}
$$

as obtained in formula (6).

When the probability refers to the survival of at least one life, the "1" is omitted from the symbol.

18. Great care must be exercised if the "Z" formulae be applied to probabilities that exactly or at least r lives *fail* within or after a certain period.

The probability that at least one of three lives (x), (y) and (z) will fail in the $(t+1)$th year was shown in paragraph 16 to be

$$
\begin{aligned}
1 - (1 - {}_{t|}q_x)&(1 - {}_{t|}q_y)(1 - {}_{t|}q_z) \\
&= {}_{t|}q_x + {}_{t|}q_y + {}_{t|}q_z - ({}_{t|}q_x \times {}_{t|}q_y + {}_{t|}q_x \times {}_{t|}q_z + {}_{t|}q_y \times {}_{t|}q_z) \\
&\qquad + {}_{t|}q_x \times {}_{t|}q_y \times {}_{t|}q_z.
\end{aligned}
$$

This probability referring to "at least" one life failing, the "Z" formula to be employed in its evaluation would be

$$\frac{Z}{1+Z} = Z - Z^2 + Z^3,$$

where Z^2 represents the sum of the probabilities of two lives *both* failing in the $(t+1)$th year for all combinations of two lives that can be made from the original number of lives.

The probability that the last survivor of three lives (x), (y) and (z) will die in the $(t+1)$th year is

$$_{t|}q_{\overline{xyz}} = {}_{t|}q_x + {}_{t|}q_y + {}_{t|}q_z - {}_{t|}q_{xy} - {}_{t|}q_{xz} - {}_{t|}q_{yz} + {}_{t|}q_{xyz}.$$

The event under consideration here may occur whether one, two or three lives fail in the $(t+1)$th year. With the provision, therefore, that the last death occurs in the $(t+1)$th year, this probability also refers to "at least" one life failing, and the Z formula to be employed in its evaluation would again be

$$\frac{Z}{1+Z} = Z - Z^2 + Z^3.$$

Here, however, Z^2 is the sum of the probabilities of the *joint* existence of two lives failing in the $(t+1)$th year, for all combinations of two lives which can be made from the original number.

In these two examples, therefore, Z^2 would have two distinct interpretations which are very easily confused, and it is advisable to avoid the risk of error thus introduced by dealing with such questions by more general reasoning.

19. If there are m lives aged x, what is the *most probable* number of deaths among them within a year?

The probability that exactly r lives fail and the rest survive is $\binom{m}{r} q_x^r \cdot p_x^{m-r}$. If therefore we make r successively equal to $0, 1, 2, \ldots m$ we shall have the following series, the successive terms of which represent the probability that there will be no deaths, exactly one death, exactly two deaths, etc. among the m persons:

$$p_x^m + mp_x^{m-1}q_x + \frac{m(m-1)}{\underline{|2}} p_x^{m-2}q_x^2 + \ldots + \binom{m}{r} p_x^{m-r}q_x^r + \ldots.$$

This series is the expansion of $(p_x + q_x)^m$ by the Binomial Theorem; and the sum of all the terms is unity, since $(p_x + q_x) = 1$.

In order to ascertain the most probable number of deaths, we must find the term in the above expansion which has the greatest numerical value.

The $(r+1)$th term > the rth term

so long as $\binom{m}{r} p_x^{m-r} q_x^r > \binom{m}{r-1} p_x^{m-r+1} q_x^{r-1}$,

$$\text{,,} \quad \frac{\dfrac{|\underline{m}}{|\underline{r}\,|\underline{m-r}} p_x^{m-r} q_x^r}{\dfrac{|\underline{m}}{|\underline{r-1}\,|\underline{m-r+1}} p_x^{m-r+1} q_x^{r-1}} > 1,$$

$$\text{,,} \quad \frac{m-r+1}{r}\frac{q}{p} > 1,$$

$$\text{,,} \quad \frac{m+1}{r} - 1 > \frac{p}{q},$$

$$\text{,,} \quad \frac{m+1}{r} > 1 + \frac{p}{q}$$

$$\text{,,} \quad (m+1)\,q > r.$$

The terms of the expansion, therefore, continue to increase until r is the greatest integer in $(m+1)\,q$, after which they decrease. The greatest term in the expansion is the $(r+1)$th, which involves q_x^r, and the most probable number of deaths is, therefore, r where r is the greatest integer in $(m+1)\,q_x$.

If, therefore, an Office have on its books at the beginning of a year m policies on lives aged x, the most probable number of claims that will arise among them in a year is the greatest integer in $(m+1)\,q_x$. If $(m+1)\,q_x$ be an integer, then $(m+1)\,q_x$ and $(m+1)\,q_x - 1$ claims are equally likely.

20. In practice it is usual to look at the *expected* deaths or expected amount of the claims during the year. In order to ascertain the *expected* claims, the probabilities of 0, 1, 2, ... deaths occurring must be multiplied by the amount that will be payable in respect of each number of claims. The series in paragraph 19 gives the probabilities of 0, 1, 2, ... deaths among m lives, and if we assume that each policy is for a sum assured of 1, the measure of the company's probable liability in respect of claims during the year will be

$$0\,.\,p_x^m + 1\,.\,mp_x^{m-1}q_x + 2\,.\,\frac{m(m-1)}{2}p_x^{m-2}q_x^2 + \ldots \text{ etc.}$$

$$= mq_x\left\{p_x^{m-1} + (m-1)\,p_x^{m-2}q_x + \frac{(m-1)(m-2)}{2}p_x^{m-3}q_x^2 + \ldots\right\}$$

$$= mq_x\,(p_x + q_x)^{m-1}$$

$$= mq_x.$$

It will be appreciated that this measure of the probable claims refers to claims by death only. In respect of endowment assurances maturing during the year the full sums assured must necessarily be made available for payments as these claims arise.

21. Joint Expectation of Life. The joint curtate expectation of life of two lives (x) and (y) is

$$e_{xy} = \sum_{t=1}^{t=\infty} {}_tp_{xy} \quad \text{......................(18)}$$

and the joint complete expectation of life of the same two lives

$$\begin{aligned} \mathring{e}_{xy} &= \int_0^\infty {}_tp_{xy}\,dt \\ &= \sum_{t=1}^{t=\infty} {}_tp_{xy} + \tfrac{1}{2} \text{ approx.} \\ &= e_{xy} + \tfrac{1}{2} \quad \text{..............................(19).} \end{aligned}$$

Also, we can write

$$\begin{aligned} e_{xy} &= p_{xy} \sum_{t=1}^{t=\infty} {}_{t-1}p_{x+1:y+1} \\ &= p_{xy}\,(1 + e_{x+1:y+1}), \end{aligned}$$

and
$$|_ne_{xy} = p_{xy}\,(1 + |_{n-1}e_{x+1:y+1}).$$

These formulae clearly follow the same lines as those for the expectation of life of a single life (x) given in Chapter XII.

22. Joint Life Probabilities under Gompertz's and Makeham's Laws. When a table follows Gompertz's Law the probability of survival of two or more lives of different ages can be expressed as the probability of survival of one life or any number of lives of equal age.

Thus, by Gompertz's Law

$$\begin{aligned} {}_tp_{xyz\ldots(m)} &= {}_tp_x \times {}_tp_y \times {}_tp_z \times \ldots\ m \text{ factors} \\ &= g^{(c^x + c^y + c^z + \ldots)\,(c^t - 1)}. \end{aligned}$$

If, therefore, an age w be found such that $rc^w = c^x + c^y + c^z + \ldots$ to m terms, where r is *any* selected number,

$$\begin{aligned} {}_tp_{xyz\ldots(m)} &= g^{rc^w(c^t-1)} \\ &= {}_tp_{www\ldots(r)} \quad \text{..................(20).} \end{aligned}$$

It is evident that r can equal unity, in which case

$$c^x + c^y + c^z + \ldots = c^w.$$

Since
$$e_{xyz\ldots(m)} = \sum_{t=1}^{t=\infty} {}_tp_{xyz\ldots(m)},$$
it follows that, when Gompertz's Law holds, we can write
$$e_{xyz\ldots(m)} = e_{www\ldots(r)},$$
where
$$rc^w = c^x + c^y + c^z + \ldots m \text{ terms}.$$

23. When a table follows Makeham's Law, the probability of survival of any number of lives of different ages can be expressed as the probability of survival of the *same number* of lives of equal age. Thus,
$$\begin{aligned} {}_tp_{xyz\ldots(m)} &= {}_tp_x \times {}_tp_y \times {}_tp_z \times \ldots m \text{ factors} \\ &= s^{mt} g^{(c^x+c^y+c^z+\ldots)\,(c^t-1)}, \end{aligned}$$
whence, if an age w can be found such that
$$mc^w = c^x + c^y + c^z + \ldots m \text{ terms},$$
we can write
$$\begin{aligned} {}_tp_{xyz\ldots(m)} &= s^{mt} g^{mc^w\,(c^t-1)} \\ &= {}_tp_{www\ldots(m)} \quad \ldots\ldots\ldots\ldots\ldots\ldots(21). \end{aligned}$$

For the joint expectation of life under Makeham's Law we can evidently write
$$e_{xyz\ldots(m)} = e_{www\ldots(m)}.$$

This property of Makeham's Law whereby the same number of lives of equal age can be substituted for a number of lives of different ages is dealt with more fully in Chapter XV on Joint Life and Last Survivor Annuities.

If in the equality $mc^w = c^x + c^y + c^z + \ldots m$ terms each side be multiplied by B, and if further mA be added to each side, we have
$$m(\text{A} + \text{B}c^w) = (\text{A} + \text{B}c^x) + (\text{A} + \text{B}c^y) + (\text{A} + \text{B}c^z) + \ldots m \text{ terms},$$
or
$$m\mu_w = \mu_x + \mu_y + \mu_z + \ldots m \text{ terms},$$
from which it is seen that the equal age w can be ascertained from a table of μ_x just as readily as from a table of c^x.

EXAMPLES

Ex. 1. Given that the probability that two persons aged 25 and 50 respectively will both live 25 years is ·27516, and that, by the same mortality table, out of 93044 persons alive at age twenty-five, 82277 attain age forty, what is the probability that a person aged 40 will survive till the attainment of age 75?

The question gives ${}_{25}p_{25} \times {}_{25}p_{50} = \cdot 27516$,

i.e. $$\frac{l_{50}}{l_{25}} \times \frac{l_{75}}{l_{50}} = \frac{l_{75}}{l_{25}} = \cdot 27516,$$

and $${}_{15}p_{25} = \frac{l_{40}}{l_{25}} = \frac{82277}{93044}.$$

It is required to find ${}_{35}p_{40}$.

$$\begin{aligned} {}_{35}p_{40} = \frac{l_{75}}{l_{40}} = \frac{l_{25}}{l_{40}} \cdot \frac{l_{75}}{l_{25}} &= \frac{93044}{82277} \times \cdot 27516 \\ &= \cdot 31117. \end{aligned}$$

Ex. 2. Find expressions for the probabilities that out of 25 persons aged x,

(*a*) exactly five will die in a year;

(*b*) not more than five will die in a year;

(*c*) five designated individuals and no more will die in a year;

(*d*) five designated individuals at least will die in a year.

(*a*) The five lives can be selected in $\binom{25}{5}$ ways, and the probability required is, therefore, $\binom{25}{5}(q_x)^5(p_x)^{20}$.

(*b*) This is the sum of the probabilities that there will be no death, one, two, three, four or five deaths in the year; and will be given by the expression

$$\begin{aligned} (p_x)^{25} + 25(p_x)^{24} \cdot q_x + \tbinom{25}{2}(p_x)^{23}(q_x)^2 + \tbinom{25}{3}(p_x)^{22}(q_x)^3 \\ + \tbinom{25}{4}(p_x)^{21}(q_x)^4 + \tbinom{25}{5}(p_x)^{20}(q_x)^5. \end{aligned}$$

(*c*) In this case there is no selection to be made: the probability is $(p_x)^{20}(q_x)^5$.

(*d*) Here it does not matter what happens to the other 20 lives, so long as we provide for the five designated individuals all dying. That is, $(q_x)^5$.

Ex. 3. Find the probabilities that amongst three lives all aged x, (*a*) the first death, (*b*) the second death, (*c*) the third death, will occur in the $(t+1)$th year.

(*a*) ${}_tp_{xxx} - {}_{t+1}p_{xxx}$,

where ${}_tp_{xxx} = ({}_tp_x)^3$.

(b) $${}_tp_{\overline{xxx}}^{\,2} - {}_{t+1}p_{\overline{xxx}}^{\,2}$$
$$= (3_tp_{xx} - 2_tp_{xxx}) - (3_{t+1}p_{xx} - 2_{t+1}p_{xxx})$$
$$= 3_{t|}q_{xx} - 2_{t|}q_{xxx},$$

where $${}_{t|}q_{xx} = \frac{l_{x+t}\,l_{x+t} - l_{x+t+1}\,l_{x+t+1}}{l_x\,l_x}.$$

(c) $${}_tp_{\overline{xxx}} - {}_{t+1}p_{\overline{xxx}}$$
$$= (3_tp_x - 3_tp_{xx} + {}_tp_{xxx}) - (3_{t+1}p_x - 3_{t+1}p_{xx} + {}_{t+1}p_{xxx})$$
$$= 3_{t|}q_x - 3_{t|}q_{xx} + {}_{t|}q_{xxx}.$$

A simpler form for the evaluation of (c) is

$$|_{t+1}Q_{\overline{xxx}} - |_tQ_{\overline{xxx}} = (1 - {}_{t+1}p_x)^3 - (1 - {}_tp_x)^3.$$

Ex. 4. A widows' annuity society pays an annuity of £10 per annum, the first payment being due at the end of the year in which the husband dies. The society is recruited at the beginning of each year by the entrance of 100 married couples, the husband being aged 30 and the wife 25. After five years from the formation of the society, how many widows will there be on the fund, and what will be the value of the pensions then payable?

Considering any one of the 100 couples who entered at the beginning of the first year, the probability that at the end of the fifth year the wife is still alive, her husband having died previously, is $(1 - {}_5p_{30})\,{}_5p_{25}$.

The number of widows, out of the first year's entrants, on the funds at the end of five years will therefore be

$$100\,(1 - {}_5p_{30})\,{}_5p_{25}.$$

Similarly from the couples who entered at the beginning of the second year, the number of widows on the funds at the end of the fifth year of the society's existence will be $100\,(1 - {}_4p_{30})\,{}_4p_{25}$; and so on for the other years.

The total number of widows on the funds at the end of the fifth year will therefore be

$$100\,(1 - {}_5p_{30})\,{}_5p_{25} + 100\,(1 - {}_4p_{30})\,{}_4p_{25} + \ldots + 100\,(1 - p_{30})\,p_{25}$$
$$= 100\,(|_5e_{25} - |_5e_{25:30}).$$

The value of the pensions then payable will be

$$100\,(1 - {}_5p_{30})\,{}_5p_{25} \times 10\mathbf{a}_{30} + 100\,(1 - {}_4p_{30})\,{}_4p_{25} \times 10\mathbf{a}_{29} + \ldots$$
$$+ 100\,(1 - p_{30})\,p_{25} \times 10\mathbf{a}_{26},$$

including the payments just due.

Ex. 5. A Life Office has the following whole-life assurances on its books, the sum assured in each case being £100:

930 policies on lives aged 25,
924 " " " 26,
917 " " " 27,
910 " " " 28,
904 " " " 29,
897 " " " 30.

On the basis of the H^M Table, what is the expected amount of claims during the following year?

The expected amount of claims is

$$100\,(930q_{25}+924q_{26}+917q_{27}+910q_{28}+904q_{29}+897q_{30})$$
$$=657{\cdot}510+665{\cdot}280+671{\cdot}244+678{\cdot}860+686{\cdot}136+691{\cdot}587$$
$$=4050{\cdot}617.$$
$$=\text{£}4050.\ 12s.\ 4d.$$

The actual amount will necessarily be a multiple of £100 and cannot therefore be exactly the "expected" amount which is however the measure employed in making provision for the liabilities that will fall due for payment during the year.

CHAPTER XIV

CONTINGENT PROBABILITIES

1. Probabilities involving two lives. To find the probability that (x) will die in the $(n+1)$th year from the present time, (y) being alive at the moment of death of (x).

Employing the argument used in Chapter I 16, ${}_tp_x$ is the probability that (x) will survive to time t, and $\mu_{x+t}\,dt$ is the probability that $(x+t)$ will die at that moment of age. The probability that (x) will die at moment of age $x+t$ is, therefore, ${}_tp_x\mu_{x+t}\,dt$.

Similarly, ${}_tp_y$ is the probability that (y) will survive to time t; and the probability that (x) will die at moment of time t, (y) being then alive, is consequently

$$\begin{aligned}&{}_tp_x\,\mu_{x+t}\,dt \times {}_tp_y\\ &= {}_tp_{xy}\,\mu_{x+t}\,dt \quad \text{.........................(1).}\end{aligned}$$

If this expression be integrated between the limits n and $n+1$ the result is the probability that (x) will die before (y) in the $(n+1)$th year. This probability being represented by ${}_{n|}q^1_{xy}$ we have

$${}_{n|}q^1_{xy} = \int_n^{n+1} {}_tp_{xy}\,\mu_{x+t}\,dt \quad \text{..................(2).}$$

Similarly, the probability that (x) will die before (y) within n years, ${}_{|n}Q^1_{xy}$, is obtained by integrating the same expression between the limits 0 and n, thus

$${}_{|n}Q^1_{xy} = \int_0^n {}_tp_{xy}\,\mu_{x+t}\,dt \quad \text{....................(3),}$$

and the total probability that (x) will die before (y) is

$$Q^1_{xy} = \int_0^\infty {}_tp_{xy}\,\mu_{x+t}\,dt \quad \text{.....................(4).}$$

Substituting for μ_{x+t} in the last two expressions the approximate value $\dfrac{l_{x+t-1} - l_{x+t+1}}{2l_{x+t}}$ the formulae become

$$\begin{aligned}{}_{|n}Q^1_{xy} &= \int_0^n \frac{l_{x+t}}{l_x}\cdot\frac{l_{y+t}}{l_y}\cdot\frac{l_{x+t-1} - l_{x+t+1}}{2l_{x+t}}\,dt\\ &= \frac{1}{2}\left\{\frac{l_{x-1}}{l_x}\int_0^n \frac{l_{y+t}}{l_y}\cdot\frac{l_{x-1+t}}{l_{x-1}}\,dt - \frac{l_{x+1}}{l_x}\int_0^n \frac{l_{y+t}}{l_y}\cdot\frac{l_{x+1+t}}{l_{x+1}}\,dt\right\}\\ &= \frac{1}{2}\left\{\frac{{}_{|n}\mathring{e}_{x-1:y}}{p_{x-1}} - p_x\cdot{}_{|n}\mathring{e}_{x+1:y}\right\} \quad \text{............................(5).}\end{aligned}$$

Similarly,

$$Q^1_{xy} = \frac{1}{2}\left\{\frac{\mathring{e}_{x-1:y}}{p_{x-1}} - p_x \cdot \mathring{e}_{x+1:y}\right\} \quad \text{..................(6).}$$

2. Another expression for the value of Q^1_{xy} is obtained by considering the differential coefficient of $\mathring{e}_{xy}$ with regard to x. Thus

$$\begin{aligned}\frac{d\mathring{e}_{xy}}{dx} &= \frac{d}{dx}\int_0^\infty {}_tp_{xy}\,dt \\ &= \int_0^\infty \left(\frac{d}{dx}\,{}_tp_x\right){}_tp_y\,dt \\ &= \int_0^\infty {}_tp_{xy}(\mu_x - \mu_{x+t})\,dt \\ &= \mu_x\,\mathring{e}_{xy} - Q^1_{xy},\end{aligned}$$

whence

$$\left.\begin{aligned}Q^1_{xy} &= \mu_x\,\mathring{e}_{xy} - \frac{d\mathring{e}_{xy}}{dx} \\ &= \mu_x\,\mathring{e}_{xy} + \tfrac{1}{2}(\mathring{e}_{x-1:y} - \mathring{e}_{x+1:y})\end{aligned}\right\} \quad \text{...............(7).}$$

The method of obtaining this expression should be compared with the method employed in Chapter VIII 6, to obtain a formula for the value of $\overline{A}_x$. A similar method is employed in Chapter XVI.

The corresponding formula for $|_nQ^1_{xy}$ is

$$|_nQ^1_{xy} = \mu_x|_n\mathring{e}_{xy} + \tfrac{1}{2}(|_n\mathring{e}_{x-1:y} - |_n\mathring{e}_{x+1:y}) \quad \text{.........(8).}$$

3. On the assumption of a uniform distribution of deaths over the year of age, (x) will on the average die in the middle of a year, and the probability that (x) will die in the $(t+1)$th year, (y) surviving him, may therefore be taken as the product of the probabilities that (i) (x) will die in the $(t+1)$th year, and (ii) (y) will be alive in the middle of that year. That is,

$${}_{t|}q^1_{xy} = \frac{d_{x+t}}{l_x} \cdot \frac{l_{y+t+\frac{1}{2}}}{l_y} \quad \text{.....................(9).}$$

The corresponding expression for the probability that (x) will die before (y) within n years is obtained by taking the finite integral of this expression between the limits 0 and $n-1$. That is,

$$|_nQ^1_{xy} = \sum_{t=0}^{t=n-1} \frac{d_{x+t}}{l_x} \cdot \frac{l_{y+t+\frac{1}{2}}}{l_y}$$

and, similarly,

$$Q^1_{xy} = \sum_{t=0}^{t=\infty} \frac{d_{x+t}}{l_x} \cdot \frac{l_{y+t+\frac{1}{2}}}{l_y}.$$

Since $d_{x+t} = l_{x+t} - l_{x+t+1}$ and $l_{y+t+\frac{1}{2}} = \frac{1}{2}(l_{y+t} + l_{y+t+1})$ these formulae become

$$\left|_n Q^1_{xy}\right. = \sum_{t=0}^{t=n-1} ({}_tp_x - {}_{t+1}p_x) \cdot \tfrac{1}{2}({}_tp_y + {}_{t+1}p_y)$$

$$= \frac{1}{2} \sum_{t=0}^{t=n-1} ({}_tp_{xy} - {}_{t+1}p_{xy} + {}_tp_x \cdot {}_{t+1}p_y - {}_{t+1}p_x \cdot {}_tp_y)$$

$$= \frac{1}{2} \sum_{t=0}^{t=n-1} \left({}_tp_{xy} - {}_{t+1}p_{xy} + \frac{{}_{t+1}p_{x-1:y}}{p_{x-1}} - \frac{{}_{t+1}p_{x:y-1}}{p_{y-1}}\right)$$

$$= \frac{1}{2}\left(1 - {}_np_{xy} + \frac{\left|_n e_{x-1:y}\right.}{p_{x-1}} - \frac{\left|_n e_{x:y-1}\right.}{p_{y-1}}\right) \quad \text{......................(10)},$$

and $$Q^1_{xy} = \sum_{t=0}^{t=\infty} ({}_tp_x - {}_{t+1}p_x) \cdot \tfrac{1}{2}({}_tp_y + {}_{t+1}p_y)$$

$$= \frac{1}{2}\left(1 + \frac{e_{x-1:y}}{p_{x-1}} - \frac{e_{x:y-1}}{p_{y-1}}\right) \quad \text{..................................(11)}.$$

4. The formulae for $\left|_n Q^1_{xy}\right.$ and Q^1_{xy} so far obtained contain the suffix $x-1$ and are accordingly unsuitable for use in connection with "Select Tables."

If, however, in formula (10) we write

$$\left|_n e_{x-1:y}\right. = p_{x-1:y}(1 + \left|_{n-1} e_{x:y+1}\right.),$$

and $$\left|_n e_{x:y-1}\right. = p_{x:y-1}(1 + \left|_{n-1} e_{x+1:y}\right.),$$

the expression becomes, inserting "select" symbols,

$$\left|_n Q^1_{[x]:[y]}\right. = \tfrac{1}{2}\{1 - {}_np_{[x]:[y]} + p_{[y]}(1 + \left|_{n-1} e_{[x]:[y]+1}\right.) - p_{[x]}(1 + \left|_{n-1} e_{[x]+1:[y]}\right.)\} \quad \text{...(12)}.$$

Formula (11) can similarly be written

$$Q^1_{[x]:[y]} = \tfrac{1}{2}\{1 + p_{[y]}(1 + e_{[x]:[y]+1}) - p_{[x]}(1 + e_{[x]+1:[y]})\} \quad \text{...(13)}.$$

Expressions (12) and (13) are of course applicable to both Select and Aggregate Tables.

In order to render formulae (5), (6), (7) and (8) applicable to Select Tables it would be necessary to employ a different approximation to the differential coefficient involved, but as the resulting formulae would not be of practical value, it is not thought necessary to extend the discussion.

5. Formulae (5) to (13) can only be used provided the appropriate values of the joint expectations of life are available, and as this is very seldom the case, the simplest method of evaluation of

a contingent probability such as Q^1_{xy} will (unless the Mortality Table follow Makeham's Law, to which reference will be made later) be by means of approximate integration.

As an example, let it be required to find the value of $Q^1_{30:60}$ by the H^M Table (Makeham Graduation). The integral for this value is

$$Q^1_{30:60} = \frac{1}{l_{30}\,l_{60}} \int_0^\infty l_{30+t}\,l_{60+t}\,\mu_{30+t}\,dt,$$

the approximate integration formula* which will be employed being

$$\int_0^\infty f(x)\,dx = n\,\{\cdot 28f(0) + 1\cdot 62f(n) + 2\cdot 2f(3n) + 1\cdot 62f(5n) + \cdot 56f(6n) + 1\cdot 62f(7n)\},$$

and as the probability must in any case terminate at the death of (60), we shall take $7n = 102 - 60$, whence $n = 6$.

The calculation is as follows:

t	0	n $=6$	$3n$ $=18$	$5n$ $=30$	$6n$ $=36$
$\log l_{30+t}$	—	4·9314	4·8748	4·7697	4·6737
$\log l_{60+t}$	—	4·6737	4·2645	3·1048	1·8513
$\log \mu_{30+t}$	$\bar{3}$·8854	$\bar{3}$·9425	$\bar{2}$·1424	$\bar{2}$·4654	$\bar{2}$·6627
$\text{colog } l_{30}\,l_{60}$	—	$\overline{10}$·2776	$\overline{10}$·2776	$\overline{10}$·2776	$\overline{10}$·2776
log coeff.	$\bar{1}$·4472	·2095	·3424	·2095	$\bar{1}$·7482
Sum =	$\bar{3}$·3326	$\bar{2}$·0347	$\bar{3}$·9017	$\bar{4}$·8270	$\bar{5}$·2135
$\log^{-1}$	·00215	·01083	·00797	·00067	·00002 = ·02164

6

$Q^1_{30:60} = \cdot 12984$

It is evident that, when $t = 0$, $\log l_{30}$ and $\log l_{60}$ added to $\text{colog } l_{30}\,l_{60}$ will give zero and these terms are accordingly omitted. The value of $f(7n)$ will also clearly be zero and there is, therefore, no object in adding to the work by extracting the various logarithms.

The method employed is equally suitable when Select Tables are employed and also when (30) and (60) are assumed to be subject to rates of mortality shown by different tables. In the latter case, $\text{colog } l_{30}$, $\log l_{30+t}$ and $\log \mu_{30+t}$ would be taken from one mortality table and $\text{colog } l_{60}$ and $\log l_{60+t}$ from another.

6. The probability that of two lives (x) and (y), (x) will die second, Q^2_{xy}, is the same as the probability that (y) will die first;

* This approximate integration formula is given on page 296 of "An Elementary Treatise on Actuarial Mathematics" by Harry Freeman, M.A., F.I.A. The formula is commonly known amongst Actuaries as "39 (a)," this being the number assigned to it in the original Institute of Actuaries Text Book, Part II.

i.e. $Q^{2}_{xy} = Q_{x\overset{1}{y}}$. Also since either (x) or (y) must die first (unless both die at the same moment, a contingency which can be neglected), $Q^{1}_{xy} + Q_{x\overset{1}{y}} = 1$, whence $Q^{1}_{xy} = 1 - Q^{2}_{xy}$ which also must be correct since (x) must die first or second.

When the probabilities are limited to a period of n years the formulae are different. Since the probability that (x) will die at moment of age $(x+t)$ is ${}_tp_x\,\mu_{x+t}\,dt$, and the probability that (y) will not survive to time t is $(1 - {}_tp_y)$; the probability that (x) will die at time t, (y) being already dead, is $(1 - {}_tp_y)\,{}_tp_x\,\mu_{x+t}\,dt$. Integrating this expression between the limits 0 and ∞ the result is the total probability that, at the moment of death of (x), (y) is already dead; that is, that (x) will die after (y); and if the limits be taken as 0 and n, the result is the probability that (x) will die after (y) within n years. That is,

$$\left|{}_nQ^{2}_{xy}\right. = \int_0^n (1 - {}_tp_y)\,{}_tp_x\,\mu_{x+t}\,dt$$

$$= \left|{}_nQ_x\right. - \left|{}_nQ^{1}_{xy}\right. \quad \text{..........................(14).}$$

7. The probability that (x) will be alive t years after the death of (y) is

$$\int_0^\infty {}_{n+t}p_x \cdot {}_np_y\,\mu_{y+n}\,dn$$

$$= {}_tp_x \int_0^\infty {}_np_{x+t:y}\,\mu_{y+n}\,dn$$

$$= {}_tp_x \cdot Q_{x+t:\overset{1}{y}} \quad \text{............................(15),}$$

or, on the assumption of a uniform distribution of deaths over the year of age,

$$\sum_{n=0}^{n=\infty} \frac{d_{y+n}}{l_y}\,\frac{l_{x+n+t+\frac{1}{2}}}{l_x}$$

$$= \frac{l_{x+t}}{l_x} \sum_{n=0}^{n=\infty} \frac{d_{y+n}}{l_y} \cdot \frac{l_{x+t+n+\frac{1}{2}}}{l_{x+t}}$$

$$= {}_tp_x \cdot Q_{x+t:\overset{1}{y}}.$$

In either case $Q_{x+t:\overset{1}{y}}$ will be evaluated by means of one of the formulae already given.

Similarly, the probability that (y) will be alive t years after the death of (x) is ${}_tp_y \cdot Q^{1}_{x:y+t}$, and the probability that at least t years will elapse between the two deaths is therefore

$${}_tp_x \cdot Q_{x+t:\overset{1}{y}} + {}_tp_y \cdot Q^{1}_{x:y+t} \quad \text{...............(16).}$$

It follows that the probability that two persons (x) and (y) will die *within* t years of each other is

$$1-({}_tp_x\,.\,Q_{x+t:\overset{1}{y}}+{}_tp_y\,.\,Q^1_{x:y+t})\quad\text{...........(17).}$$

If the lives are of the same age x, this last expression becomes $1-2{}_tp_x\,.\,Q^1_{x:x+t}$.

8. The probability that (x) will die before (y) or within t years after the death of (y) is the complement of the probability that (x) will be alive t years after the death of (y), or

$$1-{}_tp_x\,.\,Q_{x+t:\overset{1}{y}},$$

and the probability that (x) will die during the t years following the death of (y) is

$$\int_0^\infty ({}_np_x-{}_{n+t}p_x)\,{}_np_y\ \mu_{y+n}\,dn$$
$$=Q_{x\overset{1}{y}}-{}_tp_x\,.\,Q_{x+t:\overset{1}{y}},$$

which is evidently correct since the probability required is the probability that (x) survives (y) less the probability that (x) is alive t years after (y)'s death.

9. The probability that (x) will be alive *at the end of the tth year* succeeding that in which (y) dies may be found as follows·

$$\sum_{n=0}^{n=\infty}\frac{d_{y+n}}{l_y}\ \frac{l_{x+n+t+1}}{l_x}$$
$$={}_tp_x\sum_{n=0}^{n=\infty}({}_np_y-{}_{n+1}p_y)\,{}_{n+1}p_{x+t}$$
$$={}_tp_x\left\{p_{x+t}(1+e_{x+t+1:y})-e_{x+t:y}\right\}.$$

10. Probabilities involving three lives. Expressions for the values of more complicated contingent probabilities are most readily obtained, as a rule, by means of the Integral Calculus, and for the reasons stated in paragraph 5 most readily evaluated by approximate integration.

The formula for the probability that of three lives (x), (y) and (z), (x) will die first, Q^1_{xyz}, corresponding to formula (6) for Q^1_{xy}, is as follows:

$$Q^1_{xyz}=\int_0^\infty {}_tp_{xyz}\mu_{x+t}\,dt$$
$$=\int_0^\infty {}_tp_{xyz}\,\frac{l_{x+t-1}-l_{x+t+1}}{2l_{x+t}}\,dt\ \text{approx.}$$
$$=\frac{1}{2}\left(\frac{\mathring{e}_{x-1:yz}}{p_{x-1}}-p_x\,.\,\mathring{e}_{x+1:yz}\right)\quad\text{...........(18)}$$

or, commencing with $\dfrac{d\mathring{e}_{xyz}}{dx}$,

$$Q^1_{xyz} = \mu_x \mathring{e}_{xyz} - \frac{d\mathring{e}_{xyz}}{dx}$$

$$= \mu_x \mathring{e}_{xyz} + \tfrac{1}{2}(\mathring{e}_{x-1:yz} - \mathring{e}_{x+1:yz}) \quad \text{.............(19)},$$

corresponding to formula (7).

The expression for Q^1_{xyz} corresponding to formula (11) is too complicated for practical purposes.

11. When dealing with probabilities involving the order of deaths other than the first, it is instructive to reduce the formula to an expression containing only probabilities dependent on the first death, though it will frequently be quicker to obtain the required value directly from the integral by approximate integration.

The probability that of three lives (x), (y) and (z), (x) will die second, (y) having died first, is

$$Q^2_{x\underset{1}{y}z} = \int_0^\infty (1 - {}_tp_y)\, {}_tp_{xz}\, \mu_{x+t}\, dt,$$

where the condition is involved that at the moment of death of (x), (y) is already dead—$(1 - {}_tp_y)$—and (z) is still alive. Divided into two portions the expression becomes

$$Q^2_{x\underset{1}{y}z} = \int_0^\infty {}_tp_{xz}\, \mu_{x+t}\, dt - \int_0^\infty {}_tp_{xyz}\, \mu_{x+t}\, dt$$

$$= Q^1_{xz} - Q^1_{xyz} \quad \text{...............................(20)}.$$

This is evidently correct since the probability that (x) will die second, (y) having died first, must be the probability that (x) will die before (z), less the probability that he dies before (y) and (z).

12. When dealing with probabilities, the student is sometimes confused by the different ways in which the same question can be asked. For example, the problem might be to ascertain the probability that (z) will die third, (y) having died first (i.e. $Q_{x\underset{1}{y}z}^{\;3}$), but a little consideration shows that this is the same as the probability last dealt with, namely, that (x) will die second, (y) having died first. That is, $Q^2_{x\underset{1}{y}z} = Q_{x\underset{1}{y}z}^{\;3}$.

13. The probability that of three lives (x), (y) and (z), (x) will die second, regardless of the order of the other deaths, is the sum of the probabilities that (x) will die second, (y) having died first, and that (x) will die second, (z) having died first. That is,

$$\begin{aligned} Q^2_{xyz} &= Q^2_{x\underset{1}{y}z} + Q^2_{xy\underset{1}{z}} \\ &= Q^1_{xz} + Q^1_{xy} - 2Q^1_{xyz} \quad \ldots\ldots\ldots\ldots\ldots(21). \end{aligned}$$

14. The probability that (x) will die third of the three lives (x), (y) and (z) is, since at the moment of death of (x), (y) and (z) must be already dead,

$$\begin{aligned} Q^3_{xyz} &= \int_0^\infty (1 - {}_tp_y)(1 - {}_tp_z)\, {}_tp_x \mu_{x+t}\, dt \\ &= \int_0^\infty (1 - {}_tp_y - {}_tp_z + {}_tp_{yz})\, {}_tp_x \mu_{x+t}\, dt \\ &= 1 - Q^1_{xy} - Q^1_{xz} + Q^1_{xyz} \quad \ldots\ldots\ldots\ldots\ldots\ldots\ldots\ldots(22). \end{aligned}$$

This is clearly also the probability that the survivor of (y) and (z) will die before (x). That is, $Q^3_{xyz} = Q_{x:\overset{1}{\overline{yz}}}$.

15. The probability that (x) will die before the survivor of (y) and (z), $Q^1_{x:\overline{yz}}$, is the complement of the probability that (x) will die third. That is,

$$\begin{aligned} Q^1_{x:\overline{yz}} &= 1 - Q^3_{xyz} \\ &= Q^1_{xy} + Q^1_{xz} - Q^1_{xyz} \quad \ldots\ldots\ldots\ldots\ldots\ldots(23). \end{aligned}$$

Expressed in the form of an integral, this probability is

$$\begin{aligned} &\int_0^\infty {}_tp_x \mu_{x+t} \cdot {}_tp_{\overline{yz}}\, dt \\ &= \int_0^\infty {}_tp_x \mu_{x+t} ({}_tp_y + {}_tp_z - {}_tp_{yz})\, dt \\ &= Q^1_{xy} + Q^1_{xz} - Q^1_{xyz} \end{aligned}$$

as before.

The symbol for this probability might also be written $Q^{1:2}_{x:yz}$, representing the probability that of three lives (x), (y) and (z), (x) will die first or second.

16. Another probability that must be considered is that the joint existence of two lives (x) and (y) will fail during the lifetime of (z), $Q_{\overset{1}{\overline{xy}}:z}$.

This is the sum of the two probabilities, that of the three lives, firstly, (x) will die first, and secondly, (y) will die first. That is,

$$Q_{\overset{1}{\overline{xy}}:z} = Q^1_{xyz} + Q_{x\overset{1}{y}z} \quad \ldots\ldots\ldots\ldots\ldots\ldots(24).$$

17. Probabilities involving four lives. Having dealt with most of the probabilities concerning the order of dying of two or three lives it is only necessary to give one or two examples involving four lives.

Considering four lives (w), (x), (y) and (z), the probability that (x) will die second, (w) having died first, is

$$Q_{\underset{1}{w}\overset{2}{x}yz} = \int_0^\infty (1 - {}_tp_w)\, {}_tp_{xyz}\mu_{x+t}\,dt$$

$$= Q_{\overset{1}{x}yz} - Q_{w\overset{1}{x}yz} \quad \ldots\ldots\ldots\ldots\ldots\ldots\ldots\ldots\ldots(25).$$

The probability that (x) will die second, regardless of the order of the deaths of the others, is

$$Q_{w\overset{2}{x}yz} = \int_0^\infty {}_tp_{\overline{wyz}}^{[2]} \cdot {}_tp_x\mu_{x+t}\,dt,$$

since if (x) is to die second there must at the moment of his death be *exactly* two of the others still alive; whence

$$Q_{w\overset{2}{x}yz} = \int_0^\infty ({}_tp_{wy} + {}_tp_{wz} + {}_tp_{yz} - 3\,{}_tp_{wyz})\, {}_tp_x\mu_{x+t}\,dt$$

$$= Q_{w\overset{1}{x}y} + Q_{w\overset{1}{x}z} + Q_{\overset{1}{x}yz} - 3Q_{w\overset{1}{x}yz} \ldots\ldots\ldots\ldots\ldots\ldots\ldots(26).$$

Similarly, the probability that (x) will die third is

$$Q_{w\overset{3}{x}yz} = \int_0^\infty {}_tp_{\overline{wyz}}^{[1]} \cdot {}_tp_x\mu_{x+t}\,dt$$

$$= \int_0^\infty ({}_tp_w + {}_tp_y + {}_tp_z - 2\,{}_tp_{wy} - 2\,{}_tp_{wz} - 2\,{}_tp_{yz} + 3\,{}_tp_{wyz})\, {}_tp_x\mu_{x+t}\,dt$$

$$= Q_{w\overset{1}{x}} + Q_{\overset{1}{x}y} + Q_{\overset{1}{x}z} - 2Q_{w\overset{1}{x}y} - 2Q_{w\overset{1}{x}z} - 2Q_{\overset{1}{x}yz} + 3Q_{w\overset{1}{x}yz} \quad \ldots\ldots(27).$$

If the problem be to find the probability that (x) will die first, second or third of the four lives, it is necessary to provide that *one at least* of the other three survives him. That is,

$$Q^{1:2:3}_{\ \ x\ \ :wyz} = \int_0^\infty {}_tp_{\overline{wyz}} \cdot {}_tp_x\mu_{x+t}\,dt$$

$$= \int_0^\infty ({}_tp_w + {}_tp_y + {}_tp_z - {}_tp_{wy} - {}_tp_{wz} - {}_tp_{yz} + {}_tp_{wyz})\, {}_tp_x\mu_{x+t}\,dt$$

$$= Q_{w\overset{1}{x}} + Q_{\overset{1}{x}y} + Q_{\overset{1}{x}z} - Q_{w\overset{1}{x}y} - Q_{w\overset{1}{x}z} - Q_{\overset{1}{x}yz} + Q_{w\overset{1}{x}yz} \ldots\ldots\ldots(28),$$

which is equal to $\qquad Q_{w\overset{1}{x}yz} + Q_{w\overset{2}{x}yz} + Q_{w\overset{3}{x}yz}$.

18. The probability that of four lives (w), (x), (y) and (z), (y) will die third, (w) having died first and (x) second, is

$$Q_{\underset{1}{w}\underset{2}{x}\overset{3}{y}z} = \int_0^\infty (1 - {}_tp_w)\, {}_tp_{xyz}\mu_{x+t}\, Q_{\overset{1}{\overline{y+t}}:z+t}\,dt \ldots\ldots\ldots(29).$$

To evaluate this expression it would be necessary to employ an approximate summation formula, the value of $Q_{\overset{1}{y+t}:z+t}$ being separately obtained for each value of t employed in the calculation.

19. Contingent Probabilities under Gompertz's and Makeham's Laws. If a Mortality Table follow Gompertz's Law, the probability that of m lives (x), (y), (z), ... etc. (x) will die first can be expressed in a very simple form. Thus, since $\mu_{x+t} = \mathrm{B}c^{x+t}$,

$$Q^1_{xyz\ldots(m)} = \int_0^\infty {}_tp_{xyz\ldots(m)}\,\mathrm{B}c^{x+t}dt$$

$$= \frac{c^x}{c^x+c^y+c^z+\ldots(m\,\text{terms})}\int_0^\infty {}_tp_{xyz\ldots(m)}\,\mathrm{B}c^t\,(c^x+c^y+c^z+\ldots m\text{ terms})dt$$

$$\left.\begin{aligned} &= \frac{c^x}{c^x+c^y+c^z+\ldots(m\text{ terms})} \\ &= \frac{\mu_x}{\mu_x+\mu_y+\mu_z+\ldots(m\text{ terms})}\end{aligned}\right\} \quad\ldots\ldots\ldots\ldots(30),$$

since the integral represents the probability that the joint lives (x), (y), (z), ... etc. will fail, the value of which is unity.

When the lives are all of the same age x, the formula becomes

$$Q^1_{xxx\ldots(m)} = \frac{c^x}{mc^x} = \frac{1}{m},$$

which is clearly correct whatever mortality table be employed, because if all the lives are of the same age and subject to the same risk of mortality, each has the same chance of dying first.

For the probability of (x) dying first of the m lives within n years, we have, when the table follows Gompertz's Law,

$${}_n|Q^1_{xyz\ldots(m)} = \int_0^n {}_tp_{xyz\ldots(m)}\,\mathrm{B}c^{x+t}dt$$

$$= \frac{c^x}{c^x+c^y+c^z+\ldots m\text{ terms}}\int_0^n {}_tp_{xyz\ldots(m)}\,\mathrm{B}c^t(c^x+c^y+c^z+\ldots m\text{ terms})\,dt$$

$$= Q^1_{xyz\ldots(m)} \times {}_n|Q_{xyz\ldots(m)} \quad\ldots\ldots\ldots\ldots(31).$$

That is, the probability of (x) dying first within n years is equal to the probability that (x) will die first multiplied by the probability that the joint lives will fail within the n years. This equality only holds when Gompertz's Law applies, but has been occasionally made use of as sufficiently accurate in connection with mortality tables which do not follow that law.

20. If a table follow Makeham's Law, we have

$$Q^1_{xyz\dots(m)} = \int_0^\infty {}_tp_{xyz\dots(m)}\,(\mathrm{A} + \mathrm{B}c^{x+t})\,dt$$

$$= \mathrm{A}\mathring{e}_{xyz\dots(m)} + \frac{c^x}{c^x + c^y + c^z + \dots m \text{ terms}}$$

$$\times \int_0^\infty {}_tp_{xyz\dots(m)}\,\mathrm{B}c^t\,(c^x + c^y + c^z + \dots m \text{ terms})\,dt$$

$$= \mathrm{A}\mathring{e}_{xyz\dots(m)} + \frac{c^x}{c^x + c^y + c^z + \dots m \text{ terms}}$$

$$\times \int_0^\infty {}_tp_{xyz\dots(m)}\,(\mu_{x+t} + \mu_{y+t} + \mu_{z+t} + \dots m \text{ terms} - m\mathrm{A})\,dt$$

$$= \mathrm{A}\mathring{e}_{xyz\dots(m)} + \frac{c^x}{c^x + c^y + c^z + \dots(m)}\,(Q_{xyz\dots(m)} - m\mathrm{A}\mathring{e}_{xyz\dots(m)}),$$

whence, if we can find an age w, such that

$$mc^w = c^x + c^y + c^z + \dots \text{ to } m \text{ terms},$$

$$Q^1_{xyz\dots(m)} = \mathrm{A}\mathring{e}_{www\dots(m)} + \frac{c^x}{mc^w}\,(1 - m\mathrm{A}\mathring{e}_{www\dots(m)})$$

$$= \frac{c^x}{c^w}\left(\frac{1}{m} + \log_e s\,.\,\mathring{e}_{www\dots(m)}\right) - \log_e s\,.\,\mathring{e}_{www\dots(m)} \dots\dots(32).$$

This last expression does *not* give the value of $Q^1_{www\dots(m)}$ to obtain which we must write $x = y = z = \dots = w$ on the right-hand side of the equation, the result being $Q^1_{www\dots(m)} = \frac{1}{m}$.

When a table follows Makeham's Law the temporary contingent probability does not take so convenient a form as when Gompertz's Law holds. The formula when Makeham's Law holds is

$$\left|{}_nQ^1_{xyz\dots(m)} = \frac{c^x}{c^x + c^y + c^z + \dots m \text{ terms}}\right.$$

$$\times \left(\left|{}_nQ_{xyz\dots(m)} - m\mathrm{A}\,.\,\right|{}_n\mathring{e}_{xyz\dots(m)}\right) + \mathrm{A}\,.\,\left|{}_n\mathring{e}_{xyz\dots(m)}\right.$$

$$= \frac{c^x}{c^w}\left(\frac{1}{m}\cdot\left|{}_nQ_{www\dots(m)} + \log_e s\,.\,\right|{}_n\mathring{e}_{www\dots(m)}\right)$$

$$- \log_e s\,.\,\left|{}_n\mathring{e}_{www\dots(m)}\right. \dots\dots\dots\dots(33),$$

where $mc^w = c^x + c^y + c^z + \dots$ to m terms.

It is seen from formulae (32) and (33) that if expectations of life for equal ages are tabulated, the calculation of contingent probabilities by a table following Makeham's Law is very simple.

The values of e_{xx}, e_{xxx}, and e_{xxxx} for the H^{M} Table (Makeham Graduation) are given on page 413.

21. It was pointed out in Chapter XIII 10, that there are two forms of $q_{\overline{xy}}$, namely, $q_x \times q_y$ and $q_x + q_y - q_{xy}$, but that the latter form only can be applied to the deferred probability $_{t|}q_{\overline{xy}}$.

The following is an interesting example in which there is also a danger of the wrong form being employed.

The probability that two persons aged 25 and 30 will both die before reaching age 50 can be expressed as either

$$|_{25}Q_{25} + |_{20}Q_{30} - (|_{20}Q_{25:30} + {}_{20}p_{25:30} \cdot |_{5}Q_{45}),$$

or

$$|_{25}Q_{25} \times |_{20}Q_{30}.$$

But if the problem be to find the probability that both (25) and (30) will die before reaching age (50) and in the lifetime of (40) we can adopt one form only, namely:

$$|_{25}Q^{1}_{25:40} + |_{20}Q^{1}_{30:40} - (|_{20}Q^{\;\;\;\;1}_{\overline{25:30}:40} + {}_{20}p_{25:30:40} \cdot |_{5}Q^{1}_{45:60}).$$

The expression $|_{25}Q^{1}_{25:40} \times |_{20}Q^{1}_{30:40}$ is not correct, because if (40) die first both probabilities fail, and they are therefore *not* independent.

22. The integral expressing the value of $|_{n}Q_{xy}$ is

$$\int_0^n {}_tp_{xy}\,\mu_{x+t:y+t}\,dt$$

and the combined integral expressing the value of $|_{n}Q^{1}_{xy} + |_{n}Q_{x\overset{1}{y}}$ is

$$\int_0^n {}_tp_{xy}\,(\mu_{x+t} + \mu_{y+t})\,dt;$$

whence, since $\quad |_{n}Q_{xy} = |_{n}Q^{1}_{xy} + |_{n}Q_{x\overset{1}{y}},$

it follows that $\quad \mu_{x+t:y+t} = \mu_{x+t} + \mu_{y+t}$ ....(34).

That this is so can be shown as follows:

$$\mu_{x+t} = -\frac{1}{l_{x+t}} \cdot \frac{d\,l_{x+t}}{dt}$$

$$= -\frac{d\log_e l_{x+t}}{dt}$$

and

$$\mu_{x+t:y+t} = -\frac{d\log_e l_{x+t:y+t}}{dt}$$

$$= -\frac{d\log_e l_{x+t}}{dt} - \frac{d\log_e l_{y+t}}{dt}$$

$$= \mu_{x+t} + \mu_{y+t}.$$

A similar equality holds for any number of lives, and we can therefore write

$$\mu_{xyz\ldots(m)} = \mu_x + \mu_y + \mu_z + \ldots \ (m \text{ terms}) \ldots\ldots\ldots(35).$$

EXAMPLES

Ex. 1. Three persons A, B, and C are of the same age. Find the probability that between the end of the mth and the end of the $(m+n)$th years: (1) one at least will die, (2) all will die, A dying first and B second.

Find also the probability that A and B will die within this period and that C will survive the $(m+n)$th year.

(1) The probability that any one of the lives will die in the period named is ${}_mp_x - {}_{m+n}p_x$, and that he will not so die

$$1 - ({}_mp_x - {}_{m+n}p_x).$$

The probability that none of the three lives will fail in this period is therefore $\{1 - ({}_mp_x - {}_{m+n}p_x)\}^3$, and that one at least will die

$$1 - \{1 - ({}_mp_x - {}_{m+n}p_x)\}^3.$$

(2) The probability that all will die in the period named is $({}_mp_x - {}_{m+n}p_x)^3$, but since they can die in six different orders, and one specified order is mentioned, the required probability is

$$\tfrac{1}{6}({}_mp_x - {}_{m+n}p_x)^3.$$

(3) In this case the selection is already made, and the probability is

$$({}_mp_x - {}_{m+n}p_x)^2 \, {}_{m+n}p_x.$$

Ex. 2. Express in the form of integrals:

(i) the probability that (x), (y), and (z) will all die within n years in the order named, (x) within one year of (y) and (y) within one year of (z);

(ii) the probability that (x), (y), and (z) will all die within n years, at least m years separating any two deaths $(n > 2m)$.

(i) In this case the probability must be divided into three sections, namely (a) the first year, when if (y) die there is no possibility of a year having elapsed since the death of (x), (b) the period from the second year to the last but one, when there is time for a year to elapse on either side of the death of (y), and (c) the last year, when if (y) die it is not possible for a year to elapse *after* his death.

The probability required is

$$\int_0^1 {}_tp_y\,\mu_{y+t}\,(1-{}_tp_x)\,({}_tp_z-{}_{t+1}p_z)\,dt$$

$$+\int_1^{n-1} {}_tp_y\,\mu_{y+t}\,({}_{t-1}p_x-{}_tp_x)\,({}_tp_z-{}_{t+1}p_z)\,dt$$

$$+\int_{n-1}^{n} {}_tp_y\,\mu_{y+t}\,({}_{t-1}p_x-{}_tp_x)\,({}_tp_z-{}_np_z)\,dt.$$

(ii) Assume that the order of the deaths is x, y, z, then the probability is

$$\int_m^{n-m} (1-{}_{t-m}p_x)\,{}_tp_y\,\mu_{y+t}\,({}_{t+m}p_z-{}_np_z)\,dt.$$

The required probability consists of the sum of this and five similar integrals based respectively on the deaths occurring in the orders

$$z, y, x : x, z, y : y, z, x : y, x, z : z, x, y.$$

Ex. 3. The probability that a life aged 20 dies before a life aged 40 is ·2697, the probability that a life aged 20 dies within 10 years is ·0735 and that a life aged 30 dies within 10 years is 1005. Find the probability that two lives aged 20 and 30 will die within 10 years of each other.

We are given

$$Q^1_{20:40}=\cdot 2697,$$

$$_{10|}Q_{20}=\cdot 0735,$$

$$_{10|}Q_{30}=\cdot 1005.$$

The probability required is

$$1-\left(\int_0^\infty {}_tp_{20}\,\mu_{20+t}\,.\,{}_{t+10}p_{30}\,dt+\int_0^\infty {}_tp_{30}\,\mu_{30+t}\,.\,{}_{t+10}p_{20}\,dt\right)$$

$$=1-({}_{10}p_{30}\,.\,Q^1_{20:40}+{}_{10}p_{20}\,.\,Q^1_{30:30})$$

$$=1-({}_{10}p_{30}\,.\,Q^1_{20:40}+\tfrac{1}{2}\,{}_{10}p_{20})$$

$$=1-(\cdot 8995\times\cdot 2697+\tfrac{1}{2}\times\cdot 9265)$$

$$=\cdot 2942.$$

Ex. 4. Find by the H^{M} Table, in the case of two lives aged 24 and 22 respectively,

(*a*) the probability that one at least will die before attaining age 40;

(*b*) the probability that the last survivor will die aged 40.

(*a*) $$1 - {}_{16}p_{24} \times {}_{18}p_{22}$$

$$= 1 - \frac{l_{40}}{l_{24}} \cdot \frac{l_{40}}{l_{22}}$$

$$= \cdot 2388.$$

(*b*) $$\frac{d_{40}}{l_{24}}\left(1 - \frac{l_{22+16\frac{1}{2}}}{l_{22}}\right) + \frac{d_{40}}{l_{22}}\left(1 - \frac{l_{24+18\frac{1}{2}}}{l_{24}}\right)$$

$$= \cdot 00231.$$

It might, at first sight, appear that the following expression was correct, namely,

$$\frac{d_{40}}{l_{24}}\left(1 - \frac{l_{40}}{l_{22}}\right) + \frac{d_{40}}{l_{22}}\left(1 - \frac{l_{40}}{l_{24}}\right) + \frac{d_{40}}{l_{24}} \frac{d_{40}}{l_{22}}$$

$$= \frac{d_{40}}{l_{24}}\left(1 - \frac{l_{40\frac{1}{2}}}{l_{22}}\right) + \frac{d_{40}}{l_{22}}\left(1 - \frac{l_{40\frac{1}{2}}}{l_{24}}\right).$$

A little consideration will show, however, that this is incorrect. The terms of the question would be satisfied even if (24) died at age 41 or 42, so long as he died before (22) and the latter died at age 40; but the last expression does not take this into account.

CHAPTER XV

JOINT-LIFE ANNUITIES. ANNUITIES PAYABLE UNTIL THE DEATH OF THE LAST SURVIVOR OF TWO OR MORE LIVES

1. **Joint-Life Annuities.** The values of joint-life annuities, whether immediate or deferred, can be expressed in precisely similar terms to those employed in Chapter III in connection with single-life annuities.

2. The value of an endowment of 1 payable at the end of t years, if both (x) and (y) be then alive, is $v^t\,{}_tp_{xy}$, and the value of an annuity of 1 payable at the end of each year that both the lives (x) and (y) survive—that is, the value of an annuity of 1 payable annually on the joint lives of (x) and (y)—is

$$a_{xy} = \sum_{t=1}^{t=\infty} v^t\,{}_tp_{xy} \quad\ldots\ldots\ldots\ldots\ldots\ldots\ldots\ldots(1).$$

Similarly, for temporary and deferred joint-life annuities,

$$|_n a_{xy} = \sum_{t=1}^{t=n} v^t\,{}_tp_{xy} \quad\ldots\ldots\ldots\ldots\ldots\ldots\ldots\ldots(2),$$

$$_{n|}a_{xy} = \sum_{t=n+1}^{t=\infty} v^t\,{}_tp_{xy}\ldots\ldots\ldots\ldots\ldots\ldots\ldots\ldots(3).$$

Similar expressions hold whatever the number of lives involved. Thus the value of a whole-life joint-life annuity on m lives aged $w, x, y, z, \ldots$ etc. is

$$a_{wxyz\ldots(m)} = \sum_{t=1}^{t=\infty} v^t\,{}_tp_{wxyz\ldots(m)},$$

the corresponding temporary and deferred annuity values being

$$|_n a_{wxyz\ldots(m)} = \sum_{t=1}^{t=n} v^t\,{}_tp_{wxyz\ldots(m)},$$

$$_{n|}a_{wxyz\ldots(m)} = \sum_{t=n+1}^{t=\infty} v^t\,{}_tp_{wxyz\ldots(m)}.$$

Expressions for the value of $a_{xy}^{(m)}$, $a_{xyz}^{(m)}$, etc. can be found in the same manner as those for $a_x^{(m)}$ were found in Chapter VII, the variable being taken as the combined status (xy), (xyz), etc. The formulae then become, for two and three lives,

$$a_{xy}^{(m)} = a_{xy} + \frac{m-1}{2m} - \frac{m^2-1}{12m^2}(\mu_x + \mu_y + \delta) \quad \text{.........(4).}$$

$$a_{xyz}^{(m)} = a_{xyz} + \frac{m-1}{2m} - \frac{m^2-1}{12m^2}(\mu_x + \mu_y + \mu_z + \delta) \quad \text{......(5).}$$

Similarly,

$$\bar{a}_{xy} = a_{xy} + \tfrac{1}{2} - \tfrac{1}{12}(\mu_x + \mu_y + \delta) \quad \text{.........(6),}$$

$$\bar{a}_{xyz} = a_{xyz} + \tfrac{1}{2} - \tfrac{1}{12}(\mu_x + \mu_y + \mu_z + \delta) \quad \text{.........(7).}$$

3. Difficulties arise in the practical evaluation of joint-life annuities, it being clearly impossible to tabulate values of annuities on more than two lives for all combinations of lives that can occur.

In practice, unless a table follow Makeham's Law, to which special reference will be made later, the tables of values of joint-life annuities are generally limited to those on two lives, the values being given to three places of decimals.

4. Commutation columns for two joint lives have been suggested on two different plans. The form adopted by Griffith Davies is

$$D_{xy} = v^x l_x l_y \quad \text{.........(8),}$$

where (x) is the older of the two lives. The power of v is here made to depend only on the age of (x), although the lives are symmetrically involved, and where ordinary benefits only are under consideration, no inconvenience is experienced. But if the order of survivorship of the lives be in question, as for instance in the case of contingent assurances (to be discussed in Chap. XVII), we shall find that Davies's form of Joint-Life Commutation columns involves us in complexity; two cases requiring solution, namely, for $x > y$ and $x < y$. In order to avoid the necessity for so large a number of tables, De Morgan proposed another and more convenient form of commutation column, wherein the power of v would depend on the ages of (x) and (y), thus,

$$D_{xy} = v^{\frac{x+y}{2}} l_x l_y \quad \text{.........(9).}$$

In both Davies's and De Morgan's forms the power of v increases by unity for each addition of one year to the ages of both (x) and

(y). In De Morgan's form, if (x) be taken one year older, while (y) remains the same as before, we shall have

$$D_{x+1:y} = v^{\frac{x+y}{2}+\frac{1}{2}} l_{x+1} l_y,$$

while by Davies's form

$$D_{x+1:y} = v^{x+1} l_{x+1} l_y.$$

A column of N_{xy} can be formed from the values of D_{xy} in the same manner as N_x is formed from D_x. That is,

$$N_{xy} = \sum_{t=0}^{t=\infty} D_{x+t:y+t} \quad \text{.................(10)}.$$

For Select Tables, adopting De Morgan's form,

$$D_{[x][y]} = v^{\frac{x+y}{2}} l_{[x]} l_{[y]},$$

$$D_{[x]+t:[y]+t} = v^{\frac{x+y}{2}+t} l_{[x]+t} l_{[y]+t},$$

and assuming the Select Period to be five years,

$$N_{[x][y]} = \sum_{t=0}^{t=4} D_{[x]+t:[y]+t} + N_{x+5:y+5}.$$

When both lives are "select" and are subject to the same rates of mortality the two ages can be enclosed in one bracket, thus:

$$N_{[xy]} = \sum_{t=0}^{t=4} D_{[xy]+t} + N_{x+5:y+5},$$

but it might happen that $l_{[x]}$ is taken from one mortality table and $l_{[y]}$ from another, in which case the more general form $N_{[x][y]}$ etc. should be retained.

For the evaluation of varying Joint-Life Annuities a commutation function $S_{xy} = \sum_{t=0}^{t=\infty} N_{x+t:y+t}$ could also be constructed. This, however, is very seldom required and for isolated cases can be obtained by summing the requisite values of the N_{xy} column.

Expressed in Commutation Symbols the formulae for the values of whole-life and temporary joint-life annuities are

$$\mathbf{a}_{[x][y]} = \frac{N_{[x][y]}}{D_{[x][y]}} \quad \text{...................................(11)},$$

$$\mathbf{a}_{[x][y]:\overline{n}|} = \frac{N_{[x][y]} - N_{[x]+n:[y]+n}}{D_{[x][y]}} \quad \text{..................(12)},$$

$$a_{[x][y]} = \frac{N_{[x]+1:[y]+1}}{D_{[x][y]}} \quad \text{..............................(13)},$$

$$a_{[x][y]:\overline{n}|} = \frac{N_{[x]+1:[y]+1} - N_{[x]+n+1:[y]+n+1}}{D_{[x][y]}} \quad \text{........(14)}.$$

When an aggregate table is employed, the expressions will be of the same form, but the square brackets in the suffixes will be omitted.

As in the case of Commutation Functions, when both lives are select and based on the same mortality table, both the ages x and y can, if preferred, be enclosed in one bracket: for example, $\mathbf{a}_{[xy]}$.

5. Where the values of annuities on three or more joint lives are required other methods must be employed.

Thomas Simpson in 1752 suggested the rule known as *Simpson's Rule*, which may be expressed as follows:

If it be required to find the value of a_{xyz} where $x<y<z$, take w such that $a_w = a_{yz}$ and find a_{xw}; which will be the value required. That is, when $a_w = a_{yz}$,

$$a_{xyz} = a_{xw}.$$

Except when all the lives are advanced in years, Simpson's Rule gives too large a value. An age w can be found such that $a_w = a_{yz}$ exactly, no matter what may be the ages of y and z; but by making the assumption that because $a_w = a_{yz}$, therefore $a_{xw} = a_{xyz}$, we also assume that ${}_np_w = {}_np_{yz}$ for all values of n, and this latter assumption is not legitimate.

Various modifications of Simpson's Rule have been suggested, the one giving the best results being that given by Milne in his *Annuities and Assurances*. This is simply, "if (z) the oldest life proposed be under 45 years of age, let the age of the substituted life be the whole number next greater than that which expresses the age (w). But if the age of (z) be not under 45 years let the age of the substituted life be the next greater than that of (w), which does not require more than one decimal figure to express it."

6. Joint-Life Annuities when Makeham's Law holds. If Makeham's Law hold, the calculation of joint-life annuity values is materially simplified.

Considering the value of an annuity on m joint lives (x), (y), (z), etc., we have, corresponding to Chapter XIII 23,

$$a_{xyz\ldots(m)} = \sum_{t=1}^{t=\infty} v^t\, {}_tp_{xyz\ldots(m)}$$

$$= \sum_{t=1}^{t=\infty} v^t s^{mt} g^{(c^x+c^y+c^z+\ldots m \text{ terms})(c^t-1)},$$

whence, if an age w be found such that $mc^w = c^x + c^y + c^z + \ldots$ (m terms),

$$a_{xyz\ldots(m)} = \sum_{t=1}^{t=\infty} v^t s^{mt} g^{mc^w(c^t-1)}$$

$$= \sum_{t=1}^{t=\infty} v^t {}_tp_{www\ldots(m)}$$

$$= a_{www\ldots(m)} \quad \ldots\ldots\ldots\ldots\ldots\ldots\ldots\ldots(15).$$

When a table follows Makeham's Law, therefore, in the evaluation of a joint-life annuity on m lives of unequal ages, the same number of lives of equal age w can be substituted, w being such that $mc^w = c^x + c^y + c^z + \ldots$ (m terms).

In Chapter XIII 23, it was pointed out that if both sides of this equation be multiplied by Makeham's constant "B," and if, further, mA be added to each side, the result is

$$m(A + Bc^w) = (A + Bc^x) + (A + Bc^y) + (A + Bc^z) + \ldots (m \text{ terms})$$

or $$m\mu_w = \mu_x + \mu_y + \mu_z + \ldots (m \text{ terms}),$$

from which it is seen that the equal age w can be obtained just as easily from the values of μ for the various original ages, as from the appropriate powers of the constant c.

It follows from formula (15), that with a table following Makeham's Law, annuities for equal ages only need be tabulated, and the employment of such a table is thus an immense advantage in connection with all calculations into which the values of joint-life annuities of more than two lives enter. The Tables on pages 422, 430 and 438 give the values of joint-life annuities for equal ages for two, three or four lives on the basis of the H^M Table (Makeham Graduation) at rates of interest 3, $3\frac{1}{2}$, and 4 per cent.

Tables based on the true H^M Table are printed in a volume called *The Institute of Actuaries Life Tables.* That table was not graduated by Makeham's Law, but the values of joint-life annuities given on pages 422, 430 and 438 can if desired be combined with the values of other functions based on the true H^M Table without material loss of accuracy.

As examples of the method of calculating the values of joint-life annuities when Makeham's Law holds, let it be required to find the values of $a_{32:40}$ and $a_{30:35:45}$, on the basis of the H^M Table (Makeham Graduation) at 3 per cent.

For $a_{32:40}$

$$\begin{aligned} \mu_{32} &= \cdot00798 \\ \mu_{40} &= \cdot00990 \\ 2\,&|\underline{\cdot01788} \\ &\ \ \cdot00894 = \mu_{36\cdot72}, \end{aligned}$$

$$\therefore \quad a_{32:40} = a_{36\cdot72:36\cdot72},$$

whence by first difference interpolation between the values of $a_{36:36}$ and $a_{37:37}$ given on page 422 we find that $a_{32:40} = 14{\cdot}667$.

For $a_{30:35:45}$

$$\begin{aligned} \mu_{30} &= \cdot00768 \\ \mu_{35} &= \cdot00854 \\ \mu_{45} &= \cdot01204 \\ 3\,&|\underline{\cdot02826} \\ &\ \ \cdot00942 = \mu_{38\cdot48}, \end{aligned}$$

$$\therefore \quad a_{30:35:45} = a_{38\cdot48:38\cdot48:38\cdot48},$$

whence, by first difference interpolation between the values of $a_{38:38:38}$ and $a_{39:39:39}$ given on page 422 we find that

$$a_{30:35:45} = 12{\cdot}035.$$

7. The method of evaluating joint-life annuities on the basis of a table following Makeham's Law is of great practical importance. In paragraph 6 the equal age to be substituted for the original ages was calculated in each case directly from the values of μ, but a simpler method depending on what is known as the *Law of Uniform Seniority* is generally adopted. This law may be explained as follows:

When two lives of equal age w are substituted for two lives of unequal ages x and y, where y is greater than x, the seniority of the substituted age, w, over the younger of the original ages, x, will always be the same for the same *difference* between the original ages $(y - x)$ whatever the individual original ages may be.

This can be demonstrated algebraically, for,

if $$2c^w = c^x + c^y,$$

then $$c^w = \tfrac{1}{2}c^x(1 + c^{y-x}),$$

and $$w - x = \frac{\log(1 + c^{y-x}) - \log 2}{\log c},$$

which is constant so long as $y - x$ remains constant.

This law greatly facilitates the calculation of annuity and other values, because by calculating the value of $w - x$ for each value of $y - x$ a table is obtained from which the addition to be made to the age x in order to arrive at the age w is readily found by inspection, without reference to the values of μ_x or c^x.

8. A similar method can be applied when three lives are involved. Consider the three lives (x), (y), and (z) where $x < y < z$.

For the three lives of unequal ages three lives of equal age u may be substituted, provided

$$3c^u = c^x + c^y + c^z.$$

First find an age w such that

$$2c^w = c^x + c^y,$$

whence, as shown above,

$$w - x = \frac{\log(1 + c^{y-x}) - \log 2}{\log c}$$

Then
$$\begin{aligned} 3c^u &= c^x + c^y + c^z \\ &= 2c^w + c^z \\ &= c^w(2 + c^{z-w}), \end{aligned}$$

$$\therefore \quad (u - w)\log c = \log(2 + c^{z-w}) - \log 3,$$

$$u - w = \frac{\log(2 + c^{z-w}) - \log 3}{\log c}.$$

If, therefore, two tables be constructed, one giving the values of $w - x$ corresponding to the difference $y - x$, and the other giving the values of $u - w$ corresponding to the difference $z - w$, we can, by entering each of the tables in turn, ascertain without reference to the values of μ_x or c^x the equal age to be substituted for the three original ages.

Or, if $y - x = h$ and $z - y = k$, the ages thus being x, $x + h$, $x + h + k$ respectively, one table can be prepared giving for each value of h combined with each value of k, the value of t, the addition to be made to the youngest age, so that

$$a_{x:x+h:x+h+k} = a_{x+t:x+t:x+t}.$$

9. Tables of Uniform Seniority on the basis of the H^M Table (Makeham Graduation) for two and three lives respectively and on the basis of the O$^{[NM]}$ Table for two lives are given on page 478. It must, however, be borne in mind that for the former table equal ages can only be used when all the original ages involved are above 28.

The use of these tables can be illustrated by reference to the examples given in paragraph 6. For the two lives aged respectively 32 and 40, the difference between these ages being eight years, reference to the table for two lives shows that the equal age will be $32 + 4{\cdot}72 = 36{\cdot}72$. For the three lives aged respectively 30, 35 and 45, reference to the table for two lives shows that the equal age to be substituted for 30 and 35 is $30 + 2{\cdot}78 = 32{\cdot}78$. The difference between this last age and 45 is 12·22 and reference to the table for three lives shows, after interpolation, that the addition to be made to 32·78 is 5·71, giving 38·49 as the equal age to be employed in place of the three unequal ages.

The following values of annuities by the H^M Table at 3 per cent. interest are given in order that the student may test the method of using the tables of uniform seniority for himself, and also the alternative method of obtaining the equal ages directly from the values of μ:

$$\begin{aligned} a_{35:41} &= 14{\cdot}185, \\ a_{38:56} &= 10{\cdot}411, \\ a_{45:53:70} &= 5{\cdot}339, \\ a_{33:37:43} &= 12{\cdot}043. \end{aligned}$$

10. Even where a table does not follow Makeham's Law the assumption of equal ages based on a table which follows that law may give results sufficiently accurate for practical purposes.

Thus Messrs Austin and Symmons in the introduction to their volume of *Tables on Two Joint Lives of Equal Age* based on the British Offices Life Tables say:

"The $O^{M(5)}$, $O^{[M]}$ and $O^{[NM]}$ Mortality Tables follow Makeham's first modification of Gompertz's Law. The Law of Uniform Seniority, therefore, applies at all ages and for all durations of assurance under these three Tables, and for convenience of reference a Table of Uniform Seniority has been placed at the beginning of each of these Sections.

"The O^M Mortality Table does not follow Makeham's first modification of Gompertz's Law, and the Law of Uniform Seniority does not apply except at ages 85 and upwards, where the O^M and $O^{M(5)}$ tables are identical. The substitution of two lives of equal age for two lives of unequal age is, however, a great convenience in practice, and two Tables are appended indicating the error involved by assuming that the Law of Uniform Seniority holds for this Table of Mortality. The Table of Uniform Seniority used was that applicable to the other Tables."

It is not necessary to reproduce the tables here, but after giving these, the authors continue:

"It will be seen that where the difference in age is small and also where the age of the younger life is about 35 or upwards, the error involved by the assumption is small."

11. When a table follows Makeham's Law a *single* life can be substituted for two or more joint lives provided the rate of interest be changed. Thus

$$\begin{aligned} a_{xyz\ldots(m)} &= \sum_{t=1}^{t=\infty} v^t\,{}_tp_{xyz\ldots(m)} \\ &= \sum_{t=1}^{t=\infty} v^t s^{mt} g^{(c^x+c^y+c^z+\ldots m\text{ terms})\,(c^t-1)} \\ &= \sum_{t=1}^{t=\infty} (vs^{m-1})^t s^t g^{c^w(c^t-1)} \\ &= a'_w \ \ldots\ldots\ldots\ldots\ldots\ldots\ldots\ldots\ldots\ldots(16), \end{aligned}$$

where $c^w = c^x + c^y + c^z + \ldots$ to m terms, and a' is calculated at such a rate j that $v_j = v_i s^{m-1}$, or $\dfrac{1}{1+j} = \dfrac{s^{m-1}}{1+i}$, whence $j = \dfrac{1+i}{s^{m-1}} - 1$. The special rate of interest at which a' is calculated thus depends on the *number* of lives involved.

In the case of the Makeham Graduation of the H^M Table

$$\log_{10} s = -\cdot0026893.$$

Using i to denote the rate of interest at which the value of the annuity is required and $i_{(2)}, i_{(3)}, i_{(4)}$ the corresponding rates for two, three and four joint lives we have, calculating $i_{(m)}$ from $v_{(m)} = vs^{m-1}$,

i	$i_{(2)}$	$i_{(3)}$	$i_{(4)}$
·03	·0364	·0428	·0493
·035	·0414	·0479	·0544
·04	·0465	·0530	·0595
·05	·0565	·0631	·0697
·06	·0666	·0732	·0799

If this method were adopted it would not be possible to obtain the age of the single life from the value of μ directly because when

$$c^w = c^x + c^y + c^z + \ldots$$

the corresponding relation does *not* hold for the forces of mortality under Makeham's Law.

The increase in i is approximately constant for all rates of interest used in practice, and in the case of the H^M Table (Makeham Graduation) is ·0065 for each additional life involved. That is, if the value of an annuity on m lives be required it is equivalent to the value of an annuity on an equivalent single life calculated at rate $i+(m-1)\times{}$·0065 when m is not large.

12. Evaluation by Approximate Integration. When appropriate tables of annuity values are not available, whether the mortality table follow Makeham's Law or not, the simplest method of evaluation of an isolated joint-life annuity is by approximate integration.

Let it be required to find the value of $\bar{a}_{30:35:45}$ by the H^M Table (Makeham Graduation) at 3 per cent. by means of the approximate integration formula

$$\int_0^\infty f(x)\,dx = n\{\cdot28f(0)+1\cdot62f(n)+2\cdot2f(3n)+1\cdot62f(5n)+\cdot56f(6n)+1\cdot62f(7n)\}.$$

The integral to be evaluated is

$$\bar{a}_{30:35:45}=\frac{1}{l_{30}l_{35}l_{45}}\int_0^\infty v^t\,l_{30+t}\,l_{35+t}\,l_{45+t}\,dt,$$

and since the payments cease on the death of any one of the lives involved, we must take $7n=102-45$, whence $n=8$. The value of $f(0)$ is unity, so that for this term it is only necessary to insert the coefficient (·28) in the calculation, and the value of $f(7n)$ will clearly be zero to several places of decimals, and can, therefore, be omitted. The value of $f(6n)$ in this case must also be very little more than zero and might be omitted, but as this is not quite so easy to foresee as the value of $f(7n)$ the calculation of $f(6n)$ has been carried out in the same manner as the other terms.

The calculation is as follows:

t	0	n =8	$3n$ =24	$5n$ =40	$6n$ =48	
$\log v^t$ ...	—	$\bar{1}$·8973	$\bar{1}$·6919	$\bar{1}$·4865	$\bar{1}$·3838	
$\log l_{30+t}$ ...	—	4·9236	4·8320	4·5795	4·2645	
$\log l_{35+t}$ ...	—	4·9017	4·7819	4·4083	3·9235	
$\log l_{45+t}$ ...	—	4·8402	4·6060	3·7390	2·5635	
colog $l_{30}\,l_{35}\,l_{45}$	—	$\overline{15}$·2205	$\overline{15}$·2205	$\overline{15}$·2205	$\overline{15}$·2205	
log coeff. ...	$\bar{1}$·4472	·2095	·3424	·2095	$\bar{1}$·7482	
Sum =	$\bar{1}$·4472	$\bar{1}$·9928	$\bar{1}$·4747	$\bar{3}$·6433	$\bar{5}$·1040	
$\log^{-1}$ ...	·28	·9836	·2983	·0044	·0000	= 1·5663
						8
					$\bar{a}_{30:35:45}=$	12·5304

whence, to three places of decimals,

$$a_{30:35:45} = \bar{a}_{30:35:45} - \tfrac{1}{2} + \tfrac{1}{12}(\mu_{30} + \mu_{35} + \mu_{45} + \delta) = 12{\cdot}035,$$

which is the value found in paragraph 6.

The value of a temporary joint-life annuity can similarly be ascertained by approximate integration.

Let it be required, for example, to find the value of $\bar{a}_{30:35:45:\overline{20}|}$ by the H^M Table at 3 per cent.

We have

$$\bar{a}_{30:35:45:\overline{20}|} = \frac{1}{l_{30}\,l_{35}\,l_{45}} \int_0^{20} v^t\, l_{30+t}\, l_{35+t}\, l_{45+t}\, dt,$$

and the formula we shall employ is

$$\int_0^{20} f(x)\,dx = \int_0^{10} f(x)\,dx + \int_{10}^{20} f(x)\,dx$$

$$= \tfrac{5}{3}\{f(0) + 4f(5) + f(10)\} + \tfrac{5}{3}\{f(10) + 4f(15) + f(20)\}$$

$$= \tfrac{5}{3}\{f(0) + 4f(5) + 2f(10) + 4f(15) + f(20)\}.$$

The calculation is as follows:

t	0	n $=5$	$2n$ $=10$	$3n$ $=15$	$4n$ $=20$
$\log v^t$ ...	—	$\bar{1}{\cdot}9358$	$\bar{1}{\cdot}8716$	$\bar{1}{\cdot}8074$	$\bar{1}{\cdot}7433$
$\log l_{30+t}$ ...	—	4·9352	4·9153	4·8916	4·8621
$\log l_{35+t}$ ...	—	4·9153	4·8916	4·8621	4·8233
$\log l_{45+t}$ ...	—	4·8621	4·8233	4·7697	4·6929
colog $l_{30:35:45}$	—	$\overline{15}{\cdot}2205$	$\overline{15}{\cdot}2205$	$\overline{15}{\cdot}2205$	$\overline{15}{\cdot}2205$
	·0000	$\bar{1}{\cdot}8689$	$\bar{1}{\cdot}7223$	$\bar{1}{\cdot}5513$	$\bar{1}{\cdot}3421$
$\log^{-1}$ ...	1·	·7394	·5276	·3559	·2198
		4	2	4	
	1·	2·9576	1·0552	1·4236	·2198 = 6·6562

$$\bar{a}_{30:35:45:\overline{20}|} = \tfrac{5}{3}(6{\cdot}6562) = 11{\cdot}093$$

the correct value, obtained by equal ages, being 11·081.

The method of approximate integration is equally simple whether the lives involved are assumed to be subject to the same or to different rates of mortality. For example, if (30) were taken on the basis of Mortality Table A, (35) on Table B and (45) on Table C, $\log l_{30+t}$ and colog l_{30} would be taken from the first table, $\log l_{35+t}$ and colog l_{35} from the second, and $\log l_{45+t}$ and colog l_{45} from the third.

13. Annuities payable until death of Survivor. The value of an annuity of 1 payable at the end of each year that one at least of two lives (x) and (y) shall survive; that is, an annuity payable during the joint-lives and the life of the survivor of (x) and (y); is

$$a_{\overline{xy}} = \sum_{t=1}^{t=\infty} v^t\,{}_tp_{\overline{xy}} \quad\text{.............................(17)}$$

$$= \sum_{t=1}^{t=\infty} v^t ({}_tp_x + {}_tp_y - {}_tp_{xy})$$

$$= a_x + a_y - a_{xy} \quad\text{.........................(18).}$$

This formula can be obtained by general reasoning. If there be an annuity payable during the life of (x), and a second annuity payable during the life of (y), the sum of these will provide a payment of 2 so long as both survive and a payment of 1 after the first death so long as the survivor lives. If, therefore, we deduct a_{xy}, the value of an annuity payable so long as both survive, the result is the value of $a_{\overline{xy}}$.

14. To find $a_{\overline{wxyz\ldots(m)}}^{\;r}$, the value of an annuity to continue so long as at least r lives out of m lives survive.

The value of the tth payment is $v^t\,{}_tp_{\overline{wxyz\ldots(m)}}^{\;r}$ and of the annuity

$$a_{\overline{wxyz\ldots(m)}}^{\;r} = \sum_{t=1}^{t=\infty} v^t\,{}_tp_{\overline{wxyz\ldots(m)}}^{\;r}$$

$$= \sum_{t=1}^{t=\infty} v^t \left\{Z^r - rZ^{r+1} + \frac{r(r+1)}{2} Z^{r+2} - \ldots \text{etc.}\right\},$$

where each power of Z represents the sum of certain probabilities of the form ${}_tp_{wxyz\ldots(r)}$. Therefore, to obtain $\sum_{t=1}^{t=\infty} v^t\,{}_tp_{\overline{wxyz\ldots(m)}}^{\;r}$ we must take the sum, for all values of t, of v^t multiplied into the corresponding value of each of the probabilities included in each power of Z. But $\sum_{t=1}^{t=\infty} v^t\,{}_tp_{wxyz\ldots(n)} = a_{wxyz\ldots(n)}$, and therefore, when we take the sum of the discounted probabilities included in the various powers of Z, we have simply to replace the probabilities by the corresponding joint-life annuities. Extending in this sense the meaning of Z, so that, when dealing with annuities, Z^r signifies the sum of the values of the annuities on r joint lives for all the combinations of r lives that can be made out of the m lives, we have

$$a_{\overline{wxyz\ldots(m)}}^{\;r} = Z^r - rZ^{r+1} + \frac{r(r+1)}{2} Z^{r+2} - \ldots \text{etc.}$$

$$= \frac{Z^r}{(1+Z)^r} \quad\text{..................................(19),}$$

in accordance with Chapter XIII, formula (17).

As an example of this formula, let it be required to determine the values of $a_{\overline{wxyz}}$, $a_{\overline{wxyz}}^{\;2}$ and $a_{\overline{wxyz}}^{\;3}$.

$$a_{\overline{wxyz}} = \frac{Z}{1+Z}$$
$$= Z - Z^2 + Z^3 - Z^4$$
$$= (a_w + a_x + a_y + a_z) - (a_{wx} + a_{wy} + a_{wz} + a_{xy} + a_{xz} + a_{yz})$$
$$+ (a_{wxy} + a_{wxz} + a_{wyz} + a_{xyz}) - a_{wxyz} \quad \text{..............(20)},$$

$$a_{\overline{wxyz}}^{\;2} = \frac{Z^2}{(1+Z)^2}$$
$$= Z^2 - 2Z^3 + 3Z^4.$$
$$= a_{wx} + a_{wy} + a_{wz} + a_{xy} + a_{xz} + a_{yz}$$
$$- 2(a_{wxy} + a_{wxz} + a_{wyz} + a_{xyz}) + 3a_{wxyz} \quad \text{............(21)},$$

$$a_{\overline{wxyz}}^{\;3} = \frac{Z^3}{(1+Z)^3}$$
$$= Z^3 - 3Z^4$$
$$= (a_{wxy} + a_{wxz} + a_{wyz} + a_{xyz}) - 3a_{wxyz} \quad \text{.................(22)}.$$

15. Similarly, to find $a_{\overline{wxyz\ldots(m)}}^{\;[r]}$, the value of an annuity payable only while exactly r lives out of m lives survive, we have

$$a_{\overline{wxyz\ldots(m)}}^{\;[r]} = \frac{Z^r}{(1+Z)^{r+1}}$$
$$= Z^r - (r+1)Z^{r+1} + \frac{(r+1)(r+2)}{\underline{|2}} Z^{r+2} - \ldots.$$

As an example of this formula

$$a_{\overline{wxyz}}^{\;[2]} = \frac{Z^2}{(1+Z)^3}$$
$$= Z^2 - 3Z^3 + 6Z^4$$
$$= a_{wx} + a_{wy} + a_{wz} + a_{xy} + a_{xz} + a_{yz}$$
$$- 3(a_{wxy} + a_{wxz} + a_{wyz} + a_{xyz}) + 6a_{wxyz}.$$

16. It has been shown that when a table follows Makeham's Law we can find such an age w that $a_{xy} = a_{ww}$, but it does not follow that $a_{\overline{xy}} = a_{\overline{ww}}$.

If $a_{xy} = a_{ww}$, then ${}_tp_{xy} = {}_tp_{ww}$ for all values of t, and

$$\bar{a}_{xy} = \bar{a}_{ww} \quad \text{..........................}(\alpha).$$

Similarly, if $a_{\overline{xy}} = a_{\overline{ww}}$ we shall have $\bar{a}_{\overline{xy}} = \bar{a}_{\overline{ww}}$ or

$$\bar{a}_x + \bar{a}_y - \bar{a}_{xy} = 2\bar{a}_w - \bar{a}_{ww},$$

or (since $\bar{a}_{xy} = \bar{a}_{ww}$) $\qquad \bar{a}_x + \bar{a}_y = 2\bar{a}_w \quad \text{......................}(\beta).$

It is fairly obvious that as a rule these two different relationships between x, y and w cannot hold good, but a formal proof can be furnished as follows:

Differentiating (α) with respect to age, we get

$$\bar{a}_{xy}(\mu_{xy}+\delta)-1=\bar{a}_{ww}(\mu_{ww}+\delta)-1,$$

whence, remembering that $\bar{a}_{xy}=\bar{a}_{ww}$, $\mu_{xy}=\mu_{ww}$, or

$$\mu_x+\mu_y=2\mu_w \quad \text{......................}(\gamma).$$

Differentiating (β) we get

$$\bar{a}_x(\mu_x+\delta)-1+\bar{a}_y(\mu_y+\delta)-1=2\bar{a}_w(\mu_w+\delta)-2,$$

and substituting for $\bar{a}_w$ and μ_w their values in (β) and (γ),

$$\bar{a}_x\mu_x+\bar{a}_y\mu_y=(\bar{a}_x+\bar{a}_y)\left(\frac{\mu_x+\mu_y}{2}\right).$$

Multiplying out, this reduces to

$$\bar{a}_x\mu_x+\bar{a}_y\mu_y=\bar{a}_x\mu_y+\bar{a}_y\mu_x,$$

or

$$\bar{a}_x(\mu_x-\mu_y)=\bar{a}_y(\mu_x-\mu_y),$$

which cannot be true unless

$$\bar{a}_x=\bar{a}_y \text{ or } \mu_x=\mu_y,$$

and neither of these relations can hold unless $x=y$ or μ is constant. Now μ is not constant, but increases with the age, the increase being very rapid at advanced ages, therefore the equations

$$\bar{a}_{\overline{xy}}=\bar{a}_{\overline{ww}} \text{ and } \bar{a}_{xy}=\bar{a}_{ww} \text{ (or } a_{\overline{xy}}=a_{\overline{ww}} \text{ and } a_{xy}=a_{ww})$$

cannot both hold good unless $x=y$, when the two sides of each become identical. That the amount of the error may be serious is shown by the following figures taken from the H[M] Table (Makeham Graduation) at 3 per cent., the values of w being calculated to one decimal place:

x	y	w	$\bar{a}_{\overline{ww}}$	$\bar{a}_{\overline{xy}}$	Error
20	40	34	22·354	23·831	1·477
	60	52·7	16·204	22·669	6·465
	80	72·3	8·169	22·123	13·954
40	60	54	15·697	18·220	2·523
	80	72·7	8·011	17·332	9·321
60	80	74	7·507	10·682	3·175
80	90	86·1	3·545	4·221	676

It will be noticed that $\bar{a}_{\overline{ww}}$ is less than $\bar{a}_{\overline{xy}}$ in all cases, and that the difference increases rapidly as the difference between x and y becomes larger. This also appears from the following considerations. The joint-life annuity cannot continue longer than the "complement*

* The complement of life is the difference between the present age and the limiting age of the mortality table.

of life" of the older of the two lives, however young the other may be; therefore, the age of the older life is the preponderating factor in determining the joint-life annuity value a_{xy}; and this preponderance increases with the difference between x and y, until, in the limiting case, when the older life (y say) reaches the limit of life, $a_{xy} = a_y$ (both of them being zero), and the age of the younger life has no effect whatever on the value. Accordingly, the substituted age w must be nearer the older than the younger of the two lives, or $w > \frac{1}{2}(x+y)$, and the excess increases with the difference between x and y. On the other hand, the last survivor annuity may continue for the "complement of life" of the younger of the two lives, however old the other may be; and the age of the younger is therefore the preponderating factor in this case, and the preponderance increases with the difference between x and y until, in the limit, when y reaches the limit of life, $a_{\overline{xy}} = a_x$, and the value depends solely on the age of the younger life. Therefore the age z at which $a_{\overline{xy}} = a_{\overline{zz}}$ must be nearer the younger than the older life, or $z < \frac{1}{2}(x+y)$. Hence z must be less than w, and accordingly $a_{\overline{xy}}$ greater than $a_{\overline{ww}}$, and the difference between them increases with the difference between x and y.

17. The evaluation of a deferred last survivor annuity presents peculiar difficulties.

Let it be required to find the value of an annuity of 1 per annum payable during the life of the survivor of (x) and (y), the first payment to be made at the end of the $(n+1)$th year; that is, a joint and survivorship annuity of 1 to (x) and (y) deferred n years.

If (x) and (y) both survive n years the value of the annuity will then be $a_{\overline{x+n:y+n}}$ and its present value subject to this condition is $v^n {}_np_{xy} a_{\overline{x+n:y+n}}$.

The present value of the annuity subject to the condition that (x) only survives n years is $v^n {}_np_x (1 - {}_np_y) a_{x+n}$, and that ($y$) only survives, $v^n {}_np_y (1 - {}_np_x) a_{y+n}$.

These three cases exhaust the possible cases under the annuity of which the value is required, and this value is therefore

$$\begin{aligned} &v^n {}_np_x (1 - {}_np_y) a_{x+n} + v^n {}_np_y (1 - {}_np_x) a_{y+n} \\ &\qquad\qquad + v^n {}_np_{xy} (a_{x+n} + a_{y+n} - a_{x+n:y+n}) \\ &= v^n {}_np_x a_{x+n} + v^n {}_np_y a_{y+n} - v^n {}_np_{xy} a_{x+n:y+n} \\ &= {}_{n|}a_x + {}_{n|}a_y - {}_{n|}a_{xy} \quad \ldots\ldots\ldots\ldots (23), \end{aligned}$$

which can be represented by ${}_{n|}a_{\overline{xy}}$.

For this annuity to become payable it is not necessary that both (x) and (y) survive n years, and therefore it is *not* correct to write

$$_{n|}a_{\overline{xy}} = v^n {}_np_{xy}\, a_{\overline{x+n:y+n}}.$$

It is equally *incorrect* to write

$$_{n|}a_{\overline{xy}} = v^n {}_np_{\overline{xy}}\, a_{\overline{x+n:y+n}},$$

since this would provide an annuity corresponding to $a_{\overline{x+n:y+n}}$ even when only (x) or (y) survived the period of deferment.

18. An interesting problem is to find the value of an annuity of 1 payable to (x) during the life of (y) and for t years after the death of (y) should (x) live so long.

During the first t years, the payments of the annuity depend only on the survivance of (x), and the value of the annuity for this period is $a_{x:\overline{t|}}$.

Considering the period after the first t years, a payment will be made at the end of the $(t+r)$th year, if (x) be then alive, and (y) was alive t years before, i.e., at the end of the rth year. The value of this payment is, therefore, $v^{t+r}{}_{t+r}p_x \cdot {}_rp_y$ and the present value of the annuity after t years is

$$\sum_{r=1}^{r=\infty} v^{t+r}{}_{t+r}p_x \cdot {}_rp_y$$

$$= v^t {}_tp_x \sum_{r=1}^{r=\infty} v^r {}_rp_{x+t:y}$$

$$= v^t {}_tp_x a_{x+t:y}.$$

The value of the whole annuity is, therefore,

$$a_{x:\overline{t|}} + \frac{D_{x+t}}{D_x} a_{x+t:y}$$

$$= a_x - \frac{D_{x+t}}{D_x}(a_{x+t} - a_{x+t:y}) \quad \text{..............(24).}$$

19. The value of an annuity of 1 payable at the end of each year during the joint existence of (x) with the survivor of (y) and (z) and for t years after the death of such survivor should (x) live so long, can be obtained in a similar manner.

Here also the value of the annuity during the first t years is $a_{x:\overline{t|}}$. Considering the period after t years, a payment will be made at the end of the $(t+r)$th year, if (x) be then alive and the survivor of (y) and (z) was alive at the end of the rth year. The value of this payment is $v^{t+r}{}_{t+r}p_x \cdot {}_rp_{\overline{yz}}$, and the value at the outset of that part of the annuity which will fall after the first t years is

$$\sum_{r=1}^{r=\infty} v^{t+r}\,{}_{t+r}p_x \cdot {}_rp_{\overline{yz}}$$

$$= v^t\,{}_tp_x \sum_{r=1}^{r=\infty} v^r\,{}_rp_{x+t}\,({}_rp_y + {}_rp_z - {}_rp_{yz})$$

$$= v^t\,{}_tp_x\,(a_{x+t:y} + a_{x+t:z} - a_{x+t:yz}),$$

whence, the value of the whole annuity is

$$a_{x:\overline{t}|} + \frac{D_{x+t}}{D_x}(a_{x+t:y} + a_{x+t:z} - a_{x+t:yz})$$

$$= a_x - \frac{D_{x+t}}{D_x}(a_{x+t} - a_{x+t:y} - a_{x+t:z} + a_{x+t:yz}) \ldots\ldots\ldots (25).$$

Other annuities of this nature (such, for example, as an annuity payable during the joint existence of (x) and the survivor of (y) and (z) and for t years after the death of (x) should the survivor of (y) and (z) live so long) are readily dealt with in the same way.

20. The methods employed to deduce expressions for the values of various annuities are perfectly general, and can be applied however many lives are included in any status and when one of the lives is replaced by a term certain.

The value of an annuity of 1 payable at the end of each year so long as three lives (a), (b) and (c) exist jointly with three other lives (x), (y) and (z) might be represented by $a_{(abc)(xyz)}$, but this is equivalent to an annuity payable only during the joint existence of the six lives named, the value of which is a_{abcxyz}.

If the annuity is to be payable so long as the three lives (a), (b) and (c) exist jointly with the *survivor* of the three lives (x), (y) and (z), the expression for its value can be found as follows:

$$a_{abc:\overline{xyz}} = \sum_{t=1}^{t=\infty} v^t\,{}_tp_{abc} \cdot {}_tp_{\overline{xyz}}$$

$$= \sum_{t=1}^{t=\infty} v^t\,{}_tp_{abc} \cdot ({}_tp_x + {}_tp_y + {}_tp_z - {}_tp_{xy} - {}_tp_{xz} - {}_tp_{yz} + {}_tp_{xyz})$$

$$= a_{abcx} + a_{abcy} + a_{abcz} - a_{abcxy} - a_{abcxz} - a_{abcyz} + a_{abcxyz} \ldots (26).$$

21. It is required to find the value of an annuity of 1 payable at the end of each year until the survivor of (25) or (30) reaches age 50, or until his death if both lives die before attaining that age.

The value of this annuity is

$$a_{25:\overline{25}|} + a_{30:\overline{20}|} - a_{25:30:\overline{20}|}.$$

The first term provides for an annuity of 1 payable until (25) reaches age 50 or until his death before that age, and the second term provides a similar annuity to (30). But so long as both lives continue in existence and neither has reached age 50, these terms will provide for two annuities being payable, and it becomes necessary to cancel one of these by deducting the value of an annuity during the joint existence of the lives for the period that must elapse until the elder reaches age 50.

This is a particular example of the annuity the value of which can be represented as follows:

$$\left.\begin{aligned} a_{(x:\overline{n|})(y:\overline{m|})} &= a_{x:\overline{n|}} + a_{y:\overline{m|}} - a_{xy:\overline{n|}} && \text{if } m > n \\ &= a_{x:\overline{n|}} + a_{y:\overline{m|}} - a_{xy:\overline{m|}} && \text{if } n > m \\ &= a_{\overline{xy}:\overline{n|}} && \text{if } m = n \end{aligned}\right\} \quad \ldots\ldots(27).$$

22. The value is required of a deferred annuity of 1 payable so long as either of two persons now aged 25 and 30 respectively lives after age 50. This value is

$${}_{25|}a_{25} + {}_{20|}a_{30} - {}_{25|}a_{25:30}.$$

In this case if (30) lives to age 50 and receives, say, one payment of the annuity, and then dies, the payments will cease until (25) attains age 50.

This also is a particular example of an annuity the value of which can be represented as follows:

$$\left.\begin{aligned} &{}_{n|}a_x + {}_{m|}a_y - {}_{m|}a_{xy} && \text{if } m > n \\ &{}_{n|}a_x + {}_{m|}a_y - {}_{n|}a_{xy} && \text{if } n > m \\ &{}_{n|}a_{\overline{xy}} && \text{if } m = n \end{aligned}\right\} \quad \ldots\ldots\ldots\ldots(28).$$

23. Joint-Life Annuities when Gompertz's Law holds. It has already been intimated in Chapter XI that none of the mortality tables in use at the present time follows Gompertz's Law, though at the very old ages the mortality displayed is frequently very similar to that which would be shown on this basis.

For reasons which will become apparent, however, it is an advantage to consider the calculations of joint-life annuities by such a table. By a table following Gompertz's Law

$$\begin{aligned} a_{xyz\ldots(m)} &= \sum_{t=1}^{t=\infty} v^t g^{(c^x+c^y+c^z+\ldots)(c^t-1)} \\ &= \sum_{t=1}^{t=\infty} v^t g^{c^w(c^t-1)} \\ &= a_w \quad \ldots\ldots\ldots\ldots\ldots\ldots\ldots\ldots\ldots\ldots\ldots (29), \end{aligned}$$

where $c^w = c^x + c^y + c^z + \ldots$ (m terms), or $\mu_w = \mu_x + \mu_y + \mu_z + \ldots$ (m terms).

If, therefore, an age w be found such that μ_w is equal to the sum of the forces of mortality at the original ages, the value of an annuity payable during the joint existence of the original lives is equal to the value of a single-life annuity to (w).

24. The Law of Uniform Seniority holds in the case of a table following Gompertz's Law. For two lives (x) and (y), where $y > x$,

$$c^w = c^x + c^y,$$
$$\therefore \quad c^{w-x} = 1 + c^{y-x},$$
$$w - x = \frac{\log(1 + c^{y-x})}{\log c}.$$

In this case the age of the single substituted life is always greater than that of the older of the two original lives.

When three lives (x), (y) and (z) are involved, in order to construct tables of uniform seniority, we must first find an age w such that

$$c^w = c^x + c^y, \text{ or } w - x = \frac{\log(1 + c^{y-x})}{\log c},$$

and then find an age u such that

$$c^u = c^x + c^y + c^z$$
$$= c^w + c^z,$$

whence $$u - w = \frac{\log(1 + c^{z-w})}{\log c}.$$

Thus the expression is the same in each case, proving, as can be seen from general considerations, that all that is necessary is to construct one table of uniform seniority, and when three lives are involved to enter this table twice. If four lives were involved the table would have to be entered three times, and so on.

25. Approximations to the values of Joint-Life Annuities. It has been indicated that even where Makeham's Law does not hold it is frequently sufficiently accurate in calculating the values of joint-life annuities to assume equal ages based on a somewhat similar table which follows that law.

In a note in *J. I. A.* Vol. XLIV, Messrs W. P. Elderton and A. E. King investigated the question of employing an approximation to the joint-life annuity value based indirectly on Gompertz's Law. They point out that the formula $a_{xy} = a_w$ holds if $\mu_{x+n} + \mu_{y+n} = \mu_{w+n}$ for all values of n, and proceed to state that:—

"It is clear that an age w can be found at which $a_{xy}=a_w\ldots$ but the difficulty in approximating is to guess the equivalent age required without working out the whole of the joint-life annuity table. To put this difficulty in another way, we may say, that if Gompertz's Law holds, we can use the values of μ at the ages at which the annuity is calculated (i.e. x and y); if it does not hold can we use them at some other ages we have yet to find? As soon as the question is stated in this way, it occurs to one that a good result might be obtained by averaging the values of μ from the ages at entry onwards, or by taking them arbitrarily some years later."

They then point out that "The number of years to be chosen depends, so far as our investigations have gone, on the value of the joint-life annuity which it is required to find."

As an example, it is required to find the value of $a_{20:40}$ by the O^M Table at 3 per cent. on the assumption that the only tabular values available are a_x and μ_x.

The method of approximating is as follows:

$$\mu_{20}+\mu_{40}=\cdot00399+\cdot00900=\cdot01299=\mu_{47\cdot7},$$

$$a_{47\cdot7}=14\cdot861.$$

This annuity value being approximately 15, take

$$\mu_{20+15}+\mu_{40+15}=\cdot00725+\cdot02000=\cdot02725=\mu_{44\cdot5+15},$$

whence $$a_{20:40}=a_{44\cdot5}=15\cdot948,$$

which is a good approximation to the true value, 15·958.

As a second example, to find $a_{30:30}$, we have

$$\mu_{30}+\mu_{30}=\cdot01168=\mu_{45\cdot63},$$

$$a_{45\cdot63}=15\cdot570,$$

$$\mu_{30+16}+\mu_{30+16}=\cdot02378=\mu_{41\cdot557+16},$$

whence $$a_{30:30}=a_{41\cdot557}=16\cdot905,$$

the true value being 16·933.

In the case of joint-life term annuities the age of the single life to be used in the calculations is taken as the mean of the ages found for the single life when based on the ages of the joint lives at each end of the term.

Example: To find the value of $a_{20:32:\overline{10|}}$ by the O^M Table at 3 per cent.,

$$(1)\qquad \mu_{20}+\mu_{32}=\cdot01035=\mu_{43\cdot12},$$

$$(2)\quad \mu_{20+10}+\mu_{32+10}=\cdot01567=\mu_{41\cdot06+10}.$$

Therefore taking the mean of 43·12 and 41·06, the age required $=42·09$, and we have

$$a_{20:32:\overline{10}|} = a_{42·09:\overline{10}|} = 8·025,$$

the true value being 8·018. If the age had been taken as 43·12 the result would have been 7·999.

As a second example, take $a_{41:37:\overline{22}|}$,

$$(1) \qquad \mu_{41} + \mu_{37} = ·01731 = \mu_{52·72},$$

$$(2) \quad \mu_{41+22} + \mu_{37+22} = ·06160 = \mu_{48·02+22}.$$

The mean of 52·72 and 48·02 is 50·37, whence

$$a_{41:37:\overline{22}|} = a_{50·37:\overline{22}|} = 12·483,$$

the true value being 12·474.

EXAMPLES

Ex. 1. Calculate the values of $a_{\overline{30:35:40}}$ and $a_{\overline{35:35:35}}$ by the H[M] Table at 3 per cent.

$$a_{\overline{30:35:40}} = a_{30} + a_{35} + a_{40} - a_{30:35} - a_{30:40} - a_{35:40} + a_{30:35:40}$$

$$= a_{30} + a_{35} + a_{40} - a_{32·8:32·8} - a_{36·1:36·1} - a_{37·8:37·8} + a_{35·8:35·8:35·8}$$

$$= 19·895 + 18·613 + 17·177 - 15·722 - 14·841 - 14·361 + 12·756$$

$$= 23·517,$$

$$a_{\overline{35:35:35}} = 3a_{35} - 3a_{35:35} + a_{35:35:35}$$

$$= 55·839 - 45·426 + 12·964$$

$$= 23·377.$$

Ex. 2. Find the value of an annuity of 1 payable yearly so long as (x) lives with (y) and for n years after the death of (y), but in any event no payment to be made after m years from the present time. $(m > n.)$

The value during the first n years $= a_{x:\overline{n}|}$.

The value of the payments to be made after n years is

$$\sum_{t=1}^{t=m-n} v^{n+t}\,{}_{n+t}p_x \cdot {}_tp_y$$

$$= v^n\,{}_np_x \sum_{t=1}^{t=m-n} v^t\,{}_tp_{x+n:y}$$

$$= \frac{D_{x+n}}{D_x}\, a_{x+n:y:\overline{m-n}|}.$$

The total value is therefore

$$a_{x:\overline{n}|} + \frac{D_{x+n}}{D_x}\, a_{x+n:y:\overline{m-n}|}.$$

Ex. 3. Find by the H^M Table at 3 per cent. interest the value of a curtate annuity of £1 per annum, payable half-yearly, until the death of the survivor of two lives aged 30 and 35 respectively, the annuity to cease on both lives, or the survivor, attaining age 50.

The expression for the value is

$$a^{(2)}_{35:\overline{15}|} + a^{(2)}_{30:\overline{20}|} - a^{(2)}_{30:35:\overline{15}|}$$

$$= a_{35:\overline{15}|} + \frac{1}{4}\left(1 - \frac{D_{50}}{D_{35}}\right) + a_{30:\overline{20}|} + \frac{1}{4}\left(1 - \frac{D_{50}}{D_{30}}\right)$$

$$- a_{30:35:\overline{15}|} - \frac{1}{4}\left(1 - \frac{D_{45:50}}{D_{30:35}}\right).$$

To evaluate

$$a_{35:\overline{15}|} = a_{35} - \frac{N_{50}}{D_{35}}$$

$$= 18{\cdot}613 - 7{\cdot}528$$

$$= 11{\cdot}085,$$

$$a_{30:\overline{20}|} = a_{30} - \frac{N_{50}}{D_{30}}$$

$$= 19{\cdot}895 - 6{\cdot}237$$

$$= 13{\cdot}658,$$

$$a_{30:35:\overline{15}|} = a_{32\cdot8:32\cdot8} - \frac{N_{47\cdot8:47\cdot8}}{D_{32\cdot8:32\cdot8}}$$

$$= 15{\cdot}722 - 5{\cdot}302$$

$$= 10{\cdot}420,$$

$$\frac{1}{4}\left(1 - \frac{D_{50}}{D_{35}}\right) = \frac{1}{4}(1 - {\cdot}5424) = {\cdot}114,$$

$$\frac{1}{4}\left(1 - \frac{D_{50}}{D_{30}}\right) = \frac{1}{4}(1 - {\cdot}4494) = {\cdot}138,$$

$$\frac{1}{4}\left(1 - \frac{D_{45:50}}{D_{30:35}}\right) = \frac{1}{4}\left(1 - \frac{D_{47\cdot8:47\cdot8}}{D_{32\cdot8:32\cdot8}}\right)$$

$$= \tfrac{1}{4}(1 - {\cdot}4711) = {\cdot}132.$$

Therefore, the value required is

$$11{\cdot}085 + {\cdot}114 + 13{\cdot}658 + {\cdot}138 - 10{\cdot}420 - {\cdot}132$$

$$= 14{\cdot}443.$$

The values in this solution have been obtained by means of four-figure logarithms.

Ex. 4. A life aged 30 desires to purchase a deferred annuity of £100 per annum, payable yearly, to be entered upon on attainment of age 60, subject to the following conditions:

(*a*) provided (30) survives to age 60 the annuity payments are to continue for 10 years certain and so long thereafter as he survives;

(*b*) in the event of a life now aged 25 surviving until (30) attains age 60, the annuity is to continue for 10 years after the death of (30) should (25) live so long.

Find the net value of this annuity on the basis of the H^M Table with 3 per cent. interest.

The value of the annuity may be considered in two parts, namely:—(*a*) that part which depends on the life of (30) only and (*b*) that part which is also dependent on the survival of (25).

The value of (*a*) is

$$100 \times \frac{D_{60}}{D_{30}}\left[a_{\overline{10}|} + \frac{D_{70}}{D_{60}} a_{70}\right].$$

As regards the value of (*b*), provided both lives survive 30 years, a payment not included in (*a*) will be made at the end of the $(10+t)$th year thereafter if (25) be then alive, and (30) was alive at the end of the tth year but not alive at the end of the $(t+10)$th year. The value of this payment is therefore

$$v^{30}\,{}_{30}p_{25:30}\,.\,v^{10+t}\,{}_{10+t}p_{55}\left({}_tp_{60} - {}_{t+10}p_{60}\right),$$

and the value of this part of the annuity is therefore

$$100 \times \frac{D_{55:60}}{D_{25:30}}\,.\left[v^{10}\,{}_{10}p_{55} \sum_{t=1}^{t=\infty} v^t\,{}_tp_{65:60} - v^{10}\,{}_{10}p_{55:60} \sum_{t=1}^{t=\infty} v^t\,{}_tp_{65:70}\right]$$

$$= 100\left\{\frac{D_{65}}{D_{25}}\,.\,\frac{l_{60}}{l_{30}}\,a_{65:60} - \frac{D_{65:70}}{D_{25:30}}\,a_{65:70}\right\}.$$

Combining (*a*) and (*b*) the value required is

$$100\left\{\frac{D_{60}}{D_{30}}\,a_{\overline{10}|} + \frac{N_{71}}{D_{30}} + \frac{D_{65}}{D_{25}}\,.\,\frac{l_{60}}{l_{30}}\,a_{65:60} - \frac{N_{66:71}}{D_{25:30}}\right\}.$$

The equal age for ages 65 and 60 is 62·8; for 66 and 71, 68·8; and for 25 and 30, 27·8. The values of $\log D_x$, $\log D_{xx}$, $\log N_{xx}$ and a_{xx} are given in the tables on pages 418 to 422.

The numerical value, employing four-figure logarithms, is

$$100\{2{\cdot}306 + {\cdot}864 + {\cdot}671 - {\cdot}331\}$$
$$= 351.$$

Ex. 5. A man aged 35 effects a policy on the life of his son aged 2, payable at death after age 21.

The net premiums are to be returned if the son dies before age 21, and, should the father die before the son attains age 21, all premiums are to cease till the son reaches age 25, thereafter to resume and continue payable during the life of the son.

Obtain a formula for the net premium and show the value of the policy at the end of 10 years.

Let P represent the net premium, then

$$\text{Value of Benefit} = \frac{1}{D_2}[M_{21} + P\{(M_2 - M_{21}) + p_{35}(M_3 - M_{21}) + {}_2p_{35}(M_4 - M_{21}) + \ldots\ldots + {}_{18}p_{35}(M_{20} - M_{21})\}],$$

$$\text{Value of Payment} = P\left[a_{2:35:\overline{19}|} + \frac{D_{21:54}}{D_{2:35}}a_{21} + (1 - {}_{19}p_{35})\frac{D_{25}}{D_2}a_{25}\right]$$

$$= P\left[a_{2:35:\overline{19}|} + {}_{19}p_{35}\left(\frac{D_{21}}{D_2}a_{21} - \frac{D_{25}}{D_2}a_{25}\right) + \frac{D_{25}}{D_2}a_{25}\right]$$

$$= P\left[a_{2:35:\overline{19}|} + {}_{19}p_{35}\frac{D_{21}}{D_2}a_{21:\overline{4}|} + \frac{D_{25}}{D_2}a_{25}\right],$$

$$\therefore\ P = \frac{\dfrac{M_{21}}{D_2}}{\left\{\begin{array}{l} a_{2:35:\overline{19}|} + {}_{19}p_{35}\dfrac{D_{21}}{D_2}a_{21:\overline{4}|} + \dfrac{D_{25}}{D_2}a_{25} - \dfrac{1}{D_2}\{(M_2 - M_{21}) \\ \qquad + p_{35}(M_3 - M_{21}) + \ldots\ldots + {}_{18}p_{35}(M_{20} - M_{21})\} \end{array}\right\}}.$$

If (35) still alive

$$_{10}V = \frac{M_{21}}{D_{12}} + \frac{P}{D_{12}}[11(M_{12} - M_{21}) + p_{45}(M_{13} - M_{21}) + {}_2p_{45}(M_{14} - M_{21}) + \ldots\ldots + {}_8p_{45}(M_{20} - M_{21})]$$
$$- P\left[a_{12:45:\overline{9}|} + {}_9p_{45}\frac{D_{21}}{D_{12}}a_{21:\overline{4}|} + \frac{D_{25}}{D_{12}}a_{25}\right].$$

If (35) dead

$$_{10}V = \frac{M_{21}}{D_{12}} + \frac{tP}{D_{12}}[M_{12} - M_{21}] - P\frac{D_{25}}{D_{12}}a_{25},$$

where t = number of premiums paid up to death of (35).

If we neglect mortality of the child before 21

$$\text{Value of Benefit} = v^{19}A_{21},$$

$$\text{,, \quad ,, Payment} = P[a_{35:\overline{19}|} + v^{19}{}_{19}p_{35}a_{21:\overline{4}|} + v^{23}{}_4p_{21}a_{25}].$$

The policy value at the end of 10 years would then be taken as $P(s_{\overline{11}|} - 1)$.

CHAPTER XVI

JOINT-LIFE AND LAST-SURVIVOR ASSURANCES. COMPLETE JOINT-LIFE AND LAST-SURVIVOR ANNUITIES

1. The expressions for the values of joint-life assurances are precisely similar to, and obtained in the same manner as, the formulae for the corresponding single-life assurances dealt with in Chapters III and IV. For example, let it be required to find the value of an assurance of 1 payable at the end of the year in which the joint existence of two select lives (x) and (y) fails.

The probability that the joint lives (x) and (y) will fail in the ($t+1$)th year is ${}_{t|}q_{[x][y]}$, and the value of a unit payable at the end of that year, if this event happen, is $v^{t+1}{}_{t|}q_{[x][y]}$. The value of an assurance of 1 payable at the end of the year in which the first of these lives fails, represented by $A_{[x][y]}$, is therefore

$$A_{[x][y]} = \sum_{t=0}^{t=\infty} v^{t+1}{}_{t|}q_{[x][y]} \quad \text{......................(1)}$$

$$= \sum_{t=0}^{t=\infty} v^{t+1}({}_tp_{[x][y]} - {}_{t+1}p_{[x][y]})$$

$$= v(1 + a_{[x][y]}) - a_{[x][y]} \quad \text{..............(2),}$$

which corresponds to formula (1) of Chapter IV for a single-life assurance.

2. If the investment of a unit be considered in the manner employed in Chapter IV 5, we have

$$1 = d\text{a}_{[x][y]} + A_{[x][y]},$$

$$\therefore\quad A_{[x][y]} = 1 - d\text{a}_{[x][y]} \quad \text{.........................(3).}$$

3. For a temporary joint-life assurance payable at the end of the year of death provided this occurs within n years, ${}_{|n}A_{[x][y]}$ or $A_{\overset{1}{\overline{[x][y]}}:\overline{n|}}$, the formula is

$${}_{|n}A_{[x][y]} = v\text{a}_{[x][y]:\overline{n|}} - a_{[x][y]:\overline{n|}} \quad \text{..............(4),}$$

and for a joint-life endowment assurance, payable on the first death if this occur within n years, but at the end of that period if both lives survive,

$$A_{[x][y]:\overline{n|}} = v\text{a}_{[x][y]:\overline{n|}} - a_{[x][y]:\overline{n-1|}} \quad \text{..............(5)}$$

$$= 1 - d\text{a}_{[x][y]:\overline{n|}} \quad \text{......................(6).}$$

Formulae (4), (5) and (6) correspond to formulae (2), (3) and (10) of Chapter IV.

4. The value of a sum of "1" payable at time "t" if the joint existence of two lives (x) and (y) fail at that moment is

$$v^t{}_tp_{xy}\,\mu_{x+t:y+t}\,dt,$$

and the value of an assurance of "1" payable at the moment of the first death amongst these two lives, provided this occur within the next n years, is therefore

$$|_n\bar{A}_{xy} = \int_0^n v^t {}_tp_{xy}\mu_{x+t:y+t}\,dt$$

$$= -\frac{1}{l_{xy}}\int_0^n v^t \frac{dl_{x+t:y+t}}{dt}\,dt$$

$$= -\frac{1}{l_{xy}}\left[v^t l_{x+t:y+t} - \int v^t \log_e v \,.\, l_{x+t:y+t}\,dt\right]_{t=0}^{t=n}$$

$$= 1 - v^n {}_np_{xy} - \delta\bar{a}_{xy:\overline{n|}} \quad\text{.......................... (7).}$$

For the whole-life assurance, integrating between the limits 0 and ∞, the term $v^n {}_np_{xy}$ vanishes and

$$\bar{A}_{xy} = 1 - \delta\bar{a}_{xy} \quad\text{......................(8),}$$

and for the endowment assurance, since $\bar{A}_{xy:\overline{n|}} = |_n\bar{A}_{xy} + v^n {}_np_{xy}$,

$$\bar{A}_{xy:\overline{n|}} = 1 - \delta\bar{a}_{xy:\overline{n|}} \quad\text{....................(9).}$$

Formulae (8) and (9), which are equally applicable to select tables, should be compared with formulae (2) and (3) of Chapter VIII.

For practical purposes it is sufficiently accurate, and frequently convenient, to assume that

$$\bar{A}_{xy} = A_{xy} \times (1 + \tfrac{1}{2}i) \quad\text{and}\quad |_n\bar{A}_{xy} = |_nA_{xy} \times (1 + \tfrac{1}{2}i).$$

5. Considering the differential coefficient of $\bar{a}_{xy:\overline{n|}}$, the joint status (xy) being treated as the variable, we have

$$\frac{d\bar{a}_{xy:\overline{n|}}}{d(xy)} = \frac{d}{d(xy)}\int_0^n v^t {}_tp_{xy}\,dt$$

$$= \int_0^n v^t\left(\frac{d}{d(xy)}\,{}_tp_{xy}\right)dt$$

$$= \int_0^n v^t {}_tp_{xy}(\mu_{xy} - \mu_{x+t:y+t})\,dt$$

$$= \mu_{xy}\bar{a}_{xy:\overline{n|}} - |_n\bar{A}_{xy},$$

whence

$$|_n\bar{A}_{xy} = \mu_{xy}\bar{a}_{xy:\overline{n|}} - \frac{d\bar{a}_{xy:\overline{n|}}}{d(xy)}$$

$$= \mu_{xy}\bar{a}_{xy:\overline{n|}} + \tfrac{1}{2}(\bar{a}_{x-1:y-1:\overline{n|}} - \bar{a}_{x+1:y+1:\overline{n|}}) \quad\text{......(10),}$$

and similarly

$$\bar{A}_{xy} = \mu_{xy}\bar{a}_{xy} + \tfrac{1}{2}(\bar{a}_{x-1:y-1} - \bar{a}_{x+1:y+1}) \quad\text{............(11).}$$

These formulae correspond to formulae (4) and (5) of Chapter VIII, μ_{xy} being equal to $\mu_x + \mu_y$.

6. Again, by assuming $\mu_{x+t:y+t} = \dfrac{l_{x+t-1:y+t-1} - l_{x+t+1:y+t+1}}{2l_{x+t:y+t}}$ approximately, and inserting this value in the integral, formulae

corresponding to numbers (6) and (7) of Chapter VIII are obtained. Thus

$$|_n\bar{A}_{xy} = \frac{1}{2}\left(\frac{\bar{a}_{x-1:y-1:\overline{n}|}}{p_{x-1:y-1}} - p_{xy}\bar{a}_{x+1:y+1:\overline{n}|}\right) \quad \ldots\ldots\ldots(12),$$

and

$$\bar{A}_{xy} = \frac{1}{2}\left(\frac{\bar{a}_{x-1:y-1}}{p_{x-1:y-1}} - p_{xy}\bar{a}_{x+1:y+1}\right) \quad \ldots\ldots\ldots\ldots\ldots(13).$$

7. It is evident from formulae (3), (6), (8) and (9) that when the value of the whole-life or temporary annuity is known, the value of the corresponding whole-life or endowment assurance can be ascertained by means of Premium Conversion Tables. To demonstrate this point, joint-life assurances on two lives only have been considered, but the arguments employed are applicable where more lives are involved.

For example

$$\begin{aligned} A_{xyz\ldots(m)} &= v\mathbf{a}_{xyz\ldots(m)} - a_{xyz\ldots(m)} \\ &= 1 - d\,\mathbf{a}_{xyz\ldots(m)} \quad \ldots\ldots\ldots\ldots\ldots\ldots\ldots\ldots(14). \end{aligned}$$

8. The value of an assurance payable at the end of the year of death of the $(r+1)$th life to fail, out of an original number of m lives (x), (y), (z), ... etc., is

$$\left.\begin{aligned} &v\,(1 + a_{\overline{xyz\ldots(m)}}^{\,m-r}) - a_{\overline{xyz\ldots(m)}}^{\,m-r} \\ &\quad = 1 - d\,(1 + a_{\overline{xyz\ldots(m)}}^{\,m-r}) \end{aligned}\right\} \quad \ldots\ldots\ldots\ldots\ldots(15),$$

since, if the annuity be payable so long as at least $m-r$ lives continue jointly in existence, the last payment of the annuity will be made at the commencement of that year at the end of which there cannot be more than $m-r-1$ survivors, that is the year in which the $(r+1)$th death occurs.

9. Annual Premium for Joint-Life Assurances. Reasoning on the lines adopted in connection with single-life assurances, the annual premium payable throughout the duration of the contract for a joint whole-life assurance on (x) and (y), payable at the end of the year of death, can be obtained from the formula

$$P_{[x][y]} = \frac{A_{[x][y]}}{\mathbf{a}_{[x][y]}} \quad \ldots\ldots\ldots\ldots\ldots\ldots\ldots\ldots\ldots(16).$$

Similarly, for temporary and endowment assurances,

$$P_{\overset{1}{\overline{[x][y]}}:\overline{n}|} = \frac{|_nA_{[x][y]}}{\mathbf{a}_{[x][y]:\overline{n}|}} \quad \ldots\ldots\ldots\ldots\ldots\ldots\ldots(17),$$

and

$$P_{[x][y]:\overline{n}|} = \frac{A_{[x][y]:\overline{n}|}}{\mathbf{a}_{[x][y]:\overline{n}|}} \quad \ldots\ldots\ldots\ldots\ldots\ldots\ldots(18).$$

It follows also that

$$P_{[x][y]} = \frac{1}{1 + a_{[x][y]}} - d \quad \ldots\ldots\ldots\ldots\ldots\ldots (19),$$

and

$$P_{[x][y]:\overline{n}|} = \frac{1}{1 + a_{[x][y]:\overline{n-1}|}} - d \ldots\ldots\ldots\ldots\ldots (20),$$

from which it is seen that the *annual* premiums for joint-life whole-life and endowment assurances can be ascertained by entering Annual Premium Conversion Tables with joint-life whole-life and temporary annuity values in the same manner as for single lives.

Finally, for limited payment joint-life assurances,

$${}_tP_{[x][y]} = \frac{A_{[x][y]}}{\mathbf{a}_{[x][y]:\overline{t}|}} \ldots\ldots\ldots\ldots\ldots\ldots\ldots\ldots (21),$$

$${}_tP_{[x][y]:\overline{n}|} = \frac{A_{[x][y]:\overline{n}|}}{\mathbf{a}_{[x][y]:\overline{t}|}} \ldots\ldots\ldots\ldots\ldots\ldots\ldots\ldots (22),$$

$${}_tP^{\;1}_{\overline{[x][y]}:\overline{n}|} = \frac{|_n A_{[x][y]}}{\mathbf{a}_{[x][y]:\overline{t}|}} \ldots\ldots\ldots\ldots\ldots\ldots\ldots\ldots (23).$$

10. It may be mentioned that, provided the term of the assurance is short, the annual premium for a joint-life temporary assurance is very nearly equivalent to the sum of the temporary assurance premiums for the lives taken singly. That is, if n be small,

$$P^{\;1}_{\overline{xy}:\overline{n}|} = P^{1}_{x:\overline{n}|} + P^{1}_{y:\overline{n}|}$$

very nearly.

For example, by the $O^{[NM]}$ Table at $3\frac{1}{2}$ per cent.,

$$P^{\;1}_{\overline{[35:35]}:\overline{5}|} = \cdot 01573,$$

whereas

$$2P^{1}_{[35]:\overline{5}|} = \cdot 01584,$$

a difference of only ·011 for a sum assured of £100.

In *J. I. A.* XXXIII, 354, Mr Lidstone suggested that the annual premium for a joint-life endowment assurance can be approximately calculated by the formula

$$P_{xy:\overline{n}|} = P_{x:\overline{n}|} + P_{y:\overline{n}|} - P_{\overline{n}|}.$$

He pointed out that a single-life endowment assurance can be regarded as subdivided into two portions, namely:

(*a*) A sinking fund assurance providing for payment of the full sum assured at the expiration of the specified term irrespective of any life contingency.

(*b*) A varying temporary assurance, under which the sum assured in any one year is equal to the difference between (1) the sum assured by the endowment assurance policy, and (2) the reserve in respect of the sinking fund policy.

Note:—Formulae for the approximate calculation of net premiums for endowment assurances and temporary assurances on three or four joint lives are discussed in an Actuarial Note by F. W. Robertson (*J. I. A.* LIV, 96).

If a second life be now introduced it will be necessary to add a third benefit (*c*) and to subtract a fourth benefit (*d*), namely:

(*c*) A varying term assurance similar to (*b*), but on the second life instead of the first.

(*d*) A varying term assurance on the joint lives, the sum payable thereunder to be the reserve on (*c*) if the first life predecease the second, or the reserve on (*b*) if the second life predecease the first. (This benefit may be positive or negative, but will usually be negative.)

The annual premiums for the complete benefit will be the sum of the annual premiums for the partial benefits (*a*), (*b*), (*c*) and (*d*). Now it is evident that the sum assured under benefit (*d*) will be numerically small, and hence the annual premium for that benefit must be very small. We may therefore obtain an approximate result by neglecting (*d*), and we shall then have

$$P_{xy:\overline{n|}} = P_{\overline{n|}} + (P_{x:\overline{n|}} - P_{\overline{n|}}) + (P_{y:\overline{n|}} - P_{\overline{n|}}) = P_{x:\overline{n|}} + P_{y:\overline{n|}} - P_{\overline{n|}}.$$

For example, by the $O^{[NM]}$ Table at $3\frac{1}{2}$ per cent.,

$$P_{[35:35]:\overline{20|}} = \cdot 04651,$$

whereas $$2P_{[35]:\overline{20|}} - P_{\overline{20|}} = \cdot 04641,$$

a difference of ·010 for a sum assured of £100.

11. Commutation columns applicable to joint-life assurances can be constructed on the basis of either Davies's or De Morgan's form (see Chapter XV 4). By Davies's form

$$C_{xy} = v^{x+1}(l_x l_y - l_{x+1} l_{y+1}), \text{ where } x > y,$$

and by De Morgan's form

$$C_{xy} = v^{\frac{x+y}{2}+1}(l_x l_y - l_{x+1} l_{y+1}).$$

In either case, $$M_{xy} = \sum_{t=0}^{t=\infty} C_{x+t:y+t}.$$

For Select Tables, adopting De Morgan's form,

$$C_{[x][y]} = v^{\frac{x+y}{2}+1}(l_{[x]} l_{[y]} - l_{[x]+1} l_{[y]+1}),$$

$$C_{[x]+t:[y]+t} = v^{\frac{x+y}{2}+t+1}(l_{[x]+t} l_{[y]+t} - l_{[x]+t+1} l_{[y]+t+1}),$$

and assuming the "select period" to be five years,

$$M_{[x][y]} = \sum_{t=0}^{t=4} C_{[x]+t:[y]+t} + M_{x+5:y+5}.$$

In all these expressions (x) and (y) can be taken on the basis of the same or of different mortality tables. Where both lives are assumed to be subject to the same rates of mortality the ages x and y can be enclosed in brackets thus: $[xy]$.

For the evaluation of varying joint-life assurances a commutation function $R_{xy} = \sum_{t=0}^{t=\infty} M_{x+t:y+t}$ could also be constructed. This, however, is very seldom required and for isolated cases can be obtained by summing the appropriate values of the M_{xy} column.

The values of the single and annual premiums for joint-life assurances expressed in terms of commutation functions are as follows:

$$A_{[x][y]} = \frac{M_{[x][y]}}{D_{[x][y]}},$$

$$P_{[x][y]} = \frac{M_{[x][y]}}{N_{[x][y]}},$$

$$|_n A_{[x][y]} = \frac{M_{[x][y]} - M_{[x]+n:[y]+n}}{D_{[x][y]}},$$

$$P_{\overset{1}{\overline{[x][y]}}:\overline{n|}} = \frac{M_{[x][y]} - M_{[x]+n:[y]+n}}{N_{[x][y]} - N_{[x]+n:[y]+n}},$$

$$A_{[x][y]:\overline{n|}} = \frac{M_{[x][y]} - M_{[x]+n:[y]+n} + D_{[x]+n:[y]+n}}{D_{[x][y]}},$$

$$P_{[x][y]:\overline{n|}} = \frac{M_{[x][y]} - M_{[x]+n:[y]+n} + D_{[x]+n:[y]+n}}{N_{[x][y]} - N_{[x]+n:[y]+n}}.$$

12. If it be required to find the single or annual premium for a joint-life assurance for which the appropriate annuity value or commutation table is not available, the simplest plan is to ascertain the annuity value by approximate integration and enter a premium conversion table. For example, if the value of $\overline{A}_{30:35:45}$ be required, we have

$$\overline{a}_{30:35:45} = \frac{1}{l_{30}\, l_{35}\, l_{45}} \int_0^\infty v^t\, l_{30+t}\, l_{35+t}\, l_{45+t}\, dt,$$

from which the value of the annuity can be calculated in the manner shown in Chapter XV 12.

The alternative plan is to calculate the single premium directly by means of the integral

$$\overline{A}_{30:35:45} = \frac{1}{l_{30}\, l_{35}\, l_{45}} \int_0^\infty v^t\, l_{30+t}\, l_{35+t}\, l_{45+t}\, (\mu_{30+t} + \mu_{35+t} + \mu_{45+t})\, dt,$$

but as this means, for each term of the approximate integration formula, extracting three values of μ from the mortality table, adding these together and extracting the logarithm of their sum, it is clearly more expeditious to enter a premium conversion table once with the value of the annuity.

Similarly, for a joint-life endowment assurance on three lives (x) (y) and (z) for, say, 20 years, the simplest plan would be to evaluate the temporary annuity in the manner shown in Chapter XV 12, and enter a conversion table for the required single or annual premium.

In the case of a temporary joint-life assurance the necessary relation between $\overline{\text{A}}$ and $\bar{a}$ for the use of premium conversion tables does not exist and other methods must be employed.

When the term is short the single or annual premium can be calculated in detail or by an approximation such as that mentioned in paragraph 10 for two lives. The annual premium for a short term such as five years can also be readily arrived at by the formula

$$\frac{{}_{\overline{5}|}\text{A}_{xyz}}{\text{a}_{xyz:\overline{5}|}} = \frac{v\text{a}_{xyz:\overline{5}|} - a_{xyz:\overline{5}|}}{\text{a}_{xyz:\overline{5}|}}$$

$$= v - \frac{a_{xyz:\overline{5}|}}{\text{a}_{xyz:\overline{5}|}},$$

as, in the evaluation of the successive terms of $a_{xyz:\overline{5}|}$, all the terms of $a_{xyz:\overline{4}|}$ required for the denominator are obtained. With the aid of four-figure logarithms the work is not great, particularly when $\log \text{D}_x$ and $\log l_x$ are tabulated.

For a longer term such as 20 years, the endowment assurance single premium can be ascertained with the aid of conversion tables and the single premium for the temporary assurance derived therefrom by the formula

$${}_{\overline{20}|}\overline{\text{A}}_{xyz} = \overline{\text{A}}_{xyz:\overline{20}|} - v^{20}\frac{l_{x+20}\,l_{y+20}\,l_{z+20}}{l_x\,l_y\,l_z}.$$

Similarly, if the annual premium be required,

$$\text{a}_{xyz:\overline{20}|} = \bar{a}_{xyz:\overline{20}|} + \frac{1}{2}\left(1 - v^{20}\frac{l_{x+20}\,l_{y+20}\,l_{z+20}}{l_x\,l_y\,l_z}\right),$$

whence the annual premium, assuming the sum assured payable at the moment of death,

$$^{(\infty)}\text{P}_{\overset{1}{xyz}:\overline{20}|} = \frac{{}_{\overline{20}|}\overline{\text{A}}_{xyz}}{\text{a}_{xyz:\overline{20}|}}.$$

13. Policy Values for Joint-Life Assurances. The formulae for the evaluation of joint-life single and annual premiums and annuities being similar to those for single-life assurances, the expressions for joint-life policy values do not present any fresh difficulty.

Representing the values, at the end of t years, of temporary whole-life and endowment assurances on the joint lives of (x) and (y) by ${}_t\mathrm{V}_{\overset{1}{\overline{[x][y]}}:\overline{n|}}$, ${}_t\mathrm{V}_{[x][y]}$ and ${}_t\mathrm{V}_{[x][y]:\overline{n|}}$ respectively, we have

$$ {}_t\mathrm{V}_{\overset{1}{\overline{[x][y]}}:\overline{n|}} = \mathrm{A}_{\overset{1}{\overline{[x]+t:[y]+t}}:\overline{n-t|}} - \mathrm{P}_{\overset{1}{\overline{[x][y]}}:\overline{n|}}\,\mathrm{a}_{[x]+t:[y]+t:\overline{n-t|}} \quad\text{...(24)},$$

$$ {}_t\mathrm{V}_{[x][y]} = \mathrm{A}_{[x]+t:[y]+t} - \mathrm{P}_{[x][y]}\,\mathrm{a}_{[x]+t:[y]+t} \quad\text{...............(25)},$$

$$ {}_t\mathrm{V}_{[x][y]:\overline{n|}} = \mathrm{A}_{[x]+t:[y]+t:\overline{n-t|}} - \mathrm{P}_{[x][y]:\overline{n|}}\,\mathrm{a}_{[x]+t:[y]+t:\overline{n-t|}} \quad\text{...(26)}.$$

If premiums be limited to k payments we have where $t < k$

$$ {}^k_t\mathrm{V}_{\overset{1}{\overline{[x][y]}}:\overline{n|}} = \mathrm{A}_{\overset{1}{\overline{[x]+t:[y]+t}}:\overline{n-t|}} - {}_k\mathrm{P}_{\overset{1}{\overline{[x][y]}}:\overline{n|}}\,\mathrm{a}_{[x]+t:[y]+t:\overline{k-t|}} \quad\text{...(27)},$$

$$ {}^k_t\mathrm{V}_{[x][y]} = \mathrm{A}_{[x]+t:[y]+t} - {}_k\mathrm{P}_{[x][y]}\,\mathrm{a}_{[x]+t:[y]+t:\overline{k-t|}} \quad\text{.........(28)},$$

$$ {}^k_t\mathrm{V}_{[x][y]:\overline{n|}} = \mathrm{A}_{[x]+t:[y]+t:\overline{n-t|}} - {}_k\mathrm{P}_{[x][y]:\overline{n|}}\,\mathrm{a}_{[x]+t:[y]+t:\overline{k-t|}} \quad\text{...(29)},$$

and where $t \geqq k$,

$$\left.\begin{aligned} {}^k_t\mathrm{V}_{\overset{1}{\overline{[x][y]}}:\overline{n|}} &= \mathrm{A}_{\overset{1}{\overline{[x]+t:[y]+t}}:\overline{n-t|}} \\ {}^k_t\mathrm{V}_{[x][y]} &= \mathrm{A}_{[x]+t:[y]+t} \\ {}^k_t\mathrm{V}_{[x][y]:\overline{n|}} &= \mathrm{A}_{[x]+t:[y]+t:\overline{n-t|}} \end{aligned}\right\} \quad\text{.........................(30)}.$$

14. In the periodical valuation of a Life Office having a large number of joint-life assurances of any one class in force, these are generally grouped according to the corresponding "equal ages" obtained by means of Makeham's Law. If the valuation be made on a table which follows that law, this is strictly accurate; and is sufficiently accurate for practical purposes even when the table employed does not follow that law.

For special classes such as joint-life endowment assurances subject to limited payments etc. the number of policies in force is frequently so small that the assurances are valued individually.

***15. Assurances payable on the death of the survivor of two or more lives.** The value of an assurance of "1" payable at the end of the year of death of the last survivor of two lives (x) and (y) is

$$\begin{aligned} \mathrm{A}_{\overline{xy}} &= 1 - d\,\mathrm{a}_{\overline{xy}} \quad\text{...(31)} \\ &= 1 - d\,(1 + a_x + a_y - a_{xy}) \\ &= \{1 - d\,(1 + a_x)\} + \{1 - d\,(1 + a_y)\} - \{1 - d\,(1 + a_{xy})\} \\ &= \mathrm{A}_x + \mathrm{A}_y - \mathrm{A}_{xy} \quad\text{...(32)}. \end{aligned}$$

Similarly, if the assurance be payable on the death of the survivor of three lives,

$$\begin{aligned} \mathrm{A}_{\overline{xyz}} &= 1 - d\,\mathrm{a}_{\overline{xyz}} \quad\text{...(33)} \\ &= 1 - d\,(1 + a_x + a_y + a_z - a_{xy} - a_{xz} - a_{yz} + a_{xyz}) \\ &= \mathrm{A}_x + \mathrm{A}_y + \mathrm{A}_z - \mathrm{A}_{xy} - \mathrm{A}_{xz} - \mathrm{A}_{yz} + \mathrm{A}_{xyz} \quad\text{...........(34)}. \end{aligned}$$

* All the formulae in paragraphs 15 to 25 apply also to select tables.

It will be gathered from these expressions that a method similar to that employed in XIII 17 and 18 and XV 14 and 15, involving successive powers of Z, can be employed to express such assurances in terms of single and joint-life assurances. Generally speaking, however, it will be found simpler to calculate the value of the annuity involved and to ascertain the value of the assurance therefrom with the aid of Premium Conversion Tables. In the case of $A_{\overline{xyz}}$, for example, it will be simpler to calculate the value of $a_{\overline{xyz}}$ and enter a conversion table with this single value, than to enter such a table several times with the various annuity values to obtain the separate values of "A" which must be combined to give $A_{\overline{xyz}}$.

16. The annual premium for an assurance payable on the death of the survivor of two lives (x) and (y) is obtained from the formula

$$\left.\begin{aligned} P_{\overline{xy}} &= \frac{A_{\overline{xy}}}{\mathbf{a}_{\overline{xy}}} \\ &= \frac{1}{1+a_{\overline{xy}}} - d \end{aligned}\right\} \qquad (35),$$

and similarly for any number, say, n lives

$$\left.\begin{aligned} P_{\overline{xyz\ldots(n)}} &= \frac{A_{\overline{xyz\ldots(n)}}}{\mathbf{a}_{\overline{xyz\ldots(n)}}} \\ &= \frac{1}{1+a_{\overline{xyz\ldots(n)}}} - d \end{aligned}\right\} \qquad (36).$$

It is evident that for the calculation of the annual premiums also the simplest method is to obtain the value of the annuity and to enter the appropriate conversion table with this value.

17. For a last-survivor endowment assurance on (x) and (y) for n years; that is, an assurance payable on the second death in the event of both the lives dying within n years, but payable at the end of n years provided at least one of the lives survives, we have

$$A_{\overline{xy}:\overline{n|}} = 1 - d\mathbf{a}_{\overline{xy}:\overline{n|}} \qquad (37),$$

$$P_{\overline{xy}:\overline{n|}} = \frac{1}{\mathbf{a}_{\overline{xy}:\overline{n|}}} - d \qquad (38),$$

and for a temporary assurance payable only in the event of both the lives failing within n years,

$$A^{\;1}_{\overline{xy}:\overline{n|}} = A^{\;1}_{x:\overline{n|}} + A^{\;1}_{y:\overline{n|}} - A^{\;1}_{xy:\overline{n|}} \qquad (39),$$

$$\left.\begin{aligned} P^{\;1}_{\overline{xy}:\overline{n|}} &= \frac{A^{\;1}_{\overline{xy}:\overline{n|}}}{\mathbf{a}_{\overline{xy}:\overline{n|}}} \\ &= \frac{A^{\;1}_{x:\overline{n|}} + A^{\;1}_{y:\overline{n|}} - A^{\;1}_{xy:\overline{n|}}}{1 + a_{x:\overline{n-1|}} + a_{y:\overline{n-1|}} - a_{xy:\overline{n-1|}}} \end{aligned}\right\} \qquad (40).$$

18. In order to point out a further difficulty in connection with the employment of the "Z" method in the evaluation of survivorship assurances, let us consider the value of an assurance of 1 payable at the end of the year in which the third death amongst four lives (w), (x), (y) and (z) occurs. Since the third death leaves only one surviving, the assurance continues so long as two lives at least are in existence, and the "Z" formula to be employed will, therefore, be

$$\frac{Z^2}{(1+Z)^2} = Z^2 - 2Z^3 + 3Z^4,$$

whence the value is

$$A_{wx} + A_{wy} + A_{wz} + A_{xy} + A_{xz} + A_{yz} - 2(A_{wxy} + A_{wxz} + A_{wyz} + A_{xyz}) + 3A_{wxyz}.$$

But this value can also be expressed as

$$\begin{aligned} &1 - d(1 + a_{\overline{wxyz}}^{\;2}) \\ &= 1 - d\{1 + a_{wx} + a_{wy} + a_{wz} + a_{xy} + a_{xz} + a_{yz} \\ &\qquad - 2(a_{wxy} + a_{wxz} + a_{wyz} + a_{xyz}) + 3a_{wxyz}\}, \end{aligned}$$

which in terms of "A" gives the same result as before.

In this case, not only is it easier to ascertain the value of the annuity and enter a conversion table, but there is the added difficulty, when dealing with the assurance values, of determining the proper index of Z.

Moreover, since the annual premium

$$P_{\overline{wxyz}}^{\;2} = \frac{1}{1 + a_{\overline{wxyz}}^{\;2}} - d,$$

the value of the annuity being available enables the annual premium also to be ascertained by reference to a Premium Conversion Table.

It is not considered necessary to deal with further examples of this nature.

19. There is one danger in dealing with the annual premium for a joint and survivorship assurance to which attention should be drawn.

The single premium for an assurance payable on the death of the survivor of two lives (x) and (y) is

$$A_{\overline{xy}} = A_x + A_y - A_{xy},$$

and the corresponding annual premium

$$\begin{aligned} P_{\overline{xy}} &= \frac{A_{\overline{xy}}}{\mathrm{a}_{\overline{xy}}} \\ &= \frac{A_x + A_y - A_{xy}}{\mathrm{a}_x + \mathrm{a}_y - \mathrm{a}_{xy}}. \end{aligned}$$

The mistake is sometimes made of writing $P_{\overline{xy}} = P_x + P_y - P_{xy}$ which is obviously incorrect.

20. Policy Values for Last-Survivor Assurances. For assurances payable on the death of the survivor of two lives (x) and (y), the expressions for the policy values are:

(a) if both (x) and (y) be alive

$$ {}_tV_{\overset{1}{\overline{xy}}:\overline{n}|} = A_{\overset{1}{\overline{x+t:y+t}}:\overline{n-t}|} - P_{\overset{1}{\overline{xy}}:\overline{n}|}\, a_{\overline{x+t:y+t}:\overline{n-t}|} \text{ ......(41)}, $$

$$ {}_tV_{\overline{xy}} = A_{\overline{x+t:y+t}} - P_{\overline{xy}}\, a_{\overline{x+t:y+t}} \text{ ......(42)}, $$

$$ {}_tV_{\overline{xy}:\overline{n}|} = A_{\overline{x+t:y+t}:\overline{n-t}|} - P_{\overline{xy}:\overline{n}|}\, a_{\overline{x+t:y+t}:\overline{n-t}|} \text{ ......(43)}; $$

(b) if (x) be alive and (y) dead

$$ {}_tV_{\overset{1}{\overline{xy}}:\overline{n}|} = A_{\overset{1}{x+t}:\overline{n-t}|} - P_{\overset{1}{\overline{xy}}:\overline{n}|}\, a_{x+t:\overline{n-t}|} \text{ ......(44)}, $$

$$ {}_tV_{\overline{xy}} = A_{x+t} - P_{\overline{xy}}\, a_{x+t} \text{ ......(45)}, $$

$$ {}_tV_{\overline{xy}:\overline{n}|} = A_{x+t:\overline{n-t}|} - P_{\overline{xy}:\overline{n}|}\, a_{x+t:\overline{n-t}|} \text{ ......(46)}. $$

If (y) be alive and (x) dead the formulae are the same as in (b), provided $y+t$ be substituted for $x+t$ in the Assurance and Annuity factors.

21. Premiums payable m times a year. For both joint-life and last-survivor assurances the premiums payable m times a year can be found from the annual premiums in the same manner as for single-life assurances. (See Chapter VII 12 to 19.)

22. Special Cases. An assurance may be payable on the failure of the joint existence of two statuses, each of which involves a life and a term certain. If an assurance be payable at the death of either (x) before reaching age $x+m$, or (y) before reaching age $y+n$, whichever occur first, its value will be

$$ A_{\overset{1}{xy}:\overline{n}|} + v^n{}_np_{xy}\, A_{\overset{1}{x+n}:\overline{m-n}|} \quad \text{if } m > n, $$

$$ A_{\overset{1}{xy}:\overline{m}|} + v^m{}_mp_{xy}\, A_{\overset{1}{y+m}:\overline{n-m}|} \quad \text{if } m < n, $$

$$ A_{\overset{1}{xy}:\overline{m}|} \quad \text{if } m = n. $$

Taking the first case, the assurance will clearly be payable on the first death within n years, and if both (x) and (y) survive that period it will still be payable if (x) die during the remainder of the period m years, that is, before he reaches age $x+m$.

As an example, the value of an assurance payable on the death of either of two lives aged 7 and 9 respectively before reaching age 21 can be expressed thus:

$$A_{\overset{1}{7}:9:\overline{12}|} + v^{12}{}_{12}p_{7:9}A^{1}_{19:\overline{2}|}.$$

Returning to the general case, the annual premium for this assurance would be

$$\frac{A_{\overset{1}{xy}:\overline{n}|} + v^n{}_np_{xy}A_{\overset{1}{x+n}:\overline{m-n}|}}{a_{xy:\overline{n}|} + v^n{}_np_{xy}a_{x+n:\overline{m-n}|}} \quad \text{if } m > n,$$

$$= \frac{A_{\overset{1}{xy}:\overline{m}|} + v^m{}_mp_{xy}A_{\overset{1}{y+m}:\overline{n-m}|}}{a_{xy:\overline{m}|} + v^m{}_mp_{xy}a_{y+m:\overline{n-m}|}} \quad \text{if } m < n,$$

$$= \frac{A_{\overset{1}{xy}:\overline{m}|}}{a_{xy:\overline{m}|}} = P_{\overset{1}{xy}:\overline{m}|} \quad \text{if } m = n.$$

23. If the assurance be payable in the event of *both* (x) dying before age $x+m$ and (y) before $y+n$, its value will be

$$A_{\overset{1}{\overline{xy}}:\overline{n}|} + v^n{}_np_x(1 - {}_np_y)A_{\overset{1}{x+n}:\overline{m-n}|} \quad \text{if } m > n,$$

$$A_{\overset{1}{\overline{xy}}:\overline{m}|} + v^m{}_mp_y(1 - {}_mp_x)A_{\overset{1}{y+m}:\overline{n-m}|} \quad \text{if } m < n,$$

$$A_{\overset{1}{\overline{xy}}:\overline{m}|} \quad \text{if } m = n.$$

Again considering the first case, the assurance will evidently be payable if both lives fail within the shorter term, n years, $(A_{\overset{1}{\overline{xy}}:\overline{n}|})$, but if only (y) fail within that period, the assurance will still be payable in the event of (x) dying during the remainder of the period of m years.

The annual premium for this assurance will be found by dividing the single premium by

$$a_{\overline{xy}:\overline{n}|} + v^n{}_np_x(1 - {}_np_y)a_{x+n:\overline{m-n}|} \quad \text{if } m > n,$$

$$a_{\overline{xy}:\overline{m}|} + v^m{}_mp_y(1 - {}_mp_x)a_{y+m:\overline{n-m}|} \quad \text{if } m < n,$$

$$a_{\overline{xy}:\overline{m}|} \quad \text{if } m = n.$$

The Single Premium for an assurance payable only in the event of two lives aged 7 and 9 respectively both dying before reaching age 21, is

$$A_{\overset{1}{\overline{7:9}}:\overline{12}|} + v^{12}{}_{12}p_7(1 - {}_{12}p_9)A^{1}_{19:\overline{2}|}.$$

24. Complete Joint-Life and Last-Survivor Annuities. All the formulae for complete annuities discussed in Chapter IX apply equally well to joint-life annuities, the practical formulae being

$$\mathring{a}^{(m)}_{xy} = a_{xy} + \frac{m-1}{2m} + \frac{1}{2m}A_{xy} \quad \text{..............(47)},$$

$$\mathring{a}^{(m)}_{xy} = \bar{a}_{xy}\left(1 - \frac{\delta}{2m}\right) + \frac{\delta}{12m^2} \quad \text{...............(48)}$$

$$= (\tfrac{1}{2} + a_{xy})\left(1 - \frac{\delta}{2m}\right) \quad \text{..................(49)}.$$

25. In the case of last-survivor annuities the adjustment to be made in the expression for the value of an annuity to provide a proportionate payment to the date of death requires careful consideration.

For the value of a complete annuity payable m times a year until the death of the survivor of two lives (x) and (y), we have

$$\mathring{a}^{(m)}_{\overline{xy}} = a_{\overline{xy}} + \frac{m-1}{2m} + \frac{1}{2m}\bar{A}_{\overline{xy}}.$$

To find an expression for the value of a complete annuity payable m times a year so long as exactly one of three lives (x), (y) and (z) is alive, let us assume that the annuity is set up immediately so that the successive payments are made at the end of periods of $\frac{1}{m}$th of a year dating from the date of the contract, but that we are only concerned now with the payments during the life of the last survivor after the death of the others. The value of the curtate annuity will be $a^{(m)}_{\overline{xyz}}{}^{[1]}$ and the addition to provide for the proportionate payment to the date of death, which is evidently in this case the date of the last death, is $\frac{1}{2m}\bar{A}_{\overline{xyz}}$. The value is, therefore,

$$a^{(m)\,[1]}_{\overline{xyz}} + \frac{1}{2m}\bar{A}_{\overline{xyz}}$$

$$= a^{(m)}_{x} + a^{(m)}_{y} + a^{(m)}_{z} - 2a^{(m)}_{xy} - 2a^{(m)}_{xz} - 2a^{(m)}_{yz} + 3a^{(m)}_{xyz} + \frac{1}{2m}\bar{A}_{\overline{xyz}}$$

$$= a_x + a_y + a_z - 2a_{xy} - 2a_{xz} - 2a_{yz} + 3a_{xyz} + \frac{1}{2m}\bar{A}_{\overline{xyz}},$$

where we have assumed

$$a^{(m)}_{x} = a_x + \frac{m-1}{2m}, \quad a^{(m)}_{xy} = a_{xy} + \frac{m-1}{2m}, \text{ etc.}$$

For the value of a similar complete annuity payable only while exactly two out of four lives aged respectively w, x, y and z are alive, making the same assumption as to the annuity being set up immediately, we shall have

$$a^{(m)\,[2]}_{\overline{wxyz}} + \frac{1}{2m}(1 - \delta\bar{a}_{\overline{wxyz}}^{\,2})$$

$$= a^{[2]}_{\overline{wxyz}} + \frac{1}{2m}(1 - \delta\bar{a}_{\overline{wxyz}}^{\,2}).$$

In either of these cases the condition might exist that the annuity should only be entered upon at the second death, the $m$thly periods dating from that event. This introduces a further modification into the formulae, but as such annuities are more readily treated as combinations of reversionary life annuities, the further discussion of them will be deferred until Chapter XVIII.

EXAMPLES

Ex. 1. Find the annual premium, on the basis of the $O^{[NM]}$ Table at $3\frac{1}{2}$ per cent., for a joint-life whole-life assurance of £100 on the lives of (30) and (35).

$$P_{[30:35]} = \frac{1}{1 + a_{[30:35]}} - d.$$

For the value of the annuity,

$$a_{[30:35]} = a_{[32\cdot78:32\cdot78]} = 14\cdot714,$$

whence, with the aid of the premium conversion table, we find that

$$100\,P_{[30:35]} = 2\cdot982 \text{ (say £2. 19}s.\ 8d.).$$

Ex. 2. Find, by the H^M Table at 3 per cent., the net annual premium payable throughout the duration of the contract for an assurance of £100 payable at the end of the year of the second death among four lives aged 30, 35, 40 and 45 respectively.

Let P represent the annual premium required, then

$$P = \frac{1}{1 + a_{\overline{30:35:40:45}}^{\;3}} - d,$$

since, if the premium be payable so long as at least three of the lives survive, this will be until the beginning of the year in which the second death occurs.

The value of the annuity is found as follows:

$$\begin{aligned} a_{\overline{30:35:40:45}}^{\;3} &= a_{30:35:40} + a_{30:40:45} + a_{30:35:45} + a_{35:40:45} - 3a_{30:35:40:45} \\ &= a_{35\cdot8:35\cdot8:35\cdot8} + a_{39\cdot9:39\cdot9:39\cdot9} + a_{38\cdot5:38\cdot5:38\cdot5} \\ &\qquad + a_{40\cdot7:40\cdot7:40\cdot7} - 3a_{38\cdot9:38\cdot9:38\cdot9:38\cdot9} \\ &= 12\cdot756 + 11\cdot640 + 12\cdot030 + 11\cdot412 - 3(10\cdot418) \\ &= 16\cdot584, \end{aligned}$$

whence, entering the 3 per cent. annual premium conversion table with 16·584, we find that the premium required is ·0277 or 2·77 (say £2. 15s. 6d.) per cent.

CHAPTER XVII

CONTINGENT ASSURANCES

1. The simplest form of Contingent Assurance is one under which the sum assured is payable on the death of a person, say (x), known as the "failing" life, provided another person, say (y), known as the "counter" life, survive him.

The value of such an assurance, assuming both lives to be "select," is represented by $A^{\ 1}_{[x][y]}$ if the sum assured be payable at the end of the year of death, or by $\bar{A}^{\ 1}_{[x][y]}$ if payable at the moment of death; it being sufficient for practical purposes to take

$$\bar{A}^{\ 1}_{[x][y]} = A^{\ 1}_{[x][y]} \times (1 + \tfrac{1}{2}i).$$

2. It is not necessary that the same mortality table should be employed in connection with both (x) and (y). The two lives are of distinct classes, and it may be assumed that the assurance would not be effected unless (y) were a healthy life and there was some prospect of (x) dying first.

In the calculation of the value of the assurance, therefore, (y) should be taken on the basis of a table showing as favourable a mortality experience as possible, and need not be medically examined. The failing life (x) should be medically examined and even then assumed to be subject to a less favourable mortality experience than (y).

The basis generally adopted, at the present time, is to take the $O^{[NM]}$ Table for the failing life (x) and the $O^{[af]}$ Table (British Offices Life Annuitants—Females) for the counter life (y), and tables of $A^{\ 1}_{[x][y]}$ and $P^{\ 1}_{[x][y]}$ (the corresponding annual premium) at 3 per cent. on this basis are given at the end of the volume, "British Offices Life Tables 1893—Select Tables—Whole-Life Assurances—Males." The values are tabulated for every age of (x) from 20 to 75 and quinary values of (y), intervening values being obtainable by interpolation.

3. Commutation Tables for Contingent Assurances. On the assumption of a uniform distribution of deaths over each year of age, the value of a payment of "1" at the end of the $(t+1)$th year if (x) die in that year leaving (y) surviving him is, on the basis of an aggregate table, $v^{t+1}\frac{d_{x+t}}{l_x}\cdot\frac{l_{y+t+\frac{1}{2}}}{l_y}$. Whence, multiplying numerator and denominator by $v^{\frac{x+y}{2}}$, we have

$$\frac{v^{\frac{x+y}{2}+t+1}d_{x+t}\cdot l_{y+t+\frac{1}{2}}}{v^{\frac{x+y}{2}}l_x\cdot l_y}$$

$$=\frac{C_{\overset{1}{x+t}:y+t}}{D_{xy}},$$

where $$C_{\overset{1}{x+t}:y+t}=v^{\frac{x+y}{2}+t+1}d_{x+t}\cdot l_{y+t+\frac{1}{2}}.$$

The value, on the same assumption, of an assurance of "1" payable at the end of the year of death of (x) provided (y) survive him, is

$$\left.\begin{aligned}A_{\overset{1}{x}y}&=\frac{1}{D_{xy}}\sum_{t=0}^{t=\infty}C_{\overset{1}{x+t}:y+t}\\&=\frac{M_{\overset{1}{x}y}}{D_{xy}}\end{aligned}\right\}\quad\text{......................(1)},$$

where $$M_{\overset{1}{x}y}=\sum_{t=0}^{t=\infty}C_{\overset{1}{x+t}:y+t}.$$

It is clear, therefore, that assuming a uniform distribution of deaths over each year of age, commutation tables can be constructed, in the manner indicated, suitable for the calculation of Contingent Assurances.

For the evaluation of increasing contingent assurances a further commutation function $R_{\overset{1}{x}y}=\sum_{t=0}^{t=\infty}M_{\overset{1}{x+t}\,y+t}$ can also be tabulated.

4. When a Select Table is employed, the formulae become

$$C_{\overset{1}{[x]+t}:[y]+t}=v^{\frac{x+y}{2}+t+1}d_{[x]+t}\cdot l_{[y]+t+\frac{1}{2}},$$

or $$C_{\overset{1}{x+t}:y+t}\;=v^{\frac{x+y}{2}+t+1}d_{x+t}\cdot l_{y+t+\frac{1}{2}},$$

after the "select period" is passed. And, assuming the "select period" to be five years,

$$M_{[x][y]}^{1} = \sum_{t=0}^{t=4} C_{\overset{1}{[x]+t}:[y]+t} + M_{\overset{1}{x+5}:y+5},$$

and
$$A_{[x][y]}^{1} = \frac{M_{[x][y]}^{1}}{D_{[x][y]}}.$$

Commutation Tables of this description can be constructed even when the two lives are taken on the basis of different mortality tables, the only difference being that $l_{[x]}$, $l_{[x]+t}$ and $d_{[x]+t}$ are taken from one table and $l_{[y]}$, $l_{[y]+t}$ and $l_{[y]+t+\frac{1}{2}}$ from the second table. This process was adopted in connection with the tables of $A_{[x][y]}^{1}$ and $P_{[x][y]}^{1}$ on the basis of the $O^{[NM]}$ Table for (x) and $O^{[af]}$ Table for (y) to which reference has already been made.

For the annual premium payable during the joint existence of the two lives (x) and (y), values of $N_{[x][y]}$ or of $a_{[x][y]}$ are required.

Then
$$\left.\begin{aligned} P_{[x][y]}^{1} &= \frac{A_{[x][y]}^{1}}{a_{[x][y]}} \\ &= \frac{M_{[x][y]}^{1}}{N_{[x][y]}} \end{aligned}\right\} \quad \text{.........................(2).}$$

5. The commutation functions discussed in paragraphs 3 and 4 are based on De Morgan's form of joint-life commutation tables. An alternative method is to employ Davies's form, in which case

$$C_{\overset{1}{x+t}:y+t} = v^{x+t+1} d_{x+t} l_{y+t+\frac{1}{2}} \qquad \text{if } x > y,$$

or
$$C_{\overset{1}{x+t}:y+t} = v^{y+t+1} d_{x+t} l_{y+t+\frac{1}{2}} \qquad \text{if } x < y.$$

In either case
$$M_{xy}^{1} = \sum_{t=0}^{t=\infty} C_{\overset{1}{x+t}:y+t}.$$

With the adoption of this form, therefore, it is necessary to construct two sets of tables, one for $x > y$ and the other for $x < y$. In his book on *Life Contingencies*, published in 1858, David Chisholm gave extensive commutation tables for contingent assurances based on the Carlisle Mortality Table, at many rates of interest, in Davies's form for both $x > y$ and $x < y$.

Owing to the large number of female lives included in the Carlisle experience, the effect of which is to reduce the mortality experienced at older ages, this table is rather more suitable for the calculation of Contingent Assurances than the H^M Table. For example, the value of $\overline{A}^{1}_{30:60}$ by the Carlisle Table at 3 per cent. is ·1183, which, though still less than the $O^{[NM]}\ O^{[af]}$ value, is much closer to it than the value given by the H^M Table.

6. Evaluation by Approximate Integration. When the value of a contingent assurance is required on the basis of a Select Mortality Table (or Tables) for which the appropriate commutation tables are not available, and the values of $A^{1}_{[x][y]}$ are not tabulated, the simplest plan is to obtain the value of the continuous assurance by approximate integration.

The value of a unit payable at time t if (x) die at that moment, (y) surviving him, both lives being select, is $v^t {}_tp_{[x][y]}\mu_{[x]+t}dt$, and the value of an assurance of unity, payable at the moment of death of (x) provided (y) survive him, is

$$\overline{A}^{1}_{[x][y]} = \int_0^\infty v^t {}_tp_{[x][y]}\mu_{[x]+t}dt$$

$$= \frac{1}{l_{[x]}l_{[y]}}\int_0^\infty v^t l_{[x]+t}l_{[y]+t}\mu_{[x]+t}dt \quad \ldots\ldots\ldots\ldots(3).$$

Similarly, for an Aggregate Table,

$$\overline{A}^{1}_{xy} = \int_0^\infty v^t {}_tp_{xy}\mu_{x+t}dt$$

$$= \frac{1}{l_x l_y}\int_0^\infty v^t l_{x+t}l_{y+t}\mu_{x+t}dt.$$

The method of evaluation will be the same whether a Select or an Aggregate Table be employed, and as a table following Makeham's Law affords special facilities for comparing values produced by different formulae, the H^M Table (Makeham Graduation) is employed in all the calculations in this chapter (see, however, paragraph 8).

7. As an example, let it be required to find the value of $\overline{A}^{1}_{30:60}$ by the H^M Table (Makeham Graduation) at 3 per cent., the integral being

$$\overline{A}^{1}_{30:60} = \frac{1}{l_{30}l_{60}}\int_0^\infty v^t l_{30+t}l_{60+t}\mu_{30+t}dt.$$

The approximate integration formula we shall employ is

$$\int_0^\infty f(x)\,dx = n\{\cdot 28f(0) + 1\cdot 62f(n) + 2\cdot 2f(3n) + 1\cdot 62f(5n) + \cdot 56f(6n) + 1\cdot 62f(7n)\},$$

the value of n being obtained from $7n = 102 - 60 = 42$, whence $n = 6$.

The calculation is as follows:

		n	$3n$	$5n$	$6n$	
$t=$	0	6	18	30	36	
$\log v^t$	—	$\bar{1}\cdot9230$	$\bar{1}\cdot7689$	$\bar{1}\cdot6149$	$\bar{1}\cdot5379$	
$\log l_{30+t}$	—	4·9314	4·8748	4·7697	4·6737	
$\log l_{60+t}$	—	4·6737	4·2645	3·1048	1·8513	
log coeff.	$\bar{1}\cdot4472$	·2095	·3424	·2095	$\bar{1}\cdot7482$	
$\text{colog}\ l_{30}\, l_{60}$	—	$\overline{10}\cdot2776$	$\overline{10}\cdot2776$	$\overline{10}\cdot2776$	$\overline{10}\cdot2776$	
Sum	$\bar{1}\cdot4472$	·0152	$\bar{1}\cdot5282$	$\bar{3}\cdot9765$	$\bar{4}\cdot0887$	.........(α)
$\log \mu_{30+t}$	$\bar{3}\cdot8854$	$\bar{3}\cdot9425$	$\bar{2}\cdot1424$	$\bar{2}\cdot4654$	$\bar{2}\cdot6627$	
Sum	$\bar{3}\cdot3326$	$\bar{3}\cdot9577$	$\bar{3}\cdot6706$	$\bar{4}\cdot4419$	$\bar{6}\cdot7514$	
$\log^{-1}$	·00215	·00907	·00468	·00028	·00001	= ·01619
						6
						$\bar{A}^{1}_{30:60}$ = ·09714

the correct value being ·0972.

The evaluation of contingent assurances by this method is thus very accurate and is not a lengthy process. The summation line (α) can be omitted if only the single premium be required, but it has been inserted in order to demonstrate that, by deferring the inclusion of $\log \mu_{x+t}$ until the last, the factors for the evaluation of the annuity value required for the calculation of the annual premium can be ascertained in the same process as the Single Premium.

Extracting the antilogarithms of line (α), we have

$$\begin{aligned} \cdot28\ f(0) &= \ \cdot28 \\ 1\cdot62\ f(6) &= 1\cdot036 \\ 2\cdot2\ f(18) &= \ \cdot3374 \\ 1\cdot62 f(30) &= \ \cdot0095 \\ \cdot56 f(36) &= \ \cdot0001 \\ & \quad 1\cdot663 \\ & \quad\quad 6 \\ & \quad 9\cdot978 \end{aligned}$$

The value obtained with the aid of equal ages and taking

$$\bar{a}_{30:60} = a_{30:60} + \cdot5 - \tfrac{1}{12}(\mu_{30} + \mu_{60} + \delta)$$

is 9·981.

It is evident that this calculation is just as simple whether based on a Select or an Aggregate Table, and whether the mortality of the two lives be based on the same or on different tables. If it had been based on the O$^{[NM]}$ for (30) and the O$^{[af]}$ for (60) the values of $\log l_{[30]+t}$, $\log \mu_{[30]+t}$ and $\operatorname{colog} l_{[30]}$ would have been taken from the former table, and of $\log l_{[60]+t}$ and $\operatorname{colog} l_{[60]}$ from the latter.

8. **Unsuitability of Aggregate Tables.** It was pointed out in Chapter III that the employment of an Aggregate Table, as compared with a Select Table, has the effect of underestimating the mortality of young lives and of overestimating that of older lives. Consequently, as in the great majority of contingent assurances the failing life is comparatively young (say aged from 20 to 40) and the counter life more advanced in age (say, over 60), both these tendencies operate towards reducing the value; and an aggregate table, therefore, is not a suitable one on which to calculate the premiums to be charged in practice for such assurances. The value of $\overline{A}^{1}_{30:60}$ at 3 per cent., for example, on the basis of the H^{M} Table (Makeham Graduation), ·0972, compares with ·1212 by the O$^{[NM]}$ and O$^{[af]}$ combination of tables. If the failing life were advanced in age and the counter life young, the tendency of an Aggregate Table would be to give higher values than a Select Table.

9. **Formulae by an Aggregate Table.** Though aggregate tables cannot be considered suitable for the evaluation of contingent assurances in practice, it will be instructive to investigate various formulae for A^{1}_{xy} on the assumption that such tables are used, and to examine the difficulties of applying these formulae to Select Tables.

If in the integral for $\overline{A}^{1}_{xy}$ we insert for μ_{x+t} the approximation $\dfrac{l_{x+t-1}-l_{x+t+1}}{2l_{x+t}}$, we have

$$\begin{aligned}\overline{A}^{1}_{xy} &= \int_0^\infty v^t\, {}_tp_{xy}\, \frac{l_{x+t-1}-l_{x+t+1}}{2l_{x+t}}\,dt\\ &= \frac{1}{2}\left\{\frac{l_{x-1}}{l_x}\int_0^\infty v^t\,\frac{l_{x-1+t}}{l_{x-1}}\cdot\frac{l_{y+t}}{l_y}\,dt - \frac{l_{x+1}}{l_x}\int_0^\infty v^t\,\frac{l_{x+1+t}}{l_{x+1}}\cdot\frac{l_{y+t}}{l_y}\,dt\right\}\\ &= \frac{1}{2}\left\{\frac{\bar{a}_{x-1:y}}{p_{x-1}} - p_x\,.\,\bar{a}_{x+1:y}\right\} \quad\text{.................................(4).}\end{aligned}$$

The value of the assurance payable at the end of the year of death is $A^{1}_{xy} = v^{\frac{1}{2}}\overline{A}^{1}_{xy}$ approximately.

Other expressions for $\bar{A}^1_{xy}$ can be obtained by inserting different expressions for the value of μ_{x+t}, but as these lead to more complicated expressions without gain in accuracy it is not worth while to discuss them.

10. If it be assumed that $\mu_{x+t}=q_{x+t}$ for all values of t the expression becomes

$$\bar{A}^1_{xy}=\int_0^\infty v^t\,{}_tp_{xy}\,\frac{l_{x+t}-l_{x+1+t}}{l_{x+t}}\,dt$$

$$=\bar{a}_{xy}-p_x\,.\,\bar{a}_{x+1:y}\quad\ldots\ldots\ldots\ldots\ldots\ldots\ldots(5).$$

This very simple formula gives results sufficiently accurate for the cases that usually arise in practice. Some idea of the extent of the error introduced in a particular example by the assumption made can be obtained by considering the difference between the values of q_{x+t} and μ_{x+t} over the period representing the complement of life of the "counter" life (y). For the usual practical cases q is greater than μ (for the younger life) over this period, and the values given by this formula are accordingly slightly too high, and, therefore, from the point of view of the Office granting the assurance, on the safe side.

Bearing in mind that for these cases an aggregate table gives too low a value, if the circumstances were such that an aggregate table had to be employed, it would probably be advisable to use a formula which is known to give a value on the safe side.

If the failing life were, say, over 60, and the counter life much younger, the value brought out by formula (5) would be too low.

11. A formula that has been extensively employed in practice in the past, though it does not appear to possess any advantage over those already given, is based on the assumption of a uniform distribution of deaths over each year of age. On this assumption the value of a payment of "1" to be made at the end of the $(t+1)$th year if (x) die in that year, (y) surviving him, is

$$v^{t+1}\,\frac{d_{x+t}}{l_x}\,.\,\frac{l_{y+t+\frac{1}{2}}}{l_y},$$

and the value of an assurance payable *at the end of the year of death* of (x) provided (y) survive him is

$$A^1_{xy}=\sum_{t=0}^{t=\infty} v^{t+1}\,\frac{d_{x+t}}{l_x}\,.\,\frac{l_{y+t+\frac{1}{2}}}{l_y},$$

which as shown in Chapter XIV 3 can be written

$$A^1_{xy} = \tfrac{1}{2}\sum_{t=0}^{t=\infty} v^{t+1}\left\{{}_tp_{xy} - {}_{t+1}p_{xy} + \frac{{}_{t+1}p_{x-1:y}}{p_{x-1}} - \frac{{}_{t+1}p_{x:y-1}}{p_{y-1}}\right\}$$

$$= \tfrac{1}{2}\left\{v\mathrm{a}_{xy} - a_{xy} + \frac{a_{x-1:y}}{p_{x-1}} - \frac{a_{x:y-1}}{p_{y-1}}\right\}$$

$$= \tfrac{1}{2}\left\{A_{xy} + \frac{a_{x-1:y}}{p_{x-1}} - \frac{a_{x:y-1}}{p_{y-1}}\right\} \quad \ldots\ldots\ldots\ldots(6).$$

To obtain the value of the corresponding assurance payable at the moment of death the value given by this formula must be multiplied by $(1+i)^{\frac{1}{2}}$ or $(1+\frac{1}{2}i)$.

12. Another very simple formula can be obtained by a method similar to that employed in Chapter XIV 2 to obtain the value of Q^1_{xy}.

Commencing with the differential coefficient of the joint-life annuity with regard to the age of the "failing" life, we have

$$\frac{d\bar{a}_{xy}}{dx} = \frac{d}{dx}\int_0^\infty v^t\,{}_tp_{xy}\,dt$$

$$= \int_0^\infty v^t\,{}_tp_{xy}\,(\mu_x - \mu_{x+t})\,dt$$

$$= \mu_x\bar{a}_{xy} - \bar{A}^1_{xy},$$

whence

$$\left.\begin{aligned}\bar{A}^1_{xy} &= \mu_x\bar{a}_{xy} - \frac{d\bar{a}_{xy}}{dx}\\ &= \mu_x\bar{a}_{xy} + \tfrac{1}{2}(\bar{a}_{x-1:y} - \bar{a}_{x+1:y})\ \text{approximately}\end{aligned}\right\}\ldots(7).$$

13. In considering formulae (4) to (7) it must be borne in mind that the suitability of these expressions for use in connection with any particular mortality table depends on the extent to which the appropriate joint-life annuity values are available. When a table follows Makeham's Law, the law of uniform seniority enables these values to be calculated very accurately, provided the values of joint-life annuities at equal ages are tabulated, and any one of the formulae given can be very conveniently employed: but, as already mentioned, for tables for which the appropriate annuity values or commutation tables are not available, the simplest plan is to employ the method of approximate integration.

These remarks also apply to the formulae given in the following paragraph.

14. The expressions for the value of an assurance payable on the death of (x) provided two or more specified lives survive him are exactly similar to those where the condition is that only one life shall survive him.

For example, where three lives (x), (y) and (z) are involved

$$\overline{\mathrm{A}}^{\,1}_{xyz} = \int_0^\infty v^t\, {}_tp_{xyz}\, \mu_{x+t}\, dt,$$

whence, employing the methods adopted to obtain expressions for the value of $\overline{\mathrm{A}}^{\,1}_{xy}$, we have, corresponding to formulae (4), (5) and (7) respectively,

$$\overline{\mathrm{A}}^{\,1}_{xyz} = \tfrac{1}{2}\left\{\frac{\bar{a}_{x-1:yz}}{p_{x-1}} - p_x . \bar{a}_{x+1:yz}\right\} \quad \text{.................(8)},$$

$$\overline{\mathrm{A}}^{\,1}_{xyz} = \bar{a}_{xyz} - p_x . \bar{a}_{x+1:yz} \quad \text{.......................(9)},$$

$$\mathrm{A}^{1}_{xyz} = \mu_x \bar{a}_{xyz} + \tfrac{1}{2}(\bar{a}_{x-1:yz} - \bar{a}_{x+1:yz}) \quad \text{........(10)}.$$

The expression for A^{1}_{xyz} corresponding to formula (6) is too complicated for practical use.

It is evident that expressions similar to formulae (8), (9) and (10) will hold whatever the number of lives involved.

15. The expressions obtained in paragraph 14 for the value of $\overline{\mathrm{A}}^{\,1}_{xyz}$ on the basis of an Aggregate Table are equally applicable when a status such as the joint existence of two lives is substituted for the life (x), or a different status, such as the life of the survivor of (y) and (z), substituted for the joint existence of these two lives.

Thus, $$\overline{\mathrm{A}}^{\,\,1}_{\overline{xy}:z} = \int_0^\infty v^t\, {}_tp_{xyz}\, \mu_{x+t:y+t}\, dt$$

$$= \tfrac{1}{2}\left\{\frac{\bar{a}_{x-1:y-1:z}}{p_{x-1:y-1}} - p_{xy} . \bar{a}_{x+1:y+1:z}\right\} \quad \text{..............(11)},$$

or $$\overline{\mathrm{A}}^{\,\,1}_{\overline{xy}:z} = (\mu_x + \mu_y)\, \bar{a}_{xyz} + \tfrac{1}{2}(\bar{a}_{x-1:y-1:z} - \bar{a}_{x+1:y+1:z}) \quad \text{...(12)},$$

the latter expression being obtained by differentiating the annuity value $\bar{a}_{xyz}$ with regard to the joint status (xy).

Similarly

$$\overline{\mathrm{A}}^{\,1}_{x:\overline{yz}} = \tfrac{1}{2}\left\{\frac{\bar{a}_{x-1:\overline{yz}}}{p_{x-1}} - p_x . \bar{a}_{x+1:\overline{yz}}\right\} \quad \text{......................(13)},$$

or $$\overline{\mathrm{A}}^{\,1}_{x:\overline{yz}} = \mu_x . \bar{a}_{x:\overline{yz}} + \tfrac{1}{2}(\bar{a}_{x-1:\overline{yz}} - \bar{a}_{x+1:\overline{yz}}) \quad \text{.............(14)},$$

and so on.

Generally, however, it will be simpler to evaluate cases of this kind by approximate integration. (See also paragraph 32.)

16. As an example of approximate integration when three lives are involved, let it be required to find the value of $\bar{A}^1_{30:35:45}$ by the H^M Table (Makeham Graduation) at 3 per cent. by this means.

The integral for the value of the assurance is

$$\bar{A}^1_{30:35:45}=\frac{1}{l_{30}l_{35}l_{45}}\int_0^\infty v^t l_{30+t}\,l_{35+t}\,l_{45+t}\,\mu_{30+t}\,dt,$$

and, for demonstration purposes, we will employ the formula

$$\int_0^\infty f(x)\,dx=\frac{n}{3}\big[f(0)+2\{f(2n)+f(4n)+f(6n)\}+4\{f(n)+f(3n)+f(5n)\}\big].$$

Here $6n=102-45=57$ and as the final terms will be exceedingly small we may take $n=9$ rather than $n=10$.

The value of $f(6n)$ is 0, so we shall only be concerned with the terms $f(0)\ldots f(5n)$.

The calculation is as follows:

		n	$2n$	$3n$	$4n$	$5n$	
$t=$	0	9	18	27	36	45	
$\log v^t$	—	$\bar{1}\cdot8845$	$\bar{1}\cdot7689$	$\bar{1}\cdot6534$	$\bar{1}\cdot5379$	$\bar{1}\cdot4223$	
$\log l_{30+t}$	—	4·9195	4·8748	4·8040	4·6737	4·4083	
$\log l_{35+t}$	—	4·8968	4·8402	4·7424	4·5508	4·1457	
$\log l_{45+t}$	—	4·8320	4·7271	4·5195	4·0781	3·1048	
colog $l_{30}\,l_{35}\,l_{45}$	—	$\overline{15}\cdot2205$	$\overline{15}\cdot2205$	$\overline{15}\cdot2205$	$\overline{15}\cdot2205$	$\overline{15}\cdot2205$	
Sum	·0000	$\bar{1}\cdot7533$	$\bar{1}\cdot4315$	$\bar{2}\cdot9398$	$\bar{2}\cdot0610$	$\bar{4}\cdot3016$	......(a)
$\log \mu_{30+t}$	$\bar{3}\cdot8854$	$\bar{3}\cdot9809$	$\bar{2}\cdot1424$	$\bar{2}\cdot3746$	$\bar{2}\cdot6627$	$\bar{2}\cdot9855$	
Sum	$\bar{3}\cdot8854$	$\bar{3}\cdot7342$	$\bar{3}\cdot5739$	$\bar{3}\cdot3144$	$\bar{4}\cdot7237$	$\bar{5}\cdot2871$	
$\log^{-1}$	·00768	·00542	·00375	·00206	·00053	·00002	
		4	2	4	2	4	
	·00768	·02168	·00750	·00824	·00106	·00008	= ·04624
							3
						$\bar{A}^1_{30:35:45}=$	·13872

The correct value is ·1385.

The approximate integration formula employed in this calculation gives good results when the values of the successive terms are not changing very rapidly, but where this occurs the formula

$$\int_0^\infty f(x)dx=n\{\cdot28f(0)+1\cdot62f(n)+2\cdot2f(3n)+1\cdot62f(5n)+\cdot56f(6n)+1\cdot62f(7n)\}$$

is more suitable, $7n$ being so taken, as in the example in paragraph 7, that $f(7n)$ falls just within or just beyond the limits of the mortality table. This formula can, in fact, be safely used for all functions based on the mortality table and will be employed in other examples of approximate integration included in this volume.

The summation line (α) has again been included solely to indicate that the annuity value required for the calculation of the annual premium can be obtained during the process of arriving at the single premium. When the single premium only is required this line will be omitted.

17. When the lives are all of equal age, whatever the number of lives involved, say m, we have

$$\begin{aligned}\bar{A}^{1}_{xxx\ldots(m\text{ lives})} &= \int_0^\infty v^t\,{}_tp_{xxx\ldots(m)}\,\mu_{x+t}\,dt\\ &= \frac{1}{m}\int_0^\infty v^t\,{}_tp_{xxx\ldots(m)}\,.\,m\mu_{x+t}\,dt\\ &= \frac{1}{m}\bar{A}_{xxx\ldots(m)} \quad\ldots\ldots\ldots\ldots\ldots\ldots\ldots(15).\end{aligned}$$

18. Contingent Assurances when the Mortality Table follows Makeham's Law. If a mortality table follow Makeham's Law, the value of an assurance payable at the moment of death of (x) provided he die first of any number, say m, lives can be expressed as follows:

$$\begin{aligned}\bar{A}^{1}_{xyz\ldots(m)} &= \int_0^\infty v^t\,{}_tp_{xyz\ldots(m)}\,(A+Bc^{x+t})\,dt\\ &= A\bar{a}_{xyz\ldots(m)} + \frac{c^x}{c^x+c^y+c^z+\ldots m\text{ terms}}\\ &\qquad\times\int_0^\infty v^t\,{}_tp_{xyz\ldots(m)}\,Bc^t(c^x+c^y+c^z+\ldots m\text{ terms})\,dt\\ &= A\bar{a}_{xyz\ldots(m)} + \frac{c^x}{c^x+c^y+c^z+\ldots m\text{ terms}}\\ &\qquad\times(\bar{A}_{xyz\ldots(m)} - mA\bar{a}_{xyz\ldots(m)}),\end{aligned}$$

since $Bc^t(c^x+c^y+c^z+\ldots m\text{ terms}) = (\mu_{x+t}+\mu_{y+t}+\mu_{z+t}+\ldots) - mA$,

$$= A\bar{a}_{www\ldots(m)} + \frac{c^x}{mc^w}(\bar{A}_{www\ldots(m)} - mA\bar{a}_{www\ldots(m)}),$$

where $mc^w = c^x+c^y+c^z+\ldots m$ terms,

$$= c^x\,\frac{\frac{1}{m}\bar{A}_{www\ldots(m)} + \log_e s\,.\,\bar{a}_{www\ldots(m)}}{c^w} - \log_e s\,.\,\bar{a}_{www\ldots(m)} \quad (16).$$

The expressions for the assurances where $m=2$, 3 and 4 respectively are, therefore,

$$\bar{A}^{\,1}_{xy} = c^x \frac{\frac{1}{2}\bar{A}_{ww} + \log_e s \,.\, \bar{a}_{ww}}{c^w} - \log_e s \,.\, \bar{a}_{ww} \qquad \text{where } 2c^w = c^x + c^y,$$

$$\bar{A}^{1}_{xyz} = c^x \frac{\frac{1}{3}\bar{A}_{www} + \log_e s \,.\, \bar{a}_{www}}{c^w} - \log_e s . \bar{a}_{www} \qquad ,, \qquad 3c^w = c^x + c^y + c^z,$$

$$\bar{A}^{1}_{xyzb} = c^x \frac{\frac{1}{4}\bar{A}_{wwww} + \log_e s \,.\, \bar{a}_{wwww}}{c^w} - \log_e s \,.\, \bar{a}_{wwww}$$

$$\text{where } 4c^w = c^x + c^y + c^z + c^b.$$

*19. If the functions $\log c^x$, $\log \dfrac{\frac{1}{2}\bar{A}_{ww} + \log_e s . \bar{a}_{ww}}{c^w}$ and $-\log_e s . \bar{a}_{ww}$ be tabulated, the calculation of contingent assurances by a table following Makeham's Law becomes very simple. These functions are accordingly tabulated on page 479 for two, three and four lives on the basis of the H^M Table at 3 per cent. interest, $\log \dfrac{\frac{1}{2}\bar{A}_{ww} + \log_e s \,.\, \bar{a}_{ww}}{c^w}$ being represented by $\log f_1(ww)$ and $-\log_e s \,.\, \bar{a}_{ww}$ by $f_2(ww)$ and so on.

The following examples will illustrate the method of using the tables:

Ex. 1. To find $\bar{A}^{1}_{32:40}$. H^M (Text-Book) 3 per cent.

By uniform seniority table, or μ column, $w = 36{\cdot}72$.

$$\begin{array}{rl@{\qquad\qquad}rl}
\log c^{32} = & 1{\cdot}26902 & \log c^{32} = & 1{\cdot}26902 \\
\log f_1(36, 36) = & \bar{3}{\cdot}82223 & \log f_1(37, 37) = & \bar{3}{\cdot}79667 \\
\hline
& \bar{1}{\cdot}09125 & & \bar{1}{\cdot}06569 \\
\log^{-1} = & {\cdot}12338 & \log^{-1} = & {\cdot}11633 \\
f_2(36, 36) = & {\cdot}09514 & f_2(37, 37) = & {\cdot}09341 \\
\hline
& {\cdot}21852 & & {\cdot}20974 \\
& {\cdot}20974 & & \\
\hline
& {\cdot}00878 \times {\cdot}72 & & \\
= & {\cdot}00632 & & \\
\hline
\therefore\ \bar{A}^{1}_{32:40} = & {\cdot}21220 & &
\end{array}$$

* The method employed here and the table on p. 479 are taken from a note by Messrs Hume and Stott (*J. I. A.* Vol. xxxix).

Ex. 2. To find $\overline{A}^1_{30:35:45}$. H^M (Text-Book) 3 per cent.

By uniform seniority table, or μ column, $w = 38{\cdot}49$.

$$\begin{array}{rr@{\qquad}rr}
\log c^{30} = & 1{\cdot}18971 & \log c^{30} = & 1{\cdot}18971 \\
\log f_1(38, 38, 38) = & \bar{3}{\cdot}60755 & \log f_1(39, 39, 39) = & \bar{3}{\cdot}58236 \\
\hline
 & \bar{2}{\cdot}79726 & & \bar{2}{\cdot}77207 \\
\hline
\log^{-1} = & {\cdot}06270 & \log^{-1} = & {\cdot}05917 \\
f_2(38, 38, 38) = & {\cdot}07841 & f_2(39, 39, 39) = & {\cdot}07670 \\
\hline
 & {\cdot}14111 & & {\cdot}13587 \\
 & {\cdot}13587 & & \\
\hline
 & {\cdot}00524 \times {\cdot}49 & & \\
= & {\cdot}00257 & & \\
\hline
\therefore\ \overline{A}^1_{30:35:45} = & {\cdot}13854 & &
\end{array}$$

20. Numerical Values by Different Formulae. In order to show the effect of adopting the various formulae obtained in this chapter, the values of $\overline{A}^1_{30:60}$ and $\overline{A}^1_{32:40}$ by the H^M Table (Makeham Graduation) as given by formulae (4), (5), (6), (7) and (16) respectively are set out in the following table.

Number of Formula	Formula for $\overline{A}^1_{xy}$	Value by H^M $\overline{A}^1_{30:60}$	3 per cent. $\overline{A}^1_{32:40}$
(4)	$\frac{1}{2}\left\{\frac{\bar{a}_{x-1:y}}{p_{x-1}} - p_x \cdot \bar{a}_{x+1:y}\right\}$	·0972	·2121
(5)	$\bar{a}_{xy} - p_x \cdot \bar{a}_{x+1:y}$	·1008	·2130
(6)	$\frac{1}{2}\left\{A_{xy} + \frac{a_{x-1:y}}{p_{x-1}} - \frac{a_{x:y-1}}{p_{y-1}}\right\} \times 1{\cdot}015$	·0970	·2118
(7)	$\mu_x \bar{a}_{xy} + \frac{1}{2}(\bar{a}_{x-1:y} - \bar{a}_{x+1:y})$	·0972	·2120
(16)	$c^x \frac{\frac{1}{2}\overline{A}_{ww} + \log_e s \cdot \bar{a}_{ww}}{c^w} - \log_e s \cdot \bar{a}_{ww}$	·0971	·2122

The calculations have been made on the basis of annuity values to three places of decimals, $\bar{a}$ being taken as equal to $\frac{1}{2} + a$, except in the case of formula (16) which may be taken as giving the correct value. In view of the limited number of decimal places employed, the results (apart from formula (16)) cannot be depended upon to more than three places, and even the third place cannot be relied upon to be absolutely accurate. The equal ages have all been taken to two places of decimals. All the formulae dealt with give results sufficiently accurate for practical purposes. The calculations have, of course, been made on an aggregate table and a formula such as number (5) giving a rather higher value is, therefore, probably the best in this case for Office purposes.

In practice, on account of the small number of contingent assurances issued, the premiums charged are loaded much more heavily than for the more popular classes of assurances, and it is not, therefore, of great importance that extreme accuracy in the net single premium should be attained.

21. The following table shows the value of $\bar{A}^1_{30:35:45}$ by the H^M Table at 3 per cent. by the formulae given in paragraph 14 and by formula (16).

Number of Formula	Formula for $\bar{A}^1_{xyz}$	Value by H^M 3 per cent. of $\bar{A}^1_{30:35:45}$
(8)	$\frac{1}{2}\left\{\frac{\bar{a}_{x-1:yz}}{p_{x-1}} - p_x \cdot \bar{a}_{x+1:yz}\right\}$	·1375
(9)	$\bar{a}_{xyz} - p_x \cdot \bar{a}_{x+1:yz}$	·140
(10)	$\mu_x \cdot \bar{a}_{xyz} + \frac{1}{2}(\bar{a}_{x-1:yz} - \bar{a}_{x+1:yz})$	·1375
(16)	$c^x \frac{\frac{1}{3}\bar{A}_{www} + \log_e s \cdot \bar{a}_{www}}{c^w} - \log_e s \cdot \bar{a}_{www}$	·1385

22. Application of Formulae to Select Tables. Formulae (4), (6) and (7) all contain the values of annuities involving the age $x-1$, and must accordingly be modified so as to eliminate this age if they are to be applied to Select Tables.

Formula (4) does not admit of direct modification in this way, but a very close approximation will be obtained if we assume that a similar expression holds for the assurance payable at the end of the year of death, that is, if we assume

$$A^1_{xy} = \tfrac{1}{2}\left\{\frac{a_{x-1:y}}{p_{x-1}} - p_x \cdot a_{x+1:y}\right\}.$$

Then writing $a_{x-1:y} = vp_{x-1:y} \cdot \mathrm{a}_{x:y+1}$, the formula becomes

$$A^1_{xy} = \tfrac{1}{2}\{vp_y \cdot \mathrm{a}_{x:y+1} - p_x \cdot a_{x+1:y}\},$$

whence, inserting "select" symbols, and taking $\bar{A}^1_{xy} = A^1_{xy}(1+\frac{1}{2}i)$,

$$\bar{A}^1_{[x][y]} = \tfrac{1}{2}\{vp_{[y]} \cdot \mathrm{a}_{[x]:[y]+1} - p_{[x]} \cdot a_{[x]+1:[y]}\}(1+\tfrac{1}{2}i) \quad \ldots (17).$$

Formula (5) is applicable to Select Tables as it stands, that is,

$$\bar{A}^1_{[x][y]} = \bar{a}_{[x][y]} - p_{[x]} \cdot \bar{a}_{[x]+1:[y]} \quad \ldots\ldots (18).$$

Formula (7) must be modified by assuming a different approximation to the value of $\frac{d\bar{a}_x}{dx}$. Thus, we could take

$$\frac{d\bar{a}_x}{dx} = (\Delta_x - \tfrac{1}{2}\Delta^2{}_x)\,\bar{a}_x,$$

but owing to the nature of the progression of the differences of $\bar{a}_x$ when x is the variable, a more accurate as well as a simpler expression is obtained by taking $\frac{d\bar{a}_x}{dx} = \Delta_x \bar{a}_x$ approximately. With this assumption, which is equivalent to assuming that $\mu_{x+t} = q_{x+t}$ for all values of t, the formula becomes

$$\bar{A}^1_{[x][y]} = \mu_{[x]} \cdot \bar{a}_{[x][y]} + (\bar{a}_{[x][y]} - \bar{a}_{[x]+1:[y]}) \text{ .... (19).}$$

In order to adapt formula (6) to Select Tables, it is necessary to write $a_{x-1:y} = vp_{x-1:y} \cdot \mathbf{a}_{x:y+1}$ and $a_{x:y-1} = vp_{x:y-1} \cdot \mathbf{a}_{x+1:y}$, whence

$$A^1_{[x][y]} = \tfrac{1}{2}\,\{A_{[x][y]} + vp_{[y]} \cdot \mathbf{a}_{[x]:[y]+1} - vp_{[x]} \cdot \mathbf{a}_{[x]+1:[y]}\} \text{...(20).}$$

Though formulae (17) to (20) are applicable to Select Tables, they all include one, or both, of the values $a_{[x]:[y]+1}$ and $a_{[x]+1:[y]}$, neither of which would be available from published tables. The quickest way to obtain the values of these annuities would be by approximate integration, with the result that, as stated in paragraph 6, unless the necessary commutation tables or assurance values are already tabulated, the simplest method in practice is to obtain $\bar{A}^1_{[x][y]}$ itself by this means.

23. Contingent Assurances when the Mortality Table follows Gompertz's Law. If a mortality table followed Gompertz's Law, the value of an assurance payable in the event of (x) dying first of m lives aged (x), (y), (z) ... etc., could be expressed as follows:

$$\bar{A}^1_{xyz...(m)} = \int_0^\infty v^t\,{}_tp_{xyz...(m)}\,\mathrm{B}c^{x+t}\,dt$$

$$= \frac{c^x}{c^x + c^y + c^z + \text{... } m \text{ terms}} \times \int_0^\infty v^t\,{}_tp_{xyz...(m)}\,\mathrm{B}c^t\,(c^x + c^y + c^z + \text{... } (m))\,dt$$

$$= Q^1_{xyz...(m)} \times \bar{A}_{xyz...(m)} \text{ .... (21)}$$

$$= \frac{\mu_x}{\mu_x + \mu_y + \mu_z + \text{... } (m \text{ terms})}\,\bar{A}_{xyz...(m)} \text{ .... (22).}$$

If an age "w" be obtained such that $c^w = c^x + c^y + c^z + \ldots m$ terms, the formula becomes

$$\overline{A}^1_{xyz\ldots(m)} = \frac{c^x}{c^w}\overline{A}_w \quad \ldots\ldots\ldots\ldots\ldots\ldots\ldots\ldots(23).$$

24. Approximations to value of $\overline{A}^1_{xy}$. A method of obtaining an approximate value of $\overline{A}^1_{xy}$, based indirectly on formula (22), was suggested by Messrs Elderton and King, in *J. I. A.* Vol. XLIV.

By Gompertz's Law, where $\mu_x + \mu_y = \mu_w$,

$$\overline{A}^1_{xy} = \frac{\mu_x}{\mu_x + \mu_y}\overline{A}_{xy}$$

$$= \frac{\mu_x}{\mu_w}\overline{A}_w,$$

and the problem is to find the age of a single life which can be substituted for the two lives (x) and (y) so that this formula can be employed with a sufficient degree of accuracy when Gompertz's Law does not hold. As will be seen from the following examples, the method involves, for the purpose of ascertaining the age of the single life, the addition to each age (x and y) of a number of years determined by reference to the single-life annuity value at the age of the counter life.

As an example let it be required to find an approximate value for $\overline{A}^1_{30:60}$ by the H^M Table at 3 per cent. Since $a_{60} = 10{\cdot}223$, we take

$$\mu_{30+10} = {\cdot}00990,$$

$$\mu_{60+10} = {\cdot}06353$$

$${\cdot}07343 = \mu_{61\cdot7+10},$$

$$\therefore \quad \overline{A}^1_{30:60} = \frac{{\cdot}00990}{{\cdot}07343} \times A_{62} \times 1{\cdot}015$$

$$= \frac{{\cdot}00990}{{\cdot}07343} \times {\cdot}69459 \times 1{\cdot}015$$

$$= {\cdot}0951,$$

the correct value being ·0971.

It will be observed that the addition of 10 years to the ages is retained as regards the force of mortality $\left(\text{i.e. } \frac{\mu_{30+10}}{\mu_{30+10} + \mu_{60+10}} \text{ is taken}\right)$ but is discarded in connection with the assurance factor (i.e. A_{62} is taken, *not* A_{62+10}).

Similarly, to find an approximate value of $\overline{A}^{1}_{32:40}$ by the H^M Table at 3 per cent., since $a_{40} = 17{\cdot}177$, we have

$$\mu_{32+17} = {\cdot}01462,$$
$$\mu_{40+17} = {\cdot}02369$$
$${\cdot}03831 = \mu_{46\cdot16+17},$$

$$\therefore \quad \overline{A}^{1}_{32:40} = \frac{{\cdot}01462}{{\cdot}03831} \times A_{47} \times 1{\cdot}015$$
$$= \frac{{\cdot}01462}{{\cdot}03831} \times {\cdot}53633 \times 1{\cdot}015$$
$$= {\cdot}2077,$$

the correct value being ·2122.

In these examples the H^M Table (Makeham Graduation) has been employed for convenience, though it is clearly unnecessary with this table to resort to such a method. The next higher integral age has been adopted in extracting the value of A_w, but this is not necessarily the most suitable plan for other tables. With the O^M Table, for example, the next lower integral age will give better results. The method will, however, give a fairly close approximation to the true value if the actual fractional age brought out be retained in all cases.

The method is *not* applicable to Select Tables, and even with an aggregate table, as the evaluation of a contingent assurance by approximate integration is so simple, it need not be considered as supplying anything more than a rough check on the value.

***25. Contingent Assurances payable otherwise than on the first death.** When the sum assured is payable on the second, or later, death it is often a useful plan to express the assurance in terms of simple contingent assurances payable on the first death only. In the more complicated cases, however, and when A^{1}_{xy} is not tabulated, it is generally preferable to obtain the required value directly by approximate integration.

The value of an assurance of 1 payable at the moment of death of (x) if he die *after* (y), $\overline{A}^{2}_{xy}$, is

$$\overline{A}^{2}_{xy} = \int_0^\infty v^t (1 - {}_tp_y)\, {}_tp_x \mu_{x+t} dt$$
$$= \overline{A}_x - \overline{A}^{1}_{xy} \quad \ldots\ldots\ldots (24).$$

* All the formulae in paragraphs 25 to 34 apply also to Select Tables.

From general reasoning, it is evident that the value of an assurance on the life of (x) provided he die before (y) *plus* the value of an assurance on the life of (x) provided he die after (y), must give the value of an assurance payable on the death of (x). That is, $\bar{A}^1_{xy} + \bar{A}^2_{xy} = \bar{A}_x$, whence $\bar{A}^2_{xy} = \bar{A}_x - \bar{A}^1_{xy}$.

Having established this relationship for the continuous assurance, since all the terms involve the payment of a unit on the death of (x), it is evident that a similar relation will hold if it be assumed throughout that the sum assured is payable at the end of the year of death. Thus $A^2_{xy} = A_x - A^1_{xy}$.

It is a simple matter to prove this directly on the assumption of a uniform distribution of deaths over each integral year of age, on which assumption

$$A^2_{xy} = \sum_{t=0}^{t=\infty} v^{t+1} \frac{d_{x+t}}{l_x} \left(1 - \frac{l_{y+t+\frac{1}{2}}}{l_y}\right)$$

$$= A_x - A^1_{xy}.$$

26. An important difference between the arguments employed in dealing with contingent probabilities and contingent assurances respectively must be carefully noted. When dealing with contingent probabilities the order of the events only need be considered, and we can write, for example, $Q^1_{xy} = Q_{x\overset{2}{y}}$; but when dealing with contingent assurances, since the operation of discounting is introduced, the formula employed must deal with the event which determines the payment of the sum assured. Thus

$$\bar{A}^1_{xy} = \int_0^\infty v^t \, {}_tp_{xy} \, \mu_{x+t} \, dt,$$

but

$$\bar{A}_{x\overset{2}{y}} = \int_0^\infty v^t (1 - {}_tp_x) \, {}_tp_y \, \mu_{y+t} \, dt$$

$$= \bar{A}_y - \bar{A}_{x\overset{1}{y}}.$$

27. The value of an assurance payable at the moment of death of (x) if he die before (y) or within t years after the death of (y) provides a good example of the point mentioned in the last paragraph. In Chapter XIV 8, the value of the corresponding probability was obtained by reference to the moment of death of (y), but the assurance being payable on the death of (x), from which moment the sum assured must be discounted, that method cannot now be employed.

The problem does not present any difficulty, since the value required is

$\bar{A}_x-$ (the value of an assurance payable only if the death of (x) occur at least t years after the death of (y))

$$=\bar{A}_x-\int_0^\infty v^{t+n}(1-{}_np_y)\,{}_{n+t}p_x\mu_{x+n+t}dn$$

$$=\bar{A}_x-v^t\,{}_tp_x\int_0^\infty v^n(1-{}_np_y)\,{}_np_{x+t}\mu_{x+n+t}dn$$

$$=\bar{A}_x-\frac{D_{x+t}}{D_x}(\bar{A}_{x+t}-\bar{A}_{\overset{1}{\overline{x+t}}:y})\;\ldots\ldots\ldots\ldots(25),$$

or the same expression might have been obtained by taking

$$\bar{A}^1_{x:\overline{t}|}+\int_0^\infty v^{t+n}\,{}_{t+n}p_x\cdot{}_np_y\mu_{x+t+n}dn,$$

since the sum assured must be payable in the event of (x) dying during the first t years, and after that time if (y) be alive within t years of the death of (x).

Having proved formula (25) by means of the Integral Calculus it follows, as pointed out in paragraph 25, that a similar relation holds if all the assurances be assumed to be payable at the end of the year of death; that is, if "A" be substituted for "$\bar{A}$." The student can prove this independently on the assumption of a uniform distribution of deaths, from either of the expressions

$$A_x-\sum_{n=0}^{n=\infty}v^{t+n+1}\,{}_{t+n|}q_x(1-{}_{n+\frac{1}{2}}p_y)\quad\text{or}\quad A^1_{x:\overline{t}|}+\sum_{n=0}^{n=\infty}v^{t+n+1}\,{}_{t+n|}q_x\cdot{}_{n+\frac{1}{2}}p_y.$$

28. The sum of the values of two assurances, one payable in the event of (x) dying before (y), and the other in the event of (y) dying before (x), is the value of an assurance payable on the failure of the joint lives (x) and (y). Thus

$$A_{xy}=A^1_{xy}+A_{x\overset{1}{y}}\;\ldots\ldots\ldots\ldots(26).$$

Similarly,

$$A_{\overline{xy}}=A^2_{xy}+A_{x\overset{2}{y}}\;\ldots\ldots\ldots\ldots(27).$$

29. For an assurance payable on the death of (x) if he die second of three lives (x), (y) and (z), (y) having predeceased him, we have

$$\bar{A}^2_{x\underset{1}{y}z}=\int_0^\infty v^t(1-{}_tp_y)\,{}_tp_{xz}\mu_{x+t}dt$$

$$=\bar{A}^1_{xz}-\bar{A}^1_{xyz}\;\ldots\ldots\ldots\ldots(28),$$

this being equivalent to an assurance payable on the death of (x) before (z) less an assurance payable on (x) dying before both (y) and (z).

30. The value of an assurance payable simply in the event of (x) dying second of the three lives, is the sum of the values of two assurances, one payable on (x) dying second (y) having died first, and the other on (x) dying second (z) having died first. That is,

$$\begin{aligned}\bar{A}^{2}_{xyz} &= \bar{A}^{2}_{x\underset{1}{y}z} + \bar{A}^{2}_{xy\underset{1}{z}} \\ &= \bar{A}^{1}_{xy} + \bar{A}^{1}_{xz} - 2\bar{A}^{1}_{xyz} \quad\text{.....................(29).}\end{aligned}$$

Expressed in the form of an integral,

$$\bar{A}^{2}_{xyz} = \int_0^\infty v^t\,{}_tp_x\,({}_tp_y + {}_tp_z - 2\,{}_tp_{yz})\,\mu_{x+t}\,dt.$$

31. The value of an assurance payable on the death of (x) if he die third of three lives, $\bar{A}^{3}_{xyz}$, is

$$\begin{aligned}\bar{A}^{3}_{xyz} &= \int_0^\infty v^t(1 - {}_tp_y)(1 - {}_tp_z)\,{}_tp_x\mu_{x+t}\,dt \\ &= \int_0^\infty v^t(1 - {}_tp_y - {}_tp_z + {}_tp_{yz})\,{}_tp_x\mu_{x+t}\,dt \\ &= \bar{A}_x - \bar{A}^{1}_{xy} - \bar{A}^{1}_{xz} + \bar{A}^{1}_{xyz} \quad\text{.....................(30).}\end{aligned}$$

This could also have been obtained from

$$\begin{aligned}\bar{A}^{3}_{xyz} &= \bar{A}_x - \bar{A}^{1}_{xyz} - \bar{A}^{2}_{xyz} \\ &= \bar{A}_x - \bar{A}^{1}_{x:\overline{yz}}.\end{aligned}$$

32. The value of an assurance on the life of (x) payable only in the event of (x) dying before the survivor of (y) and (z) is

$$\bar{A}^{1}_{x:\overline{yz}} = \bar{A}^{1}_{xy} + \bar{A}^{1}_{xz} - \bar{A}^{1}_{xyz} \quad\text{..................(31).}$$

This assurance can also be represented by the symbol $\bar{A}^{1\,:\,2}_{x\,:\,yz}$ or may be written $\bar{A}_x - \bar{A}^{3}_{xyz}$. In the form of an integral its value is

$$\int_0^\infty v^t\,{}_tp_{\overline{yz}}\cdot{}_tp_x\mu_{x+t}\,dt.$$

33. The symbol representing the value of an assurance payable on the death of the survivor of (x) and (y) provided this occur during the lifetime of (z), is $\bar{A}^{\;1}_{\overline{xy}:z}$ or $\bar{A}_{\overline{xy}:\underset{3}{z}}$ which can be expressed

$$\begin{aligned}\bar{A}^{\;1}_{\overline{xy}:z} &= \bar{A}^{2}_{x\underset{1}{y}z} + \bar{A}^{\;2}_{\underset{1}{x}yz} \\ &= \bar{A}^{1}_{xz} + A^{1}_{yz} - \bar{A}^{1}_{xyz} - \bar{A}^{\;1}_{xyz} \quad\text{...............(32).}\end{aligned}$$

It will be observed that, though $Q_{\overline{xy}:z}^{\,1} = Q_{xyz}^{\;\;3}$, a corresponding equality does *not* exist between the assurances represented by $A_{\overline{xy}:z}^{\,1}$ and $A_{xyz}^{\;\;3}$.

34. Finally, to give an example involving four lives, the value of an assurance payable on the death of (x) if he die third of four lives (w), (x), (y) and (z) is

$$\bar{A}_{wxyz}^{\;\,3} = \int_0^\infty v^t\,{}_tp_{\overline{wyz}}^{[1]}\cdot{}_tp_x\mu_{x+t}\,dt$$

$$= \int_0^\infty v^t\,({}_tp_w + {}_tp_y + {}_tp_z - 2\,{}_tp_{wy} - 2\,{}_tp_{wz} - 2\,{}_tp_{yz} + 3\,{}_tp_{wyz})\,{}_tp_x\,\mu_{x+t}\,dt$$

$$= \bar{A}_{wx}^{\;1} + \bar{A}_{xy}^{1} + \bar{A}_{xz}^{1} - 2\bar{A}_{wxy}^{\;\,1} - 2\bar{A}_{wxz}^{\;\,1} - 2\bar{A}_{xyz}^{1} + 3\bar{A}_{wxyz}^{\;\,1} \ldots\ldots (33).$$

The values of $\bar{A}_{wxyz}^{\;\,2}$ and $\bar{A}^{1:2:3}_{\;\;x\;\;:wyz}$ will similarly be found (with the addition of the factor v^t), in the manner employed in Chapter XIV 17, to obtain the values of the corresponding probabilities.

35. In all the cases dealt with in paragraphs 29 to 34, similar relations will hold for assurances payable at the end of the year of death, "A" being substituted for "$\bar{A}$."

36. As a further example of approximate integration let it be required to find the value of $\bar{A}^{2}_{30:\underset{1}{45}:60}$ by the H^M Table (Makeham Graduation) at 3 per cent. Here

$$\bar{A}^{2}_{30:\underset{1}{45}:60} = \frac{1}{l_{30}l_{45}l_{60}}\int_0^\infty v^t l_{30+t}\,.\,l_{60+t}\,.\,(l_{45} - l_{45+t})\,\mu_{30+t}\,dt,$$

and the formula we shall use is

$$\int_0^\infty f(x)\,dx = n\,\{\cdot 28f(0) + 1\cdot 62f(n) + 2\cdot 2f(3n) + 1\cdot 62f(5n) + \cdot 56f(6n) + 1\cdot 62f(7n)\},$$

where $7n = 102 - 60 = 42$, or $n = 6$.

The annual premium for this assurance (see paragraph 43) would be made payable during the joint lifetime of (30) and (60), and the work can be so arranged as to give the value of $\bar{a}_{30:60}$ during the process. In the following calculation it is assumed that the single premium only is required:

t	n $=6$	$3n$ $=18$	$5n$ $=30$	$6n$ $=36$	
$\log v^t$	$\bar{1}\cdot9230$	$\bar{1}\cdot7689$	$\bar{1}\cdot6149$	$\bar{1}\cdot5378$	
$\log l_{30+t}$	4·9314	4·8748	4·7697	4·6737	
$\log l_{60+t}$	4·6737	4·2645	3·1048	1·8513	
$\log (l_{45}-l_{45+t})$	3·7971	4·3903	4·7187	4·8192	
$\log \mu_{30+t}$	$\bar{3}\cdot9425$	$\bar{2}\cdot1424$	$\bar{2}\cdot4654$	$\bar{2}\cdot6627$	
$\text{colog } l_{30}\, l_{45}\, l_{60}$	15·3860	$\overline{15}\cdot3860$	$\overline{15}\cdot3860$	$\overline{15}\cdot3860$	
log coeff.	·2095	·3424	·2095	$\bar{1}\cdot7482$	
Sum	$\bar{4}\cdot8632$	$\bar{3}\cdot1693$	$\bar{4}\cdot2690$	$\bar{6}\cdot6789$	
$\log^{-1}$	·00073	·00148	·00019	·00000	$=$·00240
					6
					$\overline{A}^{\,2}_{\underset{1}{30}:45:60}=$·01440

37. In each of the examples of approximate integration given in this chapter reference has been made to the arrangement of the work so as to provide, in the same process, the value of the annuity required for the purpose of deriving the annual premium from the single premium. It is, however, frequently impossible to effect this in the more complicated cases.

For example, as pointed out in paragraph 30, the value of $\overline{A}^2_{xyz}$ expressed in the form of an integral is

$$\int_0^\infty v^t\,{}_tp_x({}_tp_y + {}_tp_z - 2\,{}_tp_{yz})\,\mu_{x+t}dt,$$

whereas the annuity value that would be required for the purpose of calculating the corresponding annual premium (see paragraph 43) is $1 + a_{x:\overline{yz}}$, the integral for $\bar{a}_{x:\overline{yz}}$ being

$$\int_0^\infty v^t\,{}_tp_x({}_tp_y + {}_tp_z - {}_tp_{yz})\,dt.$$

38. Deferred Contingent Assurances. The values of deferred contingent assurances can be expressed as follows:

$${}_{n|}\overline{A}^1_{xy} = \int_0^\infty v^{n+t}\,{}_{n+t}p_{xy}\,\mu_{x+n+t}dt$$

$$= v^n\,{}_np_{xy}\,\overline{A}_{\overset{1}{x+n}:y+n} \quad \ldots\ldots\ldots\ldots\ldots\ldots\ldots\ldots(34),$$

$${}_{n|}\overline{A}^2_{xy} = \int_0^\infty v^{n+t}\,{}_{n+t}p_x(1 - {}_{n+t}p_y)\,\mu_{x+n+t}dt$$

$$= v^n\,{}_np_x\overline{A}_{x+n} - v^n\,{}_np_{xy}\,A_{\overset{1}{x+n}:y+n}$$

$$= {}_{n|}\overline{A}_x - {}_{n|}\overline{A}^1_{xy} \ldots\ldots\ldots\ldots\ldots\ldots\ldots\ldots\ldots\ldots(35).$$

It will also be seen that

$$_{n|}A^{1}_{xy} + {}_{n|}A_{xy}^{\ 1} = {}_{n|}A_{xy} \quad\text{and}\quad {}_{n|}A^{2}_{xy} + {}_{n|}A_{xy}^{\ 2} = {}_{n|}A_{\overline{xy}}.$$

In the case of an assurance deferred n years payable on the death of (x) before (y), in order that the assurance may become effective, both lives must survive until the end of n years. But this is not so with the assurances represented by $_{n|}A^{2}_{xy}$ and $_{n|}A_{\overline{xy}}$ which would become payable if, in the first case, (x) only, and in the second case either (x) or (y) only, survived that period.

39. For an assurance payable on the death of (x), provided this occur after the lapse of a period of n years and (y) has died before (x), (z) surviving (x), we have

$$_{n|}\overline{A}^{2}_{x\underset{1}{y}z} = {}_{n|}\overline{A}^{1}_{xz} - {}_{n|}\overline{A}^{1}_{xyz} \quad\text{.....................(36).}$$

In this case (y) may have died during the period of n years and the assurance still be payable on the death of (x).

Other cases can be considered in a similar manner.

40. Temporary Contingent Assurances. The values of temporary contingent assurances for, say, n years, are readily obtained by taking the value of the whole-life assurance less the value of the deferred assurance, or by integrating the expressions already obtained between the limits 0 and n (instead of 0 and ∞) and making the consequent alterations in the formulae by inserting temporary annuity values in place of those for the whole duration of the joint lives.

For example, if it be required to find the value of $|_{20}\overline{A}^{1}_{30:60}$ by the H^M Table (Makeham Graduation), this can be obtained by means of the expression

$$\overline{A}^{1}_{30:60} - \frac{D_{50:80}}{D_{30:60}}\overline{A}^{1}_{50:80},$$

where $\overline{A}^{1}_{30:60}$ and $\overline{A}^{1}_{50:80}$ can be readily calculated by the method of paragraph 18.

If the value of $|_{20}\overline{A}^{1}_{[30][60]}$ be required on the basis of the $O^{[NM]}$ Table for (30) and the $O^{[af]}$ Table for (60), this will be most readily obtained by approximate integration.

We have

$$|_{20}\overline{A}^{1}_{[x][y]} = \frac{1}{l_{[x]}l_{[y]}}\int_0^{20} v^t l_{[x]+t}\, l_{[y]+t}\, \mu_{[x]+t}\, dt,$$

and as in Chapter XV 12, the formula

$$\int_0^{20} f(x)\,dx = \tfrac{5}{3}\{f(0)+4f(5)+2f(10)+4f(15)+f(20)\}$$

can be employed. The value of $f(0)$ in this case is $\mu_{[x]}$, so only four terms would be calculated.

For use with Aggregate Tables expressions corresponding to formulae (4) to (7) can be obtained from the integral, these being of exactly the same form as the corresponding expressions for the whole-life contingent assurances, the temporary annuities $\bar{a}_{x-1:y:\overline{n}|}$, $\bar{a}_{x:y-1:\overline{n}|}$, etc. being substituted for $\bar{a}_{x-1:y}$, $\bar{a}_{x:y-1}$, etc.

The limitations to the practical value of the various formulae have already been discussed. In view of the work involved in extracting the values of temporary annuities, where these are not tabulated, the employment of the method of approximate integration is still more often an advantage in the case of temporary contingent assurances than in connection with those for the whole of life.

41. All the formulae given in paragraphs 25 to 35, expressing the values of more complicated contingent assurances in terms of assurances payable at the first death, apply also in the case of temporary assurances, $|_n\mathrm{A}$ being substituted for A.

42. Where only two lives are involved the values of temporary contingent assurances can be expressed in terms of commutation functions. Thus

$$|_n\mathrm{A}^{\,1}_{[x][y]} = \frac{\mathrm{M}^{\,1}_{[x][y]} - \mathrm{M}^{\;\;1}_{\overline{[x]+n}:[y]+n}}{\mathrm{D}_{[x][y]}} \quad \text{.............................(37),}$$

$$|_n\mathrm{A}^{\,2}_{[x][y]} = |_n\mathrm{A}_{[x]} - |_n\mathrm{A}^{\,1}_{[x][y]}$$

$$= \frac{\mathrm{M}_{[x]} - \mathrm{M}_{[x]+n}}{\mathrm{D}_{[x]}} - \frac{\mathrm{M}^{\,1}_{[x][y]} - \mathrm{M}^{\;\;1}_{\overline{[x]+n}:[y]+n}}{\mathrm{D}_{[x][y]}} \quad \text{.........(38),}$$

and so on.

43. Annual Premiums for Contingent Assurances. In connection with the annual premiums to be charged for contingent assurances, the question of the period during which the premiums are to be payable requires careful consideration.

For an assurance payable on the first death the premium would be payable during the joint existence of all the lives named in the policy, since the death of any one of them would terminate the contract; the premium for an assurance payable on (x) dying before (y) and (z) would thus be $\frac{A^1_{xyz}}{a_{xyz}}$. If one of the counter lives failed first no claim could arise under the policy, so that it is only necessary to have (x) medically examined, (y) and (z) being assumed to be select lives.

If the assurance be payable on the death of (x) provided he die *after* (y), the premium should be made payable during the lifetime of (x), both the lives being medically examined. If (y) were not medically examined and died at an early date, the Office would, in effect, be granting (x) a whole-life assurance at a lower premium than he would have paid had he effected such an assurance without the condition that (y) should predecease him. On the other hand, if the premium were made payable during the joint lives of (x) and (y), the premium would be increased and the Office would probably lose the business, which would be secured by another Office quoting the lower premium payable until the death of (x). The annual premium should therefore be $\frac{A^2_{xy}}{a_x}$.

In the case of an assurance payable on the death of (x) if he die second of three lives (x), (y) and (z), (y) having died first, the assurance must terminate on either (x) or (z) dying first, but will continue if (y) die first. The annual premium should be made payable during the joint lives of (x) and (z), and will thus be $\frac{A^{2}_{x\underset{1}{y}z}}{a_{xz}}$, (x) and (y) being medically examined.

Similarly under an assurance on the life of (x) payable only if (x) predecease the survivor of (y) and (z), the risk will determine either on the death of (x) or on the death of the survivor of (y) and (z). The annuity to be employed in calculating the annual premium is $a_{x:\overline{yz}}$, the premium being $\frac{A^1_{x:\overline{yz}}}{a_{x:\overline{yz}}}$, but in order to avoid selection against the Office, all three lives should be medically examined. If only (x) were examined and (z) were a bad life, the Office might be granting what was practically an assurance on (x) against (y) at an insufficient premium.

The annual premium to be charged for an assurance payable on the failure of the joint lives (x) and (y) before (z) is $\frac{A_{\overset{1}{xy}:z}}{a_{xyz}}$; and for an assurance payable on the death of the survivor of (x) and (y) before (z), $\frac{A_{\overset{1}{\overline{xy}}:z}}{a_{\overline{xy}:z}}$. In these cases ($x$) and ($y$) must both be medically examined but it is not necessary to take this precaution with (z), since if (z) die first the assurance terminates without a claim arising.

For an assurance payable on the death of (x) provided he die last of the three lives (x), (y) and (z) the annual premium should be made payable during the lifetime of (x), all three lives being medically examined. The annual premium to be charged is, therefore, $\frac{A^3_{xyz}}{a_x}$.

The symbols for the annual premiums have been omitted because, where the suffix for the annuity (i.e. in the denominator) differs materially from that for the assurance, the adoption of a symbol consistent with the assurance only is misleading. It is, moreover, of no importance that a particular symbol should be known so long as the student is able to calculate the required premium.

44. The annual premium for an assurance payable on (x) dying before (y) or within t years after the death of (y) may be made payable either during the joint lives of (x) and (y), the annuity value being a_{xy}; or until the risk determines, in which case the annuity value to be employed is $a_{x:\overline{t}|} + \frac{D_{x+t}}{D_x} a_{x+t:y}$.

If the latter method be adopted, it might occur that if (y) die early, (x) will be in possession of a temporary assurance for t years at an inadequate premium; while if the former method be employed the premium is increased, with the result that the proposer might decline to effect the policy. There is also the further difficulty when the premiums are payable throughout the duration of the contract, that, in the event of (x) surviving, the last annual premium would be payable on the average only six months before the termination of the contract: this difficulty can be avoided by arranging for $t-1$ payments only after the death of (y).

45. Similar formulae hold for the annual premiums for temporary contingent assurances. The annual premium for an assurance of unity payable on the death of (x) before (y) and (z) within n years is $\dfrac{|_n A^1_{xyz}}{\mathbf{a}_{xyz:\overline{n}|}}$: for an assurance payable in the event of (x) dying before (z) within n years, (y) having died before (x), $\dfrac{|_n A^{\ \,2}_{xy\overset{1}{z}}}{\mathbf{a}_{xz:\overline{n}|}}$, and so on.

46. The formulae for the annual premiums for contingent assurances involving two lives only can be expressed in terms of commutation functions. Thus,

$$\frac{A^2_{xy}}{\mathbf{a}_x} = \frac{\dfrac{M_x}{D_x} - \dfrac{M^1_{xy}}{D_{xy}}}{\dfrac{N_x}{D_x}} \text{ ....(39)},$$

$$\frac{|_n A^2_{xy}}{\mathbf{a}_{x:\overline{n}|}} = \frac{\dfrac{M_x - M_{x+n}}{D_x} - \dfrac{M^1_{xy} - M_{\overset{1}{x+n}:y+n}}{D_{xy}}}{\dfrac{N_x - N_{x+n}}{D_x}} \text{ ....(40)},$$

and so on.

47. The approximate method of paragraph 24 can be applied very conveniently to annual premiums. Thus, by the H^M Table at 3 per cent., by this method,

$$^{(\infty)}P^1_{30:60} = \frac{\cdot 00990}{\cdot 07343} \times P_{62} \times 1\cdot 015$$
$$= \frac{\cdot 00990}{\cdot 07343} \times \cdot 06624 \times 1\cdot 015$$
$$= \cdot 00906,$$

the correct value being $\cdot 00926$, and

$$^{(\infty)}P^1_{32:40} = \frac{\cdot 01462}{\cdot 03831} \times P_{47} \times 1\cdot 015$$
$$= \frac{\cdot 01462}{\cdot 03831} \times \cdot 03369 \times 1\cdot 015$$
$$= \cdot 01305,$$

the correct value being $\cdot 01354$.

48. Values of Contingent Assurance Policies. The value at the end of t years of a policy securing a payment of "1" in the event of the death of (x) before that of (y) is

$$_tV^1_{xy} = A_{\overset{1}{x+t}:y+t} - P^1_{xy}\mathbf{a}_{x+t:y+t} \text{ ....(41)}.$$

If the sum assured be payable on the death of (x) provided he dies *after* (y), and the annual premium be payable during the life of (x), the value of the policy differs according to whether (a) both (x) and (y) are still alive, (b) (x) only is alive.

The policy value is for

$$\left.\begin{array}{ll}\text{Case }(a) & A^{\;\;2}_{\overline{x+t}:y+t} - P\mathrm{a}_{x+t} \\ \text{Case }(b) & A_{x+t} \qquad - P\mathrm{a}_{x+t}\end{array}\right\} \quad \ldots\ldots\ldots\ldots\ldots\ldots\ldots(42),$$

where $P = \dfrac{A^{\;2}_{xy}}{\mathrm{a}_x}$.

When the assurance is payable on the death of (x) only if he die third of three lives (x), (y) and (z), and the value of the policy is required at the end of t years, four cases must be considered, namely:

(a) all three lives still alive,
(b) (x) and (y) alive, (z) dead,
(c) (x) and (z) alive, (y) dead,
(d) (x) only alive.

The policy values in the respective cases are:

$$\left.\begin{array}{ll}(a) & A^{\;\;3}_{\overline{x+t}:y+t:z+t} - P\mathrm{a}_{x+t} \\ (b) & A^{\;\;2}_{\overline{x+t}:y+t} \qquad - P\mathrm{a}_{x+t} \\ (c) & A^{\;\;2}_{\overline{x+t}:z+t} \qquad - P\mathrm{a}_{x+t} \\ (d) & A_{x+t} \qquad\qquad - P\mathrm{a}_{x+t}\end{array}\right\} \quad \ldots\ldots\ldots\ldots\ldots\ldots\ldots(43),$$

where $P = \dfrac{A^{\;3}_{xyz}}{\mathrm{a}_x}$.

Other policies must be similarly considered.

At the periodical valuation of the contracts of a Life Office, the contingent assurance policies are valued individually.

EXAMPLES

Ex. 1. Find an expression for the single premium for an assurance payable at the death of a person aged 30 if he die before a person aged 40 or within ten years after the death of (40), leaving another person now aged 50 surviving.

Considering an assurance payable at the moment of death, the full assurance can be divided into two parts as follows:

(1) During the first ten years the sum assured will be payable if (30) die before (50), the value of which is

$$\int_0^{10} v^t \, {}_tp_{30:50} \, \mu_{30+t} \, dt = {}_{|10}\bar{A}^{\,1}_{30:50}$$

$$= \bar{A}^{\,1}_{30:50} - \frac{D_{40:60}}{D_{30:50}} \bar{A}^{\,1}_{40:60}.$$

(2) After ten years in order that the sum assured shall be payable at the death of (30) the life aged 50 must then survive and the life aged 40 must have been alive ten years before. The value of this portion is

$$\int_0^\infty v^{10+t}\ {}_{10+t}p_{30:50}\,\mu_{40+t}\,.\,{}_tp_{40}\,dt$$
$$= v^{10}\ {}_{10}p_{30:50}\,\bar{A}^{\ 1}_{40:40:60}.$$

The value of the full assurance is, therefore,

$$\bar{A}^{\ 1}_{30:50} - \frac{D_{40:60}}{D_{30:50}}(\bar{A}^{\ 1}_{40:60} - \bar{A}^{\ 1}_{40:40:60}).$$

Ex. 2. Find an expression for the single premium with a loading of 7½ per cent. for a contingent survivorship policy payable if a life aged 30 die before a life aged 60, or within 5 years of the death of the latter, with the return of the single premium without interest five years after the death of (60) if no claim under the policy arises by the death of (30).

Let 1·075 S be the single premium required, then S (the net single premium) will be equal to an assurance payable on the death of (30) less an assurance payable on the death of (30) if (60) was not alive five years before *plus* a payment of (1·075) S five years after the death of (60) if (30) be then alive. That is,

$$S = \bar{A}_{30} - \int_0^\infty v^{t+5}(1 - {}_tp_{60})\,{}_{t+5}p_{30}\,\mu_{35+t}\,dt + (1{\cdot}075)\,S$$
$$\times \int_0^\infty v^t\,{}_tp_{30:60}\,\mu_{60+t}\,v^5\,{}_5p_{30+t}\,dt$$
$$= \bar{A}_{30} - v^5\,{}_5p_{30}\int_0^\infty v^t(1 - {}_tp_{60})\,{}_tp_{35}\,\mu_{35+t}\,dt + (1{\cdot}075)\,S\,.\,v^5\,{}_5p_{30}$$
$$\times \int_0^\infty v^t\,{}_tp_{35:60}\,\mu_{60+t}\,dt$$
$$= \bar{A}_{30} - \frac{D_{35}}{D_{30}}(\bar{A}_{35} - \bar{A}^{\ 1}_{35:60}) + (1{\cdot}075)\,S\,\frac{D_{35}}{D_{30}}\,\bar{A}_{35:\overset{1}{60}}\,;$$

$$\therefore S = \frac{\bar{A}_{30} - \dfrac{D_{35}}{D_{30}}(\bar{A}_{35} - \bar{A}^{\ 1}_{35:60})}{1 - (1{\cdot}075)\dfrac{D_{35}}{D_{30}}\bar{A}_{35:\overset{1}{60}}}.$$

To obtain the Office premium this expression must be multiplied by 1·075.

Ex. 3. Find an expression for the annual premium, payable throughout the duration of the contract, for an assurance payable in the event of both of two lives aged 30 and 35 respectively dying before reaching age 50 and in the lifetime of a third person now aged 45.

The value of the assurance can be expressed as

$$|_{15}A^{1}_{35:45} + |_{20}A^{1}_{30:45} - \left(|_{15}A^{\overbrace{}^{1}}_{30:35:45} + v^{15}\,{}_{15}p_{30:35:45}\,|_{5}A^{1}_{45:60}\right),$$

or
$$|_{15}A_{\overset{1}{\overline{30:35}}:45} + v^{15}\,{}_{15}p_{30:45}\,(1 - {}_{15}p_{35})\,|_{5}A^{1}_{45:60},$$

and the annual premium will be found by dividing this value by

$$a_{\overline{30:35}:45:\overline{15}|} + v^{15}\,{}_{15}p_{30:45}\,(1 - {}_{15}p_{35})\,a_{45:60:\overline{5}|}.$$

Ex. 4. Find an expression for the net annual premium for an assurance of unity payable in the event of (x) dying before (y) within n years, all premiums paid to be returned in the event of (y) dying before x.

Let P be the annual premium required; then:

Value of Benefit

$$= \frac{M^{1}_{xy} - M_{\overset{1}{x+n}:y+n}}{D_{xy}} + (P + c)(1 + k)\,\frac{R_{x\overset{1}{y}} - R_{\overline{x+n}:\overset{1}{\overline{y+n}}} - nM_{\overline{x+n}:\overset{1}{\overline{y+n}}}}{D_{xy}},$$

$$\text{Value of Premiums} = P\,\frac{N_{xy} - N_{x+n:y+n}}{D_{xy}},$$

whence

$$P = \frac{(M^{1}_{xy} - M_{\overset{1}{x+n}:y+n}) + c\,(1 + k)\,(R_{x\overset{1}{y}} - R_{x+n:\overset{1}{\overline{y+n}}} - nM_{x+n:\overset{1}{\overline{y+n}}})}{(N_{xy} - N_{x+n:y+n}) - (1 + k)\,(R_{x\overset{1}{y}} - R_{x+n:\overset{1}{\overline{y+n}}} - nM_{x+n:\overset{1}{\overline{y+n}}})}.$$

CHAPTER XVIII

REVERSIONARY ANNUITIES

1. A *reversionary annuity* to (x) after (y) is an annuity to commence on the death of (y) and to continue thereafter during the life of (x).

2. If the annuity be payable continuously its value can be ascertained by deducting from the value of an immediate continuous annuity payable during the life of (x), the value of a similar annuity payable during the joint existence of (x) and (y): the balance is the value of those payments to be made during the period of (x)'s survival after the death of (y).

Representing the value of this reversionary annuity by $\bar{a}_{y|x}$, we have

$$\begin{aligned}\bar{a}_{y|x} &= \bar{a}_x - \bar{a}_{xy} \\ &= \{a_x + \tfrac{1}{2} - \tfrac{1}{12}(\mu_x + \delta)\} - \{a_{xy} + \tfrac{1}{2} - \tfrac{1}{12}(\mu_x + \mu_y + \delta)\} \\ &= a_x - a_{xy} + \tfrac{1}{12}\mu_y \quad \text{...(1).}\end{aligned}$$

The value of the last term is very small, and for practical purposes can be neglected, the formula becoming

$$\bar{a}_{y|x} = a_x - a_{xy} \quad \text{........................(2).}$$

3. The value of $\bar{a}_{y|x}$ can be expressed in the form of an integral in either of two ways:

(*a*) At the death of (y), (x) will be entitled to a continuous annuity the value of which, if (y) die at time t, will then be $\bar{a}_{x+t}$. Treating this as a benefit payable at the moment of death of (y), the present value can be expressed in the form

$$\bar{a}_{y|x} = \int_0^\infty v^t \, {}_tp_{xy} \, \mu_{y+t} \, \bar{a}_{x+t} \, dt \quad \text{..............(2}a\text{).}$$

(*b*) The payment at time t will be made if (x) be then alive and (y) has died previously, the present value of this payment being $v^t(1 - {}_tp_y)\,{}_tp_x\,dt$, where dt is the infinitely small payment made under the continuous annuity. The value of the payments to be made after the death of (y); that is, the value of the reversionary annuity is, therefore,

$$\bar{a}_{y|x} = \int_0^\infty v^t (1 - {}_tp_y)\, {}_tp_x \, dt \quad \ldots\ldots\ldots\ldots\ldots(2\,b)$$

$$= \bar{a}_x - \bar{a}_{xy}.$$

That these expressions are equal can be shown in the following manner:

The first integral can be expressed in the form

$$\bar{a}_{y|x} = \int_0^\infty {}_tp_y \, \mu_{y+t} \left(\int_t^\infty v^k \, {}_kp_x \, dk \right) dt$$

$$= \int_0^\infty v^t \, {}_tp_x \left(\int_0^t {}_kp_y \, \mu_{y+k} \, dk \right) dt$$

$$= \int_0^\infty v^t \, {}_tp_x (1 - {}_tp_y) \, dt.$$

4. Turning to the practical example of a reversionary annuity payable m times a year to (x) after the death of (y), three distinct cases arise for consideration; namely,

(1) An annuity to be *entered upon* by (x) immediately on the death of (y), the first payment of $\frac{1}{m}$ to be made at the end of a period of $\frac{1}{m}$th of a year measured from the date of death of (y), later payments being made at the ends of successive periods similarly measured.

(2) An annuity to be set up immediately, the periods, at the ends of which successive payments are to be made, being measured from the present time, the first full payment of $\frac{1}{m}$ to (x) being made at the end of the $\frac{1}{m}$th period of a year, measured from the present time, in which (y) dies, so that the actual period of accrual is disregarded.

(3) An annuity similar to (2) under which, however, the proportionate payment to the death of (y) is to be made to his estate, so that (x) will only receive the amount which has accrued since the death of (y).

5. The first case is the one that arises when a Life Office grants a reversionary annuity. Unless otherwise stated in the contract the annuity will be complete, and it is required, therefore, to ascertain the value of a complete reversionary annuity of 1 per annum payable m times a year to (x), the annuity to be entered upon at the death of (y).

The symbol for the value of this annuity is $\hat{\mathring{a}}^{(m)}_{y|x}$, where the sign $\wedge$ is placed over the letter a to indicate that the annuity is *entered upon* at the death of (y).

If (y) die at time t, (x) will then be aged $x+t$ and will be entitled to a benefit, the value of which will then be $\mathring{a}^{(m)}_{x+t}$. The present value of the reversionary annuity can, therefore, be expressed as follows:

$$\hat{\mathring{a}}^{(m)}_{y|x} = \int_0^\infty v^t \, {}_tp_{xy} \, \mu_{y+t} \, \mathring{a}^{(m)}_{x+t} \, dt$$

$$= \int_0^\infty v^t \, {}_tp_{xy} \, \mu_{y+t} \left\{ \bar{a}_{x+t} \left(1 - \frac{\delta}{2m}\right) + \frac{\delta}{12m^2} \right\} dt$$

$$= \left(1 - \frac{\delta}{2m}\right) \bar{a}_{y|x} + \frac{\delta}{12m^2} \bar{A}^{\;1}_{xy} \quad \text{......................(3).}$$

The value of the last term is exceedingly small and can be neglected, the formula becoming

$$\hat{\mathring{a}}^{(m)}_{y|x} = \left(1 - \frac{\delta}{2m}\right) (\bar{a}_x - \bar{a}_{xy}) \quad \text{..................(4)}$$

$$= \left(1 - \frac{\delta}{2m}\right) (a_x - a_{xy}) \quad \text{approx.......(5).}$$

An alternative formula can be obtained by substituting for $\mathring{a}^{(m)}_{x+t}$ the value

$$\bar{a}_{x+t} - \frac{1}{2m} + \frac{1}{2m} \bar{A}_{x+t}.$$

The expression then becomes

$$\hat{\mathring{a}}^{(m)}_{y|x} = \int_0^\infty v^t \, {}_tp_{xy} \, \mu_{y+t} \left(\bar{a}_{x+t} - \frac{1}{2m} + \frac{1}{2m} \bar{A}_{x+t} \right) dt$$

$$= \bar{a}_{y|x} - \frac{1}{2m} \bar{A}^{\;1}_{xy} + \frac{1}{2m} \bar{A}^{\;2}_{xy}$$

$$= \bar{a}_{y|x} - \frac{1}{2m} \bar{A}^{\;1}_{xy} + \frac{1}{2m} (\bar{A}_x - \bar{A}^{1}_{xy})$$

$$= \bar{a}_x - \bar{a}_{xy} + \frac{1}{2m} (\bar{A}_x - \bar{A}_{xy}) \quad \text{........................(6)}$$

$$= a_x - a_{xy} + \frac{1}{2m} (A_x - A_{xy}) \quad \text{approx. ....(7).}$$

Formula (5) is more convenient for practical use.

If the reversionary annuity be curtate, the benefit on the death of (y) must be taken as $a_{x+t}^{(m)} = \bar{a}_{x+t} - \frac{1}{2m}$. With this substitution we have

$$\hat{a}_{y|x}^{(m)} = a_x - a_{xy} - \frac{1}{2m} \mathrm{A}_{xy}^{\ 1} \text{ ....(8).}$$

6. In the second case mentioned in paragraph 4 (x) is to receive a full payment of $\frac{1}{m}$ at the end of the $\frac{1}{m}$thly interval, measured from the date of the contract, in which (y) dies. Again assuming the annuity to (x) to be complete; if (y) die at time t, and it be further assumed that deaths are uniformly distributed over each year of age, so that, on the average, (y) dies in the middle of a $\frac{1}{m}$thly period, the value of the benefit to (x) at time t, will be

$$_{\frac{1}{2m}|}\mathrm{a}_{x+t}^{(m)} + \frac{1}{2m} \overline{\mathrm{A}}_{x+t}.$$

The value of the reversionary annuity will, therefore, be

$$\mathring{a}_{y|x}^{(m)} = \int_0^\infty v^t {}_tp_{xy} \mu_{y+t} \left(_{\frac{1}{2m}|}\mathrm{a}_{x+t}^{(m)} + \frac{1}{2m} \overline{\mathrm{A}}_{x+t} \right) dt$$

$$= \int_0^\infty v^t {}_tp_{xy} \mu_{y+t} \left\{ a_{x+t} + \tfrac{1}{2} + \frac{1}{2m} \overline{\mathrm{A}}_{x+t} \right\} dt$$

$$= \bar{a}_{y|x} + \frac{1}{2m} \overline{\mathrm{A}}_{xy}^{\ 2}$$

$$= a_x - a_{xy} + \frac{1}{2m} (\mathrm{A}_x - \mathrm{A}_{xy}^1) \text{ approx.............(9).}$$

If the annuity be curtate, the formula becomes

$$a_{y|x}^{(m)} = a_x - a_{xy} \text{ ....(10).}$$

7. Formula (10) is easily, and perhaps more convincingly, ascertainable by general reasoning. If the annuity be set up immediately and (x) is to receive the whole of any payment falling due during his lifetime after the death of (y), the first payment to (x) thus being made at the end of the $\frac{1}{m}$thly period (measured from the date of the contract) in which (y) dies, it is evident that the value of the curtate annuity will be found by deducting from the value of an immediate annuity payable m times a year during the life of (x), $a_x^{(m)}$, the value of a similar annuity payable during the joint existence of (x) and (y), $a_{xy}^{(m)}$. That is,

$$\begin{aligned} a_{y|x}^{(m)} &= a_x^{(m)} - a_{xy}^{(m)} \\ &= a_x + \frac{m-1}{2m} - \frac{m^2-1}{12m^2}(\mu_x + \delta) \\ &\qquad - \left\{a_{xy} + \frac{m-1}{2m} - \frac{m^2-1}{12m^2}(\mu_x + \mu_y + \delta)\right\} \\ &= a_x - a_{xy} + \frac{m^2-1}{12m^2}\mu_y \quad \text{.........................(11)}, \end{aligned}$$

whence, if we neglect the last term, the value of which is very small, we have, for all values of m, $a_{y|x}^{(m)} = a_x - a_{xy}$.

The addition to be made to formula (10) to provide for a complete annuity can also be arrived at by general reasoning. Assuming a uniform distribution of deaths over each year of age, (x) will on the average die in the middle of a $\frac{1}{m}$thly period, and the proportionate payment to the date of his death will be $\frac{1}{2m}$. It is thus necessary to add to formula (10) the value of an assurance of $\frac{1}{2m}$ payable at the death of (x) if he die after (y); whence, using A_{xy}^{2} as sufficiently approximate to $\bar{A}_{xy}^{2}$ the formula becomes

$$\mathring{a}_{y|x}^{(m)} = a_x - a_{xy} + \frac{1}{2m}A_{xy}^{2},$$

as in formula (9).

8. In the third case of paragraph 4 the value of the reversionary annuity can be ascertained as in paragraph 7 by taking

$$\begin{aligned} &\mathring{a}_x^{(m)} - \mathring{a}_{xy}^{(m)} \\ &= \left(a_x + \frac{m-1}{2m} + \frac{1}{2m}A_x\right) - \left(a_{xy} + \frac{m-1}{2m} + \frac{1}{2m}A_{xy}\right) \\ &= a_x - a_{xy} + \frac{1}{2m}(A_x - A_{xy}), \end{aligned}$$

which is formula (7).

A little consideration will show that this annuity is very similar to that represented by $\hat{\mathring{a}}_{y|x}^{(m)}$. In both cases the annuities are complete, and though the times of payment of the respective instalments differ by $\frac{1}{2m}$ of a year—in formula (7) the first payment of $\frac{1}{m}$ is made $\frac{1}{m}$th of a year after the death of (y) and in the present case the first payment of $\frac{1}{2m}$ is made $\frac{1}{2m}$th of a year after that event, later payments in each case being made at intervals of $\frac{1}{m}$th of a year after the first payment—at any moment of time the total amount *paid and accrued* will be the same in the two cases.

It will also be observed that the annuity now being considered is similar to the second case of paragraph 4 except that in respect of the period in which (y) dies (x) will receive the sum of $\frac{1}{2m}$ instead of $\frac{1}{m}$. In other words the value of this reversionary annuity will be found by deducting from $\mathring{a}^{(m)}_{y|x}$ (formula (9)) the value of an assurance of $\frac{1}{2m}$ payable in the event of (y) dying before (x).

Employing $A_{xy}^{\;1}$ in place of $\bar{A}_{xy}^{\;1}$ the expression becomes

$$\mathring{a}^{(m)}_{y|x} - \frac{1}{2m} A_{xy}^{\;1}$$

$$= a_x - a_{xy} + \frac{1}{2m} A_{xy}^{\;2} - \frac{1}{2m} A_{xy}^{\;1}$$

$$= a_x - a_{xy} + \frac{1}{2m}(A_x - A_{xy})$$

as before.

If the annuity to (x) were to be curtate the formula would become

$$a_x - a_{xy} - \frac{1}{2m} A_{xy}^{\;1}$$

which is the same as formula (8).

9. The expression $a_x - a_{xy}$ has been obtained for both $\bar{a}_{y|x}$ and $a^{(m)}_{y|x}$, while the remainder of each of the expressions for $\hat{\mathring{a}}^{(m)}_{y|x}$ reduces the value—$\left(1-\frac{\delta}{2m}\right)$ being less than unity and $A_x - A_{xy}$ being negative—and the third term in the expression for $\mathring{a}^{(m)}_{y|x}$, though positive, is very small.

The result is that in practice, whether the annuity is to be curtate or complete, and whether the first payment is to be made at the end of the interval in which (y) dies or at the end of $\frac{1}{m}$th of a year from his death, it is usual to employ the formula $a_x - a_{xy}$ without modification, whatever the value of m.

10. The values of the respective annuities payable annually are obtainable directly from the foregoing formulae by writing $m = 1$.

11. When the annuity is payable annually, the form

$$a_{y|x} = a_x - a_{xy}$$

can be employed even when combinations of lives or of lives and terms certain are substituted for the lives (x) and (y). In symbols

$$a_{s|z} = a_z - a_{sz} \quad \text{......................}(12),$$

where either s or z may represent a life or a term certain, a combination of lives, or of a life (or lives) and a term certain. When, however, the annuity is payable more frequently than annually and a term certain is involved, consideration must be given to the different type of formula thereby introduced.

For example, an annuity of 1 per annum payable annually to (x) after the expiration of a term of n years is

$$a_{\overline{n}|\,|x} = a_x - a_{x:\overline{n}|}$$

but if the annuity were payable m times a year, this would become, using only practical formulae for the annuity values,

$$\begin{aligned} a^{(m)}_{\overline{n}|\,|x} &= a^{(m)}_x - a^{(m)}_{x:\overline{n}|} \\ &= \left(a_x + \frac{m-1}{2m}\right) - \left\{a_{x:\overline{n}|} + \frac{m-1}{2m}\left(1 - \frac{D_{x+n}}{D_x}\right)\right\} \\ &= a_x - a_{x:\overline{n}|} + \frac{m-1}{2m}\frac{D_{x+n}}{D_x} \end{aligned}$$

which is the same as the ordinary formula for the deferred annuity,

$$\frac{D_{x+n}}{D_x}a^{(m)}_{x+n} = \frac{D_{x+n}}{D_x}\left(a_{x+n} + \frac{m-1}{2m}\right).$$

12. The value of an annuity to commence on the death of (x) but in no case to continue beyond n years from the present time is, if payable annually,

$$a_{x|\overline{n}|} = a_{\overline{n}|} - a_{x:\overline{n}|}.$$

But if this annuity be payable m times a year the formula becomes

$$a^{(m)}_{x|\overline{n}|} = a^{(m)}_{\overline{n}|} - a^{(m)}_{x:\overline{n}|}$$

$$= a_{\overline{n}|} \times \frac{i}{j_{(m)}} - \left\{a_{x:\overline{n}|} + \frac{m-1}{2m}\left(1 - \frac{D_{x+n}}{D_x}\right)\right\}.$$

13. Where lives only are involved it is, in the general case, safe to assume that $\hat{\mathring{a}}^{(m)}_{s|z} = \mathring{a}^{(m)}_{s|z} = a^{(m)}_{s|z} = a_z - a_{sz}$ whatever combinations are represented by s and z.

Taking cases involving three lives we have

$$\left.\begin{aligned} a_{z|xy} &= a_{xy} - a_{xyz} \\ a_{yz|x} &= a_x \;\; - a_{xyz} \\ a_{z|\overline{xy}} &= a_{\overline{xy}} - a_{\overline{xy}:z} \\ a_{\overline{yz}|x} &= a_x \;\; - a_{x:\overline{yz}} \end{aligned}\right\} \quad \ldots\ldots\ldots\ldots\ldots\ldots\ldots(13).$$

As an example, the last of these may be examined more fully, the annuity being assumed to be payable m times a year. We then have

$$a^{(m)}_{\overline{yz}|x} = a^{(m)}_x - a^{(m)}_{x:\overline{yz}}$$

$$= a^{(m)}_x - (a^{(m)}_{xy} + a^{(m)}_{xz} - a^{(m)}_{xyz})$$

which, when we write

$$a^{(m)}_x = a_x + \frac{m-1}{2m} - \frac{m^2-1}{12m^2}(\mu_x + \delta),$$

$$a^{(m)}_{xy} = a_{xy} + \frac{m-1}{2m} - \frac{m^2-1}{12m^2}(\mu_x + \mu_y + \delta),$$

etc., reduces to

$$a^{(m)}_{\overline{yz}|x} = a_x - (a_{xy} + a_{xz} - a_{xyz})$$

$$= a_x - a_{x:\overline{yz}},$$

all the terms involving m, μ and δ cancelling out.

Again if the value of $\hat{\mathring{a}}^{(m)}_{\overline{yz}|x}$ be required, following the method employed to obtain formula (3), the expression is

$$\hat{\mathring{a}}^{(m)}_{\overline{yz}|x} = \hat{\mathring{a}}^{(m)}_{y|x} + \hat{\mathring{a}}^{(m)}_{z|x} - \hat{\mathring{a}}^{(m)}_{yz|x}$$

$$= \int_0^\infty v^t \left({}_tp_y\mu_{y+t} + {}_tp_z\mu_{z+t} - {}_tp_{yz}\mu_{y+t:z+t}\right) {}_tp_x$$

$$\times \left\{\left(1 - \frac{\delta}{2m}\right)\bar{a}_{x+t} + \frac{\delta}{12m^2}\right\} dt$$

$$= \left(1 - \frac{\delta}{2m}\right)(\bar{a}_{y|x} + \bar{a}_{z|x} - \bar{a}_{yz|x}) + \frac{\delta}{12m^2}\bar{A}_{\overline{yz}:\overset{1}{x}}$$

$$= \left(1 - \frac{\delta}{2m}\right) a_{\overline{yz}|x} \text{ approx.}$$

Or following the method employed to obtain formula (6)

$$\mathring{\hat{a}}^{(m)}_{\overline{yz}|x} = \int_0^\infty v^t \left({}_tp_y\mu_{y+t} + {}_tp_z\mu_{z+t} - {}_tp_{yz}\mu_{y+t:z+t}\right){}_tp_x$$
$$\times\left(\bar{a}_{x+t} - \frac{1}{2m} + \frac{1}{2m}\bar{A}_{x+t}\right)dt$$
$$= (\bar{a}_{y|x} + \bar{a}_{z|x} - \bar{a}_{yz|x}) - \frac{1}{2m}\bar{A}_{\underset{3}{x}:\overline{yz}} + \frac{1}{2m}\bar{A}^{3}_{xyz}$$
$$= \bar{a}_x - (\bar{a}_{xy} + \bar{a}_{xz} - \bar{a}_{xyz}) + \frac{1}{2m}(\bar{A}_x - \bar{A}_{x:\overline{yz}}),$$

since $\bar{A}^{3}_{xyz} = \bar{A}_x - \bar{A}^{1}_{x:\overline{yz}}$ and $\bar{A}^{1}_{x:\overline{yz}} + \bar{A}_{\underset{3}{x}:\overline{yz}} = \bar{A}_{x:\overline{yz}}$,

$$\therefore\ \mathring{\hat{a}}^{(m)}_{\overline{yz}|x} = a_{\overline{yz}|x} + \frac{1}{2m}(A_x - A_{x:\overline{yz}}) \text{ approx.}$$

In both these cases it is evidently sufficient, in accordance with the arguments already put forward in connection with $\mathring{\hat{a}}^{(m)}_{y|x}$, to take for practical purposes

$$\mathring{\hat{a}}^{(m)}_{\overline{yz}|x} = a_{\overline{yz}|x}$$
$$= a_x - a_{x:\overline{yz}}.$$

14. In the following tabular statement the various formulae are brought together for the purpose of comparison. The general formula, number 10, is given first without a representative symbol, as this formula has been suggested for universal use (see paragraph 9): the remaining formulae are given in the order in which they appear in this chapter. The numerical results are based on the H^M Table (Makeham Graduation) at 4 per cent., the ages being taken as $x=30$ and $y=45$, while $m=4$.

Number of Formula	Formula	Numerical Example $x=30$, $y=45$, $m=4$ H^M 4 per cent.
10	$a_x - a_{xy}$	4·771
1	$\bar{a}_{y|x} = a_x - a_{xy} + \frac{1}{12}\mu_y$	4·772
3	$\mathring{\hat{a}}^{(m)}_{y|x} = \left(1-\frac{\delta}{2m}\right)\left(a_x - a_{xy} + \frac{1}{12}\mu_y\right) + \frac{\delta}{12m^2}\bar{A}^{\ 1}_{xy}$	4·749
5	$\mathring{a}^{(m)}_{y|x} = \left(1-\frac{\delta}{2m}\right)(a_x - a_{xy})$	4·748
7	$\mathring{\hat{a}}^{(m)}_{y|x} = a_x - a_{xy} + \frac{1}{2m}(A_x - A_{xy})$	4·748
8	$\hat{a}^{(m)}_{y|x} = a_x - a_{xy} - \frac{1}{2m}A^{\ 1}_{xy}$	4·729
9	$\mathring{a}^{(m)}_{y|x} = a_x - a_{xy} + \frac{1}{2m}(A_x - A^{\ 1}_{xy})$	4·766
11	$a^{(m)}_{y|x} = a_x - a_{xy} + \frac{m^2-1}{12m^2}\mu_y$	4·772

It is evident from this table that the formula $a_x - a_{xy}$ gives sufficiently accurate results for practical purposes. When applied as the value of $\hat{\mathring{a}}^{(m)}_{y|x}$ it gives a result somewhat in excess of the true value, but from the point of view of the Life Office this is on the safe side.

15. Deferred Reversionary Annuities. If the reversionary annuity to (x) after (y) be curtate and subject to the condition that no payment is to be made until after the expiration of n years —that is, a *deferred reversionary annuity*—the value can be obtained as follows:

$$
\begin{aligned}
{}_{n|}a^{(m)}_{y|x} &= {}_{n|}a^{(m)}_{x} - {}_{n|}a^{(m)}_{xy} \\
&= v^n {}_np_x \left(a_{x+n} + \frac{m-1}{2m}\right) - v^n {}_np_{xy} \left(a_{x+n:y+n} + \frac{m-1}{2m}\right) \\
&= {}_{n|}a_x - {}_{n|}a_{xy} + \frac{m-1}{2m} v^n {}_np_x (1 - {}_np_y) \quad \text{......}(14).
\end{aligned}
$$

In this case it is not necessary that both (x) and (y) should survive n years.

If the annuity be only payable to (x) after (y) subject to both lives surviving n years, the value will be

$$v^n {}_np_{xy} (a_{x+n} - a_{x+n:y+n}),$$

while if it is only to be payable to (x) from the end of n years, provided (y) die before that time, the value is

$$v^n {}_np_x (1 - {}_np_y)\, a^{(m)}_{x+n}.$$

16. The value of a complete deferred reversionary annuity to (x) after (y), to be entered upon at the end of n years if (y) has died previously or immediately on the death of (y) should he survive that period, can be found as follows:

$$
\begin{aligned}
{}_{n|}\hat{\mathring{a}}^{(m)}_{y|x} &= v^n {}_np_x (1 - {}_np_y)\, \mathring{a}^{(m)}_{x+n} + v^n {}_np_{xy}\, \hat{\mathring{a}}^{(m)}_{y+n|x+n} \\
&= v^n {}_np_x (1 - {}_np_y) \left(1 - \frac{\delta}{2m}\right) \bar{a}_{x+n} + v^n {}_np_{xy} \left(1 - \frac{\delta}{2m}\right) \\
&\qquad \times (\bar{a}_{x+n} - \bar{a}_{x+n:y+n}) \\
&= \left(1 - \frac{\delta}{2m}\right) (v^n {}_np_x \bar{a}_{x+n} - v^n {}_np_{xy} \bar{a}_{x+n:y+n}) \\
&= \left(1 - \frac{\delta}{2m}\right) \{{}_{n|}a_x - {}_{n|}a_{xy} + \tfrac{1}{2} v^n {}_np_x (1 - {}_np_y)\} \quad \text{......}(15),
\end{aligned}
$$

corresponding to formula (5).

Or, substituting for $\hat{\mathring{a}}^{(m)}_{y+n|x+n}$ the value given in formula (7)

$$
\begin{aligned}
{}_{n|}\hat{\mathring{a}}^{(m)}_{y|x} &= v^n {}_np_x(1-{}_np_y)\left(a_{x+n}+\frac{m-1}{2m}+\frac{1}{2m}\mathrm{A}_{x+n}\right)\\
&\qquad + v^n {}_np_{xy}\left\{a_{x+n}-a_{x+n:y+n}+\frac{1}{2m}(\mathrm{A}_{x+n}-\mathrm{A}_{x+n:y+n})\right\}\\
&= v^n {}_np_x\left(a_{x+n}+\frac{m-1}{2m}+\frac{1}{2m}\mathrm{A}_{x+n}\right)\\
&\qquad - v^n {}_np_{xy}\left(a_{x+n:y+n}+\frac{m-1}{2m}+\frac{1}{2m}\mathrm{A}_{x+n:y+n}\right)\\
&= {}_{n|}a_x - {}_{n|}a_{xy} + \frac{m-1}{2m}v^n {}_np_x(1-{}_np_y)+\frac{1}{2m}({}_{n|}\mathrm{A}_x-{}_{n|}\mathrm{A}_{xy})
\end{aligned}
$$

.........(16).

If $n=20$, taking as before $x=30$, $y=45$ and $m=4$, the value of ${}_{n|}\hat{\mathring{a}}^{(m)}_{y|x}$ on the basis of the $\mathrm{H^M}$ Table at 4 per cent. is by formula (15), 3·098, and by formula (16), 3·094. If formula (14) be employed the result is 3·097.

17. Temporary Reversionary Annuities. The formulae for the value of a temporary reversionary annuity to (x) after (y), no payment to be made after the expiration of n years, can be similarly ascertained. Thus

$$
\begin{aligned}
|_n a^{(m)}_{y|x} &= a^{(m)}_{x:\overline{n}|} - a^{(m)}_{xy:\overline{n}|}\\
&= (a_{x:\overline{n}|}-a_{xy:\overline{n}|}) - \frac{m-1}{2m}v^n {}_np_x(1-{}_np_y) \quad \text{...(17).}
\end{aligned}
$$

Also

$$
\begin{aligned}
|_n\hat{\mathring{a}}^{(m)}_{y|x} &= \int_0^n v^t {}_tp_{xy}\mu_{y+t}\mathring{a}^{(m)}_{x+t:\overline{n-t}|}\,dt\\
&= \int_0^n v^t {}_tp_{xy}\mu_{y+t}\bar{a}_{x+t:\overline{n-t}|}\left(1-\frac{\delta}{2m}\right)dt\\
&= \left(1-\frac{\delta}{2m}\right)|_n\bar{a}_{y|x}\\
&= \left(1-\frac{\delta}{2m}\right)(|_n\bar{a}_x - |_n\bar{a}_{xy})\\
&= \left(1-\frac{\delta}{2m}\right)\{a_{x:\overline{n}|}-a_{xy:\overline{n}|}-\tfrac{1}{2}v^n {}_np_x(1-{}_np_y)\} \quad \text{...(18),}
\end{aligned}
$$

or $$|_n\mathring{\hat{a}}^{(m)}_{y|x} = \int_0^n v^t {}_tp_{xy}\,\mu_{y+t}\,\mathring{a}^{(m)}_{x+t:\overline{n-t|}}\,dt$$

$$= \int_0^n v^t {}_tp_{xy}\,\mu_{y+t}\left\{\bar{a}_{x+t:\overline{n-t|}} - \frac{1}{2m}\left(1 - \frac{D_{x+n}}{D_{x+t}}\right) + \frac{1}{2m}|_{n-t}\bar{A}_{x+t}\right\}dt$$

$$= |_n\bar{a}_{y|x} - \frac{1}{2m}|_n\bar{A}^{\ 1}_{xy} + \frac{1}{2m}v^n {}_np_x(1 - {}_np_y) + \frac{1}{2m}|_n\bar{A}^{\ 2}_{xy}$$

$$= |_na_{y|x} - \frac{m-1}{2m}v^n {}_np_x(1 - {}_np_y) - \frac{1}{2m}(|_nA_{xy} - |_nA_x) \quad \text{.........(19).}$$

18. Taking as before $x = 30$, $y = 45$, $n = 20$ and $m = 4$, the value of $|_n\mathring{\hat{a}}^{(m)}_{y|x}$ on the basis of the H^M Table at 4 per cent. by formula (18) is 1·655 and by formula (19), 1·652. The value given by the approximate formula (17) is 1·680. It is therefore sufficiently accurate for practical purposes to use this simple form for all kinds of temporary reversionary annuities.

19. If the complete annuity is to be entered upon at the moment of death of (y) provided he dies within the first n years, but is thereafter to be payable to (x) for life, the value is

$$\mathring{\hat{a}}^{(m)}_{y|x} - v^n {}_np_{xy}\,\mathring{\hat{a}}^{(m)}_{y+n|x+n}$$

$$= (a_x - a_{xy}) - v^n {}_np_{xy}(a_{x+n} - a_{x+n:y+n}) \quad \text{.........(20).}$$

20. Another type of annuity is one to (x) after (y) which, however, in the event of (y) dying within n years is to continue until the end of n years whether (x) survive that period or not. The value of this would be

$$\hat{a}^{(m)}_{y|\overline{n|}} + {}_n|\mathring{\hat{a}}^{(m)}_{y|x}$$

$$= a_{\overline{n|}} \times \frac{i}{j_{(m)}} - \mathring{a}^{(m)}_{y:\overline{n|}} + {}_n|a_x - {}_n|a_{xy}$$

$$+ \frac{m-1}{2m}v^n {}_np_x(1 - {}_np_y) + \frac{1}{2m}({}_n|A_x - {}_n|A_{xy})$$

$$= a_{\overline{n|}} \times \frac{i}{j_{(m)}} - \left\{a_{y:\overline{n|}} + \frac{m-1}{2m}\left(1 - \frac{D_{y+n}}{D_y}\right) + \frac{1}{2m}A^{1}_{y:\overline{n|}}\right\} + ({}_n|a_x - {}_n|a_{xy})$$

$$+ \frac{m-1}{2m}v^n {}_np_x(1 - {}_np_y) + \frac{1}{2m}({}_n|A_x - {}_n|A_{xy}) \quad \text{......(21).}$$

If this annuity were payable annually and were set up now, the first payment being a full year's payment at the end of the year of death of (y), the expression would become

$$(a_{\overline{n|}} - a_{y:\overline{n|}}) + ({}_n|a_x - {}_n|a_{xy}) \quad \text{..............(22).}$$

21. General use of Formula (12). It has been stated that formula (12) is employed in practice in all normal cases whatever combinations of lives are involved.

This simple formula enables us to write down the answers to many practical questions by inspection.

Three persons (x), (y) and (z) agree to purchase an annuity of 1 payable during the longest of their lives, that is, until the death of the last survivor. It is to be shared equally between them while they are all living; on the death of one it is to be divided equally between the two survivors, and the last survivor is to have the whole. What is the value of the share of each?

The value of the share of (x) is found as follows:

(*a*) While all three are alive (x) will receive one-third of the annuity, and the value of his share during this period is, therefore, $\frac{1}{3}a_{xyz}$.

(*b*) If (y) die first, (x) will receive half the annuity so long as he survives jointly with (z): if (z) die first (x) will receive half the annuity so long as he survives jointly with (y). The value of his share of this portion of the annuity is, therefore,

$$\tfrac{1}{2}(a_{y|xz} + a_{z|xy}) = \tfrac{1}{2}a_{xz} + \tfrac{1}{2}a_{xy} - a_{xyz}.$$

(*c*) Lastly, after the death of the survivor of (y) and (z), (x) will receive the whole of the annuity during the remainder of his life. The value of this portion of his share is

$$a_{\overline{yz}|x} = a_x - a_{xy} - a_{xz} + a_{xyz}.$$

The total value of the share of (x) is, therefore,

$$\begin{aligned}&\tfrac{1}{3}a_{xyz} + (\tfrac{1}{2}a_{xz} + \tfrac{1}{2}a_{xy} - a_{xyz}) + (a_x - a_{xy} - a_{xz} + a_{xyz})\\ &= a_x - \tfrac{1}{2}(a_{xy} + a_{xz}) + \tfrac{1}{3}a_{xyz}.\end{aligned}$$

Similarly the value of the share of (y) is

$$a_y - \tfrac{1}{2}(a_{xy} + a_{yz}) + \tfrac{1}{3}a_{xyz}$$

and the share of (z) is

$$a_z - \tfrac{1}{2}(a_{xz} + a_{yz}) + \tfrac{1}{3}a_{xyz}.$$

The sum of these three shares is

$$\begin{aligned}&a_x + a_y + a_z - a_{xy} - a_{xz} - a_{yz} + a_{xyz}\\ &= a_{\overline{xyz}}\end{aligned}$$

which is the value of the whole annuity.

The value of the share of (x) might have been written down directly in its final form, by considering how far short of a whole-life annuity of the full amount his share falls.

Commencing with a whole-life annuity to (x) the value of which is a_x, if we deduct the value of an annuity of $\frac{1}{2}$ payable during the joint existence of (x) and (y) and the value of a similar annuity payable during the joint lives of (x) and (z)—giving $a_x - \frac{1}{2}a_{xy} - \frac{1}{2}a_{xz}$ —we shall have provided for (x) receiving the whole annuity after both (y) and (z) are dead, and only $\frac{1}{2}$ while one only of (y) and (z) survives jointly with him. But unless this expression be modified so long as all three are alive the two joint-life annuities will cancel the single-life annuity and no payment at all will be made: to avoid this we must add the value of the share of (x) while all three are alive, that is, $\frac{1}{3}a_{xyz}$.

We thus have, as before, $a_x - \frac{1}{2}a_{xy} - \frac{1}{2}a_{xz} + \frac{1}{3}a_{xyz}$.

Reversing the argument in this manner frequently shortens the solution of a problem, but, until he has acquired a fair amount of experience, the student is advised to employ the more straightforward though longer method, applying the reverse process as a check on his formula.

22. Suppose the three persons (x), (y) and (z) have purchased an annuity (as in paragraph 21) payable until the death of the last survivor, but that it is to be shared in the following manner:

(*a*) (x) and (y) are to take half of the annuity each during their joint lives;

(*b*) if (x) die first, (y) and (z) are to share it equally during their joint lives, and the survivor of them is to have the whole;

(*c*) if (y) die first, (x) is to enjoy the whole during his life, and after his death the whole annuity goes to (z).

The value of the share of (x) is

$$\frac{1}{2}a_{xy} + a_{y|x}$$
$$= a_x - \frac{1}{2}a_{xy}.$$

The value of the share of (y) is

$$\frac{1}{2}a_{xy} + \frac{1}{2}a_{x|yz} + a_{\overline{xz}|y}$$
$$= a_y - \frac{1}{2}a_{xy} - \frac{1}{2}a_{yz} + \frac{1}{2}a_{xyz}.$$

The value of the share of (z) is

$$\tfrac{1}{2}a_{x|yz} + a_{\overline{xy}|z}$$
$$= a_z - a_{xz} - \tfrac{1}{2}a_{yz} + \tfrac{1}{2}a_{xyz}.$$

The sum of these values is $a_{\overline{xyz}}$.

In each case the first expression is obtained by the more straightforward method, the first method employed in paragraph 21; the second expression is obtained by considering how far the share of each falls short of a whole-life annuity of the full amount. The student should in each case prove both formulae by general reasoning, and the equality of the two expressions algebraically.

A further more complicated example is given on page 340.

23. Approximate Integration. In the absence of joint-life annuity values, the values of reversionary annuities can be ascertained by approximate integration. As an example let it be required to find on the basis of the H^M Table at 4 per cent. the value of $a_{45|30}$. It has been shown that this is practically identical with $\bar{a}_{45|30}$, and it will be sufficient, therefore, if by means of the formula

$$\int_0^\infty f(x)\,dx = n\{\cdot 28f(0) + 1\cdot 62f(n) + 2\cdot 2f(3n) + 1\cdot 62f(5n) + \cdot 56f(6n) + 1\cdot 62f(7n)\}$$

we ascertain the value of

$$\bar{a}_{45|30} = \frac{1}{l_{30}l_{45}}\int_0^\infty v^t l_{30+t}\,.\,l_{45+t}\mu_{45+t}\bar{a}_{30+t}\,dt.$$

To evaluate this we must take $7n = 102 - 45 = 57$, whence $n = 8$ approximately.

t	$=0$	n $=8$	$3n$ $=24$	$5n$ $=40$	$6n$ $=48$	$7n$ $=56$	
$\log v^t$ ...	0·0000	$\bar{1}$·8637	$\bar{1}$·5912	$\bar{1}$·3187	$\bar{1}$·1824	$\bar{1}$·0461	
$\log l_{30+t}$ ...	4·9527	4·9236	4·8320	4·5795	4·2645	3·6338	
$\log l_{45+t}$ ...	4·8916	4·8402	4·6060	3·7390	2·5635	0·0000	
$\log \mu_{45+t}$ ...	$\bar{2}$·0806	$\bar{2}$·2632	$\bar{2}$·7674	$\bar{1}$·3651	$\bar{1}$·6763	$\bar{1}$·9906	
$\log(\frac{1}{2}+a_{30+t})$	1·2469	1·2065	1·0730	0·8321	0·6587	0·4487	
log coeff. ...	$\bar{1}$·4472	0·2095	0·3424	0·2095	$\bar{1}$·7482	0·2095	
colog $l_{30:45}$ ...	$\overline{10}$·1556	$\overline{10}$·1556	$\overline{10}$·1556	$\overline{10}$·1556	$\overline{10}$·1556	$\overline{10}$·1556	
Sum ...	$\bar{2}$·7746	$\bar{1}$·4623	$\bar{1}$·3676	$\bar{2}$·1995	$\bar{4}$·2492	$\bar{7}$·4843	
$\log^{-1}$ ...	·0595	·2899	·2331	·0158	·0002	·0000	= ·5985
							8
							$\bar{a}_{45|30}$ = 4·7880

The value is ·017 in excess of that given by the general formula $a_x - a_{xy}$.

24. It sometimes happens that the value of a reversionary annuity is required with the condition that during the lifetime of the life tenant both lives are subject to the rate of mortality displayed by one mortality table, but that after his death the reversioner is subject to the mortality shown by another table. For example, a reversionary annuity may be granted while a married couple are in India to be enjoyed by the wife after the death of her husband; and it may be known that so long as the husband lives, he and his wife will remain in India, but that on the death of the husband, his widow will return to reside in Europe.

In such a case, if it could be assumed that after the death of the husband the widow will be subject to the risk of death corresponding to that shown by a table based on the experience of female annuitants resident in Europe, the form of the integral to be employed would be $\int_0^\infty v^t {}_tp_{xy}\mu_{y+t}\bar{a}_{x+t}dt$. In ascertaining the value by approximate integration the values of all the functions except $\bar{a}_{x+t}$ would be taken from a mortality table applicable to residents in India, and $\bar{a}_{x+t}$ from a table of annuities on female lives in Europe.

The alternative form of the integral, namely $\int_0^\infty v^t {}_tp_x(1-{}_tp_y)\,dt$ or $\frac{1}{l_{xy}}\int_0^\infty v^t l_{x+t}(l_y - l_{y+t})\,dt$, could not be used for such a case.

25. The value may, however, be required on the assumption that the mortality experience of the two lives will be throughout that shown by two separate tables. Thus in $a_{y|x}$ it may be assumed that the mortality experience applicable to (y) is that shown by the $O^{[NM]}$ Table and (x) may be assumed to be of the class from which the experience shown by the British Offices Female Annuitants Experience—$O^{[af]}$—was drawn.

In this case either form of the integral can be used but the arithmetical work will be reduced if the form

$$\bar{a}_{\underset{O^{[NM]}O^{[af]}}{[y]|[x]}} = \frac{1}{l_{[x]}l_{[y]}}\int_0^\infty v^t l_{[x]+t}(l_{[y]} - l_{[y]+t})\,dt$$

be employed, $l_{[x]}$ and $l_{[x]+t}$ being taken from the $O^{[af]}$ Table, and $l_{[y]}$ and $l_{[y]+t}$ from the $O^{[NM]}$ Table.

If the value of $a_{[x][y]}$ on the basis of the two tables combined be available, it is only necessary to take

$$a_{[y]|[x]} = a_{[x]} - a_{[x][y]}.$$

A table of the values of $a_{[x][y]}$ at 3 per cent. for all values of $[x]$ (by O[NM] Table) from 20 to 75 and for quinary values of t, where $[y]$ (by O[af] Table) $= [x \pm t]$, and ranges between the limits of 20 and 99, is given on pages 420 to 422 of the (Blue) volume of Tables based on the "O[M] and O[NM] Select Tables—Whole-Life Participating and Non-Participating Assurances—Males." Similar tables at $3\frac{1}{2}$ per cent. are given in the *J. I. A.* Vol. XLV.

26. Annual Premiums on Reversionary Annuities. Assurance companies generally grant reversionary annuities in consideration of periodical premiums payable during the joint lives of the life tenant and the reversioner, the formula for the annual premium for a reversionary annuity to (x) after the death of (y) thus being $\dfrac{a_{y|x}}{\mathbf{a}_{xy}}$.

The annual premium for a reversionary annuity to (x) after the failure of the joint lives (y) and (z) will be payable during the joint existence of the three lives and, therefore, obtained by the formula $\dfrac{a_{yz|x}}{\mathbf{a}_{xyz}}$. Similarly the annual premium to secure a reversionary annuity to (x) after the death of the survivor of (y) and (z) would be $\dfrac{a_{\overline{yz}|x}}{\mathbf{a}_{x:\overline{yz}}}$.

Premiums payable more frequently than yearly can be obtained by dividing by the "$m$thly" annuity value, but in practice would probably be arrived at by increasing the annual premium by a fixed percentage considered sufficient to cover the extra cost and risk involved. (See Chap. VII.)

27. Alternative forms of Integrals. It will be useful to set out the two forms of the integral for the following reversionary annuities:

$$\bar{a}_{z|xy} = \frac{1}{l_x l_y l_z}\int_0^\infty v^t l_{x+t} l_{y+t} (l_z - l_{z+t})\, dt \quad \text{..............(23 } a\text{)},$$

$$= \frac{1}{l_x l_y l_z}\int_0^\infty v^t l_{x+t} l_{y+t} l_{z+t} \mu_{z+t} \bar{a}_{x+t:y+t}\, dt \quad \text{........(23 } b\text{)}.$$

$$\bar{a}_{yz|x} = \frac{1}{l_x l_y l_z}\int_0^\infty v^t l_{x+t} (l_y l_z - l_{y+t} l_{z+t})\, dt \quad \text{...........(24 } a\text{)},$$

$$= \frac{1}{l_x l_y l_z}\int_0^\infty v^t l_{x+t} l_{y+t} l_{z+t} (\mu_{y+t} + \mu_{z+t})\, \bar{a}_{x+t}\, dt \text{...(24 } b\text{)}.$$

$$\bar{a}_{z|\overline{xy}} = \int_0^\infty v^t ({}_tp_x + {}_tp_y - {}_tp_{xy})(1 - {}_tp_z)\, dt \quad \text{.....................(25 a)},$$

$$= \int_0^\infty v^t {}_tp_z \mu_{z+t} ({}_tp_x \bar{a}_{x+t} + {}_tp_y \bar{a}_{y+t} - {}_tp_{xy} \bar{a}_{x+t:y+t})\, dt \quad \text{......(25 b)}.$$

$$\bar{a}_{\overline{yz}|x} = \frac{1}{l_x l_y l_z} \int_0^\infty v^t l_{x+t} (l_y - l_{y+t})(l_z - l_{z+t})\, dt \quad \text{..................(26 a)},$$

$$= \frac{1}{l_x l_y l_z} \int_0^\infty v^t l_{x+t} \{l_{y+t} \mu_{y+t} (l_z - l_{z+t}) + l_{z+t} \mu_{z+t} (l_y - l_{y+t})\}\, \bar{a}_{x+t}\, dt \quad \text{......(26 b)}.$$

EXAMPLES

Ex. 1. Find the value of an annuity payable for n years certain and so long thereafter as (y) may live, the first payment to be made on the death of (x) or at the end of m years if (x) be then alive, the annuity to be paid yearly and to be non-apportionable to the death of (y).

The value will be ascertained in three parts:

(a) An endowment assurance on the life of (x) to secure an annuity-due for n years. The question says "on the death of (x)" but it will be sufficiently accurate to interpret this to mean that in the event of (x) dying within m years the first payment will be made at the end of the year of death of (x). The value of this portion is, therefore, $A_{x:\overline{m}|} \cdot \mathbf{a}_{\overline{n}|}$.

(b) An annuity during the life of (y), first payment to be made at the end of the nth year *after* that in which (x) dies. The value of this is $\frac{D_{y+n}}{D_y}(a_{y+n} - a_{x:y+n})$.

(c) In order to provide for payments to be made from the $(m+n)$th year onwards *within* n years of the death of (x), we must add

$$\sum_{t=0}^{t=\infty} v^{m+n+t}\, {}_{m+n+t}p_y \cdot {}_{m+t}p_x$$

$$= v^{m+n}\, {}_{m+n}p_y \cdot {}_mp_x \sum_{t=0}^{t=\infty} v^t\, {}_tp_{y+m+n} \cdot {}_tp_{x+m}$$

$$= v^{m+n}\, {}_{m+n}p_y \cdot {}_mp_x \mathbf{a}_{x+m:y+m+n}.$$

The value of the entire contract is therefore

$$A_{x:\overline{m}|} \cdot \mathbf{a}_{\overline{n}|} + \frac{D_{y+n}}{D_y}(a_{y+n} - a_{x:y+n}) + \frac{D_{y+m+n}}{D_y} \cdot {}_mp_x \cdot \mathbf{a}_{x+m:y+m+n}.$$

Ex. 2. Find the value of an annuity deferred until the failure of the joint lives (x) and (y) to be payable thereafter for a term of 20 years or until 10 years after the death of the survivor, whichever be the longer term.

The annuity can be dealt with in two parts:

(a) A joint-life assurance to secure an annuity certain for 20 years, the first payment assumed to be made at the end of the year of death. The value of this part is $A_{xy} \, . \, \mathbf{a}_{\overline{20}|}$.

(b) After 20 years from the present time a payment will be made at the end of any particular year even though 20 years have elapsed since the failure of the joint lives of (x) and (y) provided the survivor was alive 10 years prior to the date of such payment. For example, at the end of the $(20+t)$th year, a payment (which is not allowed for in (a)) will be made even if one of the lives (x) and (y) died before the end of the tth year provided the other survived to the end of the $(t+10)$th year. The probability of this happening is $(1-{}_tp_y)\,{}_{t+10}p_x + (1-{}_tp_x)\,{}_{t+10}p_y$, and the value of the payment is therefore $v^{t+20}\{(1-{}_tp_y)\,{}_{t+10}p_x + (1-{}_tp_x)\,{}_{t+10}p_y\}$.

In order to provide for these payments it is therefore necessary to add

$$\sum_{t=1}^{t=\infty} v^{t+20}\{(1-{}_tp_y)\,{}_{t+10}p_x + (1-{}_tp_x)\,{}_{t+10}p_y\}$$

$$= v^{20}\,{}_{10}p_x \sum_{t=1}^{t=\infty} v^t(1-{}_tp_y)\,{}_tp_{x+10} + v^{20}\,{}_{10}p_y \sum_{t=1}^{t=\infty} v^t(1-{}_tp_x)\,{}_tp_{y+10}$$

$$= v^{10}\frac{D_{x+10}}{D_x}(a_{x+10} - a_{x+10:y}) + v^{10}\frac{D_{y+10}}{D_y}(a_{y+10} - a_{x:y+10}).$$

The total value required is, therefore,

$$A_{xy} \, . \, \mathbf{a}_{\overline{20}|} + v^{10}\frac{D_{x+10}}{D_x}(a_{x+10} - a_{x+10:y}) + v^{10}\frac{D_{y+10}}{D_y}(a_{y+10} - a_{x:y+10}).$$

This question can also be dealt with by assuming that the annuity payable for 20 years certain or until 10 years after the death of the survivor, whichever be the longer term, is set up immediately, and having found the value of this immediate annuity, deducting a_{xy}.

By this method the expression for the value of the whole annuity will be

$$a_{\overline{20}|} + \sum_{t=1}^{t=\infty} v^{t+20} \{{}_tp_{xy} + (1 - {}_tp_y)\, {}_{t+10}p_x + (1 - {}_tp_x)\, {}_{t+10}p_y\} - a_{xy}$$

$$= (a_{\overline{20}|} + v^{20} a_{xy} - a_{xy}) + v^{10} \frac{D_{x+10}}{D_x} (a_{x+10} - a_{x+10\,:\,y})$$

$$+ v^{10} \frac{D_{y+10}}{D_y} (a_{y+10} - a_{x\,:\,y+10}).$$

It will be noticed that

$$\begin{aligned} a_{\overline{20}|} + v^{20} a_{xy} - a_{xy} &= a_{\overline{20}|} (1 - i a_{xy}) \\ &= (1 + i)\, a_{\overline{20}|} (v - d a_{xy}) \\ &= A_{xy} \,.\, \mathrm{a}_{\overline{20}|}, \end{aligned}$$

the two expressions thus being identical.

Ex. 3. A (aged 50) is in possession during his life of a perpetuity of £100 per annum for 20 years from the present time, to be increased to £200 per annum thereafter; and B (aged 35) and C (aged 25) are entitled, during their respective lives, to the perpetuity, in succession to one another, after A's death.

What is the value of C's interest by H^M Table at 3 per cent.?

The required value will be given by the expression

$$200 \{a_{\overline{35:50}}|_{25} - \tfrac{1}{2} \,.\, |_{20}\, a_{\overline{35:50}}|_{25}\}$$

$$= 200 \{a_{25} - a_{25:35} - a_{25:50} + a_{25:35:50} - \tfrac{1}{2} (a_{25:\overline{20}|} - a_{25:35:\overline{20}|}$$

$$- a_{25:50:\overline{20}|} + a_{25:35:50:\overline{20}|})\}.$$

Reference to the tables of Uniform Seniority on page 478 shows that lives of equal ages can be substituted as follows:

For two lives aged 25 and 35 : two lives aged 31·1,
" " " 25 and 50 : " " 43·5,
" three " 25, 35 and 50 : three lives aged 41·3.

Employing these ages and the annuity values tabulated, the value is found to be £657. 8*s*.

CHAPTER XIX

COMPOUND SURVIVORSHIP ANNUITIES AND ASSURANCES

1. The difference between simple and compound survivorships may be illustrated by means of a reversionary annuity to (x) after the failure of the survivor of (y) and (z). If no stipulation be made as to the order in which (y) and (z) shall die, the benefit is the ordinary reversionary annuity, $a_{\overline{yz}|x}$, of which the value was found in Chapter XVIII 13. There the conditions include only one order of survivorship, namely, that (x) shall die third. But now, let the annuity be payable to (x) after the death of the survivor of (y) and (z), only if (y) be that survivor. Here there is a compound condition of survivorship. The failure of (y) before (x) is to follow the failure of (z) before (y); and unless the double event happen, the annuity will never come into possession.

2. Instead of an annuity to (x) after the death of the survivor of (y) and (z), there may be an annuity to (x) after the failure of the joint lives (y) and (z). If there be no stipulation as to which of the lives shall fail first, the annuity is the ordinary reversionary annuity, $a_{yz|x}$, of which also the value was found in Chapter XVIII 13. But the annuity becomes a compound survivorship if the condition be added, that the failure of the joint lives shall take place by the death of (z). The annuity then depends on a double event, namely, that (x) shall survive (z), and that (z) shall die before (y).

3. It is convenient to use for compound survivorships a notation similar to that employed for contingent assurances and reversionary annuities, adding numerals to indicate the order in which the lives are to fail. The numerals are placed *above* the letter representing the life on the failure of which the benefit is to come immediately into possession, and *below* the letters representing the lives which are to fail previously in assigned orders. Thus, an annuity to (x) after the death of the survivor of (y) and (z), if (y) be that survivor, is represented by $a^{2}_{yz|x}$, or $a_{\overline{yz}|x}$ (with 1 under the z), and an annuity to (x), after the failure of the joint lives (y) and (z) caused by the death of (z), by $a_{y\overset{1}{z}|x}$.

4. In Chapter XVIII it was shown that in the case of ordinary reversionary annuities there is little difference in the numerical value whether the annuities are payable yearly or momently; that for all practical purposes $a_{y|x}=\bar{a}_{y|x}$ and $a_{yz|x}=\bar{a}_{yz|x}$. It does not numerically affect these approximate relations if another contingency be added, and we may write as a near approximate equation $a_{y\overset{1}{z}|x}=\bar{a}_{y\overset{1}{z}|x}$. This fact may be made further evident by another line of reasoning. In the case of $a_{y\overset{1}{z}|x}$, when the annuity comes into possession the first payment will be made, on the average, six months after the death of (z); and therefore at the moment of the death of (z) the value of the benefit on which (x) will then enter (his age then being, say, $x+t$) will be, on the average, ${}_{\frac{1}{2}|}\mathrm{a}_{x+t}$. In the case of the continuous annuity, $\bar{a}_{y\overset{1}{z}|x}$, at the moment of the death of (z), (x) will enter on a continuous annuity on his life, and its value will then be $\bar{a}_{x+t}$. But in Chapter VII 8 it was shown that, approximately ${}_{\frac{1}{2}|}\mathrm{a}_{x+t}=\bar{a}_{x+t}$ and therefore, approximately, $a_{y\overset{1}{z}|x}=\bar{a}_{y\overset{1}{z}|x}$.

5. To find the value of $\bar{a}_{y\overset{1}{z}|x}$. If both (x) and (y) be alive at the moment of the death of (z), (x) will then enter into possession of a continuous annuity on his life. The present value of the benefit, therefore, is

$$\left.\begin{aligned}\bar{a}_{y\overset{1}{z}|x}&=\int_0^\infty v^t\,{}_tp_{xyz}\,\mu_{z+t}\,\bar{a}_{x+t}\,dt\\&=\frac{1}{l_xl_yl_z}\int_0^\infty v^t\,l_{x+t}\,l_{y+t}\,l_{z+t}\,\mu_{z+t}\,\bar{a}_{x+t}\,dt\end{aligned}\right\}\quad\ldots\ldots(1),$$

and by means of an approximate integration formula the value may be computed. Comparing formula (1) of this chapter with formula (24 *b*) of Chapter XVIII for the value of $\bar{a}_{yz|x}$, it will be seen that only μ_{z+t} is included in the case of the compound survivorship annuity, whereas in the case of the reversionary annuity the factor $(\mu_{y+t}+\mu_{z+t})$ appears. In other respects the formulae are identical.

6. The work of obtaining the value of $\bar{a}_{y\overset{1}{z}|x}$ may be conveniently arranged to give also the value of $\bar{a}_{xyz}$; and it is desirable to do so, because if the compound survivorship annuity is to be secured by an annual premium, the divisor will be $(1+a_{xyz})$.

7. To find the value of $\bar{a}^{2}_{yz|x}$. At the moment of the death of (y), provided (z) has died previously, (x), if he be alive, will enter on a continuous annuity on his life. The present value of the benefit, therefore, is

$$\left.\begin{aligned}\bar{a}^{2}_{yz|x} &= \int_0^\infty v^t\,{}_tp_{xy}\,(1-{}_tp_z)\,\mu_{y+t}\,\bar{a}_{x+t}\,dt\\ &= \frac{1}{l_x l_y l_z}\int_0^\infty v^t l_{x+t}\,l_{y+t}\,(l_z-l_{z+t})\,\mu_{y+t}\,\bar{a}_{x+t}\,dt\end{aligned}\right\}\quad\ldots(2).$$

In using formula (2), the work may be arranged to find at the same time the value of $\bar{a}_{xy}$ which will be useful in calculating the annual premium, the divisor for which is $(1+a_{xy})$.

8. Referring again to the value of $\bar{a}_{y\overset{1}{z}|x}$, the payment at time t will be made if (x) be then alive and (z) has died previously leaving (y) surviving him. The value of this payment is therefore

$$v^t\,{}_tp_x\,.\,|_tQ_{y\overset{1}{z}}\,dt$$

and the value of the annuity can be expressed

$$\int_0^\infty v^t\,{}_tp_x\,.\,|_tQ_{y\overset{1}{z}}\,dt.$$

If, therefore, it be assumed that for all values of t,

$$|_tQ'^{1}_{yz} = Q_{y\overset{1}{z}}\,.\,|_tQ_{yz}$$

the expression becomes

$$\begin{aligned}\bar{a}_{y\overset{1}{z}|x} &= Q_{y\overset{1}{z}}\,.\int_0^\infty v^t\,{}_tp_x\,.\,|_tQ_{yz}\,dt\\ &= Q_{y\overset{1}{z}}\,.\,\bar{a}_{yz|x}\ \ldots\ldots\ldots\ldots\ldots\ldots\ldots\ldots\ldots(3).\end{aligned}$$

This expression is sometimes used to give an approximate value for $\bar{a}_{y\overset{1}{z}|x}$; and the result is not far from the truth if (y) and (z) are advanced in age. It would be strictly accurate if Gompertz's Law prevailed.

9. If the value of $a_{y\overset{1}{z}|x}$ be known, the value of $a^{1}_{yz|x}$ can be found at once, because $a_{y\overset{1}{z}|x} + a^{1}_{yz|x} = a_{yz|x}$. Whence

$$a^{1}_{yz|x} = a_{yz|x} - a_{y\overset{1}{z}|x}\quad\ldots\ldots\ldots\ldots\ldots\ldots\ldots(4).$$

10. An intimate relation subsists between the two compound survivorship annuities, $a_{y\overset{1}{z}|x}$ and $a^{2}_{yz|x}$. The annuity $a_{y\overset{1}{z}|x}$ comes into possession immediately on the death of (z), provided both (x) and (y) be then alive; but the annuity $a^{2}_{yz|x}$ is further deferred until the death of (y). The annuity $a_{yz|x}^{1}$, therefore, includes all the payments of the annuity $a_{yz|x}^{2}$, and it includes, besides, an annuity during the joint lives of (x) and (y) after the death of (z). That is

$$a_{yz|x}^{2} = a_{yz|x}^{1} - a_{z|xy} \quad \text{......................(5).}$$

11. The following numerical examples will be useful to the student:

(i) To find, by the H^{M} Table at 4 per cent. interest, the value of $\bar{a}_{45:\overset{1}{60}|30}$.

Employing the approximate integration formula

$$\int_0^\infty f(x)\,dx = n\{\cdot 28f(0) + 1\cdot 62f(n) + 2\cdot 2f(3n) + 1\cdot 62f(5n) + \cdot 56f(6n) + 1\cdot 62f(7n)\},$$

we must take $7n = 102 - 60 = 42$, whence $n = 6$. The integral for the value required being

$$\frac{1}{l_{30}l_{45}l_{60}}\int_0^\infty v^t\, l_{30+t}\, l_{45+t}\, l_{60+t}\, \mu_{60+t}\, \bar{a}_{30+t}\, dt,$$

the calculation is made as follows:

t	$=0$	n $=6$	$3n$ $=18$	$5n$ $=30$	$6n$ $=36$	
$\log v^t$ ...	—	$\bar{1}\cdot 8978$	$\bar{1}\cdot 6934$	$\bar{1}\cdot 4890$	$\bar{1}\cdot 3868$	
$\log l_{30+t}$ ...	—	4·9314	4·8748	4·7697	4·6737	
$\log l_{45+t}$ ...	—	4·8552	4·7271	4·4083	4·0781	
$\log l_{60+t}$ ...	—	4·6737	4·2645	3·1048	1·8513	
log coeff. ...	$\bar{1}\cdot 4472$	·2095	·3424	·2095	$\bar{1}\cdot 7482$	
colog $l_{30:45:60}$	—	$\overline{15}\cdot 3860$	$\overline{15}\cdot 3860$	$\overline{15}\cdot 3860$	$\overline{15}\cdot 3860$	
Sum ...	$\bar{1}\cdot 4472$	$\bar{1}\cdot 9536$	$\bar{1}\cdot 2882$	$\bar{3}\cdot 3673$	$\bar{5}\cdot 1241$	......(α)
$\log \mu_{60+t}$ ...	$\bar{2}\cdot 4654$	$\bar{2}\cdot 6627$	$\bar{1}\cdot 0977$	$\bar{1}\cdot 5591$	$\bar{1}\cdot 7939$	
$\log \bar{a}_{30+t}$ ...	1·2469	1·2179	1·1332	·9977	·9049	
Sum ...	$\bar{1}\cdot 1595$	$\bar{1}\cdot 8342$	$\bar{1}\cdot 5191$	$\bar{3}\cdot 9241$	$\bar{5}\cdot 8229$	......(β)
$\log^{-1}(\alpha)$ ...	·2800	·8988	·1942	·0023	·0000	$=1\cdot 3753$
						6
					$\bar{a}_{30:45:60}$	$=8\cdot 2518$
$\log^{-1}(\beta)$ ...	·1444	·6827	·3305	·0084	·0001	$=1\cdot 1661$
						6
					$\bar{a}_{45:\overset{1}{60}|30}$	$=6\cdot 9966$

It is not necessary to fill in the values of the various factors when $t = 0$, as it is evident that in the case of $\bar{a}_{30:45:60}$, $f(0) = 1$.

(ii) To find, by the H^{M} Table at 4 per cent., the value of

$$\bar{a}_{45:\overset{2}{60}|30} = \frac{1}{l_{30}\, l_{45}\, l_{60}}\int_0^\infty v^t\, l_{30+t}\, l_{45+t}\, (l_{60} - l_{60+t})\, \mu_{45+t}\, \bar{a}_{30+t}\, dt.$$

Employing the same approximate integration formula as in the last example, we must take $7n = 102 - 45 = 57$, whence $n = 8$. Here $(l_{60} - l_{60+t})$ vanishes when $t = 0$, and the value of $f(56)$ will be zero to several places of decimals, so that we are only concerned with the evaluation of the terms involving $f(8)$, $f(24)$, $f(40)$ and $f(48)$.

The calculation is as follows:

t	n $=8$	$3n$ $=24$	$5n$ $=40$	$6n$ $=48$	
$\log v^t$	$\bar{1}$·8637	$\bar{1}$·5912	$\bar{1}$·3187	$\bar{1}$·1824	
$\log l_{30+t}$ ...	4·9236	4·8320	4·5795	4·2645	
$\log l_{45+t}$ ...	4·8402	4·6060	3·7390	2·5635	
$\log (l_{60} - l_{60+t})$...	4·2080	4·7160	4·7696	4·7697	
$\log \mu_{45+t}$ ...	$\bar{2}$·2632	$\bar{2}$·7674	$\bar{1}$·3651	$\bar{1}$·6763	
$\log \bar{a}_{30+t}$ ...	1·2065	1·0730	·8321	·6587	
log coeff. ...	·2095	·3424	·2095	$\bar{1}$·7482	
colog $l_{30} l_{45} l_{60}$ ...	$\overline{15}$·3860	$\overline{15}$·3860	$\overline{15}$·3860	$\overline{15}$·3860	
Sum ...	$\bar{2}$·9007	$\bar{1}$·3140	$\bar{2}$·1995	$\bar{4}$·2493	
$\log^{-1}$	·0796	·2061	·0158	·0002 =	·3017
					8
				$\bar{a}^{\ 2}_{45:60\,\vert\,30} =$	2·4136

By formula (5), we have

$$a^{2}_{45:60\,|\,30} + a_{60\,|\,30:45} = a_{45:\overset{1}{60}\,|\,30}.$$

By means of equal ages it will be found that the value of $a_{60\,|\,30:45}$ by the H^{M} Table at 4 per cent. is 4·617, whence employing the usual approximations,

$$a^{2}_{45:60\,|\,30} + a_{60\,|\,30:45} = 2{\cdot}414 + 4{\cdot}617 = 7{\cdot}031,$$

as compared with 6·997 obtained by approximate integration for the value of $a_{45:\overset{1}{60}\,|\,30}$: a difference of ·034.

12. To find the value of $\bar{a}_{xy\overset{1}{z}\,|\,w}$. At the moment of the death of (z), if all the other lives still exist, (w) will come into possession of a continuous annuity on his own life. Therefore, using for conciseness the symbols ${}^tl_x$ etc., for l_{x+t} etc.

$$\left.\begin{aligned} \bar{a}_{xy\overset{1}{z}\,|\,w} &= \int_0^\infty v^t\,{}_tp_{wxyz}\,\mu_{z+t}\,\bar{a}_{w+t}\,dt \\ &= \frac{1}{l_{wxyz}}\int_0^\infty v^t\,{}^tl_w\,.\,{}^tl_x\,.\,{}^tl_y\,.\,{}^tl_z\,.\,\mu_{z+t}\,.\,\bar{a}_{w+t}\,dt \end{aligned}\right\}\dots\dots\dots(6).$$

Similarly,

$$\left.\begin{aligned}\bar{a}^{\,1}_{yz|wx} &= \int_0^\infty v^t\,{}_tp_{wxyz}\,.\,\mu_{z+t}\,\bar{a}_{w+t:x+t}\,dt\\ &= \frac{1}{l_{wxyz}}\int_0^\infty v^t\,.\,{}^tl_w\,.\,{}^tl_x\,.\,{}^tl_y\,.\,{}^tl_z\,.\,\mu_{z+t}\,.\,\bar{a}_{w+t:x+t}\,dt\end{aligned}\right\}\quad\ldots(7).$$

Also,

$$\bar{a}^{\,1}_{yz|\overline{wx}} = \bar{a}^{\,1}_{yz|w} + \bar{a}^{\,1}_{yz|x} - \bar{a}^{\,1}_{yz|wx}\quad\ldots\ldots\ldots\ldots(8),$$

where the values of the annuities on the right-hand side of the equation must be calculated separately by formulae (1) and (7).

13. To find the value of $\bar{a}_{xy\overset{2}{z}|w}$ (with 1 under y). At the moment of the death of (y), if (z) has died previously, and if (w) and (x) be still alive, (w) will come into possession of a continuous annuity on his life. Therefore

$$\left.\begin{aligned}\bar{a}_{x\underset{1}{y}\overset{2}{z}|w} &= \int_0^\infty v^t\,{}_tp_{wxy}\,(1-{}_tp_z)\,\mu_{y+t}\,.\,\bar{a}_{w+t}\,dt\\ &= \frac{1}{l_{wxyz}}\int_0^\infty v^t\,.\,{}^tl_w\,.\,{}^tl_x\,.\,{}^tl_y\,.\,(l_z-{}^tl_z)\,\mu_{y+t}\,.\,\bar{a}_{w+t}\,dt\end{aligned}\right\}\quad(9).$$

Similarly

$$\left.\begin{aligned}\bar{a}^{\,2}_{yz|wx} &= \int_0^\infty v^t\,{}_tp_{wxy}\,(1-{}_tp_z)\,\mu_{y+t}\,\bar{a}_{w+t:x+t}\,dt\\ &= \frac{1}{l_{wxyz}}\int_0^\infty v^t\,.\,{}^tl_w\,.\,{}^tl_x\,.\,{}^tl_y\,.\,(l_z-{}^tl_z)\,\mu_{y+t}\,\bar{a}_{w+t:x+t}\,dt\end{aligned}\right\}\quad(10).$$

Also

$$\bar{a}^{\,2}_{yz|\overline{wx}} = \bar{a}^{\,2}_{yz|w} + \bar{a}^{\,2}_{yz|x} - \bar{a}^{\,2}_{yz|wx}\ldots\ldots\ldots\ldots(11),$$

where the values of the annuities on the right-hand side of the equation must be calculated separately.

14. To find the value of $\bar{a}_{x}{}^{2:3}_{\,y\ \underset{1}{z}|w}$, an annuity on the life of (w) to commence at the death of (y), provided (z) die before him in the lifetime of (x). At the moment of the death of (z), if all the other lives survive, (w) will become entitled to a reversionary annuity payable to him if he survive (y). Therefore

$$\left.\begin{aligned}\bar{a}_{x}{}^{2:3}_{\,y\ \underset{1}{z}|w} &= \int_0^\infty v^t\,{}_tp_{wxyz}\,\mu_{z+t}\,(\bar{a}_{w+t}-\bar{a}_{w+t:y+t})\,dt\\ &= \frac{1}{l_{wxyz}}\int_0^\infty v^t\,.\,{}^tl_w\,.\,{}^tl_x\,.\,{}^tl_y\,.\,{}^tl_z\,.\,\mu_{z+t}\,(\bar{a}_{w+t}-\bar{a}_{w+t:y+t})\,dt\end{aligned}\right\}\quad(12).$$

15. Lastly, to find the value of $\bar{a}^{\,3}_{x\underset{2}{y}\underset{1}{z}|w}$. At the moment of the death of (y), if (z) has died previously, and if (x) be still living,

(w) will become entitled to a reversionary annuity payable to him if he survive (x). Therefore

$$\left.\begin{aligned}\bar{a}^{3}_{\underset{21}{xyz}|w} &= \int_0^\infty v^t\, {}_tp_{wxy}\,(1-{}_tp_z)\,\mu_{y+t}\,(\bar{a}_{w+t}-\bar{a}_{w+t:x+t})\,dt \\ &= \frac{1}{l_{wxyz}}\int_0^\infty v^t\,.\,{}^tl_w\,.\,{}^tl_x\,.\,{}^tl_y.(l_z-{}^tl_z)\,\mu_{y+t}\,(\bar{a}_{w+t}-\bar{a}_{w+t:x+t})dt\end{aligned}\right\}\ldots(13).$$

16. Compound Survivorship Assurances. The value of one form of compound survivorship assurance, namely $\bar{A}^{2}_{\underset{1}{xyz}}$, was dealt with in Chapter XVII 29. We can now proceed to discuss more complicated problems of this nature.

The value of an assurance payable on the death of (x) if he die third of the three lives (x), (y) and (z), (z) having died first, is represented by $\bar{A}^{3}_{xy\underset{1}{z}}$, and can be expressed in the form of an integral as follows:

$$\left.\begin{aligned}\bar{A}^{3}_{xy\underset{1}{z}} &= \int_0^\infty v^t\, {}_tp_{xy}\,(1-{}_tp_z)\,\mu_{y+t}\,\bar{A}_{x+t}\,dt \\ &= \frac{1}{l_{xyz}}\int_0^\infty v^t\,.\,{}^tl_x\,.\,{}^tl_y\,.\,(l_z-{}^tl_z)\,\mu_{y+t}\,\bar{A}_{x+t}\,dt\end{aligned}\right\}\ldots(14),$$

by means of which, with the aid of an approximate integration formula, the value can be ascertained. If the value of $A^{3}_{xy\underset{1}{z}}$ be required all that is necessary is to multiply $\bar{A}^{3}_{xy\underset{1}{z}}$ by $v^{\frac{1}{2}}$.

An examination of formula (14) will show that if the integral be divided into its component parts, the result is

$$\bar{A}^{3}_{xy\underset{1}{z}} = \bar{A}^{2}_{xy} - \bar{A}^{2:3}_{x\,\underset{1}{y}z},$$

that is, the value of an assurance payable on the death of (x) if he die third of three lives (x), (y) and (z), (z) having died first, is equal to the value of an assurance payable on the death of (x) if he die after (y) less the value of an assurance payable on his death if he die second or third of the three lives, (y) having died first. This is clearly correct but does not simplify the work of ascertaining the value required.

17. The assurance represented by $\bar{A}^{3}_{xy\underset{1}{z}}$ depends on the same sequence of events as that denoted by $\bar{A}^{2}_{x\underset{1}{y}z}$, but the payment of the sum assured is deferred from the death of (y) to the death of (x). If, therefore, we deduct from the latter assurance the value of an annuity of the interest during the period intervening between these two deaths, (y) having died after (z), the result will be the value of $\overline{A}^{3}_{x\underset{1}{y}z}$. That is,

$$\overline{A}^{3}_{x\underset{1}{y}z} = \overline{A}^{2}_{x\underset{1}{y}z} - \delta \bar{a}^{2}_{yz|x} \text{ .... (15).}$$

If the assurance be payable at the end of the year of death we can similarly write

$$A^{3}_{x\underset{1}{y}z} = A^{2}_{x\underset{1}{y}z} - d a^{2}_{yz|x} \text{ .... (16).}$$

If we were only concerned with the probabilities of the deaths of the three lives (x), (y) and (z) occurring in a certain order, we could write $Q^{3}_{x\underset{1}{y}z} = Q^{2}_{x\underset{1}{y}z}$.

18. The formulae for compound survivorship assurances are very similar to those for the corresponding annuities. Thus

$$\left.\begin{aligned}\overline{A}^{2}_{wx\underset{1}{y}z} &= \int_0^\infty v^t \, {}_tp_{wxy} (1 - {}_tp_z) \mu_{w+t} \, dt \\ &= \frac{1}{l_{wxyz}} \int_0^\infty v^t . {}^tl_w . {}^tl_x . {}^tl_y . (l_z - {}^tl_z) \mu_{w+t} dt\end{aligned}\right\} \text{...(17).}$$

19. $\overline{A}^{2:3:4}_{w\;:x\underset{1}{y}z}$ represents the value of an assurance payable at the death of (w) if (z) die first of the four lives (w), (x), (y) and (z). Immediately on the death of (z), if he die first, the assurance will become absolute on the life of (w). Therefore,

$$\left.\begin{aligned}\overline{A}^{2:3:4}_{w\;:x\underset{1}{y}z} &= \int_0^\infty v^t . {}_tp_{wxyz} . \mu_{z+t} . \overline{A}_{w+t} \, dt \\ &= \frac{1}{l_{wxyz}} \int_0^\infty v^t . {}^tl_w . {}^tl_x . {}^tl_y . {}^tl_z . \mu_{z+t} . \overline{A}_{w+t} \, dt\end{aligned}\right\} \text{...(18).}$$

20. To find the value of $\overline{A}^{3}_{wx\underset{21}{yz}}$. Immediately on the death of (y), if (z) has died previously, and if (w) and (x) both survive, the assurance will become an assurance on the life of (w) contingent on his dying before (x). Therefore,

$$\left.\begin{aligned}\overline{A}^{3}_{wx\underset{21}{yz}} &= \int_0^\infty v^t . {}_tp_{wxy} (1 - {}_tp_z) \mu_{y+t} \overline{A}_{\overset{1}{w+t}:x+t} \, dt \\ &= \frac{1}{l_{wxyz}} \int_0^\infty v^t . {}^tl_w . {}^tl_x . {}^tl_y . (l_z - {}^tl_z) \mu_{y+t} . \overline{A}_{\overset{1}{w+t}:x+t} \, dt\end{aligned}\right\} \text{...(19).}$$

21. In the case of $\overline{A}^{3:4}_{w\,:\,\overset{}{\underset{21}{xyz}}}$ the formula is the same as for $\overline{A}^{3}_{\underset{21}{wxyz}}$ except that on the death of (y) the assurance will become absolute on the life of (w), and not contingent. That is

$$\left.\begin{aligned}\overline{A}^{3:4}_{w\,:\,\underset{21}{xyz}} &= \int_0^\infty v^t\,.\,{}_tp_{wxy}\,(1-{}_tp_z)\,\mu_{y+t}\,\overline{A}_{w+t}\,dt\\ &= \frac{1}{l_{wxyz}}\int_0^\infty v^t\,.\,{}^tl_w\,.\,{}^tl_x\,.\,{}^tl_y\,.\,(l_z-{}^tl_z)\,\mu_{y+t}\,\overline{A}_{w+t}\,dt\end{aligned}\right\}\ldots(20).$$

22. To find the value of $\overline{A}^{4}_{\underset{321}{wxyz}}$. At the moment of the death of (y), (z) having died previously, and (w) and (x) being still alive, the assurance will become an assurance on the life of (w), contingent on his surviving (x). Therefore

$$\left.\begin{aligned}\overline{A}^{4}_{\underset{321}{wxyz}} &= \int_0^\infty v^t\,.\,{}_tp_{wxy}\,(1-{}_tp_z)\,\mu_{y+t}\,.\,\overline{A}^{\;2}_{\overline{w+t}:x+t}\,dt\\ &= \frac{1}{l_{wxyz}}\int_0^\infty v^t\,.\,{}^tl_w\,.\,{}^tl_x\,.\,{}^tl_y\,.\,(l_z-{}^tl_z)\,\mu_{y+t}\,(\overline{A}_{w+t}-\overline{A}^{\;1}_{\overline{w+t}:x+t})\,dt\end{aligned}\right\}$$
$$\ldots\ldots(21).$$

23. The value of every possible compound survivorship annuity or assurance involving four lives may be found by the method employed in arriving at equations (18) to (21). For example, immediately from formula (21),

$$\left.\begin{aligned}\overline{A}^{4}_{\underset{1}{wxyz}} &= \int_0^\infty v^t\,.\,{}_tp_{wxy}\,(1-{}_tp_z)\,\{\mu_{x+t}\,.\,\overline{A}^{\;2}_{\overline{w+t}\cdot y+t}+\mu_{y+t}\;\overline{A}^{\;2}_{\overline{w+t}:x+t}\}dt\\ &= \frac{1}{l_{wxyz}}\int_0^\infty v^t\,.\,{}^tl_w\,.\,{}^tl_x\,.\,{}^tl_y\,.\,(l_z-{}^tl_z)\\ &\quad\times\{\mu_{x+t}\,(\overline{A}_{w+t}-\overline{A}^{\;1}_{\overline{w+t}:y+t})+\mu_{y+t}\,(\overline{A}_{w+t}-\overline{A}^{\;1}_{\overline{w+t}:x+t})\}dt\end{aligned}\right\}.(22).$$

24. In using formulae (21) and (22), the values of contingent assurances involving two lives are required, as the probabilities can only be taken as far as the second death. If the basis of calculation is to be the Carlisle mortality table at 3 per cent. interest, a complete table of these values is given by Gray, Smith, and Orchard in their work, *Assurance and Annuity Tables.*

If the Carlisle mortality table at other rates of interest is to be used, Chisholm's Commutation Tables afford an easy means of obtaining the required values of the contingent assurances. For other mortality tables the methods of Chap. XVII must be employed.

25. In many cases the values of compound survivorships involving five or more lives may be found by formulae similar to those which are applicable to benefits embracing only four lives. Sometimes, however, one of the factors under the sign of integration will itself be a compound survivorship, in which event a process of double integration must be resorted to. Thus, for example, if the value be sought of $\bar{a}^{4}_{\underset{321}{wxyz}|u}$, an annuity to (u) to commence on the death of (w), if (x) die before (w), (y) before (x), and (z) before (y), it will be observed that on the death of (y), (z) having died first, (u) will become entitled to a compound survivorship annuity payable to him after the death of (w) if (x) die first. Throwing the benefit into the form of an integral, it becomes

$$\bar{a}^{4}_{\underset{321}{wxyz}|u} = \int_0^\infty v^t \cdot {}_tp_{uwxy}(1 - {}_tp_z)\,\mu_{y+t}\,\bar{a}_{\overset{2}{\overline{w+t}}:x+t|u+t}\,dt \quad \ldots(23).$$

In the evaluation of this integral by approximate integration, we must first of all find, by a separate summation, the value of $\bar{a}_{\overset{2}{\overline{w+t}}:x+t|u+t}$ at each of the values of t occurring in the formula employed.

26. Annual Premiums. It is not often that a compound survivorship annuity or assurance is secured by the payment of annual premiums, but when this does occur careful consideration must be given to the period during which the premiums are to be payable, and to the selection of the lives to be medically examined.

The annual premium to secure the annuity $a_{y\overset{1}{z}|x}$ should be made payable during the joint existence of the three lives (x), (y) and (z), because if (z) die first the annuity becomes payable to (x), and if either (x) or (y) die first the contract expires. The annual premium should, therefore, be $\dfrac{a_{y\overset{1}{z}|x}}{\mathrm{a}_{xyz}}$, (z) being medically examined. It is not necessary to have (x) or (y) medically examined, as if either of these lives fail before (z) the Office will make no payment of the annuity.

For the annuity $a^{2}_{yz|x}$, the annual premium should be $\dfrac{a^{2}_{yz|x}}{\mathrm{a}_{xy}}$, (y) and (z) being medically examined. In this case, if (z) die first the premiums will continue to be payable until either the death of (x) or (y), but if either (x) or (y) die first, the contract expires.

In the case of $a_{yz|\overline{wx}}^{1}$ the annual premium should be made payable during the joint lives of (y), (z) and the survivor of (w) and (x), the premium thus becoming $\dfrac{a_{yz|\overline{wx}}^{1}}{\text{a}_{yz:\overline{wx}}}$: (z) should be medically examined.

The annual premium to secure the annuity $a_{\underset{1}{x}yz|w}^{2}$ or the annuity $a_{yz|wx}^{2}$ should be payable during the joint lifetime of (w), (x) and (y), and that for $a_{yz|\overline{wx}}^{2}$ during the joint existence of (y) and the survivor of (w) and (x); the lives to be medically examined being (y) and (z) in all three instances.

For $a_{\underset{1}{x}\,y\,z|w}^{2:3}$ the period during which the annual premium should be made payable is the joint lifetime of (w), (x) and (y) *plus* the joint lifetime of (w) and (y) after the death of (x) provided (z) die first; and for $a_{\underset{21}{xyz}|w}^{3}$ the joint lifetime of (w), (x) and (y) *plus* the joint lifetime of (w) and (x) after the death of (y) provided (z) die first. In the former case (y) and (z), and in the latter (x), (y) and (z), should be medically examined.

27. Similar considerations apply to the annual premiums for compound survivorship assurances.

The annual premium for the assurance $A_{xy\underset{1}{z}}^{3}$ should be $\dfrac{A_{xy\underset{1}{z}}^{3}}{\text{a}_{xy}}$, all three lives being medically examined: for $A_{wxy\underset{1}{z}}^{2}$, $\dfrac{A_{wxy\underset{1}{z}}^{2}}{\text{a}_{wxy}}$, (w) and (z) being medically examined.

The assurance represented by $A_{w\ :xy\underset{1}{z}}^{2:3:4}$ presents greater difficulty. If (z) die first the assurance becomes a single-life assurance on the life of (w), but it is not safe to make the premiums payable during the lifetime of (w) only, because, if (x) or (y) died before (z), the assurance would terminate and the premiums received would not cover the risk incurred. On the other hand, if the premiums be made payable during the joint lifetime of (x), (y) and (w), and (z) die first, and (x) or (y) second, the assurance may continue for many years without any premiums being payable, and the assured might feel that he should have been allowed to pay a smaller premium for a longer period. The best way of dealing with the case is, however, to make the premiums payable during the joint lifetime of (w), (x) and (y), the annual premium thus being $\dfrac{A_{w\ :xy\underset{1}{z}}^{2:3:4}}{\text{a}_{wxy}}$, and to see that the assured understands the circumstances. All four lives should be medically examined.

Similarly, in the case of $A^{3}_{\underset{21}{wxyz}}$, the annual premium should be $\dfrac{A^{3}_{\underset{21}{wxyz}}}{a_{wxy}}$, and in the case of $A^{3:4}_{w:\underset{21}{xyz}}$, $\dfrac{A^{3:4}_{w:\underset{21}{xyz}}}{a_{wxy}}$; in the former case all four lives and in the latter (w), (y) and (z) should be medically examined.

In the case of $A^{3}_{\underset{1}{xyz}}$ an alternative is to make the premium payable during the joint lives of (x) and (y) and for the remainder of the life of (x) after the death of (y), provided (y) die after (z). That is, to take the annual premium as $\dfrac{A^{3}_{\underset{1}{xyz}}}{a_{xy}+a^{2}_{yz|x}}$. Similarly, the annual premium for $A^{2:3:4}_{w:\underset{1}{xyz}}$ might be taken as

$$\frac{A^{2:3:4}_{w:\underset{1}{xyz}}}{a_{wxy}+a^{2}_{xz|wy}+a^{2}_{yz|wx}+a_{\overline{xy}:\underset{1}{z}|w}};$$

for $A^{3}_{\underset{21}{wxyz}}$ as $\dfrac{A^{3}_{\underset{21}{wxyz}}}{a_{wxy}+a^{2}_{yz|wx}}$; and for $A^{3:4}_{w:\underset{21}{xyz}}$ as $\dfrac{A^{3:4}_{w:\underset{21}{xyz}}}{a_{wxy}+a^{2}_{\underset{1}{xyz}|w}}$. These refinements, however, would not be worth while entering into if the assured were prepared to pay the premiums obtained by the expressions previously given.

28. In some cases the risk of having to pay the sum assured would be so small that the premium charged by an Office would be purely arbitrary, being in fact the smallest single premium the Company was prepared to quote. For example, if the assurance were for the payment of £100 on the death of the survivor of two lives (35) and (36) before a life aged (40) within 10 years—that is, $_{|10}A^{\;\;1}_{\overline{35:36}:40}$—the probability of both (35) and (36) dying within 10 years is $(1-{}_{10}p_{35})(1-{}_{10}p_{36})$, which on the basis of the H^M Table is ·00942. If, as a rough approximation, we take the risk involved in the assurance as represented by $(1-{}_{10}p_{35})(1-{}_{10}p_{36})\,{}_{5}p_{40}$ the value of this is ·00892, which does not take interest into account. Clearly this is a case for charging the lowest single premium for which the Company is prepared to enter into a contract, and an annual premium would not be quoted. For practical purposes, no object would be served in calculating the theoretical risk premium, the whole contract being carried out on an arbitrary basis.

EXAMPLES

Ex. 1. Find by the H^M Table at 3 per cent. interest the value of an assurance of £100 payable at the second death among three lives aged 30, 35 and 40 years respectively, with the condition that if the life aged 40 die first, £50 shall be payable at the first death and £50 at the second death.

The value is

$$100\,A_{30:35:\overset{2}{40}} + 100\,A^{2}_{30:\underset{1}{35}:40} + 100\,A_{\underset{1}{30}:\overset{2}{35}:40}$$
$$+\ 50\,A^{2}_{30:35:\underset{1}{40}} + 50\,A_{30:\overset{2}{35}:\underset{1}{40}} + 50\,A_{30:35:\overset{1}{40}}.$$

Converting each of these terms into assurances payable on the first death, we have

$$100\,[A_{30:\overset{1}{40}} + A_{35:\overset{1}{40}} - 2A_{30:35:\overset{1}{40}}] + 100\,[A^{1}_{30:40} - A^{1}_{30:35:40}]$$
$$+ 100\,[A^{1}_{35:40} - A_{30:\overset{1}{35}:40}] + 50\,[A^{1}_{30:35} - A^{1}_{30:35:40}] + 50\,[A_{30:\overset{1}{35}} - A_{30:\overset{1}{35}:40}]$$
$$+\ 50A_{30:35:\overset{1}{40}}$$
$$=\ 50A_{30:35} + 100A_{30:40} + 100A_{35:40} - 150A_{30:35:40}$$
$$=\ 50A_{32{\cdot}8:32{\cdot}8} + 100A_{36{\cdot}1:36{\cdot}1} + 100A_{37{\cdot}8:37{\cdot}8} - 150A_{35{\cdot}8:35{\cdot}8:35{\cdot}8}.$$

By interpolating between the values of a_{xx} given in the tables for $a_{32{\cdot}8:32{\cdot}8}$ etc. and entering conversion tables the value is found to be

$$50\,({\cdot}5130) + 100\,({\cdot}5386 + {\cdot}5526) - 150\,({\cdot}5994)$$
$$= 44{\cdot}86.$$

Ex. 2. Find in terms, as far as possible, of contingent survivorship assurances payable on (y) dying first, the single premium for 1 payable

(a) On the death of (y) within 10 years, (x) surviving him and both (u) and (v) having died previously;

(b) On the death of (y) after 10 years, (x) surviving him, one at least of (u) and (v) having died previously, and all having survived 10 years;

(c) On the death of (y) after 10 years, (x) surviving him and one only of (u) and (v) having died previously.

$$(a)\quad \int_0^{10} v^t\,(1 - {}_tp_u)\,(1 - {}_tp_v)\,{}_tp_{xy}\,\mu_{y+t}\,dt$$
$$= \int_0^{10} v^t\,(1 - {}_tp_u - {}_tp_v + {}_tp_{uv})\,{}_tp_{xy}\,\mu_{y+t}\,dt$$
$$= |_{10}\bar{A}_{x\overset{1}{y}} - |_{10}\bar{A}_{ux\overset{1}{y}} - |_{10}\bar{A}_{vx\overset{1}{y}} + |_{10}\bar{A}_{uvx\overset{1}{y}},$$
$$(b)\quad v^{10}\,{}_{10}p_{uvxy}\int_0^{\infty} v^t\,(1 - {}_tp_{u+10:v+10})\,{}_tp_{x+10:y+10}\,\mu_{y+10+t}\,dt$$
$$= v^{10}\,{}_{10}p_{uvxy}\,(\bar{A}_{x+10:\overset{1}{\overline{y+10}}} - \bar{A}_{u+10:v+10:x+10:\overset{1}{\overline{y+10}}}),$$

$$(c)\quad \int_{10}^{\infty} v^t\,{}_tp_{xy}\,({}_tp_u + {}_tp_v - 2{}_tp_{uv})\,\mu_{y+t}\,dt$$

$$= {}_{10|}\overline{\mathrm{A}}_{ux\overset{1}{y}} + {}_{10|}\overline{\mathrm{A}}_{vx\overset{1}{y}} - 2 \times {}_{10|}\overline{\mathrm{A}}_{uvx\overset{1}{y}}$$

where, for example,

$${}_{10|}\overline{\mathrm{A}}_{ux\overset{1}{y}} = v^{10}\,{}_{10}p_{uxy}\,\overline{\mathrm{A}}_{u+10:x+10:\overset{1}{y+10}}.$$

Ex. 3. On the death of the survivor of (x) and (y) a sum of 1 is to be divided equally among such of three persons aged a, b and c respectively as may then be living, with a further condition that if (a) predecease the survivor of (x) and (y) his share is to be divided equally between such of two persons aged u and v as are living at the date of distribution.

Express in the form of an integral the value of (u)'s share.

The probability that the survivor of (x) and (y) dies at time t, (a) having already died, is

$$({}_tp_x\,\mu_{x+t} + {}_tp_y\,\mu_{y+t} - {}_tp_{xy}\,\mu_{x+t:y+t})\,(1 - {}_tp_a)\,dt.$$

The share to be divided between such of (u) and (v) as may then be alive is, the whole payment if (b) and (c) are both dead, $\frac{1}{2}$ if either (b) or (c) be alive and the other dead, and $\frac{1}{3}$ if (b) and (c) be both alive: the amount involved is, therefore,

$$(1 - \tfrac{1}{2}{}_tp_b - \tfrac{1}{2}{}_tp_c + \tfrac{1}{3}{}_tp_{bc}).$$

And there is the further condition that if (u) be alive and (v) dead, (u) will, subject to the other conditions, receive the full share, but if (v) be also alive he will only receive a half share.

The integral required is therefore

$$\int_0^{\infty} v^t\,({}_tp_x\,\mu_{x+t} + {}_tp_y\,\mu_{y+t} - {}_tp_{xy}\,\mu_{x+t:y+t})\,(1 - {}_tp_a)\,({}_tp_u - \tfrac{1}{2}{}_tp_{uv})$$
$$\times\,(1 - \tfrac{1}{2}{}_tp_b - \tfrac{1}{2}{}_tp_c + \tfrac{1}{3}{}_tp_{bc})\,dt.$$

Ex. 4. Find an expression for the net annual premium for an assurance payable on the death of the last survivor of three lives aged x, y and z respectively: should (x) die first the premium to be reduced 50 per cent., and should (z) survive (x) and (y) the premium to cease on the second death.

Value of Benefit $= \mathrm{A}_{\overline{xyz}}$.

Representing the net premium by P, the value of the premiums to be paid is

$$\mathrm{P}\,(\mathrm{a}_{\overline{xyz}} - \tfrac{1}{2}a_{x|\overline{yz}} - \tfrac{1}{2}a_{\overline{xy}|z} + \tfrac{1}{2}a^{2}_{xz|y})$$

or

$$\mathrm{P}\,(\mathrm{a}_x + \tfrac{1}{2}a_{x|yz} + \tfrac{1}{2}a^{\,2}_{xz|y} + a^{2}_{xz|y}),$$

whence, by equating the value of the premiums to the value of the benefit, P is obtained.

PART III

CHAPTERS XX AND XXI

CONSTRUCTION OF TABLES

TABLES INVOLVING TWO OR MORE CAUSES OF DECREMENT AND FUNCTIONS DEPENDENT THEREON

CHAPTER XX

CONSTRUCTION OF TABLES

1. An intimate acquaintance with the nature of the tables he may find in his hands is important to the actuary, for without that knowledge he cannot turn them to the best account. It is therefore very desirable for the student to practise the construction of tables for himself, although those he requires may be already in print.

2. For constructing a table there are generally two courses open. Each individual value may be calculated independently; or each succeeding value may be formed from the value immediately preceding it. If the first course be chosen, each value must usually be also verified independently; but if the second, verification at stated intervals will be sufficient, because if one value be correct, so also must be those that go before it.

3. Facility and certainty of verification are not the only advantages of the "Continued* Process." On account of regular sequence of operations, the calculations may generally be performed more rapidly, and with less mental effort, than when each value is computed by itself; and it also frequently happens that the actual amount of arithmetical work is less, the differences of functions, instead of the functions themselves, being employed.

4. In order that the continued process may be successfully applied there are three things essential. There must be an Initial Value, a Continued Formula, and a Verification Formula. Frequently the most obvious formulae are not the most convenient; and the formula chosen should be such as best to suit the aids to calculation that are available.

* The word "Continuous" has sometimes been used in this connection; but "Continued" appears to be preferable, in order that possible confusion with the word "Continuous," in its sense as used in the Differential Calculus, may be avoided.

5. The most powerful aid to calculation in the construction of actuarial tables is the Arithmometer, which is now so universally employed by actuaries that it is thought no student should experience any difficulty in seeing one in practical use before reading this chapter; a step he is strongly advised to take.

In case, however, any reader should not be so placed as to have ready access to one or other of the many types of this machine it has been thought advisible to give (on page 359) a reproduction of an arithmometer (the TIM) which is widely used at the present time, together with a full description of the method of employing it in actuarial calculations, particularly in the construction of tables.

There are now in use other types of arithmometers, for example, one with two slides which is particularly suitable for certain special calculations and a larger machine with a special mechanism which by placing an indicator handle against the number (0 to 9) by which it is desired to multiply, enables the multiplication to be performed by turning the motive handle once only. These, however, are the same in principle as that now to be described, and it is not thought necessary to deal with their construction or use.

***6.** The arithmometer is constructed to add and to subtract; and by means of continued addition or subtraction it can perform multiplication and division with great rapidity. The top of the machine consists of two plates, which may be called the "fixed plate" and the "slide" respectively. On the fixed plate are slots with moveable "markers," each of which can be placed against any number desired, from 0 to 9. On the left of the fixed plate is the "regulator," by means of which the machine may be set for addition or subtraction, as may be required; and on the right is the "motive handle," which can be turned only in the direction of the hands of a clock, and by means of which the machine is set in motion. In the slide is a row of "product holes," and the slide, on being lifted, can be passed from left to right or the contrary, so that the position of the product holes with respect to the slots in the fixed plate may be varied at pleasure. A number is "placed on" the machine by marking it on the fixed plate by means of the markers in the slots. The number so placed on the machine can be "thrown up" on to the slide, by

* The description of the arithmometer given in paragraphs 6 to 11 has been copied from the old Text Book, Part II.

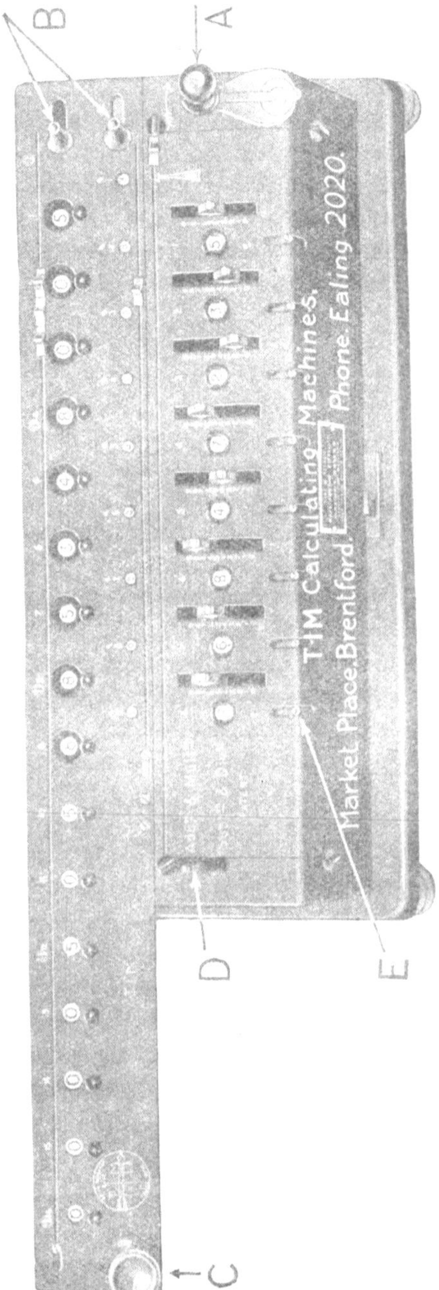

ARITHMOMETER.

A Motive handle.
B Zeroizers.
C Handle for lifting and moving slide.
D Lever for altering from multiplication to division.
E Levers for clearing keyplate, enabling whole or part of keyplate to be cleared from any point.

placing the regulator at addition, and giving one turn to the motive handle. If a second turn be given to the handle, the number is again thrown up, and added to the number already on the slide, and so on; by each turn of the motive handle the number on the fixed plate being thrown up once, and added to whatever number may already be on the slide. In this way multiplication is performed. The number on the fixed plate will be thrown up in the units place, in the tens place, etc., according to the position of the slide with regard to the fixed plate.

7. The method of procedure will best be illustrated by a numerical example. Let it be required to multiply together the numbers 76,847,235 and 6,583. Set the regulator at addition, and place the larger number on the machine by means of the moveable markers in the slots, as shown in the engraving. Let the slide be raised and drawn as far as it will go to the left, and then let it be dropped into position. Now turn the motive handle three times; this multiplies the number 76,847,235 by 3, the unit figure of the multiplier, and throws the result up on to the slide, where it will appear in the product holes. Next move the slide one station to the right, and turn the motive handle eight times for the second figure of the multiplier. This multiplies 76,847,235 by 80, and adds the result to what had already appeared in the product holes. By successively moving the slide and turning the motive handle, in the same way complete the multiplication by the remaining figures, 5 and 6, of the multiplier; and finally bring the slide into its original position. The machine is now as it appears in the engraving. The multiplicand, 76,847,235, is seen in the slots in the fixed plate where it had been placed; and the product, 505,885,348,005, is in the product holes. On the slide of the machine is a second row of holes called "quotient holes." In these are registered the number of turns given to the handle. Therefore the multiplier appears in the quotient holes, as shown in the engraving. On the slide are also the "zeroizers," by means of which the machine is set at zero before commencing an operation.

8. In order to perform division, the dividend is set as far as possible to the left upon the slide of the machine, and the slide is carried as far as it will go to the right. The divisor is placed on the fixed plate, also as far as possible to the left, and the regulator is placed at subtraction. By turning the handle and moving the slide station by station to the left, the division is effected, and the quotient appears in the quotient holes; and when the work has been completed, the remainder will be found in the product holes.

9. A great advantage of the arithmometer lies in its power to multiply two numbers together, and add the product to a third number, without recording the intermediate steps. Thus, if it be desired to find the value of $P+QR$ the number P must be placed on the slide of the machine, and the number Q, which may be called the in-factor, upon the fixed plate. The in-factor, Q, must then be multiplied by the out-factor, R, in the manner sketched above. The effect will be that the product $Q \times R$ will be formed, and added to P; and as a final result we shall have, as desired, $P+QR$.

10. This property of the arithmometer is specially useful in continued operations when Q, the in-factor, is constant, and R, the out-factor, is a series of comparatively small numbers, such as the differences of some function involved in the operation. This will abundantly appear in the illustrations to follow in this chapter.

11. By means of the arithmometer, a continued product, QR, may equally readily be subtracted from a number, P. It is only necessary for this purpose to place the regulator at subtraction, and proceed as in paragraph 9.

12. In proceeding now to treat more directly of the construction of actuarial tables, it will be convenient to deal with the various functions introduced in this volume, not necessarily in the order in which they have been so introduced, but rather in such order as will best illustrate the continued process, the use of the arithmometer with its advantages over the employment of logarithms, and the various checks that should be employed to ensure accuracy.

13. In Chapter I the construction of a column of values of l_x from q_x or p_x was dealt with. It will be remembered that starting from a convenient radix, say l_0, this was multiplied by the first value of q_0, thus obtaining d_0, which was subtracted from l_0 to produce l_1, and so on.

It is, however, simpler to construct the table with the aid of the values of p_x. Assuming values of q_x given, the values of p_x can readily be obtained from the relation $p_x = 1 - q_x$; a step which can be checked at any period of the work by summation, since for any n values $\sum_{t=1}^{t=n} p_{x+t} + \sum_{t=1}^{t=n} q_{x+t} = n$.

Employing the arithmometer, the work can then be proceeded with as follows:

1. Set up the radix (say l_0) on the fixed plate of the arithmometer, and multiply by p_0: this gives l_1 which must be copied on to the working sheet.

2. Set up l_1 on the fixed plate (it is advisable to take this from the slide and to check it against the working sheet), clear the slide, and multiply by p_1: this gives l_2 which must be copied.

3. Set up l_2 on the plate and multiply by p_2 and so on.

It is convenient to arrange the work in columns thus:

Age x	q_x	p_x	l_x
(1) 0 1 ⋮	(2)	(3)	(4)

The method of checking col. (3) has been mentioned. As regards col. (4) the process is a continued one in so far as each value depends on the one before. The initial value is l_0, the working formula $l_x \times p_x = l_{x+1}$, but each product being carried out independently makes the verification formula rather cumbersome, namely

$$l_{x+n} = l_x \times p_x \times p_{x+1} \times \ldots \times p_{x+n-1}.$$

On the whole, it is better to have this step carried out in duplicate by independent operators on different machines, and to compare the results.

The work should be carried out to at least two more places than are required in the final table in order to ensure accuracy in the "cutting down" process.

14. If we were working with logarithms, having obtained the values of p_x, we should proceed as follows:

(1) Extract the values of $\log p_x$ for all ages.

(2) Decide the radix (say l_0) and record $\log l_0$.

(3) Remembering that $\log p_x = \Delta \log l_x$, construct a column of $\log l_x$ by adding the successive values of $\log p_x$.

Thus:
$$\log l_1 = \log l_0 + \log p_0,$$
$$\log l_2 = \log l_1 + \log p_1,$$
and so on.

(4) Extract the antilogs of the last values, thus obtaining the values of l_x.

The work would be arranged as follows:

Age x	q_x	p_x	$\log p_x$ $= \Delta \log l_x$	$\log l_x$	l_x
(1)	(2)	(3)	(4)	(5)	(6)

The only part of this work that is "continued" is the construction of col. (5) with the aid of col. (4). Reference has been made to the method of checking col. (3); the extraction of $\log p_x$, and of l_x from $\log l_x$, can only be checked by the work being carried out in duplicate by independent operators or by reversing the process and extracting the antilogs and logs respectively. Col. (5) can be checked at any point by a "straight" summation of col. (4), since

$$\log l_{x+n} = \log l_x + \sum_{t=0}^{t=n-1} \log p_{x+t}.$$

This example brings out the difficulty that arises with the employment of logarithms. However careful and accurate an operator may be, it is distinctly advisable in the construction of any actuarial table, that the values tabulated should be adequately checked. The employment of logarithms necessarily introduces a step which is not "continued" and which must, therefore, be checked by some independent means. The additional work involved in this case in the employment of logarithms as against the arithmometer will be evident.

15. Commutation Columns. Turning to the construction of commutation columns, let us assume that values of l_x and d_x are available, and that it is required to construct tables of the values of D_x, N_x, $\mathbf{S}_x$, C_x, M_x, R_x.

Dealing with D_x first, the most direct method is to multiply each value of l_x by the corresponding value of v^x independently on the arithmometer.

The calculations should be checked by the work being carried out in duplicate on different machines. It would not be necessary to arrange columns of v^x and l_x, since all that is necessary is to tabulate, say, v^x on a slip card which can be placed in the required position against the page containing the values of l_x.

This process is not a "continued" one, and it will be instructive to consider other methods in which a "continued" process will be employed so far as possible.

16. For use with the arithmometer, we have

$$D_x = v^x l_x,$$
$$D_{x+1} = v^{x+1} l_{x+1} = D_x \times vp_x,$$
$$D_{x+2} = v^{x+2} l_{x+2} = D_{x+1} \times vp_{x+1},$$
and so on.

If, therefore, a table of the values of vp_x be available, the construction of a table of the values of D_x will be exactly similar to that employed in paragraph 13 to construct a table of l_x when p_x is already tabulated.

17. A column of the values of vp_x is readily obtained by means of the arithmometer, this being an example of a constant multiplied by the successive terms of a series. The first step is to extract the differences of the values of p_x: which will be checked by summation.

The work will then proceed thus:

(1) Place the value of v on the fixed plate.

(2) Multiply by the first value of p: result $= vp_x$.

(3) Without clearing the plate or the product holes, multiply by Δp_x. The result is that $v . \Delta p_x$ is added to vp_x already in the product holes, giving $v(p_x + \Delta p_x) = vp_{x+1}$.

(4) Without clearing the plate or the product holes, multiply by Δp_{x+1}, thus obtaining $v(p_{x+1} + \Delta p_{x+1}) = vp_{x+2}$, and so on.

This is a simple example of a continued process. The initial value is vp_x where x is the youngest age for which the values are required, the working formula is $vp_{x+n+1} = vp_{x+n} + v . \Delta p_{x+n}$, and verification is obtained at any step by independently multiplying

p_{x+n} by v and comparing the result with that obtained by the continued process.

In cases of this kind, when a large number of values is required, it is advisable to calculate the check values for every 10th or 15th value before commencing the construction of the column. If these check values be inserted on the working sheet before the construction of the column is commenced they will be available for comparison as each 10th or 15th value is reached by the continued process, and if an error has been made, will prevent the entire column being constructed inaccurately.

Finally, in order to detect any errors made in copying the figures from the arithmometer to the working sheet, a "summation" check should be applied. We have

$$\sum_{x}^{x+n} vp_x = v \sum_{x}^{x+n} p_x,$$

so that, if we sum the entire column of p_x and multiply by v, the result should agree with the sum of the column of values of vp_x.

A "summation" check is very important when an arithmometer is used in connection with a continued process. The figures in the product holes of some machines get rubbed with use, with the result that it is an easy matter for one occasionally to be copied down incorrectly. If the "summation" check applied to the entire column disclose a discrepancy, it can then be applied to sections of the column in order to ascertain in which section the error occurs, the error being finally located by an examination of the differences of that section.

18. Having then the values of vp_x, D_x for the youngest age is set up on the fixed plate and multiplied by vp_x to give D_{x+1}: this in turn is set up on the plate and multiplied by vp_{x+1} to give D_{x+2} and so on. The entire process will be seen by the arrangement of the following columns:

x	p_x	Δp_x	vp_x	D_x
(1)	(2)	(3)	(4)	(5)

Periodical check values should be inserted in the column of D_x before the work is started, these being obtained from the fundamental formula $D_{x+n} = v^{x+n} l_{x+n}$, but as there is no convenient summation check, it is advisable to have the construction of col. (5) carried out in duplicate.

This being so, this method possesses no advantage over the first method mentioned in paragraph 15.

If logarithms be employed, we have

$$\log D_x = x \log v + \log l_x,$$
$$\log D_{x+1} = (x+1) \log v + \log l_{x+1}$$
$$= \log D_x + \log vp_x,$$
$$\log D_{x+2} = \log D_{x+1} + \log vp_{x+1},$$
and so on.

Here the work would be arranged as follows:

x	$\log p_x$	$\log vp_x$ $= \Delta \log D_x$	$\log D_x$	D_x
(1)	(2)	(3)	(4)	(5)

If the values of $\log p_x$ have not been tabulated the extraction of these should be carried out in duplicate. The values in col. (3) are ascertained by adding $\log v$ to each value in col. (2), a simple process easily checked by summation. For col. (4) the first value must be calculated independently and successive values obtained by means of the differences given in col. (3). An independent check should be inserted periodically beforehand by means of the fundamental formula $\log D_x = x \log v + \log l_x$, or by the relation

$$\log D_{x+n} = \log D_x + \sum_{t=0}^{t=n-1} \log vp_{x+t}.$$

In this instance, since a constant, $\log v$, is added at each step, in order to prevent any accumulation of error in the last places of decimals, particular care must be taken to work to more places than are required in the final table and to observe the value of the figures discarded. Finally, for col. (5) the antilogarithms of col. (4) should be extracted by independent operators and the results compared. It is clear that this method also involves far more work than the first and more straightforward method mentioned in paragraph 15.

19. The values of D_x having been calculated, since $D_x = -\Delta \mathbf{N}_x$ the compilation of the column of values of $\mathbf{N}_x$ is a simple matter. The column will be commenced at the highest age $\omega - 1$, at which $D_{\omega-1} = N_{\omega-1}$. Then adding the value of D at the next lower age, we have $N_{\omega-1} + D_{\omega-2} = N_{\omega-2}$: similarly $N_{\omega-2} + D_{\omega-3} = N_{\omega-3}$, and so on, till the youngest age in the table is reached.

Check values will be inserted at every 10th or 15th value by means of the formula $N_x = \sum_x^{\omega-1} D_x$.

Since $\mathbb{S}_x = \sum_x^{\omega-1} N_x$ the method of construction of a column of $\mathbb{S}_x$ when N_x is available is exactly similar to that employed in constructing the column of N_x from the values of D_x.

20. The relations between C_x, M_x and R_x being similar to those existing between D_x, N_x and $\mathbb{S}_x$, it is not necessary to deal in very great detail with the methods to be employed in the construction of tables of values of these functions.

We have $C_x = v^{x+1} d_x$ by means of which each value can be calculated independently by multiplication on the arithmometer, the work being carried out in duplicate. This is exactly similar to the first method mentioned in connection with D_x.

Processes similar to the second and third methods discussed in connection with D_x can also be employed.

$$C_{x+1} = v^{x+2} d_{x+1}$$

$$= C_x \times v \frac{d_{x+1}}{d_x},$$

$$C_{x+2} = C_{x+1} \times v \frac{d_{x+2}}{d_{x+1}},$$

$$\cdots\cdots\cdots\cdots\cdots\cdots\cdots\cdots$$

and generally

$$C_{x+n+1} = C_{x+n} \times v \frac{d_{x+n+1}}{d_{x+n}}.$$

Also

$$\log C_{x+1} = \log C_x + \log v + \Delta \log d_x,$$

$$\log C_{x+2} = \log C_{x+1} + \log v + \Delta \log d_{x+1}$$

$$\cdots\cdots\cdots\cdots\cdots\cdots\cdots\cdots\cdots\cdots\cdots\cdots$$

and generally

$$\log C_{x+n+1} = \log C_{x+n} + \log v + \Delta \log d_{x+n}.$$

It is evident that the first method is the most practical.

As regards M_x and R_x, we have $M_x = \sum_x^{w-1} C_x$ and $R_x = \sum_x^{w-1} M_x$.

21. When values of C, M, R and D, N, $\mathbb{S}$ are available for the same mortality table and same rate of interest, their accuracy can be tested by comparison as follows:

$$C_x = vD_x - D_{x+1},$$

$$M_x = vN_x - N_{x+1},$$

$$R_x = v\mathbb{S}_x - \mathbb{S}_{x+1}.$$

22. Whole-Life Annuity Values. When the values of N_x and D_x are available, the simplest method of constructing a table of whole-life annuity values, $a_x = \frac{N_{x+1}}{D_x}$, is by calculating each value (in duplicate) independently on the arithmometer.

If the values of the commutation functions are not available, the simplest process is to employ the relationship

$$a_x = vp_x(1 + a_{x+1}),$$

whence, commencing with $a_{\omega-1} = 0$, and first calculating the values of vp_x, we can work backwards with the aid of the arithmometer to the youngest age. The work would be arranged thus:

x	vp_x	a_x
(1)	(2)	(3)

The value $1 = 1 + a_{\omega-1}$ would be set up on the fixed plate and multiplied by $vp_{\omega-2}$, the result being inserted in col. (3) against age $\omega - 2$. This result plus unity will be transferred from the product holes to the plate and, the slide having been cleared, multiplied by $vp_{\omega-3}$, the result being inserted in col. (3) against age $\omega - 3$: and so on. The work should be carried out in duplicate.

23. If logarithms be employed, the working formula becomes

$$\log a_x = \log vp_x + \log(1 + a_{x+1}),$$

the arrangement of the work being

x	$\log vp_x$	$\log(1+a_{x+1})$	$\log a_x$	a_x
(1)	(2)	(3)	(4)	(5)

Again working backwards from the highest age, the initial value is $a_{\omega-1} = 0$ or $\log(1 + a_{\omega-1}) = 0$, which will be placed in col. (3) against age $\omega - 2$. The value of $\log vp_x$ in col. (2) on the same line is then added to $\log(1 + a_{\omega-1})$ giving $\log a_{\omega-2}$. The remainder of the work by this method is facilitated by the employment of Gauss's Logarithms, by entering a table of which with the value of $\log a_x$ the result is $\log(1 + a_x)$. Entering such a table with $\log a_{\omega-2}$ the result is $\log(1 + a_{\omega-2})$ which is placed in col. (3) on line $\omega - 3$. The work then proceeds as before.

Finally, the antilogarithms of col. (4) must be extracted to give the values of a_x.

It will be observed that this process is a continued one only so far as the values of $\log a_x$, and it is consequently of no value to insert check values in the column of values of a_x. Periodical check values should be applied to col. (4) and if columns of N_x and D_x were available, the simplest process would be to calculate

$$\log a_x = \log N_{x+1} - \log D_x,$$

for every 10th or 15th value beforehand. If the values of these functions have been tabulated, however, the more direct method mentioned in paragraph 22 would be employed.

There is no convenient check formula for $\log a_x$ when the functions N and D have not been tabulated, and since, if the annuity values are to be calculated, it is most probable that columns of these functions will be required at some time or other, it is far preferable to construct such tables first and to calculate the annuity values therefrom by direct division of N_{x+1} by D_x for each age.

24. Sufficient examples have now been given to demonstrate three important points,

(1) The valuable assistance rendered in the construction of actuarial tables by the arithmometer:

(2) That a continued process possesses advantages, but that when the work can be carried out in a straightforward manner on the arithmometer, in duplicate, this is frequently quicker than employing a more elaborate continued process:

(3) That the employment of logarithms (unless the logs of a function only are required) *prevents* a continued process being employed throughout, since the last step necessarily involves the extraction of antilogarithms.

25. **Temporary Annuity Values.** A table of temporary annuity values is readily constructed by a simple continued process with the aid of the arithmometer.

The initial value is $a_{x:\overline{1}|} = \dfrac{D_{x+1}}{D_x}$,

the working formula $a_{x:\overline{n+1}|} = a_{x:\overline{n}|} + \dfrac{D_{x+n+1}}{D_x}$,

periodical check values can be inserted at the outset by means of the formula

$$a_{x:\overline{n}|} = \frac{N_{x+1} - N_{x+n+1}}{D_x},$$

and a summation check is provided by the expression

$$\sum_{n=1}^{n=t} a_{x.\overline{n}|} = \frac{tN_{x+1} - (\mathbb{S}_{x+2} - \mathbb{S}_{x+t+2})}{D_x}.$$

The procedure is to insert $(D_x)^{-1}$ on the fixed plate and multiply by D_{x+1} thus throwing up $a_{x:\overline{1}|}$ in the product holes. Then, without clearing the plate or the product holes, multiply by D_{x+2}, the value $\frac{D_{x+2}}{D_x}$ thus being added to $a_{x:\overline{1}|}$ giving $a_{x:\overline{2}|}$ and so on.

26. Single Premiums for Temporary Assurances. Similarly with a table of Single Premiums for Temporary Assurances:

The Initial Value is $A^1_{x:\overline{1}|} = \frac{C_x}{D_x}$.

The Working Formula is $A^1_{x:\overline{n+1}|} = A^1_{x:\overline{n}|} + \frac{C_{x+n}}{D_x}$.

Periodical Check Values are given by $A^1_{x:\overline{n}|} = \frac{M_x - M_{x+n}}{D_x}$.

The Summation Check is $\sum_{n=1}^{n=t} A^1_{x:\overline{n}|} = \frac{tM_x - (R_{x+1} - R_{x+t+1})}{D_x}$.

The process is exactly similar to that employed for $a_{x:\overline{n}|}$.

27. Annual Premiums for Temporary Assurances. To construct a table of annual premiums for temporary assurances the formula employed is $P^1_{x:\overline{n}|} = \frac{A^1_{x:\overline{n}|}}{\mathbf{a}_{x:\overline{n}|}}$, each premium being divided out independently (in duplicate) on the arithmometer.

28. Deferred Annuities. If tables of whole-life and temporary annuities are available, a table of deferred annuities can be constructed by means of the relationship

$$a_x - a_{x:\overline{n}|} = {}_{n|}a_x.$$

Or, with the aid of the arithmometer, starting with the longest period of deferment, say r, we have

$${}_{r|}a_x = \frac{N_{x+r+1}}{D_x},$$

$${}_{r-1|}a_x = {}_{r|}a_x + \frac{D_{x+r}}{D_x},$$

and generally $${}_{n|}a_x = {}_{n+1|}a_x + \frac{D_{x+n+1}}{D_x}.$$

Therefore, starting at the longest period of deferment, the value of $(D_x)^{-1}$ is placed on the fixed plate of the machine and the first value obtained by multiplying by N_{x+r+1}. Without clearing the product holes, the value on the plate is then multiplied by D_{x+r} this product being automatically added to $_{r|}a_x$ giving $_{r-1|}a_x$, and so on for other values.

Periodical check values are obtained and inserted, before constructing the table, by means of the formula

$$_{n|}a_x = \frac{N_{x+n+1}}{D_x},$$

the final value being a_x; and the summation check is

$$\sum_{n=1}^{n=t} {}_{n|}a_x = \frac{\mathbb{S}_{x+2} - \mathbb{S}_{x+t+2}}{D_x}.$$

29. Deferred Assurances. For deferred assurances, working from the longest period of deferment to the shortest, where r is the *longest* period of deferment for which the value is required,

the Initial Value is $$_{r|}A_x = \frac{M_{x+r}}{D_x},$$

the Working Formula $$_{n|}A_x = {}_{n+1|}A_x + \frac{C_{x+n}}{D_x}.$$

For the Periodical Check Values

$$_{n|}A_x = \frac{M_{x+n}}{D_x},$$

the final value being A_x.

Summation Check: $$\sum_{n=1}^{n=t} {}_{n|}A_x = \frac{R_{x+1} - R_{x+t+1}}{D_x}.$$

30. Whole-Life Policy Values. Employing the formula

$$_nV_x = 1 - \frac{1 + a_{x+n}}{1 + a_x},$$

we have $$_{n+1}V_x = 1 - \frac{1 + a_{x+n+1}}{1 + a_x}$$

$$= \left(1 - \frac{1 + a_{x+n}}{1 + a_x}\right) - \frac{a_{x+n+1} - a_{x+n}}{1 + a_x}$$

$$= {}_nV_x + \frac{(-\Delta a_{x+n})}{1 + a_x},$$

where $-\Delta a_{x+n}$ is positive.

To use this formula it is necessary to extract first the differences of a_x, which differences will be taken positively. If then $(1+a_x)^{-1}$ be set up on the fixed plate of the arithmometer this is first multiplied by $-\Delta a_x$, giving

$$\frac{a_x - a_{x+1}}{1+a_x} = {}_1V_x.$$

Without clearing the product holes $(1+a_x)^{-1}$ is then multiplied by $-\Delta a_{x+1}$, giving

$${}_1V_x + \frac{(-\Delta a_{x+1})}{1+a_x} = {}_2V_x,$$

and so on.

Here, the Initial Value is

$${}_1V_x = \frac{-\Delta a_x}{1+a_x} = \frac{a_x - a_{x+1}}{1+a_x},$$

the Working Formula is

$${}_{n+1}V_x = {}_nV_x + \frac{(-\Delta a_{x+n})}{1+a_x},$$

the Periodical Check Values, inserted beforehand, are calculated by the fundamental formula

$${}_nV_x = \frac{a_x - a_{x+n}}{1+a_x},$$

and the Summation Check is

$$\sum_{n=1}^{n=t} {}_nV_x = \frac{ta_x - \sum_{n=1}^{n=t} a_{x+n}}{1+a_x}.$$

31. Endowment Assurance Policy Values. The formulae employed in the construction of a table of Endowment Assurance Policy Values are similar to those employed for Whole-Life Values.

Taking, for example, policies on lives aged x for a period of r years, we have

Initial Value $\quad {}_1V_{x:\overline{r}|} = \dfrac{a_{x:\overline{r-1}|} - a_{x+1:\overline{r-2}|}}{1+a_{x:\overline{r-1}|}},$

Working Formula

$${}_{n+1}V_{x:\overline{r}|} = {}_nV_{x:\overline{r}|} + \frac{(-\Delta_n . a_{x+n.\overline{r-n-1}|})}{1+a_{x:\overline{r-1}|}},$$

where $(-\Delta_n . a_{x+n:\overline{r-n-1}|})$ is positive.

Periodical Check Value formula is

$${}_nV_{x:\overline{r}|} = \frac{a_{x:\overline{r-1}|} - a_{x+n:\overline{r-n-1}|}}{1+a_{x:\overline{r-1}|}},$$

Summation Check formula

$$\sum_{n=1}^{n=t} {}_n\mathrm{V}_{x:\overline{r}|} = \frac{t a_{x:\overline{r-1}|} - \sum_{n=1}^{n=t} a_{x+n:\overline{r-n-1}|}}{1 + a_{x:\overline{r-1}|}}.$$

It will be observed that in extracting the differences of the annuity values, the successive terms of the series to be differenced are $a_{x:\overline{r-1}|}$, $a_{x+1:\overline{r-2}|}$, $a_{x+2:\overline{r-3}|}$, etc.: the first term is the value of an annuity on a life of the age at which the policy was effected to run for one year less than the full term of the assurance, and the variable affects both the age and the term of the annuity, the last payment being at age $x+r-1$ in each case.

32. Limited Payment Policy Values—Whole-Life Assurances. For this type of policy the method employed in the construction of tables of Whole-Life and Endowment Assurance Policy Values is not applicable.

Examining the formula for the policy value by the prospective method, we have, where $n < t$,

$${}_n^t\mathrm{V}_x = \mathrm{A}_{x+n} - {}_t\mathrm{P}_x(1 + a_{x+n:\overline{t-n-1}|}),$$

$${}_{n+1}^{\;\;t}\mathrm{V}_x = \mathrm{A}_{x+n+1} - {}_t\mathrm{P}_x(1 + a_{x+n+1:\overline{t-n-2}|}),$$

whence $$\Delta\, {}_n^t\mathrm{V}_x = \Delta\mathrm{A}_{x+n} + {}_t\mathrm{P}_x(-\Delta_n . a_{x+n:\overline{t-n-1}|}),$$

both terms on the right-hand side being positive.

The first step is to obtain the values of ${}_t\mathrm{P}_x(-\Delta_n . a_{x+n:\overline{t-n-1}|})$ which, however, can be effected very rapidly with the aid of the arithmometer, by the method employed in paragraph 17 to construct a table of values of vp_x.

The differences of the function $-\Delta_n . a_{x+n:\overline{t-n-1}|}$ must first be extracted; ${}_t\mathrm{P}_x$ is then placed on the fixed plate and, working backwards, multiplied by the last value (namely $-\Delta_n . a_{x+t-2:\overline{1}|}$). Without clearing the product holes the quantity on the fixed plate is then multiplied by the successive terms of the series of differences $\Delta(-\Delta_n . a_{x+n:\overline{t-n-1}|})$. The values of $\Delta\mathrm{A}_{x+n}$ having been extracted by differencing, the work can be proceeded with as follows:

The Initial Value is

$${}_0^t\mathrm{V}_x = 0.$$

The Working Formula is

$${}_{n+1}^{\;\;t}\mathrm{V}_x = {}_n^t\mathrm{V}_x + \Delta\mathrm{A}_{x+n} + {}_t\mathrm{P}_x(-\Delta_n . a_{x+n:\overline{t-n-1}|}).$$

Periodical Check Values will be calculated by the original formula

$${}_{n}^{t}V_x = A_{x+n} - {}_tP_x\,(1 + a_{x+n:\overline{t-n-1}|}),$$

the value ${}_{t}^{t}V_x$ being A_{x+t}, and the Summation Check is provided by

$$\sum_{n=1}^{n=r} {}_{n}^{t}V_x = \sum_{n=1}^{n=r} A_{x+n} - {}_tP_x \sum_{n=1}^{n=r} \text{a}_{x+n:\overline{t-n}|}, \text{ where } r < t.$$

The method of setting out the work is as follows:

Age x

n	ΔA_{x+n}	${}_tP_x(-\Delta_n \cdot a_{x+n:\overline{t-n-1}|})$	${}_{n}^{t}V_x$
(1)	(2)	(3)	(4)
0			
1			
2			
⋮			

33. If tables of the values of Endowment Assurance policies are available, these can be employed to facilitate the construction of tables of the values of Whole-Life Limited Payment policies. If $n < t$,

$$\begin{aligned}
{}_{n}^{t}V_x &= A_{x+n} - {}_tP_x \cdot \text{a}_{x+n:\overline{t-n}|} \\
&= A_x + \Delta A_x^n - A_x \cdot \frac{\text{a}_{x+n:\overline{t-n}|}}{\text{a}_{x:\overline{t}|}} \quad \text{where } \Delta A_x^n = A_{x+n} - A_x \\
&= A_x \left\{1 - \frac{\text{a}_{x+n:\overline{t-n}|}}{\text{a}_{x:\overline{t}|}}\right\} + \Delta A_x^n \\
&= A_x \cdot {}_nV_{x:\overline{t}|} + \Delta A_x^n.
\end{aligned}$$

The preliminary step is to obtain the values of ΔA_x^n, a simple process, in the course of which, however, it must be remembered that $\Delta A_x^n = A_{x+n} - A_x$; $\Delta A_x^{n+1} = A_{x+n+1} - A_x$, etc.

The term $A_x \cdot {}_nV_{x:\overline{t}|}$ presents no difficulty when the arithmometer is used, being an example of a constant multiplied by a series. The differences of ${}_nV_{x:\overline{t}|}$ being available, all that is required is to set up A_x on the arithmometer, multiply by ${}_1V_{x:\overline{t}|}$, and then without clearing the product holes multiply successively by $\Delta_1V_{x:\overline{t}|}$, $\Delta_2V_{x:\overline{t}|}$, etc., thus obtaining the successive values of $A_x \cdot {}_nV_{x:\overline{t}|}$. A periodical check of this process is provided by the original formula $A_x \cdot {}_nV_{x:\overline{t}|}$ and a summation check by $\sum_{n=1}^{n=r} A_x \cdot {}_nV_{x:\overline{t}|} = A_x \sum_{n=1}^{n=r} {}_nV_{x:\overline{t}|}$ where $r < t$.

Finally, the respective values of ΔA_x^n must be added to give the policy values, ${}_n^tV_x$, required. The following columns illustrate the method:

Age x.

n	$A_x \cdot {}_nV_{x:\overline{t}\rceil}$	ΔA_x^n	${}_n^tV_x$
(1) 1 2 ⋮ t	(2)	(3)	(4)

The last value in col. (4) will be A_{x+t}.

34. Single Premiums. If a table of single-life annuity values be available a table of the Single Premiums for whole-life assurances is readily constructed by means of the formula $A_x = 1 - d(1 + a_x)$, from which we obtain $\Delta A_x = -d\Delta a_x$, which is positive.

If, therefore, the successive differences of a_x be extracted, assuming x to be the youngest age for which the Single Premium is required,

the Initial Value is $\qquad A_x = 1 - d(1 + a_x)$,

the Working Formula is $A_{x+1} = A_x + (-d\Delta a_x)$.

Periodical Checks can be inserted at the outset by the fundamental formula $A_x = 1 - d(1 + a_x)$, and the final value $A_{w-1} = v$. The arithmometer will not be employed, so it will not be necessary to have a Summation Check.

For Endowment Assurances, we have similarly

$$A_{x:\overline{t}\rceil} = 1 - d(1 + a_{x:\overline{t-1}\rceil}),$$

$$\Delta_x . A_{x:\overline{t}\rceil} = -d\Delta_x . a_{x:\overline{t-1}\rceil},$$

the process of construction being precisely similar to that indicated for whole-life assurances.

35. Annual Premiums. If a table of single-life annuity values be available, a table of Annual Premiums for single-life whole-life assurances can be constructed by means of the formula

$$P_x = \frac{1}{1 + a_x} - d.$$

Here, x being the youngest age in the table,

the Initial Value is $\qquad P_x = \dfrac{1}{1 + a_x} - d,$

the Working Formula $\Delta P_x = \Delta \dfrac{1}{1+a_x}$

or $$P_{x+1} = P_x + \Delta \frac{1}{1+a_x}.$$

Periodical Check Values are obtained by means of the original formula.

In this case it is necessary in the first place to extract the reciprocals of $(1 + a_x)$, and then to difference these, such differences being also the differences of P_x.

Similarly for Endowment Assurances,

$$P_{x:\overline{n}|} = \frac{1}{1 + a_{x:\overline{n-1}|}} - d \text{ and } \Delta_x . P_{x:\overline{n}|} = \Delta_x . \frac{1}{1 + a_{x:\overline{n-1}|}}.$$

36. Force of Mortality. The method to be employed to construct a table of the values of μ_x will depend on the formula adopted. For example, with the formula

$$\mu_x = \frac{1}{12l_x} \{7(d_{x-1} + d_x) - (d_{x-2} + d_{x+1})\},$$

the work will be arranged in columns as follows:

x	d_x	$d_{x-1}+d_x$	Col. (3) × 7	$d_{x-2}+d_{x+1}$	Col. (4) − Col. (5)	Col. (6) ÷ $12l_x$
(1)	(2)	(3)	(4)	(5)	(6)	(7)

Col. (3) is readily obtained by inspection of col. (2) and col. (4) from col. (3). To obtain col. (5) it is convenient to use a card so cut as, when placed on col. (2), to leave exposed only the two values required, which are then readily added together. Col. (6) requires no explanation, and col. (7) will be obtained by dividing out each value independently on the arithmometer. The process is not at any stage a "continued" one and it is advisable for all the work to be carried out in duplicate. Summation Checks can however be employed to compare the totals of the various columns.

If a table follow Makeham's Law, and the constants A, B and c are known, a simple continued process is available for use with the arithmometer. Assuming the youngest age to be 20, the value A is set up in the product holes and B on the fixed plate: then multiplying by c^{20} the result in the product holes is $A + Bc^{20} = \mu_{20}$. Leaving this value in the product holes, the value of μ_{21} is then obtained by multiplying B on the fixed plate by $\Delta c^{20} = c^{21} - c^{20}$, giving $A + B(c^{20} + \Delta c^{20}) = A + Bc^{21} = \mu_{21}$. Again multiplying by Δc^{21}, the result is $A + Bc^{22} = \mu_{22}$ and so on.

The columns will be as follows:

x	c^x	Δc^x	μ_x
(1)	(2)	(3)	(4)

37. Select Tables. The construction of tables has been discussed throughout this chapter on the basis of aggregate tables. The same principles apply when Select Tables are used, the only difference being that regard must be paid to the "Select Period."

For example, in constructing tables of $D_{[x]}$ and $N_{[x]}$, the columns for the Ultimate portion of the table would be constructed first. Then for the "Select Period," taken as five years, we have

$$D_{[x]} = v^x l_{[x]}, \quad D_{[x]+t} = v^{x+t} l_{[x]+t} \text{ where } t < 5,$$

$$N_{[x]} = D_{[x]} + D_{[x]+1} + \ldots + D_{[x]+4} + N_{x+5}.$$

Similarly for C and M,

$$C_{[x]} = v^{x+1} d_{[x]}, \quad C_{[x]+t} = v^{x+t+1} d_{[x]+t} \text{ where } t < 5,$$

$$M_{[x]} = C_{[x]} + C_{[x]+1} + \ldots + C_{[x]+4} + M_{x+5}.$$

For Temporary Annuities

$$a_{[x]:\overline{n+1}|} = a_{[x]:\overline{n}|} + \frac{D_{[x]+n+1}}{D_{[x]}} \text{ where } n < 4$$

$$= a_{[x]:\overline{n}|} + \frac{D_{x+n+1}}{D_{[x]}} \qquad \text{,,} \quad n > 3.$$

For Whole-Life Policy Values

$${}_{n+1}V_{[x]} = {}_{n}V_{[x]} + \frac{(-\Delta a_{[x]+n})}{1 + a_{[x]}} \text{ where } n < 5$$

$$= {}_{n}V_{[x]} + \frac{(-\Delta a_{x+n})}{1 + a_{[x]}} \qquad \text{,,} \quad n > 4,$$

and it will be observed that $-\Delta a_{[x]+4} = a_{[x]+4} - a_{x+5}$ where a_{x+5} is taken from the ultimate table.

It is thus necessary in constructing tables of monetary functions based on Select Tables to see that the values for the "Select Period" depend only on the experience of lives at each particular age at entry $[x]$, the ultimate values being used thereafter regardless of the age at entry.

38. Joint-Life and Contingent Functions. Commutation columns for two joint lives of equal age would be constructed on the basis of the formulae

$$D_{xx} = l_x D_x,$$

$$N_{xx} = \sum_{t=0}^{t=\infty} D_{x+t:x+t},$$

$$C_{xx} = v^{x+1}(l_{xx} - l_{x+1:x+1}) = vD_{xx} - D_{x+1:x+1},$$

and $$M_{xx} = \sum_{t=0}^{t=\infty} C_{x+t:x+t}.$$

Joint-life annuity values for two lives of equal age would then be tabulated with the aid of the arithmometer by means of the formula $a_{xx} = \frac{N_{xx}}{D_{xx}}$, each value being divided out independently in duplicate. Similarly $A_{xx} = \frac{M_{xx}}{D_{xx}}$.

For Contingent Assurances, where the lives will be of unequal age,

$$D_{x+n:y+n} = v^{\frac{x+n}{2}} l_{x+n} \cdot v^{\frac{y+n}{2}} l_{y+n},$$

$$\log D_{x+n:y+n} = \log v^{\frac{x+n}{2}} + \log l_{x+n} + \log v^{\frac{y+n}{2}} + \log l_{y+n},$$

$$N_{xy} = \sum_{t=0}^{t=\infty} D_{x+t:y+t},$$

$$C_{\overset{1}{x+n}:y+n} = v^{\frac{x+n+1}{2}} (l_{x+n} - l_{x+n+1}) v^{\frac{y+n+1}{2}} \tfrac{1}{2}(l_{y+n} + l_{y+n+1}),$$

$$\log C_{\overset{1}{x+n}:y+n} = \log v^{\frac{x+n+1}{2}} + \log(l_{x+n} - l_{x+n+1})$$
$$+ \log v^{\frac{y+n+1}{2}} + \log \tfrac{1}{2}(l_{y+n} + l_{y+n+1}),$$

$$M_{xy}^1 = \sum_{t=0}^{t=\infty} C_{\overset{1}{x+t}:y+t},$$

$$A_{xy}^1 = \frac{M_{xy}^1}{D_{xy}}, \quad P_{xy}^1 = \frac{M_{xy}^1}{N_{xy}}.$$

It is evident that the formulae set out above are as readily applicable where the two lives are taken on the basis of two different tables as when they are taken on the same table. In connection with select tables the columns of N_{xy} and M_{xy}^1 would be constructed for the ultimate portion of the table first. The formulae to be employed were given in Chapter XVII.

39. Special Cases. When tables of single or annual premiums for complicated forms of assurance are required, it is frequently simplest to calculate the premium independently for every fifth age or combination of fifth ages and to obtain those for intervening ages by interpolation.

It sometimes happens, however, that the numerator and denominator of the expression for an annual premium can be calculated independently for every age by a continued process, the premiums being finally ascertained by actual division carried out in duplicate on the arithmometer.

As an example, let it be required to construct a table of net annual premiums for endowment assurances maturing at age 60 with an initial sum assured of £100 increasing by £1. 10*s*. in respect of each premium paid.

The formula for the annual premium at age x is

$$\frac{100\,[M_x - M_{60} + D_{60} + {\cdot}015\,\{R_x - R_{60} + (60-x)(D_{60} - M_{60})\}]}{N_x - N_{60}}.$$

At age $x+1$ the Numerator of this expression becomes

$$100\,[M_{x+1} - M_{60} + D_{60} + {\cdot}015\,\{R_{x+1} - R_{60} + (60-x-1)(D_{60} - M_{60})\}]$$

$$= \text{Numerator at age } x + 100\,[\Delta M_x + {\cdot}015\,\{\Delta R_x - (D_{60} - M_{60})\}]$$

$$= \quad ,, \qquad ,, \qquad - 100\,[C_x + {\cdot}015\,\{M_x + D_{60} - M_{60}\}],$$

or Numerator at age x

$$= \text{Numerator at age } (x+1) + 100\,[C_x + {\cdot}015\,\{M_x + D_{60} - M_{60}\}].$$

In order to retain positive quantities it is advisable to commence the calculations at the shortest term and work backwards. For example, if the shortest term for which these policies are to be issued be ten years, we should first calculate the numerator for age 50 and add terms to obtain those for the earlier ages.

For the Denominator, we have

$$\text{at age } x \qquad N_x - N_{60},$$

$$,, \quad x+1 \qquad N_{x+1} - N_{60},$$

$\therefore$ Denominator at age x = (Denominator at age $x+1$) + D_x.

Here, also, the work would be started at the shortest term and carried on to longer terms.

The work would be arranged in columns as follows, the last column being obtained by actual division carried out in duplicate on the arithmometer.

Maturity Age 60.

x	100 C_x	1·5 M_x	(2)+(3)	Col. (4) +1·5 ($D_{60} - M_{60}$) =Δ Numerator	Numerator	D_x =Δ Denominator	$N_x - N_{60}$ Denominator	$\frac{\text{Col. (6)}}{\text{Col. (8)}}$ =P
(1)	(2)	(3)	(4)	(5)	(6)	(7)	(8)	(9)
50								
49								
48								
⋮								

CHAPTER XXI

TABLES INVOLVING TWO OR MORE CAUSES OF DECREMENT

1. In Chapters I and II, dealing with mortality tables, the discussion was limited to one decremental force (i.e. mortality) and any points which might make it more difficult for a student to grasp the principles underlying the construction of mortality tables were rigidly excluded. In Chapter II, for example, it was assumed that during the "period of observations" there were no terminations of assurance other than by death, but it was mentioned in paragraph 23 that, in practice, allowance would have to be made for other decremental forces such as withdrawal.

In this chapter it is proposed to explain how the rate of mortality can be arrived at when other decremental forces are operating, how other decremental rates (such as the rate of withdrawal) can be calculated, and the methods of evaluating monetary functions dependent on the happening of events other than those involving only death or survival.

2. **Mortality and Withdrawal.** In Chapter I the rate of mortality at age x was defined as "the probability that a person of exact age x will die within one year following the attainment of that age," its value being $\frac{d_x}{l_x}$ or $\frac{d_x}{l_{x+1}+d_x}$; the latter form showing that q_x is the ratio of the number of deaths between ages x and $x+1$ to the number of persons under observation during the whole of that year of age or until earlier death. Similarly, in Chapter II, E_x was taken as the number of persons who attained age x at such time during the period of observations that the whole of the following year of age fell within that period, and as the only cause of decrement was death this was evidently the number of persons under observation or exposed to risk of death during the whole of the year of age x to $x+1$ or until death if this occurred during that year.

3. If a number of the E_x persons aged x (say, w_x) *withdrew* from observation during the year, it would not be known whether they survived to age $x+1$ or died between the date of withdrawal and the attainment of that age. It would accordingly be incorrect to include them in the denominator of the expression representing the value of q_x as under observation, or exposed to risk of death, throughout the whole of the year; on the other hand, these lives *were* under observation for a portion of the year and it would be equally incorrect to exclude them altogether from the experience.

Assuming that the withdrawals were equally distributed throughout the year (i.e. that the w_x persons who withdrew were under observation on an average for half a year in the year of withdrawal) it will be sufficiently accurate if we take this as equivalent to $\frac{1}{2}w_x$ persons being under observation (i.e. exposed to risk of death while still in the group of persons whose experience is being extracted) for the whole year. But the number of persons (E_x) who entered on the year of age x to $x+1$ includes all the w_x persons who withdrew during that year, and if only $\frac{1}{2}w_x$ of these were observed throughout the year it follows that the number under observation throughout the year or until death must be taken as $E_x - \frac{1}{2}w_x$. Thus the rate of mortality will be obtained by taking

$$q_x = \frac{\theta_x}{E_x - \frac{1}{2}w_x}.$$

If the only object in view is to construct a mortality table, the rates of mortality can be derived from the observations by means of this formula and, commencing with a convenient radix, the table can be completed in the manner described in Chapters I and II.

4. If, instead of the rate of mortality, we require the *rate of withdrawal* (i.e. the rate per annum at which persons attaining age x withdraw from the observations, otherwise than by death, during the year of age x to $x+1$), we must obtain the ratio of the number of withdrawals (w_x) to the number of persons under observation during the whole of the year of age or until *withdrawal.* The persons who died during the year, θ_x, were not exposed to risk of withdrawal throughout the year; but if it be assumed that the deaths were uniformly distributed over the year (i.e. that they were exposed to risk of withdrawal, on the average, for half the year) it will be sufficiently accurate to take this as equivalent to $\frac{1}{2}\theta_x$ persons exposed to risk of withdrawal for the whole year. To ascertain the rate of withdrawal therefore, as the E_x persons who entered on the year of age x to $x+1$ include all those who died during the year, we must take the ratio of w_x to $E_x - \frac{1}{2}\theta_x$, i.e. the rate of withdrawal $(wq)_x = \dfrac{w_x}{E_x - \frac{1}{2}\theta_x}$.

5. Similarly, following the method of Chapter II for Select Tables, if $E_{[x]+t}$ be the number of persons who joined a Society at age x, and who completed t years of membership at such time that the whole of the following year fell within the period of observations; and if of these $E_{[x]+t}$ persons, $\theta_{[x]+t}$ died during the following year whilst still under observation, and $w_{[x]+t}$ withdrew from membership during the year; then, assuming a uniform distribution of deaths and withdrawals over the year, the rates of mortality and withdrawal would be given by the formulae:

$$q_{[x]+t} = \frac{\theta_{[x]+t}}{E_{[x]+t} - \frac{1}{2}w_{[x]+t}},$$

$$(wq)_{[x]+t} = \frac{w_{[x]+t}}{E_{[x]+t} - \frac{1}{2}\theta_{[x]+t}}.$$

6. Now let us suppose that it is required to construct a table showing the effect of deaths and withdrawals on the Staff of a Company in order to enable us to ascertain the value of certain payments to be made on the death of a person whilst in the service of the Company and of other payments to be made in the event of withdrawal from that service.

In this case we must so construct the table as to show, at each age, the *probable* number of deaths and withdrawals as displayed by the past experience of the Staff. That is, we must construct a table by means of which we can see how many, out of l_x^s persons attaining age x in the service of the Company, will probably die in the service in the following year or withdraw from the service during that year.

7. If out of E_x persons observed to attain age x, θ_x die in the service of the Company during the following year, the probability of a person aged x dying in the service within one year, which may be represented by q_x^d, is $\dfrac{\theta_x}{E_x}$. Similarly, if of these E_x persons, w_x

withdraw during the following year, the probability that a person attaining age x in the service will so withdraw, which may be represented by q_x^w, is $\frac{w_x}{E_x}$.

The records of the Company will probably supply all the information required for the calculation of these probabilities (which would have to be graduated) and having obtained these, by starting with a convenient radix (say $l_{20}^s = 10{,}000$), a table showing the probable number of deaths and withdrawals in each year of age can be compiled.

Commencing with l_{20}^s, $l_{20}^s \times q_{20}^d$ will give d_{20}^s, the probable number of deaths in the service between ages 20 and 21, and $l_{20}^s \times q_{20}^w$ will give w_{20} the probable number of withdrawals in that year.

Death and withdrawal being assumed to be the only causes of decrement, the number out of l_{20}^s persons attaining age 20 in the service of the Company who remain in the service to age 21, is

$$l_{21}^s = l_{20}^s - d_{20}^s - w_{20},$$

and so on for other ages.

The following is a specimen of a table of this kind:

SERVICE TABLE

Age x	l_x^s	w_x	d_x^s	Total Decrement
20	10,000	858	41	899
21	9,101	732	40	772
22	8,329	621	38	659

Here the probability that a person aged 20 will die in the service of the Company between ages 20 and 21 is $\frac{d_{20}^s}{l_{20}^s} = \frac{41}{10000} = \cdot 0041$, but the annual rate of mortality amongst the 10,000 persons aged 20 is $\frac{d_{20}^s}{l_{20}^s - \frac{1}{2}w_{20}} = \frac{41}{10000 - 429} = \cdot 00428$. The probability that such a person will withdraw before reaching age 21 is

$$\frac{w_{20}}{l_{20}^s} = \frac{858}{10000} = \cdot 0858,$$

but the annual rate of withdrawal amongst persons aged 20 is

$$\frac{w_{20}}{l_{20}^s - \frac{1}{2}d_{20}^s} = \frac{858}{10000 - 20\cdot 5} = \cdot 08598.$$

8. The probabilities of death in the service and of withdrawal are quite different from the annual rates of mortality and withdrawal for the reason that the persons who withdraw during the year are not exposed to the risk of death in the service for the whole year, and those who die in the service are not exposed to the risk of withdrawal for the whole year.

The total probability that a man aged 20 will cease to be in the service of the Company (i.e. by either death or withdrawal) is

$$\frac{w_{20}+d_{20}^s}{l_{20}^s}=\frac{899}{10000}=\cdot 0899,$$

which is the sum of the separate probabilities of death in the service, and of withdrawal. And as a man must either die in the service, withdraw from the service or remain in the service until the attainment of the next higher age, it follows that the sum of the probabilities of these three events must equal unity.

These conditions do not hold when the annual *rates* are considered, as is evident from the different denominators of the ratios representing these rates.*

9. Mortality, Withdrawal and Retirement. The discussion has so far been limited to two causes of decrement, but it is evident that the same principles apply however many decremental forces may be operating.

In the valuation of Pension Funds, for example, the problem that arises is to ascertain the value of certain payments to be made on death, withdrawal or retirement, and in order to evaluate these we must estimate the probable number of deaths, withdrawals and retirements on pension in year of age or service.

Representing the number of retirements between ages x and $x+1$ by r_x, the past records should supply the values of E_x, θ_x, w_x and r_x, and the probabilities required will be obtained therefrom by the formulae

$$q_x^d=\frac{\theta_x}{E_x}, \quad q_x^w=\frac{w_x}{E_x}, \quad q_x^r=\frac{r_x}{E_x}.$$

These probabilities having been obtained for each age can, after graduation, be employed in the manner already indicated to construct a "Service Table" with three decremental columns.

* The difference between *probabilities* and *annual rates* should be carefully noted. It will be seen later (paragraph 11) that in the calculation of monetary values, *probabilities* are employed.

The following is a specimen table of this kind.

SERVICE TABLE

Age x	Remaining on Active List l_x^s	Withdrawals w_x	Deaths in the Service d_x^s	Pensioned r_x	Total Decrement
20	10,000	858	41	—	899
21	9,101	732	40	—	772
22	8,329	621	38	—	659
23	7,670	521	35	—	556
24	7,114	432	33	—	465
25	6,649	356	29	2	387
26	6,262	290	27	3	320
27	5,942	239	25	4	268
28	5,674	200	23	4	227
29	5,447	171	22	4	197
30	5,250	149	22	5	176

On the basis of this table the probability that a man attaining age 26 in the service will, before reaching age 27:

(*a*) die in the service, $q_{26}^d = \frac{27}{6262} = \cdot 00431$,

(*b*) withdraw from the service, $q_{26}^w = \frac{290}{6262} = \cdot 04631$,

(*c*) retire on pension, $q_{26}^r = \frac{3}{6262} = \cdot 00048$,

the total probability that he will not remain in the service of the Company being $\frac{320}{6262} = \cdot 05110$, which is the sum of the three separate probabilities of death in the service, withdrawal or retirement.

At the same age, the

(*a*) annual rate of mortality

$$q_{26} = \frac{d_{26}^s}{l_{26}^s - \frac{1}{2}(w_{26} + r_{26})} = \frac{27}{6115 \cdot 5} = \cdot 00442,$$

(*b*) annual rate of withdrawal

$$(wq)_{26} = \frac{w_{26}}{l_{26}^s - \frac{1}{2}(d_{26}^s + r_{26})} = \frac{290}{6247} = \cdot 04642,$$

(*c*) annual rate of retirement

$$(rq)_{26} = \frac{r_{26}}{l_{26}^s - \frac{1}{2}(d_{26}^s + w_{26})} = \frac{3}{6103 \cdot 5} = \cdot 00049,$$

the total annual rate of decrement *from the service* being the same as the total probability that (26) will cease to be in the service before reaching age 27: i.e. $1 - \frac{l^s_{27}}{l^s_{26}} = 1 - \frac{5942}{6262} = \cdot 0511.$

10. The probability that a person attaining age x in the service of the Company will remain in the service until the attainment of age $x+n$ is $\frac{l^s_{x+n}}{l^s_x}$; that he will die in the service between ages $x+n$ and $x+n+1$, $\frac{d^s_{x+n}}{l^s_x}$; that he will resign (i.e. withdraw) in that year, $\frac{w_{x+n}}{l^s_x}$; and that he will retire on pension in that year $\frac{r_{x+n}}{l^s_x}$.

11. Turning to the evaluation of monetary functions, as the l^s_x column gives the (assumed) number of persons who attain exact age x *in the service of the Company*, it follows that if all those who reach age 65 while with the Company retire on pension at that age, the value at age x ($x < 65$) of an annuity due of a contribution of 1 per annum while in the service is,

$$\frac{1}{v^x l^s_x} \{v^x l^s_x + v^{x+1} l^s_{x+1} + v^{x+2} l^s_{x+2} + \ldots + v^{64} l^s_{64}\}$$

$$= \frac{N^s_x}{D^s_x},$$

where

$$N^s_x = \sum_x^{64} D^s_x = \sum_x^{64} v^x l^s_x.$$

If the contribution be payable by means of a deduction from the monthly or weekly salary, the value can be obtained by assuming that, on the average, the yearly payment is made in the middle of the year. The value would then be

$$\frac{1}{D^s_x} \sum_x^{64} D^s_{x+\frac{1}{2}}$$

$$= \frac{1}{D^s_x} \sum_x^{64} \tfrac{1}{2}(D^s_x + D^s_{x+1})$$

$$= \frac{1}{D^s_x} \{N^s_x - \tfrac{1}{2}(D^s_x - D^s_{65})\},$$

which is of the same form as

$$\bar{a}_{x:\overline{n|}} = a_{x:\overline{n|}} - \tfrac{1}{2}\left(1 - \frac{D_{x+n}}{D_x}\right).$$

The value of an assurance of 1 payable immediately on the death of (x) while in the service of the Company, is

$$\frac{1}{v^x l_x^s}\{v^{x+1} d_x^s + v^{x+2} d_{x+1}^s + v^{x+3} d_{x+2}^s + \ldots + v^{65} d_{64}^s\}(1 + \tfrac{1}{2}i)$$

$$= \frac{\overline{M}_x^s}{D_x^s},$$

where $$\overline{M}_x^s = (1 + \tfrac{1}{2}i)\sum_x^{64} C_x^s = (1 + \tfrac{1}{2}i)\sum_x^{64} v^{x+1} d_x^s,$$

the annual charge for which would be $\dfrac{\overline{M}_x^s}{N_x^s}$.

The value of a guarantee of a payment of 1 on withdrawal from the service of the Company, is

$$\frac{1}{v^x l_x^s}\{v^{x+1} w_x + v^{x+2} w_{x+1} + \ldots + v^{65} w_{64}\}(1 + \tfrac{1}{2}i)$$

$$= \frac{\overline{M}_x^w}{D_x^s},$$

where $$\overline{M}_x^w = (1 + \tfrac{1}{2}i)\sum_x^{64} C_x^w = (1 + \tfrac{1}{2}i)\sum_x^{64} v^{x+1} w_x,$$

and, of a similar payment on retirement,

$$\frac{1}{v^x l_x^s}\{v^{x+1} r_x + v^{x+2} r_{x+1} + \ldots + v^{65} r_{64}\}(1 + \tfrac{1}{2}i) + \frac{v^{65} l_{65}^s}{v^x l_x^s}$$

$$= \frac{1}{D_x^s}\{\overline{M}_x^r + D_{65}^s\}$$

where $$\overline{M}_x^r = (1 + \tfrac{1}{2}i)\sum_x^{64} C_x^r = (1 + \tfrac{1}{2}i)\sum_x^{64} v^{x+1} r_x,$$

the annual contribution for these benefits being,

$$\frac{\overline{M}_x^w}{N_x^s} \text{ and } \frac{\overline{M}_x^r + D_{65}^s}{N_x^s} \text{ respectively.}$$

In practice the allowance on retirement takes the form of a pension, for the evaluation of which it would be necessary to investigate the mortality experience amongst the pensioners in order either to construct a pensioners' mortality table or to assist in determining which mortality table can be adopted as sufficiently accurately representing that experience.

12. On the assumption that deaths, withdrawals, and retirements are uniformly distributed over each year of age, if an enumeration of the (assumed) population shown by the Service Table be made at any particular time, the number on the active list between ages x and $x+1$ will be

$$\mathrm{L}^s_x = \int_0^1 l^s_{x+t}\,dt$$
$$= \int_0^1 \{l^s_x - t(d^s_x + w_x + r_x)\}\,dt$$
$$= l^s_x - \tfrac{1}{2}(d^s_x + w_x + r_x).$$

The central death rate and central rates of withdrawal and retirement, are then

$$m_x = \frac{d^s_x}{\mathrm{L}^s_x}, \quad (wm)_x = \frac{w_x}{\mathrm{L}^s_x}, \quad (rm)_x = \frac{r_x}{\mathrm{L}^s_x}$$

and it is a simple matter to show that these central rates are related to the annual rates of mortality, withdrawal and retirement in the same manner as q_x and m_x were shown to be related in Chapter I.

Thus
$$q_x = \frac{d^s_x}{l^s_x - \frac{1}{2}(w_x + r_x)} = \frac{d^s_x}{\mathrm{L}^s_x + \frac{1}{2}d^s_x} = \frac{2m_x}{2+m_x},$$
$$(wq)_x = \frac{w_x}{l^s_x - \frac{1}{2}(d^s_x + r_x)} = \frac{w_x}{\mathrm{L}^s_x + \frac{1}{2}w_x} = \frac{2(wm)_x}{2+(wm)_x},$$
$$(rq)_x = \frac{r_x}{l^s_x - \frac{1}{2}(d^s_x + w_x)} = \frac{r_x}{\mathrm{L}^s_x + \frac{1}{2}r_x} = \frac{2(rm)_x}{2+(rm)_x}.$$

13. It may occur in some cases, that the records have been so kept that it will be found simpler to construct a Service Table by the "Census" method. If, for example, an enumeration of the Staff of a Company be made, this will provide the number of persons on the staff between any two ages, say x and $x+1$, which may be represented by $\bar{E}_x$. And if the observed numbers (per annum) of deaths, withdrawals and retirements in this year of age be θ_x, w_x and r_x, assuming a uniform distribution of each kind of decrement over the year of age, we can take $E_x = \bar{E}_x + \frac{1}{2}(\theta_x + w_x + r_x)$, thus supplying the denominator required for the calculation of the probabilities on which (after graduation) the construction of the Service Table may be based.

14. In practice, owing to lack of suitable data based on the experience of the body of persons with which it is required to deal, the Actuary, in forming estimates in connection with, for example, the formation of a pension fund, often has to employ rates of decrement derived from other sources.

When full particulars of a single experience, or the actual probabilities of death, withdrawal or retirement based on a single experience are available, no fresh difficulties are introduced, as these probabilities can be applied directly to the construction of a Service Table in the manner already described.

It may occur, however, that only the annual rates of mortality, withdrawal, etc. are obtainable, in which case a different plan might be followed.

Let us suppose, for example, that we are dealing with two causes of decrement, death and withdrawal, and that we decide to adopt the rates of mortality, q_x', disclosed by one experience, and the rates of withdrawal, $(wq)_x''$, disclosed by a second experience.

Then, l_x^s being the radix of the Service Table, assume that the number of deaths occurring in the year of age x to $x+1$ is "a", and the number of withdrawals in the same year, "b".

The number exposed to risk of death during the year of age x to $x+1$ is then $l_x^s - \frac{1}{2}b$, and the number of deaths between those ages to be shown in the Service Table is

$$(l_x^s - \tfrac{1}{2}b)\, q_x' = a,$$

whence

$$a + \tfrac{1}{2}b \, . \, q_x' = l_x^s q_x'.$$

Similarly the number of withdrawals between ages x and $x+1$ will be

$$(l_x^s - \tfrac{1}{2}a)\,(wq)_x'' = b,$$

whence

$$b + \tfrac{1}{2}a\,(wq)_x'' = l_x^s\,(wq)_x''.$$

From these two equations we find that

$$a = \frac{l_x^s \, . \, q_x' \left[1 - \frac{1}{2}(wq)_x''\right]}{1 - \frac{1}{4}q_x'\,(wq)_x''},$$

and

$$b = \frac{l_x^s\,(wq)_x''\left[1 - \frac{1}{2}q_x'\right]}{1 - \frac{1}{4}q_x'\,(wq)_x''}.$$

Then $l_{x+1}^s = l_x^s - a - b$, and the numbers of deaths and withdrawals in the following year can be found in a similar manner: and so on for later years.

If, instead of the ordinary rates of mortality and withdrawal, q_x' and $(wq)_x''$, the central rates, m_x' and $(wm)_x''$, are available, the formulae to be used in constructing the Service Table may be derived as follows:

$$\text{(i)}\quad m_x' = \frac{d_x^s}{l_x^s - \frac{1}{2}(d_x^s + w_x)}, \quad \text{and (ii)}\quad (wm)_x'' = \frac{w_x}{l_x^s - \frac{1}{2}(d_x^s + w_x)}.$$

$$\therefore\quad \frac{m_x'}{(wm)_x''} = \frac{d_x^s}{w_x}.$$

$$\therefore\quad d_x^s = \frac{m_x'}{(wm)_x''} \times w_x.$$

Inserting this expression for d_x^s in (ii), we have

$$(wm)_x'' = \frac{w_x}{l_x^s - \frac{1}{2}w_x\left\{\frac{m_x'}{(wm)_x''} + 1\right\}}.$$

$$\therefore\quad (wm)_x'' \cdot l_x^s = w_x[1 + \tfrac{1}{2}\{m_x' + (wm)_x''\}].$$

$$\therefore\quad w_x = l_x^s \times \frac{(wm)_x''}{1 + \frac{1}{2}\{m_x' + (wm)_x''\}}.$$

Similarly,
$$d_x^s = l_x^s \times \frac{m_x'}{1 + \frac{1}{2}\{m_x' + (wm)_x''\}}.$$

Whence the Service Table can be constructed.

To check the results, we have

$$\begin{aligned} l_{x+1}^s &= l_x^s - d_x^s - w_x \\ &= l_x^s\left\{1 - \frac{m_x' + (wm)_x''}{1 + \frac{1}{2}\{m_x' + (wm)_x''\}}\right\} \\ &= l_x^s \cdot \frac{1 - \frac{1}{2}\{m_x' + (wm)_x''\}}{1 + \frac{1}{2}\{m_x' + (wm)_x''\}}. \end{aligned}$$

The methods of this paragraph are introduced in order that the principles involved shall be clearly demonstrated, but it will be found, in practice, that each pension scheme presents its own special problems and that generally the employment of simpler and more arbitrary methods will give results which, so far as can be foreseen, will provide just as good a basis for estimates regarding the future.

15. Marriage and Mortality Tables. Marriage and Mortality Tables can be constructed on similar lines to those employed in the compilation of the Service Table set out in paragraph 9, or where the probabilities or rates are taken from different sources by the methods indicated in paragraph 14, the data being usually derived from statistics giving full particulars of dates of birth, marriage, etc. Selection is not generally existent in such cases, so only Aggregate Tables need be considered.

The following is a portion of a table compiled from such particulars:

Age x	Number living at exact age		Decrements caused by		
	Bachelors $(bl)_x$	Married $(ml)_x$	Bachelors dying $(bd)_x$	Bachelors marrying $(bm)_x$	Married Men dying $(md)_x$
...	...	...	...	...	...
...	...	...	...	...	...
...	...	...	...	...	...
30	536,664	377,136	4,181	39,240	2,499
31	493,243	413,877	4,323	36,138	2,680
32	452,782	447,335	4,635	32,982	2,890
...	...	...	...	...	...

From this table it is seen that of 536,664 bachelors aged 30, 4,181 die and 39,240 marry before reaching age 31. The total decrement in the number of bachelors during the year following the attainment of age 30 is, therefore,

$$(bd)_x + (bm)_x = 4{,}181 + 39{,}240 = 43{,}421,$$

the number surviving to age 31 as bachelors being

$$\begin{aligned}(bl)_{31} &= (bl)_{30} - (bd)_{30} - (bm)_{30}\\ &= 536{,}664 - 4{,}181 - 39{,}240\\ &= 493{,}243.\end{aligned}$$

The probability, on the basis of this table, that a bachelor aged 30 will die *unmarried* before reaching age 31, is

$$(bq)_{30}^{d} = \frac{(bd)_{30}}{(bl)_{30}} = \frac{4{,}181}{536{,}664} = \cdot 0078,$$

and that a bachelor aged 30 will marry before reaching age 31,

$$(bq)_{30}^{m} = \frac{(bm)_{30}}{(bl)_{30}} = \frac{39{,}240}{536{,}664} = \cdot 0731,$$

the total probability that a bachelor aged 30 will fail to survive to age 31 *still unmarried* being

$$\frac{(bd)_{30} + (bm)_{30}}{(bl)_{30}} = 1 - \frac{(bl)_{31}}{(bl)_{30}} = 1 - \frac{493{,}243}{536{,}664} = \cdot 0809.$$

These probabilities, however, are not the annual rates of mortality and marriage amongst the 536,664 bachelors aged 30. In order to obtain the annual rate of mortality amongst bachelors aged 30, assuming marriages to be uniformly spread over the year we must, in accordance with principles already laid down, take the ratio

$$(bq)_{30} = \frac{(bd)_{30}}{(bl)_{30} - \frac{1}{2}(bm)_{30}} = \frac{4,181}{536,664 - 19,620} = \frac{4,181}{517,044} = \cdot 0081.$$

Similarly the annual rate of marriage will be

$$(bmq)_{30} = \frac{(bm)_{30}}{(bl)_{30} - \frac{1}{2}(bd)_{30}} = \frac{39,240}{536,664 - 2,091} = \frac{39,240}{534,573} = \cdot 0734.$$

The total annual rate of decrement in the number of bachelors aged 30 is

$$\frac{(bd)_{30} + (bm)_{30}}{(bl)_{30}} = \frac{4,181 + 39,240}{536,664} = \cdot 0809,$$

which, however, is not equal to the sum of the separate annual rates of mortality or marriage.

The central death rate amongst bachelors aged 30 is

$$\frac{(bd)_{30}}{(bl)_{30} - \frac{1}{2}(bd)_{30} - \frac{1}{2}(bm)_{30}},$$

and the central marriage rate

$$\frac{(bm)_{30}}{(bl)_{30} - \frac{1}{2}(bd)_{30} - \frac{1}{2}(bm)_{30}}.$$

16. The value of an annuity of 1 payable at the end of each year so long as a bachelor aged x remains unmarried is

$$\frac{1}{v^x (bl)_x} \{v^{x+1}(bl)_{x+1} + v^{x+2}(bl)_{x+2} + \dots\} = \frac{(bN)_{x+1}}{(bD)_x} = (ba)_x,$$

and the value of an assurance of 1 payable at the end of the year of death of a bachelor now aged x, if he die unmarried, is

$$\frac{1}{v^x (bl)_x} \{v^{x+1}(bd)_x + v^{x+2}(bd)_{x+1} + \dots\} = \frac{(bM)_x}{(bD)_x} = (bA)_x.$$

Similarly, the value of a payment of 1 at the end of the year of marriage of a bachelor now aged x is

$$\frac{1}{v^x (bl)_x} \{v^{x+1}(bm)_x + v^{x+2}(bm)_{x+1} + \dots\} = \frac{(bm\,.\,M)_x}{(bD)_x} = (bm\,.\,E)_x.$$

17. If the number of bachelors surviving at each exact age and the number marrying or dying as bachelors at each age be available, the Marriage and Mortality Table can be constructed directly from the data.

If, however, the conditions are such that it becomes necessary to revert to the "census" method of constructing the table, we shall have from the data, subject to graduation,

Central death rate amongst bachelors $(bd\,.\,m)_x = \dfrac{(bd)_x}{(b\mathrm{L})_x}$.

Central marriage rate amongst bachelors $(bm\,.\,m)_x = \dfrac{(bm)_x}{(b\mathrm{L})_x}$.

Probability of a bachelor aged x dying unmarried within one year

$$\frac{(bd)_x}{(b\mathrm{L})_x + \frac{1}{2}(bd)_x + \frac{1}{2}(bm)_x} = \frac{(bd)_x}{(bl)_x}.$$

Probability of a bachelor aged x marrying within one year

$$\frac{(bm)_x}{(b\mathrm{L})_x + \frac{1}{2}(bd)_x + \frac{1}{2}(bm)_x} = \frac{(bm)_x}{(bl)_x}.$$

TABLES

SYNOPSIS OF TABLES

Functions Tabulated	English Life Table No. 8—Males: Mortality only	English Life Table No. 8—Males: Rate per cent. 3	English Life Table No. 8—Males: Rate per cent. $3\frac{1}{2}$	H^M Table (Makeham Graduation): Mortality only	H^M Table (Makeham Graduation): Rate per cent. 3	H^M Table (Makeham Graduation): Rate per cent. $3\frac{1}{2}$	H^M Table (Makeham Graduation): Rate per cent. 4
Single Lives	pp.	pp.	pp.	pp.	pp.	pp.	pp.
$l_x, d_x, p_x, q_x, \mu_x, L_x, T_x, \mathring{e}_x$	398–399	...	...	410–411	...	...	...
$\log l_x, \log p_x, \log \mu_x$	...	...	...	412	...	...	...
$e_{xx}, e_{xxx}, e_{xxxx}$	...	...	...	413	...	...	...
$D_x, N_x, S_x, C_x, M_x, R_x$ ...	...	400–401	404–405	...	416–417	424–425	432–433
$\log D_x, \log N_x, \log M_x$	...	...	...	...	418	426	434
a_x, A_x, P_x	...	402	406	...	419	427	435
$\bar{a}_x, \bar{A}_x, {}^{(\infty)}\bar{P}_x$	...	403	407	...	...	...	...
$\log D_{xx}, \log N_{xx}$	...	...	...	...	} 420–421	} 428–429	} 436–437
$\log D_{xxx}, \log N_{xxx}$	...	...	...	...	}	}	}
$\log D_{xxxx}, \log N_{xxxx}$	...	...	...	...	}	}	}
$a_{xx}, a_{xxx}, a_{xxxx}$	...	...	...	...	422	430	438
Contingent Assurance factors	...	...	...	...	479	...	...

British Offices Experience. *Whole-Life Non-Participating Assurances*—$O^{[NM]}$

Tabulated in respect of the *First Five years of Assurance* and of the *Ultimate Table*

Functions Tabulated	Mortality only	Rate per cent. 3	Rate per cent. $3\frac{1}{2}$
	pp.	pp.	pp.
$l_{[x]+t}$	440	...	...
$\log l_{[x]+t}$ ...	441	...	...
$d_{[x]+t}$	442	...	...
$q_{[x]+t}$	443	...	...
$p_{[x]+t}$	444	...	...
$\log p_{[x]+t}$ ...	445	...	...
$\mu_{[x]+t}$	446	...	...
$\log \mu_{[x]+t}$ ...	447	...	...
$e_{[x]+t}$ ($t=0$, and $t=5$ or more)	450	...	...

Functions Tabulated	Mortality only	Rate per cent. 3	Rate per cent. $3\frac{1}{2}$
	pp.	pp.	pp.
$D_{[x]+t}$	...	452	464
$\log D_{[x]+t}$	...	453	465
$N_{[x]+t}$	...	454	466
$\log N_{[x]+t}$	...	455	467
$M_{[x]+t}$	...	456	468
R_{x+5}	...	456	...
$\log M_{[x]+t}$	...	457	469
$a_{[x]+t}$	...	458	470

Tabulated as at Date of Assurance only

Functions Tabulated	Mortality only	Rate per cent. 3	Rate per cent. $3\frac{1}{2}$
$a_{[x]}, A_{[x]}, P_{[x]}$	...	460	472
$a_{[xx]}$	...	461	473

Tabulated in respect of the Ultimate Table only

Functions Tabulated		Mortality only	Rate per cent. 3	Rate per cent. $3\frac{1}{2}$
$l_x, d_x, p_x, q_x, \mu_x$ ... }		} 448–449	...	...
$\log l_x, \log p_x, \log \mu_x$ ... }		}		
D_x, N_x, M_x ...	} Ages 81 to 105	...	459	471
$\log D_x, \log N_x, \log M_x$	}			
a_x	}			
R_x		...	459	...
a_{xx}		...	461	473

Premium Conversion Tables

	Rate per cent. 3	Rate per cent. $3\frac{1}{2}$	Rate per cent. 4
	pp.	pp.	pp.
Single Premium }	474	475	476
Annual Premium }			
Continuous functions	477	...	...

Uniform Seniority Tables

	p.
H^M Table—Two Lives }	478
H^M ,, —Three ,, }	
$O^{[NM]}$,, —Two ,, }	

ENGLISH LIFE TABLE No. 8

MALES

NOTE ON FORCE OF MORTALITY

From age 2 upwards the value of μ_x has been calculated by the formula

$$\mu_x = \frac{7(d_{x-1}+d_x)-(d_{x-2}+d_{x+1})}{12l_x}.$$

The value of μ_0 was obtained by taking the (ratio of the number of deaths during the first day following birth in the three years 1910 to 1912 inclusive, to the number of births in the same three years) × 365. This is the closest approximation that can be made with the data available, but clearly underestimates the true value of the force of mortality at the moment of birth.

The actual figures used were

$$\frac{5950+5818+5666}{457266+448933+445004} \times 365 = 4{\cdot}70944.$$

In order to obtain μ_1, it was assumed that the deaths under age 1 in the three years 1910–1912 occurred amongst

{½ (Births in 1909) + (Births in 1910 and 1911) + ½ (Births in 1912)}.

The number of deaths occurring during each of the first twelve months of life being available, the value of m_x for each of these months was obtained by the formula

$$m_{\frac{n}{12}} = \frac{d_{\frac{n}{12}}}{l_{\frac{n}{12}} - \frac{1}{2}d_{\frac{n}{12}}} \times 12 = \mu_{\frac{n+\frac{1}{2}}{12}},$$

where $d_{\frac{n}{12}}$ represents the number of deaths occurring in the $(n+1)$th month.

By this means the values of μ_x at ages ½ month, 1½ months...4½ months were ascertained, the value of μ_1 being finally calculated by the formula

$$\begin{aligned}\mu_1 &= (1+\Delta)^{\frac{5}{2}}\mu_{\frac{9\frac{1}{2}}{12}} \\ &= \mu_{\frac{19}{24}} + \tfrac{5}{2}\Delta\mu_{\frac{19}{24}} + \tfrac{15}{8}\Delta^2\mu_{\frac{19}{24}}.\end{aligned}$$

The figures employed in the calculation of μ_0 and μ_1 were taken from pp. 43 and 44 of the *Supplement to the 75th Annual Report of the Registrar General.* The value of μ_0 is of theoretical interest only.

Assurance and Annuity factors at age 0 are not employed in practice and have accordingly been omitted from the following tables.

Interest Constants at 3 per cent. will be found on page 415 and at 3½ per cent. on page 423.

English Life Table No. 8—Males

Age x	l_x	d_x	p_x	q_x	μ_x	L_x	T_x	$\mathring{e}_x$	Age x
0	1 000 000	120 441	·879 56	·120 44	>4·709 44	911 428	51 495 315	51·50	0
1	879 559	30 115	·965 76	·034 24	0·062 08	864 501	50 583 887	57·51	1
2	849 444	11 353	·986 64	·013 37	·015 99	843 768	49 719 386	58·53	2
3	838 091	6 856	·991 82	·008 18	·009 19	834 663	48 875 618	58·32	3
4	831 235	4 959	·994 03	·005 97	·006 75	828 755	48 040 955	57·80	4
5	826 276	4 038	·995 11	·004 89	·005 33	824 257	47 212 200	57·14	5
6	822 238	3 262	·996 03	·003 97	·004 41	820 607	46 387 943	56·42	6
7	818 976	2 630	·996 79	·003 21	·003 57	817 661	45 567 336	55·64	7
8	816 346	2 141	·997 38	·002 62	·002 89	815 276	44 749 675	54·82	8
9	814 205	1 791	·997 80	·002 20	·002 39	813 309	43 934 399	53·96	9
10	812 414	1 570	·998 07	·001 93	·002 04	811 629	43 121 090	53·08	10
1	810 844	1 468	·998 19	·001 81	·001 85	810 110	42 309 461	52·18	1
2	809 376	1 469	·998 18	·001 82	·001 79	808 642	41 499 351	51·27	2
3	807 907	1 556	·998 07	·001 93	·001 86	807 129	40 690 709	50·37	3
4	806 351	1 705	·997 89	·002 11	·002 01	805 498	39 883 580	49·46	4
15	804 646	1 888	·997 65	·002 35	·002 23	803 702	39 078 082	48·57	15
6	802 758	2 077	·997 41	·002 59	·002 47	801 720	38 274 380	47·68	6
7	800 681	2 236	·997 21	·002 79	·002 69	799 563	37 472 660	46·80	7
8	798 445	2 414	·996 98	·003 02	·002 91	797 238	36 673 097	45·93	8
9	796 031	2 596	·996 74	·003 26	·003 15	794 733	35 875 859	45·07	9
20	793 435	2 762	·996 52	·003 48	·003 38	792 054	35 081 126	44·21	20
1	790 673	2 895	·996 34	·003 66	·003 59	789 225	34 289 072	43·37	1
2	787 778	2 980	·996 22	·003 78	·003 74	786 288	33 499 847	42·53	2
3	784 798	3 031	·996 14	·003 86	·003 83	783 283	32 713 559	41·68	3
4	781 767	3 068	·996 08	·003 92	·003 90	780 233	31 930 276	40·84	4
25	778 699	3 112	·996 00	·004 00	·003 96	777 143	31 150 043	40·00	25
6	775 587	3 184	·995 89	·004 11	·004 05	773 995	30 372 900	39·16	6
7	772 403	3 280	·995 75	·004 25	·004 18	770 763	29 598 905	38·32	7
8	769 123	3 388	·995 60	·004 40	·004 33	767 429	28 828 142	37·48	8
9	765 735	3 508	·995 42	·004 58	·004 50	763 981	28 060 713	36·65	9
30	762 227	3 647	·995 22	·004 78	·004 69	760 403	27 296 732	35·81	30
1	758 580	3 806	·994 98	·005 02	·004 91	756 677	26 536 329	34·98	1
2	754 774	3 987	·994 72	·005 28	·005 16	752 781	25 779 652	34·16	2
3	750 787	4 190	·994 42	·005 58	·005 44	748 692	25 026 871	33·33	3
4	746 597	4 406	·994 10	·005 90	·005 75	744 394	24 278 179	32·52	4
35	742 191	4 633	·993 76	·006 24	·006 09	739 874	23 533 785	31·71	35
6	737 558	4 864	·993 41	·006 59	·006 44	735 126	22 793 911	30·90	6
7	732 694	5 091	·993 05	·006 95	·006 79	730 149	22 058 785	30·11	7
8	727 603	5 319	·992 69	·007 31	·007 15	724 943	21 328 636	29·31	8
9	722 284	5 557	·992 31	·007 69	·007 53	719 506	20 603 693	28·53	9
40	716 727	5 813	·991 89	·008 11	·007 93	713 820	19 884 187	27·74	40
1	710 914	6 097	·991 42	·008 58	·008 37	707 866	19 170 367	26·97	1
2	704 817	6 408	·990 91	·009 09	·008 87	701 613	18 462 501	26·20	2
3	698 409	6 736	·990 36	·009 64	·009 41	695 041	17 760 888	25·43	3
4	691 673	7 083	·989 76	·010 24	·009 98	688 131	17 065 847	24·67	4
45	684 590	7 452	·989 11	·010 89	·010 61	680 864	16 377 716	23·92	45
6	677 138	7 842	·988 42	·011 58	·011 29	673 217	15 696 852	23·18	6
7	669 296	8 242	·987 69	·012 31	·012 01	665 175	15 023 635	22·45	7
8	661 054	8 647	·986 92	·013 08	·012 77	656 731	14 358 460	21·72	8
9	652 407	9 074	·986 09	·013 91	·013 57	647 870	13 701 729	21·00	9
50	643 333	9 537	·985 18	·014 82	·014 45	638 564	13 053 859	20·29	50
1	633 796	10 051	·984 14	·015 86	·015 44	628 771	12 415 295	19·59	1
2	623 745	10 610	·982 99	·017 01	·016 55	618 440	11 786 524	18·90	2
3	613 135	11 199	·981 73	·018 27	·017 78	607 535	11 168 084	18·22	3
4	601 936	11 816	·980 37	·019 63	·019 11	596 028	10 560 549	17·55	4

English Life Table No. 8—Males

Age x	l_x	d_x	p_x	q_x	μ_x	L_x	T_x	$\mathring{e}_x$	Age x
55	590 120	12 458	·978 89	·021 11	·020 56	583 891	9 964 521	16·89	55
6	577 662	13 122	·977 28	·022 72	·022 14	571 101	9 380 630	16·24	6
7	564 540	13 798	·975 56	·024 44	·023 84	557 641	8 809 529	15·61	7
8	550 742	14 477	·973 71	·026 29	·025 67	543 504	8 251 888	14·98	8
9	536 265	15 162	·971 73	·028 27	·027 63	528 684	7 708 384	14·37	9
60	521 103	15 850	·969 58	·030 42	·029 76	513 178	7 179 700	13·78	60
1	505 253	16 540	·967 26	·032 74	·032 06	496 983	6 666 522	13·19	1
2	488 713	17 206	·964 79	·035 21	·034 54	480 110	6 169 539	12·62	2
3	471 507	17 834	·962 18	·037 82	·037 17	462 590	5 689 429	12·07	3
4	453 673	18 441	·959 35	·040 65	·039 98	444 452	5 226 839	11·52	4
65	435 232	19 043	·956 25	·043 75	·043 06	425 711	4 782 387	10·99	65
6	416 189	19 646	·952 80	·047 20	·046 48	406 366	4 356 676	10·47	6
7	396 543	20 232	·948 98	·051 02	·050 30	386 427	3 950 310	9·96	7
8	376 311	20 766	·944 82	·055 18	·054 50	365 928	3 563 883	9·47	8
9	355 545	21 237	·940 27	·059 73	·059 10	344 926	3 197 955	9·00	9
70	334 308	21 629	·935 30	·064 70	·064 15	323 494	2 853 029	8·53	70
1	312 679	21 927	·929 87	·070 13	·069 70	301 715	2 529 535	8·09	1
2	290 752	22 134	·923 87	·076 13	·075 83	279 685	2 227 820	7·66	2
3	268 618	22 223	·917 27	·082 73	·082 65	257 507	1 948 135	7·25	3
4	246 395	22 146	·910 12	·089 88	·090 16	235 322	1 690 628	6·86	4
75	224 249	21 866	·902 49	·097 51	·098 29	213 316	1 455 306	6·49	75
6	202 383	21 359	·894 46	·105 54	·106 97	191 703	1 241 990	6·14	6
7	181 024	20 647	·885 94	·114 06	·116 20	170 701	1 050 287	5·80	7
8	160 377	19 758	·876 80	·123 20	·126 16	150 498	879 586	5·49	8
9	140 619	18 684	·867 13	·132 87	·136 90	131 277	729 088	5·19	9
80	121 935	17 436	·857 01	·142 99	·148 34	113 217	597 811	4·90	80
1	104 499	16 035	·846 55	·153 45	·160 36	96 481	484 594	4·64	1
2	88 464	14 526	·835 81	·164 19	·172 88	81 201	388 113	4·39	2
3	73 938	12 963	·824 67	·175 33	·185 96	67 457	306 912	4·15	3
4	60 975	11 397	·813 06	·186 94	·199 70	55 276	239 455	3·93	4
85	49 578	9 873	·800 89	·199 11	·214 33	44 642	184 179	3·72	85
6	39 705	8 416	·788 04	·211 96	·229 92	35 497	139 537	3·51	6
7	31 289	7 079	·773 74	·226 26	·246 97	27 749	104 040	3·33	7
8	24 210	5 861	·757 92	·242 08	·266 50	21 280	76 291	3·15	8
9	18 349	4 741	·741 60	·258 40	·287 97	15 978	55 011	3·00	9
90	13 608	3 728	·726 05	·273 95	·309 77	11 744	39 033	2·87	90
1	9 880	2 838	·712 73	·287 27	·329 99	8 461	27 289	2·76	1
2	7 042	2 097	·702 29	·297 71	·346 81	5 994	18 828	2·67	2
3	4 945	1 510	·694 68	·305 32	·359 69	4 190	12 834	2·60	3
4	3 435	1 067	·689 16	·310 84	·368 61	2 901	8 644	2·52	4
95	2 368	748	·684 36	·315 64	·375 63	1 994	5 743	2·43	95
6	1 620	521	·678 26	·321 74	·383 28	1 360	3 749	2·32	6
7	1 099	365	·668 25	·331 75	·394 15	916	2 389	2·18	7
8	734	256	·651 26	·348 74	·413 94	606	1 473	2·01	8
9	478	180	·624 08	·375 92	·446 83	388	867	1·82	9
100	298	124	·583 95	·416 05	·500 56	236	479	1·61	100
1	174	82	·529 27	·470 73	·580 46	133	243	1·40	1
2	92	50	·460 51	·539 49	·701 09	67	110	1·20	2
3	42	26	·380 81	·619 19	·871 03	29	43	1·02	3
4	16	11	·296 01	·703 99	1·067 71	11	14	·87	4
105	5	4	·213 69	·786 31	1·300 00	3	3	·75	105
6	1	1	·141 41	·858 59				·65	6

Note:—This table is printed as originally published, except that the values of p_x and q_x have been cut down from seven to five places of decimals. From age 82 onwards, owing to the reduction in the number of figures in the l_x and d_x columns (all decimals having been discarded in the construction of the table) the division of d_x by l_x does not exactly reproduce the tabulated value of q_x to five places of decimals. (See Chap. II 25.)

English Life Table No. 8—Males

Commutation Table. **3** *per cent.*

Age x	D_x	N_x	S_x	C_x	M_x	R_x	Age x
0	1 000 000	23 293 788	526 785 873	116 933	321 541	7 950 534	0
1	853 941	22 293 788	503 492 085	28 386·3	204 608	7 628 993	1
2	800 682	21 439 847	481 198 297	10 389·6	176 222	7 424 385	2
3	766 972	20 639 165	459 758 450	6 091·47	165 832	7 248 163	3
4	738 541	19 872 193	439 119 285	4 277·68	159 741	7 082 331	4
5	712 753	19 133 652	419 247 092	3 381·76	155 463	6 922 590	5
6	688 611	18 420 899	400 113 440	2 652·30	152 081	6 767 127	6
7	665 902	17 732 288	381 692 541	2 076·15	149 429	6 615 046	7
8	644 431	17 066 386	363 960 253	1 640·90	147 353	6 465 617	8
9	624 020	16 421 955	346 893 867	1 332·67	145 712	6 318 264	9
10	604 512	15 797 935	330 471 912	1 134·20	144 379	6 172 552	10
1	585 771	15 193 423	314 673 977	1 029·63	143 245	6 028 173	1
2	567 680	14 607 652	299 480 554	1 000·32	142 215	5 884 928	2
3	550 145	14 039 972	284 872 902	1 028·70	141 215	5 742 713	3
4	533 093	13 489 827	270 832 930	1 094·37	140 186	5 601 498	4
15	516 472	12 956 734	257 343 103	1 176·54	139 092	5 461 312	15
6	500 252	12 440 262	244 386 369	1 256·62	137 915	5 322 220	6
7	484 425	11 940 010	231 946 107	1 313·41	136 658	5 184 305	7
8	469 002	11 455 585	220 006 097	1 376·67	135 345	5 047 647	8
9	453 965	10 986 583	208 550 512	1 437·34	133 968	4 912 302	9
20	439 306	10 532 618	197 563 929	1 484·71	132 531	4 778 334	20
1	425 026	10 093 312	187 031 311	1 510·88	131 046	4 645 803	1
2	411 135	9 668 286	176 937 999	1 509·94	129 535	4 514 757	2
3	397 651	9 257 151	167 269 713	1 491·05	128 025	4 385 222	3
4	384 578	8 859 500	158 012 562	1 465·29	126 534	4 257 197	4
25	371 911	8 474 922	149 153 062	1 443·02	125 069	4 130 663	25
6	359 636	8 103 011	140 678 140	1 433·40	123 626	4 005 594	6
7	347 727	7 743 375	132 575 129	1 433·61	122 193	3 881 968	7
8	336 166	7 395 648	124 831 754	1 437·69	120 759	3 759 775	8
9	324 937	7 059 482	117 436 106	1 445·25	119 321	3 639 016	9
30	314 027	6 734 545	110 376 624	1 458·75	117 876	3 519 695	30
1	303 422	6 420 518	103 642 079	1 478·01	116 417	3 401 819	1
2	293 107	6 117 096	97 221 561	1 503·20	114 939	3 285 402	2
3	283 066	5 823 989	91 104 465	1 533·73	113 436	3 170 463	3
4	273 288	5 540 923	85 280 476	1 565·82	111 902	3 057 027	4
35	263 762	5 267 635	79 739 553	1 598·54	110 336	2 945 125	35
6	254 481	5 003 873	74 471 918	1 629·36	108 737	2 834 789	6
7	245 440	4 749 392	69 468 045	1 655·73	107 108	2 726 052	7
8	236 636	4 503 952	64 718 653	1 679·49	105 452	2 618 944	8
9	228 064	4 267 316	60 214 701	1 703·54	103 773	2 513 492	9
40	219 718	4 039 252	55 947 385	1 730·11	102 069	2 409 719	40
1	211 588	3 819 534	51 908 133	1 761·78	100 339	2 307 650	1
2	203 663	3 607 946	48 088 599	1 797·72	98 577·4	2 207 311	2
3	195 934	3 404 283	44 480 653	1 834·70	96 779·7	2 108 734	3
4	188 392	3 208 349	41 076 370	1 873·02	94 945·0	2 011 954	4
45	181 032	3 019 957	37 868 021	1 913·20	93 072·0	1 917 009	45
6	173 846	2 838 925	34 848 064	1 954·69	91 158·8	1 823 937	6
7	166 828	2 665 079	32 009 139	1 994·55	89 204·1	1 732 778	7
8	159 974	2 498 251	29 344 060	2 031·62	87 209·5	1 643 574	8
9	153 283	2 338 277	26 845 809	2 069·84	85 177·9	1 556 364	9
50	146 749	2 184 994	24 507 532	2 112·09	83 108·1	1 471 186	50
1	140 362	2 038 245	22 322 538	2 161·09	80 996·0	1 388 078	1
2	134 113	1 897 883	20 284 293	2 214·84	78 834·9	1 307 082	2
3	127 992	1 763 770	18 386 410	2 269·70	76 620·1	1 228 247	3
4	121 994	1 635 778	16 622 640	2 325·00	74 350·4	1 151 627	4

ENGLISH LIFE TABLE NO. 8—MALES

Commutation Table. **3** *per cent.*

Age x	D_x	N_x	S_x	C_x	M_x	R_x	Age x
55	116 116	1 513 784	14 986 862	2 379·93	72 025·4	1 077 277	55
6	110 354	1 397 668	13 473 078	2 433·76	69 645·5	1 005 252	6
7	104 706	1 287 314	12 075 410	2 484·60	67 211·7	935 606	7
8	99 172·0	1 182 608	10 788 096	2 530·94	64 727·1	868 394	8
9	93 752·6	1 083 436	9 605 488	2 573·49	62 196·2	803 667	9
60	88 448·4	989 683	8 522 052	2 611·91	59 622·7	741 471	60
1	83 260·3	901 235	7 532 369	2 646·23	57 010·8	681 848	1
2	78 189·0	817 975	6 631 134	2 672·60	54 364·6	624 837	2
3	73 239·1	739 786	5 813 159	2 689·47	51 692·0	570 472	3
4	68 416·5	666 547	5 073 373	2 700·01	49 002·5	518 780	4
65	63 723·8	598 131	4 406 826	2 706·94	46 302·5	469 777	65
6	59 160·8	534 407	3 808 695	2 711·31	43 595·6	423 474	6
7	54 726·3	475 246	3 274 288	2 710·86	40 884·3	379 878	7
8	50 421·5	420 520	2 799 042	2 701·37	38 173·4	338 994	8
9	46 251·5	370 099	2 378 522	2 682·18	35 472·0	300 821	9
70	42 222·2	323 847	2 008 423	2 652·12	32 789·8	265 349	70
1	38 340·3	281 624	1 684 576	2 610·35	30 137·7	232 559	1
2	34 613·3	243 284	1 402 952	2 558·25	27 527·3	202 421	2
3	31 046·9	208 671	1 159 668	2 493·72	24 969·0	174 894	3
4	27 648·9	177 624	950 997	2 412·70	22 475·3	149 925	4
75	24 430·9	149 975	773 373	2 312·81	20 062·6	127 450	75
6	21 406·5	125 544	623 398	2 193·38	17 749·8	107 387	6
7	18 589·6	104 138	497 854	2 058·51	15 556·4	89 636·9	7
8	15 989·6	85 548·1	393 716	1 912·50	13 497·9	74 080·5	8
9	13 611·4	69 558·5	308 168	1 755·87	11 585·4	60 582·6	9
80	11 459·1	55 947·1	238 609	1 590·86	9 829·57	48 997·2	80
1	9 534·48	44 488·0	182 662	1 420·42	8 238·71	39 167·6	1
2	7 836·35	34 953·5	138 174	1 249·27	6 818·29	30 928·9	2
3	6 358·84	27 117·1	103 220	1 082·38	5 569·02	24 110·6	3
4	5 091·25	20 758·3	76 103·2	923·904	4 486·64	18 541·6	4
85	4 019·07	15 667·1	55 344·9	777·048	3 562·74	14 055·0	85
6	3 124·95	11 648·0	39 677·8	643·083	2 785·69	10 492·3	6
7	2 390·86	8 523·03	28 029·8	525·166	2 142·61	7 706·62	7
8	1 796·05	6 132·17	19 506·8	422·142	1 617·44	5 564·01	8
9	1 321·60	4 336·12	13 374·6	331·528	1 195·30	3 946·57	9
90	951·578	3 014·52	9 038·48	253·098	863·776	2 751·27	90
1	670·764	2 062·94	6 023·96	187·063	610·678	1 887·49	1
2	464·164	1 392·18	3 961·02	134·195	423·615	1 276·81	2
3	316·449	928·014	2 568·84	93·816 1	289·420	853·196	3
4	213·416	611·565	1 640·83	64·361 8	195·604	563·776	4
95	142·838	398·149	1 029·26	43·805 4	131·242	368·172	95
6	94·872 7	255·311	631·106	29·622 9	87·436 5	236·930	6
7	62·486 6	160·438	375·795	20·148 6	57·813 6	149·493	7
8	40·518 0	97·951 4	215·357	13·720 0	37·665 0	91·678 9	8
9	25·617 8	57·433 4	117·406	9·365 90	23·945 0	54·013 9	9
100	15·505 8	31·815 6	59·972 1	6·264 11	14·579 1	30·068 9	100
1	8·789 96	16·309 8	28·156 5	4·021 77	8·314 97	15·489 8	1
2	4·512 23	7·519 83	11·846 7	2·380 85	4·293 20	7·174 81	2
3	1·999 91	3·007 60	4·326 86	1·202 01	1·912 35	2·881 61	3
4	·739 696	1·007 69	1·319 26	·493 724	·710 339	·969 261	4
105	·224 420	·267 997	·311 574	·174 308	·216 615	·258 922	105
6	·043 577	·043 577	·043 577	·042 307	·042 307	·042 307	6

English Life Table No. 8—Males

3 *per cent.*

Age x	a_x	A_x	P_x	Age x	a_x	A_x	P_x
1	25·107	·239 60	·009 18	55	12·037	·620 29	·047 58
2	25·777	·220 09	·008 22	6	11·665	·631 11	·049 83
3	25·910	·216 22	·008 03	7	11·295	·641 91	·052 21
4	25·907	·216 29	·008 04	8	10·925	·652 68	·054 73
5	25·845	·218 12	·008 13	9	10·556	·663 41	·057 41
6	25·751	·220 85	·008 26	60	10·189	·674 10	·060 24
7	25·629	·224 40	·008 43	1	9·824	·684 73	·063 26
8	25·483	·228 66	·008 63	2	9·462	·695 30	·066 46
9	25·316	·233 51	·008 87	3	9·101	·705 80	·069 87
10	25·133	·238 84	·009 14	4	8·742	·716 24	·073 52
1	24·937	·244 54	·009 43	65	8·386	·726 61	·077 41
2	24·732	·250 52	·009 74	6	8·033	·736 90	·081 58
3	24·520	·256 69	·010 06	7	7·684	·747 07	·086 03
4	24·305	·262 97	·010 39	8	7·340	·757 09	·090 78
15	24·087	·269 31	·010 74	9	7·002	·766 94	·095 84
6	23·868	·275 69	·011 09	70	6·670	·776 60	·101 25
7	23·648	·282 10	·011 45	1	6·345	·786 06	·107 01
8	23·425	·288 58	·011 81	2	6·029	·795 28	·113 15
9	23·201	·295 11	·012 19	3	5·721	·804 23	·119 66
20	22·976	·301 68	·012 58	4	5·424	·812 88	·126 53
1	22·748	·308 32	·012 98	75	5·139	·821 20	·133 77
2	22·516	·315 07	·013 40	6	4·865	·829 18	·141 38
3	22·280	·321 95	·013 83	7	4·602	·836 83	·149 38
4	22·037	·329 02	·014 28	8	4·350	·844 17	·157 78
25	21·788	·336 29	·014 76	9	4·110	·851 15	·166 56
6	21·531	·343 75	·015 26	80	3·882	·857 80	·175 69
7	21·269	·351 40	·015 78	1	3·666	·864 10	·185 19
8	21·000	·359 22	·016 33	2	3·460	·870 08	·195 07
9	20·726	·367 21	·016 90	3	3·264	·875 79	·205 37
30	20·446	·375 37	·017 50	4	3·077	·881 25	·216 14
1	20·160	·383 68	·018 13	85	2·898	·886 46	·227 40
2	19·870	·392 14	·018 79	6	2·727	·891 44	·239 16
3	19·575	·400 74	·019 48	7	2·565	·896 17	·251 39
4	19·275	·409 47	·020 20	8	2·414	·900 55	·263 76
35	18·971	·418 32	·020 95	9	2·281	·904 43	·275 66
6	18·663	·427 29	·021 73	90	2·168	·907 73	·286 54
7	18·351	·436 39	·022 55	1	2·076	·910 42	·296 02
8	18·033	·445 63	·023 41	2	1·999	·912 64	·304 28
9	17·711	·455 02	·024 32	3	1·933	·914 59	·311 87
40	17·384	·464 55	·025 27	4	1·866	·916 54	·319 84
1	17·052	·474 22	·026 27	95	1·787	·918 82	·329 63
2	16·715	·484 02	·027 32	6	1·691	·921 62	·342 47
3	16·375	·493 94	·028 43	7	1·568	·925 22	·360 35
4	16·030	·503 98	·029 59	8	1·417	·929 59	·384 53
45	15·682	·514 12	·030 82	9	1·242	·934 70	·416 92
6	15·330	·524 37	·032 11	100	1·052	·940 24	·458 24
7	14·975	·534 71	·033 47	1	·856	·945 96	·509 81
8	14·617	·545 15	·034 91	2	·667	·951 46	·570 92
9	14·255	·555 69	·036 43	3	·504	·956 22	·635 84
50	13·889	·566 33	·038 04	4	·362	·960 31	·704 92
1	13·521	·577 05	·039 74	105	·194	·965 22	·808 27
2	13·151	·587 82	·041 54	6		·970 86	·970 86
3	12·780	·598 63	·043 44				
4	12·409	·609 46	·045 45				

English Life Table No. 8—Males

3 per cent.

Age x	$\bar{a}_x$	$\bar{A}_x$	${}^{(\infty)}\bar{P}_x$	Age x	$\bar{a}_x$	$\bar{A}_x$	${}^{(\infty)}\bar{P}_x$
1	25·599	·243 32	·009 50	55	12·533	·629 54	·050 23
2	26·273	·223 40	·008 51	6	12·161	·640 53	·052 67
3	26·407	·219 44	·008 31	7	11·791	·651 47	·055 25
4	26·404	·219 53	·008 32	8	11·420	·662 44	·058 01
5	26·342	·221 36	·008 41	9	11·051	·673 35	·060 93
6	26·248	·224 14	·008 54	60	10·684	·684 19	·064 04
7	26·126	·227 74	·008 72	1	10·319	·694 98	·067 35
8	25·980	·232 06	·008 93	2	9·957	·705 68	·070 87
9	25·813	·237 00	·009 18	3	9·595	·716 38	·074 67
10	25·630	·242 41	·009 46	4	9·236	·726 99	·078 71
1	25·434	·248 20	·009 76	65	8·880	·737 52	·083 05
2	25·229	·254 26	·010 08	6	8·527	·747 95	·087 71
3	25·017	·260 52	·010 42	7	8·177	·758 29	·092 74
4	24·802	·266 88	·010 76	8	7·833	·768 46	·098 11
15	24·584	·273 32	·011 12	9	7·495	·778 45	·103 86
6	24·365	·279 80	·011 49	70	7·162	·788 30	·110 07
7	24·145	·286 30	·011 86	1	6·837	·797 90	·116 70
8	23·922	·292 89	·012 25	2	6·520	·807 28	·123 82
9	23·698	·299 51	·012 63	3	6·212	·816 38	·131 42
20	23·473	·306 16	·013 04	4	5·914	·825 19	·139 54
1	23·245	·312 90	·013 46	75	5·628	·833 64	·148 13
2	23·013	·319 76	·013 89	6	5·354	·841 74	·157 22
3	22·777	·326 74	·014 35	7	5·090	·849 55	·166 90
4	22·534	·333 92	·014 82	8	4·837	·857 02	·177 18
25	22·285	·341 28	·015 31	9	4·596	·864 15	·188 02
6	22·028	·348 88	·015 83	80	4·367	·870 91	·199 43
7	21·766	·356 62	·016 39	1	4·150	·877 33	·211 41
8	21·497	·364 57	·016 96	2	3·943	·883 45	·224 06
9	21·223	·372 67	·017 56	3	3·746	·889 27	·237 39
30	20·943	·380 95	·018 19	4	3·558	·894 83	·251 50
1	20·657	·389 40	·018 85	85	3·378	·900 15	·266 48
2	20·367	·397 97	·019 54	6	3·205	·905 26	·282 46
3	20·072	·406 69	·020 26	7	3·042	·910 08	·299 17
4	19·772	·415 56	·021 02	8	2·889	·914 60	·316 58
35	19·468	·424 55	·021 81	9	2·755	·918 56	·333 42
6	19·160	·433 65	·022 63	90	2·640	·921 96	·349 23
7	18·848	·442 87	·023 50	1	2·546	·924 74	·363 22
8	18·530	·452 28	·024 41	2	2·468	·927 05	·375 63
9	18·208	·461 79	·025 37	3	2·401	·929 03	·386 94
40	17·881	·471 46	·026 37	4	2·333	·931 04	·399 08
1	17·549	·481 27	·027 42	95	2·253	·933 40	·414 30
2	17·212	·491 23	·028 54	6	2·157	·936 24	·434 05
3	16·872	·501 28	·029 71	7	2·033	·939 91	·462 33
4	16·527	·511 48	·030 95	8	1·880	·944 43	·502 36
45	16·179	·521 76	·032 25	9	1·702	·949 69	·557 99
6	15·827	·532 17	·033 62	100	1·508	·955 42	·633 57
7	15·472	·542 67	·035 07	1	1·305	·961 42	·736 74
8	15·113	·553 28	·036 61	2	1·106	·967 31	·874 62
9	14·751	·563 98	·038 24	3	·929	·972 54	
50	14·385	·574 79	·039 96	4	·771	·977 21	
1	14·017	·585 67	·041 79	105	·583	·982 77	
2	13·647	·596 61	·043 72				
3	13·276	·607 57	·045 76				
4	12·905	·618 54	·047 93				

NOTE:—The values of $\bar{a}_x$ have been calculated by the formula $\bar{a}_x = a_x + \frac{1}{2} - \frac{1}{12}(\mu_x + \delta)$, the values of $\bar{A}_x$ and ${}^{(\infty)}\bar{P}_x$ being obtained by entering continuous premium conversion tables with $\bar{a}_x$.

English Life Table No. 8—Males

Commutation Table. $3\frac{1}{2}$ per cent.

Age x	D_x	N_x	S_x	C_x	M_x	R_x	Age x
0	1 000 000	21 056 654	444 436 347	116 368	287 939	6 027 417	0
1	849 815	20 056 654	423 379 693	28 112·7	171 571	5 739 478	1
2	792 965	19 206 839	403 323 039	10 239·8	143 458	5 567 907	2
3	755 910	18 413 874	384 116 200	5 974·61	133 219	5 424 449	3
4	724 373	17 657 964	365 702 326	4 175·35	127 244	5 291 230	4
5	695 702	16 933 591	348 044 362	3 284·92	123 069	5 163 986	5
6	668 891	16 237 889	331 110 771	2 563·90	119 784	5 040 917	6
7	643 708	15 568 998	314 872 882	1 997·25	117 220	4 921 133	7
8	619 943	14 925 290	299 303 884	1 570·92	115 223	4 803 913	8
9	597 407	14 305 347	284 378 594	1 269·67	113 652	4 688 690	9
10	575 936	13 707 940	270 073 247	1 075·36	112 382	4 575 038	10
1	555 384	13 132 004	256 365 307	971·498	111 307	4 462 656	1
2	535 632	12 576 620	243 233 303	939·285	110 335	4 351 349	2
3	516 579	12 040 988	230 656 683	961·268	109 396	4 241 014	3
4	498 149	11 524 409	218 615 695	1 017·70	108 435	4 131 618	4
15	480 286	11 026 260	207 091 286	1 088·82	107 417	4 023 183	15
6	462 955	10 545 974	196 065 026	1 157·31	106 328	3 915 766	6
7	446 142	10 083 019	185 519 052	1 203·78	105 171	3 809 438	7
8	429 852	9 636 877	175 436 033	1 255·66	103 968	3 704 267	8
9	414 060	9 207 025	165 799 156	1 304·66	102 712	3 600 299	9
20	398 753	8 792 965	156 592 131	1 341·15	101 407	3 497 587	20
1	383 928	8 394 212	147 799 166	1 358·19	100 066	3 396 180	1
2	369 587	8 010 284	139 404 954	1 350·79	98 707·3	3 296 114	2
3	355 738	7 640 697	131 394 670	1 327·45	97 356·6	3 197 407	3
4	342 380	7 284 959	123 753 973	1 298·21	96 029·1	3 100 050	4
25	329 504	6 942 579	116 469 014	1 272·30	94 730·9	3 004 021	25
6	317 089	6 613 075	109 526 435	1 257·72	93 458·6	2 909 290	6
7	305 109	6 295 986	102 913 360	1 251·83	92 200·9	2 815 831	7
8	293 539	5 990 877	96 617 374	1 249·32	90 949·0	2 723 630	8
9	282 363	5 697 338	90 626 497	1 249·82	89 699·7	2 632 681	9
30	271 565	5 414 975	84 929 159	1 255·41	88 449·9	2 542 981	30
1	261 126	5 143 410	79 514 184	1 265·84	87 194·5	2 454 531	1
2	251 030	4 882 284	74 370 774	1 281·19	85 928·7	2 367 336	2
3	241 260	4 631 254	69 488 490	1 300·89	84 647·5	2 281 407	3
4	231 801	4 389 994	64 857 236	1 321·70	83 346·6	2 196 759	4
35	222 640	4 158 193	60 467 242	1 342·79	82 024·9	2 113 412	35
6	213 768	3 935 553	56 309 049	1 362·07	80 682·1	2 031 387	6
7	205 177	3 721 785	52 373 496	1 377·43	79 320·0	1 950 705	7
8	196 862	3 516 608	48 651 711	1 390·45	77 942·6	1 871 385	8
9	188 814	3 319 746	45 135 103	1 403·55	76 552·2	1 793 442	9
40	181 026	3 130 932	41 815 357	1 418·55	75 148·6	1 716 890	40
1	173 485	2 949 906	38 684 425	1 437·55	73 730·0	1 641 741	1
2	166 181	2 776 421	35 734 519	1 459·78	72 292·5	1 568 011	2
3	159 102	2 610 240	32 958 098	1 482·61	70 832·7	1 495 718	3
4	152 239	2 451 138	30 347 858	1 506·27	69 350·1	1 424 885	4
45	145 584	2 298 899	27 896 720	1 531·15	67 843·8	1 355 535	45
6	139 130	2 153 315	25 597 821	1 556·79	66 312·7	1 287 691	6
7	132 868	2 014 185	23 444 506	1 580·87	64 755·9	1 221 378	7
8	126 794	1 881 317	21 430 321	1 602·46	63 175·0	1 156 622	8
9	120 904	1 754 523	19 549 004	1 624·73	61 572·5	1 093 447	9
50	115 191	1 633 619	17 794 481	1 649·89	59 947·8	1 031 874	50
1	109 646	1 518 428	16 160 862	1 680·01	58 297·9	971 926	1
2	104 258	1 408 782	14 642 434	1 713·47	56 617·9	913 628	2
3	99 018·8	1 304 524	13 233 652	1 747·43	54 904·4	857 010	3
4	93 922·9	1 205 505	11 929 128	1 781·36	53 157·0	802 106	4

English Life Table No. 8—Males

Commutation Table. 3½ per cent.

Age x	D_x	N_x	S_x	C_x	M_x	R_x	Age x
55	88 965·4	1 111 582	10 723 623	1 814·63	51 375·6	748 949	55
6	84 142·2	1 022 617	9 612 041	1 846·72	49 561·0	697 573	6
7	79 450·1	938 475	8 589 424	1 876·19	47 714·3	648 012	7
8	74 887·3	859 025	7 650 949	1 901·94	45 838·1	600 298	8
9	70 452·9	784 138	6 791 924	1 924·58	43 936·2	554 460	9
60	66 145·8	713 685	6 007 786	1 943·87	42 011·6	510 524	60
1	61 965·1	647 539	5 294 101	1 959·90	40 067·7	468 512	1
2	57 909·8	585 574	4 646 562	1 969·87	38 107·8	428 444	2
3	53 981·7	527 664	4 060 988	1 972·72	36 137·9	390 336	3
4	50 183·4	473 682	3 533 324	1 970·89	34 165·2	354 198	4
65	46 515·6	423 499	3 059 642	1 966·40	32 194·3	320 033	65
6	42 976·1	376 983	2 636 143	1 960·07	30 227·9	287 839	6
7	39 562·8	334 007	2 259 160	1 950·27	28 267·9	257 611	7
8	36 274·6	294 444	1 925 153	1 934·05	26 317·6	229 343	8
9	33 113·9	258 169	1 630 709	1 911·03	24 383·5	203 025	9
70	30 083·1	225 055	1 372 540	1 880·49	22 472·5	178 641	70
1	27 185·3	194 972	1 147 485	1 841·93	20 592·0	156 168	1
2	24 424·0	167 787	952 513	1 796·45	18 750·1	135 576	2
3	21 801·7	143 363	784 726	1 742·68	16 953·6	116 826	3
4	19 321·7	121 561	641 363	1 677·91	15 211·0	99 872·8	4
75	16 990·4	102 240	519 802	1 600·67	13 533·1	84 661·8	75
6	14 815·2	85 249·2	417 562	1 510·69	11 932·4	71 128·7	6
7	12 803·5	70 434·0	332 313	1 410·94	10 421·7	59 196·3	7
8	10 959·6	57 630·5	261 879	1 304·53	9 010·75	48 774·6	8
9	9 284·45	46 670·9	204 248	1 191·91	7 706·22	39 763·8	9
80	7 778·59	37 386·4	157 577	1 074·68	6 514·31	32 057·6	80
1	6 440·86	29 607·8	120 191	954·905	5 439·63	25 543·3	1
2	5 268·15	23 167·0	90 583·6	835·790	4 484·72	20 103·7	2
3	4 254·21	17 898·8	67 416·6	720·637	3 648·93	15 619·0	3
4	3 389·71	13 644·6	49 517·8	612·155	2 928·30	11 970·1	4
85	2 662·93	10 254·9	35 873·2	512·364	2 316·14	9 041·80	85
6	2 060·51	7 591·97	25 618·3	421·983	1 803·78	6 725·66	6
7	1 568·85	5 531·46	18 026·3	342·942	1 381·80	4 921·88	7
8	1 172·85	3 962·61	12 494·8	274·335	1 038·85	3 540·08	8
9	858·858	2 789·76	8 532·21	214·407	764·518	2 501·23	9
90	615·408	1 930·90	5 742·45	162·893	550·111	1 736·71	90
1	431·703	1 315·49	3 811·55	119·812	387·218	1 186·60	1
2	297·292	883·790	2 496·06	85·535 4	267·406	799·383	2
3	201·704	586·498	1 612·27	59·509 3	181·871	531·977	3
4	135·374	384·794	1 025·77	40·628 6	122·361	350·106	4
95	90·167 3	249·420	640·976	27·518 7	81·732 7	227·745	95
6	59·599 3	159·253	391·556	18·519 3	54·214 0	146·012	6
7	39·064 6	99·653 6	232·303	12·535 4	35·694 7	91·797 9	7
8	25·208 2	60·589 0	132·649	8·494 64	23·159 3	56·103 2	8
9	15·861 1	35·380 8	72·059 9	5·770 82	14·664 6	32·943 9	9
100	9·553 91	19·519 7	36·679 1	3·841 02	8·893 79	18·279 3	100
1	5·389 82	9·965 75	17·159 4	2·454 10	5·052 77	9·385 49	1
2	2·753 38	4·575 93	7·193 69	1·445 80	2·598 67	4·332 72	2
3	1·214 47	1·822 55	2·617 76	·726 414	1·152 87	1·734 05	3
4	·447 024	·608 075	·795 207	·296 934	·426 457	·581 179	4
105	·134 970	·161 051	·187 132	·104 324	·129 523	·154 722	105
6	·026 081	·026 081	·026 081	·025 199	·025 199	·025 199	6

English Life Table No. 8—Males

$3\frac{1}{2}$ per cent.

Age x	a_x	A_x	P_x	Age x	a_x	A_x	P_x
1	22·601	·201 89	·008 55	55	11·495	·577 48	·046 22
2	23·222	·180 91	·007 47	6	11·153	·589 01	·048 46
3	23·360	·176 24	·007 23	7	10·812	·600 56	·050 84
4	23·377	·175 66	·007 21	8	10·471	·612 09	·053 36
5	23·340	·176 90	·007 27	9	10·130	·623 63	·056 03
6	23·276	·179 08	·007 38	60	9·790	·635 14	·058 87
7	23·186	·182 10	·007 53	1	9·450	·646 62	·061 88
8	23·075	·185 86	·007 72	2	9·112	·658 05	·065 08
9	22·946	·190 24	·007 94	3	8·775	·669 45	·068 49
10	22·801	·195 13	·008 20	4	8·439	·680 81	·072 13
1	22·645	·200 41	·008 48	65	8·104	·692 12	·076 02
2	22·480	·205 99	·008 77	6	7·772	·703 37	·080 18
3	22·309	·211 77	·009 09	7	7·442	·714 51	·084 63
4	22·134	·217 68	·009 41	8	7·117	·725 51	·089 38
15	21·958	·223 65	·009 74	9	6·796	·736 35	·094 45
6	21·780	·229 67	·010 08	70	6·481	·747 01	·099 85
7	21·600	·235 73	·010 43	1	6·172	·757 47	·105 62
8	21·419	·241 87	·010 79	2	5·870	·767 69	·111 75
9	21·236	·248 06	·011 16	3	5·576	·777 63	·118 26
20	21·051	·254 31	·011 53	4	5·291	·787 25	·125 13
1	20·864	·260 64	·011 92	75	5·017	·796 51	·132 37
2	20·674	·267 07	·012 32	6	4·754	·805 42	·139 97
3	20·478	·273 68	·012 74	7	4·501	·813 97	·147 96
4	20·277	·280 48	·013 18	8	4·258	·822 18	·156 35
25	20·070	·287 50	·013 64	9	4·027	·830 01	·165 12
6	19·856	·294 74	·014 13	80	3·806	·837 47	·174 24
7	19·635	·302 19	·014 64	1	3·597	·844 55	·183 72
8	19·409	·309 84	·015 18	2	3·398	·851 29	·193 58
9	19·177	·317 68	·015 74	3	3·207	·857 72	·203 86
30	18·940	·325 70	·016 33	4	3·025	·863 88	·214 61
1	18·697	·333 92	·016 95	85	2·851	·869 77	·225 86
2	18·449	·342 30	·017 60	6	2·685	·875 40	·237 59
3	18·196	·350 86	·018 28	7	2·526	·880 77	·249 81
4	17·939	·359 56	·018 99	8	2·379	·885 75	·262 16
35	17·677	·368 42	·019 73	9	2·248	·890 16	·274 04
6	17·410	·377 43	·020 50	90	2·138	·893 90	·284 90
7	17·139	·386 59	·021 31	1	2·047	·896 95	·294 35
8	16·863	·395 93	·022 16	2	1·973	·899 47	·302 57
9	16·582	·405 44	·023 06	3	1·908	·901 67	·310 10
40	16·295	·415 13	·024 00	4	1·842	·903 87	·317 99
1	16·004	·424 99	·024 99	95	1·766	·906 46	·327 69
2	15·707	·435 02	·026 04	6	1·672	·909 64	·340 43
3	15·406	·445 20	·027 14	7	1·551	·913 74	·358 19
4	15·101	·455 53	·028 29	8	1·404	·918 72	·382 24
45	14·791	·466 01	·029 51	9	1·231	·924 56	·414 48
6	14·477	·476 62	·030 80	100	1·043	·930 91	·455 63
7	14·159	·487 37	·032 15	1	·849	·937 47	·507 01
8	13·838	·498 25	·033 58	2	·662	·943 81	·567 90
9	13·512	·509 27	·035 09	3	·501	·949 28	·632 56
50	13·182	·520 42	·036 70	4	·360	·953 99	·701 32
1	12·848	·531 69	·038 39	105	·193	·959 64	·804 24
2	12·512	·543 06	·040 19	6		·966 18	·966 18
3	12·175	·554 48	·042 09				
4	11·835	·565 96	·044 10				

English Life Table No. 8—Males

$3\frac{1}{2}$ *per cent.*

Age x	$\bar{a}_x$	$\bar{A}_x$	${}^{(\infty)}\bar{P}_x$	Age x	$\bar{a}_x$	$\bar{A}_x$	${}^{(\infty)}\bar{P}_x$
1	23·093	·205 57	·008 90	55	11·990	·587 53	·049 00
2	23·718	·184 06	·007 76	6	11·648	·599 29	·051 45
3	23·856	·179 32	·007 52	7	11·307	·611 02	·054 04
4	23·874	·178 70	·007 49	8	10·966	·622 75	·056 79
5	23·837	·179 97	·007 55	9	10·625	·634 49	·059 72
6	23·773	·182 18	·007 66	60	10·285	·646 18	·062 83
7	23·683	·185 27	·007 82	1	9·944	·657 91	·066 16
8	23·572	·189 09	·008 02	2	9·606	·669 54	·069 70
9	23·443	·193 53	·008 26	3	9·269	·681 13	·073 48
10	23·298	·198 51	·008 52	4	8·933	·692 70	·077 54
1	23·142	·203 88	·008 81	65	8·598	·704 21	·081 90
2	22·977	·209 56	·009 12	6	8·265	·715 67	·086 59
3	22·806	·215 44	·009 45	7	7·935	·727 03	·091 62
4	22·631	·221 47	·009 79	8	7·610	·738 21	·097 01
15	22·455	·227 52	·010 13	9	7·288	·749 28	·102 81
6	22·277	·233 64	·010 49	70	6·973	·760 12	·109 01
7	22·097	·239 83	·010 85	1	6·663	·770 79	·115 68
8	21·916	·246 05	·011 23	2	6·361	·781 18	·122 81
9	21·733	·252 36	·011 61	3	6·066	·791 32	·130 45
20	21·548	·258 71	·012 01	4	5·781	·801 13	·138 58
1	21·361	·265 16	·012 41	75	5·506	·810 58	·147 22
2	21·171	·271 69	·012 83	6	5·242	·819 67	·156 37
3	20·975	·278 43	·013 27	7	4·988	·828 40	·166 08
4	20·774	·285 34	·013 74	8	4·745	·836 77	·176 35
25	20·567	·292 47	·014 22	9	4·513	·844 75	·187 18
6	20·353	·299 83	·014 73	80	4·291	·852 39	·198 65
7	20·132	·307 43	·015 27	1	4·081	·859 61	·210 64
8	19·906	·315 20	·015 83	2	3·881	·866 49	·223 26
9	19·674	·323 18	·016 43	3	3·689	·873 09	·236 67
30	19·437	·331 34	·017 05	4	3·505	·879 43	·250 91
1	19·194	·339 70	·017 70	85	3·330	·885 44	·265 90
2	18·946	·348 23	·018 38	6	3·163	·891 19	·281 75
3	18·693	·356 94	·019 09	7	3·003	·896 70	·298 60
4	18·436	·365 77	·019 84	8	2·854	·901 82	·315 98
35	18·174	·374 79	·020 62	9	2·721	·906 40	·333 11
6	17·907	·383 97	·021 44	90	2·609	·910 25	·348 89
7	17·636	·393 29	·022 30	1	2·517	·913 41	·362 90
8	17·360	·402 79	·023 20	2	2·441	·916 03	·375 27
9	17·079	·412 46	·024 15	3	2·375	·918 30	·386 65
40	16·791	·422 37	·025 15	4	2·308	·920 60	·398 87
1	16·500	·432 38	·026 20	95	2·232	·923 21	·413 62
2	16·203	·442 60	·027 32	6	2·137	·926 48	·433 54
3	15·902	·452 95	·028 48	7	2·015	·930 68	·461 88
4	15·597	·463 44	·029 71	8	1·867	·935 77	·501 22
45	15·287	·474 11	·031 01	9	1·691	·941 83	·556 97
6	14·973	·484 91	·032 39	100	1·498	·948 46	·633 15
7	14·655	·495 85	·033 83	1	1·298	·955 34	·736 01
8	14·334	·506 89	·035 36	2	1·101	·962 13	·873 87
9	14·008	·518 10	·036 99	3	·926	·968 14	1·045 51
50	13·678	·529 45	·038 71	4	·768	·973 57	1·267 67
1	13·344	·540 94	·040 54	105	·582	·979 98	1·683 81
2	13·008	·552 50	·042 47				
3	12·671	·564 10	·044 52				
4	12·331	·575 80	·046 70				

NOTE:—The values of $\bar{a}_x$ have been calculated by the formula $\bar{a}_x = a_x + \frac{1}{2} - \frac{1}{12}(\mu_x + \delta)$ the values of $\bar{A}_x$ and ${}^{(\infty)}\bar{P}_x$ being obtained by entering continuous premium conversion tables with $\bar{a}_x$.

INSTITUTE OF ACTUARIES' EXPERIENCE

HEALTHY MALES

H^M TABLE (MAKEHAM GRADUATION)

GRADUATION FUNCTIONS

(Applicable from age 28 upwards)

Constant	Common Logarithm	Napierian Logarithm
c	0·039 656 86	0·091 313 3
g	$\bar{1}$·999 543 2	$\bar{1}$·998 948 2
s	$\bar{1}$·997 310 673	$\bar{1}$·993 807 7
k	5·040 472 3	9·303 531 0

Modulus of Common Logarithms, $\cdot 434\,294\,482 = \dfrac{1}{2\cdot 302\,585\,09}$.

Base of Napierian Logarithms, 2·718 281 828.

H^M Table (Makeham Graduation)

The Life Table

Age x	l_x	d_x	q_x	p_x	μ_x	$L_x = \frac{1}{2}(l_x + l_{x+1})$	$T_x = \Sigma L_x$	$\mathring{e}_x = \frac{1}{2} + e_x$	Age x
0	127 283	14 358	·112 80	·887 20	...	120 104	6 082 031	47·784	0
1	112 925	3 962	·035 08	·964 92	·079 01	110 944	5 961 927	52·796	1
2	108 963	2 375	·021 79	·978 21	·023 66	107 776	5 850 983	53·697	2
3	106 588	1 646	·015 44	·984 56	·017 87	105 765	5 743 207	53·881	3
4	104 942	1 325	·012 63	·987 37	·013 79	104 279	5 637 442	53·719	4
5	103 617	1 061	·010 24	·989 76	·011 42	103 087	5 533 163	53·401	5
6	102 556	852	·008 30	·991 70	·009 25	102 130	5 430 076	52·948	6
7	101 704	683	·006 72	·993 28	·007 48	101 362	5 327 946	52·387	7
8	101 021	557	·005 51	·994 49	·006 07	100 743	5 226 584	51·738	8
9	100 464	464	·004 62	·995 38	·005 02	100 232	5 125 841	51·022	9
10	100 000	408	·004 09	·995 91	·004 28	99 796	5 025 609	50·257	10
1	99 592	369	·003 70	·996 30	·003 88	99 408	4 925 813	49·460	1
2	99 223	346	·003 47	·996 53	·003 59	99 050	4 826 405	48·643	2
3	98 877	337	·003 42	·996 58	·003 42	98 708	4 727 355	47·810	3
4	98 540	337	·003 42	·996 58	·003 40	98 372	4 628 647	46·973	4
15	98 203	360	·003 65	·996 35	·003 53	98 023	4 530 275	46·132	15
6	97 843	384	·003 93	·996 07	·003 78	97 651	4 432 252	45·299	6
7	97 459	425	·004 37	·995 63	·004 14	97 246	4 334 601	44·476	7
8	97 034	465	·004 78	·995 22	·004 58	96 802	4 237 355	43·669	8
9	96 569	508	·005 26	·994 74	·005 04	96 315	4 140 553	42·877	9
20	96 061	548	·005 72	·994 28	·005 50	95 787	4 044 238	42·101	20
1	95 513	582	·006 08	·993 92	·005 92	95 222	3 948 451	41·339	1
2	94 931	609	·006 43	·993 57	·006 29	94 626	3 853 229	40·590	2
3	94 322	631	·006 68	·993 32	·006 59	94 007	3 758 603	39·849	3
4	93 691	647	·006 91	·993 09	·006 82	93 367	3 664 596	39·114	4
25	93 044	658	·007 07	·992 93	·007 01	92 715	3 571 229	38·382	25
6	92 386	664	·007 20	·992 80	·007 16	92 054	3 478 514	37·652	6
7	91 722	673	·007 32	·992 68	·007 29	91 386	3 386 460	36·921	7
8	91 049	678	·007 46	·992 54	·007 42	90 710	3 295 074	36·189	8
9	90 371	686	·007 59	·992 41	·007 55	90 028	3 204 364	35·458	9
30	89 685	691	·007 71	·992 29	·007 68	89 339	3 114 336	34·726	30
1	88 994	700	·007 87	·992 13	·007 82	88 644	3 024 997	33·991	1
2	88 294	709	·008 03	·991 97	·007 98	87 940	2 936 353	33·257	2
3	87 585	719	·008 21	·991 79	·008 15	87 225	2 848 413	32·521	3
4	86 866	729	·008 39	·991 61	·008 33	86 502	2 761 188	31·787	4
35	86 137	742	·008 62	·991 38	·008 54	85 766	2 674 686	31·051	35
6	85 395	756	·008 85	·991 15	·008 76	85 017	2 588 920	30·317	6
7	84 639	770	·009 10	·990 90	·009 01	84 254	2 503 903	29·584	7
8	83 869	786	·009 37	·990 63	·009 28	83 476	2 419 649	28·850	8
9	83 083	806	·009 69	·990 31	·009 57	82 680	2 336 173	28·118	9
40	82 277	823	·010 01	·989 99	·009 90	81 865	2 253 493	27·389	40
1	81 454	846	·010 38	·989 62	·010 25	81 031	2 171 628	26·661	1
2	80 608	871	·010 81	·989 19	·010 64	80 173	2 090 597	25·935	2
3	79 737	895	·011 22	·988 78	·011 06	79 289	2 010 424	25·214	3
4	78 842	924	·011 72	·988 28	·011 53	78 380	1 931 135	24·493	4
45	77 918	954	·012 24	·987 76	·012 04	77 441	1 852 755	23·778	45
6	76 964	986	·012 81	·987 19	·012 60	76 471	1 775 314	23·066	6
7	75 978	1 021	·013 45	·986 55	·013 21	75 468	1 698 843	22·360	7
8	74 957	1 061	·014 15	·985 85	·013 88	74 426	1 623 375	21·658	8
9	73 896	1 101	·014 90	·985 10	·014 62	73 346	1 548 949	20·961	9

Note :—(i) This Table does not follow Makeham's Law of Mortality below age 28.
(ii) The method employed in the construction of the Table at the younger ages does not give a suitable value for μ_0, and this value is therefore omitted.

H^M Table (Makeham Graduation)

The Life Table

Age x	l_x	d_x	q_x	p_x	μ_x	$L_x = \frac{1}{2}(l_x + l_{x+1})$	$T_x = \Sigma L_x$	$\mathring{e}_x = \frac{1}{2} + e_x$	Age x
50	72 795	1 144	·015 72	·984 28	·015 42	72 223	1 475 603	20·271	50
1	71 651	1 193	·016 65	·983 35	·016 31	71 054	1 403 380	19·587	1
2	70 458	1 243	·017 64	·982 36	·017 27	69 837	1 332 326	18·909	2
3	69 215	1 296	·018 73	·981 27	·018 33	68 567	1 262 489	18·240	3
4	67 919	1 353	·019 92	·980 08	·019 50	67 242	1 193 922	17·579	4
55	66 566	1 414	·021 23	·978 77	·020 77	65 859	1 126 680	16·926	55
6	65 152	1 475	·022 65	·977 35	·022 16	64 415	1 060 821	16·282	6
7	63 677	1 541	·024 20	·975 80	·023 69	62 906	996 406	15·648	7
8	62 136	1 612	·025 93	·974 07	·025 36	61 330	933 500	15·023	8
9	60 524	1 682	·027 79	·972 21	·027 19	59 683	872 170	14·410	9
60	58 842	1 755	·029 83	·970 17	·029 20	57 965	812 487	13·808	60
1	57 087	1 830	·032 06	·967 94	·031 40	56 172	754 522	13·217	1
2	55 257	1 906	·034 51	·965 49	·033 81	54 304	698 350	12·638	2
3	53 351	1 983	·037 17	·962 83	·036 45	52 359	644 046	12·072	3
4	51 368	2 059	·040 07	·959 93	·039 34	50 339	591 687	11·519	4
65	49 309	2 133	·043 27	·956 73	·042 51	48 242	541 348	10·979	65
6	47 176	2 204	·046 72	·953 28	·045 99	46 074	493 106	10·452	6
7	44 972	2 273	·050 53	·949 47	·049 79	43 836	447 032	9·940	7
8	42 699	2 334	·054 66	·945 34	·053 96	41 532	403 196	9·443	8
9	40 365	2 388	·059 17	·940 83	·058 53	39 171	361 664	8·960	9
70	37 977	2 434	·064 10	·935 90	·063 53	36 760	322 493	8·492	70
1	35 543	2 468	·069 43	·930 57	·069 01	34 309	285 733	8·039	1
2	33 075	2 490	·075 28	·924 72	·075 02	31 830	251 424	7·602	2
3	30 585	2 496	·081 60	·918 40	·081 60	29 337	219 594	7·180	3
4	28 089	2 487	·088 56	·911 44	·088 81	26 845	190 257	6·773	4
75	25 602	2 459	·096 04	·903 96	·096 71	24 373	163 412	6·383	75
6	23 143	2 412	·104 22	·895 78	·105 36	21 937	139 039	6·008	6
7	20 731	2 343	·113 03	·886 97	·114 85	19 559	117 102	5·649	7
8	18 388	2 255	·122 62	·877 38	·125 23	17 261	97 543	5·305	8
9	16 133	2 146	·133 04	·866 96	·136 62	15 060	80 282	4·976	9
80	13 987	2 018	·144 26	·855 74	·149 09	12 978	65 222	4·663	80
1	11 969	1 873	·156 49	·843 51	·162 75	11 033	52 244	4·365	1
2	10 096	1 712	·169 58	·830 42	·177 72	9 240	41 211	4·082	2
3	8 384	1 540	·183 68	·816 32	·194 12	7 614	31 971	3·813	3
4	6 844	1 361	·198 86	·801 14	·212 09	6 164	24 357	3·559	4
85	5 483	1 180	·215 22	·784 78	·231 77	4 893	18 193	3·318	85
6	4 303	1 002	·232 85	·767 15	·253 43	3 802	13 300	3·091	6
7	3 301	830	·251 45	·748 55	·276 97	2 886	9 498	2·877	7
8	2 471	671	·271 55	·728 45	·302 86	2 135	6 612	2·676	8
9	1 800	527	·292 77	·707 23	·331 23	1 537	4 477	2·487	9
90	1 273	402	·315 79	·684 21	·362 30	1 072	2 940	2·310	90
1	871	296	·339 84	·660 16	·396 35	723	1 868	2·145	1
2	575	209	·363 48	·636 52	·433 66	470	1 145	1·992	2
3	366	144	·393 45	·606 55	·474 53	294	675	1·844	3
4	222	93	·418 91	·581 09	·519 30	176	381	1·716	4
95	129	58	·449 61	·550 39	·568 36	100	205	1·593	95
6	71	34	·478 88	·521 12	·622 11	54	105	1·486	6
7	37	18	·486 49	·513 51	·681 00	28	51	1·392	7
8	19	10	·526 31	·473 69	·745 52	14	23	1·237	8
9	9	5	·555 55	·444 45	·816 21	6	9	1·056	9
100	4	3	·750 00	·250 00	·893 66	3	3	0·750	100
1	1	1	1·000 00	·000 00	·978 51	0	...	0·500	1
2	0	...	...	...	∞	...	...	0·000	2

H^M Table (Makeham Graduation)

Elementary Values derived from the Life Table

Age x	log l_x	Δ log l_x = log p_x	log μ_x	Age x	log l_x	Δ log l_x = log p_x	log μ_x
0	5·104 77	$\bar{1}$·948 02	...	50	4·862 10	$\bar{1}$·993 12	$\bar{2}$·188 08
1	·052 79	·984 49	$\bar{2}$·897 68	1	·855 22	·992 71	·212 45
2	·037 28	·990 43	·374 01	2	·847 93	·992 27	·237 29
3	·027 71	·993 24	·252 12	3	·840 20	·991 79	·263 16
4	·020 95	·994 48	·139 56	4	·831 99	·991 26	·290 03
5	·015 43	·995 53	·057 67	55	·823 25	·990 68	·317 44
6	·010 96	·996 38	$\bar{3}$·966 14	6	·813 93	·990 05	·345 57
7	·007 34	·997 07	·873 90	7	·803 98	·989 36	·374 57
8	·004 41	·997 60	·783 19	8	·793 34	·988 59	·404 15
9	·002 01	·997 99	·700 70	9	·781 93	·987 76	·434 41
10	·000 00	·998 22	·631 44	60	·769 69	·986 85	·465 38
1	4·998 22	·998 39	·588 83	1	·756 54	·985 85	·496 93
2	·996 61	·998 49	·555 09	2	·742 39	·984 75	·529 05
3	·995 10	·998 51	·534 03	3	·727 14	·983 55	·561 70
4	·993 61	·998 51	·531 48	4	·710 69	·982 24	·594 83
15	·992 12	·998 41	·547 77	65	·692 93	·980 79	·628 49
6	·990 53	·998 29	·577 49	6	·673 72	·979 22	·662 66
7	·988 82	·998 10	·617 00	7	·652 94	·977 48	·697 14
8	·986 92	·997 92	·660 87	8	·630 42	·975 59	·732 07
9	·984 84	·997 71	·702 43	9	·606 01	·973 51	·767 38
20	·982 55	·997 51	·740 36	70	·579 52	·971 23	·802 98
1	·980 06	·997 35	·772 32	1	·550 75	·968 75	·838 91
2	·977 41	·997 20	·798 65	2	·519 50	·966 01	·875 18
3	·974 61	·997 09	·818 89	3	·485 51	·963 03	·911 69
4	·971 70	·996 99	·833 78	4	·448 54	·959 73	·948 46
25	·968 69	·996 92	·845 72	75	·408 27	·956 15	·985 47
6	·965 61	·996 86	·854 91	6	·364 42	·952 20	$\bar{1}$·022 68
7	·962 47	·996 81	·862 73	7	·316 62	·947 91	·060 13
8	·959 28	·996 75	·870 40	8	·264 53	·943 19	·097 71
9	·956 03	·996 69	·877 95	9	·207 72	·938 00	·135 51
30	·952 72	·996 64	·885 36	80	·145 72	·932 34	·173 45
1	·949 36	·996 57	·893 21	1	·078 06	·926 09	·211 52
2	·945 93	·996 50	·902 00	2	·004 15	·919 30	·249 74
3	·942 43	·996 42	·911 16	3	3·923 45	·911 86	·288 07
4	·938 85	·996 34	·920 65	4	·835 31	·903 71	·326 52
35	·935 19	·996 24	·931 46	85	·739 02	·894 75	·365 06
6	·931 43	·996 14	·942 50	6	·633 77	·884 88	·403 70
7	·927 57	·996 03	·954 72	7	·518 65	·874 22	·442 43
8	·923 60	·995 91	·967 55	8	·392 87	·862 40	·481 24
9	·919 51	·995 77	·980 91	9	·255 27	·849 56	·520 13
40	·915 28	·995 63	·995 64	90	·104 83	·835 19	·559 07
1	·910 91	·995 47	$\bar{2}$·010 72	1	2·940 02	·819 65	·598 08
2	·906 38	·995 28	·026 94	2	·759 67	·803 81	·637 15
3	·901 66	·995 10	·043 76	3	·563 48	·782 87	·676 26
4	·896 76	·994 88	·061 83	4	·346 35	·764 24	·715 42
45	·891 64	·994 65	·080 63	95	·110 59	·740 67	·754 62
6	·886 29	·994 40	·100 37	6	1·851 26	·716 94	·793 87
7	·880 69	·994 12	·120 90	7	·568 20	·710 55	·833 15
8	·874 81	·993 81	·142 39	8	·278 75	·675 49	·872 46
9	·868 62	·993 48	·164 95	9	0·954 24	·647 82	·911 80
				100	·602 06	·397 94	·951 17
				1	·000 00	...	·990 57

H^M Table (Makeham Graduation)

Curtate Expectations of Life. Joint Lives. Equal Ages

Age x	Two Lives e_{xx}	Three Lives e_{xxx}	Four Lives e_{xxxx}	Age x	Two Lives e_{xx}	Three Lives e_{xxx}	Four Lives e_{xxxx}
0	30·716	21·291	15·270	50	13·874	10·891	9·014
1	38·023	29·488	23·646	1	13·321	10·421	8·604
2	39·839	31·823	26·278	2	12·776	9·959	8·201
3	40·634	32·997	27·699	3	12·239	9·505	7·806
4	40·919	33·576	28·479	4	11·710	9·060	7·419
5	40·972	33·881	28·964	55	11·191	8·623	7·042
6	40·824	33·944	29·182	6	10·682	8·197	6·673
7	40·512	33·803	29·171	7	10·183	7·780	6·313
8	40·061	33·494	28·968	8	9·694	7·374	5·963
9	39·507	33·054	28·616	9	9·217	6·978	5·623
10	38·874	32·516	28·151	60	8·752	6·594	5·295
1	38·194	31·918	27·616	1	8·298	6·221	4·976
2	37·477	31·275	27·029	2	7·857	5·860	4·669
3	36·740	30·603	26·407	3	7·429	5·511	4·373
4	35·992	29·920	25·772	4	7·013	5·174	4·089
15	35·240	29·229	25·128	65	6·611	4·849	3·815
6	34·499	28·552	24·499	6	6·222	4·537	3·554
7	33·771	27·891	23·887	7	5·847	4·238	3·303
8	33·069	27·260	23·309	8	5·486	3·951	3·064
9	32·387	26·654	22·760	9	5·139	3·677	2·837
20	31·730	26·080	22·246	70	4·806	3·415	2·621
1	31·096	25·531	21·761	1	4·486	3·166	2·416
2	30·478	25·003	21·299	2	4·181	2·929	2·222
3	29·874	24·492	20·856	3	3·889	2·704	2·038
4	29·277	23·989	20·422	4	3·611	2·491	1·865
25	28·686	23·493	19·996	75	3·347	2·289	1·702
6	28·095	22·998	19·571	6	3·095	2·099	1·550
7	27·504	22·503	19·147	7	2·858	1·921	1·407
8	26·912	22·004	18·716	8	2·632	1·752	1·273
9	26·317	21·504	18·285	9	2·419	1·594	1·147
30	25·722	21·000	17·851	80	2·219	1·447	1·031
1	25·123	20·493	17·412	1	2·030	1·308	0·923
2	24·522	19·985	16·971	2	1·853	1·180	·823
3	23·921	19·474	16·528	3	1·687	1·060	·731
4	23·319	18·962	16·082	4	1·532	0·949	·646
35	22·715	18·448	15·633	85	1·386	·847	·567
6	22·111	17·933	15·184	6	1·251	·751	·495
7	21·508	17·418	14·733	7	1·125	·664	·430
8	20·906	16·902	14·282	8	1·008	·584	·371
9	20·302	16·386	13·830	9	0·900	·510	·317
40	19·702	15·872	13·380	90	·800	·443	·269
1	19·102	15·358	12·929	1	·708	·382	·226
2	18·505	14·846	12·480	2	·625	·329	·189
3	17·911	14·338	12·035	3	·543	·275	·152
4	17·321	13·832	11·590	4	·477	·234	·125
45	16·734	13·330	11·150	95	·413	·194	·099
6	16·151	12·832	10·713	6	·363	·163	·079
7	15·573	12·338	10·280	7	·335	·151	·073
8	15·001	11·850	9·852	8	·271	·116	·052
9	14·434	11·367	9·430	9	·210	·089	·039
				100	·063	·016	·004
				1	·000	·000	·000

H^M TABLE (MAKEHAM GRADUATION)

THREE PER CENT.

INTEREST CONSTANTS

Constant	Number	Logarithm
i	·03	$\bar{2}$·477 121 3
$(1+i)$	1·03	0·012 837 2
$(1+i)^{\frac{1}{2}}$	1·014 889 2	0·006 418 6
$(1+i)^{\frac{1}{4}}$	1·007 417 1	0·003 209 3
v	0·970 873 8	$\bar{1}$·987 162 8
$v^{\frac{1}{2}}$	0·985 329 3	$\bar{1}$·993 581 4
$v^{\frac{1}{4}}$	0·992 637 5	$\bar{1}$·996 790 7
d	0·029 126 2	$\bar{2}$·464 284 0
δ	0·029 558 8	$\bar{2}$·470 686 8
$j_{(2)}$	0·029 778 3	$\bar{2}$·473 899 9
$j_{(4)}$	0·029 668 3	$\bar{2}$·472 292 7

H^M Table (Makeham Graduation)

Commutation Table. **3** *per cent.*

Age x	D_x	N_x	S_x	C_x	M_x	R_x	Age x
0	127 283	2 815 304	61 758 474	13 940	45 284	1 016 517	0
1	109 636	2 688 021	58 943 170	3 734·6	31 344·2	971 233·2	1
2	102 708	2 578 385	56 255 149	2 173·5	27 609·6	939 889·0	2
3	97 544	2 475 677	53 676 764	1 462·4	25 436·1	912 279·4	3
4	93 240	2 378 133	51 201 087	1 143·0	23 973·7	886 843·3	4
5	89 380	2 284 893	48 822 954	888·59	22 830·68	862 869·57	5
6	85 889	2 195 513	46 538 061	692·76	21 942·09	840 038·89	6
7	82 695	2 109 624	44 342 548	539·16	21 249·33	818 096·80	7
8	79 746	2 026 929	42 232 924	426·89	20 710·17	796 847·47	8
9	76 996	1 947 183	40 205 995	345·26	20 283·28	776 137·30	9
10	74 410	1 870 187	38 258 812	294·75	19 938·02	755 854·02	10
1	71 947	1 795 777	36 388 625	258·81	19 643·27	735 916·00	1
2	69 592	1 723 830	34 592 848	235·61	19 384·46	716 272·73	2
3	67 332	1 654 238	32 869 018	222·80	19 148·85	696 888·27	3
4	65 146	1 586 906	31 214 780	216·31	18 926·05	677 739·42	4
15	63 032	1 521 760	29 627 874	224·34	18 709·74	658 813·37	15
6	60 972	1 458 728	28 106 114	232·33	18 485·40	640 103·63	6
7	58 964	1 397 756	26 647 386	249·64	18 253·07	621 618·23	7
8	56 997	1 338 792	25 249 630	265·18	18 003·43	603 365·16	8
9	55 072	1 281 795	23 910 838	281·27	17 738·25	585 361·73	9
20	53 188	1 226 723	22 629 043	294·58	17 456·98	567 623·48	20
1	51 343	1 173 535	21 402 320	303·74	17 162·40	550 166·50	1
2	49 544	1 122 192	20 228 785	308·57	16 858·66	533 004·10	2
3	47 791	1 072 648	19 106 593	310·41	16 550·09	516 145·44	3
4	46 090	1 024 857	18 033 945	309·01	16 239·68	499 595·35	4
25	44 439	978 767	17 009 088	305·11	15 930·67	483 355·67	25
6	42 839	934 328	16 030 321	298·92	15 625·56	467 425·00	6
7	41 291	891 489	15 095 993	294·16	15 326·64	451 799·44	7
8	39 796	850 198	14 204 504	287·71	15 032·48	436 472·80	8
9	38 349	810 402	13 354 306	282·62	14 744·77	421 440·32	9
30	36 949	772 053	12 543 904	276·39	14 462·15	406 695·55	30
1	35 597	735 104	11 771 851	271·84	14 185·76	392 233·40	1
2	34 288	699 507	11 036 747	267·31	13 913·92	378 047·64	2
3	33 022	665 219	10 337 240	263·18	13 646·61	364 133·72	3
4	31 797	632 197	9 672 021	259·08	13 383·43	350 487·11	4
35	30 612	600 400	9 039 824	256·01	13 124·35	337 103·68	35
6	29 464	569 788	8 439 424	253·24	12 868·34	323 979·33	6
7	28 352	540 324	7 869 636	250·43	12 615·10	311 110·99	7
8	27 277	511 972	7 329 312	248·18	12 364·67	298 495·89	8
9	26 234	484 695	6 817 340	247·09	12 116·49	286 131·22	9
40	25 223	458 461	6 332 645	244·95	11 869·40	274 014·73	40
1	24 243	433 238	5 874 184	244·46	11 624·45	262 145·33	1
2	23 293	408 995	5 440 946	244·35	11 379·99	250 520·88	2
3	22 370	385 702	5 031 951	243·77	11 135·64	239 140·89	3
4	21 474	363 332	4 646 249	244·34	10 891·87	228 005·25	4
45	20 604	341 858	4 282 917	244·93	10 647·53	217 113·38	45
6	19 760	321 254	3 941 059	245·77	10 402·60	206 465·85	6
7	18 938	301 494	3 619 805	247·08	10 156·83	196 063·25	7
8	18 139	282 556	3 318 311	249·29	9 909·75	185 906·42	8
9	17 362	264 417	3 035 755	251·15	9 660·46	175 996·67	9

H^M Table (Makeham Graduation)

Commutation Table. **3** *per cent.*

Age x	D_x	N_x	S_x	C_x	M_x	R_x	Age x
50	16 605	247 055	2 771 338	253·36	9 409·31	166 336·21	50
1	15 868	230 450	2 524 283	256·51	9 155·95	156 926·90	1
2	15 149	214 582	2 293 833	259·48	8 899·44	147 770·95	2
3	14 449	199 433	2 079 251	262·66	8 639·96	138 871·51	3
4	13 765	184 984	1 879 818	266·23	8 377·30	130 231·55	4
55	13 098	171 219	1 694 834	270·13	8 111·07	121 854·25	55
6	12 447	158 121	1 523 615	273·57	7 840·94	113 743·18	6
7	11 810	145 674	1 365 494	277·49	7 567·37	105 902·24	7
8	11 189	133 864	1 219 820	281·82	7 289·88	98 334·87	8
9	10 581	122 675	1 085 956	285·50	7 008·06	91 044·99	9
60	9 987·6	112 093·8	963 280·6	289·21	6 722·56	84 036·93	60
1	9 407·4	102 106·2	851 186·8	292·78	6 433·35	77 314·37	1
2	8 840·6	92 698·8	749 080·6	296·05	6 140·57	70 881·02	2
3	8 286·9	83 858·2	656 381·8	299·05	5 844·52	64 740·45	3
4	7 746·6	75 571·3	572 523·6	301·47	5 545·47	58 895·93	4
65	7 219·5	67 824·7	496 952·3	303·20	5 244·00	53 350·46	65
6	6 705·9	60 605·2	429 127·6	304·17	4 940·80	48 106·46	6
7	6 206·5	53 899·3	368 522·4	304·56	4 636·63	43 165·66	7
8	5 721·2	47 692·8	314 623·1	303·62	4 332·07	38 529·03	8
9	5 251·0	41 971·6	266 930·3	301·59	4 028·45	34 196·96	9
70	4 796·3	36 720·6	224 958·7	298·46	3 726·86	30 168·51	70
1	4 358·2	31 924·3	188 238·1	293·81	3 428·40	26 441·65	1
2	3 937·5	27 566·1	156 313·8	287·79	3 134·59	23 013·25	2
3	3 535·0	23 628·6	128 747·7	280·09	2 846·80	19 878·66	3
4	3 152·0	20 093·6	105 119·1	270·95	2 566·71	17 031·86	4
75	2 789·2	16 941·6	85 025·5	260·09	2 295·76	14 465·15	75
6	2 447·9	14 152·4	68 083·9	247·69	2 035·67	12 169·39	6
7	2 128·9	11 704·5	53 931·5	233·60	1 787·98	10 133·72	7
8	1 833·3	9 575·6	42 227·0	218·28	1 554·38	8 345·74	8
9	1 561·6	7 742·3	32 651·4	201·67	1 336·10	6 791·36	9
80	1 314·4	6 180·7	24 909·1	184·12	1 134·43	5 455·26	80
1	1 092·0	4 866·3	18 728·4	165·92	950·31	4 320·83	1
2	894·33	3 774·27	13 862·06	147·23	784·39	3 370·52	2
3	721·04	2 879·94	10 087·79	128·58	637·16	2 586·13	3
4	571·45	2 158·90	7 207·85	110·33	508·58	1 948·97	4
85	444·49	1 587·45	5 048·95	92·871	398·246	1 440·392	85
6	338·66	1 142·96	3 461·50	76·565	305·375	1 042·146	6
7	252·24	804·30	2 318·54	61·574	228·810	736·771	7
8	183·31	552·06	1 514·24	48·329	167·236	507·961	8
9	129·65	368·75	962·18	36·852	118·907	340·725	9
90	89·018	239·100	593·425	27·292	82·055	221·818	90
1	59·133	150·082	354·325	19·511	54·763	139·763	1
2	37·901	90·949	204·243	13·375	35·252	85·000	2
3	23·422	53·048	113·294	8·946 6	21·876 5	49·747 6	3
4	13·793	29·626	60·246	5·609 7	12·929 9	27·871 1	4
95	7·781	15·833	30·620	3·396 7	7·320 2	14·941 2	95
6	4·158	8·052	14·787	1·933 2	3·923 5	7·621 0	6
7	2·104	3·894	6·735	·993 6	1·990 3	3·697 5	7
8	1·049	1·790	2·841	·535 9	·996 7	1·707 2	8
9	·482	·741	1·051	·260 2	·460 8	·710 5	9
100	·208	·259	·310	·151 5	·200 6	·249 7	100
1	·051	·051	·051	·049 1	·049 1	·049 1	1

H^M TABLE (MAKEHAM GRADUATION)

Logarithms of D_x, N_x, *and* M_x. **3** *per cent.*

Age x	log D_x	log N_x	log M_x	Age x	log D_x	log N_x	log M_x
0	5·104 77	6·449 53	4·655 94	50	4·220 24	5·392 80	3·973 56
1	·039 95	·429 43	·496 15	1	·200 52	·362 58	·961 71
2	·011 61	·411 35	·441 07	2	·180 39	·331 59	·949 36
3	4·989 20	·393 70	·405 45	3	·159 83	·299 79	·936 51
4	·969 60	·376 23	·379 74	4	·138 78	·267 12	·923 10
5	·951 24	·358 87	·358 52	55	·117 20	·233 55	·909 08
6	·933 94	·341 53	·341 28	6	·095 05	·198 99	·894 37
7	·917 48	·324 20	·327 34	7	·072 26	·163 37	·878 95
8	·901 71	·306 83	·316 18	8	·048 78	·126 65	·862 72
9	·886 47	·289 41	·307 13	9	·024 53	·088 77	·845 60
10	·871 63	·271 89	·299 68	60	3·999 46	·049 57	·827 54
1	·857 01	·254 26	·293 21	1	·973 47	·009 07	·808 44
2	·842 56	·236 49	·287 47	2	·946 48	4·967 08	·788 21
3	·828 22	·218 59	·282 15	3	·918 39	·923 54	·766 75
4	·813 89	·200 55	·277 06	4	·889 11	·878 36	·743 94
15	·799 56	·182 36	·272 07	65	·858 51	·831 39	·719 66
6	·785 13	·163 97	·266 82	6	·826 46	·782 51	·693 80
7	·770 59	·145 45	·261 33	7	·792 85	·731 58	·666 20
8	·755 85	·126 72	·255 34	8	·757 49	·678 45	·636 70
9	·740 93	·107 82	·248 90	9	·720 24	·622 96	·605 14
20	·725 81	·088 74	·241 97	70	·680 91	·564 91	·571 35
1	·710 48	·069 48	·234 57	1	·639 31	·504 12	·535 09
2	·694 99	·050 07	·226 83	2	·595 22	·440 37	·496 18
3	·679 35	·030 44	·218 80	3	·548 39	·373 45	·454 36
4	·663 61	·010 68	·210 59	4	·498 59	·303 07	·409 38
25	·647 76	5·990 68	·202 24	75	·445 48	·228 96	·360 93
6	·631 84	·970 50	·193 85	6	·388 79	·150 82	·308 71
7	·615 86	·950 12	·185 46	7	·328 15	·068 37	·252 37
8	·599 84	·929 52	·177 02	8	·263 23	3·981 17	·191 56
9	·583 75	·908 70	·168 64	9	·193 58	·888 87	·125 84
30	·567 60	·887 65	·160 23	80	·118 74	·791 04	·054 77
1	·551 41	·866 35	·151 86	1	·038 24	·687 20	2·977 87
2	·535 14	·844 79	·143 45	2	2·951 50	·576 84	·894 53
3	·518 80	·822 97	·135 04	3	·857 96	·459 38	·804 25
4	·502 38	·800 85	·126 55	4	·756 98	·334 23	·706 36
35	·485 89	·778 44	·118 07	85	·647 86	·200 71	·600 16
6	·469 29	·755 71	·109 51	6	·529 77	·058 05	·484 83
7	·452 59	·732 65	·100 89	7	·401 81	2·905 42	·359 48
8	·435 79	·709 24	·092 19	8	·263 19	·741 99	·223 34
9	·418 86	·685 47	·083 36	9	·112 76	·566 73	·075 22
40	·401 79	·661 30	·074 41	90	1·949 48	·378 58	1·914 11
1	·384 58	·636 73	·065 36	1	·771 83	·176 32	·738 49
2	·367 22	·611 72	·056 14	2	·578 65	1·958 80	·547 18
3	·349 66	·586 25	·046 73	3	·369 62	·724 67	·339 99
4	·331 92	·560 30	·037 11	4	·139 65	·471 67	·111 60
45	·313 96	·533 85	·027 27	95	0·891 05	·199 56	0·864 52
6	·295 78	·506 84	·017 16	6	·618 89	0·905 90	·593 67
7	·277 34	·479 27	·006 77	7	·322 99	·590 40	·298 92
8	·258 62	·451 11	3·996 06	8	·020 70	·252 85	$\bar{1}$·998 56
9	·239 60	·422 29	·985 00	9	$\bar{1}$·683 35	$\bar{1}$·869 82	·663 51
				100	·318 34	·413 30	·302 33
				1	$\bar{2}$·703 44	$\bar{2}$·703 44	$\bar{2}$·690 64

H^M Table (Makeham Graduation)

Values of Annuities, and Single and Annual Premiums for Assurance of a Unit

3 *per cent.*

Age x	a_x	A_x	P_x	Age x	a_x	A_x	P_x
1	23·517 70	·285 89	·011 66	50	13·878 28	·566 66	·038 09
2	24·104 01	·268 82	·010 71	1	13·522 86	·577 02	·039 73
3	24·380 34	·260 77	·010 27	2	13·164 39	·587 45	·041 47
4	24·505 62	·257 12	·010 08	3	12·802 83	·597 97	·043 32
5	24·563 55	·255 43	·009 99	4	12·438 53	·608 58	·045 29
6	24·562 20	·255 47	·009 99	55	12·072 10	·619 27	·047 37
7	24·511 00	·256 96	·010 07	6	11·704 13	·629 97	·049 59
8	24·417 03	·259 70	·010 22	7	11·334 50	·640 75	·051 95
9	24·288 97	·263 43	·010 42	8	10·964 07	·651 54	·054 46
10	24·133 73	·267 95	·010 66	9	10·593 76	·662 32	·057 13
1	23·959 56	·273 02	·010 94	60	10·223 49	·673 10	·059 97
2	23·770 13	·278 55	·011 25	1	9·853 91	·683 86	·063 00
3	23·568 91	·284 40	·011 58	2	9·485 66	·694 59	·066 24
4	23·359 00	·290 52	·011 93	3	9·119 29	·705 28	·069 70
15	23·142 35	·296 83	·012 29	4	8·755 46	·715 86	·073 38
6	22·924 31	·303 17	·012 67	65	8·394 70	·726 36	·077 32
7	22·705 07	·309 56	·013 06	6	8·037 48	·736 78	·081 53
8	22·488 67	·315 86	·013 45	7	7·684 33	·747 05	·086 02
9	22·274 87	·322 08	·013 84	8	7·336 19	·757 20	·090 83
20	22·064 43	·328 22	·014 23	9	6·993 19	·767 18	·095 98
1	21·856 75	·334 26	·014 63	70	6·655 91	·777 03	·101 49
2	21·650 46	·340 28	·015 02	1	6·325 07	·786 65	·107 39
3	21·443 97	·346 30	·015 43	2	6·000 94	·796 09	·113 71
4	21·236 04	·352 35	·015 85	3	5·684 18	·805 32	·120 48
25	21·025 22	·358 49	·016 28	4	5·374 95	·814 31	·127 74
6	20·810 21	·364 76	·016 72	75	5·073 99	·823 10	·135 51
7	20·589 70	·371 19	·017 19	6	4·781 51	·831 61	·143 84
8	20·364 15	·377 73	·017 68	7	4·497 96	·839 89	·152 76
9	20·132 44	·384 49	·018 19	8	4·223 23	·847 87	·162 33
30	19·895 02	·391 41	·018 73	9	3·957 94	·855 58	·172 57
1	19·650 98	·398 52	·019 30	80	3·702 15	·863 04	·183 54
2	19·400 98	·405 80	·019 89	1	3·456 13	·870 22	·195 29
3	19·144 77	·413 28	·020 52	2	3·220 23	·877 06	·207 82
4	18·882 33	·420 89	·021 17	3	2·994 13	·883 67	·221 24
35	18·613 40	·428 73	·021 86	4	2·777 89	·889 98	·235 58
6	18·338 39	·436 74	·022 58	85	2·571 45	·895 98	·250 87
7	18·057 25	·444 94	·023 35	6	2·374 90	·901 70	·267 17
8	17·769 73	·453 31	·024 15	7	2·188 66	·907 13	·284 49
9	17·475 98	·461 85	·025 00	8	2·011 54	·912 33	·302 94
40	17·176 58	·470 57	·025 89	9	1·844 24	·917 19	·322 47
1	16·870 63	·479 49	·026 83	90	1·685 96	·921 79	·343 19
2	16·559 13	·488 56	·027 82	1	1·538 02	·926 10	·364 90
3	16·242 22	·497 82	·028 87	2	1·399 66	·930 10	·387 60
4	15·919 39	·507 21	·029 98	3	1·264 88	·934 05	·412 40
45	15·591 42	·516 79	·031 15	4	1·147 91	·937 45	·436 45
6	15·258 22	·526 48	·032 38	95	1·034 73	·940 74	·462 34
7	14·919 92	·536 33	·033 69	6	·936 40	·943 58	·487 27
8	14·576 84	·546 31	·035 07	7	·850 78	·946 08	·511 12
9	14·229 71	·556 42	·036 54	8	·706 49	·950 30	·556 81
				9	·536 23	·955 34	·621 86
				100	·242 72	·963 81	·774 52
				1	...	·970 87	·970 87

H^M TABLE (MAKEHAM GRADUATION)

Logarithms of D *and* N. *Joint Lives. Equal Ages*

3 *per cent.*

Age x	Two Lives log D_{xx}	Two Lives log N_{xx}	Three Lives log D_{xxx}	Three Lives log N_{xxx}	Four Lives log D_{xxxx}	Four Lives log N_{xxxx}	Age x
0	10·209 54	11·424 55	15·314 31	16·412 41	20·419 08	21·409 16	0
1	·092 74	·397 24	·145 53	·376 30	·198 32	·362 29	1
2	·048 89	·375 15	·086 17	·350 00	·123 45	·331 45	2
3	·016 91	·354 17	·044 62	·325 66	·072 33	·303 67	3
4	9·990 55	·333 71	·011 50	·302 31	·032 45	·277 40	4
5	·966 67	·313 55	14·982 10	·279 48	19·997 53	·251 95	5
6	·944 90	·293 56	·955 86	·257 03	·966 82	·227 09	6
7	·924 82	·273 65	·932 16	·234 75	·939 50	·202 54	7
8	·906 12	·253 75	·910 53	·212 56	·914 94	·178 18	8
9	·888 48	·233 78	·890 49	·190 33	·892 50	·153 81	9
10	·871 63	·213 73	·871 63	·168 00	·871 63	·129 37	10
1	·855 23	·193 51	·853 45	·145 48	·851 67	·104 69	1
2	·839 17	·173 10	·835 78	·122 71	·832 39	·079 72	2
3	·823 32	·152 50	·818 42	·099 68	·813 52	·054 42	3
4	·807 50	·131 65	·801 11	·076 35	·794 72	·028 73	4
15	·791 68	·110 56	·783 80	·052 66	·775 92	·002 64	15
6	·775 66	·089 20	·766 19	·028 61	·756 72	20·976 07	6
7	·759 41	·067 55	·748 23	·004 24	·737 05	·949 04	7
8	·742 77	·045 68	·729 69	15·979 44	·716 61	·921 53	8
9	·725 77	·023 50	·710 61	·954 29	·695 45	·893 55	9
20	·708 36	·001 04	·690 91	·928 77	·673 46	·865 12	20
1	·690 54	10·978 31	·670 60	·902 91	·650 66	·836 25	1
2	·672 40	·955 32	·649 81	·876 70	·627 22	·806 95	2
3	·653 96	·932 07	·628 57	·850 14	·603 18	·777 25	3
4	·635 31	·908 55	·607 01	·823 25	·578 71	·747 14	4
25	·616 45	·884 77	·585 14	·796 02	·553 83	·716 63	25
6	·597 45	·860 70	·563 06	·768 44	·528 67	·685 70	6
7	·578 33	·836 34	·540 80	·740 49	·503 27	·654 34	7
8	·559 12	·811 68	·518 40	·712 16	·477 68	·622 54	8
9	·539 78	·786 69	·495 81	·683 43	·451 84	·590 25	9
30	·520 32	·761 37	·473 04	·654 28	·425 76	·557 47	30
1	·500 77	·735 69	·450 13	·624 69	·399 49	·524 15	1
2	·481 07	·709 64	·427 00	·594 61	·372 93	·490 27	2
3	·461 23	·683 20	·403 66	·564 04	·346 09	·455 79	3
4	·441 23	·656 34	·380 08	·532 93	·318 93	·420 68	4
35	·421 08	·629 03	·356 27	·501 26	·291 46	·384 87	35
6	·400 72	·601 26	·332 15	·469 00	·263 58	·348 36	6
7	·380 16	·572 99	·307 73	·436 08	·235 30	·311 08	7
8	·359 39	·544 19	·282 99	·402 50	·206 59	·272 98	8
9	·338 37	·514 84	·257 88	·368 19	·177 39	·234 01	9
40	·317 07	·484 91	·232 35	·333 14	·147 63	·194 10	40
1	·295 49	·454 36	·206 40	·297 26	·117 31	·153 24	1
2	·273 60	·423 13	·179 98	·260 52	·086 36	·111 26	2
3	·251 32	·391 20	·152 98	·222 85	·054 64	·068 19	3
4	·228 68	·358 54	·125 44	·184 21	·022 20	·023 91	4
45	·205 60	·325 08	·097 24	·144 51	18·988 88	19·978 36	45
6	·182 07	·290 77	·068 36	·103 70	·954 65	·931 42	6
7	·158 03	·255 56	·038 72	·061 68	·919 41	·883 00	7
8	·133 43	·219 40	·008 24	·018 41	·883 05	·833 01	8
9	·108 22	·182 24	13·976 84	14·973 77	·845 46	·781 31	9

H^M Table (Makeham Graduation)

Logarithms of D and N. Joint Lives. Equal Ages

3 per cent.

Age x	Two Lives		Three Lives		Four Lives		Age x
	log D_{xx}	log N_{xx}	log D_{xxx}	log N_{xxx}	log D_{xxxx}	log N_{xxxx}	
50	9·082 34	10·143 98	13·944 44	14·927 67	18·806 54	19·727 81	50
1	·055 74	·104 56	·910 96	·880 01	·766 18	·672 35	1
2	·028 32	·063 90	·876 25	·830 67	·724 18	·614 79	2
3	·000 03	·021 93	·840 23	·779 54	·680 43	·555 00	3
4	8·970 77	9·978 52	·802 76	·726 48	·634 75	·492 77	4
55	·940 45	·933 61	·763 70	·671 36	·586 95	·427 94	55
6	·908 98	·887 09	·722 91	·614 02	·536 84	·360 31	6
7	·876 24	·838 83	·680 22	·554 30	·484 20	·289 63	7
8	·842 12	·788 71	·635 46	·491 99	·428 80	·215 72	8
9	·806 46	·736 60	·588 39	·426 92	·370 32	·138 27	9
60	·769 15	·682 33	·538 84	·358 87	·308 53	·057 02	60
1	·730 01	·625 77	·486 55	·287 60	·243 09	18·971 66	1
2	·688 87	·566 72	·431 26	·212 85	·173 65	·881 84	2
3	·645 53	·504 99	·372 67	·134 37	·099 81	·787 21	3
4	·599 80	·440 39	·310 49	·051 81	·021 18	·687 35	4
65	·551 44	·372 69	·244 37	13·964 87	17·937 30	·581 84	65
6	·500 18	·301 64	·173 90	·873 18	·847 62	·470 18	6
7	·445 79	·226 99	·098 73	·776 34	·751 67	·351 85	7
8	·387 91	·148 39	·018 33	·673 92	·648 75	·226 29	8
9	·326 25	·065 62	12·932 26	·565 46	·538 27	·092 86	9
70	·260 43	8·978 22	·839 95	·450 42	·419 47	17·950 88	70
1	·190 06	·885 89	·740 81	·328 26	·291 56	·799 57	1
2	·114 72	·788 20	·634 22	·198 33	·153 72	·638 14	2
3	·033 90	·684 67	·519 41	·059 98	·004 92	·465 65	3
4	7·947 13	·574 83	·395 67	12·912 43	16·844 21	·281 12	4
75	·853 75	·458 11	·262 02	·754 88	·670 29	·083 43	75
6	·753 21	·333 93	·117 63	·586 44	·482 05	16·871 43	6
7	·644 77	·201 64	11·961 39	·406 13	·278 01	·643 79	7
8	·527 76	·060 55	·792 29	·212 88	·056 82	·399 09	8
9	·401 30	7·909 81	·609 02	·005 52	15·816 74	·135 71	9
80	·264 46	·748 61	·410 18	11·782 71	·555 90	15·851 91	80
1	·116 30	·575 98	·194 36	·543 05	·272 42	·545 80	1
2	6·955 65	·390 90	10·959 80	·284 97	14·963 95	·215 24	2
3	·781 41	·192 26	·704 86	·006 81	·628 31	14·858 05	3
4	·592 29	6·978 82	·427 60	10·706 67	·262 91	·471 69	4
85	·386 88	·749 20	·125 90	·382 50	13·864 92	·053 39	85
6	·163 54	·501 87	9·797 31	·031 97	·431 08	13·599 97	6
7	5·920 46	·235 17	·439 11	9·652 59	12·957 76	·108 09	7
8	·656 06	5·947 42	·048 93	·241 80	·441 80	12·574 38	8
9	·368 03	·636 50	8·623 30	8·796 35	11·878 57	11·994 46	9
90	·054 31	·300 27	·159 14	·313 07	·263 97	·364 06	90
1	4·711 85	4·936 18	7·651 87	7·787 91	10·591 89	10·677 58	1
2	·338 32	·541 94	·097 99	·217 54	9·857 66	9·930 59	2
3	3·933 10	·115 14	6·496 58	6·598 90	·060 06	·119 75	3
4	·486 00	3·649 72	5·832 35	5·920 91	8·178 70	8·228 43	4
95	·001 64	·146 75	·112 23	·186 82	7·222 82	7·262 59	95
6	2·470 15	2·600 11	4·321 41	4·384 93	6·172 67	6·204 74	6
7	1·891 19	·012 80	3·459 39	3·518 66	5·027 59	5·057 36	7
8	·299 45	1·400 56	2·578 20	2·624 35	3·856 95	3·878 45	8
9	0·637 59	0·718 00	1·591 83	1·627 88	2·546 07	2·562 [illegible]8	9
100	$\bar{1}$·920 40	$\bar{1}$·945 99	0·522 46	0·528 99	1·124 52	1·126 16	100
1	$\bar{2}$·703 44	$\bar{2}$·703 44	$\bar{2}$·703 44	$\bar{2}$·703 44	$\bar{2}$·703 44	$\bar{2}$·703 44	1

H^M Table (Makeham Graduation)

Values of Annuities. Joint Lives. Equal Ages

3 per cent.

Age x	Two Lives a_{xx}	Three Lives a_{xxx}	Four Lives a_{xxxx}	Age x	Two Lives a_{xx}	Three Lives a_{xxx}	Four Lives a_{xxxx}
1	19·161	16·013	13·587	50	10·525	8·621	7·342
2	20·197	17·358	15·143	1	10·190	8·312	7·057
3	20·740	18·100	16·035	2	9·854	8·004	6·774
4	21·038	18·534	16·577	3	9·517	7·696	6·491
5	21·227	18·833	16·965	4	9·180	7·389	6·211
6	21·318	19·006	17·208	55	8·844	7·085	5·934
7	21·327	19·072	17·325	6	8·509	6·783	5·660
8	21·265	19·046	17·333	7	8·175	6·483	5·389
9	21·147	18·946	17·253	8	7·843	6·187	5·122
10	20·984	18·787	17·103	9	7·514	5·895	4·861
1	20·791	18·589	16·906	60	7·188	5·607	4·604
2	20·575	18·361	16·674	1	6·866	5·325	4·353
3	20·339	18·110	16·414	2	6·548	5·048	4·107
4	20·094	17·846	16·141	3	6·235	4·777	3·869
15	19·839	17·572	15·854	4	5·928	4·512	3·636
6	19·583	17·300	15·571	65	5·626	4·254	3·411
7	19·332	17·030	15·293	6	5·331	4·004	3·193
8	19·087	16·773	15·029	7	5·042	3·760	2·983
9	18·848	16·526	14·780	8	4·761	3·525	2·780
20	18·619	16·293	14·548	9	4·487	3·297	2·586
1	18·398	16·073	14·331	70	4·221	3·078	2·399
2	18·183	15·861	14·126	1	3·964	2·868	2·221
3	17·972	15·656	13·930	2	3·715	2·665	2·051
4	17·761	15·453	13·738	3	3·475	2·472	1·889
25	17·549	15·251	13·548	4	3·243	2·287	1·735
6	17·334	15·046	13·356	75	3·021	2·111	1·589
7	17·114	14·837	13·160	6	2·808	1·943	1·451
8	16·888	14·623	12·959	7	2·605	1·784	1·322
9	16·657	14·404	12·754	8	2·410	1·634	1·199
30	16·420	14·179	12·543	9	2·225	1·492	1·084
1	16·176	13·947	12·325	80	2·049	1·358	·977
2	15·927	13·710	12·102	1	1·882	1·232	·877
3	15·671	13·467	11·874	2	1·724	1·114	·784
4	15·410	13·218	11·640	3	1·576	1·004	·697
35	15·142	12·964	11·400	4	1·435	·901	·617
6	14·869	12·704	11·156	85	1·303	·806	·543
7	14·589	12·439	10·906	6	1·179	·717	·475
8	14·304	12·167	10·652	7	1·064	·635	·414
9	14·013	11·892	10·392	8	·956	·559	·357
40	13·718	11·612	10·130	9	·856	·490	·306
1	13·417	11·327	9·862	90	·762	·425	·259
2	13·110	11·037	9·590	1	·676	·368	·218
3	12·800	10·746	9·317	2	·598	·317	·183
4	12·485	10·449	9·040	3	·521	·266	·147
45	12·167	10·150	8·761	4	·458	·226	·121
6	11·844	9·847	8·479	95	·397	·187	·096
7	11·518	9·543	8·196	6	·349	·157	·077
8	11·189	9·237	7·912	7	·323	·146	·071
9	10·858	8·930	7·627	8	·262	·112	·051
				9	·203	·087	·038
				100	·061	·015	·004

H^M TABLE (MAKEHAM GRADUATION)

THREE-AND-A-HALF PER CENT.

INTEREST CONSTANTS

Constant	Number	Logarithm
i	·035	$\bar{2}$·544 068 0
$(1+i)$	1·035	0·014 940 3
$(1+i)^{\frac{1}{2}}$	1·017 349 5	0·007 470 2
$(1+i)^{\frac{1}{4}}$	1·008 637 4	0·003 735 1
v	·966 183 6	$\bar{1}$·985 059 7
$v^{\frac{1}{2}}$	·982 946 4	$\bar{1}$·992 529 8
$v^{\frac{1}{4}}$	·991 436 5	$\bar{1}$·996 264 9
d	·033 816 4	$\bar{2}$·529 127 7
δ	·034 401 4	$\bar{2}$·536 576 5
$j_{(2)}$	·034 699 0	$\bar{2}$·540 317 0
$j_{(4)}$	·034 549 8	$\bar{2}$·538 445 4

H^M Table (Makeham Graduation)

Commutation Table. 3½ *per cent.*

Age x	D_x	N_x	S_x	C_x	M_x	R_x	Age x
0	127 280	2 553 052	52 256 901	13 872	40 948	785 908	0
1	109 110	2 425 772	49 703 849	3 698·5	27 075·5	744 959·6	1
2	101 720	2 316 662	47 278 077	2 142·1	23 377·0	717 884·1	2
3	96 137	2 214 942	44 961 415	1 434·4	21 234·9	694 507·1	3
4	91 451	2 118 805	42 746 473	1 115·6	19 800·5	673 272·2	4
5	87 243	2 027 354	40 627 668	863·14	18 684·94	653 471·69	5
6	83 430	1 940 111	38 600 314	669·67	17 821·80	634 786·75	6
7	79 939	1 856 681	36 660 203	518·68	17 152·13	616 964·95	7
8	76 717	1 776 742	34 803 522	408·70	16 633·45	599 812·82	8
9	73 714	1 700 025	33 026 780	328·94	16 224·75	583 179·37	9
10	70 892	1 626 311	31 326 755	279·46	15 895·81	566 954·62	10
1	68 215	1 555 419	29 700 444	244·20	15 616·35	551 058·81	1
2	65 664	1 487 204	28 145 025	221·24	15 372·15	535 442·46	2
3	63 224	1 421 540	26 657 821	208·19	15 150·91	520 070·31	3
4	60 877	1 358 316	25 236 281	201·15	14 942·72	504 919·40	4
15	58 615	1 297 439	23 877 965	207·61	14 741·57	489 976·68	15
6	56 426	1 238 824	22 580 526	213·96	14 533·96	475 235·11	6
7	54 304	1 182 398	21 341 702	228·80	14 320·00	460 701·15	7
8	52 238	1 128 094	20 159 304	241·87	14 091·20	446 381·15	8
9	50 231	1 075 856	19 031 210	255·30	13 849·33	432 289·95	9
20	48 277	1 025 625	17 955 354	266·09	13 594·03	418 440·62	20
1	46 378	977 348	16 929 729	273·04	13 327·94	404 846·59	1
2	44 537	930 970	15 952 381	276·05	13 054·90	391 518·65	2
3	42 754	886 433	15 021 411	276·35	12 778·85	378 463·75	3
4	41 033	843 679	14 134 978	273·77	12 502·50	365 684·90	4
25	39 371	802 646	13 291 299	269·02	12 228·73	353 182·40	25
6	37 771	763 275	12 488 653	262·29	11 959·71	340 953·67	6
7	36 231	725 504	11 725 378	256·86	11 697·42	328 993·96	7
8	34 750	689 273	10 999 874	250·01	11 440·56	317 296·54	8
9	33 324	654 523	10 310 601	244·41	11 190·55	305 855·98	9
30	31 953	621 199	9 656 078	237·86	10 946·14	294 665·43	30
1	30 634	589 246	9 034 879	232·81	10 708·28	283 719·29	1
2	29 366	558 612	8 445 633	227·83	10 475·47	273 011·01	2
3	28 145	529 246	7 887 021	223·23	10 247·64	262 535·54	3
4	26 970	501 101	7 357 775	218·69	10 024·41	252 287·90	4
35	25 839	474 131	6 856 674	215·06	9 805·72	242 263·49	35
6	24 750	448 292	6 382 543	211·70	9 590·66	232 457·77	6
7	23 702	423 542	5 934 251	208·33	9 378·96	222 867·11	7
8	22 692	399 840	5 510 709	205·47	9 170·63	213 488·15	8
9	21 719	377 148	5 110 869	203·58	8 965·16	204 317·52	9
40	20 781	355 429	4 733 721	200·84	8 761·58	195 352·36	40
1	19 877	334 648	4 378 292	199·47	8 560·74	186 590·78	1
2	19 006	314 771	4 043 644	198·42	8 361·27	178 030·04	2
3	18 165	295 765	3 728 873	196·99	8 162·85	169 668·77	3
4	17 353	277 600	3 433 108	196·49	7 965·86	161 505·92	4
45	16 570	260 247	3 155 508	196·02	7 769·37	153 540·06	45
6	15 814	243 677	2 895 261	195·74	7 573·35	145 770·69	6
7	15 083	227 863	2 651 584	195·83	7 377·61	138 197·34	7
8	14 377	212 780	2 423 721	196·63	7 181·78	130 819·73	8
9	13 694	198 403	2 210 941	197·14	6 985·15	123 637·95	9

H^M TABLE (MAKEHAM GRADUATION)

Commutation Table. **3½** *per cent.*

Age x	D_x	N_x	$\mathbf{S}_x$	C_x	M_x	R_x	Age x
50	13 034	184 709	2 012 538	197·91	6 788·01	116 652·80	50
1	12 395	171 675	1 827 829	199·41	6 590·10	109 864·79	1
2	11 777	159 280	1 656 154	200·74	6 390·69	103 274·69	2
3	11 178	147 503	1 496 874	202·22	6 189·95	96 884·00	3
4	10 598	136 325	1 349 371	203·98	5 987·73	90 694·05	4
55	10 035	125 727	1 213 046	205·96	5 783·75	84 706·32	55
6	9 490·1	115 691·8	1 087 319·3	207·58	5 577·79	78 922·57	6
7	8 961·5	106 201·7	971 627·5	209·54	5 370·21	73 344·78	7
8	8 448·9	97 240·2	865 425·8	211·78	5 160·67	67 974·57	8
9	7 951·5	88 791·3	768 185·6	213·51	4 948·89	62 813·90	9
60	7 469·1	80 839·8	679 394·3	215·24	4 735·38	57 865·01	60
1	7 001·3	73 370·7	598 554·5	216·85	4 520·14	53 129·63	1
2	6 547·7	66 369·4	525 183·8	218·21	4 303·29	48 609·49	2
3	6 108·0	59 821·7	458 814·4	219·35	4 085·08	44 306·20	3
4	5 682·1	53 713·7	398 992·7	220·06	3 865·73	40 221·12	4
65	5 270·0	48 031·6	345 279·0	220·26	3 645·67	36 355·39	65
6	4 871·5	42 761·6	297 247·4	219·89	3 425·41	32 709·72	6
7	4 486·8	37 890·1	254 485·8	219·11	3 205·52	29 284·31	7
8	4 116·0	33 403·3	216 595·7	217·38	2 986·41	26 078·79	8
9	3 759·5	29 287·3	183 192·4	214·89	2 769·03	23 092·38	9
70	3 417·4	25 527·8	153 905·1	211·62	2 554·14	20 323·35	70
1	3 090·2	22 110·4	128 377·3	207·32	2 342·52	17 769·21	1
2	2 778·4	19 020·2	106 266·9	202·09	2 135·20	15 426·69	2
3	2 482·3	16 241·8	87 246·7	195·73	1 933·11	13 291·49	3
4	2 202·7	13 759·5	71 004·9	188·43	1 737·38	11 358·38	4
75	1 939·7	11 556·8	57 245·4	180·01	1 548·95	9 621·00	75
6	1 694·1	9 617·1	45 688·6	170·60	1 368·94	8 072·05	6
7	1 466·3	7 923·0	36 071·5	160·11	1 198·34	6 703·11	7
8	1 256·6	6 456·7	28 148·5	148·89	1 038·23	5 504·77	8
9	1 065·2	5 200·1	21 691·8	136·90	889·34	4 466·54	9
80	892·26	4 134·89	16 491·72	124·38	752·44	3 577·20	80
1	737·72	3 242·63	12 356·83	111·54	628·06	2 824·76	1
2	601·23	2 504·91	9 114·20	98·503	516·521	2 196·695	2
3	482·39	1 903·68	6 609·29	85·611	418·018	1 680·174	3
4	380·47	1 421·29	4 705·61	73·102	332·407	1 262·156	4
85	294·50	1 040·82	3 284·32	61·236	259·305	929·749	85
6	223·31	746·32	2 243·50	50·241	198·069	670·444	6
7	165·52	523·01	1 497·18	40·210	147·828	472·375	7
8	119·71	357·49	974·17	31·407	107·618	324·547	8
9	84·252	237·784	616·680	23·833	76·211	216·929	9
90	57·571	153·532	378·896	17·565	52·378	140·718	90
1	38·058	95·961	225·364	12·496	34·813	88·340	1
2	24·275	57·903	129·403	8·525 1	22·317 0	53·527 2	2
3	14·929	33·628	71·500	5·675 1	13·791 9	31·210 2	3
4	8·749	18·699	37·872	3·541 2	8·116 8	17·418 3	4
95	4·912	9·950	19·173	2·133 8	4·575 6	9·301 5	95
6	2·612	5·038	9·223	1·208 6	2·441 8	4·725 9	6
7	1·315	2·426	4·185	·618 3	1·233 2	2·284 1	7
8	·653	1·111	1·759	·331 7	·614 9	1·050 9	8
9	·299	·458	·648	·160 3	·283 2	·436 0	9
100	·128	·159	·190	·093 0	·122 9	·152 8	100
1	·031	·031	·031	·029 9	·029 9	·029 9	1

H^M Table (Makeham Graduation)

Logarithms of D_x, N_x, *and* M_x. $3\frac{1}{2}$ *per cent.*

Age x	log D_x	log N_x	log M_x	Age x	log D_x	log N_x	log M_x
0	5·104 77	6·407 06	4·612 23	50	4·115 08	5·266 49	3·831 74
1	·037 85	·384 85	·432 58	1	·093 26	·234 72	·818 89
2	·007 40	·364 87	·368 79	2	·071 03	·202 16	·805 55
3	4·982 89	·345 35	·327 05	3	·048 36	·168 79	·791 69
4	·961 19	·326 09	·296 69	4	·025 21	·134 59	·777 26
5	·940 73	·306 94	·271 49	55	·001 53	·099 44	·762 21
6	·921 32	·287 82	·250 96	6	3·977 27	·063 30	·746 46
7	·902 76	·268 74	·234 31	7	·952 38	·026 12	·729 99
8	·884 89	·249 61	·220 97	8	·926 80	4·987 84	·712 71
9	·867 55	·230 45	·210 18	9	·900 45	·948 37	·694 51
10	·850 60	·211 20	·201 29	60	·873 27	·907 63	·675 36
1	·833 88	·191 84	·193 57	1	·845 18	·865 52	·655 15
2	·817 33	·172 37	·186 73	2	·816 09	·821 97	·633 80
3	·800 88	·152 75	·180 44	3	·785 90	·776 86	·611 20
4	·784 45	·133 00	·174 44	4	·754 51	·730 09	·587 23
15	·768 01	·113 07	·168 56	65	·721 81	·681 53	·561 78
6	·751 48	·093 00	·162 39	6	·687 66	·631 06	·534 71
7	·734 83	·072 76	·155 94	7	·651 94	·578 52	·505 90
8	·717 99	·052 35	·148 94	8	·614 48	·523 79	·475 15
9	·700 97	·031 77	·141 42	9	·575 13	·466 67	·442 32
20	·683 74	·010 98	·133 35	70	·533 70	·407 02	·407 24
1	·666 31	5·990 05	·124 76	1	·489 99	·344 59	·369 68
2	·648 72	·968 94	·115 78	2	·443 79	·279 21	·329 44
3	·630 98	·947 64	·106 50	3	·394 86	·210 64	·286 25
4	·613 13	·926 18	·097 01	4	·342 95	·138 62	·239 90
25	·595 18	·904 53	·087 39	75	·287 74	·062 85	·190 05
6	·577 16	·882 68	·077 73	6	·228 95	3·983 04	·136 37
7	·559 08	·860 64	·068 07	7	·166 21	·898 89	·078 57
8	·540 95	·838 39	·058 46	8	·099 18	·810 01	·016 28
9	·522 76	·815 92	·048 87	9	·027 43	·716 01	2·949 07
30	·504 51	·793 23	·039 26	80	2·950 49	·616 47	·876 47
1	·486 21	·770 30	·029 71	1	·867 89	·510 89	·798 00
2	·467 84	·747 11	·020 15	2	·779 04	·398 79	·713 09
3	·449 40	·723 66	·010 64	3	·683 40	·279 60	·621 20
4	·430 88	·699 92	·001 04	4	·580 32	·152 69	·521 67
35	·412 28	·675 90	3·991 48	85	·469 09	·017 37	·413 82
6	·393 58	·651 56	·981 85	6	·348 90	2·872 93	·296 82
7	·374 78	·626 89	·972 16	7	·218 84	·718 51	·169 76
8	·355 87	·601 89	·962 40	8	·078 12	·553 26	·031 89
9	·336 84	·576 51	·952 56	9	1·925 58	·376 18	1·882 02
40	·317 67	·550 75	·942 58	90	·760 20	·186 19	·719 15
1	·298 36	·524 59	·932 51	1	·580 45	1·982 09	·541 74
2	·278 89	·497 99	·922 27	2	·385 16	·762 70	·348 64
3	·259 23	·470 95	·911 84	3	·174 03	·526 70	·139 63
4	·239 38	·443 42	·901 23	4	0·941 96	·271 82	0·909 38
45	·219 32	·415 39	·890 39	95	·691 26	0·997 81	·660 45
6	·199 03	·386 82	·879 29	6	·416 99	·702 23	·387 71
7	·178 49	·357 67	·867 92	7	·118 99	·384 82	·091 03
8	·157 67	·327 93	·856 23	8	$\bar{1}$·814 60	·045 48	$\bar{1}$·788 87
9	·136 54	·297 54	·844 18	9	·475 15	$\bar{1}$·660 73	·452 03
				100	·108 03	·202 00	·089 41
				1	$\bar{2}$·491 03	$\bar{2}$·491 03	$\bar{2}$·476 09

H^{M} Table (Makeham Graduation)

Values of Annuities, and Single and Annual Premiums for Assurance of a Unit

3½ *per cent.*

Age x	a_x	A_x	P_x	Age x	a_x	A_x	P_x
1	21·233	·248 16	·011 16	50	13·172	·520 79	·036 75
2	21·775	·229 82	·010 09	1	12·850	·531 66	·038 39
3	22·039	·220 88	·009 59	2	12·524	·542 65	·040 12
4	22·169	·216 52	·009 35	3	12·196	·553 77	·041 97
5	22·238	·214 17	·009 22	4	11·864	·565 00	·043 92
6	22·255	·213 62	·009 19	55	11·528	·576 34	·046 00
7	22·225	·214 56	·009 24	6	11·191	·587 75	·048 21
8	22·160	·216 81	·009 36	7	10·851	·599 25	·050 57
9	22·062	·220 11	·009 54	8	10·509	·610 82	·053 07
10	21·940	·224 23	·009 77	9	10·167	·622 39	·055 74
1	21·802	·228 92	·010 04	60	9·823	·634 00	·058 58
2	21·648	·234 10	·010 34	1	9·480	·645 61	·061 61
3	21·484	·239 64	·010 66	2	9·136	·657 22	·064 84
4	21·312	·245 47	·011 00	3	8·794	·668 81	·068 29
15	21·134	·251 51	·011 36	4	8·453	·680 33	·071 97
6	20·955	·257 58	·011 73	65	8·114	·691 78	·075 90
7	20·774	·263 70	·012 11	6	7·778	·703 15	·080 10
8	20·596	·269 74	·012 49	7	7·445	·714 43	·084 60
9	20·418	·275 71	·012 87	8	7·115	·725 55	·089 40
20	20·245	·281 59	·013 25	9	6·790	·736 53	·094 55
1	20·074	·287 38	·013 64	70	6·470	·747 38	·100 05
2	19·903	·293 13	·014 02	1	6·155	·758 04	·105 95
3	19·733	·298 90	·014 42	2	5·846	·768 51	·112 26
4	19·561	·304 71	·014 82	3	5·543	·778 74	·119 02
25	19·387	·310 61	·015 24	4	5·247	·788 77	·126 26
6	19·208	·316 64	·015 67	75	4·958	·798 56	·134 03
7	19·024	·322 84	·016 12	6	4·677	·808 02	·142 34
8	18·835	·329 24	·016 60	7	4·404	·817 26	·151 24
9	18·641	·335 82	·017 10	8	4·138	·826 23	·160 79
30	18·441	·342 57	·017 62	9	3·882	·834 91	·171 03
1	18·235	·349 54	·018 17	80	3·634	·843 30	·181 97
2	18·023	·356 71	·018 75	1	3·395	·851 35	·193 69
3	17·804	·364 12	·019 36	2	3·166	·859 11	·206 21
4	17·580	·371 67	·020 00	3	2·946	·866 56	·219 58
35	17·349	·379 49	·020 68	4	2·736	·873 68	·233 87
6	17·112	·387 50	·021 39	85	2·534	·880 50	·249 14
7	16·870	·395 71	·022 14	6	2·342	·886 99	·265 39
8	16·620	·404 14	·022 94	7	2·160	·893 14	·282 65
9	16·365	·412 78	·023 77	8	1·986	·899 02	·301 04
40	16·103	·421 61	·024 65	9	1·822	·904 57	·320 51
1	15·835	·430 68	·025 58	90	1·667	·909 81	·341 16
2	15·562	·439 93	·026 56	1	1·521	·914 72	·362 79
3	15·282	·449 38	·027 60	2	1·385	·919 35	·385 43
4	14·997	·459 04	·028 70	3	1·253	·923 85	·410 14
45	14·706	·468 89	·029 85	4	1·137	·927 73	·434 07
6	14·409	·478 92	·031 08	95	1·026	·931 52	·459 88
7	14·107	·489 14	·032 38	6	·929	·934 80	·484 71
8	13·800	·499 53	·033 75	7	·844	·937 65	·508 41
9	13·488	·510 08	·035 21	8	·702	·942 48	·553 85
				9	·533	·948 16	·618 44
				100	·242	·958 03	·771 63
				1	...	·966 18	·966 18

H^M Table (Makeham Graduation)

Logarithms of D *and* N. *Joint Lives. Equal Ages*

3½ *per cent.*

Age x	Two Lives		Three Lives		Four Lives		Age x
	log D_{xx}	log N_{xx}	log D_{xxx}	log N_{xxx}	log D_{xxxx}	log N_{xxxx}	
0	10·209 54	11·387 91	15·314 31	16·380 01	20·419 08	21·380 30	0
1	·090 64	·358 11	·143 43	·340 98	·196 22	·330 01	1
2	·044 68	·333 99	·081 96	·312 52	·119 24	·296 86	2
3	·010 60	·311 08	·038 31	·286 19	·066 02	·267 01	3
4	9·982 14	·288 76	·003 09	·260 93	·024 04	·238 77	4
5	·956 16	·266 80	14·971 59	·236 26	19·987 02	·211 44	5
6	·932 28	·245 02	·943 24	·211 97	·954 20	·184 72	6
7	·910 10	·223 34	·917 44	·187 94	·924 78	·158 39	7
8	·889 30	·201 70	·893 71	·164 00	·898 12	·132 26	8
9	·869 56	·180 01	·871 57	·140 04	·873 58	·106 16	9
10	·850 60	·158 24	·850 60	·115 98	·850 60	·079 98	10
1	·832 10	·136 31	·830 32	·091 74	·828 54	·053 58	1
2	·813 94	·114 18	·810 55	·067 29	·807 16	·026 90	2
3	·795 98	·091 88	·791 08	·042 54	·786 18	20·999 90	3
4	·778 06	·069 34	·771 67	·017 49	·765 28	·972 51	4
15	·760 13	·046 53	·752 25	15·992 10	·744 37	·944 69	15
6	·742 01	·023 46	·732 54	·966 36	·723 07	·916 40	6
7	·723 65	·000 13	·712 47	·940 24	·701 29	·887 65	7
8	·704 91	10·976 52	·691 83	·913 74	·678 75	·858 40	8
9	·685 81	·952 64	·670 65	·886 87	·655 49	·828 70	9
20	·666 29	·928 49	·648 84	·859 64	·631 39	·798 53	20
1	·646 37	·904 07	·626 43	·832 05	·606 49	·767 92	1
2	·626 13	·879 39	·603 54	·804 12	·580 95	·736 89	2
3	·605 59	·854 45	·580 20	·775 85	·554 81	·705 44	3
4	·584 83	·829 25	·556 53	·747 26	·528 23	·673 61	4
25	·563 87	·803 77	·532 56	·718 32	·501 25	·641 37	25
6	·542 77	·778 03	·508 38	·689 03	·473 99	·608 72	6
7	·521 55	·751 99	·484 02	·659 40	·446 49	·575 64	7
8	·500 23	·725 67	·459 51	·629 39	·418 79	·542 13	8
9	·478 79	·699 02	·434 82	·598 98	·390 85	·508 14	9
30	·457 23	·672 05	·409 95	·568 14	·362 67	·473 65	30
1	·435 57	·644 72	·384 93	·536 87	·334 29	·438 64	1
2	·413 77	·617 03	·359 70	·505 14	·305 63	·403 07	2
3	·391 83	·588 94	·334 26	·472 90	·276 69	·366 91	3
4	·369 73	·560 44	·308 58	·440 14	·247 43	·330 11	4
35	·347 47	·531 50	·282 66	·406 80	·217 85	·292 63	35
6	·325 01	·502 10	·256 44	·372 88	·187 87	·254 43	6
7	·302 35	·472 22	·229 92	·338 32	·157 49	·215 48	7
8	·279 47	·441 81	·203 07	·303 11	·126 67	·175 71	8
9	·256 35	·410 84	·175 86	·267 15	·095 37	·135 07	9
40	·232 95	·379 29	·148 23	·230 45	·063 51	·093 53	40
1	·209 27	·347 12	·120 18	·192 93	·031 09	·050 96	1
2	·185 27	·314 29	·091 65	·154 58	18·998 03	·007 36	2
3	·160 89	·280 76	·062 55	·115 28	·964 21	19·962 63	3
4	·136 14	·246 50	·032 90	·075 00	·929 66	·916 70	4
45	·110 96	·211 44	·002 60	·033 67	·894 24	·869 48	45
6	·085 32	·175 54	13·971 61	14·991 23	·857 90	·820 88	6
7	·059 18	·138 71	·939 87	·947 60	·820 56	·770 81	7
8	·032 48	·100 96	·907 29	·902 69	·782 10	·719 15	8
9	·005 16	·062 21	·873 78	·856 41	·742 40	·665 80	9

H^M TABLE (MAKEHAM GRADUATION)

Logarithms of D *and* N. *Joint Lives. Equal Ages*

$3\frac{1}{2}$ *per cent.*

Age x	Two Lives		Three Lives		Four Lives		Age x
	log D_{xx}	log N_{xx}	log D_{xxx}	log N_{xxx}	log D_{xxxx}	log N_{xxxx}	
50	8·977 18	10·022 35	13·839 28	14·808 68	18·701 38	19·610 63	50
1	·948 48	9·981 32	·803 70	·759 39	·658 92	·553 52	1
2	·918 96	·939 05	·766 89	·708 42	·614 82	·494 29	2
3	·888 56	·895 47	·728 76	·655 65	·568 96	·432 83	3
4	·857 20	·850 48	·689 19	·600 95	·521 18	·368 92	4
55	·824 78	·803 97	·648 03	·544 19	·471 28	·302 42	55
6	·791 20	·755 84	·605 13	·485 20	·419 06	·233 10	6
7	·756 36	·705 97	·560 34	·423 82	·364 32	·160 74	7
8	·720 14	·654 22	·513 48	·359 85	·306 82	·085 15	8
9	·682 38	·600 49	·464 31	·293 12	·246 24	·006 00	9
60	·642 96	·544 60	·412 65	·223 39	·182 34	18·923 03	60
1	·601 72	·486 40	·358 26	·150 45	·114 80	·835 95	1
2	·558 48	·425 71	·300 87	·074 01	·043 26	·744 41	2
3	·513 04	·362 35	·240 18	13·993 84	17·967 32	·648 05	3
4	·465 20	·296 09	·175 89	·909 59	·886 58	·546 46	4
65	·414 74	·226 73	·107 67	·820 94	·800 60	·439 19	65
6	·361 38	·154 03	·035 10	·727 53	·708 82	·325 78	6
7	·304 88	·077 70	12·957 82	·628 97	·610 76	·205 69	7
8	·244 90	8·997 42	·875 32	·524 81	·505 74	·078 35	8
9	·181 14	·912 93	·787 15	·414 61	·393 16	17·943 13	9
70	·113 22	·823 85	·692 74	·297 80	·272 26	·799 34	70
1	·040 74	·729 81	·591 49	·173 86	·142 24	·646 23	1
2	7·963 29	·630 40	·482 79	·042 18	·002 29	·482 97	2
3	·880 37	·525 14	·365 88	12·902 01	16·851 39	·308 65	3
4	·791 49	·413 55	·240 03	·752 67	·688 57	·122 28	4
75	·696 01	·295 08	·104 28	·593 31	·512 55	16·922 75	75
6	·593 37	·169 15	11·957 79	·423 05	·322 21	·708 89	6
7	·482 83	·035 07	·799 45	·240 90	·116 07	·479 36	7
8	·363 71	7·892 18	·628 24	·045 83	15·892 77	·232 77	8
9	·235 15	·739 66	·442 87	11·836 59	·650 59	15·967 50	9
80	·096 21	·576 64	·241 93	·611 90	·387 65	·681 79	80
1	6·945 95	·402 19	·024 01	·370 37	·102 07	·373 76	1
2	·783 19	·215 29	10·787 34	·110 39	14·791 49	·041 27	2
3	·606 85	·014 81	·530 30	10·830 32	·453 75	14·682 14	3
4	·415 63	6·799 49	·250 94	·528 27	·086 25	·293 83	4
85	·208 11	·567 99	9·947 13	·202 19	13·686 15	13·873 54	85
6	5·982 67	·318 77	·616 44	9·849 72	·250 21	·418 17	6
7	·737 49	·050 19	·256 14	·468 38	12·774 79	12·924 31	7
8	·470 99	5·760 52	8·863 86	·055 61	·256 73	·388 60	8
9	·180 85	·447 69	·436 12	8·608 19	11·691 39	11·806 67	9
90	4·865 03	·109 54	7·969 86	·122 94	·074 69	·174 26	90
1	·520 47	4·743 49	·460 49	7·595 79	10·400 51	10·485 75	1
2	·144 83	·347 29	6·904 50	·023 42	9·664 17	9·736 73	2
3	3·737 51	3·918 54	·300 99	6·402 78	8·864 47	8·923 87	3
4	·288 31	·451 13	5·634 66	5·722 76	7·981 01	·030 48	4
95	2·801 85	2·946 16	4·912 44	4·986 64	·023 03	7·062 62	95
6	·268 25	·397 51	·119 51	·182 70	5·970 77	6·002 68	6
7	1·687 19	1·808 16	3·255 39	3·314 35	4·823 59	4·853 21	7
8	·093 35	·193 96	2·372 10	2·418 02	3·650 85	3·672 25	8
9	0·429 39	0·509 44	1·383 63	1·419 51	2·337 87	2·354 01	9
100	$\bar{1}$·710 09	$\bar{1}$·735 56	0·312 15	0·318 67	0·914 21	0·915 85	100
1	$\bar{2}$·491 02	$\bar{2}$·491 02	$\bar{2}$·491 02	$\bar{2}$·491 02	$\bar{2}$·491 02	$\bar{2}$·491 02	1

H^{M} Table (Makeham Graduation)

Values of Annuities. Joint Lives. Equal Ages

$3\frac{1}{2}$ *per cent.*

Age x	Two Lives a_{xx}	Three Lives a_{xxx}	Four Lives a_{xxxx}
1	17·513	14·760	12·608
2	18·467	16·004	14·053
3	18·974	16·696	14·885
4	19·260	17·107	15·396
5	19·447	17·393	15·765
6	19·546	17·567	16·003
7	19·570	17·642	16·124
8	19·530	17·633	16·145
9	19·439	17·555	16·084
10	19·307	17·424	15·958
1	19·146	17·257	15·789
2	18·964	17·060	15·586
3	18·765	16·843	15·358
4	18·555	16·612	15·115
15	18·337	16·372	14·860
6	18·118	16·132	14·608
7	17·901	15·895	14·359
8	17·690	15·669	14·124
9	17·486	15·452	13·901
20	17·289	15·248	13·694
1	17·101	15·055	13·502
2	16·917	14·870	13·320
3	16·736	14·691	13·146
4	16·555	14·514	12·976
25	16·374	14·337	12·808
6	16·189	14·159	12·637
7	16·000	13·976	12·464
8	15·805	13·787	12·284
9	15·605	13·593	12·100
30	15·399	13·394	11·912
1	15·187	13·189	11·716
2	14·968	12·978	11·515
3	14·744	12·761	11·309
4	14·513	12·538	11·097
35	14·277	12·309	10·879
6	14·035	12·075	10·656
7	13·787	11·836	10·428
8	13·532	11·590	10·195
9	13·272	11·339	9·958
40	13·007	11·084	9·715
1	12·736	10·824	9·468
2	12·459	10·559	9·217
3	12·179	10·291	8·964
4	11·893	10·018	8·706
45	11·603	9·742	8·446
6	11·308	9·462	8·183
7	11·010	9·180	7·918
8	10·709	8·895	7·651
9	10·404	8·608	7·383
50	10·096	8·320	7·114
1	9·785	8·030	6·845
2	9·474	7·740	6·577
3	9·161	7·451	6·309
4	8·847	7·161	6·043
55	8·532	6·873	5·779
6	8·218	6·587	5·517
7	7·904	6·303	5·258
8	7·592	6·021	5·002
9	7·282	5·742	4·751
60	6·973	5·468	4·504
1	6·668	5·197	4·262
2	6·366	4·931	4·025
3	6·068	4·671	3·794
4	5·775	4·416	3·570
65	5·486	4·167	3·351
6	5·204	3·925	3·140
7	4·927	3·690	2·935
8	4·656	3·462	2·738
9	4·393	3·241	2·548
70	4·136	3·028	2·366
1	3·887	2·823	2·191
2	3·646	2·626	2·025
3	3·413	2·437	1·866
4	3·189	2·256	1·715
75	2·973	2·083	1·572
6	2·765	1·919	1·436
7	2·567	1·764	1·308
8	2·377	1·616	1·188
9	2·195	1·476	1·075
80	2·023	1·344	·969
1	1·859	1·220	·869
2	1·705	1·104	·777
3	1·558	·995	·692
4	1·420	·894	·613
85	1·290	·799	·540
6	1·168	·711	·472
7	1·055	·630	·411
8	·948	·555	·355
9	·849	·486	·304
90	·756	·423	·258
1	·671	·366	·217
2	·594	·315	·182
3	·517	·264	·147
4	·455	·225	·121
95	·394	·186	·095
6	·347	·157	·076
7	·321	·145	·071
8	·261	·112	·050
9	·202	·086	·038
100	·060	·015	·004

H^M TABLE (MAKEHAM GRADUATION)

FOUR PER CENT.

INTEREST CONSTANTS

Constant	Number	Logarithm
i	·04	$\bar{2}$·602 060 0
$(1+i)$	1·04	0·017 033 3
$(1+i)^{\frac{1}{2}}$	1·019 803 9	0·008 516 7
$(1+i)^{\frac{1}{4}}$	1·009 853 4	0·004 258 3
v	·961 538 5	$\bar{1}$·982 966 7
$v^{\frac{1}{2}}$	·980 580 7	$\bar{1}$·991 483 3
$v^{\frac{1}{4}}$	·990 242 7	$\bar{1}$·995 741 7
d	·038 461 5	$\bar{2}$·585 026 7
δ	·039 220 7	$\bar{2}$·593 515 5
$j_{(2)}$	·039 607 8	$\bar{2}$·597 780 7
$j_{(4)}$	·039 413 6	$\bar{2}$·595 646 4

H^M Table (Makeham Graduation)

Commutation Table. 4 per cent.

Age x	D_x	N_x	S_x	C_x	M_x	R_x	Age x
0	127 280	2 332 017	44 612 595	13 806	37 590	616 157	0
1	108 580	2 204 737	42 280 578	3 663·0	23 784·0	578 567·3	1
2	100 740	2 096 157	40 075 841	2 111·3	20 121·0	554 783·3	2
3	94 757	1 995 417	37 979 684	1 407·0	18 009·7	534 662·3	3
4	89 706	1 900 660	35 984 267	1 089·1	16 602·7	516 652·6	4
5	85 165	1 810 954	34 083 607	838·53	15 513·57	500 049·89	5
6	81 051	1 725 789	32 272 653	647·46	14 675·04	484 536·32	6
7	77 288	1 644 738	30 546 864	499·06	14 027·58	469 861·28	7
8	73 814	1 567 450	28 902 126	391·35	13 528·52	455 833·70	8
9	70 585	1 493 636	27 334 676	313·47	13 137·17	442 305·18	9
10	67 557	1 423 051	25 841 040	265·03	12 823·70	429 168·01	10
1	64 692	1 355 494	24 417 989	230·48	12 558·67	416 344·31	1
2	61 974	1 290 802	23 062 495	207·80	12 328·19	403 785·64	2
3	59 384	1 228 828	21 771 693	194·61	12 120·39	391 457·45	3
4	56 904	1 169 444	20 542 865	187·12	11 925·78	379 337·06	4
15	54 528	1 112 540	19 373 421	192·21	11 738·66	367 411·28	15
6	52 240	1 058 012	18 260 881	197·13	11 546·45	355 672·62	6
7	50 032	1 005 772	17 202 869	209·79	11 349·32	344 126·17	7
8	47 898	955 740	16 197 097	220·71	11 139·53	332 776·85	8
9	45 836	907 842	15 241 357	231·84	10 918·82	321 637·32	9
20	43 841	862 006	14 333 515	240·48	10 686·98	310 718·50	20
1	41 914	818 165	13 471 509	245·58	10 446·50	300 031·52	1
2	40 057	776 251	12 653 344	247·09	10 200·92	289 585·02	2
3	38 268	736 194	11 877 093	246·17	9 953·83	279 384·10	3
4	36 551	697 926	11 140 899	242·70	9 707·66	269 430·27	4
25	34 903	661 375	10 442 973	237·33	9 464·96	259 722·61	25
6	33 323	626 472	9 781 598	230·29	9 227·63	250 257·65	6
7	31 810	593 149	9 155 126	224·43	8 997·34	241 030·02	7
8	30 363	561 339	8 561 977	217·40	8 772·91	232 032·68	8
9	28 977	530 976	8 000 638	211·50	8 555·51	223 259·77	9
30	27 652	501 999	7 469 662	204·86	8 344·01	214 704·26	30
1	26 383	474 347	6 967 663	199·54	8 139·15	206 360·25	1
2	25 169	447 964	6 493 316	194·33	7 939·61	198 221·10	2
3	24 007	422 795	6 045 352	189·50	7 745·28	190 281·49	3
4	22 894	398 788	5 622 557	184·74	7 555·78	182 536·21	4
35	21 828	375 894	5 223 769	180·80	7 371·04	174 980·43	35
6	20 808	354 066	4 847 875	177·13	7 190·24	167 609·39	6
7	19 831	333 258	4 493 809	173·47	7 013·11	160 419·15	7
8	18 894	313 427	4 160 551	170·26	6 839·64	153 406·04	8
9	17 997	294 533	3 847 124	167·88	6 669·38	146 566·40	9
40	17 138	276 536	3 552 591	164·83	6 501·50	139 897·02	40
1	16 313	259 398	3 276 055	162·92	6 336·67	133 395·52	1
2	15 523	243 085	3 016 657	161·28	6 173·75	127 058·85	2
3	14 765	227 562	2 773 572	159·35	6 012·47	120 885·10	3
4	14 038	212 797	2 546 010	158·19	5 853·12	114 872·63	4
45	13 340	198 759	2 333 213	157·04	5 694·93	109 019·51	45
6	12 670	185 419	2 134 454	156·07	5 537·89	103 324·58	6
7	12 026	172 749	1 949 035	155·39	5 381·82	97 786·69	7
8	11 408	160 723	1 776 286	155·27	5 226·43	92 404·87	8
9	10 814	149 315	1 615 563	154·92	5 071·16	87 178·44	9

H^M Table (Makeham Graduation)

Commutation Table. **4** *per cent.*

Age x	D_x	N_x	S_x	C_x	M_x	R_x	Age x
50	10 243	138 501	1 466 248	154·79	4 916·24	82 107·28	50
1	9 694·4	128 258·0	1 327 747·3	155·21	4 761·45	77 191·04	1
2	9 166·4	118 563·6	1 199 489·3	155·49	4 606·24	72 429·59	2
3	8 658·2	109 397·2	1 080 925·7	155·89	4 450·75	67 823·35	3
4	8 169·4	100 739·0	971 528·5	156·48	4 294·86	63 372·60	4
55	7 698·7	92 569·6	870 789·5	157·25	4 138·38	59 077·74	55
6	7 245·4	84 870·9	778 219·9	157·72	3 981·13	54 939·36	6
7	6 808·9	77 625·5	693 349·0	158·44	3 823·41	50 958·23	7
8	6 388·7	70 816·6	615 723·5	159·37	3 664·97	47 134·82	8
9	5 983·6	64 427·9	544 906·9	159·89	3 505·60	43 469·85	9
60	5 593·6	58 444·3	480 479·0	160·42	3 345·71	39 964·25	60
1	5 218·1	52 850·7	422 034·7	160·83	3 185·29	36 618·54	1
2	4 856·5	47 632·6	369 184·0	161·07	3 024·46	33 433·25	2
3	4 508·6	42 776·1	321 551·4	161·14	2 863·39	30 408·79	3
4	4 174·1	38 267·5	278 775·3	160·88	2 702·25	27 545·40	4
65	3 852·7	34 093·4	240 507·8	160·25	2 541·37	24 843·15	65
6	3 544·2	30 240·7	206 414·4	159·21	2 381·12	22 301·78	6
7	3 248·7	26 696·5	176 173·7	157·88	2 221·91	19 920·66	7
8	2 965·9	23 447·8	149 477·2	155·88	2 064·03	17 698·75	8
9	2 695·9	20 481·9	126 029·4	153·36	1 908·15	15 634·72	9
70	2 438·9	17 786·0	105 547·5	150·30	1 754·79	13 726·57	70
1	2 194·7	15 347·1	87 761·5	146·54	1 604·49	11 971·78	1
2	1 963·8	13 152·4	72 414·4	142·16	1 457·95	10 367·29	2
3	1 746·1	11 188·6	59 262·0	137·02	1 315·79	8 909·34	3
4	1 541·9	9 442·5	48 073·4	131·27	1 178·77	7 593·55	4
75	1 351·4	7 900·6	38 630·9	124·80	1 047·50	6 414·78	75
6	1 174·6	6 549·2	30 730·3	117·71	922·70	5 367·28	6
7	1 011·7	5 374·6	24 181·1	109·94	804·99	4 444·58	7
8	862·84	4 362·91	18 806·47	101·75	695·05	3 639·59	8
9	727·93	3 500·07	14 443·56	93·102	593·299	2 944·536	9
80	606·81	2 772·14	10 943·49	84·182	500·197	2 351·237	80
1	499·30	2 165·33	8 171·35	75·129	416·015	1 851·040	1
2	404·97	1 666·03	6 006·02	66·028	340·886	1 435·025	2
3	323·36	1 261·06	4 339·99	57·111	274·858	1 094·139	3
4	253·81	937·70	3 078·93	48·532	217·747	819·281	4
85	195·52	683·89	2 141·23	40·459	169·215	601·534	85
6	147·54	488·37	1 457·34	33·035	128·756	432·319	6
7	108·83	340·83	968·97	26·312	95·721	303·563	7
8	78·332	232·001	628·136	20·453	69·409	207·842	8
9	54·866	153·669	396·135	15·446	48·956	138·433	9
90	37·310	98·803	242·466	11·329	33·510	89·477	90
1	24·547	61·493	143·663	8·020 8	22·181 1	55·966 8	1
2	15·581	36·946	82·170	5·445 7	14·160 3	33·785 7	2
3	9·536	21·365	45·224	3·607 7	8·714 6	19·625 4	3
4	5·562	11·829	23·859	2·240 3	5·106 9	10·910 8	4
95	3·108	6·267	12·030	1·343 5	2·866 6	5·803 9	95
6	1·645	3·159	5·763	·757 3	1·523 1	2·937 3	6
7	·824	1·514	2·604	·385 5	·765 8	1·414 2	7
8	·407	·690	1·090	·205 9	·380 3	·648 4	8
9	·185	·283	·400	·099 0	·174 4	·268 1	9
100	·079	·098	·117	·057 1	·075 4	·093 7	100
1	·019	·019	·019	·018 3	·018 3	·018 3	1

H^{M} Table (Makeham Graduation)

Logarithms of D_x, N_x, *and* M_x. 4 *per cent.*

Age x	log D_x	log N_x	log M_x	Age x	log D_x	log N_x	log M_x
0	5·104 77	6·367 73	4·575 07	50	4·010 43	5·141 45	3·691 63
1	·035 76	·343 35	·376 28	1	3·986 52	·108 09	·677 74
2	·003 21	·321 43	·303 65	2	·962 20	·073 94	·663 34
3	4·976 61	·300 03	·255 51	3	·937 43	·039 02	·648 44
4	·952 82	·278 91	·220 19	4	·912 19	·003 20	·632 95
5	·930 26	·257 92	·190 72	55	·886 42	4·966 47	·616 83
6	·908 76	·236 99	·166 58	6	·860 06	·928 76	·600 00
7	·888 11	·216 09	·147 00	7	·833 08	·890 01	·582 45
8	·868 14	·195 21	·131 27	8	·805 41	·850 14	·564 07
9	·848 71	·174 23	·118 50	9	·776 96	·809 07	·544 76
10	·829 67	·153 24	·108 02	60	·747 69	·766 74	·524 49
1	·810 85	·132 10	·098 96	1	·717 51	·723 05	·503 15
2	·792 21	·110 86	·090 89	2	·686 32	·677 91	·480 65
3	·773 67	·089 48	·083 50	3	·654 04	·631 20	·456 88
4	·755 14	·067 96	·076 49	4	·620 56	·582 84	·431 73
15	·736 62	·046 30	·069 63	65	·585 76	·532 67	·405 07
6	·718 00	·024 49	·062 43	6	·549 52	·480 60	·376 78
7	·699 25	·002 51	·054 96	7	·511 71	·426 46	·346 72
8	·680 32	5·980 34	·046 89	8	·472 15	·370 11	·314 71
9	·661 21	·958 01	·038 18	9	·430 71	·311 37	·280 62
20	·641 88	·935 51	·028 86	70	·387 19	·250 08	·244 23
1	·622 36	·912 84	·018 99	1	·341 38	·186 02	·205 34
2	·602 68	·890 00	·008 64	2	·293 10	·118 99	·163 76
3	·582 84	·866 99	3·997 99	3	·242 08	·048 79	·119 19
4	·562 90	·843 81	·987 12	4	·188 07	3·975 09	·071 44
25	·542 86	·820 45	·976 12	75	·130 77	·897 66	·020 15
6	·522 74	·796 90	·965 09	6	·069 89	·816 19	2·965 06
7	·502 57	·773 16	·954 11	7	·005 05	·730 35	·905 79
8	·482 35	·749 23	·943 14	8	2·935 93	·639 78	·842 02
9	·462 06	·725 08	·932 25	9	·862 09	·544 08	·773 27
30	·441 72	·700 70	·921 37	80	·783 05	·442 81	·699 14
1	·421 33	·676 10	·910 58	1	·698 36	·335 52	·619 11
2	·400 86	·651 24	·899 80	2	·607 42	·221 68	·532 61
3	·380 33	·626 14	·889 04	3	·509 68	·100 75	·439 11
4	·359 72	·600 74	·878 28	4	·404 51	2·972 06	·337 96
35	·339 02	·575 06	·867 53	85	·291 19	·834 99	·228 45
6	·318 23	·549 09	·856 74	6	·168 90	·688 75	·109 78
7	·297 34	·522 78	·845 91	7	·036 75	·532 54	1·981 01
8	·276 33	·496 14	·835 03	8	1·893 94	·365 49	·841 42
9	·255 21	·469 13	·824 09	9	·739 30	·186 59	·689 81
40	·233 95	·441 76	·813 01	90	·571 83	1·994 77	·525 17
1	·212 54	·413 97	·801 86	1	·389 99	·788 83	·345 98
2	·190 98	·385 77	·790 55	2	·192 60	·567 57	·151 06
3	·169 23	·357 10	·779 06	3	0·979 38	·329 70	0·940 25
4	·147 29	·327 97	·767 39	4	·745 22	·072 95	·708 16
45	·125 14	·298 33	·755 49	95	·492 42	0·797 04	·457 37
6	·102 76	·268 16	·743 35	6	·216 06	·499 56	·182 73
7	·080 12	·237 42	·730 93	7	$\bar{1}$·915 97	·180 27	$\bar{1}$·884 13
8	·057 21	·206 07	·718 20	8	·609 48	$\bar{1}$·839 14	·580 17
9	·033 99	·174 12	·705 11	9	·267 94	·452 66	·241 60
				100	$\bar{2}$·898 73	$\bar{2}$·992 28	$\bar{2}$·877 49
				1	·279 63	·279 63	·262 60

H^M Table (Makeham Graduation)

Value of Annuities, and Single and Annual Premiums for Assurance of a Unit

4 *per cent.*

Age x	a_x	A_x	P_x
1	19·305	·219 04	·010 79
2	19·807	·199 73	·009 60
3	20·059	·190 06	·009 03
4	20·188	·185 08	·008 74
5	20·264	·182 16	·008 57
6	20·292	·181 06	·008 50
7	20·282	·181 51	·008 53
8	20·234	·183 29	·008 63
9	20·162	·186 12	·008 80
10	20·065	·189 82	·009 01
1	19·953	·194 14	·009 27
2	19·828	·198 92	·009 55
3	19·692	·204 09	·009 86
4	19·551	·209 58	·010 20
15	19·403	·215 28	·010 55
6	19·254	·221 02	·010 91
7	19·102	·226 84	·011 28
8	18·954	·232 58	·011 66
9	18·806	·238 22	·012 03
20	18·662	·243 77	·012 40
1	18·520	·249 25	·012 77
2	18·379	·254 66	·013 14
3	18·238	·260 11	·013 52
4	18·095	·265 60	·013 91
25	17·949	·271 18	·014 31
6	17·800	·276 92	·014 73
7	17·647	·282 84	·015 17
8	17·488	·288 93	·015 63
9	17·324	·295 25	·016 11
30	17·155	·301 75	·016 62
1	16·979	·308 50	·017 16
2	16·799	·315 46	·017 72
3	16·612	·322 63	·018 32
4	16·419	·330 04	·018 95
35	16·221	·337 68	·019 61
6	16·016	·345 55	·020 31
7	15·805	·353 65	·021 04
8	15·588	·361 99	·021 82
9	15·366	·370 58	·022 64
40	15·136	·379 37	·023 51
1	14·902	·388 44	·024 43
2	14·660	·397 71	·025 40
3	14·413	·407 22	·026 42
4	14·159	·416 97	·027 51
45	13·900	·426 92	·028 65
6	13·635	·437 11	·029 87
7	13·364	·447 52	·031 15
8	13·089	·458 13	·032 52
9	12·807	·468 94	·033 96

Age x	a_x	A_x	P_x
50	12·522	·479 95	·035 50
1	12·230	·491 16	·037 12
2	11·935	·502 50	·038 85
3	11·635	·514 06	·040 68
4	11·331	·525 73	·042 63
55	11·024	·537 54	·044 71
6	10·714	·549 47	·046 91
7	10·401	·561 53	·049 25
8	10·085	·573 67	·051 75
9	9·767	·585 87	·054 41
60	9·448	·598 14	·057 25
1	9·129	·610 44	·060 27
2	8·808	·622 77	·063 50
3	8·488	·635 10	·066 94
4	8·168	·647 40	·070 61
65	7·850	·659 64	·074 54
6	7·533	·671 83	·078 74
7	7·218	·683 93	·083 23
8	6·906	·695 92	·088 02
9	6·597	·707 80	·093 16
70	6·293	·719 52	·098 66
1	5·993	·731 07	·104 55
2	5·698	·742 44	·110 86
3	5·408	·753 55	·117 60
4	5·124	·764 49	·124 84
75	4·846	·775 14	·132 58
6	4·576	·785 54	·140 89
7	4·313	·795 68	·149 78
8	4·057	·805 55	·159 31
9	3·808	·815 04	·169 51
80	3·568	·824 31	·180 44
1	3·337	·833 20	·192 13
2	3·114	·841 76	·204 61
3	2·900	·850 02	·217 95
4	2·695	·857 93	·232 22
85	2·498	·865 49	·247 43
6	2·310	·872 73	·263 65
7	2·132	·879 55	·280 85
8	1·962	·886 09	·299 18
9	1·801	·892 30	·318 58
90	1·648	·898 13	·339 16
1	1·505	·903 63	·360 70
2	1·371	·908 78	·383 26
3	1·240	·913 84	·407 90
4	1·127	·918 21	·431 73
95	1·017	·922 47	·457 44
6	·921	·926 13	·482 14
7	·838	·929 31	·505 66
8	·697	·934 74	·550 85
9	·530	·941 15	·615 09
100	·240	·952 27	·767 73
1	...	·961 54	·961 54

H^M Table (Makeham Graduation)

Logarithms of D *and* N. *Joint Lives. Equal Ages*

4 *per cent.*

Age x	Two Lives log D_{xx}	Two Lives log N_{xx}	Three Lives log D_{xxx}	Three Lives log N_{xxx}	Four Lives log D_{xxxx}	Four Lives log N_{xxxx}	Age x
0	10·209 54	11·353 74	15·314 31	16·349 74	20·419 08	21·353 26	0
1	·088 55	·321 41	·141 34	·307 75	·194 13	·299 53	1
2	·040 49	·295 24	·077 77	·277 08	·115 05	·264 04	2
3	·004 32	·270 38	·032 03	·248 73	·059 74	·232 08	3
4	9·973 77	·246 18	14·994 72	·221 52	·015 67	·201 86	4
5	·945 69	·222 35	·961 12	·194 99	19·976 55	·172 60	5
6	·919 72	·198 74	·930 68	·168 85	·941 64	·144 01	6
7	·895 45	·175 28	·902 79	·143 01	·910 13	·115 88	7
8	·872 55	·151 86	·876 96	·117 27	·881 37	·087 96	8
9	·850 72	·128 40	·852 73	·091 56	·854 74	·060 09	9
10	·829 67	·104 86	·829 67	·065 77	·829 67	·032 14	10
1	·809 07	·081 17	·807 29	·039 77	·805 51	·004 02	1
2	·788 82	·057 32	·785 43	·013 55	·782 04	20·975 61	2
3	·768 77	·033 26	·763 87	15·987 09	·758 97	·946 86	3
4	·748 75	·008 98	·742 36	·960 31	·735 97	·917 74	4
15	·728 74	10·984 45	·720 86	·933 19	·712 98	·888 17	15
6	·708 53	·959 65	·699 06	·905 70	·689 59	·858 15	6
7	·688 07	·934 58	·676 89	·877 84	·665 71	·827 64	7
8	·667 24	·909 24	·654 16	·849 60	·641 08	·796 64	8
9	·646 05	·883 62	·630 89	·820 98	·615 73	·765 18	9
20	·624 43	·857 74	·606 98	·792 01	·589 53	·733 25	20
1	·602 42	·831 58	·582 48	·762 67	·562 54	·700 88	1
2	·580 09	·805 17	·557 50	·733 00	·534 91	·668 09	2
3	·557 45	·778 51	·532 06	·702 99	·506 67	·634 89	3
4	·534 60	·751 59	·506 30	·672 66	·478 00	·601 30	4
25	·511 55	·724 40	·480 24	·641 99	·448 93	·567 31	25
6	·488 35	·696 95	·453 96	·610 99	·419 57	·532 92	6
7	·465 04	·669 21	·427 51	·579 64	·389 98	·498 10	7
8	·441 63	·641 20	·400 91	·547 90	·360 19	·462 85	8
9	·418 09	·612 86	·374 12	·515 78	·330 15	·427 13	9
30	·394 44	·584 20	·347 16	·483 26	·299 88	·390 94	30
1	·370 69	·555 19	·320 05	·450 30	·269 41	·354 20	1
2	·346 79	·525 82	·292 72	·416 86	·238 65	·316 91	2
3	·322 76	·496 07	·265 19	·382 94	·207 62	·279 05	3
4	·298 57	·465 92	·237 42	·348 48	·176 27	·240 55	4
35	·274 21	·435 32	·209 40	·313 49	·144 59	·201 37	35
6	·249 66	·404 27	·181 09	·277 88	·112 52	·161 49	6
7	·224 91	·372 73	·152 48	·241 67	·080 05	·120 87	7
8	·199 93	·340 66	·123 53	·204 77	·047 13	·079 40	8
9	·174 72	·308 07	·094 23	·167 17	·013 74	·037 11	9
40	·149 23	·274 87	·064 51	·128 82	18·979 79	19·993 85	40
1	·123 45	·241 07	·034 36	·089 66	·945 27	·949 63	1
2	·097 36	·206 64	·003 74	·049 64	·910 12	·904 36	2
3	·070 89	·171 46	13·972 55	·008 69	·874 21	·857 95	3
4	·044 05	·135 58	·940 81	14·966 76	·837 57	·810 35	4
45	·016 78	·098 89	·908 42	·923 79	·800 06	·761 46	45
6	8·989 05	·061 38	·875 34	·879 71	·761 63	·711 20	6
7	·960 01	·022 96	·841 50	·834 43	·722 19	·659 46	7
8	·932 02	9·983 57	·806 83	·787 89	·681 64	·606 13	8
9	·902 61	·943 18	·771 23	·739 97	·639 85	·551 12	9

H^M Table (Makeham Graduation)

Logarithms of D *and* N. *Joint Lives. Equal Ages*

4 *per cent.*

Age x	Two Lives		Three Lives		Four Lives		Age x
	log D_{xx}	log N_{xx}	log D_{xxx}	log N_{xxx}	log D_{xxxx}	log N_{xxxx}	
50	8·872 53	9·901 71	13·734 63	14·690 59	18·596 73	19·494 28	50
1	·841 74	·859 08	·696 96	·639 66	·552 18	·435 49	1
2	·810 13	·815 21	·658 06	·587 04	·505 99	·374 60	2
3	·777 63	·770 00	·617 83	·532 63	·458 03	·311 44	3
4	·744 18	·723 39	·576 17	·476 28	·408 16	·245 86	4
55	·709 67	·675 26	·532 92	·417 85	·356 17	·177 68	55
6	·673 99	·625 51	·487 92	·357 21	·301 85	·106 67	6
7	·637 06	·574 02	·441 04	·294 16	·245 02	·032 62	7
8	·598 75	·520 65	·392 09	·228 55	·185 43	18·955 32	8
9	·558 89	·465 28	·340 82	·160 14	·122 75	·874 46	9
60	·517 38	·407 76	·287 07	·088 74	·056 76	·789 80	60
1	·474 05	·347 92	·230 59	·014 10	17·987 13	·701 01	1
2	·428 71	·285 58	·171 10	13·936 00	·913 49	·607 74	2
3	·381 18	·220 58	·108 32	·854 12	·835 46	·509 65	3
4	·331 25	·152 66	·041 94	·768 16	·752 63	·406 32	4
65	·278 69	·081 64	12·971 62	·677 81	·664 55	·297 30	65
6	·223 24	·007 28	·896 96	·582 68	·570 68	·182 13	6
7	·164 65	8·929 25	·817 59	·482 39	·470 53	·060 28	7
8	·102 57	·847 30	·732 99	·376 50	·363 41	17·931 17	8
9	·036 72	·761 12	·642 73	·264 56	·248 74	·794 17	9
70	7·966 71	·670 34	·546 23	·146 00	·125 75	·648 59	70
1	·892 13	·574 59	·442 88	·020 28	16·993 63	·493 68	1
2	·812 60	·473 46	·332 10	12·886 82	·851 60	·328 62	2
3	·727 59	·366 46	·213 10	·744 88	·698 61	·152 47	3
4	·636 61	·253 14	·085 15	·593 74	·533 69	16·964 26	4
75	·539 04	·132 93	11·947 31	·432 57	·355 58	·762 88	75
6	·434 31	·005 22	·798 73	·260 50	·163 15	·547 16	6
7	·321 67	7·869 38	·638 29	·076 53	15·954 91	·315 76	7
8	·200 46	·724 70	·464 99	11·879 60	·729 52	·067 29	8
9	·069 81	·570 38	·277 53	·668 52	·485 25	15·800 13	9
80	6·928 77	·405 55	·074 49	·441 96	·220 21	·512 51	80
1	·776 42	·229 27	10·854 48	·198 55	14·932 54	·202 57	1
2	·611 57	·040 52	·615 72	10·936 68	·619 87	14·868 15	2
3	·433 13	6·838 19	·356 58	·654 72	·280 03	·507 07	3
4	·239 82	·621 03	·075 13	·350 77	13·910 44	·116 81	4
85	·030 21	·387 66	9·769 23	·022 76	·508 25	13·694 58	85
6	5·802 67	·136 56	·436 44	9·668 34	·070 21	·237 24	6
7	·555 40	5·866 10	·074 05	·285 06	12·592 70	12·741 40	7
8	·286 81	·574 54	8·679 68	8·870 34	·072 55	·203 71	8
9	4·994 57	·259 78	·249 84	·420 96	11·505 11	11·619 78	9
90	·676 66	4·919 70	7·781 49	7·933 74	10·886 32	10·985 37	90
1	·330 01	·551 72	·270 03	·404 59	·210 05	·294 86	1
2	3·952 27	·153 57	6·711 94	6·830 23	9·471 61	9·543 81	2
3	·542 86	3·722 87	·106 34	·207 58	8·669 82	8·728 92	3
4	·091 57	·253 48	5·437 92	5·525 58	7·784 27	7·833 50	4
95	2·603 01	2·746 54	4·713 60	4·787 43	6·824 19	6·863 58	95
6	·067 32	·195 90	3·918 58	3·981 45	5·769 84	5·801 61	6
7	1·484 17	1·604 51	·052 37	·111 06	4·620 57	4·650 05	7
8	0·888 23	0·988 32	2·166 98	2·212 69	3·445 73	3·467 02	8
9	·222 18	·301 83	1·176 42	1·212 11	2·130 66	2·146 72	9
100	$\bar{1}$·500 79	$\bar{1}$·526 13	0·102 85	0·109 31	0·704 91	0·706 54	100
1	$\bar{2}$·279 63	$\bar{2}$·279 63	$\bar{2}$·279 63	$\bar{2}$·279 63	$\bar{2}$·279 63	$\bar{2}$·279 63	1

H^M Table (Makeham Graduation)

Values of Annuities. Joint Lives. Equal Ages

4 per cent.

Age x	Two Lives a_{xx}	Three Lives a_{xxx}	Four Lives a_{xxxx}	Age x	Two Lives a_{xx}	Three Lives a_{xxx}	Four Lives a_{xxxx}
1	16·095	13·669	11·747	50	9·695	8·036	6·899
2	16·978	14·824	13·093	1	9·407	7·764	6·644
3	17·453	15·470	13·871	2	9·117	7·492	6·389
4	17·725	15·859	14·353	3	8·826	7·219	6·135
5	17·908	16·134	14·705	4	8·533	6·945	5·882
6	18·012	16·305	14·936	55	8·238	6·673	5·630
7	18·047	16·386	15·060	6	7·944	6·401	5·380
8	18·024	16·391	15·091	7	7·649	6·131	5·132
9	17·953	16·332	15·045	8	7·354	5·862	4·887
10	17·844	16·222	14·940	9	7·061	5·597	4·646
1	17·711	16·079	14·794	60	6·769	5·334	4·408
2	17·557	15·910	14·616	1	6·479	5·075	4·175
3	17·386	15·720	14·414	2	6·193	4·820	3·946
4	17·207	15·518	14·197	3	5·909	4·569	3·723
15	17·018	15·305	13·969	4	5·629	4·324	3·505
6	16·829	15·093	13·742	65	5·353	4·084	3·293
7	16·641	14·884	13·519	6	5·082	3·850	3·088
8	16·458	14·683	13·308	7	4·816	3·622	2·888
9	16·281	14·492	13·108	8	4·556	3·401	2·696
20	16·112	14·312	12·923	9	4·302	3·186	2·511
1	15·950	14·142	12·751	70	4·054	2·979	2·333
2	15·791	13·979	12·589	1	3·814	2·779	2·163
3	15·637	13·823	12·435	2	3·580	2·587	1·999
4	15·481	13·668	12·283	3	3·354	2·402	1·844
25	15·325	13·513	12·134	4	3·136	2·226	1·695
6	15·166	13·356	11·982	75	2·925	2·057	1·555
7	15·002	13·194	11·827	6	2·723	1·896	1·421
8	14·833	13·028	11·666	7	2·530	1·743	1·295
9	14·659	12·857	11·502	8	2·344	1·598	1·177
30	14·479	12·681	11·332	9	2·166	1·460	1·065
1	14·293	12·497	11·156	80	1·998	1·331	·960
2	14·102	12·309	10·975	1	1·837	1·208	·862
3	13·905	12·114	10·788	2	1·685	1·094	·771
4	13·701	11·914	10·595	3	1·541	·987	·687
35	13·491	11·708	10·397	4	1·406	·886	·608
6	13·276	11·497	10·194	85	1·278	·793	·536
7	13·054	11·280	9·985	6	1·157	·706	·469
8	12·827	11·057	9·772	7	1·045	·626	·408
9	12·594	10·829	9·552	8	·940	·551	·353
40	12·355	10·596	9·329	9	·842	·483	·302
1	12·111	10·358	9·101	90	·750	·420	·256
2	11·860	10·115	8·868	1	·666	·363	·216
3	11·606	9·868	8·633	2	·590	·313	·181
4	11·346	9·616	8·393	3	·514	·263	·146
45	11·082	9·360	8·150	4	·452	·224	·120
6	10·812	9·101	7·904	95	·392	·185	·095
7	10·538	8·839	7·655	6	·345	·156	·076
8	10·260	8·573	7·404	7	·319	·145	·070
9	9·979	8·305	7·152	8	·259	·111	·050
				9	·201	·086	·038
				100	·060	·015	·004

BRITISH OFFICES LIFE TABLES, 1893

WHOLE-LIFE NON-PARTICIPATING ASSURANCES

MALE LIVES

$O^{[NM]}$

SELECT TABLES

GRADUATION FUNCTIONS

$t=$	0	1	2
A_t	·002 720 1	·004 617 2	·005 767 9
B_t	·000 072 150	·000 075 981	·000 085 117
a_t	·001 623 6	·002 278 7	·002 650 1
β_t	·000 033 393	·000 036 503	·000 041 183
$\log_{10} B_t$	$\bar{5}$·858 234 4	$\bar{5}$·880 703 9	$\bar{5}$·930 014 1
$\log_{10} \beta_t$	$\bar{5}$·523 655 4	$\bar{5}$·562 328 6	$\bar{5}$·614 718 0
$\log_{10} k_t$	5·060 845 6	5·062 091 5	5·062 682 5
$\log_{10} g_t$	−·000 573 064	−·000 554 370	−·000 540 126

$t=$	3	4	5 or more
A_t	·006 358 8	·006 576 5	·006 607 6
B_t	·000 096 021	·000 105 156	·000 108 987
a_t	·002 819 0	·002 866 2	·002 869 6
β_t	·000 045 873	·000 048 933	·000 049 523
$\log_{10} B_t$	$\bar{5}$·982 364 2	$\bar{4}$·021 835 3	$\bar{4}$·037 376 4
$\log_{10} \beta_t$	$\bar{5}$·661 557 1	$\bar{5}$·689 601 8	$\bar{5}$·694 806 9
$\log_{10} k_t$	5·062 901 9	5·062 952 5	5·062 956 0
$\log_{10} g_t$	−·000 531 381	−·000 527 674	−·000 527 087

ABSOLUTE CONSTANTS

$c=$ 1·093 956 4; $\log_{10} c=$ ·039; $\log_e c=$ ·089 800 8; $\log_{10} s = -a_5 = -$ ·002 869 6

$$\log l_{[x]+t} = \log k_t + (x+t)\log s + c^{x+t}\log g_t$$

$$\mu_{[x]+t} = A_t + B_t c^{x+t}$$

$$\mathrm{col}_{10}\,(p_{[x]+t}) = a_t + \beta_t c^{x+t}$$

Age at Entry $[x]$	Years elapsed since Date of Assurance						Age Attained $x+5$
	0	1	2	3	4	5 or more	
	$l_{[x]}$	$l_{[x]+1}$	$l_{[x]+2}$	$l_{[x]+3}$	$l_{[x]+4}$	l_{x+5}	
20	100 000	99 580	99 003	98 333	97 616	96 879	25
1	99 264	98 844	98 267	97 596	96 877	96 137	6
2	98 530	98 109	97 530	96 857	96 135	95 392	7
3	97 794	97 369	96 790	96 115	95 389	94 641	8
4	97 055	96 630	96 048	95 370	94 639	93 886	9
25	96 316	95 887	95 302	94 619	93 884	93 124	30
6	95 567	95 135	94 547	93 862	93 122	92 355	1
7	94 818	94 382	93 791	93 100	92 353	91 578	2
8	94 059	93 618	93 023	92 327	91 574	90 790	3
9	93 300	92 854	92 253	91 550	90 788	89 995	4
30	92 529	92 079	91 472	90 763	89 991	89 187	35
1	91 749	91 294	90 682	89 964	89 183	88 365	6
2	90 962	90 500	89 879	89 154	88 361	87 529	7
3	90 163	89 693	89 066	88 330	87 525	86 678	8
4	89 355	88 877	88 241	87 494	86 674	85 810	9
35	88 536	88 048	87 402	86 642	85 806	84 924	40
6	87 700	87 203	86 545	85 771	84 918	84 016	1
7	86 850	86 342	85 670	84 881	84 010	83 085	2
8	85 981	85 459	84 775	83 971	83 079	82 130	3
9	85 092	84 559	83 861	83 039	82 124	81 148	4
40	84 188	83 639	82 924	82 081	81 141	80 136	45
1	83 257	82 693	81 962	81 096	80 131	79 095	6
2	82 300	81 720	80 969	80 081	79 086	78 017	7
3	81 319	80 720	79 948	79 035	78 010	76 904	8
4	80 310	79 691	78 897	77 956	76 897	75 753	9
45	79 267	78 627	77 807	76 837	75 743	74 557	50
6	78 192	77 528	76 683	75 682	74 549	73 318	1
7	77 083	76 394	75 520	74 483	73 308	72 029	2
8	75 931	75 216	74 312	73 239	72 019	70 690	3
9	74 736	73 993	73 057	71 945	70 679	69 296	4
50	73 499	72 724	71 753	70 599	69 284	67 845	55
1	72 212	71 405	70 398	69 199	67 831	66 333	6
2	70 878	70 036	68 989	67 744	66 319	64 759	7
3	69 483	68 606	67 518	66 225	64 743	63 118	8
4	68 036	67 120	65 989	64 644	63 102	61 409	9
55	66 527	65 571	64 395	62 997	61 392	59 629	60
6	64 952	63 954	62 732	61 279	59 610	57 776	1
7	63 315	62 274	61 004	59 494	57 758	55 851	2
8	61 610	60 523	59 202	57 634	55 832	53 852	3
9	59 830	58 698	57 327	55 699	53 829	51 777	4
60	57 982	56 802	55 380	53 693	51 756	49 632	65
1	56 060	54 831	53 357	51 611	49 608	47 414	6
2	54 059	52 784	51 259	49 456	47 389	45 130	7
3	51 991	50 669	49 093	47 233	45 106	42 785	8
4	49 845	48 476	46 853	44 942	42 757	40 382	9
65	47 630	46 218	44 549	42 589	40 355	37 932	70
6	45 348	43 894	42 185	40 182	37 904	35 445	1
7	43 002	41 512	39 766	37 726	35 415	32 929	2
8	40 603	39 080	37 304	35 235	32 901	30 401	3
9	38 152	36 602	34 803	32 717	30 372	27 874	4
70	35 662	34 092	32 280	30 186	27 845	25 365	75
1	33 146	31 564	29 747	27 659	25 336	22 893	6
2	30 615	29 030	27 221	25 152	22 864	20 476	7
3	28 083	26 506	24 717	22 682	20 448	18 135	8
4	25 570	24 012	22 255	20 271	18 108	15 889	9
75	23 091	21 564	19 854	17 936	15 863	13 758	80

Age at Entry $[x]$	Years elapsed since Date of Assurance: 0 — $\log l_{[x]}$	1 — $\log l_{[x]+1}$	2 — $\log l_{[x]+2}$	3 — $\log l_{[x]+3}$	4 — $\log l_{[x]+4}$	5 or more — $\log l_{x+5}$	Age Attained $x+5$
20	5·000 00	4·998 17	4·995 65	4·992 70	4·989 52	4·986 23	25
1	4·996 79	·994 95	·992 41	·989 43	·986 22	·982 89	6
2	·993 57	·991 71	·989 14	·986 13	·982 88	·979 51	7
3	·990 31	·988 42	·985 83	·982 79	·979 50	·976 08	8
4	·987 02	·985 11	·982 49	·979 41	·976 07	·972 60	9
25	·983 70	·981 76	·979 10	·975 98	·972 59	·969 06	30
6	·980 31	·978 34	·975 65	·972 49	·969 05	·965 46	1
7	·976 89	·974 89	·972 16	·968 95	·965 45	·961 79	2
8	·973 40	·971 36	·968 59	·965 33	·961 77	·958 04	3
9	·969 88	·967 80	·964 98	·961 66	·958 03	·954 22	4
30	·966 28	·964 16	·961 29	·957 91	·954 20	·950 30	35
1	·962 60	·960 44	·957 52	·954 07	·950 28	·946 28	6
2	·958 86	·956 65	·953 66	·950 14	·946 26	·942 15	7
3	·955 03	·952 76	·949 71	·946 11	·942 13	·937 91	8
4	·951 12	·948 79	·945 67	·941 98	·937 89	·933 54	9
35	·947 12	·944 72	·941 52	·937 73	·933 52	·929 03	40
6	·943 00	·940 53	·937 24	·933 34	·929 00	·924 36	1
7	·938 77	·936 22	·932 83	·928 81	·924 33	·919 52	2
8	·934 40	·931 76	·928 27	·924 13	·919 49	·914 50	3
9	·929 89	·927 16	·923 56	·919 28	·914 47	·909 28	4
40	·925 25	·922 41	·918 68	·914 24	·909 24	·903 83	45
1	·920 42	·917 47	·913 61	·909 00	·903 80	·898 15	6
2	·915 40	·912 33	·908 32	·903 53	·898 10	·892 19	7
3	·910 19	·906 98	·902 81	·897 82	·892 15	·885 95	8
4	·904 77	·901 41	·897 06	·891 85	·885 91	·879 40	9
45	·899 09	·895 57	·891 02	·885 57	·879 34	·872 49	50
6	·893 16	·889 46	·884 70	·878 99	·872 44	·865 21	1
7	·886 96	·883 06	·878 06	·872 06	·865 15	·857 51	2
8	·880 42	·876 31	·871 06	·864 74	·857 45	·849 36	3
9	·873 53	·869 19	·863 66	·857 00	·849 29	·840 71	4
50	·866 28	·861 68	·855 84	·848 80	·840 63	·831 52	55
1	·858 61	·853 73	·847 56	·840 10	·831 43	·821 73	6
2	·850 51	·845 32	·838 78	·830 87	·821 64	·811 30	7
3	·841 88	·836 36	·829 42	·821 02	·811 19	·800 15	8
4	·832 74	·826 85	·819 47	·810 53	·800 04	·788 23	9
55	·823 00	·816 71	·808 85	·799 32	·788 11	·775 46	60
6	·812 59	·805 87	·797 49	·787 31	·775 32	·761 75	1
7	·801 51	·794 31	·785 36	·774 47	·761 61	·747 03	2
8	·789 65	·781 92	·772 34	·760 68	·746 88	·731 20	3
9	·776 92	·768 62	·758 36	·745 85	·731 02	·714 14	4
60	·763 29	·754 36	·743 35	·729 92	·713 96	·695 76	65
1	·748 65	·739 03	·727 19	·712 74	·695 55	·675 91	6
2	·732 87	·722 50	·709 77	·694 22	·675 68	·654 47	7
3	·715 93	·704 74	·691 02	·674 25	·654 23	·631 29	8
4	·697 62	·685 53	·670 74	·652 65	·631 01	·606 19	9
65	·677 88	·664 81	·648 84	·629 30	·605 90	·579 01	70
6	·656 56	·642 41	·625 16	·604 03	·578 69	·549 55	1
7	·633 49	·618 17	·599 51	·576 64	·549 19	·517 58	2
8	·608 56	·591 95	·571 75	·546 98	·517 21	·482 89	3
9	·581 52	·563 50	·541 62	·514 77	·482 47	·445 20	4
70	·552 21	·532 65	·508 93	·479 81	·444 74	·404 24	75
1	·520 43	·499 19	·473 45	·441 84	·403 74	·359 70	6
2	·485 94	·462 85	·434 91	·400 58	·359 16	·311 25	7
3	·448 44	·423 34	·392 99	·355 69	·310 65	·258 51	8
4	·407 73	·380 42	·347 43	·306 87	·257 86	·201 09	9
75	·363 45	·333 73	·297 85	·253 73	·200 38	·138 55	80

Age at Entry $[x]$	Years elapsed since Date of Assurance						Age Attained $x+5$
	0	1	2	3	4	5 or more	
	$d_{[x]}$	$d_{[x]+1}$	$d_{[x]+2}$	$d_{[x]+3}$	$d_{[x]+4}$	d_{x+5}	
20	420	577	670	717	737	742	25
1	420	577	671	719	740	745	6
2	421	579	673	722	743	751	7
3	425	579	675	726	748	755	8
4	425	582	678	731	753	762	9
25	429	585	683	735	760	769	30
6	432	588	685	740	767	777	1
7	436	591	691	747	775	788	2
8	441	595	696	753	784	795	3
9	446	601	703	762	793	808	4
30	450	607	709	772	804	822	35
1	455	612	718	781	818	836	6
2	462	621	725	793	832	851	7
3	470	627	736	805	847	868	8
4	478	636	747	820	864	886	9
35	488	646	760	836	882	908	40
6	497	658	774	853	902	931	1
7	508	672	789	871	925	955	2
8	522	684	804	892	949	982	3
9	533	698	822	915	976	1 012	4
40	549	715	843	940	1 005	1 041	45
1	564	731	866	965	1 036	1 078	6
2	580	751	888	995	1 069	1 113	7
3	599	772	913	1 025	1 106	1 151	8
4	619	794	941	1 059	1 144	1 196	9
45	640	820	970	1 094	1 186	1 239	50
6	664	845	1 001	1 133	1 231	1 289	1
7	689	874	1 037	1 175	1 279	1 339	2
8	715	904	1 073	1 220	1 329	1 394	3
9	743	936	1 112	1 266	1 383	1 451	4
50	775	971	1 154	1 315	1 439	1 512	55
1	807	1 007	1 199	1 368	1 498	1 574	6
2	842	1 047	1 245	1 425	1 560	1 641	7
3	877	1 088	1 293	1 482	1 625	1 709	8
4	916	1 131	1 345	1 542	1 693	1 780	9
55	956	1 176	1 398	1 605	1 763	1 853	60
6	998	1 222	1 453	1 669	1 834	1 925	1
7	1 041	1 270	1 510	1 736	1 907	1 999	2
8	1 087	1 321	1 568	1 802	1 980	2 075	3
9	1 132	1 371	1 628	1 870	2 052	2 145	4
60	1 180	1 422	1 687	1 937	2 124	2 218	65
1	1 229	1 474	1 746	2 003	2 194	2 284	6
2	1 275	1 525	1 803	2 067	2 259	2 345	7
3	1 322	1 576	1 860	2 127	2 321	2 403	8
4	1 369	1 623	1 911	2 185	2 375	2 450	9
65	1 412	1 669	1 960	2 234	2 423	2 487	70
6	1 454	1 709	2 003	2 278	2 459	2 516	1
7	1 490	1 746	2 040	2 311	2 486	2 528	2
8	1 523	1 776	2 069	2 334	2 500	2 527	3
9	1 550	1 799	2 086	2 345	2 498	2 509	4
70	1 570	1 812	2 094	2 341	2 480	2 472	75
1	1 582	1 817	2 088	2 323	2 443	2 417	6
2	1 585	1 809	2 069	2 288	2 388	2 341	7
3	1 577	1 789	2 035	2 234	2 313	2 246	8
4	1 558	1 757	1 984	2 163	2 219	2 131	9
75	1 527	1 710	1 918	2 073	2 105	1 998	80

Age at Entry [x]	Years elapsed since Date of Assurance: 0	1	2	3	4	5 or more	Age Attained x+5
	$q_{[x]}$	$q_{[x]+1}$	$q_{[x]+2}$	$q_{[x]+3}$	$q_{[x]+4}$	q_{x+5}	
20	·004 20	·005 79	·006 77	·007 30	·007 55	·007 66	25
1	·004 23	·005 83	·006 84	·007 36	·007 64	·007 75	6
2	·004 27	·005 90	·006 91	·007 46	·007 73	·007 87	7
3	·004 34	·005 95	·006 98	·007 55	·007 84	·007 98	8
4	·004 39	·006 01	·007 07	·007 66	·007 96	·008 12	9
25	·004 46	·006 11	·007 16	·007 78	·008 10	·008 26	30
6	·004 53	·006 17	·007 25	·007 89	·008 23	·008 41	1
7	·004 59	·006 27	·007 36	·008 03	·008 39	·008 60	2
8	·004 69	·006 36	·007 48	·008 16	·008 55	·008 76	3
9	·004 78	·006 47	·007 62	·008 32	·008 73	·008 99	4
30	·004 87	·006 59	·007 75	·008 51	·008 94	·009 21	35
1	·004 96	·006 70	·007 91	·008 69	·009 17	·009 46	6
2	·005 08	·006 86	·008 07	·008 89	·009 42	·009 72	7
3	·005 21	·007 00	·008 25	·009 12	·009 67	·010 01	8
4	·005 35	·007 16	·008 46	·009 37	·009 97	·010 33	9
35	·005 51	·007 34	·008 69	·009 65	·010 29	·010 70	40
6	·005 67	·007 55	·008 94	·009 94	·010 63	·011 08	1
7	·005 85	·007 78	·009 21	·010 26	·011 01	·011 49	2
8	·006 06	·008 00	·009 49	·010 63	·011 42	·011 95	3
9	·006 27	·008 26	·009 81	·011 01	·011 88	·012 47	4
40	·006 52	·008 55	·010 17	·011 45	·012 38	·012 99	45
1	·006 77	·008 85	·010 56	·011 90	·012 93	·013 63	6
2	·007 04	·009 19	·010 97	·012 43	·013 52	·014 27	7
3	·007 36	·009 56	·011 42	·012 97	·014 17	·014 97	8
4	·007 71	·009 97	·011 92	·013 58	·014 88	·015 78	9
45	·008 07	·010 42	·012 47	·014 24	·015 65	·016 62	50
6	·008 48	·010 90	·013 06	·014 97	·016 51	·017 57	1
7	·008 94	·011 45	·013 72	·015 78	·017 44	·018 59	2
8	·009 42	·012 02	·014 45	·016 65	·018 46	·019 72	3
9	·009 94	·012 65	·015 22	·017 60	·019 56	·020 94	4
50	·010 54	·013 36	·016 08	·018 64	·020 76	·022 29	55
1	·011 17	·014 11	·017 03	·019 77	·022 09	·023 73	6
2	·011 88	·014 95	·018 05	·021 03	·023 53	·025 35	7
3	·012 63	·015 85	·019 16	·022 38	·025 10	·027 07	8
4	·013 47	·016 85	·020 37	·023 86	·026 83	·028 98	9
55	·014 38	·017 94	·021 70	·025 48	·028 71	·031 08	60
6	·015 35	·019 11	·023 17	·027 23	·030 76	·033 33	1
7	·016 44	·020 40	·024 76	·029 18	·033 01	·035 79	2
8	·017 64	·021 82	·026 49	·031 28	·035 46	·038 52	3
9	·018 93	·023 35	·028 39	·033 57	·038 12	·041 44	4
60	·020 35	·025 03	·030 45	·036 08	·041 04	·044 68	65
1	·021 91	·026 89	·032 72	·038 81	·044 22	·048 17	6
2	·023 59	·028 89	·035 17	·041 79	·047 66	·051 97	7
3	·025 44	·031 10	·037 88	·045 05	·051 45	·056 16	8
4	·027 45	·033 48	·040 80	·048 61	·055 55	·060 67	9
65	·029 65	·036 10	·044 00	·052 45	·060 04	·065 58	70
6	·032 06	·038 94	·047 49	·056 68	·064 90	·070 97	1
7	·034 66	·042 06	·051 30	·061 25	·070 20	·076 77	2
8	·037 52	·045 45	·055 44	·066 25	·075 98	·083 13	3
9	·040 64	·049 13	·059 95	·071 68	·082 24	·090 00	4
70	·044 04	·053 15	·064 85	·077 58	·089 04	·097 47	75
1	·047 73	·057 55	·070 20	·083 99	·096 43	·105 56	6
2	·051 78	·062 31	·076 00	·090 97	·104 45	·114 35	7
3	·056 16	·067 50	·082 30	·098 51	·113 13	·123 85	8
4	·060 95	·073 15	·089 16	·106 72	·122 53	·134 12	9
75	·066 14	·079 30	·096 60	·115 60	·132 70	·145 25	80

Age at Entry [x]	Years elapsed since Date of Assurance						Age Attained x+5
	0	1	2	3	4	5 or more	
	$p_{[x]}$	$p_{[x]+1}$	$p_{[x]+2}$	$p_{[x]+3}$	$p_{[x]+4}$	p_{x+5}	
20	·995 80	·994 21	·993 23	·992 70	·992 45	·992 34	25
1	·995 77	·994 17	·993 16	·992 64	·992 36	·992 25	6
2	·995 73	·994 10	·993 09	·992 54	·992 27	·992 13	7
3	·995 66	·994 05	·993 02	·992 45	·992 16	·992 02	8
4	·995 61	·993 99	·992 93	·992 34	·992 04	·991 88	9
25	·995 54	·993 89	·992 84	·992 22	·991 90	·991 74	30
6	·995 47	·993 83	·992 75	·992 11	·991 77	·991 59	1
7	·995 41	·993 73	·992 64	·991 97	·991 61	·991 40	2
8	·995 31	·993 64	·992 52	·991 84	·991 45	·991 24	3
9	·995 22	·993 53	·992 38	·991 68	·991 27	·991 01	4
30	·995 13	·993 41	·992 25	·991 49	·991 06	·990 79	35
1	·995 04	·993 30	·992 09	·991 31	·990 83	·990 54	6
2	·994 92	·993 14	·991 93	·991 11	·990 58	·990 28	7
3	·994 79	·993 00	·991 75	·990 88	·990 33	·989 99	8
4	·994 65	·992 84	·991 54	·990 63	·990 03	·989 67	9
35	·994 49	·992 66	·991 31	·990 35	·989 71	·989 30	40
6	·994 33	·992 45	·991 06	·990 06	·989 37	·988 92	1
7	·994 15	·992 22	·990 79	·989 74	·988 99	·988 51	2
8	·993 94	·992 00	·990 51	·989 37	·988 58	·988 05	3
9	·993 73	·991 74	·990 19	·988 99	·988 12	·987 53	4
40	·993 48	·991 45	·989 83	·988 55	·987 62	·987 01	45
1	·993 23	·991 15	·989 44	·988 10	·987 07	·986 37	6
2	·992 96	·990 81	·989 03	·987 57	·986 48	·985 73	7
3	·992 64	·990 44	·988 58	·987 03	·985 83	·985 03	8
4	·992 29	·990 03	·988 08	·986 42	·985 12	·984 22	9
45	·991 93	·989 58	·987 53	·985 76	·984 35	·983 38	50
6	·991 52	·989 10	·986 94	·985 03	·983 49	·982 43	1
7	·991 06	·988 55	·986 28	·984 22	·982 56	·981 41	2
8	·990 58	·987 98	·985 55	·983 35	·981 54	·980 28	3
9	·990 06	·987 35	·984 78	·982 40	·980 44	·979 06	4
50	·989 46	·986 64	·983 92	·981 36	·979 24	·977 71	55
1	·988 83	·985 89	·982 97	·980 23	·977 91	·976 27	6
2	·988 12	·985 05	·981 95	·978 97	·976 47	·974 65	7
3	·987 37	·984 15	·980 84	·977 62	·974 90	·972 93	8
4	·986 53	·983 15	·979 63	·976 14	·973 17	·971 02	9
55	·985 62	·982 06	·978 30	·974 52	·971 29	·968 92	60
6	·984 65	·980 89	·976 83	·972 77	·969 24	·966 67	1
7	·983 56	·979 60	·975 24	·970 82	·966 99	·964 21	2
8	·982 36	·978 18	·973 51	·968 72	·964 54	·961 48	3
9	·981 07	·976 65	·971 61	·966 43	·961 88	·958 56	4
60	·979 65	·974 97	·969 55	·963 92	·958 96	·955 32	65
1	·978 09	·973 11	·967 28	·961 19	·955 78	·951 83	6
2	·976 41	·971 11	·964 83	·958 21	·952 34	·948 03	7
3	·974 56	·968 90	·962 12	·954 95	·948 55	·943 84	8
4	·972 55	·966 52	·959 20	·951 39	·944 45	·939 33	9
65	·970 35	·963 90	·956 00	·947 55	·939 96	·934 42	70
6	·967 94	·961 06	·952 51	·943 32	·935 10	·929 03	1
7	·965 34	·957 94	·948 70	·938 75	·929 80	·923 23	2
8	·962 48	·954 55	·944 56	·933 75	·924 02	·916 87	3
9	·959 36	·950 87	·940 05	·928 32	·917 76	·910 00	4
70	·955 96	·946 85	·935 15	·922 42	·910 96	·902 53	75
1	·952 27	·942 45	·929 80	·916 01	·903 57	·894 44	6
2	·948 22	·937 69	·924 00	·909 03	·895 55	·885 65	7
3	·943 84	·932 50	·917 70	·901 49	·886 87	·876 15	8
4	·939 05	·926 85	·910 84	·893 28	·877 47	·865 88	9
75	·933 86	·920 70	·903 40	·884 40	·867 30	·854 75	80

Age at Entry [x]	Years elapsed since Date of Assurance: 0	1	2	3	4	5 or more	Age Attained x+5
	$\log p_{[x]}$	$\log p_{[x]+1}$	$\log p_{[x]+2}$	$\log p_{[x]+3}$	$\log p_{[x]+4}$	$\log p_{x+5}$	
20	$\bar{1}$·998 17	$\bar{1}$·997 48	$\bar{1}$·997 05	$\bar{1}$·996 82	$\bar{1}$·996 71	$\bar{1}$·996 66	25
1	·998 16	·997 46	·997 02	·996 79	·996 67	·996 62	6
2	·998 14	·997 43	·996 99	·996 75	·996 63	·996 57	7
3	·998 11	·997 41	·996 96	·996 71	·996 58	·996 52	8
4	·998 09	·997 38	·996 92	·996 66	·996 53	·996 46	9
25	·998 06	·997 34	·996 88	·996 61	·996 47	·996 40	30
6	·998 03	·997 31	·996 84	·996 56	·996 41	·996 33	1
7	·998 00	·997 27	·996 79	·996 50	·996 34	·996 25	2
8	·997 96	·997 23	·996 74	·996 44	·996 27	·996 18	3
9	·997 92	·997 18	·996 68	·996 37	·996 19	·996 08	4
30	·997 88	·997 13	·996 62	·996 29	·996 10	·995 98	35
1	·997 84	·997 08	·996 55	·996 21	·996 00	·995 87	6
2	·997 79	·997 01	·996 48	·996 12	·995 89	·995 76	7
3	·997 73	·996 95	·996 40	·996 02	·995 78	·995 63	8
4	·997 67	·996 88	·996 31	·995 91	·995 65	·995 49	9
35	·997 60	·996 80	·996 21	·995 79	·995 51	·995 33	40
6	·997 53	·996 71	·996 10	·995 66	·995 36	·995 16	1
7	·997 45	·996 61	·995 98	·995 52	·995 19	·994 98	2
8	·997 36	·996 51	·995 86	·995 36	·995 01	·994 78	3
9	·997 27	·996 40	·995 72	·995 19	·994 81	·994 55	4
40	·997 16	·996 27	·995 56	·995 00	·994 59	·994 32	45
1	·997 05	·996 14	·995 39	·994 80	·994 35	·994 04	6
2	·996 93	·995 99	·995 21	·994 57	·994 09	·993 76	7
3	·996 79	·995 83	·995 01	·994 33	·993 80	·993 45	8
4	·996 64	·995 65	·994 79	·994 06	·993 49	·993 09	9
45	·996 48	·995 45	·994 55	·993 77	·993 15	·992 72	50
6	·996 30	·995 24	·994 29	·993 45	·992 77	·992 30	1
7	·996 10	·995 00	·994 00	·993 09	·992 36	·991 85	2
8	·995 89	·994 75	·993 68	·992 71	·991 91	·991 35	3
9	·995 66	·994 47	·993 34	·992 29	·991 42	·990 81	4
50	·995 40	·994 16	·992 96	·991 83	·990 89	·990 21	55
1	·995 12	·993 83	·992 54	·991 33	·990 30	·989 57	6
2	·994 81	·993 46	·992 09	·990 77	·989 66	·988 85	7
3	·994 48	·993 06	·991 60	·990 17	·988 96	·988 08	8
4	·994 11	·992 62	·991 06	·989 51	·988 19	·987 23	9
55	·993 71	·992 14	·990 47	·988 79	·987 35	·986 29	60
6	·993 28	·991 62	·989 82	·988 01	·986 43	·985 28	1
7	·992 80	·991 05	·989 11	·987 14	·985 42	·984 17	2
8	·992 27	·990 42	·988 34	·986 20	·984 32	·982 94	3
9	·991 70	·989 74	·987 49	·985 17	·983 12	·981 62	4
60	·991 07	·988 99	·986 57	·984 04	·981 80	·980 15	65
1	·990 38	·988 16	·985 55	·982 81	·980 36	·978 56	6
2	·989 63	·987 27	·984 45	·981 46	·978 79	·976 82	7
3	·988 81	·986 28	·983 23	·979 98	·977 06	·974 90	8
4	·987 91	·985 21	·981 91	·978 36	·975 18	·972 82	9
65	·986 93	·984 03	·980 46	·976 60	·973 11	·970 54	70
6	·985 85	·982 75	·978 87	·974 66	·970 86	·968 03	1
7	·984 68	·981 34	·977 13	·972 55	·968 39	·965 31	2
8	·983 39	·979 80	·975 23	·970 23	·965 68	·962 31	3
9	·981 98	·978 12	·973 15	·967 70	·962 73	·959 04	4
70	·980 44	·976 28	·970 88	·964 93	·959 50	·955 46	75
1	·978 76	·974 26	·968 39	·961 90	·955 96	·951 55	6
2	·976 91	·972 06	·965 67	·958 58	·952 09	·947 26	7
3	·974 90	·969 65	·962 70	·954 96	·947 86	·942 58	8
4	·972 69	·967 01	·959 44	·950 99	·943 23	·937 46	9
75	·970 28	·964 12	·955 88	·946 65	·938 17	·931 84	80

$\mu_{[x]+t}$

Age at Entry $[x]$	Years elapsed since Date of Assurance: 0	1	2	3	4	5 or more	Age Attained $x+5$
	$\mu_{[x]}$	$\mu_{[x]+1}$	$\mu_{[x]+2}$	$\mu_{[x]+3}$	$\mu_{[x]+4}$	μ_{x+5}	
20	·003 16	·005 12	·006 38	·007 12	·007 48	·007 64	25
1	·003 20	·005 17	·006 44	·007 19	·007 57	·007 73	6
2	·003 24	·005 22	·006 50	·007 27	·007 66	·007 84	7
3	·003 29	·005 27	·006 57	·007 35	·007 76	·007 96	8
4	·003 34	·005 33	·006 65	·007 44	·007 88	·008 08	9
25	·003 40	·005 40	·006 73	·007 55	·008 00	·008 22	30
6	·003 47	·005 48	·006 82	·007 66	·008 13	·008 37	1
7	·003 54	·005 56	·006 92	·007 78	·008 28	·008 54	2
8	·003 61	·005 64	·007 03	·007 91	·008 44	·008 72	3
9	·003 70	·005 74	·007 15	·008 06	·008 61	·008 92	4
30	·003 79	·005 85	·007 28	·008 22	·008 80	·009 13	35
1	·003 89	·005 96	·007 42	·008 39	·009 01	·009 37	6
2	·004 00	·006 09	·007 57	·008 58	·009 24	·009 63	7
3	·004 12	·006 23	·007 74	·008 79	·009 49	·009 92	8
4	·004 25	·006 38	·007 93	·009 02	·009 77	·010 23	9
35	·004 39	·006 54	·008 13	·009 27	·010 07	·010 57	40
6	·004 55	·006 72	·008 35	·009 55	·010 39	·010 94	1
7	·004 72	·006 92	·008 59	·009 85	·010 75	·011 34	2
8	·004 91	·007 14	·008 86	·010 17	·011 14	·011 79	3
9	·005 12	·007 38	·009 15	·010 53	·011 57	·012 28	4
40	·005 34	·007 64	·009 47	·010 92	·012 04	·012 81	45
1	·005 59	·007 92	·009 81	·011 35	·012 56	·013 39	6
2	·005 86	·008 23	·010 19	·011 82	·013 12	·014 03	7
3	·006 15	·008 57	·010 61	·012 33	·013 73	·014 73	8
4	·006 47	·008 94	·011 07	·012 90	·014 41	·015 49	9
45	·006 82	·009 35	·011 56	·013 51	·015 14	·016 32	50
6	·007 21	·009 79	·012 11	·014 18	·015 95	·017 23	1
7	·007 63	·010 28	·012 70	·014 92	·016 83	·018 23	2
8	·008 09	·010 81	·013 35	·015 72	·017 79	·019 33	3
9	·008 60	·011 39	·014 07	·016 60	·018 85	·020 52	4
50	·009 15	·012 03	·014 85	·017 56	·020 00	·021 83	55
1	·009 75	·012 72	·015 70	·018 62	·021 26	·023 26	6
2	·010 42	·013 48	·016 63	·019 77	·022 64	·024 82	7
3	·011 14	·014 32	·017 65	·021 03	·024 15	·026 53	8
4	·011 93	·015 23	·018 77	·022 41	·025 80	·028 40	9
55	·012 80	·016 22	·019 99	·023 91	·027 61	·030 45	60
6	·013 74	·017 31	·021 33	·025 56	·029 58	·032 69	1
7	·014 78	·018 51	·022 79	·027 37	·031 74	·035 14	2
8	·015 91	·019 81	·024 39	·029 34	·034 11	·037 82	3
9	·017 15	·021 24	·026 14	·031 50	·036 70	·040 76	4
60	·018 50	·022 80	·028 05	·033 86	·039 53	·043 97	65
1	·019 99	·024 51	·030 15	·036 45	·042 62	·047 48	6
2	·021 61	·026 38	·032 44	·039 27	·046 01	·051 32	7
3	·023 39	·028 42	·034 94	·042 36	·049 71	·055 52	8
4	·025 33	·030 66	·037 68	·045 75	·053 77	·060 11	9
65	·027 45	·033 11	·040 68	·049 45	·058 20	·065 14	70
6	·029 77	·035 78	·043 96	·053 50	·063 05	·070 64	1
7	·032 32	·038 71	·047 55	·057 93	·068 36	·076 65	2
8	·035 10	·041 92	·051 48	·062 77	·074 16	·083 24	3
9	·038 14	·045 42	·055 77	·068 07	·080 51	·090 43	4
70	·041 47	·049 26	·060 47	·073 87	·087 46	·098 31	75
1	·045 11	·053 45	·065 61	·080 21	·095 06	·106 93	6
2	·049 09	·058 04	·071 23	·087 15	·103 37	·116 35	7
3	·053 45	·063 06	·077 38	·094 74	·112 47	·126 66	8
4	·058 21	·068 55	·084 11	·103 04	·122 42	·137 94	9
75	·063 43	·074 55	·091 47	·112 13	·133 30	·150 28	80

Age at Entry $[x]$	Years elapsed since Date of Assurance: 0	1	2	3	4	5 or more	Age Attained $x+5$
	$\log \mu_{[x]}$	$\log \mu_{[x]+1}$	$\log \mu_{[x]+2}$	$\log \mu_{[x]+3}$	$\log \mu_{[x]+4}$	$\log \mu_{x+5}$	
20	$\bar{3}$·499 69	$\bar{3}$·709 27	$\bar{3}$·804 82	$\bar{3}$·852 48	$\bar{3}$·873 90	$\bar{3}$·883 09	25
1	·505 15	·713 49	·808 89	·856 73	·879 10	·888 18	6
2	·510 55	·717 67	·812 91	·861 53	·884 23	·894 32	7
3	·517 20	·721 81	·817 57	·866 29	·889 86	·900 91	8
4	·523 75	·726 73	·822 82	·871 57	·896 53	·907 41	9
25	·531 48	·732 39	·828 02	·877 95	·903 09	·914 87	30
6	·540 33	·738 78	·833 78	·884 23	·910 09	·922 73	1
7	·549 00	·745 07	·840 11	·890 98	·918 03	·931 46	2
8	·557 51	·751 28	·846 96	·898 18	·926 34	·940 52	3
9	·568 20	·758 91	·854 31	·906 34	·935 00	·950 36	4
30	·578 64	·767 16	·862 13	·914 87	·944 48	·960 47	35
1	·589 95	·775 25	·870 40	·923 76	·954 72	·971 74	6
2	·602 06	·784 62	·879 10	·933 49	·965 67	·983 63	7
3	·614 90	·794 49	·888 74	·943 99	·977 27	·996 51	8
4	·628 39	·804 82	·899 27	·955 21	·989 89	$\bar{2}$·009 88	9
35	·642 46	·815 58	·910 09	·967 08	$\bar{2}$·003 03	·024 08	40
6	·658 01	·827 37	·921 69	·980 00	·016 62	·039 02	1
7	·673 94	·840 11	·933 99	·993 44	·031 41	·054 61	2
8	·691 08	·853 70	·947 43	$\bar{2}$·007 32	·046 89	·071 51	3
9	·709 27	·868 06	·961 42	·022 43	·063 33	·089 20	4
40	·727 54	·883 09	·976 35	·038 22	·080 63	·107 55	45
1	·747 41	·898 73	·991 67	·055 00	·098 99	·126 78	6
2	·767 90	·915 40	$\bar{2}$·008 17	·072 62	·117 93	·147 06	7
3	·788 88	·932 98	·025 72	·090 96	·137 67	·168 20	8
4	·810 90	·951 34	·044 15	·110 59	·158 66	·190 05	9
45	·833 78	·970 81	·062 96	·130 66	·180 13	·212 72	50
6	·857 94	·990 78	·083 14	·151 68	·202 76	·236 29	1
7	·882 52	$\bar{2}$·011 99	·103 80	·173 77	·226 08	·260 79	2
8	·907 95	·033 83	·125 48	·196 45	·250 18	·286 23	3
9	·934 50	·056 52	·148 29	·220 11	·275 31	·312 18	4
50	·961 42	·080 27	·171 73	·244 52	·301 03	·339 05	55
1	·989 00	·104 49	·195 90	·269 98	·327 56	·366 61	6
2	$\bar{2}$·017 87	·129 69	·220 89	·296 01	·354 88	·394 80	7
3	·046 89	·155 94	·246 74	·322 84	·382 92	·423 74	8
4	·076 64	·182 70	·273 46	·350 44	·411 62	·453 32	9
55	·107 21	·210 05	·300 81	·378 58	·441 07	·483 59	60
6	·137 99	·238 30	·328 99	·407 56	·471 00	·514 41	1
7	·169 67	·267 41	·357 74	·437 27	·501 61	·545 80	2
8	·201 67	·296 88	·387 21	·467 46	·532 88	·577 72	3
9	·234 26	·327 15	·417 31	·498 31	·564 67	·610 23	4
60	·267 17	·357 93	·447 93	·529 69	·596 93	·643 16	65
1	·300 81	·389 34	·479 29	·561 70	·629 61	·676 51	6
2	·334 65	·421 27	·511 08	·594 06	·662 85	·710 29	7
3	·369 03	·453 62	·543 32	·626 96	·696 44	·744 45	8
4	·403 64	·486 57	·576 11	·660 39	·730 54	·778 95	9
65	·438 54	·519 96	·609 38	·694 17	·764 92	·813 85	70
6	·473 78	·553 64	·643 06	·728 35	·799 69	·849 05	1
7	·509 47	·587 82	·677 15	·762 90	·834 80	·884 51	2
8	·545 31	·622 42	·711 64	·797 75	·870 17	·920 33	3
9	·581 38	·657 25	·746 40	·832 96	·905 85	·956 31	4
70	·617 73	·692 49	·781 54	·868 47	·941 81	·992 60	75
1	·654 27	·727 95	·816 97	·904 23	·978 00	$\bar{1}$·029 10	6
2	·690 99	·763 73	·852 66	·940 27	$\bar{1}$·014 39	·065 77	7
3	·727 95	·799 75	·888 63	·976 53	·051 04	·102 64	8
4	·765 00	·836 01	·924 85	$\bar{1}$·013 01	·087 85	·139 69	9
75	·802 29	·872 45	·961 28	·049 72	·124 83	·176 90	80

ULTIMATE VALUES

Age x	l_x	d_x	p_x	q_x	μ_x	$\log l_x$	$\log p_x$	$\log \mu_x$	Age x
25	96 879	742	·992 34	·007 66	·007 64	4·986 23	$\bar{1}$·996 66	$\bar{3}$·883 09	25
6	96 137	745	·992 25	·007 75	·007 73	·982 89	·996 62	·888 18	6
7	95 392	751	·992 13	·007 87	·007 84	·979 51	·996 57	·894 32	7
8	94 641	755	·992 02	·007 98	·007 96	·976 08	·996 52	·900 91	8
9	93 886	762	·991 88	·008 12	·008 08	·972 60	·996 46	·907 41	9
30	93 124	769	·991 74	·008 26	·008 22	·969 06	·996 40	·914 87	30
1	92 355	777	·991 59	·008 41	·008 37	·965 46	·996 33	·922 73	1
2	91 578	788	·991 40	·008 60	·008 54	·961 79	·996 25	·931 46	2
3	90 790	795	·991 24	·008 76	·008 72	·958 04	·996 18	·940 52	3
4	89 995	808	·991 01	·008 99	·008 92	·954 22	·996 08	·950 36	4
35	89 187	822	·990 79	·009 21	·009 13	·950 30	·995 98	·960 47	35
6	88 365	836	·990 54	·009 46	·009 37	·946 28	·995 87	·971 74	6
7	87 529	851	·990 28	·009 72	·009 63	·942 15	·995 76	·983 63	7
8	86 678	868	·989 99	·010 01	·009 92	·937 91	·995 63	·996 51	8
9	85 810	886	·989 67	·010 33	·010 23	·933 54	·995 49	$\bar{2}$·009 88	9
40	84 924	908	·989 30	·010 70	·010 57	·929 03	·995 33	·024 08	40
1	84 016	931	·988 92	·011 08	·010 94	·924 36	·995 16	·039 02	1
2	83 085	955	·988 51	·011 49	·011 34	·919 52	·994 98	·054 61	2
3	82 130	982	·988 05	·011 95	·011 79	·914 50	·994 78	·071 51	3
4	81 148	1 012	·987 53	·012 47	·012 28	·909 28	·994 55	·089 20	4
45	80 136	1 041	·987 01	·012 99	·012 81	·903 83	·994 32	·107 55	45
6	79 095	1 078	·986 37	·013 63	·013 39	·898 15	·994 04	·126 78	6
7	78 017	1 113	·985 73	·014 27	·014 03	·892 19	·993 76	·147 06	7
8	76 904	1 151	·985 03	·014 97	·014 73	·885 95	·993 45	·168 20	8
9	75 753	1 196	·984 22	·015 78	·015 49	·879 40	·993 09	·190 05	9
50	74 557	1 239	·983 38	·016 62	·016 32	·872 49	·992 72	·212 72	50
1	73 318	1 289	·982 43	·017 57	·017 23	·865 21	·992 30	·236 29	1
2	72 029	1 339	·981 41	·018 59	·018 23	·857 51	·991 85	·260 79	2
3	70 690	1 394	·980 28	·019 72	·019 33	·849 36	·991 35	·286 23	3
4	69 296	1 451	·979 06	·020 94	·020 52	·840 71	·990 81	·312 18	4
55	67 845	1 512	·977 71	·022 29	·021 83	·831 52	·990 21	·339 05	55
6	66 333	1 574	·976 27	·023 73	·023 26	·821 73	·989 57	·366 61	6
7	64 759	1 641	·974 65	·025 35	·024 82	·811 30	·988 85	·394 80	7
8	63 118	1 709	·972 93	·027 07	·026 53	·800 15	·988 08	·423 74	8
9	61 409	1 780	·971 02	·028 98	·028 40	·788 23	·987 23	·453 32	9
60	59 629	1 853	·968 92	·031 08	·030 45	·775 46	·986 29	·483 59	60
1	57 776	1 925	·966 67	·033 33	·032 69	·761 75	·985 28	·514 41	1
2	55 851	1 999	·964 21	·035 79	·035 14	·747 03	·984 17	·545 80	2
3	53 852	2 075	·961 48	·038 52	·037 82	·731 20	·982 94	·577 72	3
4	51 777	2 145	·958 56	·041 44	·040 76	·714 14	·981 62	·610 23	4

$O^{[NM]}$ l_x, d_x, p_x, q_x, μ_x, $\log l_x$, $\log p_x$, $\log \mu_x$ $O^{[NM]}$

ULTIMATE VALUES

Age x	l_x	d_x	p_x	q_x	μ_x	$\log l_x$	$\log p_x$	$\log \mu_x$	Age x
65	49 632	2 218	·955 32	·044 68	·043 97	4·695 76	$\bar{1}$·980 15	$\bar{2}$·643 16	65
6	47 414	2 284	·951 83	·048 17	·047 48	·675 91	·978 56	·676 51	6
7	45 130	2 345	·948 03	·051 97	·051 32	·654 47	·976 82	·710 29	7
8	42 785	2 403	·943 84	·056 16	·055 52	·631 29	·974 90	·744 45	8
9	40 382	2 450	·939 33	·060 67	·060 11	·606 19	·972 82	·778 95	9
70	37 932	2 487	·934 42	·065 58	·065 14	·579 01	·970 54	·813 85	70
1	35 445	2 516	·929 03	·070 97	·070 64	·549 55	·968 03	·849 05	1
2	32 929	2 528	·923 23	·076 77	·076 65	·517 58	·965 31	·884 51	2
3	30 401	2 527	·916 87	·083 13	·083 24	·482 89	·962 31	·920 33	3
4	27 874	2 509	·910 00	·090 00	·090 43	·445 20	·959 04	·956 31	4
75	25 365	2 472	·902 53	·097 47	·098 31	·404 24	·955 46	·992 60	75
6	22 893	2 417	·894 44	·105 56	·106 93	·359 70	·951 55	$\bar{1}$·029 10	6
7	20 476	2 341	·885 65	·114 35	·116 35	·311 25	·947 26	·065 77	7
8	18 135	2 246	·876 15	·123 85	·126 66	·258 51	·942 58	·102 64	8
9	15 889	2 131	·865 88	·134 12	·137 94	·201 09	·937 46	·139 69	9
80	13 758	1 998	·854 75	·145 25	·150 28	·138 55	·931 84	·176 90	80
1	11 760	1 849·2	·842 79	·157 21	·163 78	·070 39	·925 72	·214 26	1
2	9 910·8	1 686·3	·829 85	·170 15	·178 55	3·996 11	·919 00	·251 76	2
3	8 224·5	1 513·8	·815 94	·184 06	·194 70	·915 11	·911 66	·289 37	3
4	6 710·7	1 335·4	·801 00	·199 00	·212 38	·826 77	·903 63	·327 11	4
85	5 375·3	1 155·9	·784 96	·215 04	·231 71	·730 40	·894 85	·364 94	85
6	4 219·4	979·9	·767 77	·232 23	·252 86	·625 25	·885 23	·402 88	6
7	3 239·5	811·7	·749 43	·250 57	·275 99	·510 48	·874 73	·440 89	7
8	2 427·8	655·9	·729 83	·270 17	·301 31	·385 21	·863 22	·479 01	8
9	1 771·9	515·7	·708 99	·291 01	·328 99	·248 43	·850 64	·517 18	9
90	1 256·2	393·32	·686 88	·313 12	·359 28	·099 07	·836 88	·555 43	90
1	862·88	290·39	·663 47	·336 53	·392 42	2·935 95	·821 82	·593 75	1
2	572·49	206·79	·638 78	·361 22	·428 67	·757 77	·805 35	·632 12	2
3	365·70	141·60	·612 82	·387 18	·468 33	·563 12	·787 33	·670 55	3
4	224·10	92·86	·585 61	·414 39	·511 71	·350 45	·767 61	·709 02	4
95	131·24	58·106	·557 26	·442 74	·559 16	·118 06	·746 06	·747 54	95
6	73·134	34·535	·527 79	·472 21	·611 08	1·864 12	·722 46	·786 10	6
7	38·599	19·402	·497 35	·502 65	·667 87	·586 58	·696 66	·824 69	7
8	19·197	10·250	·466 04	·533 96	·730 00	·283 24	·668 42	·863 32	8
9	8·947	5·064	·434 06	·565 94	·797 97	0·951 66	·637 55	·901 99	9
100	3·883	2·324	·401 56	·598 44	·892 33	·589 21	·603 75	·950 53	100
1	1·559	·984	·368 81	·631 19	·953 67	·192 96	·566 80	·979 40	1
2	·575	·382	·336 02	·663 98	1·042 65	$\bar{1}$·759 76	·526 36	0·018 14	2
3	·193	·134	·303 48	·696 52	1·139 99	·286 12	·482 13	·056 90	3
4	·059	·043	·271 48	·728 52	1·246 48	$\bar{2}$·768 25	·433 74	·095 68	4
105	·016	·016	·000 00	1·000 00	1·362 97	·201 99	...	·134 49	105

$O^{[NM]}$ $e_{[x]+t}$ $O^{[NM]}$

Age Attained $[x]+t$	$t=0$	$t=5$ or more	Age Attained $[x]+t$	$t=0$	$t=5$ or more
20	40·980	...	65	10·750	10·356
1	40·277	...	6	10·244	9·841
2	39·571	...	7	9·752	9·339
3	38·864	...	8	9·273	8·851
4	38·155	...	9	8·809	8·377
25	37·441	37·228	70	8·360	7·918
6	36·728	36·515	1	7·924	7·474
7	36·012	35·800	2	7·503	7·045
8	35·297	35·084	3	7·098	6·631
9	34·578	34·366	4	6·707	6·232
30	33·859	33·648	75	6·330	5·849
1	33·141	32·928	6	...	5·480
2	32·420	32·206	7	...	5·127
3	31·700	31·487	8	...	4·789
4	30·980	30·765	9	...	4·466
35	30·259	30·043	80	...	4·158
6	29·539	29·322	1	...	3·864
7	28·820	28·603	2	...	3·585
8	28·103	27·884	3	...	3·320
9	27·388	27·166	4	...	3·069
40	26·674	26·450	85	...	2·831
1	25·962	25·735	6	...	2·607
2	25·254	25·024	7	...	2·395
3	24·548	24·314	8	...	2·196
4	23·846	23·609	9	...	2·009
45	23·148	22·906	90	...	1·833
6	22·455	22·209	1	...	1·669
7	21·765	21·514	2	...	1·515
8	21·082	20·826	3	...	1·371
9	20·405	20·143	4	...	1·238
50	19·732	19·466	95	...	1·114
1	19·069	18·795	6	...	·999
2	18·411	18·131	7	...	·892
3	17·761	17·475	8	...	·793
4	17·120	16·826	9	...	·703
55	16·488	16·185	100	...	·619
6	15·866	15·555	1	...	·541
7	15·251	14·933	2	...	·466
8	14·648	14·321	3	...	·386
9	14·056	13·720	4	...	·271
60	13·474	13·130	105	...	·000
1	12·904	12·550			
2	12·347	11·956			
3	11·801	11·428			
4	11·269	10·886			

O[NM]

THREE PER CENT.

INTEREST CONSTANTS

Constant	Number	Logarithm
i	·03	$\bar{2}$·477 121 3
$(1+i)$	1·03	0·012 837 2
$(1+i)^{\frac{1}{2}}$	1·014 889 2	0·006 418 6
$(1+i)^{\frac{1}{4}}$	1·007 417 1	0·003 209 3
v	·970 873 8	$\bar{1}$·987 162 8
$v^{\frac{1}{2}}$	·985 329 3	$\bar{1}$·993 581 4
$v^{\frac{1}{4}}$	·992 637 5	$\bar{1}$·996 790 7
d	·029 126 2	$\bar{2}$·464 284 0
δ	·029 558 8	$\bar{2}$·470 686 8

Age at Entry $[x]$	Years elapsed since Date of Assurance: 0 $D_{[x]}$	1 $D_{[x]+1}$	2 $D_{[x]+2}$	3 $D_{[x]+3}$	4 $D_{[x]+4}$	5 or more D_{x+5}	Age Attained $x+5$
20	55 368	53 529	51 669	49 824	48 021	46 270	25
1	53 359	51 586	49 791	48 011	46 269	44 578	6
2	51 422	49 711	47 979	46 259	44 577	42 944	7
3	49 551	47 899	46 227	44 568	42 943	41 366	8
4	47 745	46 151	44 537	42 934	41 365	39 840	9
25	46 001	44 462	42 903	41 356	39 839	38 365	30
6	44 314	42 828	41 325	39 830	38 365	36 941	1
7	42 685	41 252	39 800	38 356	36 940	35 563	2
8	41 111	39 726	38 324	36 930	35 561	34 230	3
9	39 591	38 254	36 900	35 552	34 229	32 942	4
30	38 121	36 831	35 522	34 220	32 940	31 696	35
1	36 699	35 453	34 189	32 931	31 694	30 489	6
2	35 324	34 121	32 900	31 684	30 487	29 320	7
3	33 994	32 831	31 653	30 477	29 319	28 190	8
4	32 708	31 586	30 446	29 309	28 189	27 095	9
35	31 464	30 379	29 278	28 179	27 094	26 034	40
6	30 259	29 211	28 147	27 083	26 032	25 005	1
7	29 093	28 081	27 051	26 021	25 003	24 008	2
8	27 963	26 984	25 988	24 992	24 007	23 041	3
9	26 868	25 922	24 959	23 995	23 039	22 102	4
40	25 808	24 893	23 962	23 027	22 100	21 191	45
1	24 779	23 895	22 994	22 088	21 189	20 307	6
2	23 782	22 926	22 054	21 176	20 304	19 446	7
3	22 813	21 986	21 141	20 291	19 445	18 611	8
4	21 874	21 073	20 256	19 431	18 609	17 798	9
45	20 961	20 186	19 394	18 594	17 796	17 007	50
6	20 075	19 325	18 557	17 782	17 005	16 237	1
7	19 214	18 487	17 744	16 990	16 235	15 487	2
8	18 375	17 672	16 951	16 220	15 485	14 757	3
9	17 559	16 878	16 179	15 469	14 754	14 044	4
50	16 766	16 106	15 428	14 738	14 042	13 350	55
1	15 992	15 353	14 696	14 025	13 347	12 672	6
2	15 239	14 620	13 982	13 330	12 670	12 011	7
3	14 505	13 904	13 285	12 651	12 008	11 366	8
4	13 789	13 207	12 606	11 990	11 363	10 736	9
55	13 090	12 527	11 943	11 344	10 733	10 121	60
6	12 408	11 862	11 296	10 713	10 118	9 520·9	1
7	11 743	11 214	10 665	10 098	9 517·9	8 935·5	2
8	11 094	10 581	10 049	9 497·5	8 932·4	8 364·7	3
9	10 460	9 963·0	9 446·9	8 911·3	8 361·2	7 808·4	4
60	9 841·5	9 360·3	8 860·1	8 340·1	7 805·1	7 266·7	65
1	9 238·0	8 772·4	8 287·8	7 783·2	7 263·2	6 739·8	6
2	8 648·9	8 198·8	7 730·2	7 241·0	6 736·3	6 228·5	7
3	8 075·7	7 641·2	7 187·9	6 714·1	6 225·0	5 732·7	8
4	7 516·9	7 097·6	6 660·1	6 202·4	5 729·0	5 253·2	9
65	6 973·6	6 569·8	6 148·2	5 706·5	5 249·6	4 790·7	70
6	6 446·1	6 057·9	5 652·4	5 227·1	4 787·2	4 346·2	1
7	5 934·7	5 562·1	5 173·0	4 764·6	4 342·6	3 920·1	2
8	5 440·4	5 083·7	4 711·3	4 320·6	3 916·8	3 513·7	3
9	4 963·1	4 622·6	4 267·6	3 894·8	3 510·3	3 127·9	4
70	4 504·0	4 180·3	3 842·8	3 488·9	3 124·6	2 763·4	75
1	4 064·3	3 757·6	3 438·2	3 103·8	2 760·3	2 421·4	6
2	3 644·7	3 355·3	3 054·6	2 740·2	2 418·4	2 102·7	7
3	3 245·8	2 974·3	2 692·8	2 399·2	2 099·8	1 808·0	8
4	2 869·3	2 616·0	2 354·0	2 081·6	1 805·3	1 538·0	9
75	2 515·7	2 280·9	2 038·8	1 788·3	1 535·5	1 292·9	80

Age at Entry [x]	Years elapsed since Date of Assurance: 0	1	2	3	4	5 or more	Age Attained x+5
	$\log D_{[x]}$	$\log D_{[x]+1}$	$\log D_{[x]+2}$	$\log D_{[x]+3}$	$\log D_{[x]+4}$	$\log D_{x+5}$	
20	4·743 26	4·728 59	4·713 23	4·697 44	4·681 43	4·665 30	25
1	·727 21	·712 53	·697 15	·681 34	·665 29	·649 12	6
2	·711 15	·696 45	·681 05	·665 20	·649 11	·632 90	7
3	·695 05	·680 33	·664 90	·649 02	·632 89	·616 64	8
4	·678 93	·664 18	·648 72	·632 80	·616 63	·600 32	9
25	·662 77	·647 99	·632 49	·616 54	·600 31	·583 94	30
6	·646 54	·631 73	·616 21	·600 21	·583 93	·567 51	1
7	·630 28	·615 45	·599 88	·583 83	·567 50	·551 00	2
8	·613 96	·599 08	·583 47	·567 38	·550 98	·534 41	3
9	·597 60	·582 68	·567 03	·550 87	·534 40	·517 75	4
30	·581 16	·566 21	·550 50	·534 28	·517 73	·501 00	35
1	·564 65	·549 65	·533 89	·517 60	·500 98	·484 14	6
2	·548 07	·533 02	·517 19	·500 84	·484 12	·467 17	7
3	·531 40	·516 29	·500 41	·483 97	·467 15	·450 10	8
4	·514 65	·499 49	·483 53	·467 00	·450 08	·432 89	9
35	·497 82	·482 58	·466 54	·449 92	·432 87	·415 54	40
6	·480 86	·465 55	·449 43	·432 69	·415 51	·398 03	1
7	·463 79	·448 41	·432 18	·415 32	·398 00	·380 36	2
8	·446 59	·431 11	·414 78	·397 80	·380 33	·362 50	3
9	·429 24	·413 67	·397 23	·380 12	·362 47	·344 44	4
40	·411 76	·396 08	·379 52	·362 24	·344 40	·326 15	45
1	·394 09	·378 31	·361 61	·344 16	·326 12	·307 64	6
2	·376 24	·360 33	·343 48	·325 85	·307 59	·288 84	7
3	·358 19	·342 14	·325 13	·307 31	·288 80	·269 76	8
4	·339 93	·323 73	·306 55	·288 50	·269 72	·250 38	9
45	·321 41	·305 06	·287 67	·269 38	·250 32	·230 63	50
6	·302 65	·286 11	·268 51	·249 97	·230 58	·210 51	1
7	·283 61	·266 87	·249 04	·230 20	·210 45	·189 97	2
8	·264 23	·247 29	·229 20	·210 04	·189 91	·168 99	3
9	·244 51	·227 33	·208 96	·189 46	·168 92	·147 50	4
50	·224 42	·206 98	·188 30	·168 43	·147 42	·125 47	55
1	·203 91	·186 19	·167 19	·146 89	·125 38	·102 85	6
2	·182 97	·164 95	·145 57	·124 82	·102 76	·079 58	7
3	·161 51	·143 15	·123 37	·102 14	·079 47	·055 59	8
4	·139 53	·120 80	·100 59	·078 81	·055 48	·030 83	9
55	·116 95	·097 83	·077 13	·054 76	·030 71	·005 23	60
6	·093 71	·074 15	·052 93	·029 91	·005 09	3·978 68	1
7	·069 79	·049 75	·027 96	·004 24	3·978 54	·951 12	2
8	·045 09	·024 52	·002 11	3·977 61	·950 97	·922 45	3
9	·019 52	3·998 39	3·975 29	·949 94	·922 27	·892 56	4
60	3·993 06	·971 29	·947 44	·921 17	·892 38	·861 34	65
1	·965 58	·943 12	·918 44	·891 16	·861 13	·828 65	6
2	·936 96	·913 75	·888 19	·859 80	·828 42	·794 38	7
3	·907 18	·883 16	·856 60	·826 99	·794 14	·758 36	8
4	·876 04	·851 11	·823 48	·792 56	·758 08	·720 42	9
65	·843 46	·817 55	·788 75	·756 37	·720 13	·680 40	70
6	·809 30	·782 32	·752 23	·718 26	·680 08	·638 11	1
7	·773 40	·745 24	·713 74	·678 03	·637 75	·593 30	2
8	·735 63	·706 18	·673 14	·635 54	·592 93	·545 77	3
9	·695 75	·664 89	·630 18	·590 49	·545 35	·495 25	4
70	·653 60	·621 21	·584 65	·542 69	·494 79	·441 45	75
1	·608 99	·574 91	·536 33	·491 89	·440 95	·384 07	6
2	·561 66	·525 73	·484 96	·437 79	·383 53	·322 78	7
3	·511 32	·473 39	·430 20	·380 06	·322 18	·257 21	8
4	·457 78	·417 63	·371 80	·318 40	·256 56	·186 95	9
75	·400 66	·358 10	·309 38	·252 43	·186 24	·111 57	80

Age at Entry $[x]$	Years elapsed since Date of Assurance: 0	1	2	3	4	5 or more	Age Attained $x+5$
	$N_{[x]}$	$N_{[x]+1}$	$N_{[x]+2}$	$N_{[x]+3}$	$N_{[x]+4}$	N_{x+5}	
20	1 265 826	1 210 458	1 156 929	1 105 260	1 055 436	1 007 415	25
1	1 210 161	1 156 802	1 105 216	1 055 425	1 007 414	961 145	6
2	1 156 515	1 105 093	1 055 382	1 007 403	961 144	916 567	7
3	1 104 811	1 055 260	1 007 361	961 134	916 566	873 623	8
4	1 054 989	1 007 244	961 093	916 556	873 622	832 257	9
25	1 006 978	960 977	916 515	873 612	832 256	792 417	30
6	960 714	916 400	873 572	832 247	792 417	754 052	1
7	916 144	873 459	832 207	792 407	754 051	717 111	2
8	873 200	832 089	792 363	754 039	717 109	681 548	3
9	831 844	792 253	753 999	717 099	681 547	647 318	4
30	792 010	753 889	717 058	681 536	647 316	614 376	35
1	753 646	716 947	681 494	647 305	614 374	582 680	6
2	716 707	681 383	647 262	614 362	582 678	552 191	7
3	681 145	647 151	614 320	582 667	552 190	522 871	8
4	646 919	614 211	582 625	552 179	522 870	494 681	9
35	613 980	582 516	552 137	522 859	494 680	467 586	40
6	582 284	552 025	522 814	494 667	467 584	441 552	1
7	551 796	522 703	494 622	467 571	441 550	416 547	2
8	522 473	494 510	467 526	441 538	416 546	392 539	3
9	494 281	467 413	441 491	416 532	392 537	369 498	4
40	467 186	441 378	416 485	392 523	369 496	347 396	45
1	441 150	416 371	392 476	369 482	347 394	326 205	6
2	416 140	392 358	369 432	347 378	326 202	305 898	7
3	392 128	369 315	347 329	326 188	305 897	286 452	8
4	369 084	347 210	326 137	305 881	286 450	267 841	9
45	346 974	326 013	305 827	286 433	267 839	250 043	50
6	325 780	305 705	286 380	267 823	250 041	233 036	1
7	305 469	286 255	267 768	250 024	233 034	216 799	2
8	286 015	267 640	249 968	233 017	216 797	201 312	3
9	267 394	249 835	232 957	216 778	201 309	186 555	4
50	249 591	232 825	216 719	201 291	186 553	172 511	55
1	232 574	216 582	201 229	186 533	172 508	159 161	6
2	216 330	201 091	186 471	172 489	159 159	146 489	7
3	200 831	186 326	172 422	159 137	146 486	134 478	8
4	186 067	172 278	159 071	146 465	134 475	123 112	9
55	172 013	158 923	146 396	134 453	123 109	112 376	60
6	158 652	146 244	134 382	123 086	112 373	102 254·7	1
7	145 972	134 229	123 015	112 350	102 251·7	92 733·8	2
8	133 952	122 858	112 277	102 228·2	92 730·7	83 798·3	3
9	122 576	112 116	102 153·0	92 706·1	83 794·8	75 433·6	4
60	111 832·3	101 990·8	92 630·5	83 770·4	75 430·3	67 625·2	65
1	101 703·1	92 465·1	83 692·7	75 404·9	67 621·7	60 358·5	6
2	92 173·9	83 525·0	75 326·2	67 596·0	60 355·0	53 618·7	7
3	83 234·1	75 158·4	67 517·2	60 329·3	53 615·2	47 390·2	8
4	74 863·5	67 346·6	60 249·0	53 588·9	47 386·5	41 657·5	9
65	67 052·0	60 078·4	53 508·6	47 360·4	41 653·9	36 404·3	70
6	59 784·3	53 338·2	47 280·3	41 627·9	36 400·8	31 613·6	1
7	53 044·4	47 109·7	41 547·6	36 374·6	31 610·0	27 267·4	2
8	46 820·1	41 379·7	36 296·0	31 584·7	27 264·1	23 347·3	3
9	41 092·0	36 128·9	31 506·3	27 238·7	23 343·9	19 833·6	4
70	35 846·3	31 342·3	27 162·0	23 319·2	19 830·3	16 705·7	75
1	31 066·5	27 002·2	23 244·6	19 806·4	16 702·6	13 942·3	6
2	26 734·1	23 089·4	19 734·1	16 679·5	13 939·3	11 520·9	7
3	22 830·1	19 584·3	16 610·0	13 917·2	11 518·0	9 418·2	8
4	19 336·4	16 467·1	13 851·1	11 497·1	9 415·5	7 610·2	9
75	16 231·4	13 715·7	11 434·8	9 396·0	7 607·7	6 072·2	80

Age at Entry [x]	Years elapsed since Date of Assurance: 0	1	2	3	4	5 or more	Age Attained $x+5$
	$\log N_{[x]}$	$\log N_{[x]+1}$	$\log N_{[x]+2}$	$\log N_{[x]+3}$	$\log N_{[x]+4}$	$\log N_{x+5}$	
20	6·102 38	6·082 95	6·063 31	6·043 46	6·023 43	6·003 21	25
1	·082 84	·063 26	·043 45	·023 43	·003 21	5·982 79	6
2	·063 15	·043 40	·023 41	·003 20	5·982 79	·962 17	7
3	·043 28	·023 36	·003 18	5·982 78	·962 17	·941 32	8
4	·023 25	·003 14	5·982 76	·962 16	·941 32	·920 26	9
25	·003 02	5·982 71	·962 14	·941 32	·920 26	·898 96	30
6	5·982 59	·962 09	·941 30	·920 25	·898 96	·877 40	1
7	·961 96	·941 24	·920 23	·898 95	·877 40	·855 59	2
8	·941 11	·920 17	·898 92	·877 39	·855 59	·833 50	3
9	·920 04	·898 86	·877 37	·855 58	·833 50	·811 12	4
30	·898 73	·877 31	·855 56	·833 49	·811 12	·788 44	35
1	·877 17	·855 49	·833 46	·811 11	·788 43	·765 43	6
2	·855 34	·833 39	·811 08	·788 42	·765 43	·742 09	7
3	·833 24	·811 01	·788 39	·765 42	·742 09	·718 39	8
4	·810 85	·788 32	·765 39	·742 08	·718 39	·694 32	9
35	·788 15	·765 31	·742 05	·718 39	·694 32	·669 87	40
6	·765 13	·741 96	·718 34	·694 32	·669 86	·644 98	1
7	·741 78	·718 25	·694 27	·669 85	·644 98	·619 67	2
8	·718 06	·694 18	·669 81	·644 97	·619 67	·593 88	3
9	·693 97	·669 70	·644 92	·619 65	·593 88	·567 61	4
40	·669 49	·644 81	·619 60	·593 86	·567 61	·540 83	45
1	·644 59	·619 48	·593 82	·567 59	·540 82	·513 49	6
2	·619 24	·593 68	·567 53	·540 80	·513 48	·485 58	7
3	·593 43	·567 40	·540 74	·513 47	·485 58	·457 05	8
4	·567 12	·540 59	·513 40	·485 55	·457 05	·427 88	9
45	·540 29	·513 23	·485 48	·457 02	·427 88	·398 02	50
6	·512 92	·485 31	·456 94	·427 85	·398 01	·367 42	1
7	·484 97	·456 76	·427 76	·397 98	·367 42	·336 06	2
8	·456 39	·427 55	·397 89	·367 38	·336 05	·303 87	3
9	·427 15	·397 65	·367 27	·336 02	·303 87	·270 81	4
50	·397 23	·367 03	·335 90	·303 82	·270 81	·236 81	55
1	·366 56	·335 62	·303 69	·270 76	·236 81	·201 83	6
2	·335 12	·303 39	·270 61	·236 76	·201 83	·165 81	7
3	·302 83	·270 27	·236 59	·201 77	·165 80	·128 65	8
4	·269 67	·236 23	·201 59	·165 74	·128 65	·090 30	9
55	·235 56	·201 19	·165 53	·128 57	·090 29	·050 67	60
6	·200 45	·165 08	·128 34	·090 21	·050 66	·009 68	1
7	·164 27	·127 85	·089 96	·050 57	·009 67	4·967 24	2
8	·126 95	·089 40	·050 29	·009 57	4·967 22	·923 23	3
9	·088 40	·049 66	·009 25	4·967 11	·923 22	·877 57	4
60	·048 57	·008 56	4·966 76	·923 09	·877 54	·830 11	65
1	·007 33	4·965 98	·922 69	·877 40	·830 09	·780 74	6
2	4·964 61	·921 82	·876 94	·829 92	·780 71	·729 32	7
3	·920 30	·875 98	·829 41	·780 53	·729 29	·675 69	8
4	·874 27	·828 32	·779 95	·729 08	·675 66	·619 70	9
65	·826 41	·778 72	·728 43	·675 41	·619 66	·561 15	70
6	·776 59	·727 04	·674 68	·619 39	·561 11	·499 88	1
7	·724 64	·673 11	·618 55	·560 80	·499 82	·435 64	2
8	·670 43	·616 79	·559 86	·499 48	·435 59	·368 24	3
9	·613 76	·557 86	·498 40	·435 19	·368 18	·297 40	4
70	·554 44	·496 13	·433 96	·367 71	·297 33	·222 86	75
1	·492 30	·431 40	·366 32	·296 81	·222 78	·144 34	6
2	·427 06	·363 41	·295 22	·222 19	·144 24	·061 49	7
3	·358 51	·291 91	·220 37	·143 56	·061 38	3·973 97	8
4	·286 38	·216 61	·141 48	·060 58	3·973 84	·881 40	9
75	·210 36	·137 22	·058 23	3·972 94	·881 25	·783 35	80

Age at Entry [x]	Years elapsed since Date of Assurance: 0	1	2	3	4	5 or more		Age Attained x+5
	$M_{[x]}$	$M_{[x]+1}$	$M_{[x]+2}$	$M_{[x]+3}$	$M_{[x]+4}$	M_{x+5}	R_{x+5}	
20	18 498·87	18 273·10	17 971·97	17 632·49	17 279·77	16 927·77	501 941·69	25
1	18 111·88	17 892·69	17 600·33	17 270·24	16 926·84	16 583·71	485 013·92	6
2	17 737·17	17 523·86	17 239·03	16 917·60	16 582·81	16 248·32	468 430·21	7
3	17 372·43	17 163·36	16 886·83	16 573·84	16 247·00	15 920·07	452 181·89	8
4	17 016·81	16 813·83	16 543·96	16 238·74	15 919·23	15 599·69	436 261·82	9
25	16 671·57	16 472·64	16 209·28	15 910·76	15 598·86	15 285·75	420 662·13	30
6	16 331·98	16 137·50	15 880·50	15 589·82	15 284·95	14 978·15	405 376·38	1
7	16 002·20	15 811·63	15 560·84	15 276·16	14 977·37	14 676·41	390 398·23	2
8	15 677·98	15 490·84	15 245·71	14 967·32	14 674·90	14 379·31	375 721·82	3
9	15 363·01	15 179·27	14 938·88	14 665·88	14 378·58	14 088·31	361 342·51	4
30	15 052·50	14 872·51	14 636·79	14 369·48	14 086·89	13 801·16	347 254·20	35
1	14 747·57	14 570·88	14 340·14	14 077·33	13 799·77	13 517·54	333 453·04	6
2	14 448·95	14 274·77	14 047·46	13 789·80	13 516·19	13 237·49	319 935·50	7
3	14 154·67	13 982·63	13 759·80	13 505·85	13 236·19	12 960·72	306 698·01	8
4	13 865·69	13 695·81	13 476·37	13 226·14	12 959·45	12 686·64	293 737·29	9
35	13 581·33	13 412·95	13 196·55	12 949·38	12 685·41	12 415·03	281 050·65	40
6	13 299·61	13 133·12	12 919·12	12 674·73	12 413·24	12 144·78	268 635·62	1
7	13 021·56	12 856·34	12 644·15	12 402·28	12 143·05	11 875·76	256 490·84	2
8	12 745·63	12 580·81	12 371·12	12 131·83	11 874·08	11 607·84	244 615·08	3
9	12 471·57	12 308·17	12 100·43	11 862·90	11 606·20	11 340·37	233 007·24	4
40	12 201·06	12 037·66	11 831·05	11 594·55	11 338·52	11 072·76	221 666·87	45
1	11 930·58	11 767·61	11 562·53	11 326·66	11 071·48	10 805·50	210 594·11	6
2	11 660·80	11 498·08	11 293·53	11 058·71	10 803·26	10 536·80	199 788·61	7
3	11 392·29	11 229·14	11 024·99	10 790·59	10 535·10	10 267·45	189 251·81	8
4	11 124·18	10 960·49	10 756·64	10 522·09	10 265·81	9 997·02	178 984·36	9
45	10 855·21	10 690·90	10 486·51	10 251·77	9 994·73	9 724·20	168 987·34	50
6	10 586·07	10 420·56	10 216·07	9 980·88	9 722·43	9 449·81	159 263·14	1
7	10 316·52	10 149·78	9 944·43	9 707·88	9 447·66	9 172·66	149 813·33	2
8	10 044·71	9 876·72	9 670·51	9 432·88	9 170·57	8 893·14	140 640·67	3
9	9 771·05	9 601·57	9 394·28	9 155·19	8 890·91	8 610·62	131 747·53	4
50	9 496·08	9 324·45	9 115·67	8 874·77	8 608·26	8 325·11	123 136·91	55
1	9 218·33	9 044·82	8 834·61	8 591·61	8 322·43	8 036·26	114 811·80	6
2	8 938·83	8 763·06	8 550·86	8 305·89	8 033·66	7 744·33	106 775·54	7
3	8 655·15	8 477·41	8 263·33	8 016·32	7 741·45	7 448·84	99 031·21	8
4	8 369·47	8 189·23	7 973·17	7 723·71	7 446·05	7 150·07	91 582·37	9
55	8 080·27	7 897·64	7 679·52	7 427·78	7 147·18	6 847·94	84 432·30	60
6	7 787·25	7 602·15	7 382·11	7 128·09	6 844·80	6 542·58	77 584·36	1
7	7 491·55	7 304·10	7 082·08	6 825·78	6 539·70	6 234·60	71 041·78	2
8	7 192·59	7 002·56	6 778·34	6 519·95	6 231·65	5 924·10	64 807·18	3
9	6 889·63	6 697·49	6 471·56	6 211·10	5 920·64	5 611·18	58 883·08	4
60	6 584·20	6 389·75	6 162·25	5 900·21	5 608·10	5 297·12	53 271·90	65
1	6 275·86	6 079·23	5 850·28	5 586·97	5 293·71	4 981·84	47 974·78	6
2	5 964·22	5 766·18	5 536·20	5 272·21	4 978·39	4 666·62	42 992·94	7
3	5 651·47	5 452·10	5 221·35	4 956·96	4 663·41	4 352·42	38 326·32	8
4	5 336·44	5 136·00	4 905·29	4 641·55	4 348·78	4 039·83	33 973·90	9
65	5 020·69	4 819·98	4 589·64	4 327·02	4 036·41	3 730·40	29 934·07	70
6	4 704·87	4 504·21	4 275·22	4 014·66	3 726·96	3 425·44	26 203·67	1
7	4 389·66	4 190·01	3 962·88	3 705·24	3 421·87	3 125·92	22 778·23	2
8	4 076·66	3 878·54	3 654·24	3 400·54	3 122·68	2 833·73	19 652·31	3
9	3 766·18	3 570·42	3 349·83	3 101·50	2 830·47	2 550·16	16 818·58	4
70	3 459·93	3 267·42	3 051·71	2 809·69	2 547·00	2 276·82	14 268·42	75
1	3 159·47	2 971·14	2 761·13	2 526·83	2 273·75	2 015·35	11 991·60	6
2	2 865·98	2 682·79	2 479·79	2 254·38	2 012·37	1 767·15	9 976·25	7
3	2 580·87	2 403·91	2 209·01	1 993·77	1 764·36	1 533·75	8 209·10	8
4	2 306·11	2 136·37	1 950·53	1 746·79	1 531·13	1 316·34	6 675·35	9
75	2 042·90	1 881·39	1 705·79	1 514·56	1 313·90	1 116·08	5 359·01	80

Age at Entry $[x]$	Years elapsed since Date of Assurance: 0	1	2	3	4	5 or more	Age Attained $x+5$
	$\log M_{[x]}$	$\log M_{[x]+1}$	$\log M_{[x]+2}$	$\log M_{[x]+3}$	$\log M_{[x]+4}$	$\log M_{x+5}$	
20	4·267 15	4·261 81	4·254 60	4·246 31	4·237 54	4·228 60	25
1	·257 97	·252 67	·245 52	·237 30	·228 58	·219 68	6
2	·248 88	·243 63	·236 51	·228 34	·219 66	·210 81	7
3	·239 86	·234 60	·227 55	·219 43	·210 77	·201 94	8
4	·230 88	·225 67	·218 64	·210 55	·201 92	·193 11	9
25	·221 98	·216 76	·209 77	·201 69	·193 10	·184 29	30
6	·213 04	·207 84	·200 87	·192 84	·184 27	·175 45	1
7	·204 18	·198 98	·192 04	·184 01	·175 43	·166 62	2
8	·195 29	·190 08	·183 15	·175 14	·166 58	·157 74	3
9	·186 48	·181 25	·174 32	·166 31	·157 72	·148 86	4
30	·177 61	·172 39	·165 44	·157 44	·148 82	·139 91	35
1	·168 72	·163 49	·156 55	·148 52	·139 87	·130 90	6
2	·159 84	·154 57	·147 59	·139 55	·130 86	·121 80	7
3	·150 90	·145 59	·138 61	·130 52	·121 77	·112 63	8
4	·141 94	·136 58	·129 57	·121 43	·112 59	·103 35	9
35	·132 94	·127 53	·120 46	·112 25	·103 30	·093 95	40
6	·123 84	·118 36	·111 23	·102 94	·093 89	·084 39	1
7	·114 66	·109 12	·101 89	·093 50	·084 33	·074 66	2
8	·105 36	·099 71	·092 40	·083 92	·074 60	·064 75	3
9	·095 92	·090 20	·082 80	·074 19	·064 69	·054 62	4
40	·086 40	·080 54	·073 02	·064 25	·054 56	·044 26	45
1	·076 66	·070 69	·063 05	·054 10	·044 21	·033 65	6
2	·066 73	·060 62	·052 83	·043 71	·033 55	·022 71	7
3	·056 61	·050 35	·042 38	·033 04	·022 64	·011 46	8
4	·046 27	·039 83	·031 68	·022 10	·011 39	3·999 87	9
45	·035 64	·029 02	·020 63	·010 80	3·999 77	·987 85	50
6	·024 73	·017 89	·009 28	3·999 17	·987 77	·975 42	1
7	·013 53	·006 46	3·997 58	·987 13	·975 33	·962 50	2
8	·001 94	3·994 61	·985 45	·974 65	·962 40	·949 05	3
9	3·989 94	·982 34	·972 86	·961 67	·948 95	·935 03	4
50	·977 55	·969 63	·959 79	·948 16	·934 92	·920 39	55
1	·964 65	·956 40	·946 19	·934 07	·920 25	·905 06	6
2	·951 28	·942 66	·932 01	·919 39	·904 92	·888 98	7
3	·937 28	·928 26	·917 15	·903 97	·888 83	·872 09	8
4	·922 70	·913 24	·901 63	·887 83	·871 93	·854 31	9
55	·907 43	·897 50	·885 33	·870 86	·854 14	·835 56	60
6	·891 39	·880 94	·868 18	·852 97	·835 36	·815 75	1
7	·874 57	·863 57	·850 16	·834 15	·815 56	·794 81	2
8	·856 89	·845 26	·831 12	·814 25	·794 61	·772 62	3
9	·838 19	·825 91	·811 01	·793 17	·772 37	·749 06	4
60	·818 50	·805 49	·789 74	·770 87	·748 82	·724 04	65
1	·797 68	·783 85	·767 18	·747 18	·723 76	·697 39	6
2	·775 55	·760 89	·743 21	·721 99	·697 09	·669 00	7
3	·752 16	·736 56	·717 79	·695 22	·668 70	·638 73	8
4	·727 25	·710 63	·690 67	·666 67	·638 37	·606 36	9
65	·700 76	·683 05	·661 77	·636 19	·605 99	·571 76	70
6	·672 55	·653 62	·630 96	·603 65	·571 36	·534 71	1
7	·642 43	·622 21	·598 01	·568 81	·534 26	·494 98	2
8	·610 31	·588 67	·562 79	·531 55	·494 53	·452 36	3
9	·575 90	·552 72	·525 02	·491 57	·451 86	·406 57	4
70	·539 07	·514 20	·484 54	·448 66	·406 03	·357 32	75
1	·499 61	·472 92	·441 09	·402 58	·356 74	·304 35	6
2	·457 28	·428 59	·394 42	·353 03	·303 70	·247 28	7
3	·411 76	·380 92	·344 20	·299 67	·246 59	·185 76	8
4	·362 88	·329 67	·290 16	·242 24	·185 01	·119 37	9
75	·310 25	·274 48	·231 93	·180 29	·118 56	·047 69	80

Age at Entry $[x]$	Years elapsed since Date of Assurance						Age Attained $x+5$
	0	1	2	3	4	5 or more	
	$a_{[x]}$	$a_{[x]+1}$	$a_{[x]+2}$	$a_{[x]+3}$	$a_{[x]+4}$	a_{x+5}	
20	21·862	21·613	21·391	21·183	20·979	20·773	25
1	21·680	21·425	21·197	20·983	20·773	20·561	6
2	21·491	21·230	20·997	20·777	20·562	20·343	7
3	21·296	21·031	20·791	20·566	20·344	20·120	8
4	21·096	20·825	20·580	20·348	20·120	19·890	9
25	20·890	20·613	20·362	20·124	19·891	19·654	30
6	20·680	20·397	20·139	19·895	19·655	19·412	1
7	20·463	20·173	19·910	19·659	19·413	19·165	2
8	20·240	19·945	19·675	19·418	19·165	18·911	3
9	20·011	19·710	19·433	19·170	18·911	18·650	4
30	19·776	19·469	19·186	18·916	18·651	18·384	35
1	19·536	19·223	18·933	18·656	18·384	18·111	6
2	19·290	18·970	18·674	18·390	18·112	17·833	7
3	19·037	18·711	18·408	18·118	17·834	17·548	8
4	18·779	18·446	18·136	17·840	17·549	17·258	9
35	18·514	18·175	17·859	17·555	17·258	16·961	40
6	18·243	17·897	17·575	17·265	16·962	16·659	1
7	17·967	17·614	17·285	16·969	16·660	16·350	2
8	17·684	17·326	16·990	16·667	16·351	16·037	3
9	17·397	17·031	16·689	16·359	16·038	15·718	4
40	17·102	16·731	16·381	16·046	15·719	15·394	45
1	16·803	16·425	16·069	15·728	15·395	15·064	6
2	16·498	16·114	15·751	15·404	15·066	14·730	7
3	16·189	15·798	15·429	15·075	14·732	14·392	8
4	15·873	15·476	15·101	14·742	14·393	14·049	9
45	15·553	15·150	14·769	14·405	14·051	13·702	50
6	15·228	14·819	14·432	14·062	13·704	13·352	1
7	14·898	14·484	14·091	13·716	13·354	12·999	2
8	14·565	14·145	13·746	13·366	13·001	12·642	3
9	14·228	13·802	13·399	13·014	12·644	12·283	4
50	13·887	13·456	13·047	12·658	12·285	11·922	55
1	13·543	13·107	12·693	12·300	11·925	11·560	6
2	13·196	12·754	12·336	11·940	11·562	11·196	7
3	12·846	12·401	11·978	11·579	11·199	10·832	8
4	12·494	12·045	11·619	11·216	10·835	10·467	9
55	12·141	11·687	11·257	10·853	10·470	10·103	60
6	11·786	11·329	10·896	10·489	10·106	9·740	1
7	11·431	10·970	10·534	10·126	9·743	9·378	2
8	11·074	10·611	10·173	9·764	9·381	9·018	3
9	10·719	10·253	9·813	9·403	9·022	8·661	4
60	10·363	9·896	9·455	9·044	8·664	8·306	65
1	10·009	9·541	9·098	8·688	8·310	7·956	6
2	9·657	9·187	8·744	8·335	7·960	7·609	7
3	9·307	8·836	8·393	7·986	7·613	7·267	8
4	8·959	8·489	8·046	7·640	7·271	6·930	9
65	8·615	8·145	7·703	7·299	6·935	6·599	70
6	8·274	7·805	7·365	6·964	6·604	6·274	1
7	7·938	7·470	7·032	6·634	6·279	5·956	2
8	7·606	7·140	6·704	6·310	5·961	5·645	3
9	7·280	6·816	6·383	5·994	5·650	5·341	4
70	6·959	6·498	6·068	5·684	5·347	5·045	75
1	6·644	6·186	5·761	5·381	5·051	4·758	6
2	6·335	5·882	5·461	5·087	4·764	4·479	7
3	6·034	5·584	5·168	4·801	4·485	4·209	8
4	5·739	5·295	4·884	4·523	4·215	3·948	9
75	5·452	5·013	4·609	4·254	3·955	3·697	80

Age x	D_x	N_x	M_x	R_x	a_x	Age x
81	1 072·9	4 779·3	933·78	4 242·93	3·455	81
2	877·93	3 706·44	769·97	3 309·15	3·222	2
3	707·33	2 828·51	624·95	2 539·18	2·999	3
4	560·33	2 121·18	498·55	1 914·23	2·786	4
85	435·75	1 560·85	390·291	1 415·676	2·582	85
6	332·09	1 125·10	299·316	1 025·385	2·388	6
7	247·54	793·01	224·440	726·069	2·204	7
8	180·11	545·47	164·223	501·629	2·029	8
9	127·62	365·36	116·981	337·406	1·863	9
90	87·846	237·743	80·919	220·425	1·706	90
1	58·581	149·897	54·216	139·506	1·559	1
2	37·735	91·316	35·075	85·290	1·420	2
3	23·402	53·581	21·841 8	50·214 5	1·290	3
4	13·924	30·179	13·044 3	28·372 7	1·168	4
95	7·916 3	16·254 9	7·443 0	15·328 4	1·053	95
6	4·283 0	8·338 6	4·040 1	7·885 4	·947	6
7	2·194 7	4·055 6	2·076 5	3·845 3	·848	7
8	1·059 7	1·860 9	1·005 5	1·768 8	·756	8
9	·479 5	·801 2	·456 2	·763 3	·671	9
100	·202 1	·321 7	·192 7	·307 1	·592	100
1	·078 8	·119 6	·075 3	·114 4	·518	1
2	·028 2	·040 8	·027 0	·039 1	·448	2
3	·009 2	·012 6	·008 8	·012 1	·372	3
4	·002 7	·003 4	·002 6	·003 3	·264	4
105	·000 7	·000 7	·000 7	·000 7	·000	105

Age x	log D_x	log N_x	log M_x	Age x	log D_x	log N_x	log M_x
81	3·030 57	3·679 36	2·970 24	95	0·898 52	·210 99	0·871 75
2	2·943 46	·568 95	·886 47	6	·631 75	0·921 09	·606 39
3	·849 62	·451 56	·795 85	7	·341 37	·608 06	·317 33
4	·748 44	·326 58	·697 71	8	·025 19	·269 72	·002 38
85	·639 24	·193 37	·591 39	9	$\bar{1}$·680 77	$\bar{1}$·903 71	$\bar{1}$·659 12
6	·521 25	·051 19	·476 13	100	·305 49	·507 41	·284 81
7	·393 64	2·899 28	·351 10	1	$\bar{2}$·896 40	·077 78	$\bar{2}$·876 64
8	·255 53	·736 77	·215 44	2	·450 36	$\bar{2}$·611 03	·431 56
9	·105 92	·562 72	·068 11	3	$\bar{3}$·963 89	·101 33	$\bar{3}$·945 57
90	1·943 72	·376 11	1·908 05	4	·433 18	$\bar{3}$·534 77	·419 49
1	·767 76	·175 79	·734 13	105	$\bar{4}$·854 08	$\bar{4}$·854 08	$\bar{4}$·843 37
2	·576 75	1·960 55	·545 00				
3	·369 26	·729 01	·339 29				
4	·143 75	·479 70	·115 42				

The ultimate values for ages below 81 are given in the final columns of the corresponding tables of values for the first five years of assurance.

$O^{[NM]}$ $a_{[x]}$, $A_{[x]}$, $P_{[x]}$—SELECT VALUES 3 PER CENT.

Age [x]	$a_{[x]}$	$A_{[x]}$	$P_{[x]}$	Age [x]	$a_{[x]}$	$A_{[x]}$	$P_{[x]}$
20	21·862	·334 11	·014 61	50	13·887	·566 41	·038 05
1	21·680	·339 44	·014 97	1	13·543	·576 42	·039 64
2	21·491	·344 93	·015 34	2	13·196	·586 56	·041 32
3	21·296	·350 60	·015 73	3	12·846	·596 72	·043 10
4	21·096	·356 41	·016 13	4	12·494	·606 97	·044 98
25	20·890	·362 42	·016 56	55	12·141	·617 28	·046 98
6	20·680	·368 55	·017 00	6	11·786	·627 60	·049 08
7	20·463	·374 89	·017 47	7	11·431	·637 94	·051 32
8	20·240	·381 36	·017 96	8	11·074	·648 34	·053 70
9	20·011	·388 04	·018 47	9	10·719	·658 67	·056 21
30	19·776	·394 87	·019 01	60	10·363	·669 02	·058 88
1	19·536	·401 86	·019 57	1	10·009	·679 36	·061 71
2	19·290	·409 04	·020 16	2	9·657	·689 59	·064 71
3	19·037	·416 39	·020 78	3	9·307	·699 81	·067 90
4	18·779	·423 93	·021 43	4	8·959	·709 92	·071 28
35	18·514	·431 64	·022 12	65	8·615	·719 95	·074 88
6	18·243	·439 52	·022 84	6	8·274	·729 88	·078 70
7	17·967	·447 58	·023 60	7	7·938	·739 66	·082 75
8	17·684	·455 80	·024 40	8	7·606	·749 34	·087 07
9	17·397	·464 17	·025 23	9	7·280	·758 84	·091 65
40	17·102	·472 76	·026 12	70	6·959	·768 19	·096 52
1	16·803	·481 47	·027 04	1	6·644	·777 36	·101 70
2	16·498	·490 33	·028 02	2	6·335	·786 36	·107 21
3	16·189	·499 37	·029 05	3	6·034	·795 13	·113 04
4	15·873	·508 56	·030 14	4	5·739	·803 71	·119 26
45	15·553	·517 88	·031 29	75	5·452	·812 06	·125 86
6	15·228	·527 33	·032 50				
7	14·898	·536 93	·033 77				
8	14·565	·546 65	·035 12				
9	14·228	·556 45	·036 54				

JOINT LIFE ANNUITIES

Two Lives

Select Values		Ultimate Values			
Age $[x]$	$a_{[xx]}$	Age x	a_{xx}	Age x	a_{xx}
20	18·363	25	17·213	65	5·537
1	18·184	6	17·004	6	5·249
2	17·999	7	16·789	7	4·967
3	17·808	8	16·567	8	4·692
4	17·611	9	16·340	9	4·425
25	17·407	30	16·107	70	4·166
6	17·200	1	15·867	1	3·914
7	16·985	2	15·622	2	3·671
8	16·765	3	15·371	3	3·436
9	16·538	4	15·114	4	3·210
30	16·306	35	14·850	75	2·993
1	16·069	6	14·581	6	2·785
2	15·825	7	14·307	7	2·585
3	15·576	8	14·027	8	2·395
4	15·321	9	13·741	9	2·213
35	15·059	40	13·451	80	2·041
6	14·792	1	13·156	1	1·877
7	14·520	2	12·856	2	1·722
8	14·243	3	12·551	3	1·575
9	13·962	4	12·242	4	1·437
40	13·674	45	11·930	85	1·307
1	13·383	6	11·613	6	1·185
2	13·087	7	11·295	7	1·071
3	12·787	8	10·973	8	0·965
4	12·482	9	10·648	9	·865
45	12·175	50	10·322	90	·773
6	11·864	1	9·994	1	·687
7	11·550	2	9·665	2	·608
8	11·234	3	9·336	3	·536
9	10·916	4	9·007	4	·469
50	10·596	55	8·678	95	·408
1	10·275	6	8·351	6	·352
2	9·953	7	8·024	7	·302
3	9·632	8	7·701	8	·256
4	9·311	9	7·379	9	·216
55	8·990	60	7·061	100	·180
6	8·671	1	6·747	1	·148
7	8·353	2	6·437	2	·120
8	8·037	3	6·131	3	·096
9	7·725	4	5·831	4	·072
60	7·416			105	·000
1	7·110				
2	6·809				
3	6·512				
4	6·221				
65	5·935				
6	5·654				
7	5·380				
8	5·113				
9	4·853				
70	4·599				
1	4·353				
2	4·115				
3	3·884				
4	3·661				
75	3·446				

O[NM]

THREE-AND-A-HALF PER CENT.

INTEREST CONSTANTS

Constant	Number	Logarithm
i	·035	$\bar{2}$·544 068 0
$(1+i)$	1·035	0·014 940 3
$(1+i)^{\frac{1}{2}}$	1·017 349 5	0·007 470 2
$(1+i)^{\frac{1}{4}}$	1·008 637 4	0·003 735 1
v	·966 183 6	$\bar{1}$·985 059 7
$v^{\frac{1}{2}}$	·982 946 4	$\bar{1}$·992 529 8
$v^{\frac{1}{4}}$	·991 436 5	$\bar{1}$·996 264 9
d	·033 816 4	$\bar{2}$·529 127 7
δ	·034 401 4	$\bar{2}$·536 576 5

Age at Entry $[x]$	Years elapsed since Date of Assurance: 0	1	2	3	4	5 or more	Age Attained $x+5$
	$D_{[x]}$	$D_{[x]+1}$	$D_{[x]+2}$	$D_{[x]+3}$	$D_{[x]+4}$	D_{x+5}	
20	50 256	48 353	46 447	44 573	42 751	40 994	25
1	48 199	46 372	44 543	42 743	40 993	39 304	6
2	46 225	44 471	42 714	40 985	39 303	37 681	7
3	44 328	42 643	40 956	39 295	37 680	36 120	8
4	42 506	40 888	39 268	37 672	36 119	34 620	9
25	40 756	39 202	37 645	36 112	34 619	33 178	30
6	39 071	37 579	36 084	34 611	33 177	31 791	1
7	37 454	36 021	34 585	33 170	31 791	30 458	2
8	35 898	34 522	33 142	31 782	30 457	29 175	3
9	34 404	33 082	31 756	30 449	29 174	27 942	4
30	32 966	31 696	30 423	29 166	27 940	26 754	35
1	31 583	30 363	29 140	27 932	26 753	25 611	6
2	30 253	29 082	27 906	26 744	25 610	24 511	7
3	28 973	27 848	26 718	25 601	24 510	23 452	8
4	27 743	26 661	25 575	24 501	23 451	22 432	9
35	26 559	25 519	24 475	23 442	22 431	21 450	40
6	25 419	24 420	23 416	22 422	21 448	20 503	1
7	24 321	23 361	22 395	21 439	20 501	19 590	2
8	23 263	22 340	21 412	20 492	19 588	18 710	3
9	22 244	21 357	20 465	19 579	18 709	17 861	4
40	21 264	20 411	19 552	18 699	17 859	17 042	45
1	20 317	19 498	18 672	17 849	17 040	16 251	6
2	19 405	18 617	17 821	17 030	16 250	15 488	7
3	18 525	17 766	17 002	16 239	15 486	14 751	8
4	17 676	16 947	16 211	15 476	14 749	14 038	9
45	16 857	16 155	15 446	14 738	14 037	13 350	50
6	16 066	15 391	14 708	14 025	13 348	12 684	1
7	15 302	14 653	13 995	13 336	12 682	12 040	2
8	14 564	13 939	13 306	12 670	12 038	11 416	3
9	13 850	13 249	12 639	12 025	11 414	10 813	4
50	13 160	12 581	11 993	11 401	10 811	10 228	55
1	12 493	11 935	11 369	10 797	10 226	9 662·1	6
2	11 847	11 310	10 765	10 213	9 660·1	9 113·8	7
3	11 221	10 705	10 179	9 646·3	9 111·5	8 582·4	8
4	10 616	10 119	9 611·9	9 097·7	8 580·3	8 067·7	9
55	10 030	9 551·0	9 062·5	8 566·0	8 065·5	7 569·0	60
6	9 460·8	9 000·6	8 530·0	8 050·6	7 566·6	7 085·8	1
7	8 910·7	8 467·8	8 014·6	7 551·8	7 083·5	6 618·0	2
8	8 377·4	7 951·3	7 514·8	7 068·4	6 615·8	6 165·4	3
9	7 860·3	7 450·8	7 030·7	6 600·1	6 162·8	5 727·4	4
60	7 359·9	6 966·3	6 562·2	6 147·2	5 725·1	5 304·4	65
1	6 875·3	6 497·3	6 108·7	5 709·0	5 301·9	4 896·1	6
2	6 405·8	6 043·1	5 670·1	5 285·7	4 893·5	4 502·7	7
3	5 952·4	5 604·8	5 246·9	4 877·4	4 500·2	4 124·3	8
4	5 513·7	5 181·0	4 838·2	4 483·8	4 121·6	3 761·1	9
65	5 090·5	4 772·5	4 444·7	4 105·4	3 758·5	3 413·4	70
6	4 682·7	4 379·4	4 066·5	3 742·4	3 410·9	3 081·7	1
7	4 290·3	4 001·6	3 703·7	3 394·8	3 079·1	2 766·1	2
8	3 914·0	3 639·7	3 356·8	3 063·5	2 763·8	2 467·4	3
9	3 553·4	3 293·7	3 025·9	2 748·3	2 465·0	2 185·8	4
70	3 209·2	2 964·1	2 711·6	2 450·0	2 183·5	1 921·8	75
1	2 881·8	2 651·4	2 414·3	2 169·0	1 919·6	1 675·8	6
2	2 571·8	2 356·1	2 134·6	1 905·7	1 673·7	1 448·2	7
3	2 279·2	2 078·5	1 872·7	1 660·4	1 446·2	1 239·3	8
4	2 005·1	1 819·2	1 629·1	1 433·7	1 237·4	1 049·1	9
75	1 749·5	1 578·6	1 404·2	1 225·7	1 047·3	877·65	80

Age at Entry [x]	Years elapsed since Date of Assurance: 0	1	2	3	4	5 or more	Age Attained x+5
	$\log D_{[x]}$	$\log D_{[x]+1}$	$\log D_{[x]+2}$	$\log D_{[x]+3}$	$\log D_{[x]+4}$	$\log D_{x+5}$	
20	4·701 19	4·684 42	4·666 96	4·649 07	4·630 95	4·612 72	25
1	·683 04	·666 26	·648 78	·630 86	·612 71	·594 44	6
2	·664 88	·648 08	·630 57	·612 62	·594 43	·576 12	7
3	·646 68	·629 85	·612 32	·594 34	·576 11	·557 75	8
4	·628 45	·611 60	·594 04	·576 02	·557 74	·539 33	9
25	·610 19	·593 31	·575 71	·557 65	·539 32	·520 85	30
6	·591 86	·574 95	·557 32	·539 22	·520 84	·502 31	1
7	·573 50	·556 56	·538 89	·520 74	·502 30	·483 70	2
8	·555 07	·538 09	·520 38	·502 18	·483 68	·465 01	3
9	·536 61	·519 59	·501 83	·483 57	·465 00	·446 25	4
30	·518 07	·501 01	·483 20	·464 88	·446 23	·427 39	35
1	·499 45	·482 35	·464 49	·446 10	·427 37	·408 43	6
2	·480 77	·463 62	·445 69	·427 23	·408 41	·389 36	7
3	·462 00	·444 79	·426 80	·408 26	·389 34	·370 18	8
4	·443 15	·425 88	·407 82	·389 19	·370 16	·350 87	9
35	·424 21	·406 87	·388 73	·370 00	·350 85	·331 42	40
6	·405 15	·387 74	·369 51	·350 67	·331 39	·311 81	1
7	·385 98	·368 49	·350 16	·331 20	·311 78	·292 03	2
8	·366 67	·349 09	·330 66	·311 58	·292 00	·272 07	3
9	·347 22	·329 55	·311 01	·291 79	·272 04	·251 90	4
40	·327 64	·309 86	·291 19	·271 81	·251 86	·231 51	45
1	·307 87	·289 98	·271 18	·251 62	·231 48	·210 89	6
2	·287 91	·269 90	·250 94	·231 21	·210 84	·189 99	7
3	·267 76	·249 60	·230 49	·210 56	·189 95	·168 81	8
4	·247 39	·229 09	·209 80	·189 65	·168 77	·147 32	9
45	·226 77	·208 31	·188 82	·168 43	·147 26	·125 47	50
6	·205 90	·187 26	·167 56	·146 91	·125 42	·103 25	1
7	·184 76	·165 92	·145 98	·125 04	·103 19	·080 61	2
8	·163 28	·144 23	·124 04	·102 78	·080 55	·057 52	3
9	·141 45	·122 17	·101 70	·080 10	·057 45	·033 93	4
50	·119 26	·099 72	·078 94	·056 96	·033 85	·009 80	55
1	·096 65	·076 83	·055 72	·033 32	·009 71	3·985 07	6
2	·073 61	·053 48	·032 00	·009 15	3·984 98	·959 70	7
3	·050 04	·029 58	·007 70	3·984 36	·959 59	·933 61	8
4	·025 96	·005 13	3·982 81	·958 93	·933 50	·906 75	9
55	·001 28	3·980 05	·957 25	·932 78	·906 63	·879 04	60
6	3·975 93	·954 27	·930 95	·905 83	·878 90	·850 39	1
7	·949 91	·927 77	·903 88	·878 05	·850 25	·820 73	2
8	·923 11	·900 44	·875 92	·849 32	·820 58	·789 96	3
9	·895 44	·872 20	·847 00	·819 55	·789 78	·757 96	4
60	·866 87	·843 00	·817 05	·788 68	·757 78	·724 64	65
1	·837 29	·812 73	·785 95	·756 56	·724 43	·689 85	6
2	·806 57	·781 26	·753 59	·723 10	·689 62	·653 47	7
3	·774 69	·748 56	·719 90	·688 19	·653 23	·615 35	8
4	·741 44	·714 41	·684 68	·651 65	·615 07	·575 31	9
65	·706 76	·678 75	·647 84	·613 36	·575 02	·533 19	70
6	·670 50	·641 41	·609 22	·573 15	·532 87	·488 79	1
7	·632 49	·602 23	·568 63	·530 82	·488 43	·441 87	2
8	·592 62	·561 07	·525 93	·486 22	·441 50	·392 24	3
9	·550 64	·517 68	·480 86	·439 06	·391 82	·339 61	4
70	·506 39	·471 89	·433 22	·389 16	·339 15	·283 71	75
1	·459 67	·423 48	·382 80	·336 25	·283 21	·224 23	6
2	·410 23	·372 20	·329 32	·280 05	·223 69	·160 84	7
3	·357 79	·317 75	·272 46	·220 22	·160 24	·093 16	8
4	·302 14	·259 89	·211 96	·156 46	·092 51	·020 80	9
75	·242 92	·198 26	·147 44	·088 38	·020 09	2·943 32	80

Age at Entry [x]	Years elapsed since Date of Assurance: 0 $N_{[x]}$	1 $N_{[x]+1}$	2 $N_{[x]+2}$	3 $N_{[x]+3}$	4 $N_{[x]+4}$	5 or more N_{x+5}	Age Attained $x+5$
20	1 059 109	1 008 853	960 500	914 053	869 480	826 729	25
1	1 008 585	960 386	914 014	869 471	826 728	785 735	6
2	960 129	913 904	869 433	826 719	785 734	746 431	7
3	913 652	869 324	826 681	785 725	746 430	708 750	8
4	869 083	826 577	785 689	746 421	708 749	672 630	9
25	826 344	785 588	746 386	708 741	672 629	638 010	30
6	785 354	746 283	708 704	672 620	638 009	604 832	1
7	746 062	708 608	672 587	638 002	604 832	573 041	2
8	708 384	672 486	637 964	604 822	573 040	542 583	3
9	672 273	637 869	604 787	573 031	542 582	513 408	4
30	637 657	604 691	572 995	542 572	513 406	485 466	35
1	604 483	572 900	542 537	513 397	485 465	458 712	6
2	572 696	542 443	513 361	485 455	458 711	433 101	7
3	542 240	513 267	485 419	458 701	433 100	408 590	8
4	513 069	485 326	458 665	433 090	408 589	385 138	9
35	485 132	458 573	433 054	408 579	385 137	362 706	40
6	458 381	432 962	408 542	385 126	362 704	341 256	1
7	432 770	408 449	385 088	362 693	341 254	320 753	2
8	408 258	384 995	362 655	341 243	320 751	301 163	3
9	384 807	362 563	341 206	320 741	301 162	282 453	4
40	362 377	341 113	320 702	301 150	282 451	264 592	45
1	340 926	320 609	301 111	282 439	264 590	247 550	6
2	320 422	301 017	282 400	264 579	247 549	231 299	7
3	300 829	282 304	264 538	247 536	231 297	215 811	8
4	282 119	264 443	247 496	231 285	215 809	201 060	9
45	264 255	247 398	231 243	215 797	201 059	187 022	50
6	247 210	231 144	215 753	201 045	187 020	173 672	1
7	230 956	215 654	201 001	187 006	173 670	160 988	2
8	215 465	200 901	186 962	173 656	160 986	148 948	3
9	200 709	186 859	173 610	160 971	148 946	137 532	4
50	186 665	173 505	160 924	148 931	137 530	126 719	55
1	173 311	160 818	148 883	137 514	126 717	116 491	6
2	160 624	148 777	137 467	126 702	116 489·0	106 828·9	7
3	148 578	137 357	126 652	116 472·9	106 826·6	97 715·1	8
4	137 158	126 542	116 422·6	106 810·7	97 713·0	89 132·7	9
55	126 340	116 310·0	106 759·0	97 696·5	89 130·5	81 065·0	60
6	116 104·6	106 643·8	97 643·2	89 113·2	81 062·6	73 496·0	1
7	106 438·6	97 527·9	89 060·1	81 045·5	73 493·7	66 410·2	2
8	97 319·9	88 942·5	80 991·2	73 476·4	66 408·0	59 792·2	3
9	88 731·5	80 871·2	73 420·4	66 389·7	59 789·6	53 626·8	4
60	80 660·1	73 300·2	66 333·9	59 771·7	53 624·5	47 899·4	65
1	73 087·2	66 211·9	59 714·6	53 605·9	47 896·9	42 595·0	6
2	65 997·1	59 591·3	53 548·2	47 878·1	42 592·4	37 698·9	7
3	59 377·9	53 425·5	47 820·7	42 573·8	37 696·4	33 196·2	8
4	53 210·2	47 696·5	42 515·5	37 677·3	33 193·5	29 071·9	9
65	47 482·4	42 391·9	37 619·4	33 174·7	29 069·3	25 310·8	70
6	42 179·3	37 496·6	33 117·2	29 050·7	25 308·3	21 897·4	1
7	37 285·2	32 994·9	28 993·3	25 289·6	21 894·8	18 815·7	2
8	32 787·4	28 873·4	25 233·7	21 876·9	18 813·4	16 049·6	3
9	28 668·5	25 115·1	21 821·4	18 795·5	16 047·2	13 582·2	4
70	24 914·8	21 705·6	18 741·5	16 029·9	13 579·9	11 396·4	75
1	21 510·7	18 628·9	15 977·5	13 563·2	11 394·2	9 474·6	6
2	18 440·7	15 868·9	13 512·8	11 378·2	9 472·5	7 798·8	7
3	15 687·6	13 408·4	11 329·9	9 457·2	7 796·8	6 350·6	8
4	13 235·8	11 230·7	9 411·5	7 782·4	6 348·7	5 111·3	9
75	11 067·5	9 318·0	7 739·4	6 335·2	5 109·5	4 062·24	80

Age at Entry [x]	Years elapsed since Date of Assurance: 0	1	2	3	4	5 or more	Age Attained $x+5$
	$\log N_{[x]}$	$\log N_{[x]+1}$	$\log N_{[x]+2}$	$\log N_{[x]+3}$	$\log N_{[x]+4}$	$\log N_{x+5}$	
20	6·024 94	6·003 83	5·982 50	5·960 97	5·939 26	5·917 36	25
1	·003 71	5·982 45	·960 95	·939 25	·917 36	·895 28	6
2	5·982 33	·960 90	·939 23	·917 36	·895 27	·872 99	7
3	·960 78	·939 18	·917 34	·895 27	·872 99	·850 49	8
4	·939 06	·917 28	·895 25	·872 98	·850 49	·827 78	9
25	·917 16	·895 20	·872 97	·850 49	·827 78	·804 83	30
6	·895 06	·872 90	·850 46	·827 77	·804 83	·781 63	1
7	·872 77	·850 41	·827 75	·804 82	·781 63	·758 18	2
8	·850 27	·827 69	·804 79	·781 63	·758 18	·734 46	3
9	·827 54	·804 73	·781 60	·758 18	·734 46	·710 46	4
30	·804 59	·781 53	·758 15	·734 46	·710 46	·686 16	35
1	·781 38	·758 08	·734 43	·710 46	·686 16	·661 54	6
2	·757 93	·734 35	·710 42	·686 15	·661 54	·636 59	7
3	·734 19	·710 35	·686 12	·661 53	·636 59	·611 29	8
4	·710 18	·686 04	·661 50	·636 58	·611 29	·585 62	9
35	·685 86	·661 41	·636 54	·611 28	·585 62	·559 56	40
6	·661 23	·636 45	·611 23	·585 61	·559 55	·533 08	1
7	·636 26	·611 14	·585 56	·559 54	·533 08	·506 17	2
8	·610 94	·585 46	·559 50	·533 06	·506 17	·478 80	3
9	·585 25	·559 38	·533 02	·506 15	·478 80	·450 95	4
40	·559 16	·532 90	·506 10	·478 78	·450 94	·422 57	45
1	·532 66	·505 98	·478 73	·450 93	·422 57	·393 66	6
2	·505 72	·478 59	·450 86	·422 56	·393 66	·364 18	7
3	·478 32	·450 72	·422 49	·393 64	·364 17	·334 07	8
4	·450 43	·422 33	·393 57	·364 15	·334 07	·303 33	9
45	·422 03	·393 40	·364 07	·334 04	·303 33	·271 89	50
6	·393 07	·363 88	·333 96	·303 29	·271 89	·239 73	1
7	·363 53	·333 76	·303 20	·271 85	·239 72	·206 79	2
8	·333 38	·302 98	·271 75	·239 69	·206 79	·173 03	3
9	·302 57	·271 52	·239 57	·206 74	·173 03	·138 41	4
50	·271 06	·239 31	·206 62	·172 98	·138 40	·102 85	55
1	·238 82	·206 33	·172 85	·138 35	·102 84	·066 29	6
2	·205 81	·172 54	·138 20	·102 79	·066 29	·028 69	7
3	·171 95	·137 85	·102 62	·066 22	·028 68	4·989 96	8
4	·137 22	·102 24	·066 04	·028 61	4·989 95	·950 04	9
55	·101 54	·065 62	·028 41	4·989 88	·950 03	·908 83	60
6	·064 85	·027 94	4·989 64	·949 94	·908 82	·866 26	1
7	·027 09	4·989 13	·949 68	·908 73	·866 25	·822 23	2
8	4·988 20	·949 11	·908 44	·866 15	·822 22	·776 64	3
9	·948 08	·907 79	·865 81	·822 10	·776 63	·729 38	4
60	·906 66	·865 10	·821 74	·776 50	·729 37	·680 33	65
1	·863 84	·820 94	·776 08	·729 21	·680 31	·629 36	6
2	·819 52	·775 18	·728 74	·680 14	·629 33	·576 33	7
3	·773 63	·727 75	·679 62	·629 14	·576 30	·521 09	8
4	·725 99	·678 49	·628 55	·576 08	·521 06	·463 47	9
65	·676 53	·627 28	·575 41	·520 81	·463 44	·403 31	70
6	·625 10	·573 99	·520 05	·463 16	·403 27	·340 39	1
7	·571 53	·518 45	·462 30	·402 94	·340 34	·274 52	2
8	·515 70	·460 50	·401 98	·339 99	·274 47	·205 47	3
9	·457 41	·399 93	·338 88	·274 06	·205 40	·132 97	4
70	·396 46	·336 57	·272 81	·204 93	·132 90	·056 77	75
1	·332 65	·270 19	·203 51	·132 37	·056 69	3·976 56	6
2	·265 77	·200 55	·130 74	·056 08	3·976 46	·892 03	7
3	·195 56	·127 38	·054 23	3·975 76	·891 92	·802 81	8
4	·121 75	·050 41	3·973 66	·891 11	·802 68	·708 53	9
75	·044 05	3·969 32	·888 71	·801 76	·708 38	·608 76	80

Age at Entry [x]	Years elapsed since Date of Assurance: 0	1	2	3	4	5 or more	Age Attained x+5
	$M_{[x]}$	$M_{[x]+1}$	$M_{[x]+2}$	$M_{[x]+3}$	$M_{[x]+4}$	M_{x+5}	
20	14 441·34	14 237·40	13 966·70	13 663·00	13 348·99	13 037·13	25
1	14 093·02	13 895·98	13 634·43	13 340·56	13 036·32	12 733·78	6
2	13 757·35	13 566·52	13 312·94	13 028·16	12 732·98	12 439·49	7
3	13 432·22	13 246·09	13 001·09	12 725·13	12 438·35	12 152·87	8
4	13 116·72	12 936·88	12 698·94	12 431·12	12 152·13	11 874·46	9
25	12 811·91	12 636·52	12 405·44	12 144·77	11 873·74	11 602·97	30
6	12 513·57	12 342·93	12 118·52	11 865·93	11 602·28	11 338·25	1
7	12 225·25	12 058·85	11 840·92	11 594·73	11 337·59	11 079·83	2
8	11 943·19	11 780·57	11 568·58	11 328·99	11 078·55	10 826·61	3
9	11 670·45	11 511·55	11 304·67	11 070·86	10 825·99	10 579·78	4
30	11 402·88	11 247·98	11 046·10	10 818·27	10 578·58	10 337·40	35
1	11 141·43	10 990·10	10 793·44	10 570·52	10 336·24	10 099·16	6
2	10 886·64	10 738·18	10 545·37	10 327·88	10 098·04	9 865·05	7
3	10 636·74	10 490·81	10 302·72	10 089·40	9 863·97	9 634·80	8
4	10 392·52	10 249·13	10 064·79	9 855·61	9 633·75	9 407·89	9
35	10 153·39	10 011·95	9 831·05	9 625·42	9 406·88	9 184·11	40
6	9 917·64	9 778·46	9 600·43	9 398·10	9 182·65	8 962·53	1
7	9 686·07	9 548·62	9 372·95	9 173·67	8 961·12	8 743·02	2
8	9 457·39	9 320·93	9 148·17	8 951·96	8 741·65	8 525·46	3
9	9 231·35	9 096·73	8 926·39	8 732·58	8 524·14	8 309·32	4
40	9 009·33	8 875·36	8 706·77	8 514·73	8 307·83	8 094·11	45
1	8 788·42	8 655·44	8 488·91	8 298·30	8 093·08	7 880·22	6
2	8 569·15	8 437·02	8 271·72	8 082·88	7 878·44	7 666·22	7
3	8 351·96	8 220·12	8 055·95	7 868·36	7 664·88	7 452·74	8
4	8 136·15	8 004·52	7 841·38	7 654·57	7 451·45	7 239·44	9
45	7 920·71	7 789·21	7 626·43	7 440·38	7 237·64	7 025·29	50
6	7 706·18	7 574·36	7 412·28	7 226·78	7 023·91	6 810·95	1
7	7 492·35	7 360·20	7 198·23	7 012·55	6 809·28	6 595·50	2
8	7 277·80	7 145·30	6 983·44	6 797·81	6 593·89	6 379·26	3
9	7 062·83	6 929·79	6 767·86	6 581·99	6 377·54	6 161·75	4
50	6 847·87	6 713·80	6 551·50	6 365·13	6 159·94	5 943·00	55
1	6 631·81	6 496·92	6 334·29	6 147·20	5 940·96	5 722·76	6
2	6 415·39	6 279·41	6 116·04	5 928·35	5 720·79	5 501·25	7
3	6 196·85	6 060·01	5 895·98	5 707·64	5 499·07	5 278·11	8
4	5 977·81	5 839·71	5 674·97	5 485·68	5 276·01	5 053·59	9
55	5 757·13	5 617·88	5 452·38	5 262·29	5 051·43	4 827·65	60
6	5 534·68	5 394·23	5 228·07	5 037·18	4 825·32	4 600·39	1
7	5 311·24	5 169·69	5 002·84	4 811·17	4 598·26	4 372·29	2
8	5 086·44	4 943·63	4 775·95	4 583·65	4 370·12	4 143·43	3
9	4 859·72	4 716·03	4 547·89	4 354·98	4 140·89	3 913·90	4
60	4 632·27	4 487·55	4 319·05	4 125·91	3 911·65	3 684·65	65
1	4 403·77	4 258·14	4 089·38	3 896·25	3 682·18	3 455·62	6
2	4 173·92	4 027·95	3 859·26	3 666·56	3 453·12	3 227·74	7
3	3 944·38	3 798·15	3 629·71	3 437·64	3 225·43	3 001·69	8
4	3 714·27	3 567·96	3 400·37	3 209·71	2 999·08	2 777·88	9
65	3 484·78	3 338·98	3 172·46	2 983·52	2 775·45	2 557·41	70
6	3 256·32	3 111·26	2 946·52	2 759·97	2 554·98	2 341·18	1
7	3 029·40	2 885·77	2 723·16	2 539·59	2 338·66	2 129·83	2
8	2 805·17	2 663·32	2 503·50	2 323·61	2 127·55	1 924·65	3
9	2 583·81	2 444·33	2 287·92	2 112·69	1 922·37	1 726·49	4
70	2 366·53	2 230·03	2 077·82	1 907·87	1 724·30	1 536·40	75
1	2 154·36	2 021·47	1 874·00	1 710·27	1 534·27	1 355·44	6
2	1 948·14	1 819·50	1 677·64	1 520·88	1 353·39	1 184·49	7
3	1 748·75	1 625·09	1 489·55	1 340·58	1 182·58	1 024·52	8
4	1 557·53	1 439·49	1 310·87	1 170·55	1 022·74	876·23	9
75	1 375·24	1 263·46	1 142·51	1 011·44	874·57	740·29	80

Age at Entry $[x]$	Years elapsed since Date of Assurance: 0	1	2	3	4	5 or more	Age Attained $x+5$
	$\log M_{[x]}$	$\log M_{[x]+1}$	$\log M_{[x]+2}$	$\log M_{[x]+3}$	$\log M_{[x]+4}$	$\log M_{x+5}$	
20	4·159 61	4·153 43	4·145 09	4·135 55	4·125 45	4·115 18	25
1	·149 00	·142 89	·134 64	·125 18	·115 15	·104 95	6
2	·138 53	·132 47	·124 28	·114 88	·104 93	·094 80	7
3	·128 15	·122 08	·113 98	·104 66	·094 76	·084 68	8
4	·117 82	·111 83	·103 77	·094 51	·084 65	·074 61	9
25	·107 62	·101 63	·093 61	·084 39	·074 59	·064 57	30
6	·097 38	·091 42	·083 45	·074 30	·064 54	·054 55	1
7	·087 26	·081 31	·073 39	·064 26	·054 52	·044 53	2
8	·077 12	·071 17	·063 28	·054 19	·044 48	·034 49	3
9	·067 09	·061 13	·053 26	·044 18	·034 47	·024 48	4
30	·057 02	·051 08	·043 21	·034 16	·024 42	·014 41	35
1	·046 94	·041 00	·033 16	·024 10	·014 36	·004 29	6
2	·036 90	·030 93	·023 06	·014 01	·004 24	3·994 10	7
3	·026 81	·020 81	·012 95	·003 87	3·994 05	·983 84	8
4	·016 72	·010 69	·002 80	3·993 68	·983 80	·973 49	9
35	·006 61	·000 52	3·992 60	·983 42	·973 45	·963 04	40
6	3·996 41	3·990 27	·982 29	·973 04	·962 97	·952 43	1
7	·986 15	·979 94	·971 88	·962 54	·952 36	·941 66	2
8	·975 77	·969 46	·961 34	·951 92	·941 60	·930 72	3
9	·965 27	·958 88	·950 68	·941 14	·930 65	·919 56	4
40	·954 69	·948 19	·939 86	·930 17	·919 49	·908 17	45
1	·943 91	·937 29	·928 85	·918 99	·908 11	·896 54	6
2	·932 94	·926 19	·917 59	·907 57	·896 44	·884 58	7
3	·921 79	·914 88	·906 12	·895 89	·884 51	·872 31	8
4	·910 42	·903 33	·894 39	·883 92	·872 24	·859 70	9
45	·898 76	·891 49	·882 32	·871 60	·859 59	·846 66	50
6	·886 84	·879 35	·869 95	·858 95	·846 58	·833 21	1
7	·874 62	·866 89	·857 22	·845 88	·833 10	·819 25	2
8	·862 00	·854 02	·844 07	·832 37	·819 14	·804 77	3
9	·848 98	·840 72	·830 45	·818 36	·804 65	·789 71	4
50	·835 56	·826 97	·816 34	·803 81	·789 57	·774 01	55
1	·821 63	·812 71	·801 70	·788 68	·773 86	·757 61	6
2	·807 22	·797 92	·786 47	·772 94	·757 46	·740 47	7
3	·792 17	·782 47	·770 56	·756 45	·740 29	·722 48	8
4	·776 54	·766 39	·753 97	·739 23	·722 30	·703 60	9
55	·760 20	·749 57	·736 59	·721 18	·703 41	·683 74	60
6	·743 09	·731 93	·718 34	·702 19	·683 52	·662 80	1
7	·725 19	·713 47	·699 21	·682 25	·662 60	·640 71	2
8	·706 41	·694 04	·679 06	·661 22	·640 49	·617 36	3
9	·686 61	·673 57	·657 81	·638 99	·617 09	·592 61	4
60	·665 80	·652 01	·635 39	·615 52	·592 36	·566 40	65
1	·643 83	·629 22	·611 66	·590 65	·566 11	·538 52	6
2	·620 54	·605 09	·586 51	·564 26	·538 21	·508 90	7
3	·595 98	·579 58	·559 87	·536 26	·508 59	·477 37	8
4	·569 88	·552 42	·531 53	·506 46	·476 99	·443 72	9
65	·542 18	·523 62	·501 40	·474 73	·443 34	·407 80	70
6	·512 72	·492 94	·469 31	·440 90	·407 39	·369 44	1
7	·481 36	·460 26	·435 07	·404 77	·368 97	·328 35	2
8	·447 96	·425 42	·398 55	·366 16	·327 88	·284 35	3
9	·412 26	·388 16	·359 44	·324 84	·283 83	·237 17	4
70	·374 11	·348 31	·317 60	·280 55	·236 61	·186 50	75
1	·333 32	·305 66	·272 77	·233 06	·185 90	·132 08	6
2	·289 62	·259 95	·224 70	·182 09	·131 43	·073 54	7
3	·242 73	·210 88	·173 06	·127 29	·072 83	·010 52	8
4	·192 44	·158 21	·117 56	·068 39	·009 77	2·942 62	9
75	·138 38	·101 56	·057 86	·004 94	2·941 79	·869 40	80

O[NM] $a_{[x]+t}$ 3½ PER CENT.

Age at Entry [x]	Years elapsed since Date of Assurance: 0 ($a_{[x]}$)	1 ($a_{[x]+1}$)	2 ($a_{[x]+2}$)	3 ($a_{[x]+3}$)	4 ($a_{[x]+4}$)	5 or more (a_{x+5})	Age Attained x+5
20	20·074	19·865	19·679	19·507	19·338	19·167	25
1	19·926	19·710	19·520	19·342	19·168	18·991	6
2	19·771	19·550	19·355	19·171	18·992	18·809	7
3	19·611	19·386	19·184	18·995	18·810	18·622	8
4	19·446	19·215	19·008	18·814	18·623	18·429	9
25	19·276	19·040	18·827	18·626	18·429	18·230	30
6	19·100	18·859	18·640	18·434	18·230	18·025	1
7	18·920	18·672	18·447	18·234	18·025	17·814	2
8	18·734	18·480	18·249	18·030	17·815	17·597	3
9	18·540	18·281	18·045	17·819	17·598	17·374	4
30	18·343	18·078	17·834	17·603	17·375	17·145	35
1	18·140	17·868	17·619	17·380	17·146	16·911	6
2	17·930	17·652	17·396	17·152	16·911	16·670	7
3	17·715	17·431	17·168	16·917	16·671	16·423	8
4	17·494	17·204	16·934	16·676	16·423	16·169	9
35	17·266	16·970	16·694	16·429	16·170	15·910	40
6	17·033	16·730	16·448	16·176	15·911	15·644	1
7	16·794	16·484	16·195	15·918	15·646	15·373	2
8	16·550	16·233	15·937	15·653	15·374	15·097	3
9	16·299	15·976	15·673	15·382	15·098	14·814	4
40	16·042	15·712	15·402	15·105	14·815	14·526	45
1	15·780	15·444	15·127	14·823	14·527	14·233	6
2	15·512	15·169	14·846	14·536	14·234	13·934	7
3	15·239	14·890	14·560	14·243	13·935	13·631	8
4	14·960	14·604	14·268	13·945	13·632	13·322	9
45	14·677	14·314	13·971	13·643	13·324	13·009	50
6	14·387	14·018	13·669	13·335	13·011	12·692	1
7	14·093	13·718	13·362	13·022	12·694	12·371	2
8	13·794	13·413	13·051	12·706	12·373	12·047	3
9	13·492	13·104	12·736	12·386	12·049	11·720	4
50	13·184	12·791	12·418	12·063	11·722	11·389	55
1	12·873	12·474	12·096	11·736	11·391	11·057	6
2	12·558	12·154	11·770	11·406	11·059	10·722	7
3	12·241	11·832	11·442	11·074	10·724	10·386	8
4	11·920	11·506	11·112	10·740	10·388	10·048	9
55	11·597	11·178	10·780	10·405	10·051	9·710	60
6	11·272	10·849	10·447	10·069	9·713	9·372	1
7	10·945	10·517	10·112	9·732	9·375	9·035	2
8	10·617	10·186	9·778	9·395	9·038	8·698	3
9	10·288	9·854	9·443	9·059	8·702	8·363	4
60	9·959	9·522	9·109	8·724	8·367	8·030	65
1	9·631	9·191	8·775	8·390	8·034	7·700	6
2	9·303	8·861	8·444	8·058	7·704	7·373	7
3	8·976	8·532	8·114	7·729	7·377	7·049	8
4	8·651	8·206	7·788	7·403	7·053	6·730	9
65	8·328	7·882	7·464	7·081	6·734	6·415	70
6	8·007	7·562	7·144	6·763	6·420	6·106	1
7	7·691	7·246	6·828	6·449	6·111	5·802	2
8	7·377	6·933	6·517	6·141	5·807	5·505	3
9	7·068	6·625	6·212	5·839	5·510	5·214	4
70	6·764	6·323	5·912	5·543	5·219	4·930	75
1	6·464	6·026	5·618	5·253	4·936	4·654	6
2	6·171	5·735	5·330	4·971	4·660	4·385	7
3	5·883	5·451	5·050	4·696	4·391	4·125	8
4	5·601	5·173	4·777	4·428	4·131	3·872	9
75	5·326	4·903	4·512	4·169	3·879	3·629	80

Age x	D_x	N_x	M_x	Age x	log D_x	log N_x	log M_x
81	724·80	3 184·59	617·14	81	2·860 22	3·503 05	2·790 38
2	590·20	2 459·79	507·019	2	·771 00	·390 90	·705 03
3	473·22	1 869·59	409·995	3	·675 06	·271 75	·612 78
4	373·06	1 396·37	325·840	4	·571 78	·145 00	·513 00
85	288·72	1 023·31	254·113	85	·460 47	·010 01	·405 03
6	218·97	734·59	194·127	6	·340 38	2·866 05	·288 08
7	162·43	515·62	144·994	7	·210 67	·712 33	·161 35
8	117·61	353·19	105·671	8	·070 46	·548 01	·023 95
9	82·935	235·582	74·970	9	1·918 74	·372 14	1·874 89
90	56·812	152·647	51·648	90	·754 44	·183 69	·713 05
1	37·703	95·835	34·462	1	·576 38	1·981 52	·537 34
2	24·169	58·132	22·203 2	2	·383 26	·764 42	·346 41
3	14·917	33·963	13·768 3	3	·173 67	·531 01	·138 88
4	8·832 0	19·045 8	8·187 8	4	0·946 06	·279 80	0·913 17
95	4·997 2	10·213 8	4·651 9	95	·698 73	·009 19	·667 63
6	2·690 6	5·216 6	2·514 2	6	·429 85	0·717 39	·400 40
7	1·372 1	2·526 0	1·286 6	7	·137 37	·402 43	·109 45
8	·659 3	1·153 9	·620 3	8	$\bar{1}$·819 09	·062 15	$\bar{1}$·792 59
9	·296 9	·494 5	·280 2	9	·472 57	$\bar{1}$·694 20	·447 41
100	·124 5	·197 7	·117 8	100	·095 18	·295 94	·071 17
1	·048 3	·073 2	·045 8	1	$\bar{2}$·683 98	$\bar{2}$·864 34	$\bar{2}$·661 04
2	·017 2	·024 9	·016 4	2	·235 84	·395 64	·214 00
3	·005 6	·007 7	·005 3	3	$\bar{3}$·747 26	$\bar{3}$·884 02	$\bar{3}$·726 05
4	·001 6	·002 1	·001 6	4	·214 45	·315 61	·198 11
105	·000 4	·000 4	·000 4	105	$\bar{4}$·633 25	$\bar{4}$·633 25	$\bar{4}$·620 44

a_x—ULTIMATE VALUES

Age x	a_x	Age x	a_x
81	3·394	95	1·044
2	3·168	6	·939
3	2·951	7	·841
4	2·743	8	·750
85	2·544	9	·666
6	2·355	100	·588
7	2·174	1	·515
8	2·003	2	·445
9	1·841	3	·370
90	1·687	4	·262
1	1·542	105	·000
2	1·405		
3	1·277		
4	1·157		

The ultimate values for ages below 81 are given in the final columns of the corresponding tables of values for the first five years of assurance.

$O^{[NM]}$ $a_{[x]}$, $A_{[x]}$, $P_{[x]}$—SELECT VALUES 3½ PER CENT.

Age $[x]$	$a_{[x]}$	$A_{[x]}$	$P_{[x]}$	Age $[x]$	$a_{[x]}$	$A_{[x]}$	$P_{[x]}$
20	20·074	·287 36	·013 64	50	13·184	·520 36	·036 69
1	19·926	·292 39	·013 97	1	12·873	·530 86	·038 27
2	19·771	·297 61	·014 33	2	12·558	·541 51	·039 94
3	19·611	·303 02	·014 70	3	12·241	·552 24	·041 71
4	19·446	·308 58	·015 09	4	11·920	·563 09	·043 58
25	19·276	·314 36	·015 51	55	11·597	·574 01	·045 57
6	19·100	·320 27	·015 93	6	11·272	·585 01	·047 67
7	18·920	·326 41	·016 39	7	10·945	·596 05	·049 90
8	18·734	·332 70	·016 86	8	10·617	·607 16	·052 27
9	18·540	·339 22	·017 36	9	10·288	·618 26	·054 77
30	18·343	·345 90	·017 88	60	9·959	·629 40	·057 43
1	18·140	·352 77	·018 43	1	9·631	·640 53	·060 26
2	17·930	·359 86	·019 01	2	9·303	·651 58	·063 24
3	17·715	·367 12	·019 62	3	8·976	·662 66	·066 43
4	17·494	·374 60	·020 26	4	8·651	·673 66	·069 81
35	17·266	·382 30	·020 93	65	8·328	·684 57	·073 39
6	17·033	·390 18	·021 64	6	8·007	·695 38	·077 20
7	16·794	·398 26	·022 38	7	7·691	·706 11	·081 25
8	16·550	·406 54	·023 17	8	7·377	·716 70	·085 56
9	16·299	·415 00	·023 99	9	7·068	·727 14	·090 13
40	16·042	·423 69	·024 86	70	6·764	·737 43	·094 98
1	15·780	·432 55	·025 78	1	6·464	·747 57	·100 15
2	15·512	·441 60	·026 74	2	6·171	·757 51	·105 65
3	15·239	·450 85	·027 76	3	5·883	·767 26	·111 47
4	14·960	·460 29	·028 84	4	5·601	·776 78	·117 68
45	14·677	·469 88	·029 97	75	5·326	·786 07	·124 26
6	14·387	·479 67	·031 17				
7	14·093	·489 62	·032 44				
8	13·794	·499 71	·033 78				
9	13·492	·509 95	·035 19				

Two Lives

Select Values		Ultimate Values			
Age $[x]$	$a_{[xx]}$	Age x	a_{xx}	Age x	a_{xx}
20	17.069	25	16.075	65	5.400
1	16.918	6	15.896	6	5.124
2	16.761	7	15.710	7	4.854
3	16.599	8	15.519	8	4.590
4	16.431	9	15.322	9	4.333
25	16.257	30	15.119	70	4.082
6	16.079	1	14.909	1	3.839
7	15.893	2	14.694	2	3.604
8	15.704	3	14.473	3	3.376
9	15.506	4	14.246	4	3.156
30	15.305	35	14.013	75	2.945
1	15.098	6	13.774	6	2.742
2	14.884	7	13.530	7	2.548
3	14.666	8	13.280	8	2.362
4	14.440	9	13.024	9	2.184
35	14.209	40	12.763	80	2.015
6	13.973	1	12.496	1	1.854
7	13.731	2	12.225	2	1.702
8	13.484	3	11.949	3	1.558
9	13.232	4	11.669	4	1.422
40	12.973	45	11.384	85	1.294
1	12.711	6	11.095	6	1.174
2	12.445	7	10.802	7	1.062
3	12.173	8	10.506	8	0.956
4	11.897	9	10.207	9	.858
45	11.617	50	9.906	90	.767
6	11.334	1	9.602	1	.682
7	11.046	2	9.297	2	.604
8	10.756	3	8.990	3	.532
9	10.464	4	8.683	4	.466
50	10.168	55	8.376	95	.405
1	9.872	6	8.069	6	.350
2	9.573	7	7.762	7	.300
3	9.275	8	7.457	8	.255
4	8.975	9	7.153	9	.215
55	8.675	60	6.852	100	.179
6	8.377	1	6.554	1	.147
7	8.079	2	6.259	2	.120
8	7.782	3	5.968	3	.095
9	7.488	4	5.682	4	.071
60	7.195			105	.000
1	6.906				
2	6.620				
3	6.338				
4	6.060				
65	5.787				
6	5.519				
7	5.257				
8	5.000				
9	4.750				
70	4.506				
1	4.268				
2	4.038				
3	3.815				
4	3.598				
75	3.389				

PREMIUM CONVERSION TABLE

Single Premiums: *Interest* 3 *per cent.*

Annuity Value a	Single Premium $[A = 1 - d(1 + a)]$									
	0	1	2	3	4	5	6	7	8	9
1	·941 75	·938 83	·935 92	·933 01	·930 10	·927 18	·924 27	·921 36	·918 45	·915 53
2	·912 62	·909 71	·906 80	·903 88	·900 97	·898 06	·895 15	·892 23	·889 32	·886 41
3	·883 50	·880 58	·877 67	·874 76	·871 84	·868 93	·866 02	·863 11	·860 19	·857 28
4	·854 37	·851 46	·848 54	·845 63	·842 72	·839 81	·836 89	·833 98	·831 07	·828 16
5	·825 24	·822 33	·819 42	·816 50	·813 59	·810 68	·807 77	·804 85	·801 94	·799 03
6	·796 12	·793 20	·790 29	·787 38	·784 47	·781 55	·778 64	·775 73	·772 82	·769 90
7	·766 99	·764 08	·761 17	·758 25	·755 34	·752 43	·749 51	·746 60	·743 69	·740 78
8	·737 86	·734 95	·732 04	·729 13	·726 21	·723 30	·720 39	·717 48	·714 56	·711 65
9	·708 74	·705 83	·702 91	·700 00	·697 09	·694 17	·691 26	·688 35	·685 44	·682 52
10	·679 61	·676 70	·673 79	·670 87	·667 96	·665 05	·662 14	·659 22	·656 31	·653 40
11	·650 49	·647 57	·644 66	·641 75	·638 83	·635 92	·633 01	·630 10	·627 18	·624 27
12	·621 36	·618 45	·615 53	·612 62	·609 71	·606 80	·603 88	·600 97	·598 06	·595 15
13	·592 23	·589 32	·586 41	·583 50	·580 58	·577 67	·574 76	·571 84	·568 93	·566 02
14	·563 11	·560 19	·557 28	·554 37	·551 46	·548 54	·545 63	·542 72	·539 81	·536 89
15	·533 98	·531 07	·528 16	·525 24	·522 33	·519 42	·516 50	·513 59	·510 68	·507 77
16	·504 85	·501 94	·499 03	·496 12	·493 20	·490 29	·487 38	·484 47	·481 55	·478 64
17	·475 73	·472 82	·469 90	·466 99	·464 08	·461 17	·458 25	·455 34	·452 43	·449 51
18	·446 60	·443 69	·440 78	·437 86	·434 95	·432 04	·429 13	·426 21	·423 30	·420 39
19	·417 48	·414 56	·411 65	·408 74	·405 83	·402 91	·400 00	·397 09	·394 17	·391 26
20	·388 35	·385 44	·382 52	·379 61	·376 70	·373 79	·370 87	·367 96	·365 05	·362 14
21	·359 22	·356 31	·353 40	·350 49	·347 57	·344 66	·341 75	·338 83	·335 92	·333 01
22	·330 10	·327 18	·324 27	·321 36	·318 45	·315 53	·312 62	·309 71	·306 80	·303 88
23	·300 97	·298 06	·295 15	·292 23	·289 32	·286 41	·283 50	·280 58	·277 67	·274 76
24	·271 84	·268 93	·266 02	·263 11	·260 19	·257 28	·254 37	·251 46	·248 54	·245 63
25	·242 72	·239 81	·236 89	·233 98	·231 07	·228 16	·225 24	·222 33	·219 42	·216 50
	0	1	2	3	4	5	6	7	8	9
Proportional Parts	29	58	87	116	146	175	204	233	262	

Annual Premiums: *Interest* 3 *per cent.*

Annuity Value a	Annual Premium $\left[P = \frac{1}{1+a} - d\right]$									
	0	1	2	3	4	5	6	7	8	9
1	·470 87	·447 06	·425 42	·405 66	·387 54	·370 87	·355 49	·341 24	·328 02	·315 70
2	·304 21	·293 45	·283 37	·273 90	·264 99	·256 59	·248 65	·241 14	·234 03	·227 28
3	·220 87	·214 78	·208 97	·203 43	·198 15	·193 10	·188 27	·183 64	·179 21	·174 96
4	·170 87	·166 95	·163 18	·159 55	·156 06	·152 69	·149 45	·146 31	·143 29	·140 37
5	·137 54	·134 81	·132 16	·129 60	·127 12	·124 72	·122 39	·120 13	·117 93	·115 80
6	·113 73	·111 72	·109 76	·107 86	·106 01	·104 21	·102 45	·100 74	·099 08	·097 46
7	·095 87	·094 33	·092 83	·091 36	·089 92	·088 52	·087 15	·085 82	·084 51	·083 23
8	·081 98	·080 76	·079 57	·078 40	·077 26	·076 14	·075 04	·073 97	·072 91	·071 88
9	·070 87	·069 88	·068 91	·067 96	·067 03	·066 11	·065 21	·064 33	·063 47	·062 62
10	·061 78	·060 96	·060 16	·059 37	·058 59	·057 83	·057 08	·056 34	·055 62	·054 91
11	·054 21	·053 52	·052 84	·052 17	·051 52	·050 87	·050 24	·049 61	·049 00	·048 39
12	·047 80	·047 21	·046 63	·046 06	·045 50	·044 95	·044 40	·043 87	·043 34	·042 82
13	·042 30	·041 80	·041 30	·040 80	·040 32	·039 84	·039 37	·038 90	·038 44	·037 99
14	·037 54	·037 10	·036 66	·036 23	·035 81	·035 39	·034 98	·034 57	·034 16	·033 77
15	·033 37	·032 99	·032 60	·032 22	·031 85	·031 48	·031 11	·030 75	·030 40	·030 05
16	·029 70	·029 35	·029 01	·028 68	·028 35	·028 02	·027 69	·027 37	·027 05	·026 74
17	·026 43	·026 12	·025 82	·025 52	·025 22	·024 93	·024 64	·024 35	·024 07	·023 78
18	·023 51	·023 23	·022 96	·022 69	·022 42	·022 16	·021 89	·021 64	·021 38	·021 13
19	·020 87	·020 63	·020 38	·020 13	·019 89	·019 65	·019 42	·019 18	·018 95	·018 72
20	·018 49	·018 27	·018 04	·017 82	·017 60	·017 39	·017 17	·016 96	·016 75	·016 54
21	·016 33	·016 12	·015 92	·015 72	·015 52	·015 32	·015 12	·014 93	·014 73	·014 54
22	·014 35	·014 16	·013 98	·013 79	·013 61	·013 43	·013 25	·013 07	·012 89	·012 71
23	·012 54	·012 37	·012 20	·012 03	·011 86	·011 69	·011 52	·011 36	·011 20	·011 03
24	·010 87	·010 71	·010 56	·010 40	·010 24	·010 09	·009 94	·009 78	·009 63	·009 48
25	·009 34	·009 19	·009 04	·008 90	·008 75	·008 61	·008 47	·008 33	·008 19	·008 05
	0	1	2	3	4	5	6	7	8	9

PREMIUM CONVERSION TABLE

Single Premiums: *Interest 3½ per cent.*

Annuity Value a	Single Premium $[A = 1 - d(1 + a)]$									
	0	**1**	**2**	**3**	**4**	**5**	**6**	**7**	**8**	**9**
1	·932 37	·928 99	·925 60	·922 22	·918 84	·915 46	·912 08	·908 70	·905 31	·901 93
2	·898 55	·895 17	·891 79	·888 41	·885 02	·881 64	·878 26	·874 88	·871 50	·868 12
3	·864 73	·861 35	·857 97	·854 59	·851 21	·847 83	·844 44	·841 06	·837 68	·834 30
4	·830 92	·827 54	·824 15	·820 77	·817 39	·814 01	·810 63	·807 25	·803 86	·800 48
5	·797 10	·793 72	·790 34	·786 96	·783 57	·780 19	·776 81	·773 43	·770 05	·766 67
6	·763 29	·759 90	·756 52	·753 14	·749 76	·746 38	·743 00	·739 61	·736 23	·732 85
7	·729 47	·726 09	·722 71	·719 32	·715 94	·712 56	·709 18	·705 80	·702 42	·699 03
8	·695 65	·692 27	·688 89	·685 51	·682 13	·678 74	·675 36	·671 98	·668 60	·665 22
9	·661 84	·658 45	·655 07	·651 69	·648 31	·644 93	·641 55	·638 16	·634 78	·631 40
10	·628 02	·624 64	·621 26	·617 87	·614 49	·611 11	·607 73	·604 35	·600 97	·597 58
11	·594 20	·590 82	·587 44	·584 06	·580 68	·577 29	·573 91	·570 53	·567 15	·563 77
12	·560 39	·557 00	·553 62	·550 24	·546 86	·543 48	·540 10	·536 71	·533 33	·529 95
13	·526 57	·523 19	·519 81	·516 43	·513 04	·509 66	·506 28	·502 90	·499 52	·496 14
14	·492 75	·489 37	·485 99	·482 61	·479 23	·475 85	·472 46	·469 08	·465 70	·462 32
15	·458 94	·455 56	·452 17	·448 79	·445 41	·442 03	·438 65	·435 27	·431 88	·428 50
16	·425 12	·421 74	·418 36	·414 98	·411 59	·408 21	·404 83	·401 45	·398 07	·394 69
17	·391 30	·387 92	·384 54	·381 16	·377 78	·374 40	·371 01	·367 63	·364 25	·360 87
18	·357 49	·354 11	·350 72	·347 34	·343 96	·340 58	·337 20	·333 82	·330 43	·327 05
19	·323 67	·320 29	·316 91	·313 53	·310 14	·306 76	·303 38	·300 00	·296 62	·293 24
20	·289 86	·286 47	·283 09	·279 71	·276 33	·272 95	·269 57	·266 18	·262 80	·259 42
21	·256 04	·252 66	·249 28	·245 89	·242 51	·239 13	·235 75	·232 37	·228 99	·225 60
22	·222 22	·218 84	·215 46	·212 08	·208 70	·205 31	·201 93	·198 55	·195 17	·191 79
23	·188 41	·185 02	·181 64	·178 26	·174 88	·171 50	·168 12	·164 73	·161 35	·157 97
24	·154 59	·151 21	·147 83	·144 44	·141 06	·137 68	·134 30	·130 92	·127 54	·124 15
25	·120 77	·117 39	·114 01	·110 63	·107 25	·103 86	·100 48	·097 10	·093 72	·090 34
	0	**1**	**2**	**3**	**4**	**5**	**6**	**7**	**8**	**9**
Proportional Parts		34	68	101	135	169	203	237	270	304

Annual Premiums: *Interest 3½ per cent.*

Annuity Value a	Annual Premium $\left[P = \frac{1}{1+a} - d\right]$									
	0	**1**	**2**	**3**	**4**	**5**	**6**	**7**	**8**	**9**
1	·466 18	·442 37	·420 73	·400 97	·382 85	·366 18	·350 80	·336 55	·323 33	·311 01
2	·299 52	·288 76	·278 68	·269 21	·260 30	·251 90	·243 96	·236 45	·229 34	·222 59
3	·216 18	·210 09	·204 28	·198 74	·193 46	·188 41	·183 57	·178 95	·174 52	·170 27
4	·166 18	·162 26	·158 49	·154 86	·151 37	·148 00	·144 76	·141 62	·138 60	·135 68
5	·132 85	·130 12	·127 47	·124 91	·122 43	·120 03	·117 70	·115 44	·113 24	·111 11
6	·109 04	·107 03	·105 07	·103 17	·101 32	·099 52	·097 76	·096 05	·094 39	·092 77
7	·091 18	·089 64	·088 13	·086 67	·085 23	·083 83	·082 46	·081 13	·079 82	·078 54
8	·077 29	·076 07	·074 88	·073 71	·072 57	·071 45	·070 35	·069 28	·068 22	·067 19
9	·066 18	·065 19	·064 22	·063 27	·062 34	·061 42	·060 52	·059 64	·058 78	·057 93
10	·057 09	·056 27	·055 47	·054 68	·053 90	·053 14	·052 39	·051 65	·050 93	·050 22
11	·049 52	·048 83	·048 15	·047 48	·046 83	·046 18	·045 55	·044 92	·044 31	·043 70
12	·043 11	·042 52	·041 94	·041 37	·040 81	·040 26	·039 71	·039 18	·038 65	·038 13
13	·037 61	·037 11	·036 61	·036 11	·035 63	·035 15	·034 68	·034 21	·033 75	·033 30
14	·032 85	·032 41	·031 97	·031 54	·031 12	·030 70	·030 29	·029 88	·029 47	·029 08
15	·028 68	·028 30	·027 91	·027 53	·027 16	·026 79	·026 42	·026 06	·025 71	·025 36
16	·025 01	·024 66	·024 32	·023 99	·023 65	·023 33	·023 00	·022 68	·022 36	·022 05
17	·021 74	·021 43	·021 13	·020 83	·020 53	·020 24	·019 95	·019 66	·019 38	·019 09
18	·018 82	·018 54	·018 27	·018 00	·017 73	·017 47	·017 20	·016 94	·016 69	·016 43
19	·016 18	·015 93	·015 69	·015 44	·015 20	·014 96	·014 73	·014 49	·014 26	·014 03
20	·013 80	·013 58	·013 35	·013 13	·012 91	·012 70	·012 48	·012 27	·012 06	·011 85
21	·011 64	·011 43	·011 23	·011 03	·010 83	·010 63	·010 43	·010 24	·010 04	·009 85
22	·009 66	·009 47	·009 29	·009 10	·008 92	·008 74	·008 56	·008 38	·008 20	·008 02
23	·007 85	·007 68	·007 51	·007 34	·007 17	·007 00	·006 83	·006 67	·006 51	·006 34
24	·006 18	·006 02	·005 87	·005 71	·005 55	·005 40	·005 25	·005 09	·004 94	·004 79
25	·004 65	·004 50	·004 35	·004 21	·004 06	·003 92	·003 78	·003 64	·003 50	·003 36
	0	**1**	**2**	**3**	**4**	**5**	**6**	**7**	**8**	**9**

PREMIUM CONVERSION TABLE

Single Premiums: *Interest 4 per cent.*

Annuity Value a	Single Premium $[A = 1 - d(1+a)]$ 0	1	2	3	4	5	6	7	8	9
1	·923 08	·919 23	·915 38	·911 54	·907 69	·903 85	·900 00	·896 15	·892 31	·888 46
2	·884 62	·880 77	·876 92	·873 08	·869 23	·865 38	·861 54	·857 69	·853 85	·850 00
3	·846 15	·842 31	·838 46	·834 62	·830 77	·826 92	·823 08	·819 23	·815 38	·811 54
4	·807 69	·803 85	·800 00	·796 15	·792 31	·788 46	·784 62	·780 77	·776 92	·773 08
5	·769 23	·765 38	·761 54	·757 69	·753 85	·750 00	·746 15	·742 31	·738 46	·734 62
6	·730 77	·726 92	·723 08	·719 23	·715 38	·711 54	·707 69	·703 85	·700 00	·696 15
7	·692 31	·688 46	·684 62	·680 77	·676 92	·673 08	·669 23	·665 38	·661 54	·657 69
8	·653 85	·650 00	·646 15	·642 31	·638 46	·634 62	·630 77	·626 92	·623 08	·619 23
9	·615 38	·611 54	·607 69	·603 85	·600 00	·596 15	·592 31	·588 46	·584 62	·580 77
10	·576 92	·573 08	·569 23	·565 38	·561 54	·557 69	·553 85	·550 00	·546 15	·542 31
11	·538 46	·534 62	·530 77	·526 92	·523 08	·519 23	·515 38	·511 54	·507 69	·503 85
12	·500 00	·496 15	·492 31	·488 46	·484 62	·480 77	·476 92	·473 08	·469 23	·465 38
13	·461 54	·457 69	·453 85	·450 00	·446 15	·442 31	·438 46	·434 62	·430 77	·426 92
14	·423 08	·419 23	·415 38	·411 54	·407 69	·403 85	·400 00	·396 15	·392 31	·388 46
15	·384 62	·380 77	·376 92	·373 01	·369 23	·365 38	·361 54	·357 69	·353 85	·350 00
16	·346 15	·342 31	·338 46	·334 62	·330 77	·326 92	·323 08	·319 23	·315 38	·311 54
17	·307 69	·303 85	·300 00	·296 15	·292 31	·288 46	·284 62	·280 77	·276 92	·273 08
18	·269 23	·265 38	·261 54	·257 69	·253 85	·250 00	·246 15	·242 31	·238 46	·234 62
19	·230 77	·226 92	·223 08	·219 23	·215 38	·211 54	·207 69	·203 85	·200 00	·196 15
20	·192 31	·188 46	·184 62	·180 77	·176 92	·173 08	·169 23	·165 38	·161 54	·157 69
21	·153 85	·150 00	·146 15	·142 31	·138 46	·134 62	·130 77	·126 92	·123 08	·119 23
22	·115 38	·111 54	·107 69	·103 85	·100 00	·096 15	·092 31	·088 46	·084 62	·080 77
23	·076 92	·073 08	·069 23	·065 38	·061 54	·057 69	·053 85	·050 00	·046 15	·042 31
24	·038 46	·034 62	·030 77	·026 92	·023 08	·019 23	·015 38	·011 54	·007 69	·003 85
	0	1	2	3	4	5	6	7	8	9
Proportional Parts		39	77	116	154	193	231	270	308	347

Annual Premiums: *Interest 4 per cent.*

Annuity Value a	Annual Premium $\left[P = \frac{1}{1+a} - d\right]$ 0	1	2	3	4	5	6	7	8	9
1	·461 54	·437 73	·416 08	·396 32	·378 21	·361 54	·346 15	·331 91	·318 68	·306 37
2	·294 87	·284 12	·274 04	·264 57	·255 66	·247 25	·239 32	·231 81	·224 70	·217 95
3	·211 54	·205 44	·199 63	·194 10	·188 81	·183 76	·178 93	·174 30	·169 87	·165 62
4	·161 54	·157 62	·153 85	·150 22	·146 72	·143 36	·140 11	·136 98	·133 95	·131 03
5	·128 21	·125 47	·122 83	·120 27	·117 79	·115 38	·113 05	·110 79	·108 60	·106 47
6	·104 40	·102 38	·100 43	·098 52	·096 67	·094 87	·093 12	·091 41	·089 74	·088 12
7	·086 54	·085 00	·083 49	·082 02	·080 59	·079 19	·077 82	·076 48	·075 17	·073 90
8	·072 65	·071 43	·070 23	·069 07	·067 92	·066 80	·065 71	·064 63	·063 58	·062 55
9	·061 54	·060 55	·059 58	·058 63	·057 69	·056 78	·055 88	·055 00	·054 13	·053 28
10	·052 45	·051 63	·050 82	·050 03	·049 26	·048 49	·047 75	·047 01	·046 28	·045 57
11	·044 87	·044 18	·043 51	·042 84	·042 18	·041 54	·040 90	·040 28	·039 66	·039 06
12	·038 46	·037 87	·037 30	·036 73	·036 17	·035 61	·035 07	·034 53	·034 00	·033 48
13	·032 97	·032 46	·031 96	·031 47	·030 98	·030 50	·030 03	·029 57	·029 11	·028 65
14	·028 21	·027 76	·027 33	·026 90	·026 47	·026 05	·025 64	·025 23	·024 83	·024 43
15	·024 04	·023 65	·023 27	·022 89	·022 51	·022 14	·021 78	·021 42	·021 06	·020 71
16	·020 36	·020 02	·019 68	·019 34	·019 01	·018 68	·018 36	·018 04	·017 72	·017 40
17	·017 09	·016 79	·016 48	·016 18	·015 89	·015 59	·015 30	·015 01	·014 73	·014 45
18	·014 17	·013 89	·013 62	·013 35	·013 08	·012 82	·012 56	·012 30	·012 04	·011 79
19	·011 54	·011 29	·011 04	·010 80	·010 56	·010 32	·010 08	·009 85	·009 62	·009 39
20	·009 16	·008 93	·008 71	·008 49	·008 27	·008 05	·007 83	·007 62	·007 41	·007 20
21	·006 99	·006 79	·006 58	·006 38	·006 18	·005 98	·005 79	·005 59	·005 40	·005 21
22	·005 02	·004 83	·004 64	·004 46	·004 27	·004 09	·003 91	·003 73	·003 56	·003 38
23	·003 21	·003 03	·002 86	·002 69	·002 52	·002 35	·002 19	·002 02	·001 86	·001 70
24	·001 54	·001 38	·001 22	·001 06	·000 91	·000 75	·000 60	·000 45	·000 30	·000 15
	0	1	2	3	4	5	6	7	8	9

PREMIUM CONVERSION TABLE

CONTINUOUS FUNCTIONS

SINGLE PREMIUMS: *Interest* 3 *per cent.*

Annuity Value $\bar{a}$	Single Premium $[\bar{A} = 1 - \delta\bar{a}]$									
	0	1	2	3	4	5	6	7	8	9
1	·970 44	·967 49	·964 53	·961 57	·958 62	·955 66	·952 71	·949 75	·946 79	·943 84
2	·940 88	·937 93	·934 97	·932 01	·929 06	·926 10	·923 15	·920 19	·917 24	·914 28
3	·911 32	·908 37	·905 41	·902 46	·899 50	·896 54	·893 59	·890 63	·887 68	·884 72
4	·881 76	·878 81	·875 85	·872 90	·869 94	·866 99	·864 03	·861 07	·858 12	·855 16
5	·852 21	·849 25	·846 29	·843 34	·840 38	·837 43	·834 47	·831 51	·828 56	·825 60
6	·822 65	·819 69	·816 74	·813 78	·810 82	·807 87	·804 91	·801 96	·799 00	·796 04
7	·793 09	·790 13	·787 18	·784 22	·781 26	·778 31	·775 35	·772 40	·769 44	·766 49
8	·763 53	·760 57	·757 62	·754 66	·751 71	·748 75	·745 79	·742 84	·739 88	·736 93
9	·733 97	·731 01	·728 06	·725 10	·722 15	·719 19	·716 24	·713 28	·710 32	·707 37
10	·704 41	·701 46	·698 50	·695 54	·692 59	·689 63	·686 68	·683 72	·680 76	·677 81
11	·674 85	·671 90	·668 94	·665 99	·663 03	·660 07	·657 12	·654 16	·651 21	·648 25
12	·645 29	·642 34	·639 38	·636 43	·633 47	·630 51	·627 56	·624 60	·621 65	·618 69
13	·615 74	·612 78	·609 82	·606 87	·603 91	·600 96	·598 00	·595 04	·592 09	·589 13
14	·586 18	·583 22	·580 27	·577 31	·574 35	·571 40	·568 44	·565 49	·562 53	·559 57
15	·556 62	·553 66	·550 71	·547 75	·544 79	·541 84	·538 88	·535 93	·532 97	·530 02
16	·527 06	·524 10	·521 15	·518 19	·515 24	·512 28	·509 32	·506 37	·503 41	·500 46
17	·497 50	·494 54	·491 59	·488 63	·485 68	·482 72	·479 77	·476 81	·473 85	·470 90
18	·467 94	·464 99	·462 03	·459 07	·456 12	·453 16	·450 21	·447 25	·444 29	·441 34
19	·438 38	·435 43	·432 47	·429 52	·426 56	·423 60	·420 65	·417 69	·414 74	·411 78
20	·408 82	·405 87	·402 91	·399 96	·397 00	·394 04	·391 09	·388 13	·385 18	·382 22
21	·379 27	·376 31	·373 35	·370 40	·367 44	·364 49	·361 53	·358 57	·355 62	·352 66
22	·349 71	·346 75	·343 79	·340 84	·337 88	·334 93	·331 97	·329 02	·326 06	·323 10
23	·320 15	·317 19	·314 24	·311 28	·308 32	·305 37	·302 41	·299 46	·296 50	·293 54
24	·290 59	·287 63	·284 68	·281 72	·278 77	·275 81	·272 85	·269 90	·266 94	·263 99
25	·261 03	·258 07	·255 12	·252 16	·24 921	·246 25	·243 29	·240 34	·237 38	·234 43
	0	1	2	3	4	5	6	7	8	9
Proportional Parts		30	59	89	118	148	177	207	237	266

ANNUAL PREMIUMS: *Interest* 3 *per cent.*

Annuity Value $\bar{a}$	Annual Premium $\left[{}^{(\infty)}\bar{P} = \frac{1}{\bar{a}} - \delta\right]$									
	0	1	2	3	4	5	6	7	8	9
1	·970 44	·879 53	·803 77	·739 67	·684 73	·637 11	·595 44	·558 68	·526 00	·496 76
2	·470 44	·446 63	·424 99	·405 22	·387 11	·370 44	·355 06	·340 81	·327 58	·315 27
3	·303 77	·293 02	·282 94	·273 47	·264 56	·256 16	·248 22	·240 71	·233 60	·226 85
4	·220 44	·214 34	·208 54	·203 00	·197 71	·192 66	·187 83	·183 21	·178 77	·174 52
5	·170 44	·166 52	·162 75	·159 12	·155 63	·152 26	·149 01	·145 88	·142 85	·139 93
6	·137 11	·134 38	·131 73	·129 17	·126 69	·124 29	·121 96	·119 69	·117 50	·115 37
7	·113 30	·111 29	·109 33	·107 43	·105 58	·103 77	·102 02	·100 31	·098 65	·097 02
8	·095 44	·093 90	·092 39	·090 92	·089 49	·088 09	·086 72	·085 38	·084 08	·082 80
9	·081 55	·080 33	·079 14	·077 97	·076 82	·075 70	·074 61	·073 53	·072 48	·071 45
10	·070 44	·069 45	·068 48	·067 53	·066 60	·065 68	·064 78	·063 90	·063 03	·062 18
11	·061 35	·060 53	·059 73	·058 94	·058 16	·057 40	·056 65	·055 91	·055 19	·054 47
12	·053 77	·053 09	·052 41	·051 74	·051 09	·050 44	·049 81	·049 18	·048 57	·047 96
13	·047 36	·046 78	·046 20	·045 63	·045 07	·044 52	·043 97	·043 43	·042 90	·042 38
14	·041 87	·041 36	·040 86	·040 37	·039 89	·039 41	·038 93	·038 47	·038 01	·037 56
15	·037 11	·036 67	·036 23	·035 80	·035 38	·034 96	·034 54	·034 14	·033 73	·033 33
16	·032 94	·032 55	·032 17	·031 79	·031 42	·031 05	·030 68	·030 32	·029 97	·029 61
17	·029 26	·028 92	·028 58	·028 24	·027 91	·027 58	·027 26	·026 94	·026 62	·026 31
18	·026 00	·025 69	·025 39	·025 09	·024 79	·024 50	·024 20	·023 92	·023 63	·023 35
19	·023 07	·022 80	·022 52	·022 25	·021 99	·021 72	·021 46	·021 20	·020 95	·020 69
20	·020 44	·020 19	·019 95	·019 70	·019 46	·019 22	·018 98	·018 75	·018 52	·018 29
21	·018 06	·017 83	·017 61	·017 39	·017 17	·016 95	·016 74	·016 52	·016 31	·016 10
22	·015 90	·015 69	·015 49	·015 28	·015 08	·014 89	·014 69	·014 49	·014 30	·014 11
23	·013 92	·013 73	·013 54	·013 36	·013 18	·012 99	·012 81	·012 64	·012 46	·012 28
24	·012 11	·011 93	·011 76	·011 59	·011 42	·011 26	·011 09	·010 93	·010 76	·010 60
25	·010 44	·010 28	·010 12	·009 97	·009 81	·009 66	·009 50	·009 35	·009 20	·009 05
	0	1	2	3	4	5	6	7	8	9

UNIFORM SENIORITY

H^M TABLE (MAKEHAM GRADUATION)

Equal Ages—Two Lives

Table showing the number of years (t) to be added to the age of the younger of two lives, (x), ($x+h$), to obtain the age of the two equivalent lives of equal ages, ($x+t$), ($x+t$).

$$c^x + c^{x+h} = 2c^{x+t}$$

$$a_{x:x+h} = a_{x+t:x+t}$$

h	t	h	t
1	0·51	26	19·38
2	1·05	27	20·30
3	1·60	28	21·23
4	2·18	29	22·16
5	2·78	30	23·09
6	3·41	31	24·04
7	4·05	32	24·98
8	4·72	33	25·93
9	5·40	34	26·89
10	6·10	35	27·85
11	6·83	36	28·81
12	7·57	37	29·78
13	8·33	38	30·75
14	9·10	39	31·72
15	9·89	40	32·69
16	10·69	41	33·67
17	11·51	42	34·64
18	12·34	43	35·62
19	13·19	44	36·60
20	14·04	45	37·59
21	14·91	46	38·57
22	15·79	47	39·56
23	16·67	48	40·55
24	17·57	49	41·53
25	18·47	50	42·52

Equal Ages—Three Lives

Table showing the number of years (t) to be added to the age of the two lives, (x), (x), to obtain the age of the three lives of equal ages, ($x+t$), ($x+t$), ($x+t$), to be substituted for the three lives, (x), (x), ($x+h$).

$$2c^x + c^{x+h} = 3c^{x+t}$$

$$a_{x:x:x+h} = a_{x+t:x+t:x+t}$$

h	t	h	t
0	0·00		
1	0·35	26	15·84
2	0·71	27	16·69
3	1·09	28	17·55
4	1·50	29	18·42
5	1·93	30	19·30
6	2·38	31	20·19
7	2·86	32	21·09
8	3·36	33	22·00
9	3·88	34	22·91
10	4·42	35	23·83
11	4·99	36	24·76
12	5·58	37	25·69
13	6·19	38	26·63
14	6·82	39	27·57
15	7·47	40	28·52
16	8·14	41	29·48
17	8·84	42	30·43
18	9·55	43	31·39
19	10·28	44	32·36
20	11·03	45	33·32
21	11·79	46	34·29
22	12·57	47	35·26
23	13·37	48	36·24
24	14·18	49	37·22
25	15·00	50	38·19

$O^{[NM]}$ TABLE

Equal Ages—Two Lives

Table showing the number of years (t) to be added to the age of the younger of two lives, (x), ($x+h$), to obtain the age of the two equivalent lives of equal ages, ($x+t$), ($x+t$).

General Relation: $a_{[x-n]+n:[x-n+h]+n} = a_{[x-n+t]+n:[x-n+t]+n}$

Select Values: $a_{[x][x+h]} = a_{[x+t][x+t]}$

Ultimate Values: $a_{x:x+h} = a_{x+t:x+t}$

h	t	h	t	h	t	h	t
0	0·00	15	9·86	30	23·01	45	37·48
1	0·51	16	10·66	31	23·95	46	38·46
2	1·05	17	11·47	32	24·89	47	39·44
3	1·60	18	12·30	33	25·84	48	40·43
4	2·18	19	13·14	34	26·80	49	41·42
5	2·78	20	13·99	35	27·75	50	42·41
6	3·40	21	14·85	36	28·71		
7	4·04	22	15·73	37	29·68		
8	4·70	23	16·61	38	30·64		
9	5·39	24	17·50	39	31·61		
10	6·09	25	18·40	40	32·58		
11	6·81	26	19·31	41	33·56		
12	7·54	27	20·23	42	34·54		
13	8·30	28	21·15	43	35·51		
14	9·07	29	22·08	44	36·50		

H^M TABLE (MAKEHAM GRADUATION)

Factors for Contingent Assurances—**3** *per cent.*

(For method of employing this table see pp. 301 and 302)

x	$\log c^x$	w	$\log f_1(ww)$	$f_2(ww)$	$\log f_1(www)$	$f_2(www)$	$\log f_1(wwww)$	$f_2(wwww)$
20	·793 14	20	$\bar{2}$·202 98	·118 37	$\bar{2}$·012 70	·103 96	$\bar{3}$·866 49	·093 16
21	·832 79	21	·183 16	·117 00	$\bar{3}$·996 39	·102 60	·854 03	·091 81
22	·872 45	22	·162 10	·115 66	·978 07	·101 29	·838 68	·090 54
23	·912 11	23	·139 78	·114 36	·958 12	·100 02	·820 93	·089 32
24	·951 76	24	·116 87	·113 05	·937 15	·098 76	·801 67	·088 14
25	·991 42	25	·093 41	·111 74	·915 29	·097 51	·781 41	·086 96
26	1·031 08	26	·069 57	·110 41	·892 99	·096 24	·760 47	·085 77
27	1·070 74	27	·045 50	·109 05	·870 32	·094 95	·739 02	·084 56
28	1·110 39	28	·021 32	·107 65	·847 46	·093 62	·717 43	·083 31
29	1·150 05	29	$\bar{3}$·996 91	·106 22	·824 23	·092 27	·695 36	·082 04
30	1·189 71	30	·972 38	·104 75	·800 94	·090 87	·673 08	·080 74
31	1·229 36	31	·947 77	·103 24	·777 49	·089 44	·650 77	·079 39
32	1·269 02	32	·922 93	·101 70	·753 78	·087 97	·628 06	·078 01
33	1·308 68	33	·898 01	·100 11	·729 98	·086 46	·605 19	·076 59
34	1·348 33	34	·872 90	·098 49	·705 94	·084 91	·582 06	·075 14
35	1·387 99	35	·847 66	·096 83	·681 61	·083 34	·558 66	·073 66
36	1·427 65	36	·822 23	·095 14	·657 11	·081 73	·534 96	·072 15
37	1·467 30	37	·796 67	·093 41	·632 38	·080 09	·511 11	·070 60
38	1·506 96	38	·770 92	·091 65	·607 55	·078 41	·486 96	·069 02
39	1·546 62	39	·745 04	·089 84	·582 36	·076 70	·462 62	·067 41
40	1·586 27	40	·718 89	·088 02	·556 96	·074 97	·437 81	·065 79
41	1·625 93	41	·692 61	·086 15	·531 35	·073 21	·412 85	·064 13
42	1·665 59	42	·666 16	·084 25	·505 55	·071 41	·387 64	·062 44
43	1·705 24	43	·639 47	·082 33	·479 37	·069 61	·362 02	·060 75
44	1·744 90	44	·612 60	·080 38	·453 01	·067 77	·336 12	·059 04
45	1·784 56	45	·585 47	·078 41	·426 37	·065 92	·309 91	·057 31
46	1·824 22	46	·558 21	·076 41	·399 56	·064 03	·283 46	·055 56
47	1·863 87	47	·530 70	·074 39	·372 39	·062 15	·256 64	·053 81
48	1·903 53	48	·502 96	·072 35	·344 91	·060 26	·229 50	·052 05
49	1·943 19	49	·474 96	·070 30	·317 17	·058 36	·202 07	·050 28
50	1·982 84	50	·446 73	·068 24	·289 19	·056 44	·174 31	·048 51
51	2·022 50	51	·418 28	·066 16	·260 94	·054 52	·146 20	·046 75
52	2·062 16	52	·389 58	·064 08	·232 28	·052 62	·117 74	·044 99
53	2·101 81	53	·360 68	·061 99	·203 41	·050 71	·089 03	·043 23
54	2·141 47	54	·331 46	·059 91	·174 21	·048 81	·059 87	·041 50
55	2·181 13	55	·301 99	·057 82	·144 71	·046 92	·030 34	·039 79
56	2·220 78	56	·272 25	·055 75	·114 88	·045 05	·000 56	·038 08
57	2·260 44	57	·242 26	·053 68	·084 78	·043 19	$\bar{4}$·970 42	·036 40
58	2·300 10	58	·212 02	·051 62	·054 35	·041 35	·939 92	·034 75
59	2·339 75	59	·181 49	·049 58	·023 62	·039 54	·909 08	·033 12
60	2·379 41	60	·150 69	·047 56	$\bar{4}$·992 58	·037 76	·877 88	·031 53
61	2·419 07	61	·119 62	·045 56	·961 20	·036 01	·846 38	·029 97
62	2·458 73	62	·088 27	·043 59	·929 53	·034 29	·814 55	·028 44
63	2·498 38	63	·056 64	·041 65	·897 58	·032 60	·782 36	·026 96
64	2·538 04	64	·024 70	·039 75	·865 27	·030 96	·749 87	·025 51
65	2·577 70	65	$\bar{4}$·992 54	·037 87	·832 67	·029 36	·717 03	·024 11
66	2·617 35	66	·960 05	·036 05	·799 77	·027 80	·683 85	·022 76
67	2·657 01	67	·927 33	·034 25	·766 60	·026 29	·650 38	·021 45
68	2·696 67	68	·894 28	·032 51	·733 08	·024 83	·616 61	·020 19
69	2·736 32	69	·861 00	·030 81	·699 33	·023 41	·582 56	·018 97
70	2·775 98	70	·827 46	·029 15	·665 28	·022 04	·548 22	·017 80
71	2·815 64	71	·793 60	·027 56	·630 91	·020 73	·513 53	·016 69
72	2·855 29	72	·759 52	·026 01	·596 33	·019 47	·478 60	·015 63
73	2·894 95	73	·725 15	·024 52	·561 45	·018 26	·443 43	·014 61
74	2·934 61	74	·690 56	·023 07	·526 32	·017 10	·407 97	·013 64
75	2·974 26	75	·655 71	·021 69	·490 93	·016 00	·372 29	·012 72
76	3·013 92	76	·620 61	·020 36	·455 31	·014 95	·336 35	·011 85
77	3·053 58	77	·585 26	·019 09	·419 44	·013 95	·300 16	·011 03
78	3·093 24	78	·549 67	·017 88	·383 36	·013 00	·263 78	·010 25
79	3·132 89	79	·513 89	·016 72	·347 06	·012 11	·227 21	·009 51
80	3·172 55	80	·477 86	·015 62	·310 55	·011 26	·190 40	·008 82

For EU product safety concerns, contact us at Calle de José Abascal, 56–1°, 28003 Madrid, Spain or eugpsr@cambridge.org.

www.ingramcontent.com/pod-product-compliance
Lightning Source LLC
LaVergne TN
LVHW090256210926
848480LV00001B/37

* 9 7 8 1 1 0 7 6 4 8 0 9 8 *